THE MILITARY TRANSPORT BOOK

THE MILITARY TRANSPORT BOOK

THE DEFINITIVE VISUAL HISTORY

Contents

INTRODUCTION 8

TO 1830: WHEELS, SAILS, AND GUNS

Armies have always needed to be mobile. For thousands of years, the most basic form of transport was marching on foot, and from around 4000 BCE until the industrial era, military transport was dominated by horses on land, and on water by ships powered with oars and sails.

The Rise of Battlefield Mobility	12
Chariots and War Wagons	14
Leonardo da Vinci's "Tank"	16
The Sea as a Battlefield	18
Olympias Greek Trireme	20
Early Warships	22
HMS *Victory*	24
End of an Era	26
The Great Age of Sail	28

1830–1918: THE MECHANIZATION OF WAR

The steam engine revolutionized transport, and military forces were quick to adapt it to ships, trains, and later, road vehicles. Improvements in the internal combustion engine further accelerated the development of military transport, and World War I ushered in a new generation of vehicles such as tanks and fighter planes.

Engines of War	32
Military Trains and Railway Guns	34
Battleships and Cruisers	36
Mikasa	38
Torpedo Boats, Destroyers, and Submarines	42
Steamboat Battles in the American Civil War	44
World War I: Mobile Warfare on Land	46
Utility and Troop Trucks	48
Pierce-Arrow R Type	50
World War I Locomotives	54
World War I Tanks	56
Mark IV	58
Tank Battles in World War I	62

World War I Armoured Cars	64
War Takes to the Air	66
Reconnaissance Aircraft	68
Fighter Aircraft	70
RAF S.E.5a	72
Airship Bombing Raids	76
Bomber Aircraft	78
Sea Battles in World War I	80
Dreadnoughts and Battleships	82
USS *Texas*	84
Destroyers and Escorts	88
Submarine Warfare in World War I	90
World War I Submarines	92

1918–1945: THE BATTLEFIELD REDEFINED

After World War I, armies explored technological advances in the air and on land. As the world plunged once more into conflict in World War II, a period of dramatically swift progress took place in military technology.

The Era of Manoeuvre	96
Interwar Armoured Cars	98
Light, Medium, and Heavy Tanks	100
Vickers Medium Mark II	102
The Age of Monoplanes	106
The Warplane Evolves	108
World War II: Mass Mobility on Land	110
Logistics Trains	112
Military Motorcycles	114
Harley-Davidson WLC	116
Trucks, Half-tracks, and Light Vehicles	120
Rise of the "Jeep"	122
Axis Tanks	124
Tiger I	126
Allied Tanks	130
M4 Sherman	132
Engineering and Specialist Vehicles	136
Allied and Axis Tank Destroyers	138
Soviet Tanks	140
T-34/85	142
Armoured Cars and Troop Carriers	146
Aerial Combat Takes Centre Stage	148

Bombers	**150**
Boeing B-17	**152**
Fighter Planes	**156**
Supermarine Spitfire	**158**
The Gliders of World War II	**162**
Early Jets	**164**
Sea Battles in World War II	**166**
Battleships and Cruisers	**168**
HMS *Belfast*	**170**
Destroyers and Escorts in World War II	**174**
World War II Submarines	**176**
U-995 Submarine	**178**
Aircraft Carriers	**182**
Carrier and Maritime Strike Aircraft	**184**
The Normandy Landings	**186**

1945–1989: THE COLD WAR

In the postwar world, transport platforms for nuclear arms became paramount, including long-range bomber aircraft and nuclear submarines. Many already powerful weapons systems increased their threat and lethality.

The Age of Technology	**190**
Transporting Missiles	**192**
Communist Bloc Tanks	**194**
T-72	**196**
NATO Tanks	**200**
Prague Spring	**202**
Leopard I	**204**
Troop Carriers	**208**
Infantry Fighting Vehicles	**210**
Transporting Special Forces	**212**
Tanks of Non-aligned Nations	**214**
Cold War Land Vehicles	**216**
Entering the Jet Age	**218**
Jet Fighters	**220**
Military Transport Planes	**222**
F-86 Sabre	**224**
Bombers and Ground-attack Aircraft	**228**
Military Helicopters	**230**
The Helicopter Comes of Age	**232**
AH-64 Apache	**234**
Front-line Aircraft	**236**
Mikoyan MiG-29	**238**

Stealth Technology	**242**
The Changing Role of Navies	**244**
Cold War Frigates and Destroyers	**246**
Nuclear-powered Submarines	**248**
USS *Nautilus*	**250**
Military Patrol Boats	**252**

1989–PRESENT: THE HIGH-TECH AGE

The modern era has seen the deployment of massive aircraft carriers and nuclear submarines. The invasion of Ukraine brought a return of trench warfare and tank combat, as well as the use of drones. Future battlefields seem likely to be dominated by digital technology and increasing numbers of unmanned vehicles.

Present War, Future War	**256**
Counterinsurgency Vehicles	**258**
Buffel	**260**
Modern Tank Warfare	**264**
Troop Carriers	**266**

Post-Cold War Tanks	**268**
M1A2 Abrams	**270**
Amphibious Warfare	**274**
Warships in the Digital Age	**276**
21st-century Aircraft Carriers	**278**
USS *George Washington*	**280**
Modern Destroyers and Frigates	**284**
Nuclear-powered Submarines	**286**
Tech in the Sky and Beyond	**288**
High-tech Fighters	**290**
Eurofighter Typhoon	**292**
Drones in Modern Warfare	**296**
Drones	**298**
MQ-9 Reaper	**300**

REFERENCE

Seafaring Technology	**302**
Protective Technology	**304**
Flight Technology	**306**

GLOSSARY	**308**
INDEX	**312**
ACKNOWLEDGMENTS	**318**

Introduction

War has been a part of human history since records began. Throughout this time, military forces have had three basic requirements, which remain as pressing today as they were in ancient times: weapons, protection, and mobility. The third necessity is particularly notable – for military forces, a means of getting to the fight, or taking the fight to the enemy, is the key to victory.

The Military Transport Book illustrates and explains the technology that has made this possible. Covering land, sea, and air, it features military vehicles and mobile weapons platforms from antiquity to the present day, from the first chariots and the earliest warships to the latest nuclear submarines, jet fighters, and drones. The book explains these machines' roles and uses, and looks at key inventions and technological milestones.

War on the move

The need for transport in war is universal. In static (or attritional) warfare, armies meet and remain in relatively fixed positions, and try to wear each other down with repeated attacks and counterattacks. Mobile warfare, by contrast, employs speed to achieve strategic advantage. However, both types of warfare require vehicles to move troops and munitions – and on the battlefield, the more mobile an army is, the more easily it can out-manoeuvre or surround its opponent. Mobility makes it easier for an army to retreat to fight another day, rather than remaining to be defeated by an enemy's overwhelming force. Mobile warfare can also particularly benefit smaller armies that cannot match an enemy soldier-for-soldier or weapon-for-weapon. It enables the swift concentration of force on vulnerable areas, or on key targets such as headquarters, transport hubs, and supply centres.

Across land and sea

On land, for much of history, the distance a soldier could march in a day, and still be able to fight, was the limit of military mobility. The domestication of the horse in around 4,000 BCE revolutionized land warfare. A horse – which could carry not only its rider, but also his supplies – had far greater range, speed, and endurance than a foot soldier. These animals enabled mounted warriors to ride forward and scout for the enemy, charge into battle to fight as archers, swordsmen, and lancers, or dismount in a location that gave a tactical advantage. Horses could also pull chariots – the first vehicles used in an offensive role – and supply wagons.

The industrial revolution that took hold during the 19th century further transformed land warfare. The arrival of steam power and the internal combustion engine introduced railways and motor vehicles that sped up troop mobilization, while in World War I (1914–18), the first tanks brought mobile firepower to the battlefield.

> "Since the **dawn of history**, the **mobility of combat forces** has always been a **decisive element** in warfare."
> COL. ROBERT E. MCMAHON, US ARMY, "AIRMOBILE OPERATIONS", 1959

At sea and on waterways, boats provided a way of transporting soldiers swiftly to engage with the enemy, often over great distances, while avoiding land obstacles. They were also an efficient way to carry supplies. Boats soon opened up seas and rivers as a theatre of war, with the first recorded naval battle, the Battle of the Delta, taking place around 1175 BCE in Ancient Egypt.

Over the next millennia, fleets of vessels were able to bring whole armies ashore or evacuate them to safety, notably during the era of the Western Roman Empire (c. 27 BCE–476 CE). The "age of sail" (mid-1600s to mid-1800s) saw European sail-powered, ocean-going warships take centre stage. These were vital for protecting trade routes, while naval blockades of ports could starve an enemy into submission or prevent escape or rescue by water. In the early 1900s, the invention of the submarine took naval warfare beneath the waves, and these stealthy vessels rapidly became a mainstay of navies.

Taking to the skies

The sky, too, eventually became a battlefield. In the late 18th century, the French army first deployed balloons carrying observers to monitor enemy forces, and in 1804 Napoleon Bonaparte considered using balloons to invade Britain (he was advised against the idea due to the variable winds in the English Channel). Balloons also delivered military messages, and in 1849 Austrian forces attempted to use balloons to drop explosives onto Venice. Just over one decade after the first powered, heavier-than-air flight by the Wright brothers' *Flyer* in 1903, purpose-built aircraft were taking to the skies during World War I in reconnaissance, bomber, and fighter roles; this era also saw the first takeoff from an aircraft carrier.

During World War II (1939–45), both Axis and Allied powers realized that air power could bring destruction to cities and industrial centres far from the front line, which necessitated the creation of fleets of aeroplanes for defence. It also resulted in the movement and dispersal of factories out of bomber range, or even underground. Planes were also used to supply ground forces, and to drop or land ground troops by parachute or glider. From the 1940s, helicopters took on supply and transport roles, being well-suited to landing in difficult terrain; when equipped with weapons, they could defend themselves and carry out attacks on ground targets. From the jet age in the 1950s onwards, the need to fly faster to outpace enemy defences, to extend the range and altitude of flight, and to carry greater loads, has produced rapid technological developments in military aircraft. In the early 21st century, a new generation of remotely piloted drone aircraft is reshaping strategy and tactics.

Spotlighting these examples and many more, *The Military Transport Book* showcases in detail the numerous types of vehicles that humanity has invented to aid mobility in warfare. Often ingenious and groundbreaking, and in many cases lethal, these machines have shaped the world we live in today, and their successors will continue to do so in the centuries ahead.

To 1830
WHEELS, SAILS, AND GUNS

The Rise of Battlefield Mobility

By the end of the 4th millennium BCE, the foundations of military mobility for the next few thousand years were already in place – the foot, the horse, the wheel, the oar, and the sail. Based on these elements, a slow process of innovation paved the way for modern warfare.

For much of human history, the primary means of transport for land armies were the soldiers' own legs. Although simple, this could be very effective: a well-trained and fit army could traverse long distances and difficult terrain. In 218 BCE, for example, the Carthaginian commander Hannibal famously led his army across Spain, through Gaul, and into Italy to fight the Romans. During the ordeal of this five-month trek, the soldiers maintained an average daily distance of 21 km (13 miles), a figure made even more impressive because they crossed the Alps in the process. There are numerous other historical examples of epic military marches, some even in the 20th century. However, there are clear limits to foot mobility. The fastest walking pace is about 8 km/h (5 mph), but it can drop considerably depending on the nature of the landscape, the amount of load carried, and the physical wellbeing of the soldiers.

Horses in warfare

Horses were critical to improving military mobility (other animals used in similar capacities included mules, camels, and, occasionally, elephants). From the domestication of the horse in the 4th millennium BCE, horses provided armies with three main benefits. Firstly, they functioned as mounts for cavalry, which by the 1st millennium BCE was being used for fast manoeuvres and shock battlefield attacks, as well as offering mobile reconnaissance, screening, and other tactical functions. Secondly, horses could pull wheeled combat platforms such as chariots, war wagons, siege engines, and gun carriages,

> **TALKING POINT**
>
> ### Wheels
> Predated by crude log rollers, the first vehicular wheels are dated to around 3500 BCE. Wheels not only transformed human social and commercial history, but also revolutionized military logistics and tactics. Spoked wheels emerged around 2000 BCE. Lighter and with better shock-absorbing properties than their solid predecessors, they made possible the development of fast horse-drawn battle chariots. Chariot engineers in the ancient Near East and Middle East perfected the manoeuvrability of battle chariots by adjusting the placement of the axle relative to the centreline of the box (the chariot "carriage"). After this, solid wheels were reserved for drawing unusually heavy loads.
>
>
>
> **Egyptian pharaoh Ramesses II** takes aim with bow and arrow from the back of his war chariot during the Battle of Kadesh, in 1274 BCE, between Egyptian and Hittite armies.

enabling armies to deploy heavy fighting equipment. Thirdly, they greatly improved the logistical side of war. A powerful draught horse, for example, could pull a wheeled load of supplies weighing as much as 4,500 kg (9,000 lb).

However, employing horses in large numbers could require the transportation of immense volumes of forage, itself a logistical challenge – particularly if the campaign passed through land with poor grazing. During the autumn and winter months, a horse needed approximately 10 kg (22 lb) of grass, oats, or hay each day. Campaigns such as Napoleon's invasion of Russia in 1812, which used around 250,000 horses, give a sense of the potential scale of the amount of supplies that might be needed.

Galley warfare
The Battle of Lepanto in 1571 between the Holy League and the Ottoman Turks mainly involved galleys and galleasses – ships that were still driven in battle by oars rather than by sails.

Timeline
It did not take long for humans to utilize horses, wheels, oars, and sails as tools of warfare. In the first millennia of recorded history, chariots provided nimble mobile platforms for archers, warships evolved from oar-powered galleys into multi-gundeck galleons, and soldiers even made their first forays into the air.

- **c.3000 BCE** Egypt and Crete develop rowed galleys intended purely for warfare
- **c.2500 BCE** Mesopotamian armies deploy four-wheeled war wagons, drawn by donkeys or onagers
- **c.700 BCE** The Phoenicians introduce the bireme, with two banks of oars on each side
- **c.250 BCE** The Chinese use *Muyuan* military kites for signalling, communications, and weather observations
- **c.1600 BCE** Two-wheeled horse-drawn chariots appear in the Middle East, Africa, and Asia
- **c.600 BCE** War elephants are fielded by Indian Imperial armies as "living tanks"
- **c.480 BCE** The Greek trireme (three banks of oars) transforms Mediterranean warfare
- **c.119 BCE** Armoured wagons are utilized as mobile fortifications at the Battle of Mobei, China

THE RISE OF BATTLEFIELD MOBILITY · 13

Battle of Waterloo, 1815
At Waterloo, Napoleon's French forces were defeated by a coalition of European armies. As in ancient times, the battle was fought on foot and on horseback. Horses also drew field artillery.

On water, from ancient times until the 19th century, naval mobility relied on two devices: oars and sails. Oars propelled galleys, longships, and many small riverine craft. Speed was dictated by the numbers of oars in the water, but more rowers necessarily meant a heavier vessel. A Greek trireme of the 5th century BCE, for example, could achieve a maximum speed of about 9 knots (17 km/h) for short fighting distances, driven by 170 oars. Oar propulsion was ultimately restricted by the finite power of human muscle.

Harnessing the wind

Sails, by contrast, drew on the vast but often unpredictable power of the wind. Ships were fitted with masted sails by around 3500 BCE, but for centuries these sails were basic designs with limited efficiency, suitable mainly for short coastal journeys. Improvements in sail and ship design eventually gave rise to sail warships, which became instruments of global strategic power. These developments included the introduction of lateen sails (triangular sails that enabled ships to tack forward into even light winds); increases in the numbers and efficiency of both masts and sails, supported by extensive rigging; improvements in hull shape and construction, especially the shift from clinker-built (overlapping planks) to caravel-built (smoothly joined planks) hull profiles; and the introduction of centrally aligned rudders at the stern, fitted to a sternpost. These advances, and many others, allowed ships to increase dramatically in size – by the 15th century, a fully rigged galleon might weigh around 470 tonnes (518 tons) – and cross entire oceans laden with guns, cargo, and crew. They also gave warships better manoeuvring capabilities in battle, albeit at slow pace – 10 knots (18.5 km/h) would have been considered a good speed for a 17th-century ship-of-the-line.

The great "age of sail", which ran from the 16th to the 19th century, revolutionized naval mobility in terms of range, carrying capacity, and gunnery. Towards the end of the 19th century, the first steam boats entered civilian service. Spotting the potential, in 1814 the US Navy launched the *Demologos*, a floating battery that was the first military steamship. The future promised mobility for navies that was not dependent on the wind.

> "An aptitude for **war** is an aptitude for **movement**."
> NAPOLEON BONAPARTE, IN *MAXIMS FOR WAR*, 1831

c.350 CE The first Viking longships are built in Scandinavia

1400 Civilian masted sailing vessels, such as cogs and carracks, are converted to warships

1485 Leonardo da Vinci designs a prototype wheeled armoured fighting vehicle

1520 Three- or four-masted galleons emerge as the defining vessels of the age of sail warships

1794 The French Aerostatic Corps flies manned observation balloons at the Battle of Fleurus

1420 In central Europe, the Hussites use heavy war wagons at the Battle of Sudomer

1450 Limbers are developed in Europe to help tow wheeled artillery pieces

1765 French artillery officer Gribeauval standardizes artillery caissons to transport ammunition

1792 French surgeon Dominique-Jean Larrey designs military horse-drawn "flying ambulances"

1814 *Demologos*, a steam-powered floating battery, is launched in the US

Chariots and War Wagons

Horse-drawn chariots were first used as weapons of war in the 2nd millennium BCE, notably in southern Europe, the Near East, Central Asia, and the Indian subcontinent. The ancient equivalent of modern armoured fighting vehicles (AFVs), chariots carried archers, spear-throwers, or other soldiers in a small, low, open carriage called a box. They provided mobile fighting platforms that, directed by a skilled commander, could break up enemy troop formations, leaving them unable to resist a follow-up infantry assault. Chariots were less effective over rough ground, and they tended to fight at the speed of a brisk canter, since at a gallop they became difficult to control.

◁ Hittite chariot
Date 10th–8th century BCE
Origin Türkiye

The Hittites were pioneers of chariot warfare. As seen here, they manned their chariots with three warriors: a charioteer, an archer, and a third man who would dismount and fight on foot in close action. Here, the occupants carry shields to protect themselves against incoming arrows.

▽ Egyptian war carriage
Date 13th century BCE
Origin Egypt

Over time, Egyptian chariots moved the axle to the rear of the box to give a tight turning cycle and better performance at speed. They had two-man or three-man crews and operated in large chariot formations composed of a "host" of 250 chariots divided into five squadrons.

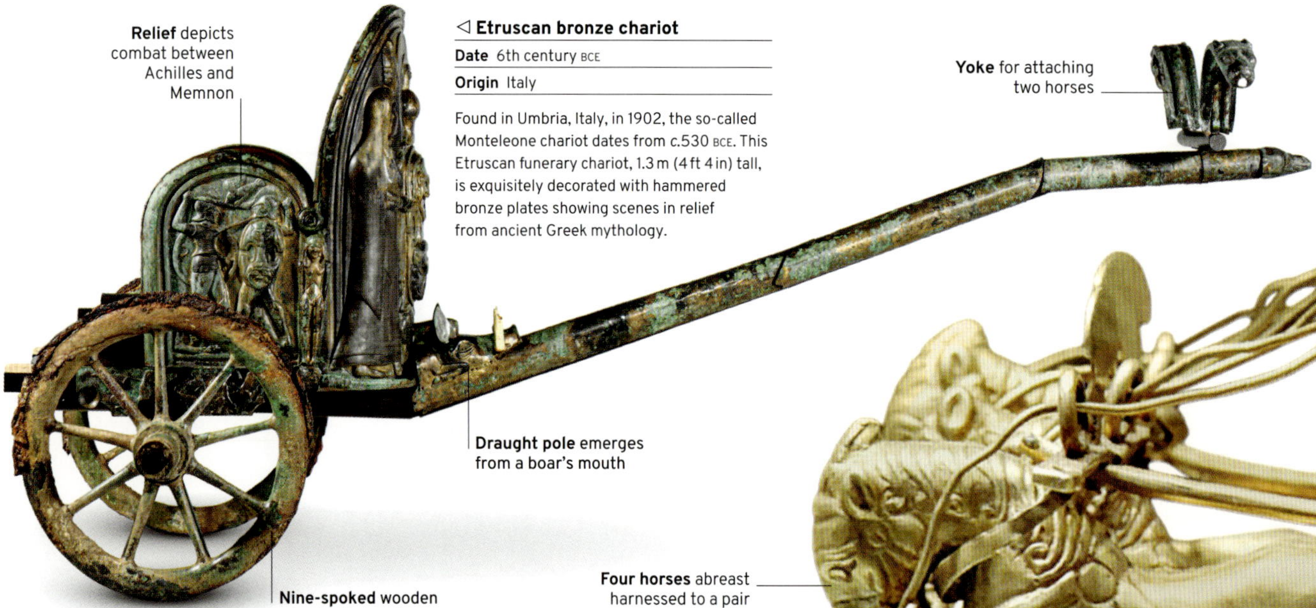

◁ Etruscan bronze chariot
Date 6th century BCE
Origin Italy

Found in Umbria, Italy, in 1902, the so-called Monteleone chariot dates from c.530 BCE. This Etruscan funerary chariot, 1.3 m (4 ft 4 in) tall, is exquisitely decorated with hammered bronze plates showing scenes in relief from ancient Greek mythology.

Relief depicts combat between Achilles and Memnon

Yoke for attaching two horses

Draught pole emerges from a boar's mouth

Nine-spoked wooden wheel with iron tyre

Four horses abreast harnessed to a pair of draught poles

◁ Greek chariot
Date 6th century BCE
Origin Greece

Greek chariots were generally of unsophisticated design, with simple, four-spoked wheels and the axle running under the centre of the box. This axle position improved stability, but it also reduced manoeuvrability compared to chariots that had their axle at the rear of the box.

△ **Indian chariot**

Date 3rd century BCE

Origin India

Depictions of ancient Indian chariots show vehicles with either spoked or solid wheels. The chariot box, known as a *kosha*, was made of either wicker or a leather-coated wooden framework. This scene from the Great Stupa at Sanchi shows King Ashoka on his chariot.

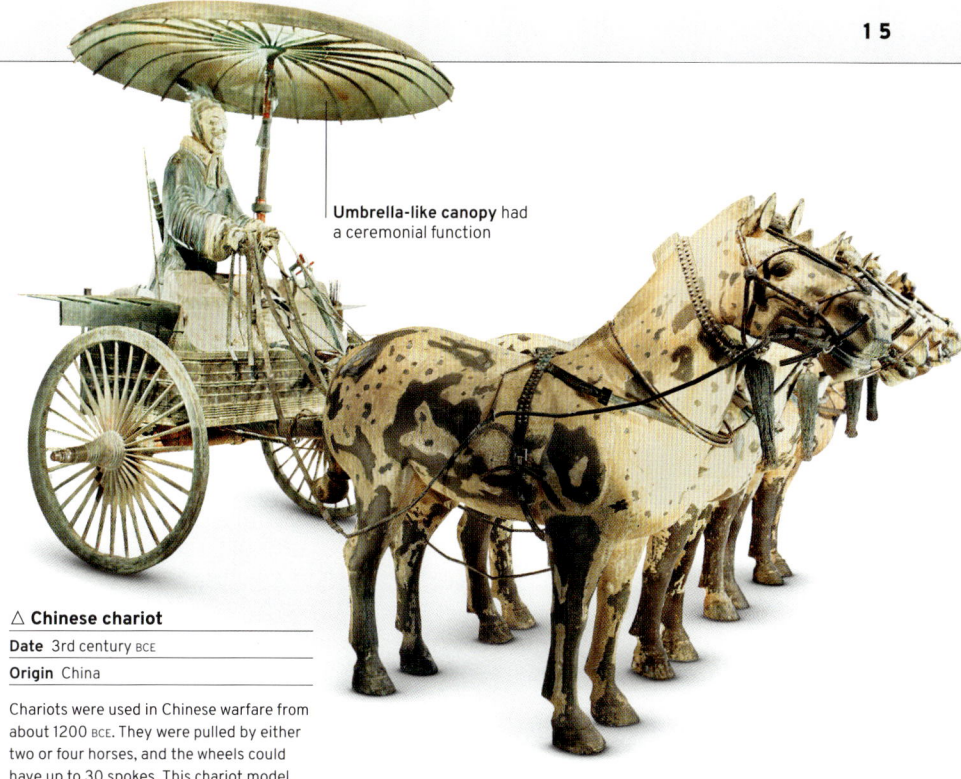

Umbrella-like canopy had a ceremonial function

△ **Chinese chariot**

Date 3rd century BCE

Origin China

Chariots were used in Chinese warfare from about 1200 BCE. They were pulled by either two or four horses, and the wheels could have up to 30 spokes. This chariot model dates from the Qin Dynasty (221–206 BCE).

◁ **Persian chariot**

Date 4th–5th century CE

Origin Persia

Less than 8 cm (3 in) tall, this finely detailed gold model of a square-fronted Persian chariot carries a driver and a robed figure, possibly a satrap (a governor of the Persian Empire). The chariot is drawn by four horses under a single four-bay yoke, rather than the more typical two-horse arrangement.

Wheel studs were attachment points for a tyre and bronze sheath

▽ **War wagon**

Date 2600 BCE–16th century

Origin Mesopotamia

The Standard of Ur – a Sumerian wooden box from the 3rd millennium BCE inlaid with shell, red limestone, and lapis lazuli – bears depictions of war wagons with four solid wheels. War wagons were used in battle by various cultures in Asia and Europe until around the 1500s.

▽ **Roman chariot**

Date Unknown

Origin Rome

Roman chariots were designed for speed; chariot teams often competed against one another in public races. Iron tyres might be applied to the wheels to enhance their grip. Chariots also featured in triumphal processions, but the Roman Army did not use them for warfare.

Ram's head motif atop draught pole

Leonardo da Vinci's "Tank"

"I can make armoured cars, safe and unassailable, which will enter the closed ranks of the enemy… behind these our infantry will be able to follow quite unharmed". So boasted Italian artist and inventor Leonardo da Vinci in 1482, in a letter to Ludovico Sforza, Duke of Milan, in an attempt to win the patronage of the powerful nobleman.

Around 1485, da Vinci made sketches for military inventions, including a "war car". Regarded as one of the precursors of the tank, Da Vinci's vehicle comprised a protective wooden shell reinforced by metal plates, with holes around the perimeter through which light cannons could fire in all directions. Two cranks, turned manually, would have driven four wheels to propel the vehicle. With angled surfaces to deflect incoming projectiles, the design looks surprisingly modern.

Da Vinci's sketch was primarily a concept to win favour with the duke. It contains a flaw, possibly intentionally, to protect his work: the cranks would have turned the wheels in opposite directions, making the vehicle undriveable. The technology to make the "tank" a reality did not exist at the time, but modern recreations (with the flaw corrected) have shown it could only have travelled over very flat surfaces, rendering it unsuitable for the rugged terrain of contemporary battlefields.

Leonardo da Vinci's sketches of his "war car" (lower left and right) show the crank mechanism and the vehicle's exterior, below his idea for a chariot armed with rotating scythes.

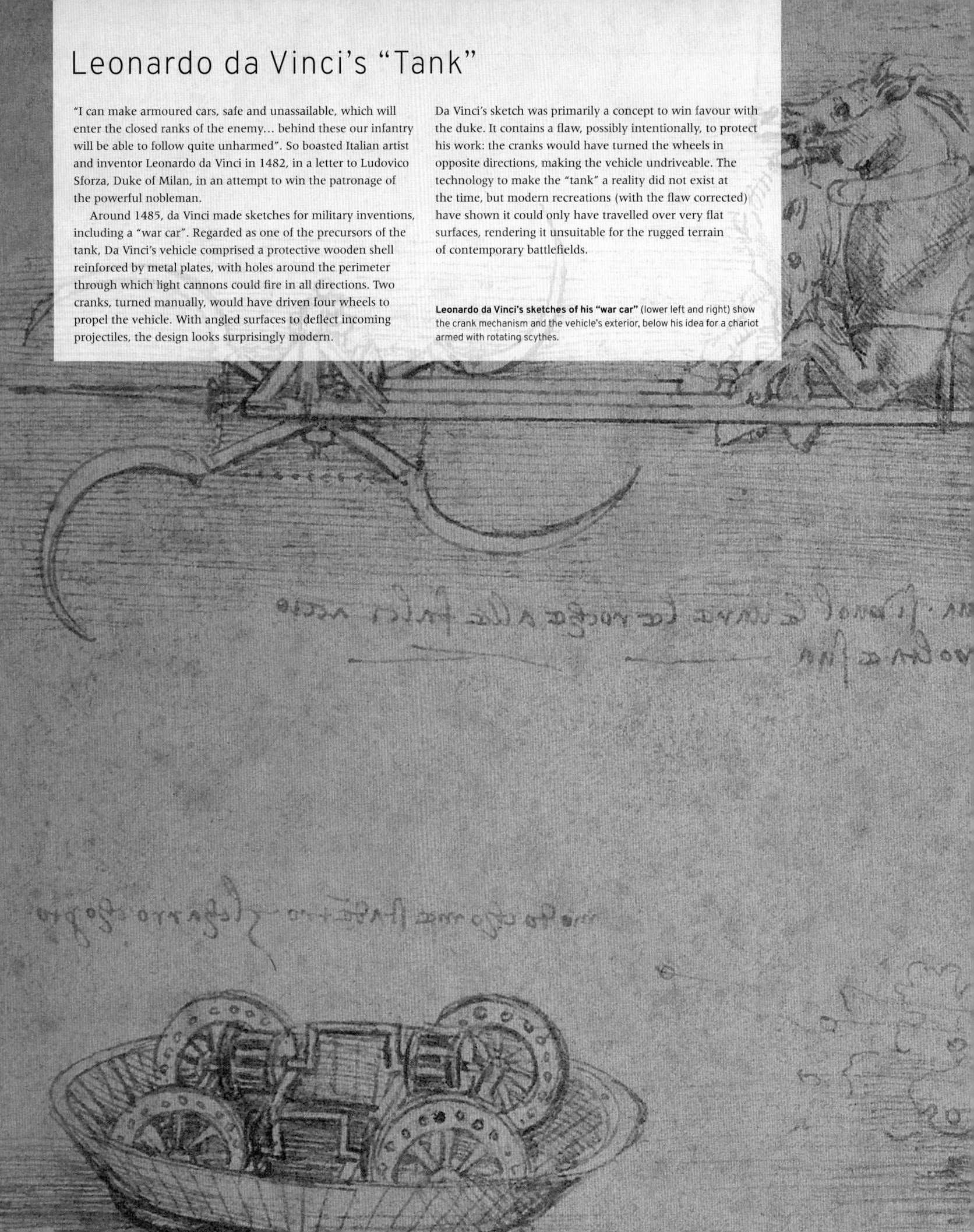

The Sea as a Battlefield

For over two millennia, naval warfare was dominated by galleys, which were propelled into combat by oars and often supported by merchant sailing ships that delivered logistics and could land troops ashore. The rise of the great fleets of sail warships, which began in the 1500s, transformed the strategic potential of navies from largely coastal forces into blue-water fleets able to traverse the oceans.

Ancient galley battle
This depiction of the Battle of Actium in 31 BCE provides a window into the reality of galley warfare, which often involved infantry combat taking place on floating platforms. At Actium, the Roman triumvir Octavian defeated the fleets of Mark Antony and Cleopatra.

From the start of recorded military history until the Renaissance, naval forces had a limited operational range. The primary instrument of war across this entire period was the galley – a vessel propelled by banks of oars with the assistance of two or three masts rigged with triangular lateen sails.

Muscle-powered navies

Galley-design variations were largely limited to the numbers of oars, the size of the vessel, and displacement. For example, an Athenian trireme of the 5th century BCE had 170 oarsmen manning three banks of oars, with the ship itself measuring about 37 m (120 ft) long and displacing about 45 tonnes (49 tons). A typical Roman quinquereme of the 1st century BCE was significantly upscaled – it had five banks of oars powered by 300 rowers, was around 45 m (148 ft) in length, and had a displacement of around 100 tonnes (110 tons) with its full complement. However, the overall design principle changed very little.

In fact, the galleys fighting in the Battle of Salamis in 480 BCE and the Battle of Lepanto, over 2,000 years later, in 1571 CE shared the same core design. Used at Lepanto, the Venetian innovation of the "galleass" was essentially a double-sized galley. Naval combat at this time was basic: enemy ships were typically sunk by ramming or captured after a successful boarding action.

The predominance of shallow-draft, oar-and-sail-powered galleys meant that prior to the 1500s, battles at sea were typically fought relatively close to coastlines (especially across the Mediterranean and its adjacent seas) or within reach of home or friendly ports. Of course, some vessels did travel long distances, notably the sail-powered Viking longships, which had made transatlantic journeys by the 10th century.

Raising the sails

From around the 1500s, multiple revolutions in the design of warships transformed naval tactics and maritime strategy. In Europe, the rise of the three-masted galleon, with raised "castles" fore and aft and broadside cannon arranged across multiple decks, ushered in the age of fighting sail. Properly provisioned and with favourable winds, these formidable vessels eventually gave nations hemispheric range. As well as range, protection also saw advances in this era. In Korea, Admiral Yi Sun-sin (1545–98) developed the *kŏbuksŏn* ("turtle ship"), essentially a cannon-armed wooden galley, but fully enclosed by iron plates. Turtle ships were, in effect, the first armoured warships.

The great fleets

The English, Spanish, Portuguese, Dutch, French, and others built vast fleets of sail warships to establish, maintain, and protect their empires and oceanic shipping lanes. Naval warfare was now fought ever further from home and the shore, although the needs of provisioning meant that coastlines were usually kept

Viking longship
The longships of the Vikings were ideal raiding vessels. Powered by oars and a single square sail, longships had a slender design and a shallow-draft hull that made them fast, manoeuvrable, and easy to beach.

The age of sail ships
Unleashing broadsides as they fight in the "line of battle", French and British warships engage at the Battle of the Chesapeake on 5 September 1781, during the American Revolutionary War. Victory went to the French.

within comfortable range. By the 18th century, the British Royal Navy had built the world's largest and most formidable fleet, eclipsing those of Spain and the Netherlands. France challenged for the naval crown in the Napoleonic age, but Britain retained the edge through its command professionalism and its superior seamanship and gunnery.

The frequent and lengthy wars between 1500 and 1830 saw naval tactics honed and tested, especially through the debate between those who advocated rigid lines of attack and those who favoured a less structured "melee" approach to engaging enemy vessels. By 1830, the world's first steamships had also made an appearance, inaugurating the next revolution in naval warfare.

> "… **no Captain** can do very wrong if he **places his ship** alongside that of the **enemy**."
> BRITISH ADMIRAL HORATIO NELSON, MEMORANDUM TO SHIP COMMANDERS BEFORE THE BATTLE OF TRAFALGAR, OCTOBER 1805

TALKING POINT

Greek fire

An incendiary composition, "Greek fire" was developed by the Byzantine Greeks during the 7th century CE as an anti-ship weapon. Its exact formula is unknown, but it probably included naphtha or petroleum mixed with sulphur or pitch. The result was a viscous substance that glued itself to wooden ships and burned ferociously; according to the accounts of ancient writers, it even flamed away on the water's surface. Either ejected under air pressure from metal tubes or hurled in pottery grenades, Greek fire was highly effective. It played a key role in repelling the first Arab siege of Constantinople in 674–78 CE and in several major battles thereafter, and it was still being used as late as the 13th century.

This Byzantine manuscript depicts Greek fire being launched under pressure from a metal tube mounted at the prow of an attacking ship, engulfing an enemy vessel in flames.

Olympias Greek Trireme

Light, speedy, manoeuvrable galleys called triremes helped the ancient Greeks extend their influence and power throughout the Mediterranean. While no trireme has survived from antiquity, a full-scale reconstruction based on historical evidence, the *Olympias*, was built at Piraeus, Athens, between 1985 and 1987.

Full speed ahead
In trials under sail, and with a favourable wind, the *Olympias* achieved speeds of around 9 knots (17 km/h).

APPROXIMATELY 37 M (120 FT) LONG and 5.5 m (18 ft) wide, the shallow-draught *Olympias* proved to be agile and fast in sea trials, turning about in twice its own length and reaching almost 9 knots (17 km/h) under oar. Steered by a helmsman operating a pair of tillers, a trireme like *Olympias* would have cruised under sail but relied on oarsmen for propulsion in battle. The 170 rowers sat in three staggered tiers, each with its own type of oarsmen: 54 thalamians at the bottom, 54 zygians in the middle, and 62 thranites on top. Thranites were paid the most, since the steep angle at which their oars entered the water made for harder work. Around 30 other men, including marine hoplites and archers, completed the crew. There was room for only a few basic supplies and insufficient space for everyone to sleep on board.

In battle, a well-trained, disciplined trireme crew could use the ship's bronze prow ram to hole an enemy vessel, or ride over its oars and then reverse to render it helpless. If its own hull was pierced, a trireme would not sink because it was made of buoyant wood such as pine, poplar, or fir.

SPECIFICATIONS	
Model	*Olympias*
Origin	Greece
Date	Built 1985–87; replica of a c.5th century BCE trireme
Displacement	47 tonnes (51.8 tons)
Length	36.9 m (121 ft 1 in)
Propulsion	Two sails; 170 oarsmen
Armament	Bronze prow ram, 10 spears, 4 archers
Maximum speed	Approx. 9 knots (17 km/h)

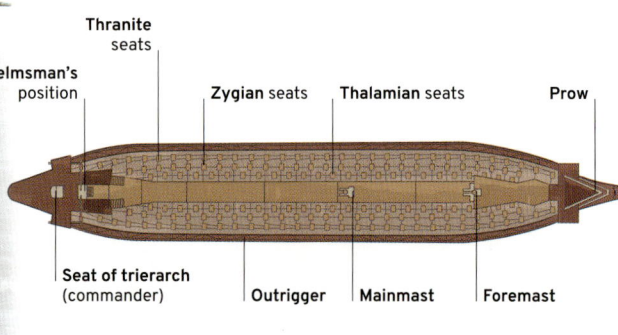

EXTERIOR

Sailors dropped and weighed anchor from platforms called *epotides* (ears) near the prow. Oars on the lowest tier had leather sheaths to keep water of the hull. Outriggers on the top tier allowed the thranites to row in a position outboard of the tiers below. The two steering oars (rudders) could also be used as a brake.

1. Bronze prow ram **2.** Ear and anchor **3.** Tiers of oars (showing leather sheaths) **4.** Outrigger **5.** Steering oar

INTERIOR

Each rower sat level with the shoulders of the oarsman on the tier below. The helmsman at the stern overlooked the slot between the decks, where the mast was stowed. *Olympias* tested various rowing techniques, securing one foot to the stretcher.

6. Thranites' benches **7.** Stretcher (to push against when rowing) **8.** Oarsmen's seats **9.** View from the stern **10.** Tiller

▷ Greek trireme

Date 7th–4th century BCE   **Origin** Greece
Displacement c.50 tonnes (55 tons)
Length 37 m (121 ft)
Propulsion 7–9 knots (13–17 km/h)

The defining warship of the Mediterranean and adjacent seas in ancient times was the trireme, a type of galley. Most of a trireme's crew of 200 were oarsmen. Triremes played a major role in the wars of the 5th century BCE.

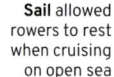

Sail allowed rowers to rest when cruising on open sea

Three tiers of oars propelled boat in battle

Prow ram for holing enemy ships

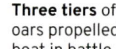

◁ Viking longship

Date 3rd century BCE–9th century CE   **Origin** Scandinavia
Displacement c.20 tonnes (22 tons)
Length Up to 23 m (75 ft)
Propulsion 10–12 knots (19–22 km/h)

A design so successful that it lasted for more than 1,000 years, the Viking longship had excellent sailing abilities in rough, open seas. Its shallow draught also allowed it to sail up rivers and onto beaches, making it an ideal raiding vessel.

Clinker-built hull, made of overlapping planks

Shields placed over the oar holes to protect the rowers

△ Roman troop ship

Date 27 BCE–476 CE   **Origin** Rome
Displacement c.150 tonnes (165 tons)
Length 30 m (98 ft)
Propulsion 5–6 knots (9–11 km/h)

The Roman Army ferried its soldiers across the sea in merchant ships, or *navis oneraria*, that it repurposed for military transport. Large examples of these vessels could carry up to 300 troops, although with limited space for cargo and equipment.

◁ Venetian galley

Date 15th–16th century CE   **Origin** Italy
Displacement c.120 tonnes (132 tons)
Length 42 m (138 ft)
Propulsion 6–7 knots (11–13 km/h)

This large Venetian galley has lateen-sail masts in addition to its banks of oars, indicative of the fact that when such ships were not at war they were often used for long-distance trading voyages.

▽ Algerian xebec

Date 16th century CE   **Origin** Algeria
Displacement c.150 tonnes (165 tons)
Length 30 m (98 ft)
Propulsion 12–14 knots (22–26 km/h)

The *xebec* (or *chebec*) was a trade ship that operated in the Mediterranean Sea. The Barbary corsairs of the North African coast converted xebecs into warships by adding up to 40 guns, although 15–30 guns was a more typical armament.

Early Warships

Purpose-built warships took to the waves in the Mediterranean during the 1st millennium BCE, in the form of fighting galleys. In combat, these vessels were powered by banks of oars, the number of oars increasing over time depending on the period and the culture. Galley warfare prevailed until the medieval era, when sail power gradually took over. In Europe, simple cargo sailing ships known as cogs were converted for warfare, with high "castles" added fore and aft as fighting platforms for archers and other missile troops. From such ships evolved the large cannon-armed carracks, galleons, and other vessels of the age of sail.

Overhanging bowsprit for anchoring sail of foremast

Oar holes along sides of ship

EARLY WARSHIPS · 23

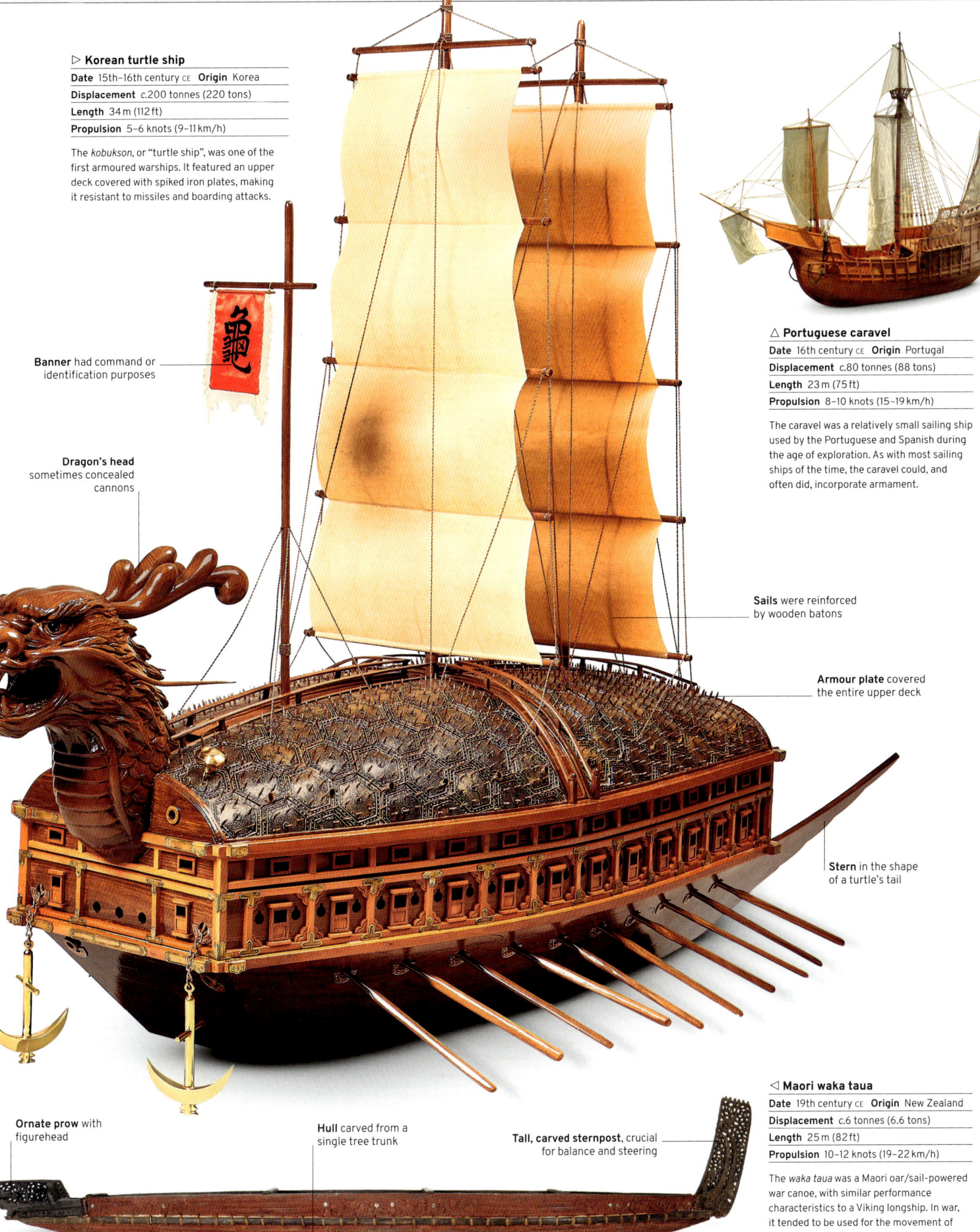

▷ Korean turtle ship
Date 15th–16th century CE **Origin** Korea
Displacement c.200 tonnes (220 tons)
Length 34 m (112 ft)
Propulsion 5–6 knots (9–11 km/h)

The *kobukson*, or "turtle ship", was one of the first armoured warships. It featured an upper deck covered with spiked iron plates, making it resistant to missiles and boarding attacks.

Banner had command or identification purposes

Dragon's head sometimes concealed cannons

Sails were reinforced by wooden batons

Armour plate covered the entire upper deck

Stern in the shape of a turtle's tail

Ornate prow with figurehead

Hull carved from a single tree trunk

Tall, carved sternpost, crucial for balance and steering

△ Portuguese caravel
Date 16th century CE **Origin** Portugal
Displacement c.80 tonnes (88 tons)
Length 23 m (75 ft)
Propulsion 8–10 knots (15–19 km/h)

The caravel was a relatively small sailing ship used by the Portuguese and Spanish during the age of exploration. As with most sailing ships of the time, the caravel could, and often did, incorporate armament.

◁ Maori waka taua
Date 19th century CE **Origin** New Zealand
Displacement c.6 tonnes (6.6 tons)
Length 25 m (82 ft)
Propulsion 10–12 knots (19–22 km/h)

The *waka taua* was a Maori oar/sail-powered war canoe, with similar performance characteristics to a Viking longship. In war, it tended to be used for the movement of warriors along the New Zealand coastline to achieve tactical advantage.

HMS Victory

Built from the wood of around 6,000 trees, mostly oak, this first-rate British ship of the line was launched in 1765. The *Victory* was the flagship of Admiral Horatio Nelson at the Battle of Trafalgar, in 1805, when the Royal Navy defeated the combined Spanish and French fleets. It is the world's oldest ship still officially in naval service.

LAUNCHED IN 1765 but held in reserve for its first 13 years, the *Victory* first saw action in 1778, when the British fleet engaged the French at the Battle of Ushant. It later became the Royal Navy's flagship in the Mediterranean, and spearheaded the action that destroyed the Spanish fleet at the Battle of Cape St Vincent in 1797. It played a key role in the Battle of Trafalgar, and remained in active service until 1812. The *Victory*'s 104 smoothbore, muzzle-loading cannon gave it phenomenal firepower. For stability, the *Victory*'s heaviest guns, the 32-pounders, were positioned on the lower gun deck. The middle gun deck held the 24-pounders, while the 12-pounders were located on the upper gun deck. To keep its cannon fed with ammunition, the ship carried about 122 tonnes (134 tons) of cast-iron shot, the largest weighing 14.5 kg (32 lb).

SPECIFICATIONS	
Name	HMS *Victory*
Commissioned	1778
Displacement	3,556 tonnes (3,920 tons)
Length	69.34 m (227 ft 6 in)
Depth of hold	6.55 m (21 ft 6 in)
Propulsion	Sail
Armament	At Trafalgar: 104 guns, including 32-, 24-, and 12-pounders
Maximum speed	Up to 11 knots (20 km/h)

Warship at rest
The *Victory* has gone through five major repairs since its launch in 1765; it had been almost entirely rebuilt by the time of Trafalgar in 1805. Now restored to its pre-Trafalgar condition, HMS *Victory* sits in dry dock at Portsmouth, England.

EXTERIOR

Men climbed along the yards (horizontal spars) of the three masts to set or furl the sails. The masts are supported by ropes known as standing rigging; running rigging refers to the ropes that raise, lower, and manipulate sails. In total, the *Victory*'s 42 km (26 miles) of rigging used 768 blocks, or pulleys, the biggest of which are called jeer blocks. Ropes were also used to open and close the gun ports along the hull. Two powerful, short-barrelled carronade guns were mounted on the forecastle. The *Victory* had seven anchors; the largest and heaviest required 144 men to raise it. The double wheel was located aft on the quarterdeck, under the poop.

1. Stern **2.** Wheel and binnacle holding a lantern and two compasses **3.** Gun ports **4.** Mainmast and rigging **5.** Carronade **6.** Figurehead

INTERIOR

The *Victory* carried 820 men, including 146 marines, most of whom lived among the cannon on the gun decks. The men slept in hammocks slung from the beams; meals were taken at mess tables suspended between the guns. The magazines were on the orlop deck and in the hold, which both lay below the water line, safe from enemy fire. The hold also held stores and ballast. In the stern were cabins for the admiral, captain, and other officers.

7. 32-pounder guns **8.** Nelson's sleeping cabin **9.** Sick berth **10.** Captain's day cabin

End of an Era

The Battle of Navarino on 20 October 1827, during the Greek War of Independence (1821–29), was the last great action of the age of sail. The Treaty of London in July had committed Britain, Russia, and France to work together for Greek independence from Ottoman rule. Under the British vice-admiral Sir Edward Codrington, a combined fleet from the three nations entered the bay at Navarino (modern Pylos in southern Greece), where a larger Ottoman fleet was anchored. Codrington tried to open negotiations, but firing broke out. The ensuing battle was utterly one-sided: the allies' achieved a decisive victory through superior firepower, skill, and tactics, losing no ships but destroying much of the opposing fleet. A pivotal moment in the war, the battle ended Ottoman naval dominance in the region and helped pave the way for an independent Greek state.

With cannons blazing and ships burning, this engraving conveys the drama of the battle. Navarino caught the public imagination: many prints and souvenirs were made, and Codrington became a national hero.

28 • TO 1830

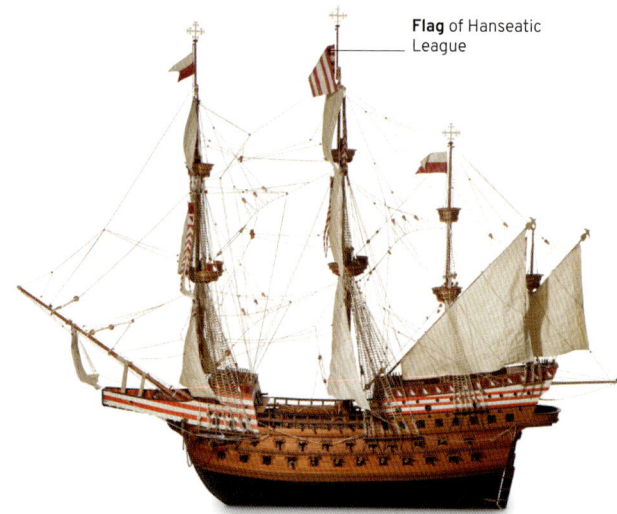

△ **Adler von Lübeck**
Date 1567 **Origin** Lübeck
Displacement 3,050 tonnes (3,360 tons)
Length 78 m (256 ft)
Propulsion Sail (4 masts)

Built as a warship to protect trade between ports of the Hanseatic League during the Northern Seven Years War (1563–70), *Adler von Lübeck* was one of the largest sea-going vessels of its day. Converted into a merchant vessel when peace was declared, the ship carried cargo until 1588.

△ **HMS Revenge**
Date 1577 **Origin** England
Displacement 447 tonnes (492 tons)
Length 43 m (140 ft)
Propulsion Sail (4 masts)

The 46-gun *Revenge* fought in numerous actions, including the defeat of the Spanish Armada in 1588 under the command of Sir Francis Drake. The ship was captured by the Spanish after a long fight off the Azores in 1591, but then sank after running into cliffs.

◁ **Spanish galleon**
Date 1698 **Origin** Iberian Peninsula
Displacement 500–1,000 tonnes (550–1,100 tons)
Length 40–60 m (130–200 ft)
Propulsion Sail (3 or 4 masts)

Developed in Spain and Portugal in the 16th and 17th centuries, galleons were armed cargo ships with a raised rear quarterdeck. Their armament depended on the period of their use and the threats they might encounter. Galleons transported wealth from colonies in the Americas to the Iberian Peninsula, braving encounters with enemy navies, privateers, and pirates, as well as the Atlantic weather.

△ **Santisima Trinidad**
Date 1769 **Origin** Cuba
Displacement 5,030 tonnes (5,545 tons)
Length 61 m (200 ft)
Propulsion Sail (3 masts)

Designed by an Irishman, Michael Mullan, working for the Spanish in Havana, Cuba, the *Santisima Trinidad* carried 136 guns, more than any other ship of its day. After fighting in numerous engagements against the British Royal Navy, sometimes as the Spanish flagship, *Santisima Trinidad* was captured at Trafalgar in 1805, and eventually scuttled off Cadiz. A full-sized replica is shown here.

The Great Age of Sail

The development of large, well-armed, sail-powered warships gave navies the ability to protect trade routes around the world and extend their power. Ships designed to line up and engage the enemy in broadsides during battle were known as ships of the line. The British Royal Navy classed the largest of these ships, which carried over 100 guns of varying calibres, as first-rate ships; second-rate and third-rate ships carried correspondingly fewer guns. Frigates were fourth-rate ships not considered suitable for the line of battle; they were less well armed than ships of the line, but significantly faster.

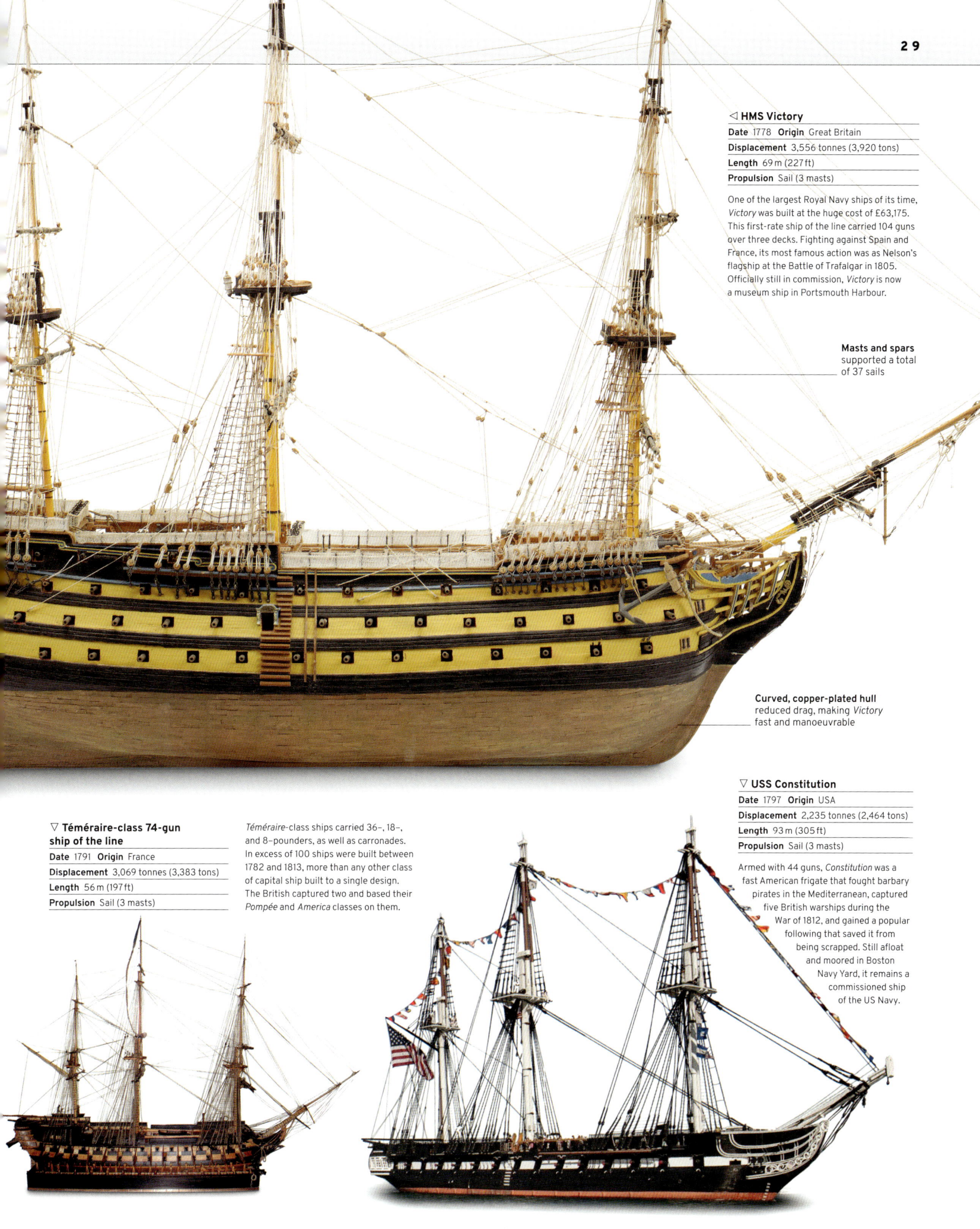

◁ HMS Victory

Date 1778	**Origin** Great Britain
Displacement 3,556 tonnes (3,920 tons)	
Length 69 m (227 ft)	
Propulsion Sail (3 masts)	

One of the largest Royal Navy ships of its time, *Victory* was built at the huge cost of £63,175. This first-rate ship of the line carried 104 guns over three decks. Fighting against Spain and France, its most famous action was as Nelson's flagship at the Battle of Trafalgar in 1805. Officially still in commission, *Victory* is now a museum ship in Portsmouth Harbour.

Masts and spars supported a total of 37 sails

Curved, copper-plated hull reduced drag, making *Victory* fast and manoeuvrable

▽ Téméraire-class 74-gun ship of the line

Date 1791	**Origin** France
Displacement 3,069 tonnes (3,383 tons)	
Length 56 m (197 ft)	
Propulsion Sail (3 masts)	

Téméraire-class ships carried 36–, 18–, and 8–pounders, as well as carronades. In excess of 100 ships were built between 1782 and 1813, more than any other class of capital ship built to a single design. The British captured two and based their *Pompée* and *America* classes on them.

▽ USS Constitution

Date 1797	**Origin** USA
Displacement 2,235 tonnes (2,464 tons)	
Length 93 m (305 ft)	
Propulsion Sail (3 masts)	

Armed with 44 guns, *Constitution* was a fast American frigate that fought barbary pirates in the Mediterranean, captured five British warships during the War of 1812, and gained a popular following that saved it from being scrapped. Still afloat and moored in Boston Navy Yard, it remains a commissioned ship of the US Navy.

1830–1918
THE MECHANIZATION OF WAR

Engines of War

The age of mechanically driven military vehicles emerged between 1830 and 1918. The invention of engines fuelled by coal, oil, petrol, and diesel heralded new types of transport, from huge dreadnought battleships to military aircraft.

The transformative force in military transportation during the 19th century was steam power. Steam engines were initially developed in the 18th century for industrial and agricultural applications. As power outputs and efficiency increased, the new engines gave rise to steam-powered trains and ships, which in turn quickly found military applications.

The first steam locomotives were designed by Englishman John Blenkinsop in 1812–13 to haul coal in mines, and by 1822 Britain had its first passenger railway line, the Stockton and Darlington Railway. Rail networks subsequently spread across Britain and its empire, Europe, the US, and, eventually, the rest of the world. In trains and railways there was great potential for scaling up military mobilization and deployment. Railways could concentrate the mass movement of men and materiel in timetabled, reliable journeys, less constrained by terrain and free from the challenges of overland horse logistics.

Navies under steam

The steam revolution soon found its way onto ships. Sails remained in use throughout the 19th century, and continuing improvements in sail layouts and hull design raised the speed of sail vessels. However, by 1840, steamships were making unassisted crossings of the Atlantic. Civilian steam ships, like civilian railways, were soon repurposed as troop transports. The first transatlantic steamer, Isambard Kingdom Brunel's *Great Western*, made its maiden voyage in April 1838, but by 1856 it was being used to ferry British soldiers to the Crimean War. Furthermore, from 1859, "ironclad" warships began to emerge, steam-powered and clad in steel or iron armour. In 1860, the inaugural steam-powered, fully iron-hulled warship, HMS *Warrior*, took to the waves. This

> **TALKING POINT**
>
> ### Rail and War
>
> The first major use of rail in warfare occurred in the late 1840s. During the European revolutions of 1848, trains were used to move soldiers rapidly to contested cities, and Prussia deployed thousands of troops by rail during its war against Denmark of 1848–51. While the Prussians refined military rail transportation to a high degree of efficiency during the Franco-Prussian War of 1870–71, the American Civil War of 1861–65 stakes its claim to being history's first large-scale "railway war". In the autumn of 1863 alone, around 20,000 men were transferred 1,930 km (1,200 miles) by rail to the front lines. The war also featured the first railway guns and armoured rail cars that could function as mobile fortifications.
>
>
>
> **The "Dictator"** was a heavy mortar used by Union forces in 1864, during the American Civil War. It fired from a rail flatcar, although the recoil of its first firing destroyed the platform.

began the rise of the steel-and-steam warship, which by the "dreadnought" age of the early 20th century included powerful battleships with transoceanic range, heavy turreted guns, and crews of more than 1,000.

Land vehicles

On land, steam power was not just adopted by locomotives. In Britain, the first steam traction engine purpose-built to pull artillery was developed in 1870. Such vehicles became relatively common in the late 19th century and during World War I, not least because field artillery pieces were growing considerably heavier. These vehicles had serious limitations, being slow and cumbersome, and their smoking chimneys could act as markers for enemy artillery. There was, however, an alternative power source available in this era.

Battle of Tsushima, 1905
Tsushima, fought in the waters between Korea and Japan during the Russo-Japanese War, was a crushing defeat for the Russian fleet against a confident Japanese Navy.

Timeline
As the 19th century progressed, literal horse power progressively gave way to the mechanical "horsepower" that engines could generate by steam and internal combustion. As a result, by the beginning of World War I, armies had entered a new industrial age. It was an era of iron, motorization, armour, and the early stages of combat aviation.

- **1846** The Prussian Army pioneers the use of trains for military transportation
- **1859** The French launch the first ironclad warship, the *Gloire*
- **1860** The British launch HMS *Warrior*, the first iron-hulled, armoured warship
- **1861** A rail baggage wagon is converted to an armoured carriage during the American Civil War
- **1864** In the American Civil War, a Confederate submarine CSS *Hunley* becomes the first submarine to sink another ship in combat
- **1870s** Fast torpedo boats enter service in European navies

ENGINES OF WAR · 33

World War I railway gun
US Navy gunners pose for the camera, distributed along a 357 mm (14 in) railway gun on a Mark 1 Army mount. Able to engage targets beyond the range of traditional artillery, the gun was used to support US troops on the Meuse-Argonne battlefield in northern France.

By World War I, modern armies had embraced the possibilities of the internal combustion engine (ICE), which had been invented in Germany in the 1870s. The ICE gave birth to the civilian car, motorbike, and truck, and it gradually became clear that all three modes of transport could be adapted for military use. The first steps into the mechanization and motorization of armed forces began around 1910, principally using trucks as supply vehicles. During World War I, many thousands of trucks, including types designed specifically for military use, performed logistical and support roles on all fronts.

The conflict also saw the rise of ICE-powered armoured fighting vehicles (AFVs), including armoured cars and the first tanks. The performance and reliability of military vehicles at this time were poor. British Mk IV tanks of World War I, for example, had a top speed of just 6.4 km/h (4 mph), were deafening and suffocating to operate, and broke down constantly. They did, however, demonstrate the shock value of mobile, armoured firepower, particularly when used en masse.

Airborne warfare

The early 20th century saw a completely new addition to vehicular warfare: the aeroplane. Powered, pilot-controlled aeroplane flight was born in 1903, and just a decade later planes had developed sufficiently to be useful for military purposes. At first these purposes were mainly reconnaissance and observation, but aircraft types soon diversified, producing bombers, fighters, and ground-attack aircraft. As with early tanks, performance was limited. A typical biplane fighter had a top speed of around 177 km/h (110 mph) and a range of around 482 km (300 miles). Although dangerous to fly, let alone to fight in, the impact of these warplanes was profound: they opened up a new kind of warfare, and the use of military technology in the skies would become one of the defining features of warfare in the 20th century and beyond.

> "We need **bold and free flight,** we need **mobility!**"
> SOVIET REVOLUTIONARY AND MILITARY COMMANDER MIKHAIL FRUNZE, 1921

1884 Driven by an electric motor, *La France* makes the world's first fully controlled airship flight near Paris

1903 The American Wright brothers' *Flyer* makes the first flight of a manned, powered, controllable, heavier-than-air aircraft

1904 The French vessel *Aigrette* becomes history's first diesel-electric powered submarine

1909 In the US, the Wright Military Flyer, the world's first military aircraft, enters service

1914 Introduction of the first bomber aircraft

1880s The destroyer emerges as a new type of warship

1902 Design of the first armoured car, the French Charron, Girardot et Voigt

1906 French and Austrian armies develop petrol-powered artillery tractors

1915 The armies of World War I use increasing numbers of military trucks

1916 The first use of tanks in combat – British Mark Is at the Battle of Flers-Courcelette

Military Trains and Railway Guns

The use of railways for military purposes began in the 1840s and became well-established during the second half of the 19th century. At first, civilian freight and passenger trains were repurposed to transport military materiel and personnel. However, such trains became high-profile targets for sabotage, ambush, and artillery strikes, particularly trains that ran through contested regions or came close to the frontlines. As a result, many military trains were fitted with armour and defensive weaponry. During World War I, some combatants produced enormous railway guns. These outsized artillery pieces were too heavy and logistically complex to move by any other means than rail.

◁ B&O L Class No.57 Memnon
Date 1848 **Origin** USA
Wheel arrangement 0-8-0
Boiler pressure 5 kg/sq cm (75 psi)
Driving wheel diameter 1,118 mm (44 in)
Top speed approx. 48 km/h (30 mph)

With eight driving wheels for extra traction and power, *Memnon* was originally used by the Baltimore & Ohio Railroad to haul freight. During the American Civil War, it transported supplies and troops for the Union Army.

Tall stack created strong draught for better combustion and helped capture sparks

△ Railroad battery
Date 1861 **Origin** USA
Wheel arrangement Four axles
Armament 1 x 24-pounder cannon; infantry muskets
Crew Up to 60 infantrymen
Armour Heavy boilerplate

This boxy, boilerplate mobile battery was developed in the first year of the American Civil War (1861–65) to protect engineers repairing railway bridges that had been damaged or destroyed by Confederate forces. It had a 24-pounder cannon as its main armament; the infantry inside could fire their muskets through hinged firing ports.

Cowcatcher (also called a pilot) deflected objects on track

Eight driving wheels, with no leading or trailing wheels

▷ American Standard locomotive
Date 1862 **Origin** USA
Wheel arrangement 4-4-0
Boiler pressure Up to 9.8 kg/sq cm (140 psi)
Driving wheel diameter Up to 1,676 mm (66 in)
Top speed c. 97 km/h (60 mph)

The American Standard was an iconic steam locomotive type put to work during the American Civil War in troop transport and logistical roles. This particular train, the *W. H. Whiton*, pulled President Abraham Lincoln's rail car, which was later converted to his funerary car.

Headlights were powered by oil or kerosene

MILITARY TRAINS AND RAILWAY GUNS · 35

◁ **Armoured train (British)**

Date 1900	Origin South Africa
Wheel arrangement	4–8 axles total
Armament	1 x 12-pounder QF gun; multiple machine-guns; infantry rifles and carbines
Crew	40–60
Armour	Boilerplate and steel cladding on gun trucks and engine cab

The British forces in the Boer War (1899–1902) made extensive use of armoured trains. The trains were essentially railway wagons fitted with steel plating for protection and firing ports and gun positions for defence. They proved to be vulnerable to well-planned Boer ambushes.

Tender carried on two four-wheel bogies

△ **British Imperial Military Railways armoured CSAR Class E 4-10-2T**

Date 1902	Origin UK
Wheel arrangement	4-10-2T
Boiler pressure	12.3 kg/sq cm (175 psi)
Driving wheel diameter	1,143 mm (45 in)
Top speed	c.45–50 km/h (28–31 mph)

During the Boer War, the British Imperial Military Railways (IMR) commissioned the construction of 35 armoured variants of the "Reid Tenwheeler" locomotive designed by George W. Reid. The engines, which became the Class E 4-10-2T, had good traction and were ideal for pulling heavy loads up the steep inclines common in South Africa.

△ **280 cm SK L/40 "Bruno"**

Date 1916	Origin Germany
Wheel arrangement	2 x 5-axle bogies (10 axles total)
Armament	1 x 280 mm naval gun
Crew	c.25–30 artillery personnel, plus support and security troops
Armour	Minimal

The "Bruno" was a 280 mm railway gun that operated on the Western Front during World War I, where it bombarded targets up to a maximum range of 18 km (11 miles). The gun was actually a type used on German Navy warships, adapted to rail in 1916.

Barrel measured 17 m (54 ft) in length

▽ **Ordnance BL 12 in gun Mk IX**

Date 1916	Origin UK
Wheel arrangement	11 axles total
Armament	1 x 12 in Mk IX W naval gun
Crew	c.30–55
Armour	None

The British deployed four of these heavy railway guns to the Western Front between 1915 and 1918. The guns were surplus Royal Navy 12 in Mk IX W naval models set on railway mountings; shown here is a Mk II mounting made by the Elswick Ordnance Company of Newcastle-upon-Tyne.

△ **M1895 railway gun**

Date 1917	Origin USA
Wheel arrangement	2 x 8-axle bogies (16 axles total)
Armament	1 x 16 in M1895 coastal defence gun
Crew	c.40–50
Armour	None

This mighty American railway gun was constructed in 1902 as a mobile coastal defence weapon, being deployed around Panama in 1917. It married an M1895 406 mm (16 in) gun to two eight-axle bogies. The total weight of the entire assembly was a hefty 129,000 kg (284,000 lb).

Battleships and Cruisers

Britain's Royal Navy was seen by many rival nations as the bedrock of the country's success in expanding the British Empire during the 19th century. Nations wanting to acquire colonies overseas felt compelled to boost their naval strength with increasingly powerful warships. Of all fighting ships, cruisers and battleships carried the biggest guns and had the best armour protection; consequently, they became part of a technological arms race – and a symbol of the global power struggles of the late 19th and early 20th centuries.

88 mm gun for defence against torpedo boats

24 cm gun (was main armament)

△ **HMS Trafalgar**

Date 1890	Origin UK
Displacement	12,792 tonnes (14,100 tons)
Length	105 m (345 ft)
Top speed	16.7 knots (31 km/h)

This was the last of a series of British low-freeboard battleships. With a short distance from waterline to main deck, the hull sat low in the water, so the ship presented a smaller target. Such ships were best suited for calmer waters, like the Mediterranean.

▽ **USS Atlanta**

Date 1886	Origin USA
Displacement	3,240 tonnes (3,570 tons)
Length	86.3 m (283 ft)
Top speed	16.3 knots (30 km/h)

Atlanta was a cruiser with 5 cm (2 in) of armour protection, one of the first four steel ships built for the US Navy as part of its "New Navy" drive in the 1880s. *Atlanta*'s armament included two 8 in and six 6 in guns, and a range of smaller weapons.

 **Rigging** supported the masts and was used to raise and lower the sails

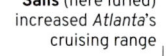 **Sails** (here furled) increased *Atlanta*'s cruising range

BATTLESHIPS AND CRUISERS · 37

◁ **Siegfried-class ship**

Date 1890 Origin Germany

Displacement 3,500 tonnes (3,860 tons)

Length 79 m (259 ft)

Top speed 14 knots (26 km/h)

The six *Siegfried*-class ships, built 1888–94, were designed to patrol and protect the German coast and the entry to the Kiel Canal. Armament was three 24 cm main guns (able to fire two rounds per minute), eight 88 mm guns, and torpedo tubes.

▷ **USS Indiana**

Date 1895 Origin USA

Displacement 10,453 tonnes (11,522 tons)

Length 107 m (350 ft)

Top speed 15 knots (28 km/h)

The US Navy's first battleship, *Indiana* was built for coastal protection work (with its low freeboard, it would have struggled in heavy open seas). In the Spanish-American War, *Indiana* took part in the 1898 Battle of Santiago de Cuba, a decisive US victory.

Turret housing two 6 in guns (two more in aft turret)

△ **Navarin**

Date 1896 Origin Russia

Displacement 10,370 tonnes (11,430 tons)

Length 107 m (351 ft)

Top speed 15 knots (28 km/h)

Ordered in 1890 by the Imperial Russian Navy, changes in design and delays in construction meant this battleship did not enter service until 1896. *Navarin* saw action in the Russo-Japanese War, being sunk in 1905 at the Battle of Tsushima by mines laid in its path by Japanese destroyers. Only three of her crew of over 600 survived.

▷ **Fuji**

Date 1897 Origin Japan

Displacement 12,430 tonnes (13,700 tons)

Length 125 m (412 ft)

Top speed 18 knots (33 km/h)

Fuji was one of two British-built battleships ordered by Japan in response to the Chinese acquiring two new battleships from Germany. *Fuji* was involved in the battles of the Yellow Sea (1904) and Tsushima (1905) during the Russo-Japanese War. Later used for coastal patrols, it ended its life as a training ship.

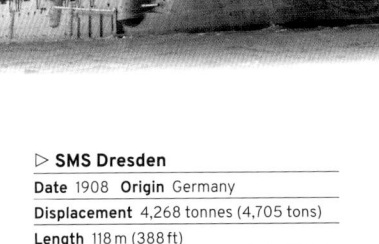

◁ **HMS Leviathan**

Date 1903 Origin UK

Displacement 14,380 tonnes (15,850 tons)

Length 162 m (533 ft)

Top speed 23 knots (43 km/h)

One of four *Drake*-class armoured cruisers, with two 9 in and sixteen 6 in guns, *Leviathan* served in East Asia and the Mediterranean before being put in reserve. Recommissioned in 1914, *Leviathan* chased commerce raiders and escorted convoys across the Atlantic during World War I.

▷ **SMS Dresden**

Date 1908 Origin Germany

Displacement 4,268 tonnes (4,705 tons)

Length 118 m (388 ft)

Top speed 24 knots (44 km/h)

Built as part of the Imperial German navy's efforts to rival the Royal Navy, the light cruiser *Dresden* saw action in World War I as a commerce raider in the South Atlantic. It fought at the battles of Coronel and the Falkland Islands (1914), but was cornered and scuttled off the Chilean coast in 1915.

Mikasa

Renowned as the Japanese flagship at the 1905 Battle of Tsushima, which saw the fleet of the Imperial Russian Navy virtually annihilated, the *Mikasa* is the only surviving example of a pre-dreadnought battleship. The *Mikasa* was one of the first ships to be fitted with "Krupp Cemented" steel armour. This armour proved highly effective at Tsushima, when some 30 hits from Russian guns failed to put the *Mikasa* out of action.

BASED ON THE ROYAL NAVY'S Majestic class, the *Mikasa* was built by Vickers at Barrow-in-Furness – the last of four similar battleships made in British yards for the Imperial Japanese Navy. Powered by 25 coal-burning boilers, the *Mikasa* entered service in 1902.

The ship's main armament consisted of four 12in guns mounted in twin centre-line turrets fore and aft; these guns could be fired at a rate of three rounds every two minutes. The *Mikasa*'s array of secondary armaments included fourteen 6in quick-firing guns, lighter guns to defend against destroyers and torpedo-boats, and four torpedo tubes submerged below the waterline.

In addition to forming the main deck, Krupp cemented armour was fitted in belts around the waterline up to 23 cm (9in) thick, and in 356mm (14in)-thick barbettes around the 12in gun installations. Other features that proved influential at Tsushima included up-to-date wireless communication and superior rangefinders, which gave the Japanese fleet long-range firepower superiority. Ironically, having survived the Russian guns at Tsushima, the ship sank in harbour four months later, following an accidental explosion in a magazine. Raised in 1906 and repaired, the *Mikasa* never fought again. Decommissioned in 1923, it is now a museum ship at Yokosuka.

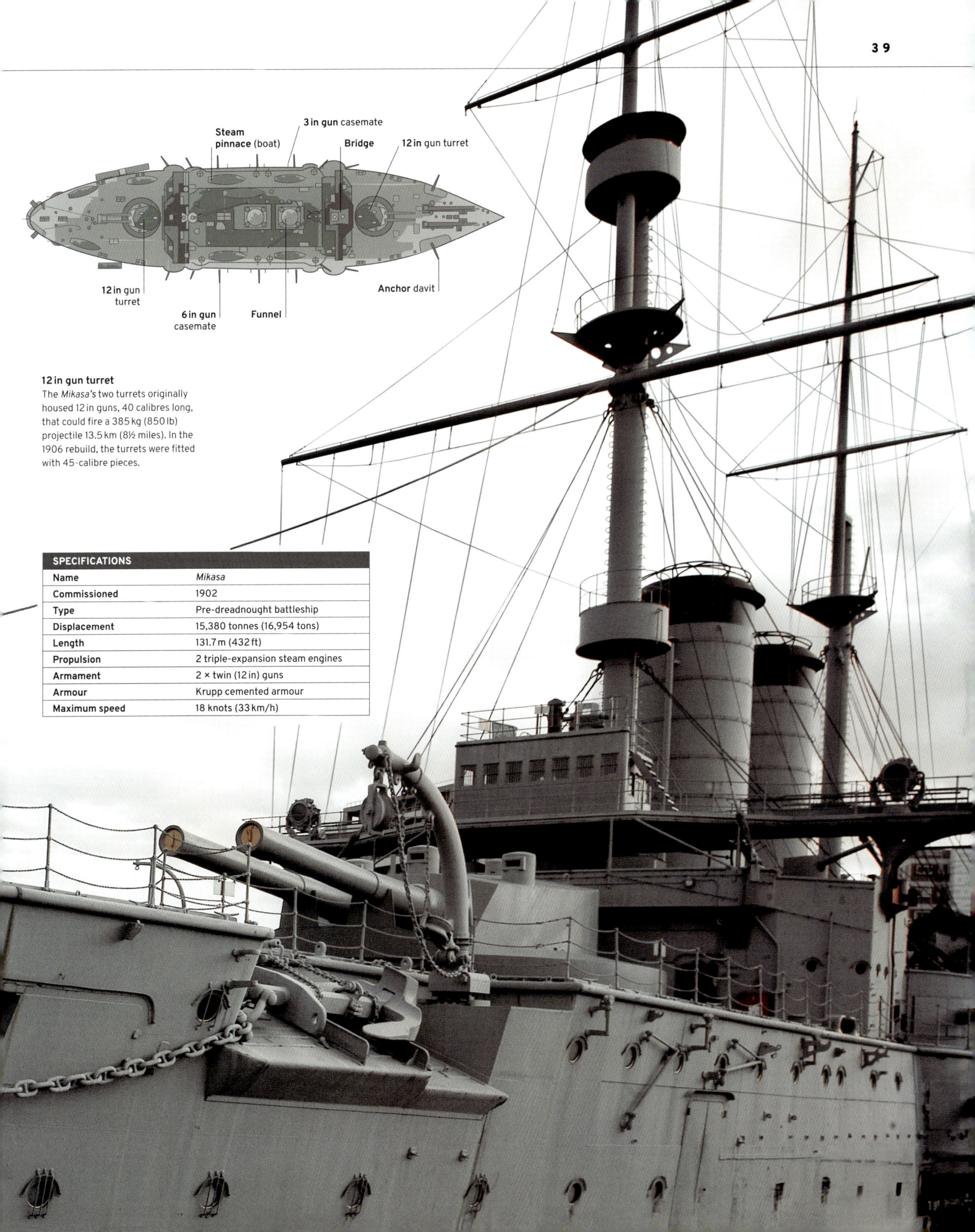

12 in gun turret
The *Mikasa's* two turrets originally housed 12 in guns, 40 calibres long, that could fire a 385 kg (850 lb) projectile 13.5 km (8½ miles). In the 1906 rebuild, the turrets were fitted with 45-calibre pieces.

SPECIFICATIONS	
Name	*Mikasa*
Commissioned	1902
Type	Pre-dreadnought battleship
Displacement	15,380 tonnes (16,954 tons)
Length	131.7 m (432 ft)
Propulsion	2 triple-expansion steam engines
Armament	2 × twin (12 in) guns
Armour	Krupp cemented armour
Maximum speed	18 knots (33 km/h)

EXTERIOR

The *Mikasa* supplemented its main armament with a variety of smaller-calibre weapons, ranging from 6in guns for use against cruisers and destroyers, to 12-, 3-, and 1-pounders, in addition to machine-guns. From the command post on top of the bridge, which gave uninterrupted views to the front and sides, orders were passed to the pilot house via a speaking tube beside the compass. The gilded characters on the railings of the walkway to the admiral's cabin spell out *Mi-ka-sa*.

1. Rear view of bridge **2.** Bridge searchlight **3.** Fore anchor **4.** Bridge **5.** Stern walkway **6.** Porthole **7.** Mainmast **8.** Aft skylight **9.** Hotchkiss 3-pounder gun **10.** Funnels **11.** Command post with speaking tube **12.** 6in guns **13.** Rangefinder **14.** Port to 3in battery **15.** 6in gun breech

INTERIOR

The ship was controlled, or "conned", from the pilot house, whose wheel, compass, and engine-room telegraphs (used to indicate the speed required) were duplicated in an armoured conning tower one deck below. Living conditions for the crew were almost unchanged from the days of sail, with the men sleeping in hammocks and eating at fold-away tables. Officers dined in the wardroom, which also hosted meetings; the admiral, who had his own bathroom, took formal meals in his saloon.

16. 3in gun casemate   **17.** Pilot house   **18.** Pantry   **19.** Admiral's cabin
20. Wireless Morse key   **21.** Admiral's saloon   **22.** Officer's wardroom
23. Admiral's bathroom

Torpedo Boats, Destroyers, and Submarines

A new chapter in naval warfare began in 1866, when the English engineer Robert Whitehead, working at Fiume (modern-day Rijeka in Croatia), perfected the self-propelled torpedo. Soon, boats were being designed specifically to deploy the revolutionary weapon; this, in turn, prompted the production of torpedo-boat "destroyers" to combat the new threat. Able to defend other ships and also take on the offensive role of torpedo boats if needed, destroyers became an indispensable element of the fleet. The torpedo gave the emerging generation of submarines a powerful weapon to use against surface vessels while remaining underwater.

▽ **HMS Lightning**
Date 1876 Origin UK
Displacement 33.5 tonnes (37 tons)
Length 26.7 m (87½ ft)
Top speed 18.5 knots (34 km/h)

Built at the urging of constructor John Thornycroft, *Lightning* was the British Royal Navy's first torpedo boat. This experimental craft incorporated a variety of innovative features, including a divided rudder ahead of the single propeller.

Torpedo launch tube

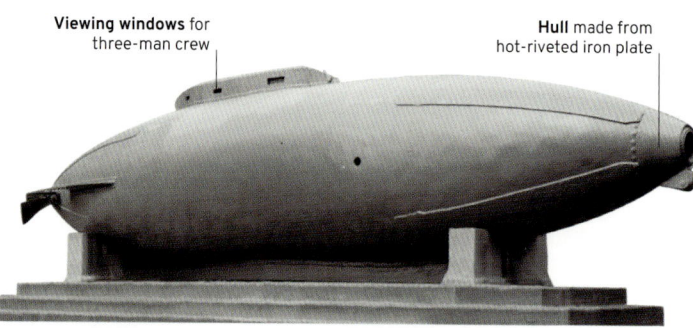

Viewing windows for three-man crew

Hull made from hot-riveted iron plate

△ **Fenian Ram**
Date 1881 Origin USA
Displacement 17.2 tonnes (19 tons)
Length 9.4 m (31 ft)
Top speed 9 knots (17 km/h)

Designed by Irish émigré John Philip Holland and funded by the Irish Republican Brotherhood in America for use against British ships in Ireland, *Fenian Ram* was armed with a 9 in pneumatic gun for firing explosive projectiles from its bow. It never saw action. Holland later designed the USS *Holland*, the US Navy's first commissioned submarine.

Two torpedo tubes between funnels

Single torpedo tube between the bridge and forecastle

△ **HMS Havock**
Date 1893 Origin UK
Displacement 279 tonnes (308 tons)
Length 56 m (185 ft)
Top speed 27 knots (50 km/h)

Havock and its sister ship, *Hornet*, were the first operational Royal Navy destroyers. *Havock* carried a 12-pounder gun, three 6-pounders, and three torpedo tubes – a fixed bow tube and a pair of deck tubes on a rotating mount.

△ **SMS S90**
Date 1899 Origin Germany
Displacement 396 tonnes (437 tons)
Length 63 m (207 ft)
Top speed 26.5 knots (49 km/h)

Armed with a trio of 5 cm guns and three torpedo tubes, *S90* was the lead vessel of a class of large torpedo boats built from 1898 to 1907. In 1914, during the siege of the German port of Tsingtao (Qindao) in China, *S90* sank the Japanese cruiser *Takachiho*, before being scuttled to avoid capture.

▷ **Sokol**
Date 1895 Origin Russia
Displacement 240 tonnes (265 tons)
Length 57.9 m (190 ft)
Top speed 29 knots (54 km/h)

Constructed by British shipbuilder Yarrow, *Sokol* – Russia's first destroyer – was claimed to be the fastest warship of its day. Renamed *Pruitki* in 1902, it served with the Imperial Russian Navy in World War I, then, after the October Revolution, with the Bolshevik Red Fleet, fighting White Army forces during the Russian Civil War (1917–22).

Two torpedo tubes between funnels

Porthole windows for admitting light and ventilation

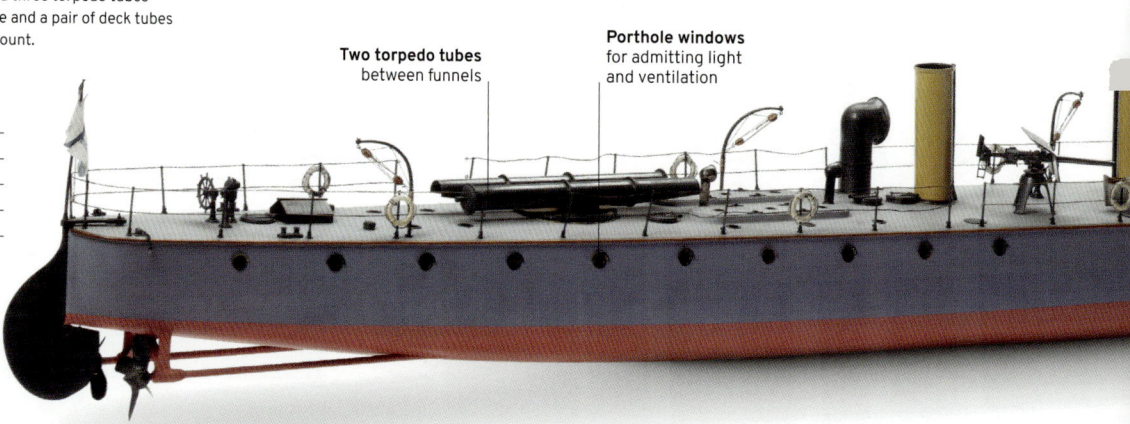

▷ Kagerō

Date 1899 **Origin** Japan
Displacement 366 tonnes (403 tons)
Length 64 m (210 ft)
Top speed 30 knots (56 km/h)

Kagerō was one of six *Murakano*-class destroyers built for Japan in the late 1890s by Thornycroft in the UK, based on Thornycroft's design for HMS *Angler*. Kagerō featured in the Battle of Tsushima and other engagements of the Russo-Japanese War of 1904–05, and saw action in World War I.

"Four-stack" (four funnel) arrangement

△ USS Hull (DD-7)

Date 1903 **Origin** USA
Displacement 415 tonnes (457 tons)
Length 75.8 m (249 ft)
Top speed 29 knots (54 km/h)

Hull and other *Bainbridge* class vessels were the inaugural US destroyers. *Hull* was equipped with two torpedo tubes, a pair of 3 in guns, and five 6-pounders. Put into reserve in 1912, the ship was recommissioned in 1917. It took part in patrols, escorts, and training exercises during World War I.

Divided rudder for improved manoeuvrability

△ USS Tarantula (B-3)

Date 1907 **Origin** USA
Displacement 147 tonnes (162 tons)
Length 25.1 m (82½ ft)
Top speed 9 knots (17 km/h)

Tarantula was one of three B-class US Navy vessels, the last submarines directly designed by John Holland. With a 10-man crew, it carried four torpedoes and could dive to around 46 m (150 ft). It sailed with the US Atlantic and Asiatic Fleets, ending its operational life in the Philippines.

Steamboat Battles in the American Civil War

The American Civil War (1861–65) generated a range of new weapons. On the water, the first engagements of "ironclads" took place, with iron-hulled ships at sea and armoured monitor vessels sporting turrets operating nearer to shore. Both types were powered by effective steam engines, meaning that fighting was no longer dictated by the wind's direction. Early ironclads were converted wooden sailing ships, but innovative designs soon appeared, spawning new maritime battle tactics. Since armour plate was effective at protecting a vessel against cannon fire, ships were fitted with rams to hole and sink their adversaries. Submarines were used with varying degrees of success, along with torpedoes and mines. The blockading of ports by Union forces prevented the Confederate South from trading or importing weaponry – a major factor in its defeat.

The Battle of Mobile Bay by J.O. Davidson depicts the victorious assault by Union ships on a smaller Confederate fleet and three defensive forts around Mobile Bay in the Gulf of Mexico in 1864.

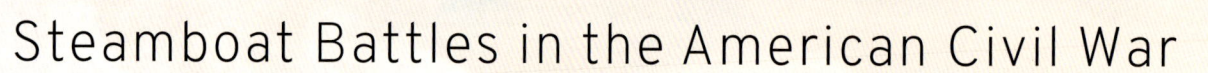

World War I: Mobile Warfare on Land

World War I was a conflict forged in the industrial age. The vast material requirements of the war depended heavily upon railway logistics, plus an ever-growing fleet of motor vehicles. On the front line, the war saw the introduction of history's first armoured fighting vehicles, which provided mobile firepower. However, horses and mules were also widely used for logistics.

Motorcycle unit
Britain's Motor Machine-Gun Service (MMGS) used motorbikes (here a 532 cc Scott) and sidecars armed with Vickers guns to provide mobile anti-aircraft defence and suppress ground fire.

British historian A.J.P. Taylor described World War I as being "imposed on the statesmen of Europe by railway timetables". Trains made possible the swift, mass transportation of soldiers and materials. Taylor argued that, pre-war, nations believed the ability to mobilize by rail faster than their adversaries would act as a deterrent, but in reality planning for such rapid mobilization made war inevitable.

Home front to front line

When the conflict began in 1914, continental Europe – including western Russia – was connected by over 300,000 km (186,400 miles) of railway. Rail tracks allowed newly mobilized armies to be sent rapidly to major rail hubs close to emerging battlefields. Above all, railways offered logistical scale. An infantry division of 12,000 men required around 1,000 tonnes (1,100 tons) of supplies each day just to meet its non-combat demands, equivalent to two 50-wagon supply trains.

For this reason, railways were integral to the strategic and operational planning of the war. Germany's opening offensive, the so-called "Schlieffen Plan", was developed closely around rail timetables and transportation volumes, underpinning the belief that the German Army would be able to secure a quick victory in the west before moving its forces east to face the Russians. In France, the mobilization of 3.7 million men in August 1914 was converted into a practical offensive–defensive response by 63,000 km (39,150 miles) of rail (including local lines).

In matters of logistics, rail power enabled armies to build up vast supply dumps located several miles from the fighting front. To take those stores forward to the troops, the French and Germans in particular, and later the British, laid thousands of miles of 60 cm (24 in) gauge railway track, across which small, lightweight engines pulling supply trains rolled endlessly.

Beyond the rails

World War I demonstrated rail's limitations, as well as its usefulness. The chaos and destruction wrought by fighting could disrupt rail traffic, especially near the artillery-ravaged front lines, and ultimately trains had to stop short of the combat zone, with the final miles of supply movement often being undertaken by horse and mules (see panel below).

However, the war also saw the first substantial military use of mechanical horsepower, especially by the British and, later, the Americans. Cars, buses, and trucks were requisitioned and sent to the front line, while steam-, petrol-, and diesel-driven tracked tractors were used to haul heavy artillery pieces. By 1915–16, large fleets of purpose-built military trucks were in use, such as the British 3-ton AEC Type Y and the US 3- and 5-ton "Liberty" trucks. Although these vehicles were limited in reliability, speed, and off-road performance, they nevertheless demonstrated the viability of military motorization.

Armoured warfare

Another World War I innovation was mobile, mechanized armour. The first crude iterations of armoured cars were little more than actual road cars with some sheet metal protection and a machine-gun. Particularly on the Western Front, however, heavier armoured vehicles were developed as a means to break the trench deadlock. While there were many precursors, Britain led the way with the first tank, the prototype "Little Willie", in 1915. More significantly, in September 1916 Britain launched the lozenge-shaped Mark I tank into action at the Somme, followed in June 1917 by the more capable Mark IV at the Battle of Messines. The Germans and French developed their own tanks, and in April 1918 the first tank vs tank duel was fought between a Mark IV and a German A7V – the former prevailed. The age of armour had begun.

Modes of transport
Here, at the Second Battle of Bapaume, August–September 1918, the full spectrum of World War I mobility can be seen: horse-drawn logistics, military trucks, and British Mark IV tanks alongside Canadian infantry.

Artillery tractor
During the British retreat on the Western Front in spring 1918, an artillery gun and assorted personnel are pulled by what appears to be a US-built Holt tracked artillery tractor.

"Employment of tanks in mass is our greatest enemy."
GENERAL ERICH LUDENDORFF, FIRST QUARTERMASTER GENERAL OF THE GERMAN GENERAL STAFF

TALKING POINT

Horses in World War I

Across the many fronts of World War I, millions of horses and mules were drafted into war service (as well as camels in the Middle East). In the UK alone, the British Army's Remount Department sent more than 368,000 domestic and agricultural horses to the Western Front between 1914 and 1917. Although there were still some horse-mounted cavalry units in service during the war, particularly on the Eastern Front, horses were mainly employed in logistical work, moving heavy loads over rough terrain that proved impassable to military vehicles. Their roles included carrying ammunition between forward rail hubs and front-line troops, drawing field ambulances, and pulling heavy artillery pieces. Often, the requisitioned horses were terribly unsuited for the hard labour at the front lines – it is estimated that around eight million horses died, most of them on the Western Front.

Horses, like their handlers, needed protection from sudden gas attacks. British equine gas masks consisted of a dual-layer flannelette bag, impregnated with a "Komplexene" chemical treatment and expanded out from the horse's nose and mouth by a canvas frame.

△ **Nash Quad**

Date 1913	Origin USA

Engine 4-cylinder petrol, 39 kW (52 hp)

Payload 1.4 tonnes (1.5 tons)

A versatile and durable utility truck, the Nash Quad was developed specifically for military use by the Thomas B. Jeffery Company, itself acquired by the Nash Motors Company in 1916. More than 11,500 vehicles were produced by 1919.

▷ **Fiat 15 Ter**

Date 1912	Origin Italy

Engine 4-cylinder petrol, 30 kW (40 hp)

Payload 1.5 tonnes (1.65 tons)

The Fiat 15 Ter, Italy's first military truck, served initially in the Italo-Turkish War. The Italian, British, French, and Russian armies all used the light truck in large numbers throughout World War I.

Bulkhead and engine firewall

△ **Latil TAR**

Date 1913	Origin France

Engine 4-cylinder petrol, 22.5 kW (30 hp)

Payload 4 tonnes (4.4 tons)

During World War I, the 4x4 Latil TAR took the place of horses to pull heavy artillery, including 13-tonne (14.3-ton) 155 mm field guns. By 1922, more than 3,000 trucks had been built and many were still in service at the start of World War II.

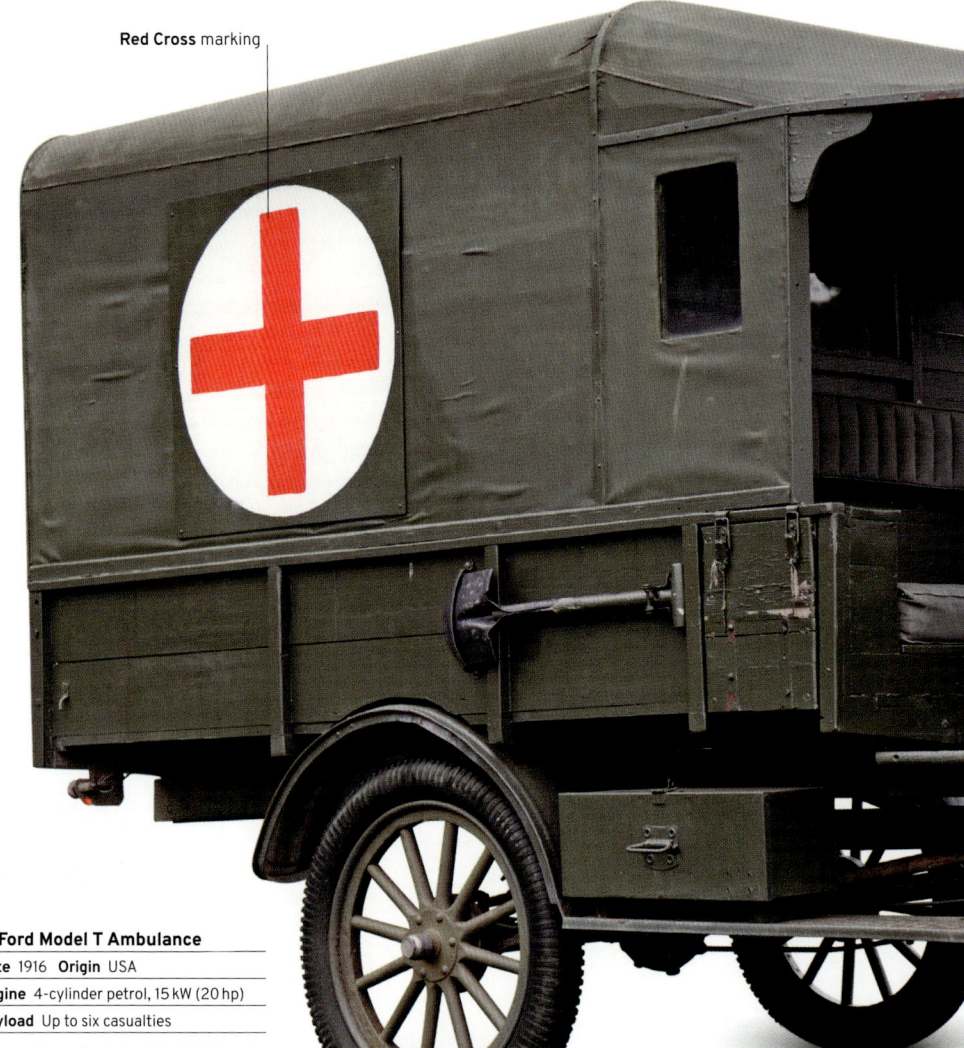

Red Cross marking

△ **Ford Model T Ambulance**

Date 1916	Origin USA

Engine 4-cylinder petrol, 15 kW (20 hp)

Payload Up to six casualties

The readily available Ford Model T chassis offered a practical battlefield ambulance platform in World War I. The back cabin could transport three litters or four seated casualties, with two more wounded carried in the front cabin.

Utility and Troop Trucks

World War I heralded the arrival of industrialized, highly mechanized conflict. Horses struggled to haul the larger artillery pieces or carry the sheer weight of soldiers, equipment, and supplies that modern warfare demanded. As war broke out in 1914, huge numbers of trucks were needed, but development time was limited, so civilian vehicles, such as London buses and Paris taxis, were drafted in, hastily painted green or brown, and sent to the front to supply and transport troops, including the wounded. Even purpose-built trucks were often ill-suited to the shell-blasted terrain, struggling to steer through the mud and terrifyingly vulnerable to attack. The lessons from such extreme conditions were quickly learned, leading to a new generation of robust battlefield trucks – and drivers who could carry their skills into transport roles at home.

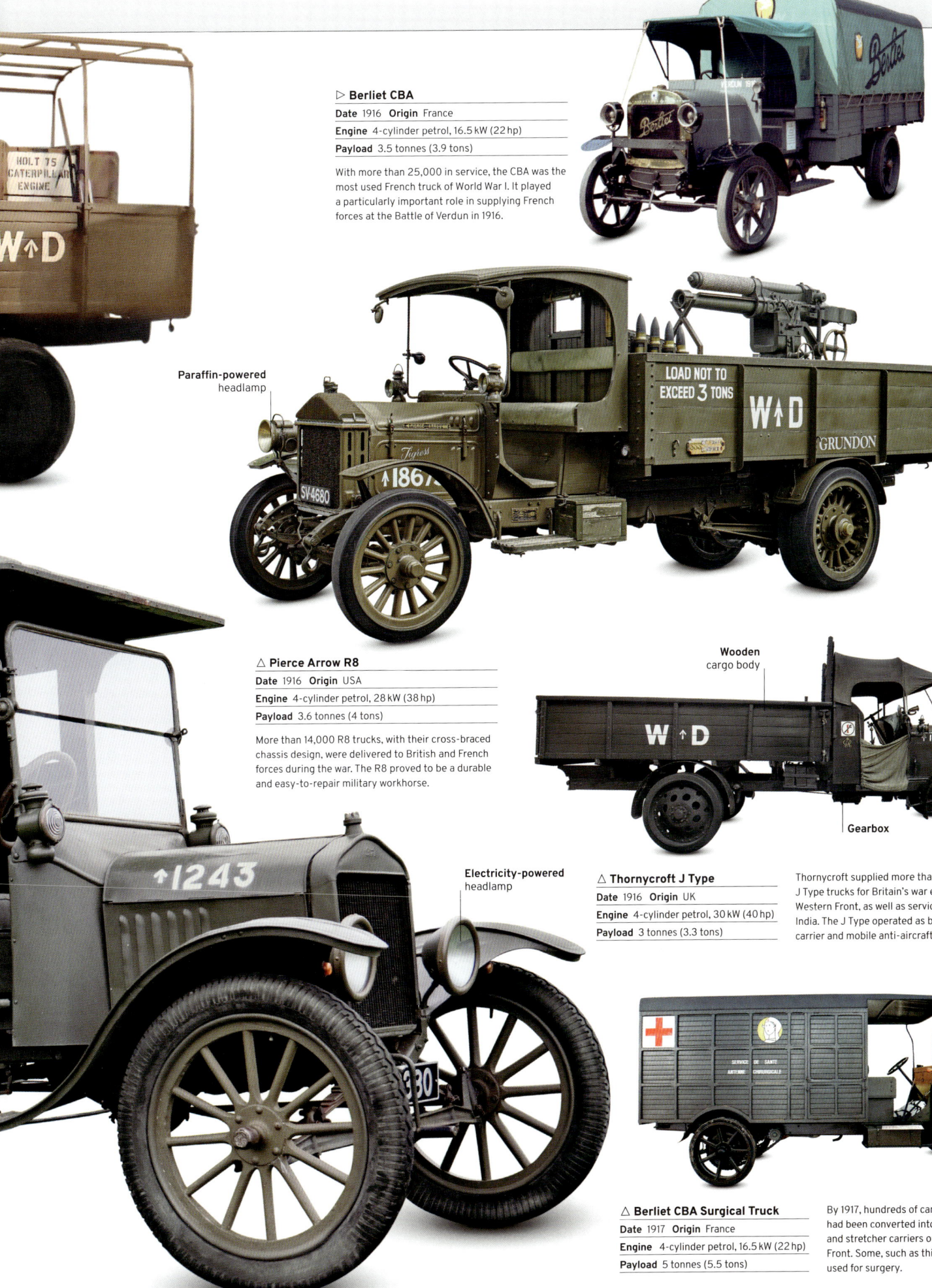

▷ **Berliet CBA**
Date 1916 **Origin** France
Engine 4-cylinder petrol, 16.5 kW (22 hp)
Payload 3.5 tonnes (3.9 tons)

With more than 25,000 in service, the CBA was the most used French truck of World War I. It played a particularly important role in supplying French forces at the Battle of Verdun in 1916.

△ **Pierce Arrow R8**
Date 1916 **Origin** USA
Engine 4-cylinder petrol, 28 kW (38 hp)
Payload 3.6 tonnes (4 tons)

More than 14,000 R8 trucks, with their cross-braced chassis design, were delivered to British and French forces during the war. The R8 proved to be a durable and easy-to-repair military workhorse.

△ **Thornycroft J Type**
Date 1916 **Origin** UK
Engine 4-cylinder petrol, 30 kW (40 hp)
Payload 3 tonnes (3.3 tons)

Thornycroft supplied more than 5,000 J Type trucks for Britain's war effort on the Western Front, as well as service in Egypt and India. The J Type operated as both a cargo carrier and mobile anti-aircraft gun platform.

△ **Berliet CBA Surgical Truck**
Date 1917 **Origin** France
Engine 4-cylinder petrol, 16.5 kW (22 hp)
Payload 5 tonnes (5.5 tons)

By 1917, hundreds of cars and trucks had been converted into ambulances and stretcher carriers on the Western Front. Some, such as this Berliet, were used for surgery.

Pierce-Arrow R Type

Between 1901 and 1938, Pierce-Arrow of Buffalo, New York, was one of the leading US manufacturers of luxury automobiles, its models used by presidents and movie stars alike. After the outbreak of World War I, the company switched its focus from expensive cars for the rich and famous to trucks for military use. The high quality of the Pierce-Arrow R type truck made it a popular choice for the Allied war effort.

PIERCE-ARROW described its R type as the "American Rolls-Royce of trucks". During World War I, over 14,000 Pierce-Arrow trucks were produced for the French and British armed forces. Most were general cargo types, but some were fully equipped workshop trucks, and a few were even armoured and equipped with guns.

The R8 truck pictured here was one of many delivered to the French government in 1916. Transporting the trucks from the US to France was a perilous affair: the vehicles were hoisted onto barges at the docks in New York and towed across the ocean to Le Havre, but many did not survive the rough Atlantic voyage.

CLOSED REAR VIEW

OPEN REAR VIEW

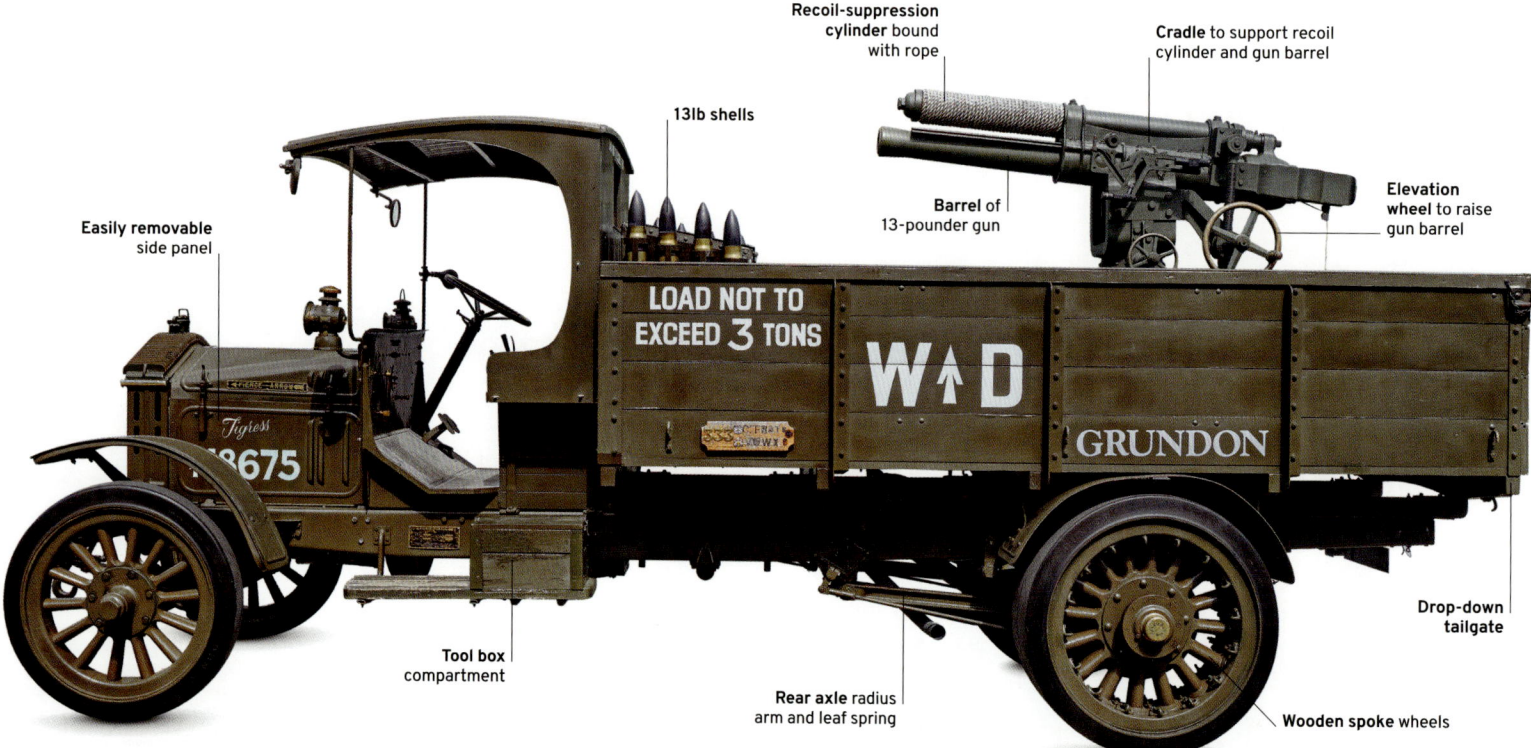

PIERCE-ARROW R TYPE · 51

SPECIFICATIONS	
Model	Pierce-Arrow R Type
Origin	USA
Assembly	Buffalo, New York
Production run	1911–19, approx. 16,500
Weight	4.5 tonnes (4.95 tons)
Payload	3 tonnes (3.3 tons)
Engine	4-cylinder petrol, 3880 cc, 22 kW (30 hp)
Transmission	3-speed manual
Maximum speed	29 km/h (18 mph)

Restored survivor
After wartime service, this cargo truck remained in military use until the late 1920s, when it was sold for civilian purposes in the south of France. In 1991, it was brought to the UK in 1991 and restored. Sporting British Army paintwork, this R type now has a 13-pounder anti-aircraft gun mounted on the truck bed.

Radiator filling cap

Radiator design inspired by British Dennis lorries

Brass side lamp burned paraffin

Front mudguard

Solid-rubber tyre

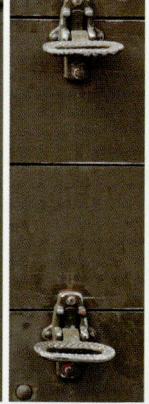

EXTERIOR

With no windscreen or doors, the driver and passenger were at the mercy of the elements. While glass was forbidden, due to the risk of shell bursts causing shattering, some trucks were fitted with a canvas apron that at least gave the crew some protection from wind and rain – as well as a small measure of warmth. Except for the bonnet and wings, the truck's bodywork is mostly wood, painted a drab army-camouflage green.

1. Maker's badge **2.** Chassis plate with identification numbers **3.** Bonnet catch **4.** Main headlamp, fitted for wartime use **5.** War Department vehicle number and adopted name **6.** Footplates to gain access **7.** Fuel feed from tank selector lever **8.** Heavy-duty wooden spoked wheel with detachable rim **9.** Rear spring hanger bracket

PIERCE-ARROW R TYPE • 53

ENGINE

The R type's four-cylinder engine consists of two blocks bolted on to a shared alloy crankcase, with each block housing a pair of cylinders. A handle protruding from the front of the vehicle is turned to start the engine. External metal engine parts in trucks of this period were often made of brass – the water pump (seen bottom centre in image 11) being one such example. Having a pump at all made the engine relatively sophisticated compared to many truck-engines of the time.

10. Engine bay, showing the magneto – an early form of ignition system **11.** Engine bay; the bonnet hinges upwards to provide access to the engine

 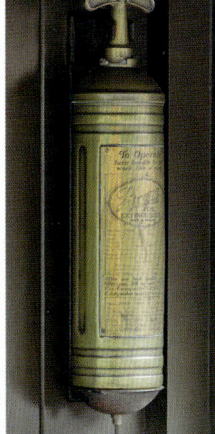 

INTERIOR

The simple, doorless cab design has little that could get in the way and impede access, allowing for rapid entry and exit – a great asset in wartime. The foot pedals are typical of the era, with a clutch pedal on the left, a centre throttle pedal, and a brake pedal on the right. Only one light (if any) was used for night driving during the war: that would be the light closest to the driver, so that it could be extinguished quickly.

12. Ignition switch and engine starter button **13.** Dashboard and driving controls layout **14.** Cab-mounted fire extinguisher **15.** Handbrake lever and gear lever selector **16.** Steering wheel and advance/retard ignition control levers **17.** Sight glass for fuel tank **18.** Foot pedals: clutch left, accelerator centre, brake right

World War I Locomotives

Formed in 1915, the Railway Operating Division (ROD) of the British Royal Engineers was set up to operate railways in the European and Middle East theatres during World War I. The British network of narrow-gauge trench railways was operated by the War Department Light Railways. The French had already standardized portable, 600 mm (1 ft 11⅝ in) gauge, military Decauville equipment to supply ammunition and stores to their forces on the Western Front; German trench railways used a similar system, the Heeresfeldbahn. After the US entered the war in 1917, many American-built locomotives were shipped across the Atlantic for wartime service in France.

▷ GWR Class 2301 "Dean Goods"

Date 1883	**Origin** UK
Wheel arrangement 0-6-0	
Cylinders 2 (inside)	
Boiler pressure 12.65 kg/sq cm (180 psi)	
Driving wheel diameter 1,575 mm (62 in)	
Top speed 72 km/h (45 mph)	

Between 1883 and 1899, the Great Western Railway's Swindon Works produced 260 William Dean-designed standard-gauge Class 2301 freight locomotives. The ROD shipped 62 to northern France in 1917 to haul supply trains, with 16 later transferred to Salonika, Greece. Some engines also served in France during World War II.

◁ O&K Feldbahn

Date 1903	**Origin** Germany
Wheel arrangement 0-8-0T	
Cylinders 2	
Boiler pressure 12.65 kg/sq cm (180 psi)	
Driving wheel diameter Approx. 580 mm (22¾ in)	
Top speed 24 km/h (15 mph)	

Several German companies made these 600 mm (1 ft 11⅝ in) gauge "Brigadelok" locomotives, with around 2,500 produced in total. The engines were widely used on the military light railways constructed by the Germans to supply their forward army positions. Shown here is No. 7999, a 1915 Orenstein & Koppel engine with Klein–Lindner articulation of the front and rear axles.

▷ GCR Class 8K

Date 1911	**Origin** UK
Wheel arrangement 2-8-0	
Cylinders 2	
Boiler pressure 12.65 kg/sq cm (180 psi)	
Driving wheel diameter 1,422 mm (56 in)	
Top speed 97 km/h (60 mph)	

The Great Central Railway's Class 8K freight engine entered service in Britain in 1911 and served as the ROD's standard 2-8-0 locomotive during World War I. Many of the 521 Class 8Ks built for ROD were used to haul troop and freight trains in wartime France, and during World War II a number were sent on active service to the Middle East.

WORLD WAR I LOCOMOTIVES · 55

◁ **Henschel metre-gauge**

Date 1914	Origin Germany
Wheel arrangement	0-6-0T
Cylinders	2
Boiler pressure	14 kg/sq cm (200 psi)
Driving wheel diameter	800 mm (31½ in)
Top speed	30 km/h (19 mph)

In 1914, the Henschel company supplied a pair of 1m (3 ft 3⅜ in) gauge locomotives to Germany's Army Technical Research Institute. The two engines were later transferred to the Harz Mountains in central Germany, where they ran on the Nordhausen–Wernigerode Railway, put to work hauling trains of standard-gauge freight wagons.

△ **Baldwin Class 10-12-D**

Date 1916	Origin USA
Wheel arrangement	4-6-0PT
Cylinders	2
Boiler pressure	12.5 kg/sq cm (178 psi)
Driving wheel diameter	597 mm (23½ in)
Top speed	30 km/h (19 mph)

These 600 m (1 ft 11⅝ in) gauge pannier tank locomotives, based on a French design, were built by the Baldwin Locomotive Works in the US. They were supplied to Britain's War Office for front-line use on railways in northern France and the Middle East. The engine above joined the Glyn Valley Tramway, Wales, after the war.

▷ **Pershing Nord**

Date 1917	Origin UK
Wheel arrangement	2-8-0
Cylinders	2
Boiler pressure	13.4 kg/sq cm (190 psi)
Driving wheel diameter	1,422 mm (56 in)
Top speed	90 km/h (56 mph)

The Glasgow-based North British Locomotive Company supplied 113 Consolidation Pershings to France for wartime use by the Compagnie des Chemins de fer du Nord. The railway (often referred to simply as Nord) operated these large engines at up to 90 km/h (56 mph); other French railways preferred to run them at lower speeds.

◁ **Baldwin "Spider"**

Date 1917	Origin USA
Wheel arrangement	4-6-0
Cylinders	2
Boiler pressure	13.4 kg/sq cm (190 psi)
Driving wheel diameter	1,570 mm (61¾ in)
Top speed	105 km/h (65 mph)

Between 1917 and 1918, America's Baldwin Locomotive Works built 70 of these mixed-traffic, bar-frame locomotives for Western Front service. Nicknamed "Spiders" by British soldiers, they later became Class 40 engines on the Belgian State Railways.

World War I Tanks

On 15 September 1916, during the Battle of the Somme, the tank – a British Mark I – made its battlefield debut. The heavy Mark I and its successors, with tracks around their entire rhomboid-shaped bodies and armed with 6-pounder guns and machine-guns, were designed to cross trenches and support infantry. The French developed their own tanks, and in 1918, as fighting became more open, sent large numbers of light FT-17s into battle to support cavalry. The British did the same, in smaller numbers, with the Whippet medium tank. Germany built only one tank, the A7, as did Italy, the Fiat 2000.

△ "Little Willie"
Date 1915 **Origin** UK
Weight 16.3 tonnes (18 tons)
Engine Daimler 6-cylinder petrol, 78 kW (105 hp)
Main armament None

"Little Willie" was a prototype armoured, tracked fighting vehicle, built to prove the viability of the concept to British military chiefs.

Track made up of hardened steel plates

△ Mark I
Date 1916 **Origin** UK
Weight 28.4 tonnes (31.3 tons)
Engine Daimler 6-cylinder petrol, 78 kW (105 hp)
Main armament 2 x 6-pounder guns

Of the 150 Mark I tanks built, half were Male (as shown here) and half Female, the latter replacing each of the Male's 6-pounder guns with two .303 Vickers machine-guns. The crew of eight – four to drive and steer, four to fire the weapons – were protected by armour 12 mm (½ in) thick.

"Sabot" for crushing barbed wire

△ Schneider CA-1
Date 1917 **Origin** France
Weight 13.5 tonnes (14.9 tons)
Engine Schneider 4-cylinder petrol, 45 kW 45 kW (60 hp)
Main armament 75 mm Schneider Blockhaus gun

Based on the American Holt tractor, the six-crew CA-1 was the first French tank to go into battle – on 14 April 1917. It struggled to cross trenches, and its field of fire was limited by a gun offset to the right, but the tank fared better in the more open advances of 1918, by which time 400 CA-1s had been built.

Dome-shaped rotating turret

Front armour

△ Fiat 2000
Date 1917 **Origin** Italy
Weight 40 tonnes (44 tons)
Engine Fiat 6-cylinder petrol, 179 kW (240 hp)
Main armament 65 mm Turin Arsenal M.1910/M.1913 mountain howitzer

The FIAT 2000 was conceived as a "mobile fortress". It was a true heavyweight, weighing in at 40 tonnes (44 tons), heavily armoured, and bristling with guns from its hull and top cupola. However, it was ponderously slow, and the tank never entered series production, with only two examples being produced.

High angle for crossing trenches

◁ Mark IV
Date 1917 **Origin** UK
Weight 28.4 tonnes (31.3 tons)
Engine Daimler 6-cylinder petrol, 78 kW (105 hp)
Main armament 2 x 6-pounder guns

More than 1,200 Mark IVs were built, seeing action from June 1917 until the end of the war. The Mark IV was better protected than Britain's earlier tanks, and its mobility was enhanced by shortening the guns and shrinking the sponsons. Larger, armoured petrol tanks, now vacuum- rather than gravity-fed, increased the Mark IV's operational range.

WORLD WAR I TANKS · 57

37 mm main gun

Vertical spring suspension

Rear drive sprocket

△ Renault FT-17
Date 1918 **Origin** France
Weight 6.5 tonnes (7.2 tons)
Engine Renault 4-cylinder petrol, 26 kW (35 hp)
Main armament 37 mm SA18 Puteaux gun

The FT-17, which played a major role in the French victories of 1918, departed radically from earlier tanks. It was smaller, lighter, and followed what is now the standard layout of a fully rotating turret, the driver positioned at the front, and the engine and gearbox at the rear. More than 3,000 FT-17s were built, with many still in use in 1940.

△ Mark VIII "International"
Date 1918 **Origin** UK, USA
Weight 37.6 tonnes (41.4 tons)
Engine Ricardo or Liberty V-12 petrol, 224 kW (300 hp)
Main armament 2 x 6-pounder guns

Designed jointly by Britain and the US, the Mark VIII "International" was longer and more powerful than previous tanks, with thicker 16 mm (2/3 in) armour. It improved conditions by separating the crew from the engine. After the war, 100 Mark VIIIs were built in the US, serving until 1930.

Allied insignia

57 mm Maxim-Nordenfelt gun

△ A7V Sturmpanzerwagen
Date 1918 **Origin** Germany
Weight 32 tonnes (35.3 tons)
Engine 2 x Daimler 4-cylinder petrol, 74.5 kW (100 hp) each
Main armament 57 mm Maxim-Nordenfelt gun

Based on the running gear of the American Holt tractor, the A7V – a kind of mobile fortress – had a crew of at least 18 and was armed with six machine-guns and a 57 mm gun. The image above shows a replica.

◁ M1918 3 Ton Tank
Date 1918 **Origin** USA
Weight 2.8 tonnes (3.1 tons)
Engine 2 x Ford Model T 4-cylinder petrol, 33.5 kW (45 hp) each
Main armament .30-calibre machine-gun

A light tank with a crew of two sitting side by side, the M1918 was designed for mass production by the Ford Motor Company using Ford car parts. Of a planned 15,000 tanks, just 15 examples were built and only two arrived in France, with the US Tank Corps preferring the Renault F-17 for its superior combat capability.

▷ Medium Mark A Whippet
Date 1918 **Origin** UK
Weight 14.2 tonnes (15.7 tons)
Engine 2 x Tylor JB4 four-cylinder petrol, 33.5 kW (45 hp) each
Main armament 4 x .303 Hotchkiss machine-guns

Named the "Whippet" for its top speed of 13.4 km/h (8 1/3 mph), which was more than twice that of Britain's heaviest tanks, the Medium Mark A played a significant role in the open warfare of late 1918. Each track had its own engine, and steering was controlled by adjusting the two throttles.

Ventilation louvres for engine compartment

Mark IV

The British Mark IV made its impact at the Battle of Cambrai in November 1917, the first effective massed tank attack. More than 450 tanks – moved at night by rail to the quiet front line at Cambrai – launched an assault that cut deep into the German Hindenburg line. This attack demonstrated the potential destructive power of heavy tanks. More Mark IVs were made than any other British tank during World War I.

THE MARK IV featured improvements on the earlier, similar-looking Mark I, including thicker 12 mm (0.5 in) frontal armour to protect against armour-piercing bullets and an armoured rear fuel tank. The gun sponsons, one on either side, could be pushed inside the tank for transport by train; those on the Mark I had to be removed.

Mark IVs came in "male" and "female" variants: males carried two 6-pounder guns and four machine-guns; females had six machine-guns. Females were thought more useful, as their machine-guns could pin down the enemy while troops advanced; males had to stop so the 6-pounder gunners could aim. "Hermaphrodites", with one male and one female sponson, were introduced after April 1918.

Training vehicle
Having served in World War I, this Mark IV male tank was transferred to a Royal Navy facility at Whale Island, Portsmouth, UK. Tank gunners were trained at Whale Island by naval personnel who were skilled at firing weapons from moving platforms.

Commander and driver's cab

SPECIFICATIONS	
Name	Tank, Mark IV
Date	1917
Origin	UK
Production	1,222
Engine	Daimler/Knight straight six, 78 kW (105 hp)
Weight	28.4 tonnes (31.4 tons)
Armament (male)	2 x 6-pounder guns; 4 x .303 Lewis machine-guns
Armament (female)	6 x .303 Lewis machine-guns
Crew	8
Armour thickness	12 mm (0.5 in)

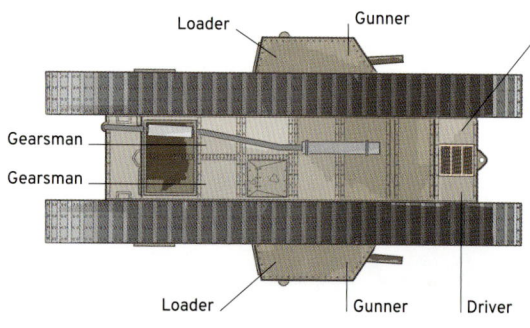

2324

Serial number
A unique four-digit number – often at the rear behind the sponsons – stayed with the tank, regardless of moves between units.

MARK IV · 59

FRONT VIEW

REAR VIEW

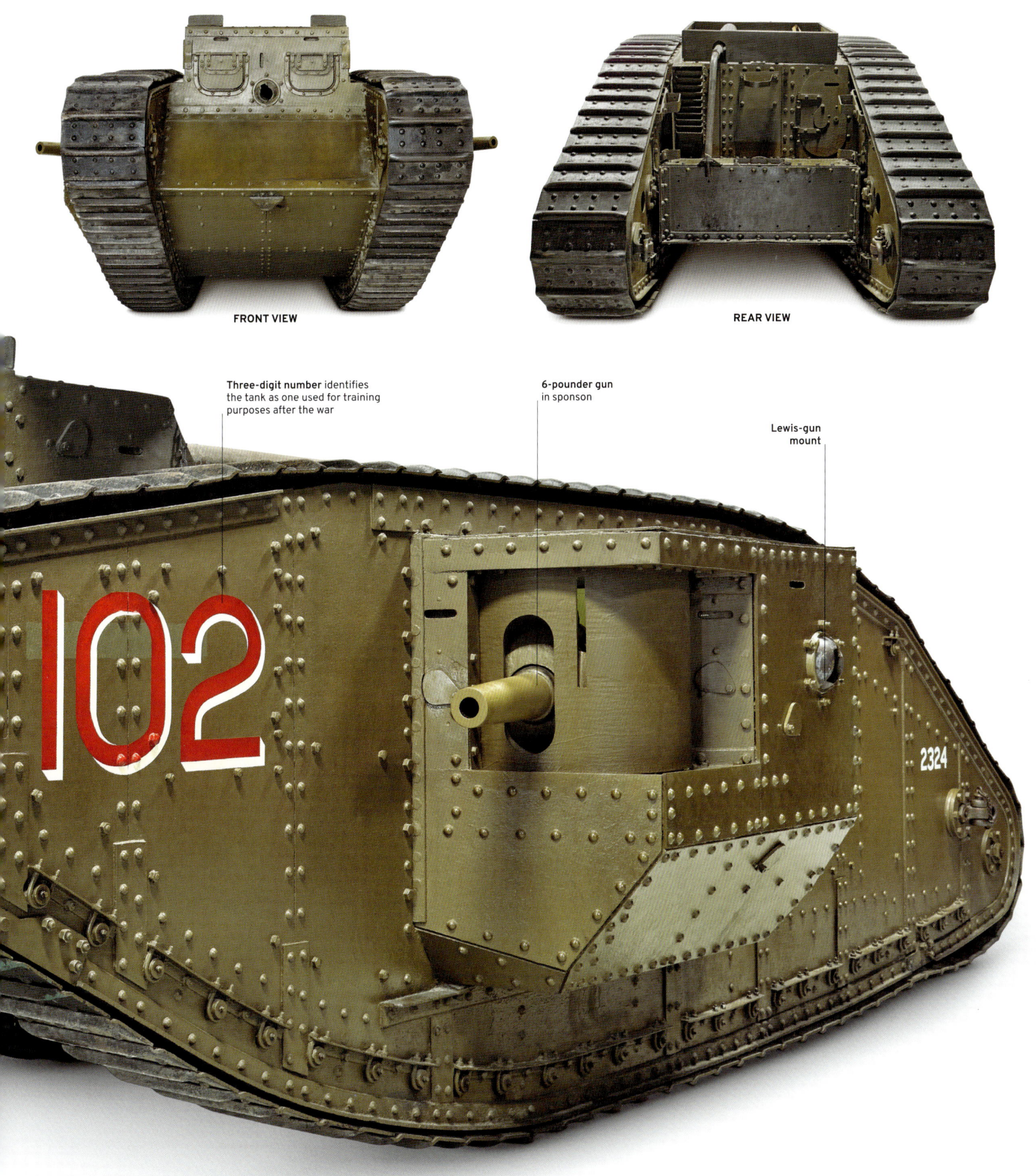

Three-digit number identifies the tank as one used for training purposes after the war

6-pounder gun in sponson

Lewis-gun mount

EXTERIOR

The Mark IV's construction – a metal framework with armour plates hot-riveted or bolted on – is characteristic of early tanks. However, this riveted build allowed bullet "splash" to enter through small gaps. To protect their faces from hot metal splinters, tank crews were issued with leather-covered steel masks.

1. Training number **2.** Driver's vision port (closed) **3.** Ventilation louvres **4.** Male sponson with 6-pounder gun **5.** Rear escape hatch **6.** Towing eye **7.** Track tensioner **8.** Location of final drive **9.** Sponson ball machine-gun mount (without gun) **10.** Track plates

1

2

3

11

4
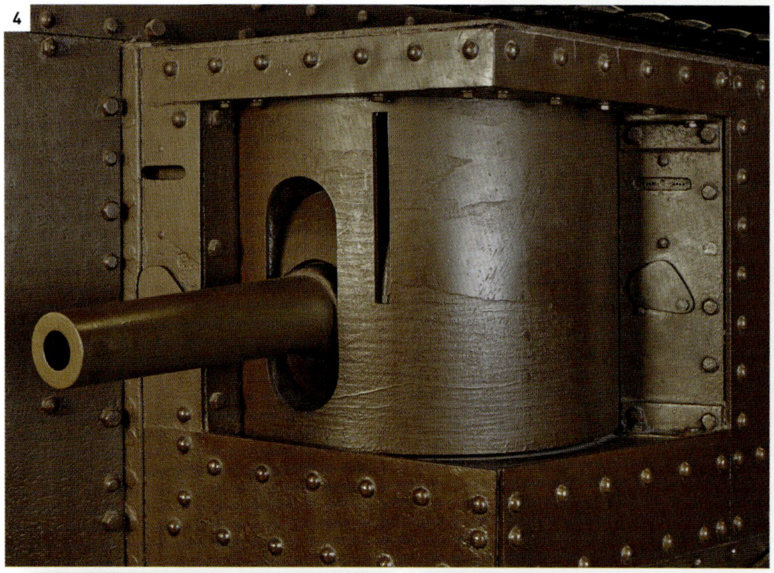

5
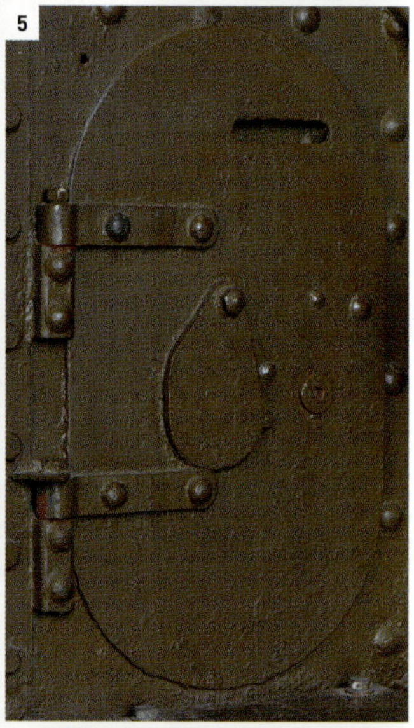

16

17

6
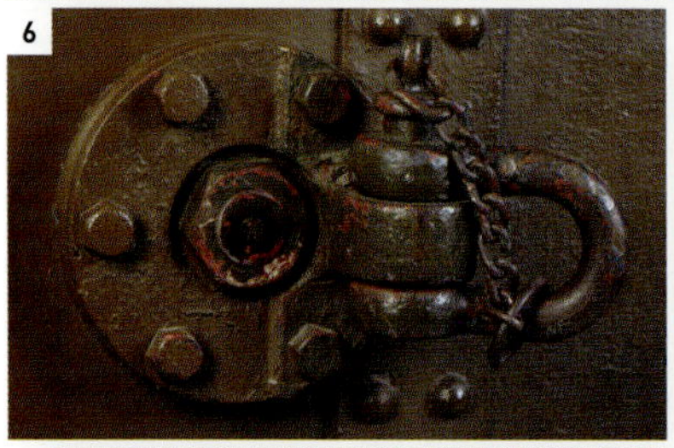

7
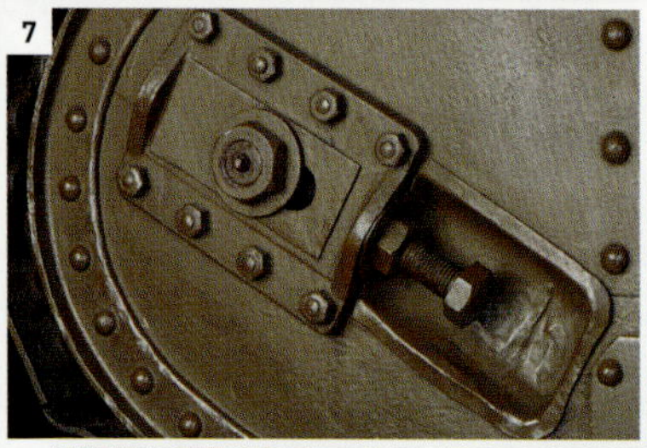

8
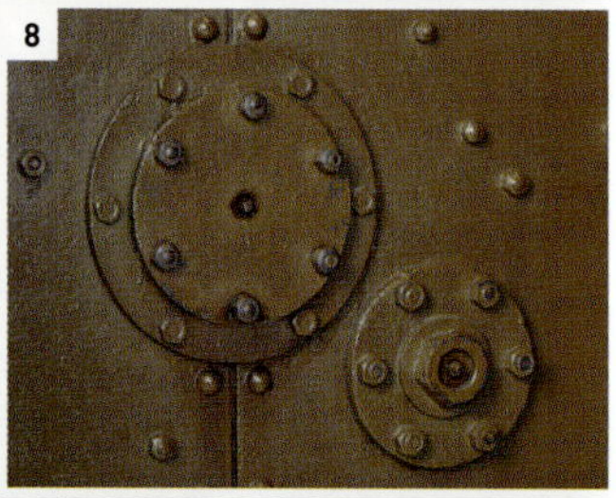

20

9
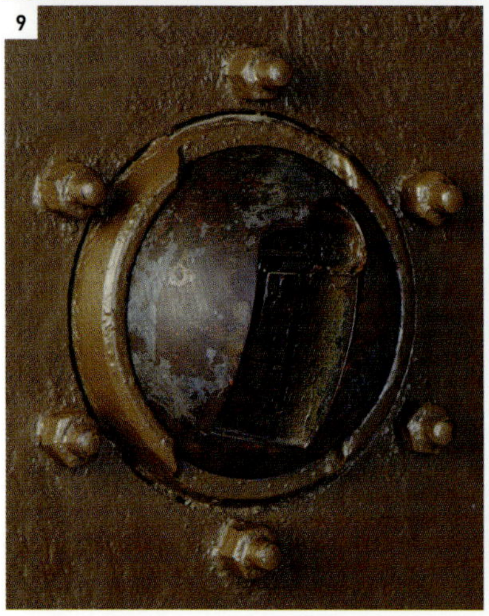

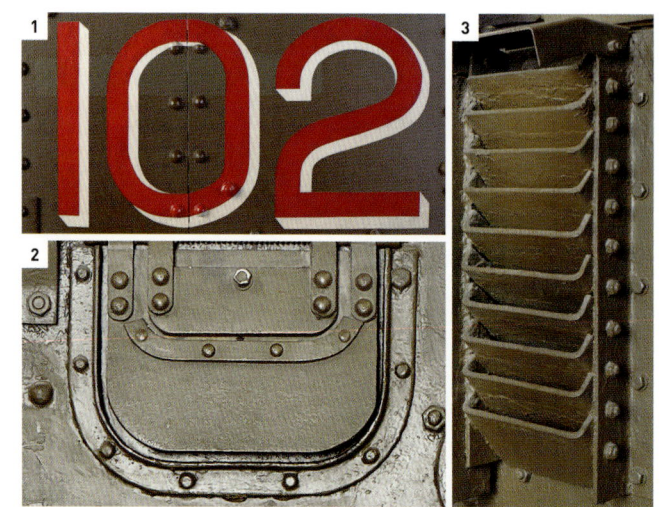

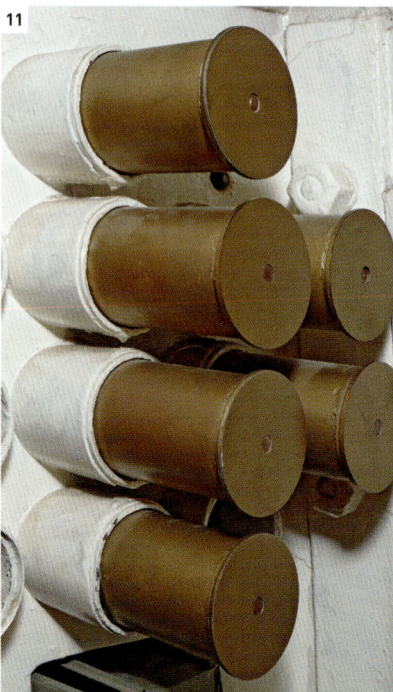

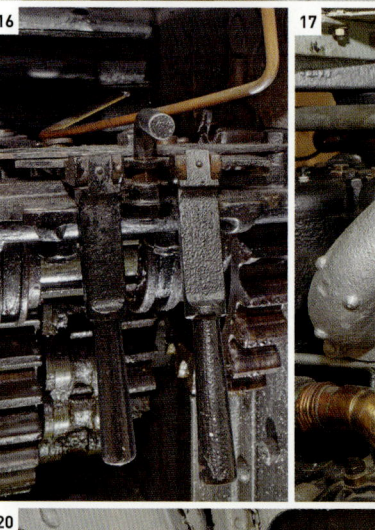

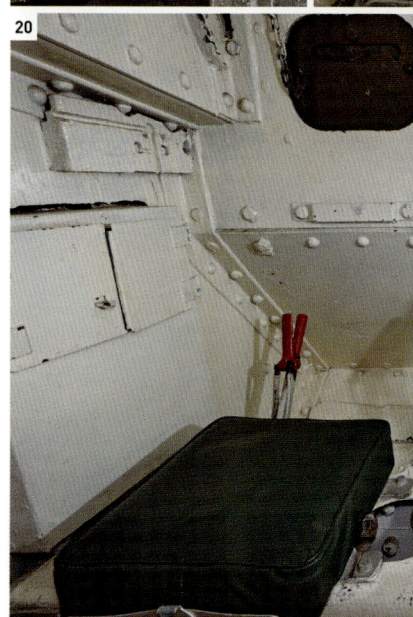

10
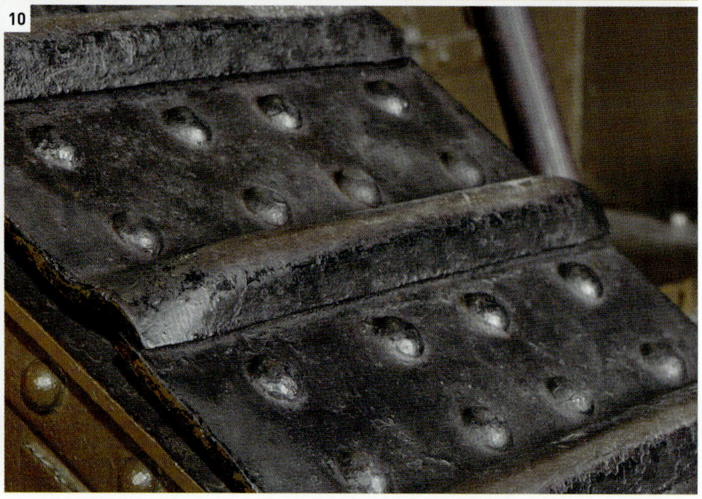

12
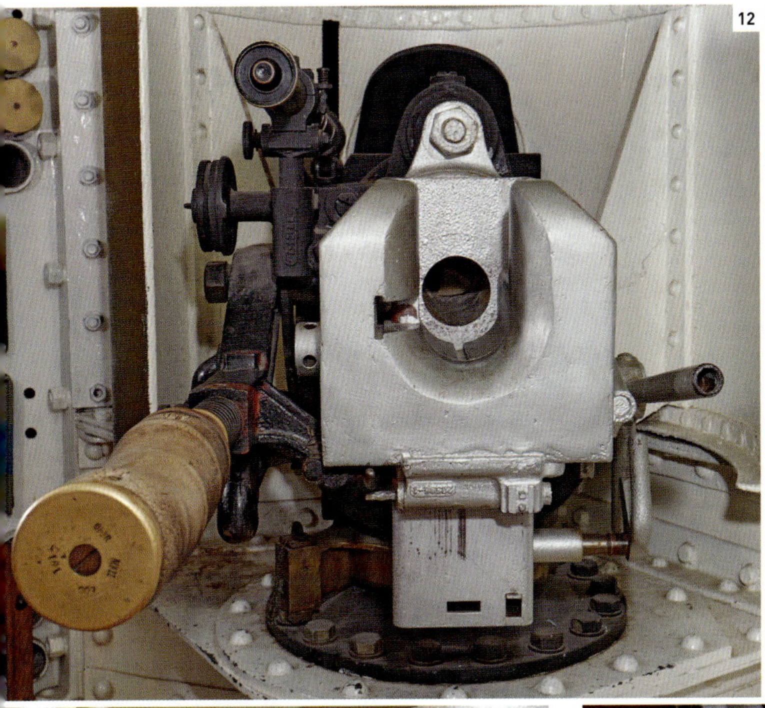

13
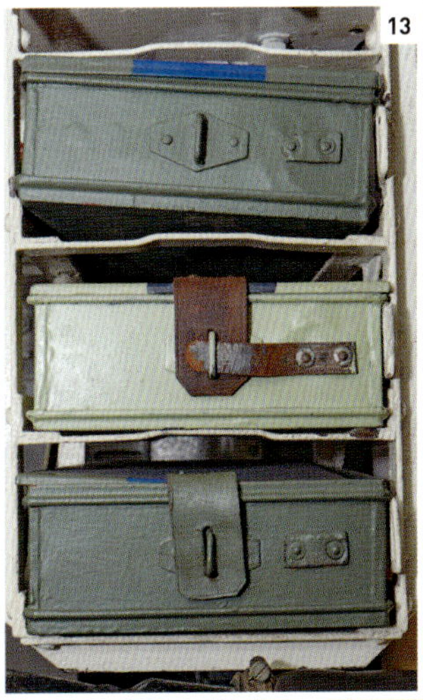

14
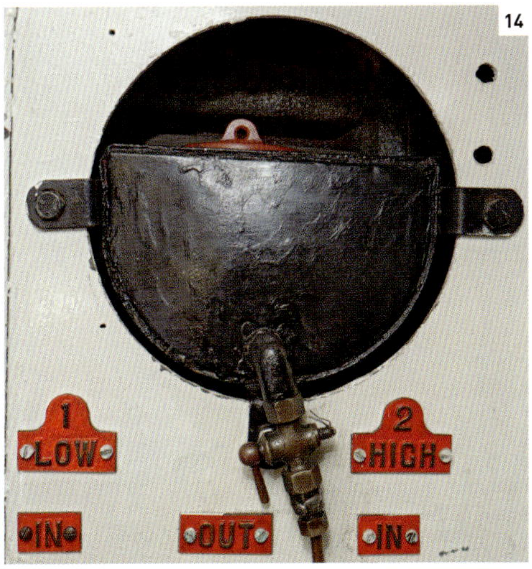

15
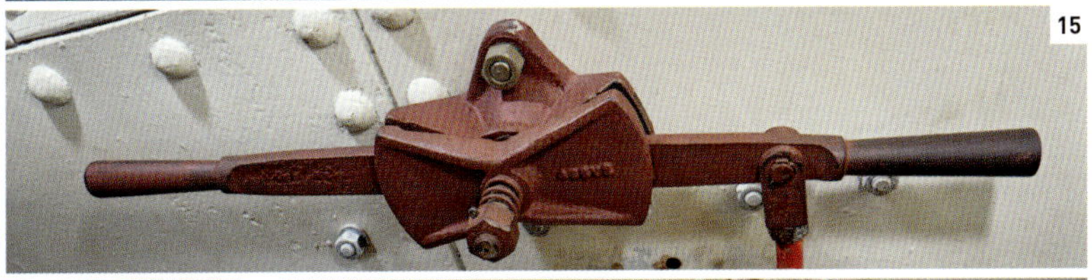

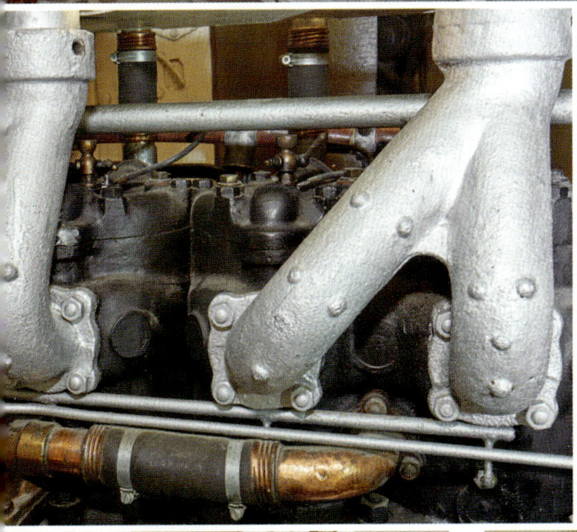

18
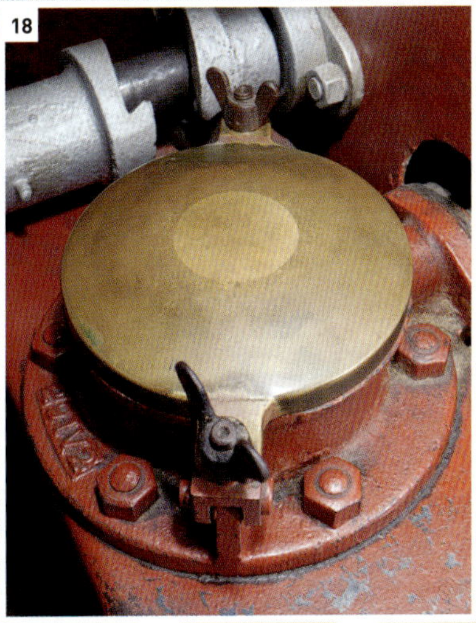

19
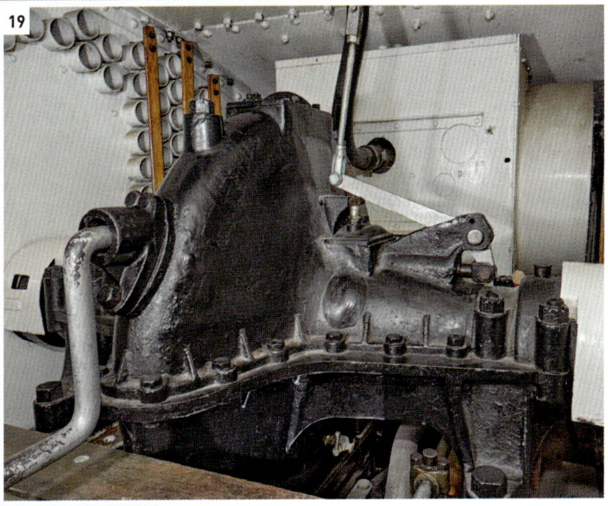

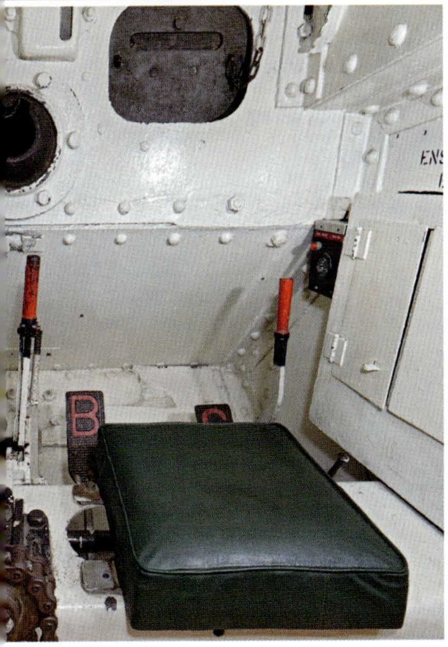

21
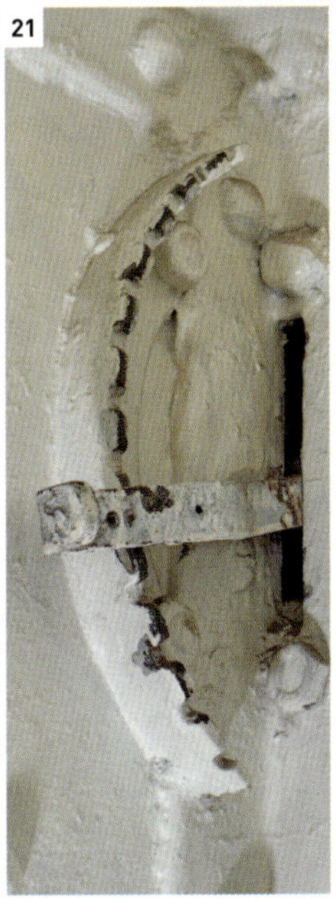

22
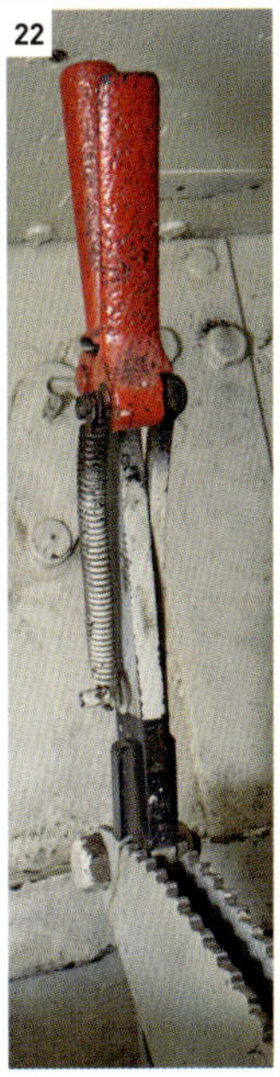

23
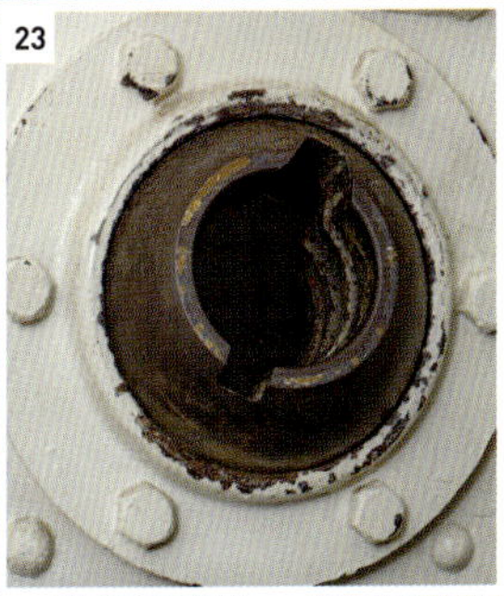

24
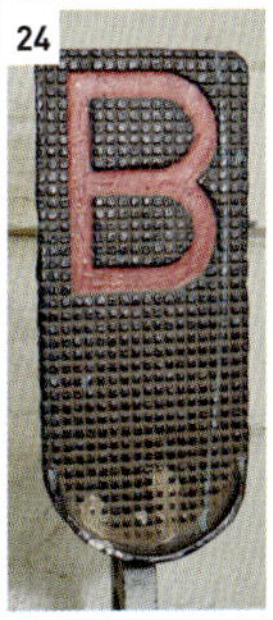

25
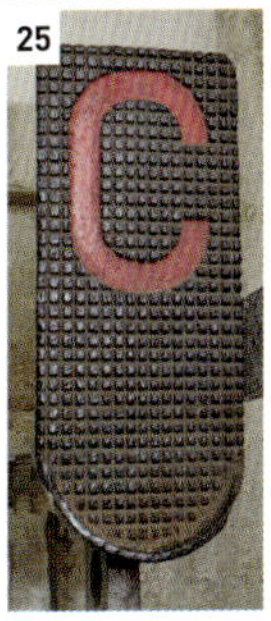

INTERIOR

With the Daimler 105 hp engine positioned in the centre of the interior compartment, conditions for the crew were cramped, hot, noisy, and fume-filled. It was also a rough ride, since the Mark IV lacked suspension. There were no seats for gunners or loaders, so they often rode on top or walked beside the tank when not in action.

11. 6-pounder ammunition stowage **12.** Starboard side 6-pounder gun breech **13.** Machine-gun ammunition stowage **14.** Oil tank to lubricate secondary gears **15.** Differential lock lever **16.** Secondary gear levers **17.** Engine **18.** Oil filler cover **19.** Differential housing **20.** Front commander and driver's positions **21.** Vision port lever **22.** Steering lever **23.** Front machine-gun ball mount (without gun) **24.** Brake pedal **25.** Clutch pedal

Tank Battles in World War I

The need to cross "no man's land" – the barbed-wire-strewn and machine-gun-swept ground between entrenched armies – led to the invention of the tank during World War I. Both Britain and France developed the idea of an armour-plated vehicle with caterpillar tracks to help it cross rough terrain. With armament fitted to suppress enemy machine guns, the tank would crush the wire to allow infantry to advance. Britain deployed 49 tanks towards the end of the Battle of the Somme in September 1916. They were not a great success, but Douglas Haig, the British Commander-in-Chief, saw their potential and ordered 1,000.

Tanks were a work in progress during World War I, with each new model incorporating improvements learnt from battlefield experience. They undoubtedly had an impact on German forces, and were used to best effect when combined in an "all arms battle" – that is, with artillery, air power, and infantry working in cohesion, such as at Cambrai in 1917 and Amiens in 1918. Britain was determined to exploit the new armoured vehicle's potential, designing armoured personnel carrier, self-propelled artillery, and engineer variants, as well as faster light tanks, although not all made it into service before the war's end. In contrast, the Germans made only 20 tanks of their own design, and used captured British and French tanks on the battlefield.

British Mark V tanks carry roof mounted "cribs" to help cross trenches as they advance ready for the Battle of St Quentin Canal in September 1918.

World War I Armoured Cars

Belgium pioneered the combat deployment of armoured cars in World War I, using them to engage German forces around Antwerp in August 1914 and operate behind enemy lines. The earliest vehicles of this type were civilian cars with improvised armour and weaponry – such as the Belgian Minerva and, later, the British Rolls-Royce – but specialist versions soon appeared. Trench warfare and stalemate on the Western Front limited the effectiveness of armoured cars, but where combat was more mobile, their value as fighting machines increased.

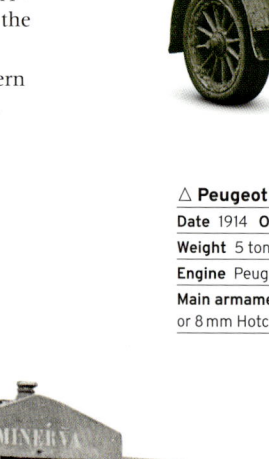

Front-mounted engine

△ **Peugeot modèle AC**
Date 1914	Origin France
Weight 5 tonnes (5.5 tons)	
Engine Peugeot 4-cylinder petrol, 30 kW (40 hp)	
Main armament 37 mm Puteaux SA 18 cannon or 8 mm Hotchkiss machine-gun	

Cannon-carrying Peugeots were given the designation AC (*autocannon*); AM (*automitrailleuse*) denoted those armed with machine-guns. Not suited to trench warfare, Peugeots were few in number by 1918; some vehicles later served with the Polish and Serbian armies.

△ **Minerva Armoured Car**
Date 1914	Origin Belgium
Weight 4.1 tonnes (4.5 tons)	
Engine Minerva 4-cylinder petrol, 30 kW (40 hp)	
Main armament 8 mm Hotchkiss machine-gun	

In 1914, the Belgian car manufacturer Minerva converted around 30 of its civilian vehicles into armoured cars. The earliest model, with a top speed of 40 km/h (25 mph), had no doors or roof. More armour, including a roof and machine-gun protection, was added later. Minervas were the first armoured cars to see combat in World War I.

▽ **Lanchester Armoured Car**
Date 1915	Origin UK
Weight 4.9 tonnes (5.4 tons)	
Engine Lanchester 6-cylinder petrol, 45 kW (60 hp)	
Main arm ament .303 Vickers machine-gun	

Around 36 Lanchesters were built, initially for the Royal Naval Air Service (RNAS) to serve in Belgium, harassing German forces and carrying out reconnaissance missions. A detachment of Lanchesters was deployed to the Caucasus in 1916, reaching as far as Persia and Turkey. Some Lanchesters took part in the Russian Civil War from 1918.

Riveted steel armour

Spoked wheels

△ **Mgebrov-Renault**
Date 1915	Origin Russia
Weight 3.4 tonnes (3.7 tons)	
Engine Renault 4-cylinder petrol, 22.5 kW (30 hp)	
Main armament 2 x 7.62 mm Maxim M1910 machine-guns	

A Russian army captain, Vladimir Mgebrov, designed the Mgebrov-Renault's distinctive sloped armour to deflect enemy fire or minimize damage without adding excessive weight. The original hand-cranked triple-turret arrangement proved too heavy for the Renault chassis, and it was replaced in 1916 by two smaller turrets.

WORLD WAR I ARMOURED CARS · 65

△ **Lancia Ansaldo 1Z**
Date 1916 **Origin** Italy
Weight 3.8 tonnes (4.2 tons)
Engine Lancia V-6 petrol, 30 kW (40 hp)
Main armament 3 x 6.5 mm FIAT-Revelli M1914 machine-guns

Only 10 double-turreted 1Z armoured cars – based on a Lancia frame – were built by the Ansaldo engineering firm. In 1917, the company developed the 1ZM ("M" for *modificato*), producing 110 armoured cars similar to the 1Z, but with a single, more stable turret housing two machine-guns. The 1ZM remained in use in Italy's African colonies until World War II.

Vision ports for driver

Armoured skirt to protect rear wheels

△ **Ehrhardt E-V/4**
Date 1917 **Origin** Germany
Weight 7.3 tonnes (8 tons)
Engine Daimler 6-cylinder petrol, 60 kW (80 hp)
Main armament 3 x 7.92 mm MG08 or MG15 machine-guns

Developed in 1915, Germany's E-V/4 was purpose-built for military action, rather than converted from a civilian vehicle like most World War I armoured cars. A lighter version with enhanced armour served on the more mobile Eastern Front from 1917, and was used in 1919 by German police and paramilitary to subdue urban rioting.

Forward-left turret

Armour-plated chassis

Double-wheels at rear to support weight of armour

△ **Izhorski Fiat**
Date 1917 **Origin** Russia
Weight 4.8 tonnes (5.3 tons)
Engine FIAT 6-cylinder petrol, 54 kW (72 hp)
Main armament 2 x 7.62 mm Maxim M1910 machine-guns

The Russian Izhorski company used a Fiat chassis to create this five-man armoured car, which featured two turrets, each armed with a machine-gun. Around 70 of these vehicles were built, many serving with the Bolsheviks from 1918 in the Russian Civil War.

◁ **White Model AEF Armoured Car**
Date 1918 **Origin** USA
Weight 6 tonnes (6.6 tons)
Engine White 4-cylinder petrol, 33.5 kW (45 hp)
Main armament M1895 Colt-Browning machine-gun

The White Motor Company of Cleveland, Ohio, had been providing chassis for French and American armoured cars since 1915. The White AEF was a variant produced from 1918 for the American Expeditionary Force.

War Takes to the Air

The first flight of a piloted heavier-than-air vehicle took place in December 1903, and little more than a decade later the first combat aircraft were in military service. Strategists were quick to see the potential of this new form of transport. By the end of World War I, air power had become the most important emerging arm of modern warfare.

Flight jacket
Most early military aircraft had open cockpits, so a fur-lined leather flight jacket was an essential item of clothing for airmen. Also vital was a silk scarf to prevent the neck from rubbing raw against the jacket collar.

When World War I began in 1914, the aircraft had already been tested as a tool of destruction. On 1 November 1911, Italian aviator Giulio Gavotti had hand-dropped four bulky grenades over the side of his Etrich Taube monoplane, targeting Ottoman troops around the Ain Zara oasis in Libya during the Italo-Turkish War (1911–12) – the first known example of aerial bombing. However, early military aircraft were primarily used for reconnaissance and observation.

The first fighters

The majority of World War I military aircraft were biplanes. The biplane layout – two wings, one over the other, linked by struts – provided structural rigidity to aircraft made largely of wood and canvas, gave greater lift for short takeoffs with typically under-powered engines, and delivered superb manoeuvrability. The trade-offs were low speed, poor range, and slow climb rates, but these limitations did not hamper the early reconnaissance and observation planes, which operated above battle lines that, especially on the Western Front, were often static and close together. As they overflew the combat zone, aircraft such as Britain's B.E.2 and Germany's Aviatik B.I carried out tasks including deep reconnaissance, battle-damage assessment, artillery spotting, and intelligence gathering.

Rival reconnaissance pilots soon began trading shots using hand-held pistols, rifles, and, eventually, flexibly mounted machine-guns. More martially significant was the rise of "interceptors" – aircraft purpose-built to catch and shoot down observation planes. By 1916, interceptors had become "fighters" that engaged one another with fixed machine-guns in twisting dogfights as they attempted to gain air supremacy.

Fighters became the most important and numerous combat aircraft type of World War I. An important technical innovation came in 1915, with the invention of the synchronizer, or interrupter gear, which enabled machine-guns to fire safely through the arc of the propeller without hitting the spinning blades. The synchronizer put the fighter pilot in a line-of-sight relationship with his weapons; crudely put, his bullets went where his aircraft was pointed. This German invention, which was soon copied in detail or principle by the other combatants, turned aerial duels between fighters into a lethal battle of firepower and pilot skill.

Strategic bombing

World War I also saw the birth of what is now known as "strategic bombing" – the use of bomber aircraft to attack significant industrial or military targets at long ranges. The tactic was pioneered by Germany, primarily because air power was one of the few ways in which it could strike at the distant British homeland.

The first aerial bombardments were delivered by large, slow Zeppelin airships. In 1915 and 1916, Zeppelins made regular raids, particularly over England's north and Midlands. From 1917, however, twin-engined Gotha bomber aeroplanes also began hitting targets in southern England. The Zeppelin and Gotha raids caused comparatively light damage, but it was enough to shock the British public. In total, German bombing raids killed 1,414 people and injured another 3,416. It was in developing a coherent response to these air raids that Britain formed history's first independent air force – the Royal Air Force (RAF).

Anti-aircraft defences
Four gas-mask-clad German infantrymen operate a heavy anti-aircraft machine-gun in World War I. By the war's end, ground fire from automatic weapons had become a significant threat to air operations.

Fighters and pilots
Pilots of No. 1 Squadron, RAF, pose alongside their British S.E.5a biplanes at Clairmarais aerodrome, near Ypres, July 1918. Life expectancy for young combat aviators was appallingly low, often measured in weeks.

Military planners continued to find new battlefield roles for aircraft. Between December 1915 and April 1916, the Royal Flying Corps (RFC), the RAF's predecessor, made air-drops of food and materials to besieged British troops at Kut-el-Amara (in what is now Iraq). Although these clumsy efforts could not save the garrison, they did show that resupplying ground forces by air was possible. Similarly, in 1917–18, the Germans began using aircraft for ground-attack missions, making tactical aerial strikes against enemy targets on the battlefield in support of infantry manoeuvres.

Military leaders were just beginning to exploit the potential of aircraft, but it was already clear that warfare had gained a completely new dimension.

> **"Fight on** and **fly on** to the last drop of **blood**... the last drop of **fuel**... the last beat of the **heart**."
> MANFRED VON RICHTHOFEN, WORLD WAR I GERMAN AIR ACE

TALKING POINT

Manfred von Richthofen

World War I gave rise to the fighter "ace": a pilot who had shot down five or more aircraft in aerial combat. Manfred Freiherr (Baron) von Richthofen was the greatest ace, officially credited with downing 80 enemy aircraft. Born in 1892 in Kleinburg, Lower Silesia, von Richthofen served in the cavalry and infantry before joining the Imperial Air Service from September 1916. Having shown astonishing skill and courage as a fighter pilot, he was given the command of Jagdgeschwader 1 (Fighter Wing 1), known as "Richthofen's Flying Circus" because of its plane's bright colours. The Allies nicknamed von Richthofen the "Red Baron", for his red-painted Fokker triplane. Fate caught up with von Richthofen on 21 April 1918, when he was shot down and killed over Morlancourt Ridge, northern France.

Manfred von Richthofen, the "Red Baron", stands in front of his famous Fokker Dr.I (Dr = Dreidecker, "triplane") on the Western Front.

Reconnaissance Aircraft

When World War I began, the primary roles of military aircraft were observation and reconnaissance, not combat. On the Western Front, with no open flanks for land-based reconnaissance troops to penetrate, aircraft provided an invaluable means to monitor enemy activities, increasingly using aerial photography to map trench systems. These two-seater aircraft could maintain surveillance for two to four hours, flying up to 90 km (56 miles) behind the front line at altitudes above 6,000 m (19,700 ft). Although messages continued to be hand-dropped throughout the war, from 1915 some aircraft were fitted with wireless radios for airborne artillery observations.

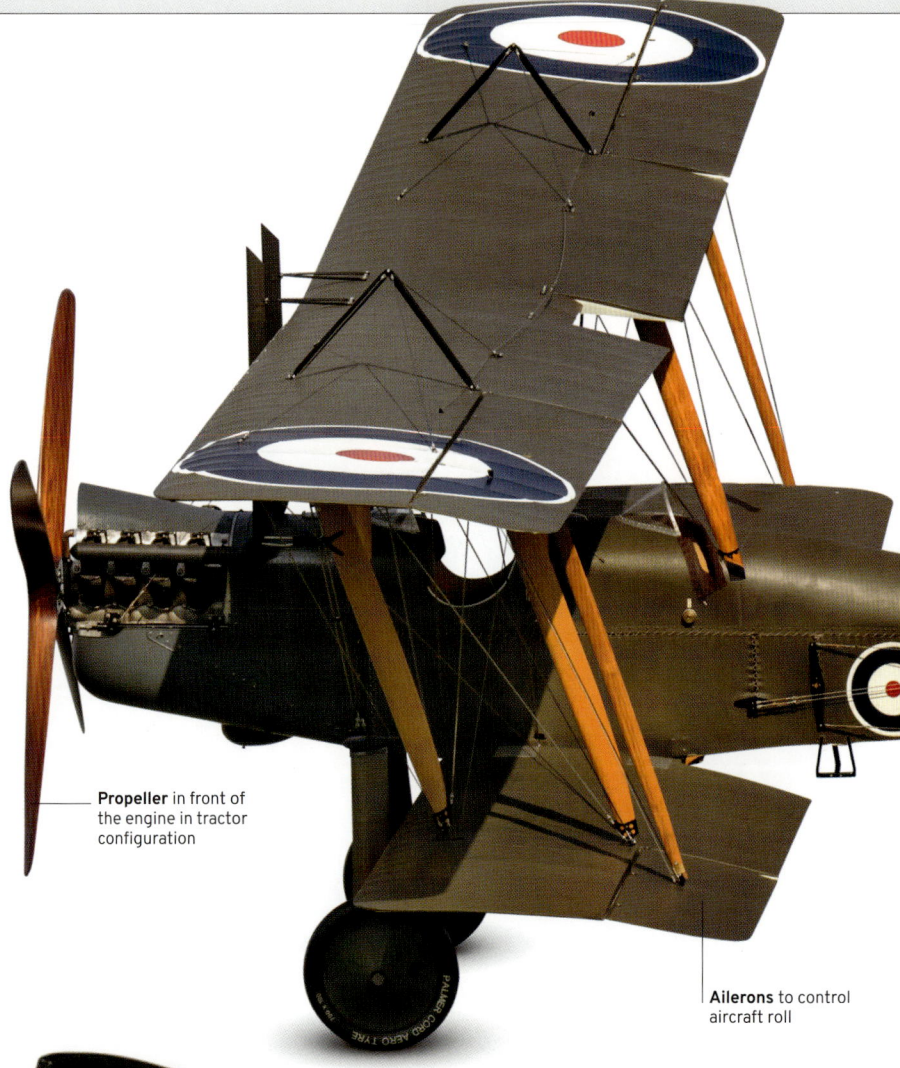

Propeller in front of the engine in tractor configuration

Ailerons to control aircraft roll

▷ **Royal Aircraft Factory B.E.2**
Date 1912 **Origin** UK
Engine 67 kW (90 hp) RAF 1a air-cooled V8 (B.E.2c onwards)
Length 8.3 m (27 ft)
Top speed 116 km/h (72 mph)

Although primarily a reconnaissance aircraft, the B.E.2 was also one of the first aircraft in the Royal Flying Corps (RFC) to be fitted with a machine gun. It was a stable platform for observation and aerial photography, but poor manoeuvrability made the aircraft an easy target for enemy fighters.

△ **Nieuport 12**
Date 1915 **Origin** France
Engine 82 kW (110 hp) Clerget 9Z 9-cylinder rotary
Length 7 m (23 ft)
Top speed 146 km/h (91 mph)

The Nieuport 12 was a sesquiplane – meaning that its lower wing was smaller than the upper wing. This layout reduced drag and so improved performance, and also gave the pilot and observer better downwards visibility, which was especially useful for a reconnaissance aircraft.

Fabric-covered wings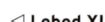

◁ **Lebed XII**
Date 1916 **Origin** Russia
Engine 112 kW (150 hp) Salmson water-cooled radial
Length 8 m (26 ft)
Top speed 135 km/h (84 mph)

The Lebed XII was one of few aircraft produced indigenously by Russia in World War I. Although it drew inspiration from captured German aircraft, the two-seater XII was notoriously unreliable and underpowered, and losses in both combat and training were high.

△ **DFW C.V**
Date 1916 **Origin** Germany
Engine 149 kW (200 hp) Benz Bz IV 6-cylinder in-line water-cooled
Length 7.9 m (26 ft)
Top speed 155 km/h (96 mph)

Reliable, structurally sound, easy to control, and a nimble performer, the DFW C.V was also heavily armed for a reconnaissance aircraft. The pilot had a fixed forward-firing LMG 08 machine-gun, while the observer had a flexible-mount LMG 14 machine-gun for rear and side defence.

△ **LFG Roland C.II**
Date 1916 **Origin** Germany
Engine 119 kW (160 hp) Mercedes D.III 6-cylinder in-line water-cooled
Length 7.7 m (25 ft)
Top speed 165 km/h (103 mph)

Despite its popular name of *Walfisch* ("Whale"), the LFG Roland C.II actually had a low-drag design, partly achieved by limiting the number of wing struts. This gave the aircraft a relatively high top speed, which enabled it to outrun many enemy interceptors.

RECONNAISSANCE AIRCRAFT · 69

▷ **Royal Aircraft Factory R.E.8**

Date 1917	Origin UK

Engine 112 kW (150 hp) RAF 4a 12-cylinder in-line air-cooled

Length 8.5 m (28 ft)

Top speed 164 km/h (102 mph)

Nicknamed the "Harry Tate" after a popular music-hall comedian, the R.E.8 was an artillery-spotting, reconnaissance, and light bomber aircraft. Early variants were plagued by a series of fatal spins, but this fault was rectified by fitting a ventral fin to the base of the tail.

Wired-braced linen-covered fuselage

Curved tailplane to aid flying stability

▽ **Salmson 2**

Date 1917	Origin France

Engine 172 kW (230 hp) Salmson 9Za 9-cylinder water-cooled radial

Length 8.5 m (28 ft)

Top speed 188 km/h (117 mph)

In the final two years of World War I, around 3,200 Salmson 2s were built – the majority for the French Air Force and about 700 for the American Expeditionary Force. The aircraft was also used in daylight bombing and ground attacks.

△ **Armstrong Whitworth F.K.8**

Date 1917	Origin UK

Engine 119 kW (160 hp) Beardmore 6-cylinder in-line water-cooled

Length 9.6 m (31½ ft)

Top speed 153 km/h (95 mph)

The F.K.8 (nicknamed the "Big Ack") was a stable aircraft to fly, which made it ideally suited for a reconnaissance role in World War I. It was also used for ground-attack and bombing missions, and could carry up to 118 kg (260 lb) of bombs.

◁ **LVG C.VI**

Date 1918	Origin Germany

Engine 150 kW (200 hp) Benz Bz.IV 6-cylinder in-line water-cooled

Length 7.45 m (24½ ft)

Top speed 170 km/h (106 mph)

A distinctive feature of the LVG C.VI was the top-mounted exhaust pipe, which projected above the engine like a chimney. The aircraft was also fitted with wireless Morse code transmission equipment, useful for transferring real-time coordinates and information.

70 • 1830–1918

▷ Sopwith F.1 Camel
Date 1917 **Origin** UK
Wingspan 8.53 m (28 ft)
Length 5.72 m (18¾ ft)
Engine 130 hp Clerget 9B/150 hp Bentley BR1 air-cooled 9-cylinder rotary
Top speed 185 km/h (115 mph)

Though difficult to fly, this highly agile aircraft was the first British fighter armed with twin Vickers machine guns. The Sopwith Camel shot down 1,294 aircraft – more than any other fighter in World War I. Some 5,490 Camels were built, giving Allied forces air superiority.

Cut-out section of wing gives pilot better visibility above

Two forward-firing synchronized Vickers machine-guns

Fuselage has wire-braced wooden box-girder design covered with fabric

Welded steel-tube fuselage, cross-braced with cables and covered with fabric and plywood

Two 7.92 mm LMG 08/15 machine-guns

◁ Fokker Dr.1
Date 1917 **Origin** Germany
Wingspan 7.2 m (23½ ft)
Length 5.77 m (19 ft)
Engine 82 kW (110 hp) Oberursel UR II or Le Rhône 9J single-bank 9-cylinder rotary
Top speed 165 km/h (103 mph)

Noting the success of the Sopwith Triplane, the Luftstreitkräfte (German Air Force) adopted the three-wing format for its Fokker Dr.1, flown by air ace Manfred von Richthofen, the "Red Baron" (see p.67).

Short ailerons on upper wings

▷ Bristol Fighter F.2b
Date 1917 **Origin** UK
Wingspan 11.96 m (39¼ ft)
Length 7.87 m (25¾ ft)
Engine 205 kW (275 hp) Rolls-Royce Falcon III in-line V-12
Top speed 198 km/h (123 mph)

The F.2b, the second model of the Bristol Fighter, was one of the few two-seater fighters that was a match against single-seaters, largely thanks to its powerful engine.

Observer's Lewis gun – or sometimes a pair – mounted on a Scarff ring

Exhaust pipe extends behind observer's position

Fighter Aircraft

In their initial reconnaissance roles, as opposing planes encountered one another, the desire to control the airspace above the combat zone resulted in the first "dogfights", fought with pistols and rifles. These encounters proved largely inconclusive until aircraft began to be fitted with machine-guns. Enabling such weapons to follow the pilot's natural sightline and fire through the propeller's arc – without destroying the propeller blades – led to the evolution of dedicated fighter aircraft. Early efforts involved fitting the blades with steel strips to deflect bullets; these were soon superseded by "interrupter" mechanisms, which shut off the gun as the blade passed through the line of fire.

△ AVRO 504K
Date 1917 **Origin** UK
Wingspan 10.97 m (36 ft)
Length 8.97 m (29½ ft)
Engine 82 kW (110 hp) Le Rhône 9Ja single-bank 9-cylinder rotary
Top speed 145 km/h (90 mph)

The 504 enjoyed a production run of nearly 20 years, during which time over 10,000 were built. Initially a reconnaissance and combat plane, the 504's greatest success was as a trainer in its K variant.

FIGHTER AIRCRAFT • 71

▷ **Albatros D.V**

Date 1917	Origin Germany
Wingspan 9 m (29½ ft)	
Length 7.33 m (24 ft)	
Engine 149.13 kW (200 hp) Daimler-Benz D.III in-line 6-cylinder	
Top speed 175 km/h (110 mph)	

The Albatros Type D's semi-monocoque, plywood-skinned fuselage made it more rigid than frame-and-fabric aircraft. The D.V was disliked by pilots, because a fault in the lower wing design was never successfully corrected.

▽ **S.E.5A**

Date 1917	Origin UK
Wingspan 8.11 m (26½ ft)	
Length 6.38 m (21 ft)	
Engine 149.13 kW (200 hp) Hispano-Suiza 8b or Wolseley W4a "Viper" in-line V-8	
Top speed 225 km/h (140 mph)	

This upgraded version of the S.E.5 – already an extremely powerful aircraft – surpassed the Fokker D.VII, its German rival, in terms of stability and speed. The S.E.5a also boasted superior high-altitude performance.

△ **Fokker D.VII**

Date 1918	Origin Germany
Wingspan 8.93 m (29¼ ft)	
Length 6.93 m (22¾ ft)	
Engine 140 kW (185 hp) BMW IIIa in-line 6-cylinder	
Top speed 190 km/h (118 mph)	

Designed by Reinhold Platz, the D.VII – the last of Germany's WWI Fokkers – was viewed by some as the war's best fighter. However, it struggled against the Sopwith Snipe and the Spad XII.

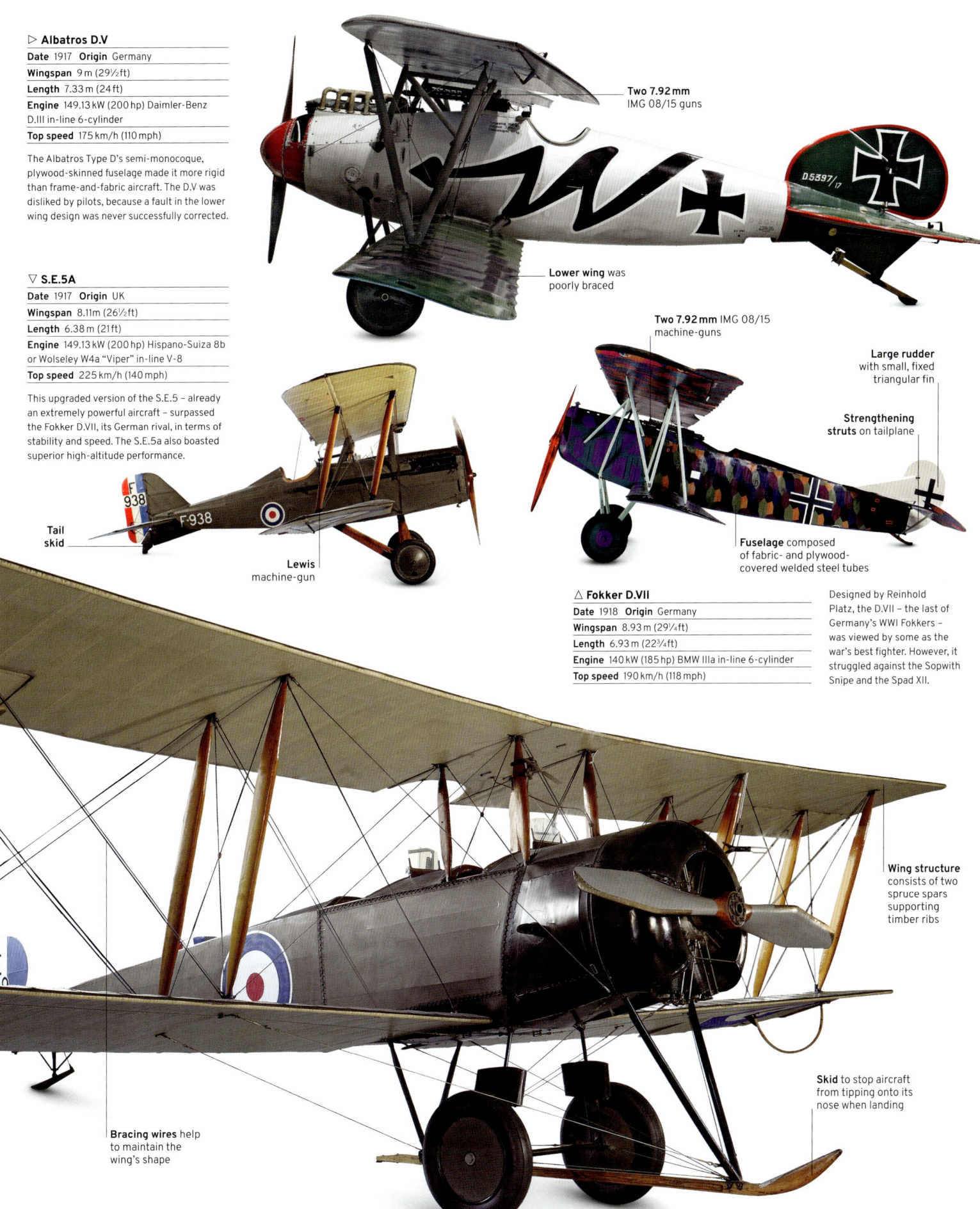

- Two 7.92 mm lMG 08/15 guns
- Lower wing was poorly braced
- Two 7.92 mm lMG 08/15 machine-guns
- Large rudder with small, fixed triangular fin
- Strengthening struts on tailplane
- Fuselage composed of fabric- and plywood-covered welded steel tubes
- Tail skid
- Lewis machine-gun
- Wing structure consists of two spruce spars supporting timber ribs
- Skid to stop aircraft from tipping onto its nose when landing
- Bracing wires help to maintain the wing's shape

RAF S.E.5a

Developed from the S.E.5, the square-nosed Royal Aircraft Factory (RAF) S.E.5a was an exceptionally robust single-seat fighter. In the hands of such World War I Victoria-Cross aces as Albert Ball, Billy Bishop, "Mick" Mannock, and James McCudden, the S.E.5 and S.E.5a proved formidable aerial weapons, valued by pilots for their strength and steadiness, superior speed, excellent all-round field of vision from the cockpit, and good levels of performance – even at high altitude.

THE S.E.5 ("S.E." stood for "Scout Experimental"), which first flew in November 1916, was designed under Henry Folland at the Royal Aircraft Factory in Farnborough, Hampshire. Early Royal Flying Corps fighters, such as the DH2 and FE8, were "pushers" – biplanes with their engines and propellers mounted behind the pilot. The S.E.5's "tractor" configuration, with front-mounted engine and propeller, allowed for a more streamlined design. The upgraded S.E.5a entered service in June 1917 with a powerful 200 hp engine in place of the S.E.5's 150 hp unit, making it one of the fastest aircraft of the war.

The S.E.5a is often seen as the World War I equivalent of the later Hawker Hurricane, of Battle of Britain fame, since both were very stable gun platforms. Likewise, the lighter, more manoeuvrable Sopwith Camel is equated with World War II's Supermarine Spitfire. Together, the S.E.5a and Camel dominated the skies over the Western Front from mid-1917 until the war's end.

SPECIFICATIONS	
Model	Royal Aircraft Factory S.E.5a, 1916 (in service from 1917)
Origin	UK
Production	5,205 (including the S.E.5)
Construction	Wooden frames, fabric covering
Maximum weight	898 kg (1,980 lb)
Engine	149 kW (200 hp) Hispano-Suiza/Wolseley Viper water-cooled V8
Wingspan	8.1 m (26 ft 7 in)
Length	6.38 m (20 ft 11 in)
Range	483 km (300 miles)

Perfect blend
The S.E.5a combined a powerful engine with a simple, slab-sided fuselage and single-bay, strut-and-wire-braced biplane wings. The result was a fast, easily maintained, reliable fighting machine that blended strength with practicality.

Fin is wire-braced to tailplane

Rear decking made of fabric over wooden stringers

Tail is wood and steel-tube frame, fabric-covered

Side panel of fabric fuselage can be opened for maintenance and inspection

FRONT VIEW

REAR VIEW

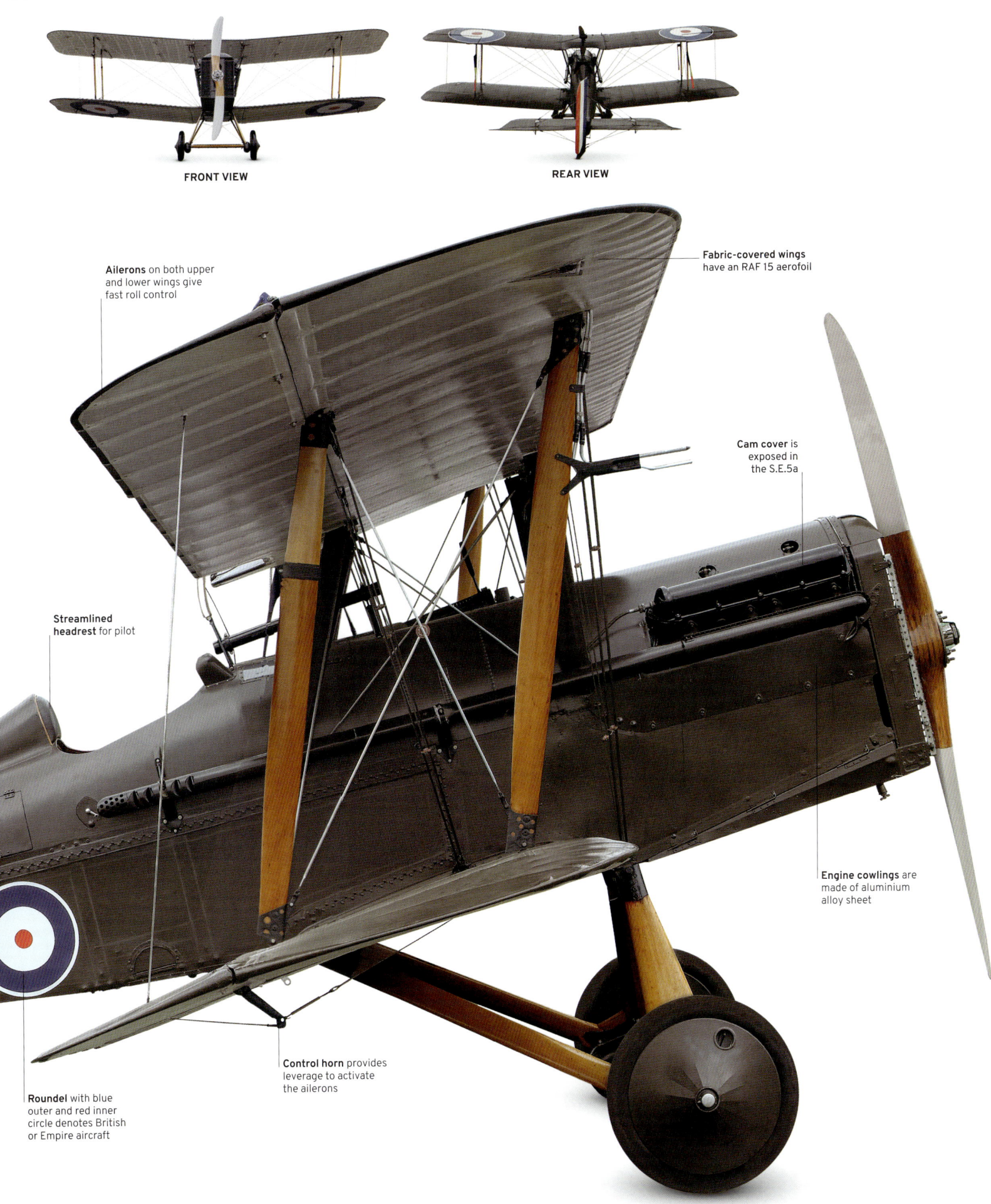

EXTERIOR

With an urgent need for aircraft that could be got to the front line quickly and kept combat-ready, the design of the S.E.5a emphasized simplicity, durability, ease of manufacture, and practical serviceability. Problems with the thin structures of the wings and tail on the S.E.5 were ironed out, and a weakness in the aircraft's steel-tube undercarriage struts was solved by replacing them with wooden struts, which were more resilient.

1. Radiator shutters 2. Radiator drain 3. Oil filler 4. Bullet spacer on bracing wires 5. Leather "boots" on bracing-wire ends 6. Perforated exhaust 7. Control pulley inspection panel 8. Wing strut end 9. Fabric panel join 10. Control horn 11. Bungee suspension 12. Gun sight 13. Control-wire grommet 14. Lewis machine gun

COCKPIT

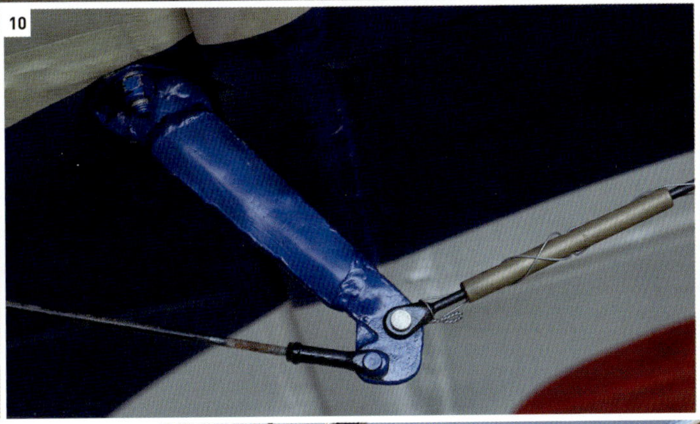

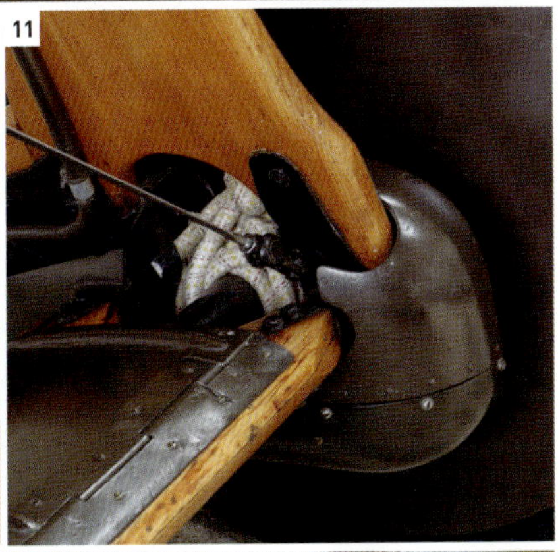

All varnished wood, copper tubes, and brass fittings, the S.E.5a's no-frills "office", which looks spartan by today's standards, was typical of the period. Instruments and controls are seemingly positioned wherever they would fit, with few concessions to pilot comfort or ease of use. The cockpit gave the pilot in-flight access to the aircraft's two machine guns – the movable, rail-mounted Lewis over the wing and the fixed internal Vickers – in order to clear jams and, in the case of the Lewis, change the drum-shaped ammunition magazine.

15. Cockpit general view   16. Fuel pump control
17. Fuel cock   18. Compass   19. Airspeed indicator
20. Control column "spade" with gun firing buttons
21. Rudder bar   22. Radiator shutter lever

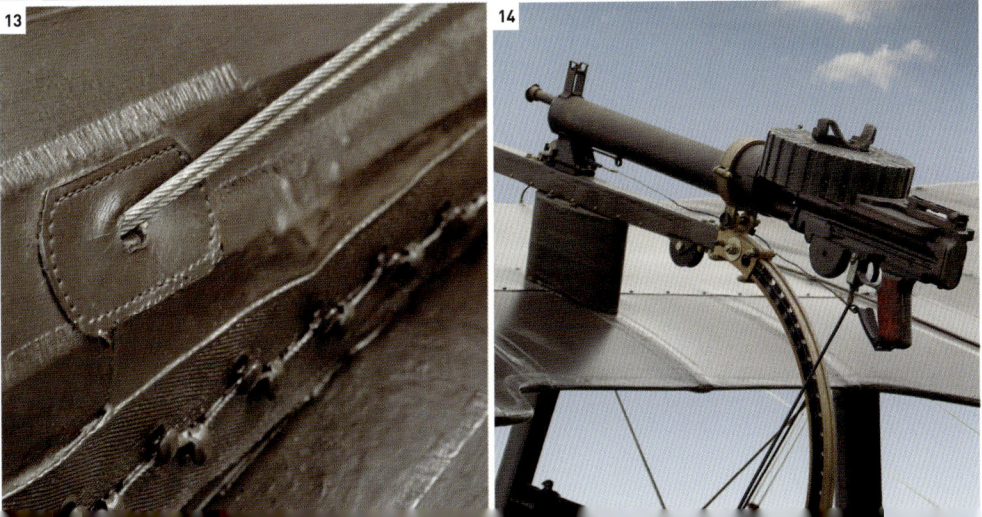

Airship Bombing Raids

Balloons had been deployed to overlook enemy forces on the battlefield during the Napoleonic Wars at the start of the 19th century. Their first use to drop munitions came in 1849, when the Austrians launched paper balloons to send explosive charges over the besieged city of Venice. Many militaries established balloon sections, mainly to assist artillery by spotting targets and observing the fall of shot, but it was World War I that saw the real debut of the airship as a weapon. The designs of Germany's Count Ferdinand von Zeppelin were used to bomb London, creating a great deal of alarm but little actual damage for the effort involved. The Royal Navy saw the need for airships to use as blimps, known as Sea Scouts, that could remain in the air for up to 24 hours and keep watch for German submarines around the coast of Britain. As the war progressed, it gradually became clear to military commanders that aeroplanes were better suited to the tasks performed by airships, which were vulnerable to adverse weather conditions and presented a large, slow target to their enemies.

The British Army airship Beta II at Aldershot in World War I. A rebuilt version of the Beta I airship, Beta II, was an experimental craft tested for a potential role observing troop movements and photographing ground positions. Beta II ended its service life as a training airship for the Royal Naval Air Service in 1916.

78 • 1830–1918

△ **RAF F.E.2b**
"Pusher" propeller behind the crew
Date 1915 Origin UK
Wingspan 14.5 m (47¾ ft)
Length 9.8 m (32¼ ft)
Engine 119 kW (160 hp) Beardmore 6-cylinder
Top speed 147 km/h (91 mph)

Although an unusual configuration, the "pusher" propeller of the F.E.2 series of biplanes allowed the gunner an uninterrupted field of fire. Intended as a fighter, the F.E.2b later found success as a night bomber. Nearly 2,000 of the aircraft were produced.

△ **RAF R.E.8**
Observer had one or two Lewis guns
Tail skid
Date 1916 Origin UK
Wingspan 13 m (42½ ft)
Length 8.5 m (27¾ ft)
Engine 104 kW (140 hp) RAF 4a in-line V12
Top speed 165 km/h (103 mph)

The R.E.8 was better armed and carried a heavier payload than the B.E.2, its predecessor. Although slow, cumbersome, and difficult to fly, it performed well in the hands of skilled pilots and remained in service until the war's end. More than 4,000 R.E.8s were built.

▽ **AEG G.IV**
Date 1916 Origin Germany
Wingspan 18.4 m (60⅓ ft)
Length 9.7 m (31¾ ft)
Engine 2 x 194 kW (260 hp) Daimler-Benz D.IVa in-line 6-cylinder
Top speed 165 km/h (103 mph)

The G.IV's advanced equipment included an all-metal welded-tube frame, radios, and heated suits for the crew. Lacking range, it was used mainly as a tactical bomber to attack battlefield targets, although on the Italian front it also bombed cities, including Padua, Venice, and Verona.

Parabellum LMG14 machine-gun
Machine-gun mounting
Under-wing racks could carry around 400 kg (880 lb) of bombs

Under-wing racks could carry around 180 kg (397 lb) of bombs

△ **Voisin 8**
Date 1916 Origin France
Wingspan 18.2 m (59¾ ft)
Length 10.4 m (34 ft)
Engine 164 kW (220 hp) Peugeot 8Aa in-line V8
Top speed 132 km/h (82 mph)

The first purpose-built night bomber of the French air service (*Aéronautique Militaire*), the Voisin 8 was hampered by the limited capabilities of its Peugeot engine. Changing the engine to a 220.6 kW (300 hp) Renault V-12 improved performance, but the Voisin 8 was never more than mediocre.

Bomber Aircraft

In November 1911, an Italian pilot dropped grenades on ground targets during Italy's campaign to wrest Libya from Ottoman Empire control. This was the first use of an aircraft as a bomber. World War I showed that there was a need to design machines specifically for this role, but progress in producing dedicated bomber aircraft was slow. By the war's end, only the bombing of built-up areas had proven at all effective. The large aircraft needed to carry bomb payloads over long distances were easy prey for fighters, so they quickly became restricted to nighttime operations.

△ **Zeppelin-Staaken R.IV**
Date 1916 Origin Germany
Wingspan 42.2 m (138½ ft)
Length 22.1 m (72½ ft)
Engine 4 x 164 kW (220 hp) Benz Bz.IV in wing nacelles; 2 x 119 kW (160 hp) Mercedes D.III in nose
Top speed 135 km/h (84 mph)

The giant R-series Zeppelins were the most remarkable aircraft built for the *Luftstreitkräfte* (the German Air Force). Equipped with four, five, or six engines, they could accurately deliver up to 2,000 kg (4,410 lb) of bombs to targets in Britain.

BOMBER AIRCRAFT • 79

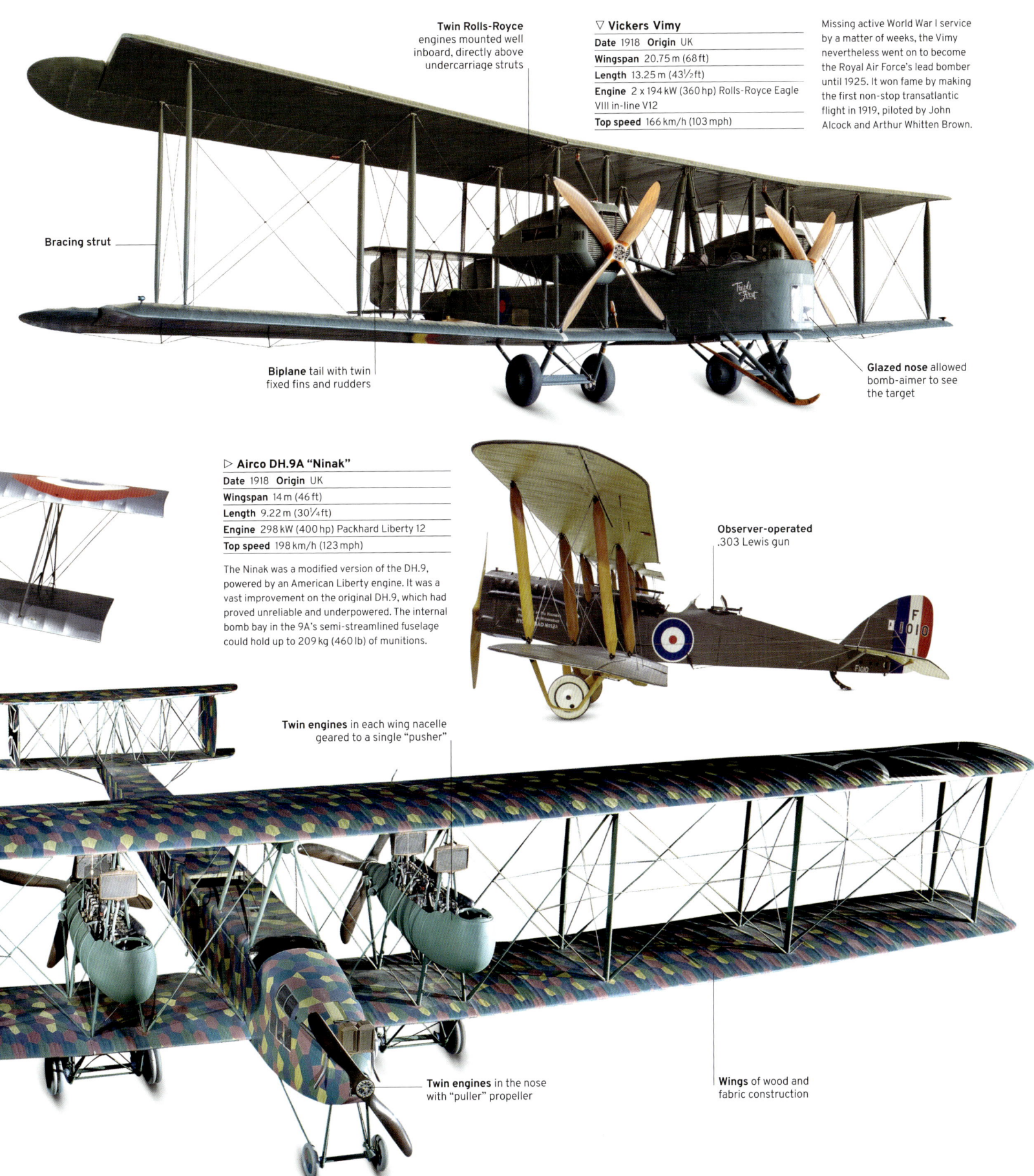

Twin Rolls-Royce engines mounted well inboard, directly above undercarriage struts

▽ Vickers Vimy
Date	1918
Origin	UK
Wingspan	20.75 m (68 ft)
Length	13.25 m (43½ ft)
Engine	2 x 194 kW (360 hp) Rolls-Royce Eagle VIII in-line V12
Top speed	166 km/h (103 mph)

Missing active World War I service by a matter of weeks, the Vimy nevertheless went on to become the Royal Air Force's lead bomber until 1925. It won fame by making the first non-stop transatlantic flight in 1919, piloted by John Alcock and Arthur Whitten Brown.

Bracing strut

Biplane tail with twin fixed fins and rudders

Glazed nose allowed bomb-aimer to see the target

▷ Airco DH.9A "Ninak"
Date	1918
Origin	UK
Wingspan	14 m (46 ft)
Length	9.22 m (30¼ ft)
Engine	298 kW (400 hp) Packhard Liberty 12
Top speed	198 km/h (123 mph)

The Ninak was a modified version of the DH.9, powered by an American Liberty engine. It was a vast improvement on the original DH.9, which had proved unreliable and underpowered. The internal bomb bay in the 9A's semi-streamlined fuselage could hold up to 209 kg (460 lb) of munitions.

Observer-operated .303 Lewis gun

Twin engines in each wing nacelle geared to a single "pusher"

Twin engines in the nose with "puller" propeller

Wings of wood and fabric construction

Sea Battles in World War I

The navies of World War I were initially dominated by enormous battleships. However, the reality of the conflict gradually undermined the rationale of these great vessels. As the war progressed, submarines, torpedo boats, and sea mines emerged to challenge the battleships' supremacy, both tactically and strategically.

U-boat engine room
German engineers monitor the operation of a U-boat powerplant. The typical submerged speed of a U-boat was about 9 knots (17 km/h), and about 17 knots (31 km/h) on the surface, where the U-boats spent most of their time.

Recruitment poster
This stirring US Navy poster is a bold attempt to attract new recruits. The US Navy began combat operations from 6 April 1917, with its principal roles being convoy escort duties and antisubmarine warfare.

When World War I began, the power of a navy was mainly determined by the numbers of battleships it had in service. Fitted with turreted heavy guns, plated in armour, and with oceanic reach, these powerful ships projected influence and security around the globe. In battle, they could engage enemies with massive shells at ranges beyond the horizon, relying on complicated (and often fallible) fire-control technologies. The British Royal Navy – at the time, the most powerful navy in the world – entered hostilities with 52 battleships against the 34 capital vessels of the German Kaiserliche Marine.

Big-gun battles

The first year of the war produced a few major clashes between opposing battleships and cruisers at disparate points on the globe. On 28 August 1914, the Germans lost three light cruisers and a torpedo boat during the Battle of Heligoland Bight near Germany's northern coast. The tide turned on 1 November at the Battle of Coronel off Chile, when the formidable German battlecruisers *Scharnhorst* and *Gneisenau* sank two British armoured cruisers. However, both German warships were later destroyed, along with a pair of light cruisers accompanying them, in the retaliatory Battle of the Falkland Islands on 8 December. The Germans also lost an armoured cruiser, *Blücher*, on 24 January 1915 during a huge North Sea gun battle at Dogger Bank.

The zenith of battleship warfare was the Battle of Jutland, fought on 31 May–1 June 1916. This large-scale action brought the full might of the German High Seas Fleet and the British Grand Fleet into contact off the coast of Denmark; the objective was potential control of the North Sea. In a chaotic, rather random engagement, the British came off worst materially, with three of their battlecruisers, three armoured cruisers, and eight destroyers being sunk. Although the Germans lost two battleships, four light cruisers, and five destroyers, the bulk of their fleet made it safely home to port. The Kaiser's government declared a victory, but in reality no strategic advantage had been gained.

Changing threats

While surface actions such as this were awe-inspiring events, with huge shells arcing from billowing heavy guns across miles of ocean, the battleships had already begun their slide towards obsolescence. New threats meant that for much of the war, many battleships spent their time at anchor in protected ports.

Among the emerging threats were sea mines: contact-detonated canisters of explosive that were deployed in their tens of thousands off enemy coasts and along contested sea lanes. These passive weapons sank many warships and merchant vessels. At the Battle of the Dardanelles on 18 March 1915, for example, three Allied warships were lost to mines during an Allied attempt to force passage up the Dardanelles Strait.

Light and fast torpedo boats also posed a serious challenge to heavier vessels; at Jutland, the British

HMS *Ramillies*
One of five British *Revenge*-class battleships, HMS *Ramillies* was launched in September 1916. It survived the war, and one of its 15 in main guns now stands on permanent display outside the Imperial War Museum in London.

SEA BATTLES IN WORLD WAR I · 81

"Our losses were heavy, and we miss many most gallant comrades"

ADMIRAL SIR JOHN JELLICOE, IN A MESSAGE TO THE BRITISH FLEET AFTER THE BATTLE OF JUTLAND IN 1916

commander, Admiral Sir John Jellicoe, felt sufficiently intimidated by torpedo-boat attacks to break off pursuit of the German fleet.

Submarine war

As successful as the new sea mines were, arguably the most important development of World War I naval warfare was the submarine, which Germany used to great strategic effect, unleashing its growing fleet of U-boats against Allied vessels. On 22 September 1914, a single U-boat, *U-9*, sank three British armoured cruisers in less than an hour in the southern North Sea. The submarines of the Central Powers also began preying on merchant ships, sinking approximately 5,000 such vessels and killing 15,000 sailors by the end of the war.

Losses to submarines eventually compelled the Allies to adopt a system of escorted convoys to elevate the statistical likelihood of merchant ships reaching transatlantic shores without being intercepted and sunk. With the rise of the submarine, the battleship was no longer the most influential vessel on the high seas.

> **TALKING POINT**
>
> ### The Blockade of Europe
>
> The British naval blockade of Germany and its allies is considered one of the most controversial aspects of World War I. The blockade was established in August 1914 and ran until June 1919, not finishing until seven months after the signing of the Armistice. Britain used mine-laying ships to deploy vast numbers of sea mines off enemy coastlines, while its warships attempted to cut off access to the English Channel and the North Sea. By early 1915, all merchant vessels bound for Germany could be stopped and their cargoes seized. The impact of the blockade by the end of the war was profound. Estimates of deaths from malnutrition and associated diseases range from about 400,000 to more than 700,000. The blockade was not impenetrable, but it made a significant contribution to Germany's final defeat.
>
>
>
> **German submarine captains** Paul Konig, left, (*Deutschland*) and Wolfgang Schwartzkopf, right, (*Bremen*) became famous for blockade-running exploits.

Dreadnoughts and Battleships

The launch of HMS *Dreadnought* in 1906 began an international arms race to build new generations of fast and thickly armoured "all-big-gun" warships. By 1914, these had evolved into "super-dreadnought" monsters such as the British *Queen Elizabeth* class, with a steam-turbine-driven top speed of 24 knots (44 km/h), armour plate 330 mm (13 in) thick, and guns with a maximum range of around 26 km (16 miles). Battlecruisers also emerged as a new type of battleship – heavily armed but more lightly armoured for greater speed.

▷ HMS Dreadnought

Date 1906 **Origin** UK
Displacement 21,845 tonnes (24,080 tons)
Length 160.6 m (527 ft)
Top speed 21 knots (39 km/h)

Armed with 10 big guns in five turrets and no "intermediates", and propelled by turbines, which saved weight, increased speed, and improved reliability, *Dreadnought* broke new ground in warship design. It was also better armoured than previous ships.

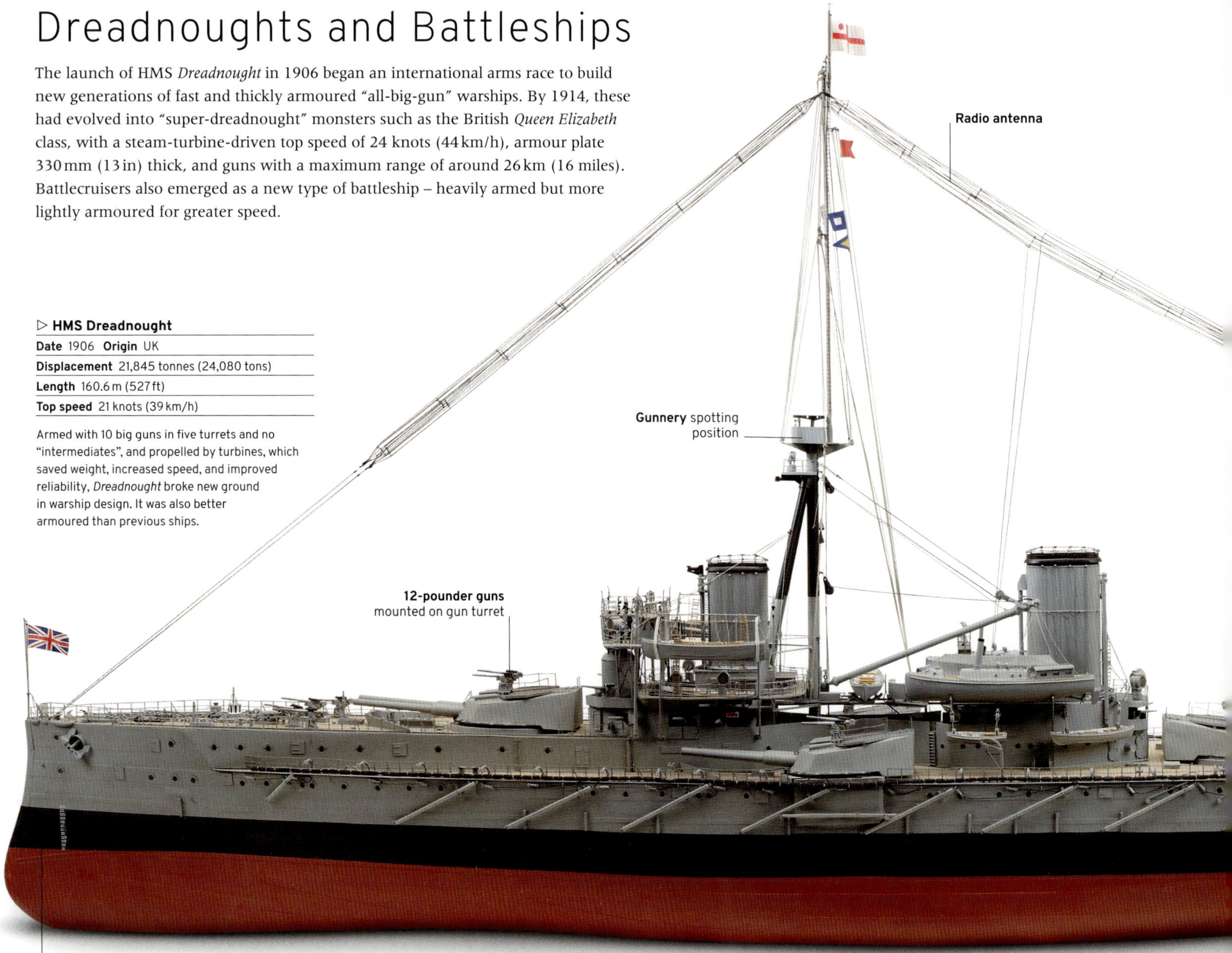

- Radio antenna
- Gunnery spotting position
- 12-pounder guns mounted on gun turret
- Waterline belt armour was 178–279 mm (7–11 in) thick

▽ Courbet

Date 1913 **Origin** France
Displacement 25,579 tonnes (28,196 tons)
Length 166 m (545 ft)
Top speed 21 knots (39 km/h)

Courbet was an early French contribution to the dreadnought arms race, the lead ship of a class of four vessels. It had six twin 305 mm guns and 22 single 138 mm guns as its main armament.

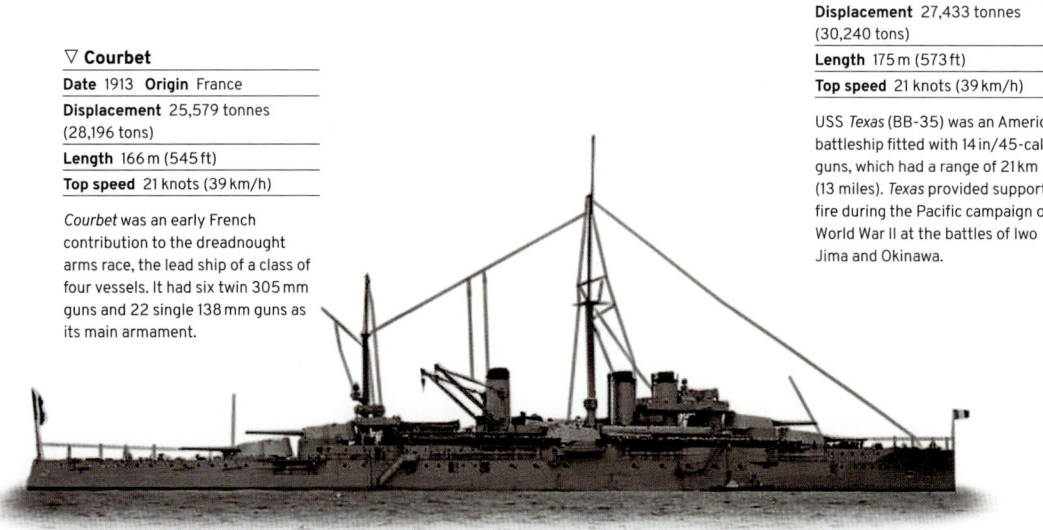

▷ USS Texas

Date 1914 **Origin** USA
Displacement 27,433 tonnes (30,240 tons)
Length 175 m (573 ft)
Top speed 21 knots (39 km/h)

USS *Texas* (BB-35) was an American battleship fitted with 14 in/45-calibre guns, which had a range of 21 km (13 miles). *Texas* provided support fire during the Pacific campaign of World War II at the battles of Iwo Jima and Okinawa.

DREADNOUGHTS AND BATTLESHIPS · 83

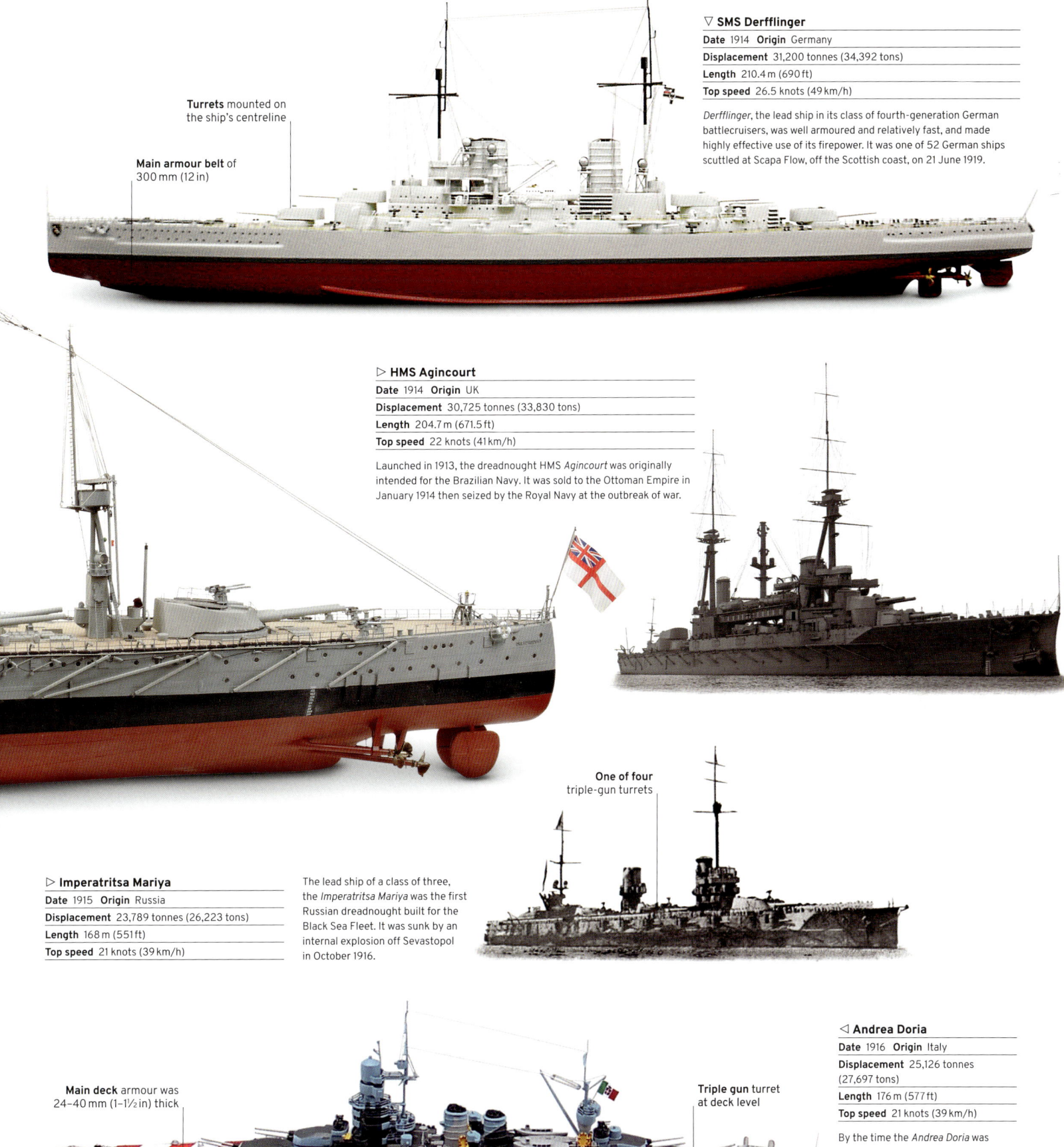

Turrets mounted on the ship's centreline

Main armour belt of 300 mm (12 in)

▽ **SMS Derfflinger**
Date 1914 **Origin** Germany
Displacement 31,200 tonnes (34,392 tons)
Length 210.4 m (690 ft)
Top speed 26.5 knots (49 km/h)

Derfflinger, the lead ship in its class of fourth-generation German battlecruisers, was well armoured and relatively fast, and made highly effective use of its firepower. It was one of 52 German ships scuttled at Scapa Flow, off the Scottish coast, on 21 June 1919.

▷ **HMS Agincourt**
Date 1914 **Origin** UK
Displacement 30,725 tonnes (33,830 tons)
Length 204.7 m (671.5 ft)
Top speed 22 knots (41 km/h)

Launched in 1913, the dreadnought HMS *Agincourt* was originally intended for the Brazilian Navy. It was sold to the Ottoman Empire in January 1914 then seized by the Royal Navy at the outbreak of war.

One of four triple-gun turrets

▷ **Imperatritsa Mariya**
Date 1915 **Origin** Russia
Displacement 23,789 tonnes (26,223 tons)
Length 168 m (551 ft)
Top speed 21 knots (39 km/h)

The lead ship of a class of three, the *Imperatritsa Mariya* was the first Russian dreadnought built for the Black Sea Fleet. It was sunk by an internal explosion off Sevastopol in October 1916.

Main deck armour was 24–40 mm (1–1½ in) thick

Triple gun turret at deck level

◁ **Andrea Doria**
Date 1916 **Origin** Italy
Displacement 25,126 tonnes (27,697 tons)
Length 176 m (577 ft)
Top speed 21 knots (39 km/h)

By the time the *Andrea Doria* was completed, its main armament of 305 mm guns had been outclassed by heavier armaments on other international battleships. The ship was rebuilt in 1937–40 and served in the Italian navy until 1956.

USS Texas

With a main armament of ten 14 in guns, the USS *Texas* entered service in 1914 as the world's most powerful warship. This *New York*-class battleship, which cost around $6 million to build, was the product of the naval arms race that preceded World War I.

DESPITE THE HEAVY FIREPOWER of this "superdreadnought", the *Texas* was behind the times as it used coal-fired reciprocating engines rather than oil-fired steam turbines. Oil-fired boilers were installed in 1927 as part of a major overhaul, with the ship's armour and fire-control systems also being upgraded. Anti-aircraft guns and fire-control and air-defence radars were added at a later date.

By the outbreak of World War II, the *Texas* was no longer fast enough to keep up with more modern capital ships in combat. Before the US entered the war, the *Texas* escorted merchant convoys across the Atlantic. Subsequently, it was used for shore bombardment, since its 14 in guns could fire 680 kg (1,500 lb) shells at targets more than 20 km (12 miles) away, at a rate of one round every 45 seconds. In this role, the *Texas* provided fire support for landings in North Africa, Normandy, Iwo Jima, and Okinawa.

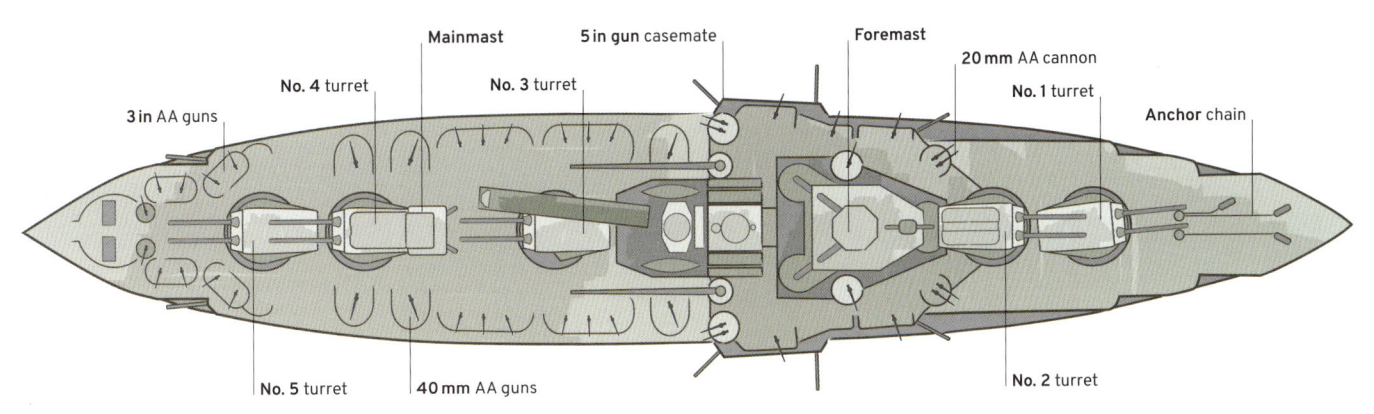

SPECIFICATIONS	
Name	USS *Texas*
Commissioned	1914
Class and type	*New York*-class battleship
Displacement	27,433 tonnes (30,240 tons)
Length	175 m (573 ft)
Propulsion	2 × triple-expansion steam engines
Armament	10 × 14 in/45-calibre guns
Armour	356 mm (14 in) max.
Maximum speed	21 knots (39 km/h)

Illustrious career
Having served with the Grand Fleet in World War I, the *Texas* earned five battle stars during World War II, before being decommissioned in 1946. The last surviving dreadnought-era battleship, it is now a museum ship at San Jacinto, Texas.

EXTERIOR

Observers in the battery control, situated at the top of the foremast, relayed readings of range, speed, and bearing that were used to instruct the gunners. Below the battery control sat other areas that needed a high, clear line of sight, such as the bridge and lookout platforms. The *Texas* carried two paravanes, which were towed behind the ship to snag or cut the lines of submerged mines.

1. Rear view of foremast **2.** Anchor capstans
3. Battery control **4.** Ship's bell **5.** Anti-aircraft guns
6. Bofors 40mm anti-aircraft gun **7.** Forward gun turrets **8.** 20mm anti-aircraft cannon **9.** Paravane
10. Line cutter of paravane **11.** Breech of 14in gun

USS TEXAS • 87

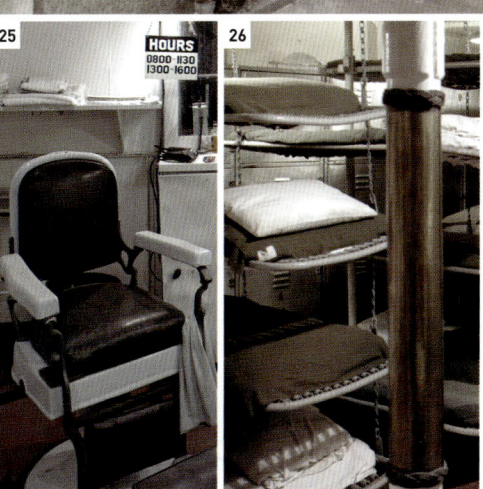
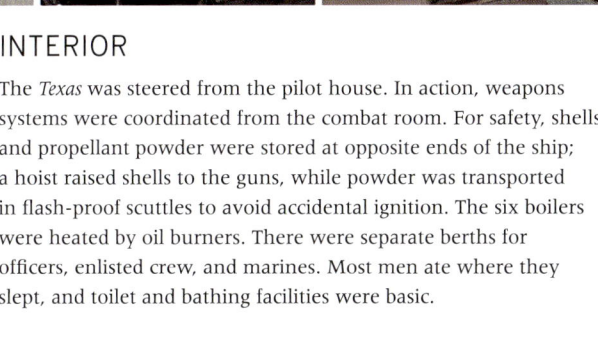

INTERIOR

The *Texas* was steered from the pilot house. In action, weapons systems were coordinated from the combat room. For safety, shells and propellant powder were stored at opposite ends of the ship; a hoist raised shells to the guns, while powder was transported in flash-proof scuttles to avoid accidental ignition. The six boilers were heated by oil burners. There were separate berths for officers, enlisted crew, and marines. Most men ate where they slept, and toilet and bathing facilities were basic.

12. Combat room **13.** Pilot house **14.** Chart room **15.** Below-deck 14in shell hoist **16.** Powder scuttles **17.** Oil burner nozzle detail **18.** Emergency steering position **19.** Oil-fired boiler **20.** Enlisted men's galley **21.** Bakery **22.** Cafeteria **23.** Post office **24.** Crew locker **25.** Barber's shop **26.** Marine berths

Destroyers and Escorts

Essentially coastal vessels, early destroyers displaced around 200 tonnes (220 tons), but by 1914 destroyers had grown in size, with some displacing over 1,000 tonnes (1,100 tons). Although much bigger, these ships were still fast, some with speeds in excess of 30 knots (56 km/h), and they typically carried 4-inch guns or larger, in addition to torpedoes. Shipping losses to German U-boats during World War I diverted Allied destroyers from defending the fleet to protecting convoys and hunting submarines. Built for speed and with limited range, these destroyers were not ideal for long-range duties, so specialist escort destroyers with depth charges and hydrophones were developed to counter the U-boat threat.

△ HMS Hornet
Date 1911 **Origin** UK
Displacement 1,006 tonnes (1,109 tons)
Length 75 m (246 ft)
Top speed 28 knots (52 km/h)

Armed with two 4 in guns, two 12-pounders, and a pair of torpedo tubes, *Hornet* was one of 23 *Acheron*-class destroyers built for the British Royal Navy. *Hornet* served throughout World War I, screening battle squadrons and carrying out antisubmarine work. In 1918, it survived serious damage inflicted by fire from Austro-Hungarian destroyers.

△ Novik
Date 1913 **Origin** Russia
Displacement 3,129 tonnes (3,450 tons)
Length 110 m (361 ft)
Top speed 25 knots (46 km/h)

The *Novik* was a German-built Russian armoured cruiser. It was damaged and scuttled during the Russo-Japanese War (1904–05), but subsequently salvaged, repaired, and heavily modified for the Japanese Navy. It served Japan from 1906 to 1913 as the *Suzuya*, albeit with reduced performance.

△ SMS S19
Date 1913 **Origin** Germany
Displacement 697 tonnes (768.3 tons)
Length 71 m (233 ft)
Top speed 32 knots (59.3 km/h)

This torpedo boat of the Imperial German Navy was designed to be smaller than previous iterations. It fought in the Battle of Jutland in 1916, and survived World War I to be kept in reserve until 1931.

DESTROYERS AND ESCORTS • 89

French tricolor naval ensign (blue, white, and red)

△ **Bisson**
Date 1913 **Origin** France
Displacement 800 tonnes (882 tons)
Length 78 m (256 ft)
Top speed 30 knots (56 km/h)

Six *Bisson*-class destroyers were constructed for the French Navy. *Bisson*, the lead ship of the class, was commissioned in September 1913. It was armed with two 100 mm guns, four 65 mm guns, and two twin 450 mm torpedo tubes. *Bisson* saw action in World War I, and served until 1933.

▽ **HMAS Geranium**
Date 1915 (Royal Navy) **Origin** UK
Displacement 1,270 tonnes (1,400 tons)
Length 81.6 m (268 ft)
Top speed 16.5 knots (30.6 km/h)

Built for use in World War I, this *Arabis*-class sloop (the term was used in this era for specialized convoy-defence ships) was a minesweeper used by Britain's Royal Navy until 1919, when it was transferred to the Royal Australian Navy.

Cowl vent let air flow below deck but kept out seawater

△ **SMS V43**
Date 1915 **Origin** Germany
Displacement 1,106 tonnes (1,219 tons)
Length 79.5 m (261 ft)
Top speed 33.5 knots (62 km/h)

This *V25*-class *Großes Torpedoboot* (Large Torpedo Boat) survived numerous wartime engagements, but was one of the many German warships scuttled at Scapa Flow on 21 June 1919. British crews managed to beach and save the sinking *V43*, however, and it ended its service in 1921 as a target ship.

102 mm/60-calibre Pattern 1911 gun (one of four)

Three smokestacks served five British-made Thornycroft boilers

△ **Kerch**
Date 1917 **Origin** Russia
Displacement 1,347 tonnes (1,485 tons)
Length 92.5 m (304 ft)
Top speed 31 knots (57 km/h)

The *Kerch* belonged to the *Fidonisy*-class of Russian destroyer. It was built from October 1915, launched in May 1916, and commissioned in June 1917. In June 1918, however, it was scuttled by its crew to prevent it falling into German hands as part of the Treaty of Brest-Litovsk.

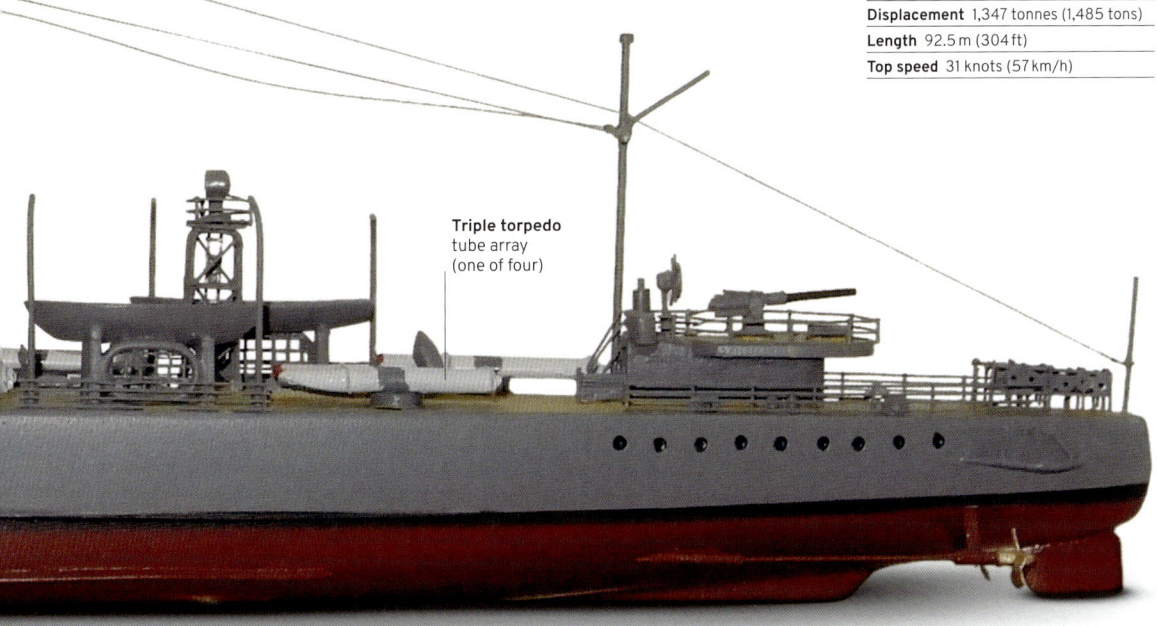

Triple torpedo tube array (one of four)

◁ **USS Ward**
Date 1918 **Origin** USA
Displacement 1,267 tonnes (1,397 tons)
Length 95.8 m (314 ft)
Top speed 35 knots (65 km/h)

USS *Ward*, a *Wickes*-class destroyer, was commissioned in July 1918, having been built in just over three months. It achieved fame in World War II by sinking a Japanese midget submarine at Pearl Harbor just prior to the air attack on 7 December 1941. *Ward* sank after kamikaze attacks in 1944.

Submarine Warfare in World War I

More than 5,000 Allied ships were sunk by German submarines during World War I. In September 1915, complaints from a neutral US after the sinking of passenger liners and the loss of its citizens' lives caused Germany to cease its unrestricted sinking of ships. The potential to starve Britain into submission spurred the German navy to argue for a resumption of unrestricted attacks in 1917. The German high command understood that allowing such attacks would bring the US into the conflict. Assessing that they could defeat Britain and France before the American military could influence events, they recommenced attacks. The Allies responded with new convoy tactics that limited the effectiveness of the submarines and prevented the Germans from achieving their aims. Nevertheless, the potential of submarine warfare to have strategic results on a conflict had been realized, and it would be used again in World War II.

One of the 15 UC-1 Class submarines built by Germany early in World War I surfaces. These submarines were used solely to deploy mines.

World War I Submarines

On 5 September 1914, the German submarine *U-21* sank the British cruiser HMS *Pathfinder* off eastern Scotland – the first warship ever sunk by a submarine-fired torpedo. Although the ease with which capital ships could be sunk by submarines had been predicted before World War I, Allied naval commanders sometimes disastrously failed to shield large warships with destroyer screens. Fear of submarines came to inhibit the operation of surface fleets, and the Royal Navy's Grand Fleet spent much of the war out of German U-boat range. The most effective role for U-boats, however, was as commerce raiders: attacks on merchant shipping almost succeeded in crippling Britain's war effort. The Allies eventually adopted an effective solution – a system of protected merchant convoys.

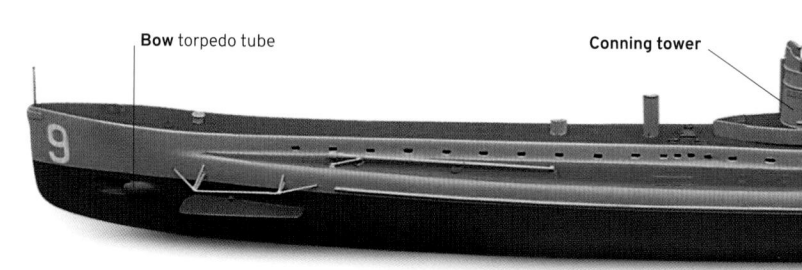

△ **SM U-9**
Date 1910 **Origin** Germany
Displacement 493 tonnes (543 tons)
Length 57.4 m (188 ft)
Top speed 14 knots (26 km/h)

Like all pre-1912 U-boats, the four Type *U-9* coastal submarines (of which *U-9* was the lead boat) had both electric motors and petrol engines, rather than diesels. In September 1914, in one of the most famous submarine actions, *U-9* sank the British armoured cruisers *Hogue*, *Aboukir*, and *Cressy* in the same engagement.

△ **SM U-10**
Date 1911 **Origin** Germany
Displacement 493 tonnes (543 tons)
Length 57.4 m (188 ft)
Top speed 14 knots (26 km/h)

Armed with four torpedo tubes, two in the bow, two in the stern, this Type *U-9* submarine took part in Germany's Atlantic campaign against merchant vessels. It disappeared in 1916 while travelling from Latvia to the Swedish coast, and was presumed sunk.

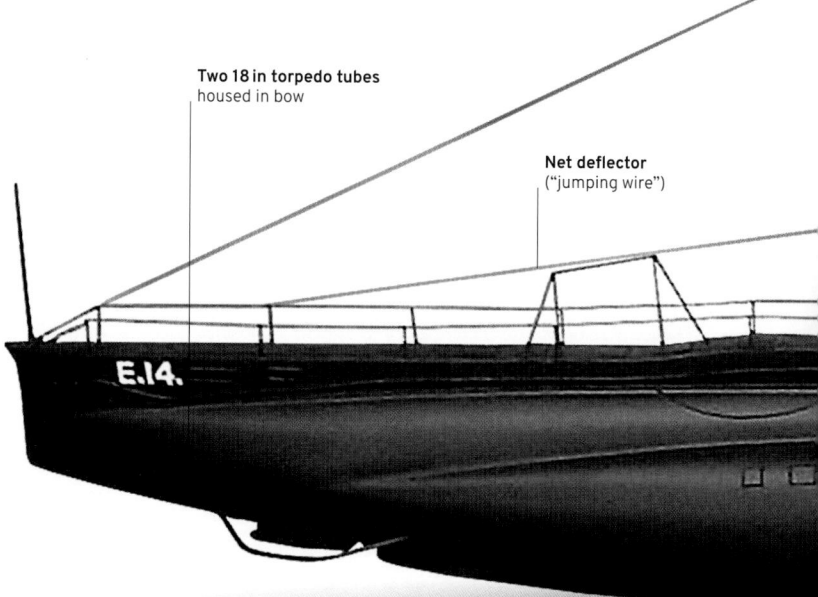

△ **RN E-class submarine**
Date 1915 **Origin** UK
Displacement Approx. 675 tonnes (744 tons)
Length Approx. 55 m (180 ft)
Top speed 15 knots (28 km/h)

The 56 E-class boats – the backbone of Britain's World War I submarine fleet – were ocean-going vessels with a range of 5,556 km (3,000 nautical miles). The first Royal Navy submarines with internal watertight bulkheads, they had five torpedo tubes: two fore, one aft, and a pair of transverse tubes amidships to fire side-on. Six were built as minelayers; these had just fore and aft torpedo tubes to accommodate 20 mines.

△ **SM U-35**
Date 1914 **Origin** Germany
Displacement 685 tonnes (755 tons)
Length 64.7 m (212 ft)
Top speed 16.4 knots (30 km/h)

One of 11 German *U-31*-class submarines, *U-35* operated in the Mediterranean during World War I and became the most successful U-boat of the war, sinking 220 Allied merchant vessels, 3 warships and 3 auxiliary ships. The submarine survived to the end of the war, after which it was transferred to the UK; it was broken up in 1920.

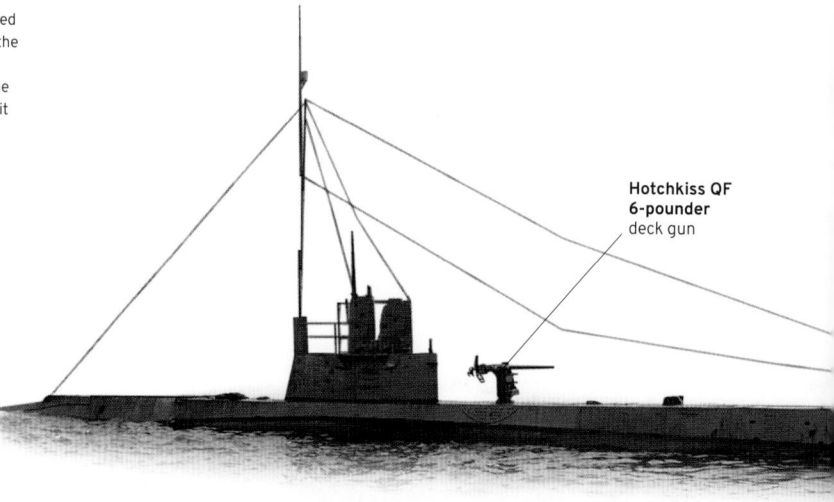

▷ **H-class submarine**
Date 1915 **Origin** UK
Displacement 369–430 tonnes (407–474 tons)
Length 46–52 m (150–170 ft)
Top speed 11.5–13 knots (21–24 km/h)

Over 40 H-class submarines were built for the British Royal Navy between 1915 and 1919. Most entered service too late to have any impact on the war. HMS *H4*, shown here, sank the German submarine *UB-52* in 1918. H-class submarines remained in service as training vessels, some until the end of World War II.

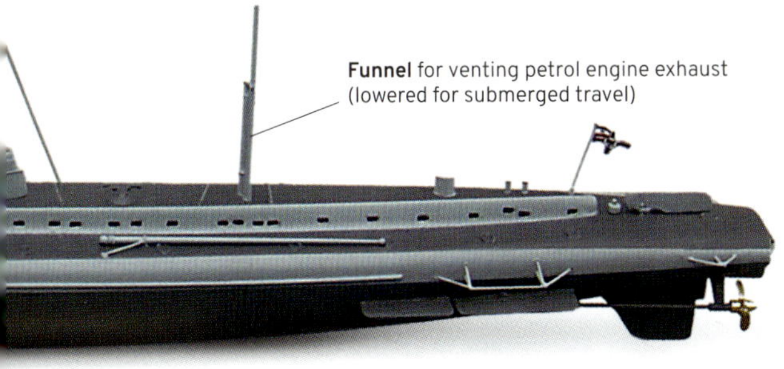

Funnel for venting petrol engine exhaust (lowered for submerged travel)

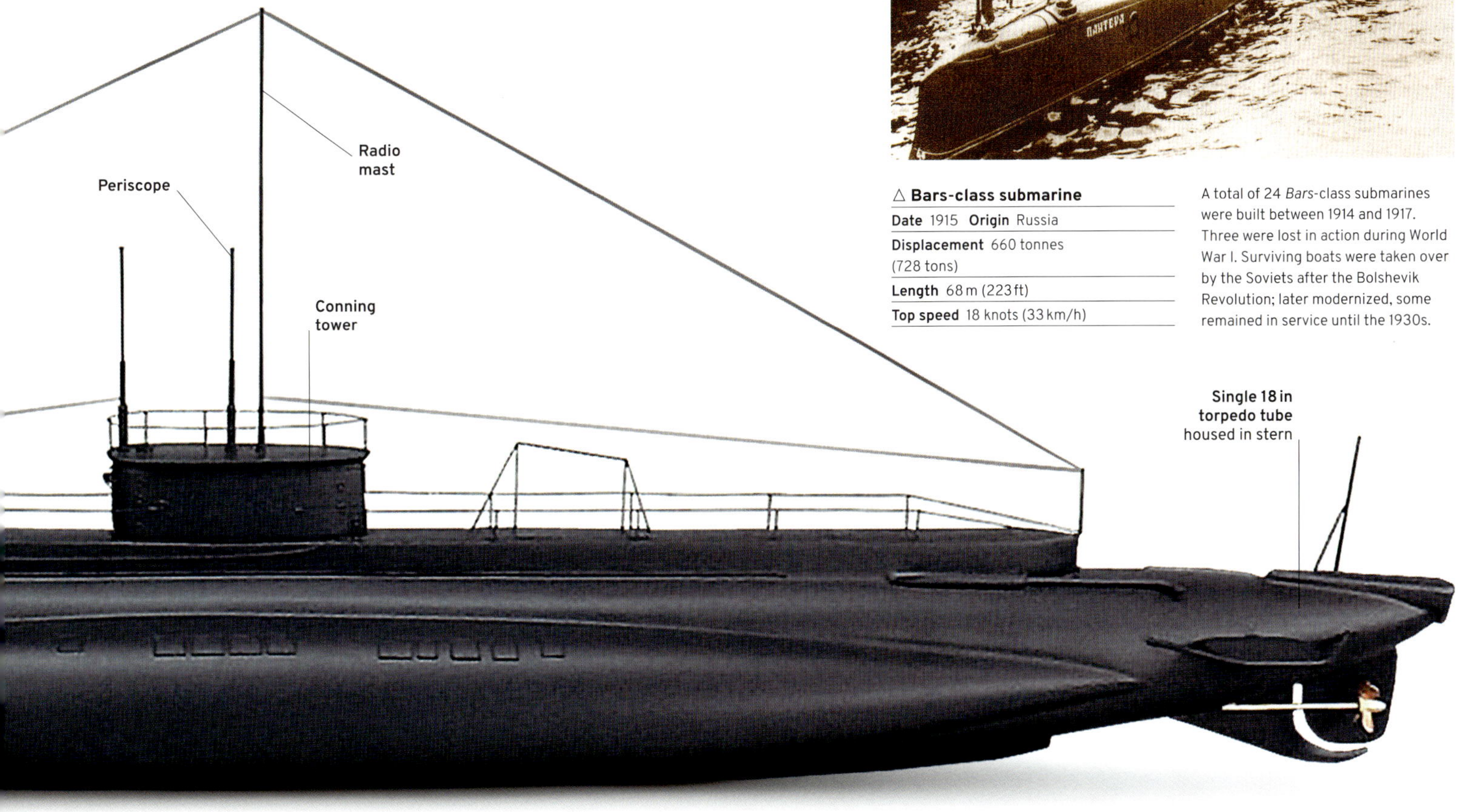

Periscope

Radio mast

Conning tower

△ **Bars-class submarine**

Date 1915	Origin Russia
Displacement 660 tonnes (728 tons)	
Length 68 m (223 ft)	
Top speed 18 knots (33 km/h)	

A total of 24 *Bars*-class submarines were built between 1914 and 1917. Three were lost in action during World War I. Surviving boats were taken over by the Soviets after the Bolshevik Revolution; later modernized, some remained in service until the 1930s.

Single 18 in torpedo tube housed in stern

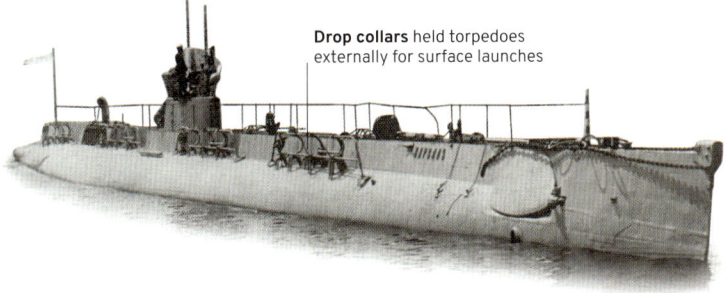

Drop collars held torpedoes externally for surface launches

△ **Narval-class submarine**

Date 1915	Origin Russia
Displacement 631 tonnes (696 tons)	
Length 70 m (230 ft)	
Top speed 9.5 knots (17.5 km/h)	

The three *Narval*-class vessels of the Black Sea Fleet were the largest Russian submarines of the war; with crash-diving tanks for faster diving, watertight bulkheads, and ballast tanks filled by natural water flow (rather than by pumps), they were also the most advanced. As well as internal torpedo tubes, they had external "drop collars" for surface torpedo launches.

▽ **L-class submarine**

Date 1916–1923	Origin USA
Displacement Approx. 457 tonnes (504 tons)	
Length Approx. 50 m (165 ft)	
Top speed 14 knots (26 km/h)	

The US built 11 L-class coastal defence submarines between 1914 and 1917. Some vessels had a semi-retractable deck gun. Wartime service showed the boats to be under-powered and not suited to long North Atlantic patrols. After the war, they were used for trials of torpedoes and hydrophone systems, before being decommissioned in the early 1920s.

Canvas surround was erected around conning tower for extended surface travel

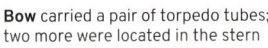

Bow carried a pair of torpedo tubes; two more were located in the stern

1918–1945
THE BATTLEFIELD REDEFINED

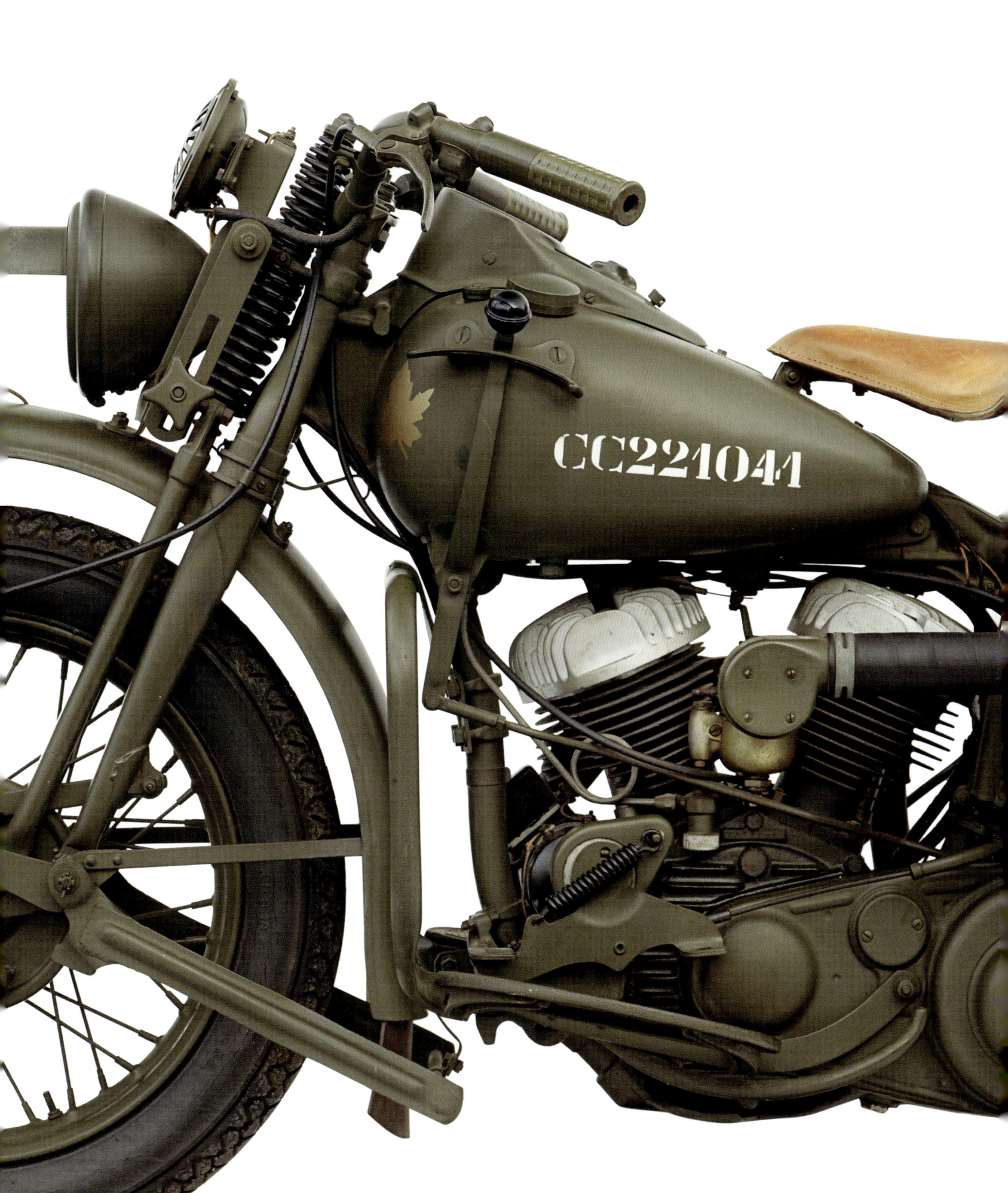

The Era of Manoeuvre

The changes in vehicle technology between 1919 and 1945 were immense. In every theatre – land, sea, and air – military vehicle design and performance were upgraded dramatically, giving rise to entirely new approaches to warfare.

Aftermath of battle
A disabled US M4 Sherman medium tank stands on the island of Iwo Jima, March 1945. Its sides clearly show shell impacts, and the tank has lost its right track.

World War II is regarded as one of the greatest tragedies in human history, with unimaginable loss of life in theatres around the world. However, it also represents a six-year period of unmatched and rapid innovation in military technology, particularly in the case of vehicles. The wave of technological revolutions had begun in the interwar period, aided by continuing improvements in engine design, materials science, mechanical and electric engineering, aerodynamics, and fluid mechanics.

The path to war

The development of military vehicles during the interwar period was erratic, heavily dependent upon economics and politics. During the 1920s, postwar austerity restrained the spending of many national armed forces, while Germany's military research and development was hampered under the tight restrictions imposed by the 1919 Treaty of Versailles. On the seas, warship construction was limited by the Washington Naval Treaty of 1922. However, there was still future-looking innovation. Important steps forward in this era included the development of tanks with rotating gun turrets; improved generations of armoured cars; the first half-track prototypes; the first aircraft carriers; and the progressive shift from biplanes to all-metal monoplanes. As new vehicle types emerged, they required fresh tactics to go with them. Land-warfare innovators such as J.F.C. Fuller (UK) and Heinz Guderian (Germany) outlined bold visions of armoured warfare, while William "Billy" Mitchell (USA) and Giulio Douhet (Italy) predicted futures in which air power would be dominant, both strategically and tactically. The world's navies began discussions about future sea warfare, including topics such as improved interservice cooperation, and the roles of submarines and aircraft carriers.

All these technologies and ideas became more relevant during the 1930s, when the world found itself rushing to rearm, facilitated by new efficiencies in industrial production. The propaganda material of this era projected the idea that martial spirit was synonymous with advanced military technologies,

Timeline
The interwar period and World War II transformed the tactical influence of military vehicles. Land armies focused on motorization, mechanization, and armoured vehicles; navies invested in aircraft carriers and submarines; and air forces created new generations of monoplanes, including the first jet fighters.

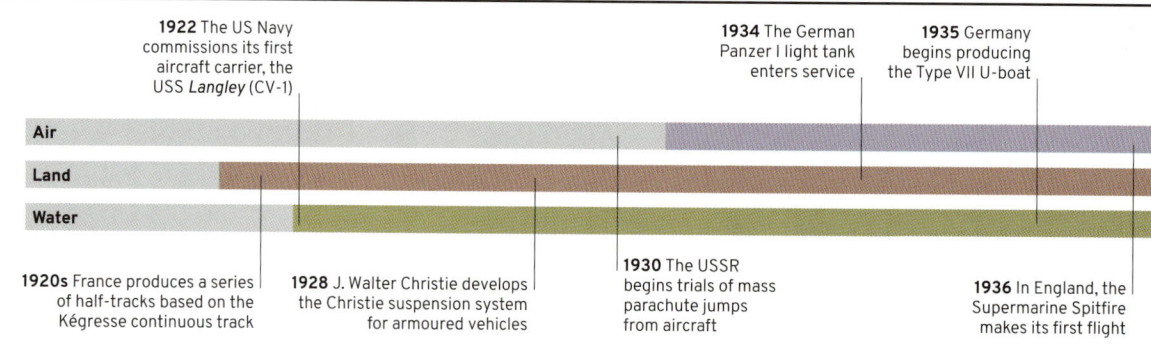

- **1922** The US Navy commissions its first aircraft carrier, the USS *Langley* (CV-1)
- **1934** The German Panzer I light tank enters service
- **1935** Germany begins producing the Type VII U-boat
- **1920s** France produces a series of half-tracks based on the Kégresse continuous track
- **1928** J. Walter Christie develops the Christie suspension system for armoured vehicles
- **1930** The USSR begins trials of mass parachute jumps from aircraft
- **1936** In England, the Supermarine Spitfire makes its first flight

particularly vehicles such as tanks and combat aircraft. It was clear that the idea of warfare had changed. Static warfare based around trenches and fixed positions was now largely a thing of the past. Warfare's future clearly lay with mobility and manoeuvre.

A new era

World War II saw major contrasts in the scale, capability, and destructive effect of vehicular warfare compared to its predecessor. In terms of ground warfare, infantry and artillery were still centre-stage as they had been in the previous conflict, but tactically armour led the way in Europe, while amphibious landing craft did the same in the Pacific. Supply was now dependent on trucks instead of horses, particularly on the well-equipped Allied side from 1942. At sea, navies retained battleships and cruisers, but it was submarines, aircraft carriers, and merchant ships that were most influential in the naval war. In the air, biplanes had almost disappeared, replaced by high-performance monoplanes, in types ranging from light reconnaissance aircraft to long-range heavy bombers and even the first generations of jet aircraft. The pressures of total war brought constant innovation and improvement at an unprecedented speed.

The consequences of these changes were far-reaching. War was now, quite literally, faster. While World War I biplanes flew at speeds of about 177 km/h (110 mph), a monoplane fighter such as a P-51D Mustang flew at 703 km/h (437 mph). Likewise, a T-34 tank ran at 53 km/h (33 mph), instead of the walking pace of a tank in the previous war. Fighting was also conducted across greater distances. US and British strategic bombers regularly made bomb runs from the UK to Germany; from late 1944, American B-29 Superfortress bombers attacked Tokyo from Guam, a round-trip of 5,000 km (3,100 miles).

Last of the biplanes
Britain's Fairey Swordfish was one of the few biplanes to see combat in World War II. These slow-moving, carrier-launched torpedo bombers sunk or damaged Axis capital ships.

Naval war was now fought as vigorously in the air and underwater as it was on the surface. Submarines patrolled further, faster, and with more lethal weaponry, including the first generations of programmable torpedoes. A US *Lexington*-class aircraft carrier such as the USS *Saratoga* (CV-3) could carry 78 combat aircraft, the equivalent of roughly six squadrons. Naval warfare and maritime logistics were also transformed by industry. When US shipyards reached their peak output, for example, some were building an individual "Liberty" merchant vessel every four-and-a-half days.

World War II was as much a clash of machines as it was of personnel. Manning these machines required immense courage and skill, since the continued reliance upon direct-fire weaponry meant that soldiers, sailors, and airmen still fought within visual range of their enemies. Communications were also key: having assembled vast fleets of military vehicles, strategists and commanders still needed to control and coordinate them. The new age of combined-arms warfare (multiple types of military force working together) was made possible by equal advances in wireless communications, command-and-control processes, and even administrative staff work.

TALKING POINT

Deploying the atomic bombs

The two atomic bombs dropped on Japan in August 1945 were delivered by the most advanced aircraft in the US arsenal at that time, the B-29 Superfortress. This gleaming, four-engine bomber had several highly advanced features: fully pressurized crew compartments; a high-aspect-ratio wing design that gave excellent performance at both high and low altitudes; remote-controlled gun turrets; and advanced avionics. It also had an astonishing range of 6,598 km (4,100 miles) and a bomb capacity of 9,072 kg (20,000 lb), which made it the only US aircraft capable of carrying the atomic loads: the single "Fat Man" bomb released above the city of Nagasaki on 9 August weighed 4,909 kg (10,800 lb).

Enola Gay, a Boeing B-29 Superfortress, dropped the first of the atomic bombs, nicknamed "Little Boy", which detonated over the city of Hiroshima on 6 August 1945.

> "Two fundamental lessons... **never to check momentum;** never to resume mere pushing."
>
> CAPTAIN SIR BASIL LIDDEL HART, BRITISH SOLDIER, STRATEGIST, AND MILITARY HISTORIAN, *THOUGHTS ON WAR*, 1944

1939 Germany's Heinkel He 178 is the first turbojet-powered aircraft to take to the air

1940 The USSR introduces the T-34 medium tank

1941 Production of the US GMC CCKW military truck and Willys MB Jeep begins

1942 Avro Lancaster bombers enter service with the British Royal Air Force (RAF)

1944 Germany deploys the Me 262, history's first operational jet fighter

1939 Germany launches the battleship *Bismarck*

1940 Japan launches the *Yamato*-class battleships *Yamato* and *Musashi*

1941 US shipyards begin producing "Liberty" merchant ships

1942 The Allies utilize a range of specialist landing craft to invade North Africa

▽ Peerless Armoured Car

Date 1919	Origin UK
Weight 7 tonnes (7.7 tons)	
Engine Peerless 4-cylinder petrol, 30 kW (40 hp)	
Main armament 2 x .303 Hotchkiss Mark I machine-guns	

Pairing a Peerless truck chassis with an Austin-built armoured body was not a great success: this British Army vehicle was big, cumbersome, and slow – and uncomfortable to ride in, due to its solid-rubber tyres. Transferred to the Territorial Army, it was retained until the late 1930s.

▷ Rolls-Royce Armoured Car

Date 1920	Origin UK
Weight 4.3 tonnes (4.7 tons)	
Engine Rolls-Royce 6-cylinder petrol, 60 kW (80 hp)	
Main armament .303 Vickers machine-gun	

A modernization of the Royal Navy's 1914 Pattern Rolls-Royce, the 1920 Pattern armoured car served with the British Army and Royal Air Force around the world, including in Ireland, Egypt, Iraq, and Shanghai. Some modified 1920 and 1924 Pattern cars took part in the North African Desert Campaign in 1940–41.

Step to driver's cabin

Storage space for equipment

△ Lanchester Armoured Car

Date 1931	Origin UK
Weight 7.1 tonnes (7.8 tons)	
Engine Lanchester 6-cylinder petrol, 67 kW (90 hp)	
Main armament .50 Vickers machine-gun	

Larger and heavier than its namesake of World War I, this armoured car had two additional .303 Vickers machine-guns, four driven wheels at the rear, and a second, rear-facing driver's space at the back. Of the 39 examples built, 10 replaced the Vickers hull gun with a radio. Some vehicles survived to fight the Japanese in Malaya in 1941–42.

Sloped bodywork deflects projectiles

△ Sd Kfz 231 6 rad Armoured Car

Date 1932	Origin Germany
Weight 5.4 tonnes (6 tons)	
Engine Magirus M206 petrol, 52 kW (70 hp)	
Main armament 2 cm KwK 30 L/55 cannon	

Germany's six-wheeled Sd Kfz 231 was based on a number of different 6x4 truck chassis. Its crew of four included a second driver, who faced rearwards. Used in Austria, Poland, Czechoslovakia, and France, poor off-road mobility led to its withdrawal in 1940. A total of 151 were built; the one seen here is a replica.

37 mm Bofors m/38 gun

Wheels in raised position

◁ Stridsvagn fm/31

Date 1935	Origin Sweden
Weight 11.7 tonnes (12.9 tons)	
Engine Maybach DSO 8 petrol, 112 kW (150 hp)	
Main armament 37 mm Bofors m/38 gun	

To overcome the short lifespan of tracks on early tanks, some countries experimented with tanks that also carried a set of wheels for road runs and to reduce track wear. Sweden's unique Stridsvagn fm/31 could raise or lower its wheels in 30 seconds. The 1930s brought improvements in the longevity of tracks, rendering such complex "convertibles" unnecessary.

Interwar Armoured Cars

Wheeled military vehicles retained some advantages over tanks, whose tracks could soon wear out and cost much more to build and maintain. Armoured cars could often be equipped with similar firepower and protection to tanks, and they were typically more reliable and quieter – and usually faster, except across the roughest ground. These qualities made armoured cars ideal as patrol vehicles or for reconnaissance duties ahead of advancing tank forces.

.303 Vickers machine-gun

Armour was up to 8.5 mm (⅓ in) thick

Running-board

◁ **Leyland Armoured Car**

Date 1937	Origin Ireland

Weight 13.2 tonnes (14.6 tons)

Engine Ford V8 type 317 petrol, 116 kW (155 hp)

Main armament 20 mm Madsen cannon

This vehicle was an amalgamation of a 6x4 Leyland truck chassis, armour salvaged from Peerless cars, and a turret made by Landsverk of Sweden. The four examples built served with the Irish army alongside eight similar Swedish L-180s; in 1957, the front armour was rebuilt, and they were re-engined.

△ **Automitrailleuse de Découverte (AMD) Panhard modèle 1935**

Date 1937	Origin France

Weight 8.2 tonnes (9 tons)

Engine Panhard ISK 4-cylinder petrol, 78 kW (105 hp)

Main armament 25 mm Hotchkiss SA 35 cannon

The quiet, fast AMD 35 was popular with crews, despite poor off-road performance. This reconnaissance vehicle had a second, rear-facing driver, who also acted as a radio operator. Production continued after France surrendered in 1940, and after the war's end in 1945; over 1,100 AMD 35s were built.

▽ **Crossley-Chevrolet Armoured Car**

Date 1939	Origin UK

Weight 5.1 tonnes (5.6 tons)

Engine Chevrolet 6-cylinder petrol, 58 kW (78 hp)

Main armament 2 x Vickers .303 machine-guns

Crossley armoured cars were first built in the 1920s and used for patrols by the British Army in India and the North West Frontier. The vehicles were built to "Indian Pattern", which included a domed turret with a "clamshell" cupola and an asbestos lining to limit temperatures inside. By 1939, the cars, now seriously in need of upgrading, were given a new Chevrolet chassis.

Cupola with "clamshell" opening

Domed turret

△ **Pansarbil m/40 (Lynx)**

Date 1939	Origin Sweden

Weight 7.1 tonnes (7.8 tons)

Engine Volvo 6-cylinder petrol, 101 kW (135 hp)

Main armament 20 mm Bofors m/40 cannon

Both front and rear wheels of Sweden's symmetrical Lynx could steer, and its forward and reverse speeds were identical. It was operated by a six-man crew of front and rear drivers and gunners. Built for Danish export, only three of the initial 18 vehicles were delivered before Germany invaded Denmark in 1940. Sweden kept the other 15 and ordered 30 more.

Light, Medium, and Heavy Tanks

Advances in automotive and military technology in the 1920s and 1930s made tanks more reliable and capable. Most light tanks of the time carried machine-guns, while medium and heavy tanks emphasized armour and firepower over mobility. A key development was American engineer J. Walter Christie's suspension system: each tank wheel had independent suspension – a "helicoil" spring mounted inside the hull – which improved agility and speed over broken ground. Tank development in Germany during this era was theoretically forbidden by the Treaty of Versailles.

▽ Leichter Kampfwagen LK II
Date 1918 **Origin** Germany
Engine Daimler-Benz 4-cylinder, 45 kW (60 hp)
Weight 8.8 tonnes (9.7 tons)
Main armament 57 mm Maxim-Nordenfelt

This light German tank was designed in the last year of World War I but never made it into production. Sweden secretly bought parts for 10 tanks, which were illegally imported labelled as tractor components. Assembled, they became the four-man m/21 – the very first Swedish tank.

△ Vickers Mark E, 6 Ton
Date 1928 **Origin** UK
Engine Armstrong-Siddeley 4-cylinder petrol, 60 kW (80 hp)
Weight 7.5 tonnes (8.3 tons)
Main armament QF 3-pounder gun

Although only 150 Mark Es were built, the tank was an export success. Vickers made sales to 12 countries, including Finland, Thailand, and Bolivia, with Poland buying 38 tanks – the largest single order. The Mark E's design was also highly influential, being the starting point for the development of the Polish 7TP and Soviet T-26 tanks. The Mark E had two variants: Type A was fitted with two machine-gun turrets; Type B, shown here, had just one.

▽ Leichttraktor Vs.Kfz.31
Date 1930 **Origin** Germany
Engine Daimler-Benz petrol, 75 kW (100 hp)
Weight 9.7 tonnes (10.7 tons)
Main armament 3.7 cm KwK 36 L/45 gun

To circumvent post-World War I restrictions, Germany worked covertly with the Soviet Union's Kama Tank School in Russia to gain experience of designing, building, and operating tanks. It built a small number of tanks, including the Vs.Kfz.31, described as a "light tractor" to maintain secrecy.

△ T-26
Date 1931 **Origin** USSR
Engine T-26 4-cylinder petrol, 68 kW (91 hp)
Weight 9.4 tonnes (10.4 tons)
Main armament .45 mm 20K Model 1934 L/46 gun

More T-26s were produced than any other tank of the interwar era: 12,000 in all, including 2,000 twin-turreted versions and 1,700 variants. The tank's weaknesses quickly became apparent when it was first exposed to combat during the Spanish Civil War of 1936–39. Despite upgrades, it was outclassed by 1939. Some T-26s continued operating in the Far East until 1945.

▷ Christie M1931
Date 1931	Origin USA

Engine Liberty V12 petrol, 252 kW (338 hp)
Weight 10.7 tonnes (11.8 tons)
Main armament .50 Browning M2 machine-gun

The J. Walter Christie-designed M1931 could achieve high speeds, even on rough ground, thanks to its flexible suspension and light armour. It could run either on tracks or its wheels alone. It was purchased by the US Army, which had rejected its predecessor, the turretless M1928. The Soviet Union bought two tanks and used them to develop its BT series and the T-34.

Camouflage colour scheme

Drive sprocket

Twin turrets for machine-guns

△ Light Tank M2A3
Date 1936	Origin USA

Engine Continental R-670-9A petrol, 186 kW (250 hp)
Weight 9.7 tonnes (10.7 tons)
Main armament .50 Browning M2 machine-gun

Only machine-guns were considered necessary for the infantry support role of tanks in the M2 series. The M2A3 had twin turrets, one with a .50 machine-gun, the other with a .30. The war in Europe showed that extra firepower was vital, so the M2A4, the version that went into combat with US forces, was given a 37 mm gun.

△ T-35
Date 1936	Origin USSR

Engine Mikulin M17T petrol, 485 kW (650 hp)
Weight 45.7 tonnes (50.4 tons)
Main armament 76.2 mm Model 1927/32 gun

The only five-turret tank ever to enter service was the T-35. One turret was equipped with a 76.2 mm gun, two with 45 mm 20K guns, and two with DT machine-guns. Just 61 examples of this slow, unreliable heavy tank were built; most were lost when Germany invaded the Soviet Union.

Driver's mirror gives view behind tank

△ Vickers Light Tank Mark VIB
Date 1937	Origin UK

Weight 5.3 tonnes (5.8 tons)
Engine Meadows ESTB 6-cylinder petrol, 66 kW (88 hp)
Main armament .50 Vickers machine-gun

The two-man crew of Vickers' Mark IV light tank was increased to three on the Mark V by the introduction of a two-man turret armed with .50 and .303 machine-guns. The Mark VI added a radio. Nearly 1,000 Mark VIBs – the most common variant – were built, but combat in France, North Africa, and Greece showed the tanks to be inadequate.

Angled sides to turret

Machine-guns cover 360 degrees

Vertical volute suspension

◁ Medium Tank M2A1
Date 1939	Origin USA

Weight 23.4 tonnes (25.8 tons)
Engine Wright Continental R-975 petrol, 298 kW (400 hp)
Main armament 37 mm M3 L/56.6 gun

Designed to support infantry, the M2 carried six .30 machine-guns arranged to allow all-round fire. In 1939, the M2 became the first US medium tank to enter production, but by 1940 it was obsolete. However, the M2's Vertical Volute Spring Suspension (VVSS) system and R-975 engine were reused on its M3 and M4 successors.

Vickers Medium Mark II

With greater mobility and range than the tanks of World War I, the Vickers Medium was designed to fight on the move. The mainstay of the Royal Tank Corps from 1923 to 1935, the Medium – Marks I, II, and III – was the first British tank to enter service with a rotating turret and sprung suspension.

THE MEDIUM MARK I was the first variant to enter service, in 1923. Its turret was equipped with a 3-pounder main gun and Hotchkiss light machine-guns. Two Vickers machine-guns, one on either side of the hull, completed its weaponry. The Mark II* replaced the Hotchkiss turret guns with a coaxial Vickers machine-gun. In addition to the gun tanks, the Medium was also produced in command-post and bridge-laying versions. Vickers Mediums formed the core of the British Army's Experimental Mechanized Force, which was set up in 1927 to explore how vehicles might be used in combat. After manoeuvres on Salisbury Plain showed the potential of armoured formations, the mechanization of the British Army continued into and throughout the 1930s.

The Vickers Medium's importance went beyond its influence on battlefield tactics: it was also an export success, being sold to numerous countries, including Russia, which bought 15. The lone Medium purchased by Japan became the model for the country's own Type 89 tank design.

Light shroud

Covered sprung suspension

FRONT VIEW

REAR VIEW

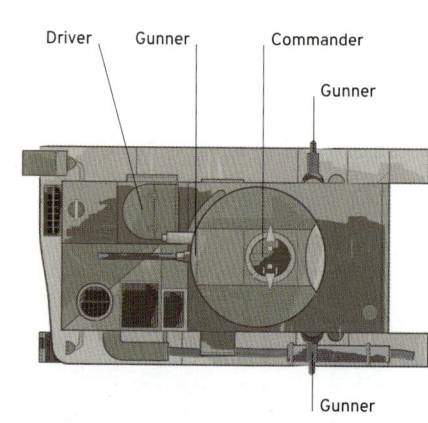

SPECIFICATIONS	
Name	Tank, Vickers Medium Mark II*
Date	1927
Origin	UK
Production	56
Engine	Armstrong Siddeley V8, 67 kW (90 hp)
Weight	12.4 tonnes (13.7 tons)
Main armament	3-pounder
Secondary armament	3 x Vickers .303 machine-guns
Crew	5
Armour thickness	6.35–8 mm (1/4–3/10 in)

Battlefield adaptation
The Medium's main gun could tackle contemporary tanks, but it was ineffective against field fortifications, and the thin armour was vulnerable to antitank guns. In response, a more powerfully armed close-support version of the tank was built.

Training vehicle
Mark IIs were used to train drivers in the early years of World War II. Identifying marks indicate that this was one such tank.

Horse-less cavalry
A World War II propaganda poster uses Medium tanks to emphasize how much the British Army had changed since World War I. By the 1940s, British cavalry regiments were mostly mechanized.

3-pounder main gun

Vickers .303 machine-gun, one on either side of the hull

Regimental HQ tank tactical symbol

Metal track with cast links

INTERIOR

Crew space inside the tank was relatively generous. The commander and main gunner occupied the turret, while the driver sat forward, beside the engine. Two more gunners, one on each side, operated the Vickers .303 hull machine-guns, completing the five-man crew.

15. View through rear door **16.** Fighting compartment interior **17.** 3-pounder gun breach **18.** Vickers .303 machine-gun **19.** Fire extinguisher **20.** Coaxial Vickers machine-gun **21.** Hull machine-gun position **22.** Gun elevation wheel **23.** Turret traverse wheel **24.** Driver's position from above **25.** Driver's controls **26.** Manufacturer's date plate **27.** Engine oil gauge

VICKERS MEDIUM MARK II · 105

EXTERIOR
The riveted armour-plate construction – just 6.35 mm (0.25 in) thick at the front – gave little protection against anything other than bullets. To compensate, crews of the Royal Tank Corps, formed in 1923, became expert at firing the 3-pounder gun while on the move, making it difficult for enemy gunners to target the fast, highly mobile Mediums.

1. HQ Command tank tactical sign **2.** Headlight **3.** Light shroud **4.** Driver's hatch **5.** Engine air intake **6.** Coaxial Vickers machine-gun mount **7.** Hull wall ball-mount Vickers machine-gun **8.** Turret vision port **9.** Main armament sight aperture **10.** "Mitre"-type commander's hatch **11.** Track tensioner **12.** Track return roller **13.** Exhaust **14.** Drive sprocket

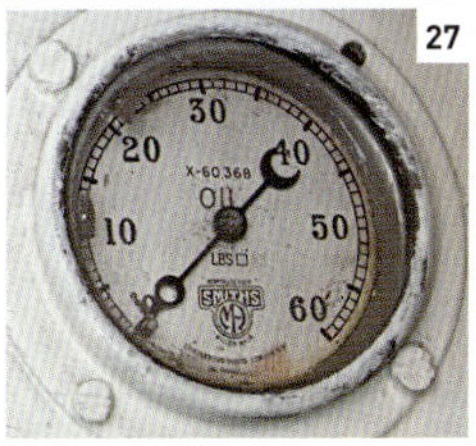

The Age of Monoplanes

The lowest drag and highest efficiency for an aircraft is achieved with a monoplane (single-winged) design. Monoplane aircraft also have the advantage of being easier to build than biplanes. During World War I, a few monoplane aircraft saw action, such as Germany's Fokker Eindecker fighter, but it was not until the interwar period, when more powerful engines became available, that monoplane designs came to dominate. The greater power provided by the new engines generated sufficient airspeed and lift that a second wing – despite the additional surface area it gave – was unnecessary. Extra power also enabled more weight to be carried, which in turn facilitated new construction techniques, such as using riveted thin metal sheets. By the late 1930s, most nations with a modern air force had introduced fast, low-wing monoplane fighters. When World War II broke out, the mass production of monoplanes such as the Hawker Hurricane and Messerschmitt Bf 109 became a priority for combatant nations.

British pilots of Fighter Command's No.111 Squadron make a practice "scramble" to board their Hawker Hurricane Mk.I aircraft from their base at RAF Northolt, London, on 26 August 1939.

△ **Bristol Bulldog**

Date 1929 **Origin** UK

Engine 328–365 kW (440–490 hp) Bristol Jupiter VII supercharged air-cooled 9-cylinder radial

Top speed 287 km/h (178 mph)

The Bristol Bulldog was the RAF's foremost interwar fighter. Fast, armed with twin guns, and with light bomb capability, Frank Barnwell's design was also cheap to maintain.

▽ **Polikarpov Po-2**

Date 1930 **Origin** USSR

Engine 93 kW (125 hp) Shvetsov M-11D air-cooled 5-cylinder radial

Top speed 152 km/h (94 mph)

Employed by the Soviets as trainers, night bombers, and reconnaissance and liaison aircraft in World War II, Nikolai Polikarpov's Po-2s proved difficult to shoot down. Over 40,000 Po-2s are thought to have been built.

Aerodynamic fuselage with sharply tapered tail

△ **Seversky P-35/AT-12 Guardsman**

Date 1935 **Origin** USA

Engine 783 kW (1,050 hp) Pratt & Whitney R-1830-45 Twin Wasp air-cooled 14-cylinder radial

Top speed 467 km/h (290 mph)

The single-seat P-35 fighter was advanced for its time, with all-metal construction, retractable undercarriage, and an enclosed cockpit. This two-seat AT-12 was a trainer variant.

▷ **Dewoitine D27**

Date 1930 **Origin** France

Engine 317 kW (425 hp) Gnome-Rhone Jupiter VII air-cooled 9-cylinder radial

Top speed 312 km/h (194 mph)

Having moved to Switzerland in 1927, French aero-engineer Émile Dewoitine built 66 parasol-wing monoplane D27 fighters for the Swiss Air Force. The D27 was also built in Romania and Yugoslavia.

The Warplane Evolves

At the start of the 1930s, military aircraft still looked much like the fighting biplanes of late World War I. However, the decade saw rapid developments in warplane technology – especially from 1935, as war loomed again. Advanced monoplane wing designs, all-metal construction, monocoque fuselages, and enclosed cockpits became standard.

△ **Hawker Hurricane Mk1**

Date 1936 **Origin** UK

Engine 768 kW (1,030 hp) Rolls-Royce Merlin supercharged liquid-cooled V12

Top speed 528 km/h (328 mph)

Credited with 60 per cent of RAF victories during World War II's Battle of Britain, Sydney Camm's Hurricane served in interceptor, fighter-bomber, night fighter, and ground-attack roles.

THE WARPLANE EVOLVES • 109

△ **Gloster Gladiator**

Date 1936 Origin UK

Engine 619 kW (830 hp) Bristol Mercury IX air-cooled 9-cylinder radial

Top speed 410 km/h (255 mph)

The last biplane fighter to see front-line action with the RAF, the Gladiator took part in the 1940 defence of Malta. Though outdated, it served in the air forces of China, Finland, and numerous other countries.

△ **Supermarine Spitfire MK1a**

Date 1936 Origin UK

Engine 768–876 kW (1,030–1,175 hp) Rolls-Royce Merlin supercharged liquid-cooled V12

Top speed 580 km/h (360 mph)

Designer R.J. Mitchell's Spitfire, which first took to the skies in 1936, played a huge part in the Allies' aerial success during World War II. In all, 20,351 Spitfires were built, in 13 main variants.

△ **Westland Lysander**

Date 1936 Origin UK

Engine 604 kW (810 hp) Bristol Mercury XX supercharged air-cooled 9-cylinder radial

Top speed 341 km/h (212 mph)

During World War II, the Lysander earned a reputation for carrying out daring army missions, landing in fields at night behind enemy lines to insert or retrieve agents. A total of 1,786 were built.

△ **Curtiss P-40 Warhawk**

Date 1938 Origin USA

Engine 776 kW (1,040 hp) Allison V-1710 supercharged liquid-cooled V12

Top speed 580 km/h (360 mph)

In service throughout World War II, the Warhawk was respected for its agility, but it was not the fastest aircraft of its kind. Durable and cheap to make, the Warhawk served with 28 air forces. Production totalled 13,738.

▽ **Messerschmitt Bf 109E**

Date 1938 Origin Germany

Engine 746 kW (1,000 hp) DB601A supercharged liquid-cooled inverted V12

Top speed 572 km/h (355 mph)

Light, fast, and agile in flight – although tricky in takeoff – the all-metal Bf 109E was the foremost German fighter of its day. First flown in 1935, the early Bf 109 models saw combat during the Spanish Civil War.

World War II: Mass Mobility on Land

World War II was primarily a conflict of manoeuvres. Armoured fighting vehicles (AFVs) such as tanks and self-propelled guns paved the way for mechanized infantry units that went into battle in their own protected vehicles, particularly half-tracks. Elsewhere, trucks and light infantry vehicles delivered logistics and broader troop movement.

The mass mobility of World War II reflected two key trends. The first was the continuing improvement of the internal combustion engine, and the performance and reliability of the vehicles it powered. The other element was mass production: a great acceleration in manufacturing output that enabled military vehicles to be produced in enormous numbers. This surge in the number of vehicles resulted in a transformation of land warfare tactics, offering unprecedented possibilities for manoeuvres and logistics.

Armour

The AFVs of World War I, primarily tanks and armoured cars, had been an adjunct to infantry and artillery whose combat role was still very much evolving. In World War II, by contrast, AFVs were central to the manoeuvre-warfare tactics that were used on many fronts. Germany pioneered this form of warfare, having developed its Panzer arm technologically and tactically in the 1920s and 1930s to be the leading element of its newly mobile army. Wehrmacht Panzer units proved the efficacy of the tactics in the campaigns of 1939–41, spurring efforts by the rest of world to catch up or develop their own visions for armour. Tanks, self-propelled guns, and AFVs of all varieties subsequently proliferated at a scale unimaginable in World War I. At the Battle of Kursk in July–August 1943, for example, the Soviets and Germans fielded approximately 6,000 tanks.

The downside to this revolution in mobile armour was that AFVs placed a huge logistical burden on armies. By the last two years of the war, a US armoured division required between 1,000 and 1,500 tonnes (1,100 and 1,650 tons) of supplies every day. The logistically robust Americans could cope with this demand, but the Axis forces were more stretched and increasingly struggled to maintain large armoured units in the field.

Tank production
US factory workers assemble M3 Lee tanks during the early 1940s. The most mass-produced American tank was the M4 Sherman – more than 50,000 were made between 1942 and 1945.

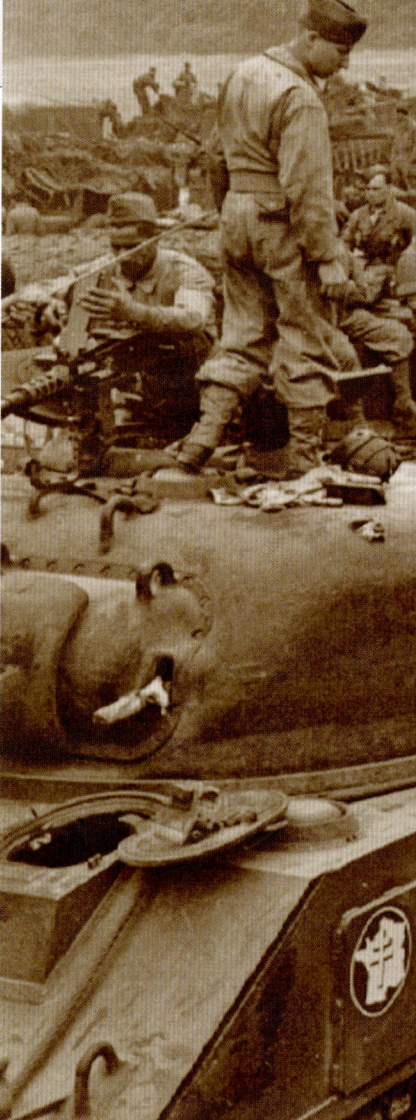

Armoured column
US-supplied M4 Sherman tanks of the 2nd French Armoured Division form up in a powerful column ready for the advance through France during the summer of 1944. Supply trucks under camouflage netting line up beside them to deliver logistics.

Logistics

Horses were still used in significant numbers for logistical roles during World War II, particularly on the Eastern Front, but trucks and light vehicles changed the way armies moved their personnel and supplies. New generations of military trucks, such as the GMC CCKW-352 (US), Opel Blitz (Germany), and Bedford QL (UK), proved rugged and reliable workhorses. Crucial to their impact were the volumes in which they could be produced, and it was here that the Allies established an advantage. Germany produced around 346,000 trucks between 1939 and 1945, and Japan 166,000; Britain made 480,000 and the Soviet Union 197,000, but the US, which became an industrial behemoth during the war years, rolled out in excess of 2.3 million trucks. American vehicles provided through the Lend-Lease scheme became central to the wider Allied war effort; the Soviet Union alone received 400,000 US trucks, more than double its own total.

The Allies also dwarfed the Axis in the manufacture of AFVs: Germany produced 46,857 tanks and SP guns during the war, against the 88,410 manufactured by the US and 105,251

Logistics in action
A heavy US truck draws a mobile field kitchen through the bow doors of a Landing Ship, Tank (LST), during embarkation at an English port for the invasion of Normandy in June 1944.

> "The **higher** the concentration of tanks, the **faster, greater,** and more sweeping will be the **success.**"
>
> GENERALOBERST HEINZ GUDERIAN, IN *PANZER MARCSH!* (1937)

by the Soviet Union. Some historians have argued that American, Soviet, and British factories won the war.

Specialist vehicles

The motorization of armies spawned many specialist vehicles, including a wide array of engineering types largely dedicated to keeping the fleets of AFVs and trucks on the road. They included vehicles that could lay bridges and temporary roads, fill ditches and demolish obstacles, or recover disabled vehicles for return to repair depots. Motor vehicles also performed a host of support and combat duties. They became mobile command posts, ambulances, radio trucks, workshops, flamethrowers, and anti-aircraft platforms.

However, not all soldiers travelled into battle on vehicles. Even in the US Army, only five of many dozens of infantry divisions were classified as motorized divisions, although the supply chain was fully motorized. The humble infantryman, as ever, would travel long distances on his own two feet.

TALKING POINT

Blitzkrieg

A combined-arms approach to warfare was developed between the wars by German military thinkers such as Oswald Lutz, Erwin Rommel, and Heinz Guderian. Backed by mechanized infantry and air power, armoured vanguards would make fast, deep breakthroughs at front-line weak points, bypass strongholds, and cause disruption in the enemy's rear. The strategy, called *Blitzkrieg* (Lightning War) in the West and *Bewegungskrieg* (War of Movement) in Germany, worked well in Poland and Western Europe in 1939–40, but from June 1941 German forces became logistically overstretched across the vast distances of the Soviet Union.

Mock battle: Panzers and infantry take part in a demonstration of combined-arms warfare at the Nuremberg Nazi Party parade grounds in 1938.

Logistics Trains

The US, Britain, and Germany mass-produced freight locomotives during World War II. Inexpensively built yet powerful, these engines provided vital logistical support. In wartime, they transported countless troops and huge quantities of equipment, ammunition, and raw materials; in the war's aftermath, large numbers ran on European national railways, either as replacements for lost stock or as war reparations. Many locomotives built for the United States Army Transportation Corps (USATC) were sent to Asia under lease-lend agreements and, after the war, by the UN Relief and Rehabilitation Administration (UNRAA).

△ **LMS Stanier 8F**
Date 1935	Origin UK
Wheel arrangement	2-8-0
Cylinders	2
Boiler pressure	15.82 kg/sq cm (225 psi)
Driving wheel diameter	1,430 mm (56¼ in)
Top speed	97 km/h (60 mph)

The London, Midland & Scottish Railway's 8F was the standard British freight locomotive during the early part of World War II. Designed by William Stanier, it was deployed by the War Department in Egypt, Palestine, Iran, and Italy. Of the 852 built, 25 were sold to Turkey in 1941. LMS 8Fs stayed in British service until 1968, and in Turkey even into the 1980s.

△ **Class V36 Shunter**
Date 1937	Origin Germany
Wheel arrangement	0-6-0
Transmission	Hydraulic
Engine	Deutsche Werke/MAK diesel
Total power output	268 kW (360 hp)
Top speed	55 km/h (34 mph)

Axle lacking driving wheels

Class V36 diesels performed shunting duties for the Wehrmacht (German armed forces). Although fitted with four axles, they only had three pairs of driving wheels. After the war, the engines were used extensively in Europe and North Africa.

◁ **USATC S100**
Date 1942	Origin USA
Wheel arrangement	0-6-0
Cylinders	2
Boiler pressure	14.8 kg/sq cm (210 psi)
Driving wheel diameter	1,372 mm (54 in)
Top speed	50 km/h (31 mph)

Nearly 400 S100s built for the USATC were transported to Britain and used in Europe after the Allied invasion of France in June 1944; 15 were later bought as shunters by Britain's Southern Railway.

◁ **USATC S160**
Date 1942	Origin USA
Wheel arrangement	2-8-0
Cylinders	2
Boiler pressure	15.82 kg/sq cm (225 psi)
Driving wheel diameter	1,448 mm (57 in)
Top speed	65 km/h (40 mph)

The USATC commissioned 2,120 "austerity" (cheaper) versions of the Consolidation-type heavy freight locomotive; 800 were shipped to Britain for use in Europe after D-Day. S160s saw postwar service on many European railways, as well as in North Africa, China, India, and North and South Korea.

▷ **DR Class 52 "Kriegslok"**
Date 1942	Origin Germany
Wheel arrangement	2-10-0
Cylinders	2
Boiler pressure	16.3 kg/sq cm (232 psi)
Driving wheel diameter	1,400 mm (55 in)
Top speed	80 km/h (50 mph)

Deutsche Reichsbahn built about 7,000 of these heavy freight locomotives in World War II, primarily for Eastern Front service. A few working engines still operate in Bosnia today, and many others have been preserved, including this Class 52 No. 52.8184-5 rebuild.

LOGISTICS TRAINS · 113

△ **Armoured Car**
Date 1942 Origin Germany
Type 4-wheel
Capacity 130 (whole train)
Construction Armour-plated steel
Railway Wehrmacht

Railcars equipped with gun turrets, as on this replica, formed part of German BP42 armoured trains that operated in the Balkans and Russia. Driven by an armour-clad Class 57 0-10-0 steam engine in the centre, the trains comprised infantry, anti-aircraft, and artillery wagons.

△ **SR Class Q1**
Date 1942 Origin UK
Wheel arrangement 0-6-0
Cylinders 2 (inside)
Boiler pressure 16.17 kg/sq cm (230 psi)
Driving wheel diameter 1,549 mm (61 in)
Top speed 120 km/h (75 mph)

Shown here is No. C1, the first of a series of 40 wartime economy freight locomotives made for Britain's Southern Railway. Oliver Bulleid's lightweight design enabled the Class Q1 engines to operate over most of the company's rail network, and they remained in service on the Southern Region of British Railways until the 1960s.

▷ **Indian Class AWE**
Date 1943 Origin USA
Wheel arrangement 2-8-2
Cylinders 2
Boiler pressure 14.76 kg/sq cm (210 psi)
Driving wheel diameter 1,562 mm (61½ in)
Top speed 100 km/h (62 mph)

The USATC commissioned Baldwin Locomotive Works to build a number of huge locomotives with 7-ft- (2,134-mm-) diameter boilers for hauling heavy freight trains in India. Forty of them became Indian Railways Class AWE engines. No. 22907 *Virat*, shown here, has been restored to working order at the Rewari Steam Loco Shed.

Central headlamp

△ **WD Austerity**
Date 1943 Origin UK
Wheel arrangement 2-8-0
Cylinders 2
Boiler pressure 15.82 kg/sq cm (225 psi)
Driving wheel diameter 1,435 mm (56½ in)
Top speed 72 km/h (45 mph)

This austerity version of the LMS 8F freighter, designed by R.A. Riddles, was ordered by Britain's War Department – hence the designation "WD". After D-Day, many were put to work in mainland Europe. Of 935 engines built, 733 saw postwar service with British Railways; others operated in the Netherlands, Hong Kong, and Sweden.

Bren gun mounted on sidecar

△ **Norton Big Four SWD**
Date 1938 **Origin** UK
Engine 633 cc, side-valve single-cylinder
Top speed 105 km/h (65 mph)

Norton's sidecar outfit – a personnel, ammunition, and gun carrier – had good mobility over uneven terrain, since both its rear and sidecar wheel were driven.

◁ **Velocette MAC-MDD**
Date 1940 **Origin** UK
Engine 349 cc, ohv single-cylinder
Top speed 120 km/h (75 mph)

The MAC-MDD was militarized for a cancelled French army order that was subsequently taken over by the British. It was succeeded by the improved MAP, used by the RAF.

△ **Harley-Davidson Model U US Navy version**
Date 1940 **Origin** USA
Engine 1,213 cc, side-valve V-twin
Top speed 120 km/h (75 mph)

Supplied in limited numbers to the US Army, and later the US Navy (for shore patrol), during World War II, Harley's U range had a higher specification and bigger capacity than its WLA models.

◁ **Zündapp KS750**
Date 1941 **Origin** Germany
Engine 751 cc, ohv flat-twin
Top speed 95 km/h (59 mph)

The KS750 had eight forward gears and two reverse, plus a driven sidecar wheel that permitted cross-country travel. It carried three soldiers plus weaponry.

▽ **Triumph 3TW**
Date 1940 **Origin** UK
Engine 349 cc, ohv parallel-twin
Top speed 113 km/h (70 mph)

This light, nippy army motorcycle never entered service, since the only batch made was destroyed when Triumph's Coventry factory was bombed in 1940.

Military Motorcycles

In the military, motorcycles were most often used for delivering messages and orders, especially when no other means of communication was available. Despatch riders needed robust, reliable machines that could handle difficult terrain and – because some riders were inexperienced – were simple to use. Military motorcycles were typically no-frills versions of existing civilian models fitted with accessories to suit their military use, such as racks, special lighting equipment, sump guards, and, in some cases, even gun mountings or holsters.

▽ **Matchless G3/L**
North Africa version
Date 1941 Origin UK
Engine 347 cc, ohv single-cylinder
Top speed 113 km/h (70 mph)

The G3/L's hydraulically damped telescopic forks were a significant improvement on other British military motorcycles. This example is painted for desert service.

▽ **Harley-Davidson WLA**
Date 1942 Origin USA
Engine 739 cc, side-valve V-twin
Top speed 105 km/h (65 mph)

This was a modified military version of Harley's WL civilian model, with a bash plate fitted under the engine, modified mudguards, and a gun holster.

Leather holster for Thompson submachine gun

▽ **Harley-Davidson XA**
Date 1942 Origin USA
Engine 738 cc, side-valve flat-twin
Top speed 105 km/h (65 mph)

A single batch of 1,000 of these BMW-inspired, shaft-drive flat-twins was made, but the arrival of the Jeep meant that no more were produced.

△ **Triumph 3HW**
Date 1941 Origin UK
Engine 343 cc, ohv single-cylinder
Top speed 115 km/h (70 mph)

After its Coventry site was bombed, Triumph built a new factory at nearby Meriden, where it made more than 30,000 military 3HWs, based on its civilian Tiger 80.

Heavy-duty luggage rack

△ **Harley-Davidson WLC**
Date 1942 Origin USA
Engine 739 cc, side-valve V-twin
Top speed 105 km/h (65 mph)

The WLC was a version of Harley's WLA made for the Canadian military. Harley supplied around 90,000 bikes to Allied forces during World War II.

△ **NSU Kettenkrad HK 101**
Date 1940 Origin Germany
Engine 1,478 cc, ohv in-line four
Top speed 70 km/h (44 mph)

Widely used in Germany's 1941 Russian campaign, the handlebar-steered Kettenkrad resembled a motorcycle/half-track hybrid. It carried troops and loads over rough terrain.

Harley-Davidson WLC

Rugged, practical, and utterly dependable, Harley-Davidson's WL military motorcycles were some of World War II's finest mechanical workhorses. Most of these 739cc V-twins were used by the US armed forces in WLA form, but a significant number, designated WLCs, were adopted by the Canadian military. Thanks to the simplicity of Harley's side-valve engine, the WLC, and its US cousin, the WLA, were well able to withstand the demands of wartime operation.

IN 1937, Milwaukee-based Harley-Davidson launched its W-series of motorcycles with V-twin engines (two cylinders in a V-configuration sharing a common crankshaft). Three years later, it turned its attention to manufacturing motorcycles for the US Army. The W-series bikes were an obvious choice for military adaptation due to the uncomplicated nature of their side-valve power plants. Among the specifications for the army's WLA variant were drab olive camouflage paint, blackout lighting, longer forks for rough-terrain riding, and – on some examples – a rifle holster on the front forks.

When British manufacturers Norton and BSA found themselves struggling to meet the demand for military bikes from Britain and Canada, Harley stepped in to bridge the gap. The WLC, a close variant of the WLA, was produced for Canadian forces between 1941 and 1944. It was used at the Normandy landings and in many other key conflict zones across Europe. By the war's end, more than 80,000 WLA and WLC bikes had been deployed by the Allies, with both versions recognized as valuable combat motorcycles. Many continued to be used by civilians in the postwar years.

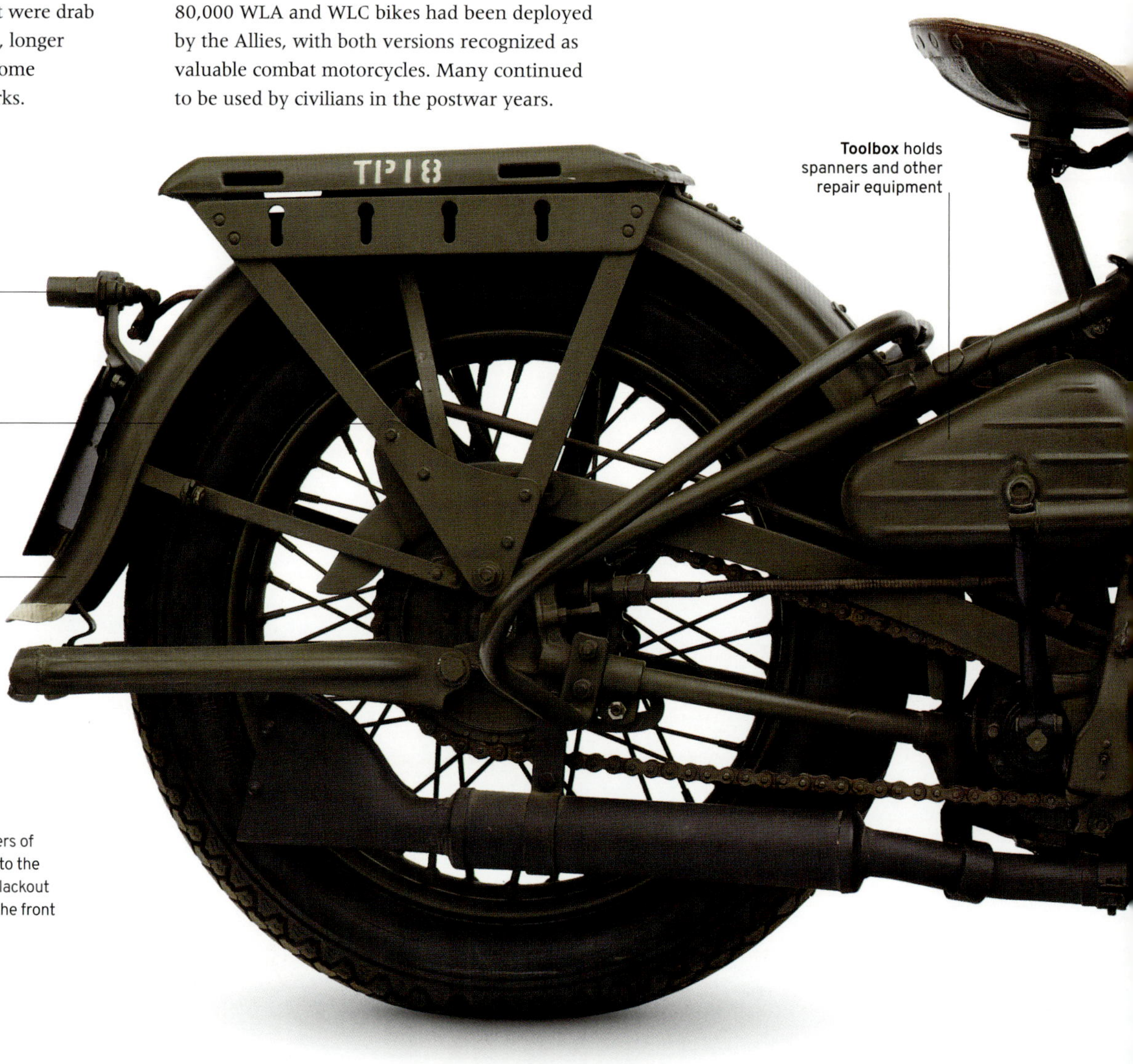

Toolbox holds spanners and other repair equipment

Rear marker light mounted on mudguard

Rear rack for attaching panniers

Olive-drab paint with non-reflective matt finish

Blackout bike
A "blackout kit" was carried by Canadian Army riders of the WLC. It contained shrouds that could be fitted to the front and rear lights to direct light downwards in blackout conditions. Small marker lights were mounted on the front and rear mudguards to compensate.

HARLEY-DAVIDSON WLC • 117

SPECIFICATIONS	
Model	Harley-Davidson WLC, 1942
Assembly	Milwaukee, USA
Production	More than 80,000
Construction	Tubular cradle frame
Engine	739 cc, side valve V-twin
Power output	17 kW (23 hp)
Transmission	Three-speed
Suspension	Leading-link front forks, rigid rear
Brakes	Drums, front and rear
Maximum speed	105 km/h (65 mph)

FRONT VIEW

REAR VIEW

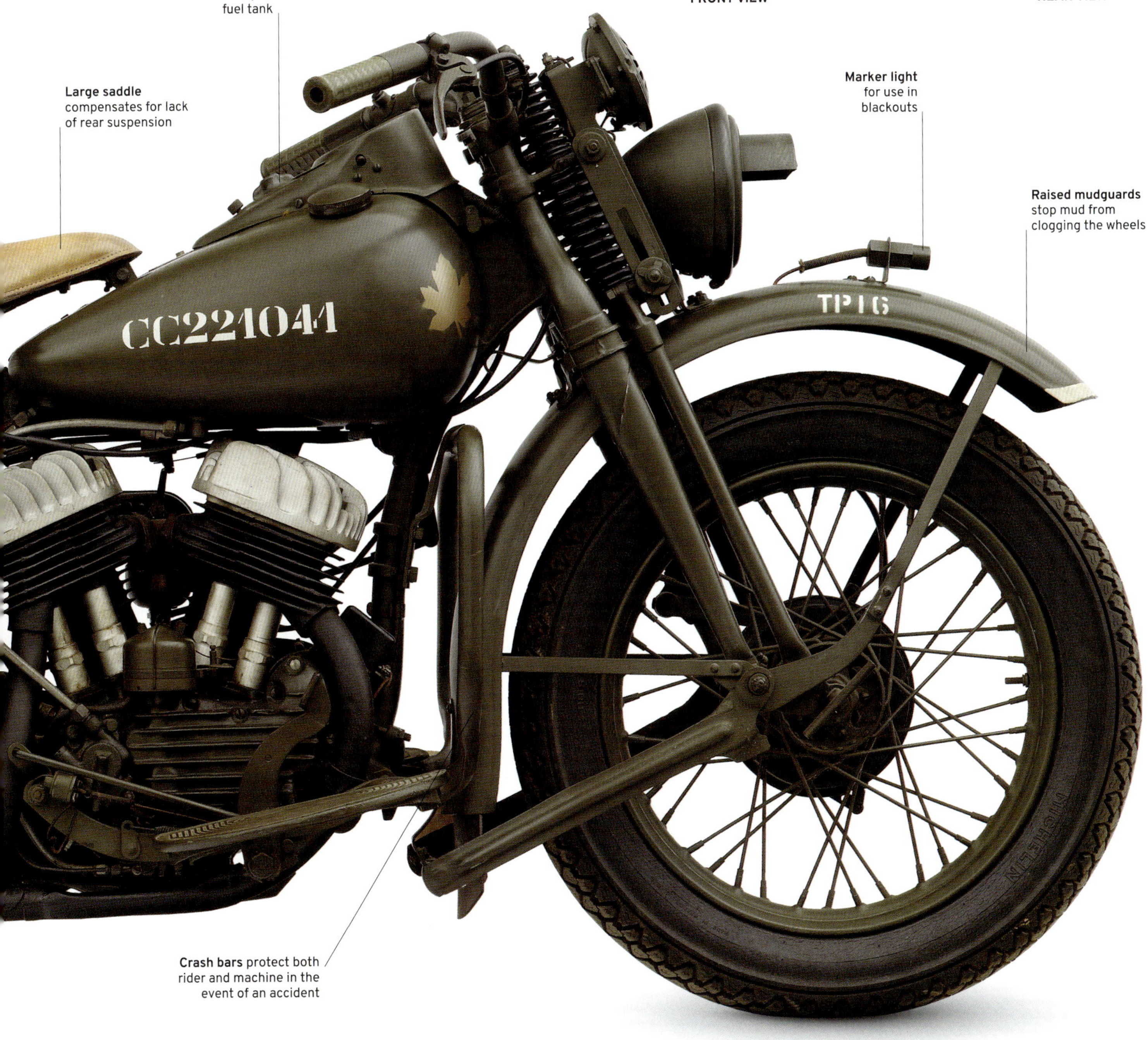

Dash panel sits on top of fuel tank

Large saddle compensates for lack of rear suspension

Marker light for use in blackouts

Raised mudguards stop mud from clogging the wheels

Crash bars protect both rider and machine in the event of an accident

BIKE

Adaptations to transform Harley-Davidson's civilian W Series of "flathead" V-twins into WL military bikes included revising Harley's traditional leading-link forks to give greater ground clearance, as well as adding footboards and protective crash bars. The Canadian WLC variant also differed in having an alternative throttle-lever position, an auxiliary clutch hand lever, and interchangeable wheels.

1. Identification number **2.** Horn **3.** Fork spring **4.** Speedometer **5.** Gear change **6.** Headlamp mask revealing only a small rectangle of light **7.** Kick-starter **8.** Rear sprocket **9.** Front marker lamp **10.** Data plate attached to top of tank **11.** Clutch control **12.** Front fork-ride adjuster knob **13.** Canadian emblem displayed on either side of tank **14.** Rear lights **15.** Fuel filler

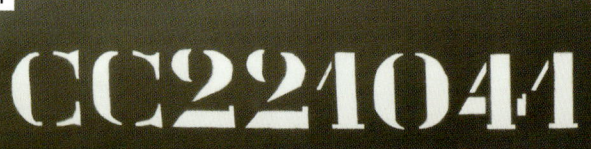

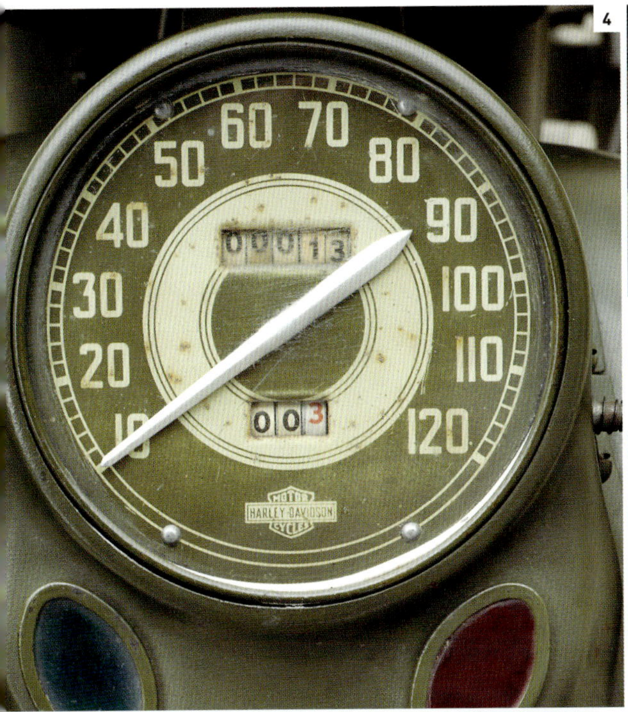

4

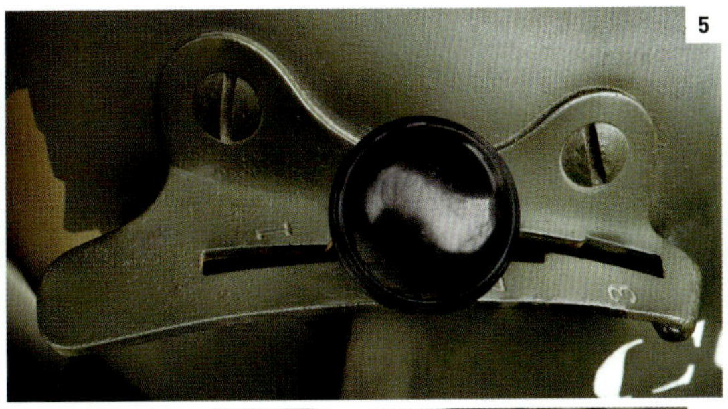
5

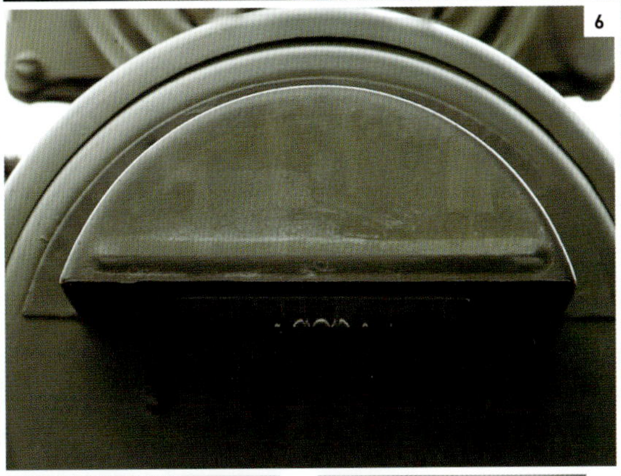
6

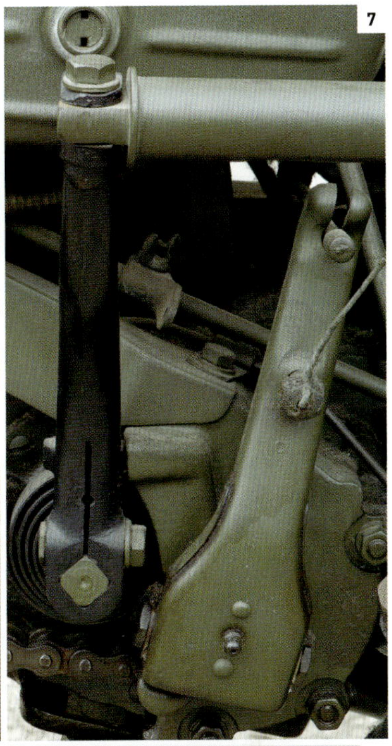
7

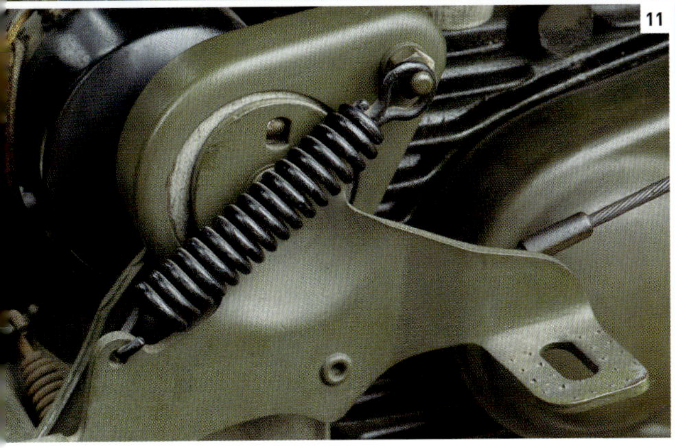
11

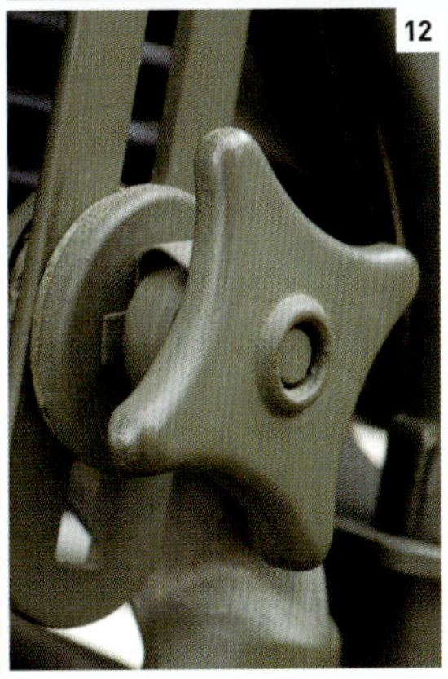
12

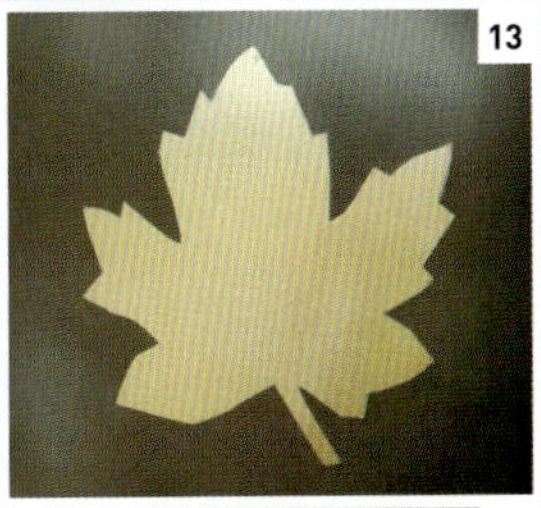
13

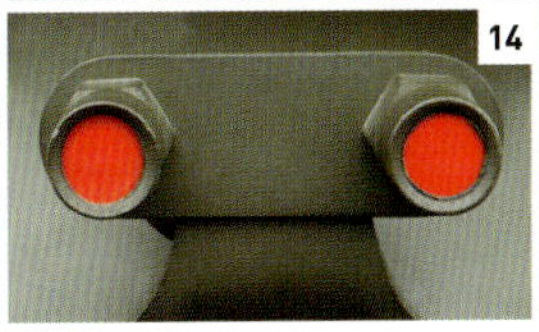
14

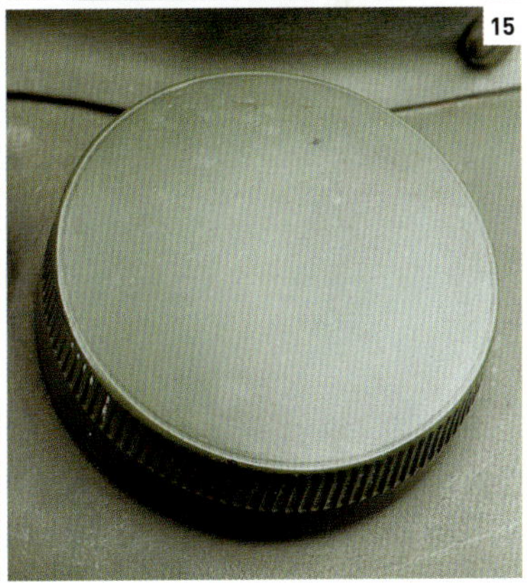
15

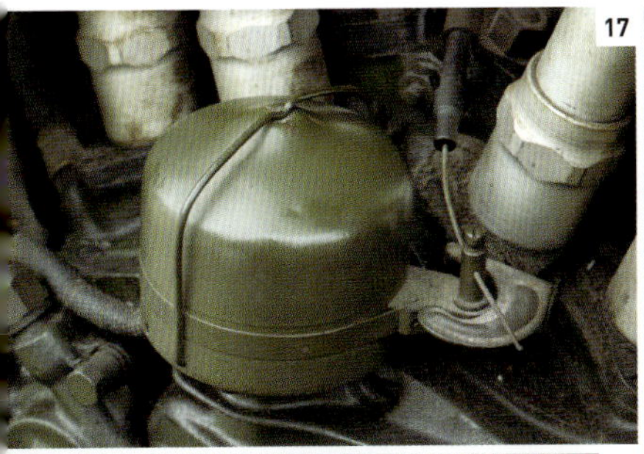
17

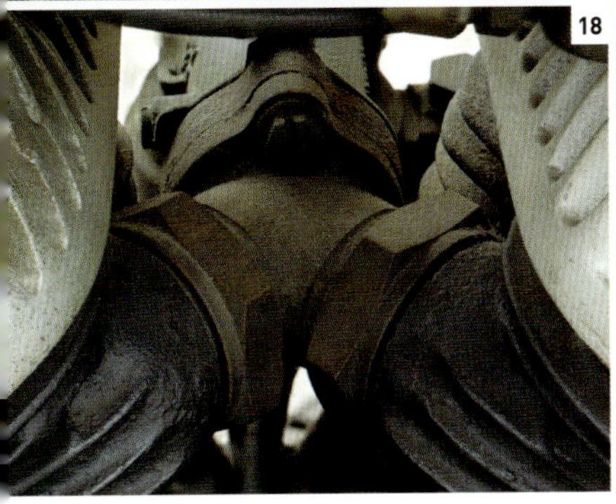
18

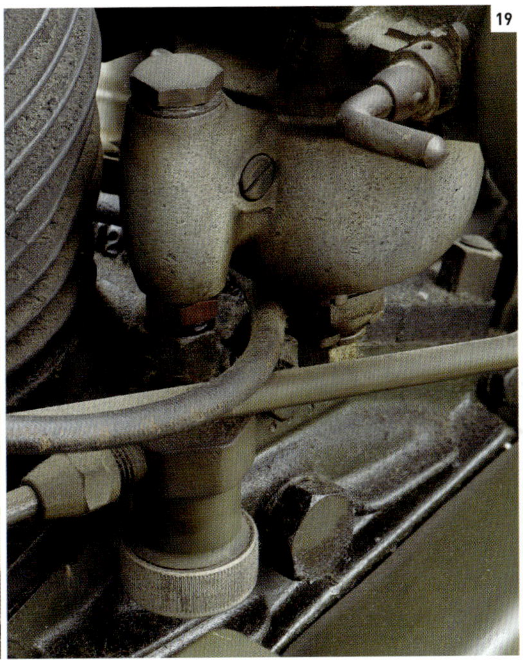
19

ENGINE

Ease of maintenance in combat conditions, due to the absence of moving parts in the cylinder head, was key to the military success of Harley's side-valve (or "flathead") V-twin engine. Reliability was enhanced by an oil-bath air filter to keep out dust, grit, or sand and an upgraded lubrication system.

16. Rugged side-valve engine **17.** Ignition timing unit **18.** Inlet manifold **19.** Carburettor floatbowl **20.** Air intake hose

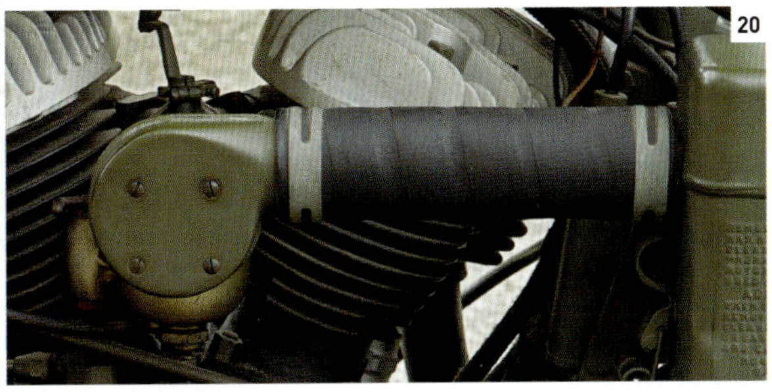
20

Trucks, Half-tracks, and Light Vehicles

During World War II, a host of trucks, half-tracks, cars, and other light vehicles provided essential logistical support. They enabled the vast Allied and Axis-power armies to function, and allowed tanks and other armoured vehicles to be as effective as they were on the battlefield. Auxiliary personnel now began to outnumber troops in front-line roles for the first time in military history. Specific models in this plethora of vehicles could come in a wide range of variants, with each version designed to suit a particular military role or situation.

△ **SdKfz 251-8 Ausf C Half-track**

Date 1940	Origin Germany
Weight 7.8 tonnes (8.6 tons)	
Engine Maybach HL 42 6-cylinder 74.6 kW (100 hp) petrol engine	
Top speed 52.5 km/h (33 mph)	

Angled armour plate

This half-track initially entered service with the German Army as an armoured personnel carrier. It proved so successful that it spawned at least 22 variants, including the 251-8 battlefield ambulance shown here, as well as rocket-launcher, anti-aircraft, and antitank versions.

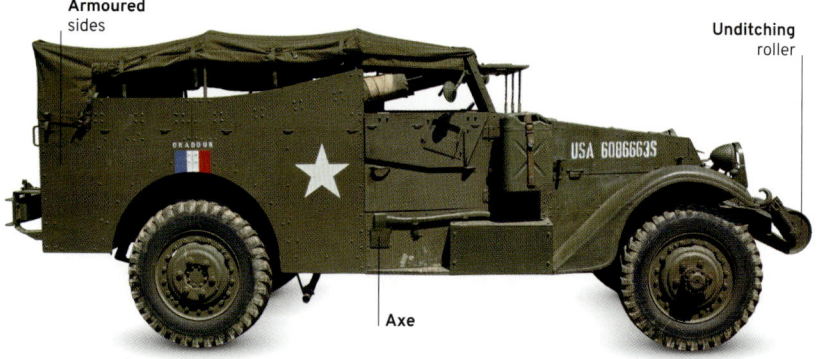

Armoured sides

Unditching roller

Axe

△ **M3A1 Scout Car**

Date 1940	Origin US
Weight 4.03 tonnes (4.4 tons)	
Engine Hercules JXD 6-cylinder 82 kW (110 hp) petrol engine	
Top speed 89 km/h (55 mph)	

Poor off-road mobility limited the effectiveness of this light armoured car, which was used to support American mechanized formations. The half-tracks that succeeded it, however, incorporated the best design features of the M3A1.

△ **Austin K3**

Date 1940	Origin UK
Weight 5.3 tonnes (5.8 tons)	
Engine Straight 6-cylinder petrol, 45 kW (60 hp)	
Top speed 80 km/h (50 mph)	

Around 17,000 K3s were built, most serving as supply trucks, ambulances, and fire engines. Many vehicles were abandoned at Dunkirk in 1940. Robust and reliable, K3s also saw action in North Africa.

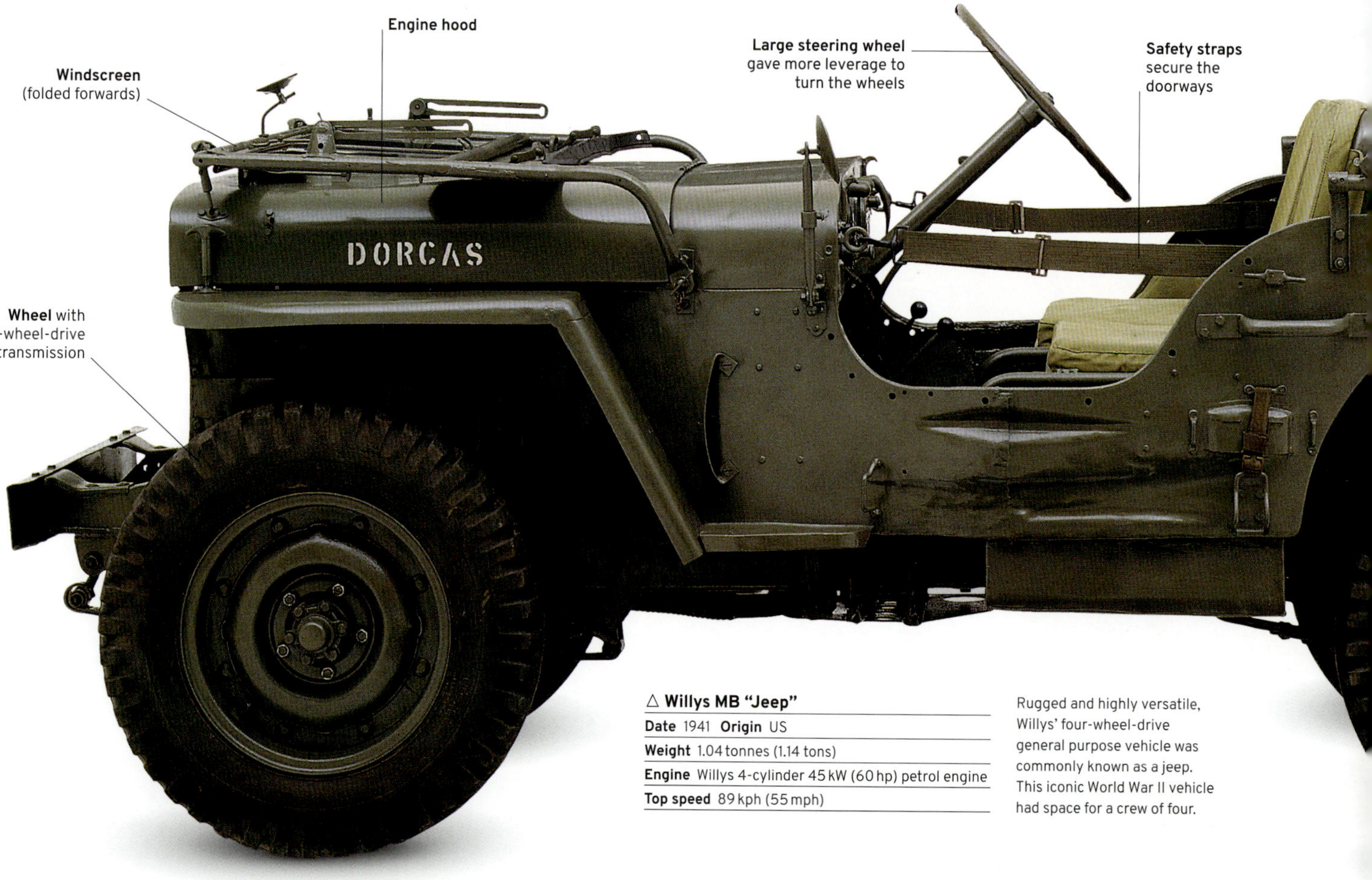

Engine hood

Large steering wheel gave more leverage to turn the wheels

Safety straps secure the doorways

Windscreen (folded forwards)

Wheel with four-wheel-drive transmission

△ **Willys MB "Jeep"**

Date 1941	Origin US
Weight 1.04 tonnes (1.14 tons)	
Engine Willys 4-cylinder 45 kW (60 hp) petrol engine	
Top speed 89 kph (55 mph)	

Rugged and highly versatile, Willys' four-wheel-drive general purpose vehicle was commonly known as a jeep. This iconic World War II vehicle had space for a crew of four.

TRUCKS, HALF-TRACKS, AND LIGHT VEHICLES • 121

▷ **GMC CCKW 352**
Date 1941 Origin USA
Weight 4 tonnes (4.4 tons)
Engine 6-cylinder petrol, 77.5 kW (104 hp)
Top speed 72 km/h (45 mph)

Featuring the cab of a 1930s Chevrolet, this truck and its variants were widely used by US and Allied forces in World War II. Its many roles included fuel transportation, mobile surgery, radio communications, and more.

Garwood winch powered by the engine

Heavy-duty leaf springs between twin axles

△ **Opel Blitz**
Date 1942 Origin Germany
Weight 2.1–3.35 tonnes (2.3–3.7 tons)
Engine 6-cylinder petrol, 41 kW (55 hp)
Top speed 80 km/h (50 mph)

The most widely used and successful of all World War II German trucks was the Blitz. Thanks to its nimble size and the ready availability of spares, it saw action in all theatres in its cargo and 88mm-gun versions.

Desert/Normandy camouflage colours

▽ **Schwimmwagen**
Date 1942 Origin Germany
Weight 910 kg (2,006 lb)
Engine 4-cylinder air-cooled 18.4 kW (25 hp) petrol engine
Top speed 80 km/h (50 mph); 10 km/h (6 mph) on water

The Schwimmwagen (swimming car) was an amphibious four-wheel-drive vehicle derived from the Volkswagen. In water, it was propelled by a screw propeller at the rear, while the front wheels acted as rudders.

Fold-down windscreen

Tow hook

Watertight hull

Paddle in case of engine failure

Spare wheel

Rear machine-gun

Leaf suspension

▽ **M5 Half-track**
Date 1942 Origin US
Weight 9.3 tonnes (10.2 tons)
Engine International Harvester RED-450-B 6-cylinder 105 kW (141 hp) petrol engine
Top speed 68 km/h (42 mph)

During World War II, the US used more than 40,000 half-tracks of various specifications. These vehicles provided mobility and protection for troops in combat situations. The M5, shown here, differed little from the M3, its more famous cousin.

Haversacks slung over external rail

Fuel can

Caterpillar tracks

Rise of the "Jeep"

In the early 1930s, the US Army looked at the British Army's conversion of the small Austin 7 car into a "military tourer" and saw the potential for a tough but lightweight vehicle that could act as a battlefield runabout. Underfunded at the time, the US military concentrated on civilian trucks that could be used in wartime, but nothing quite matched its requirement for a four-wheel drive "light reconnaissance vehicle" with a 0.27 tonne (0.3 ton) payload. So, in summer 1940 a group of manufacturers, including Bantam, Willys, and Ford, along with US Army engineers, put together the design that became known as the "Jeep". More than 600,000 Jeeps were made for the US Army and its allies, including 50,000 for the Soviet Red Army. General George C. Marshall, Chief of Staff of the US Army, called the Jeep "America's greatest contribution to modern warfare", and it is widely regarded as a design and engineering classic.

Columns of Jeeps head a parade of US Army troops along the Champs Élysées in Paris on 28 August 1944 to celebrate the city's liberation.

Axis Tanks

After Hitler's Nazi Party came to power in 1933, Germany flouted international restrictions and began openly building tanks. The experience gained in tank technology enabled the Germans to produce formidable tank designs in World War II, although some models were plagued by mechanical issues. The German tank manufacturers were unable to exploit the mass production methods used in Allied countries, since their vehicles were costly and time-consuming to build. Some effective tanks had been built by Italy and Japan, Germany's Axis partners, in the 1930s, but they were not improved sufficiently as the war progressed, and were soon surpassed by more advanced Allied vehicles.

△ **Panzerkampfwagen I Ausf A**
Date 1934 **Origin** Germany
Weight 5.5 tonnes (6.1 tons)
Engine Krupp M305 petrol, 43 kW (57 hp)
Main armament 2 x 7.92 mm MG13 machine-guns

The two-man Panzer I was designed as a training vehicle. The Ausf A model shown here, though underpowered and not really suited for combat roles, was ideal for instructing tank crews. Due to a shortage of other tanks, Panzer I variants did ultimately see action in Spain, Poland, France, Denmark, Norway, Russia, and North Africa.

△ **Type 95 Ha-Go**
Date 1936 **Origin** Japan
Weight 7.5 tonnes (8.3 tons)
Engine Mitsubishi 6-cylinder diesel, 82 kW (110 hp)
Main armament 37 mm Type 98 gun

Popular with crews, the Type 95's lightweight construction gave good mobility on difficult terrain, and its engine was powerful for its size. Despite success against Chinese forces in the late 1930s and in the early Japanese campaigns of 1942, the Type 95 found itself outclassed when Allied tanks entered the fray. It served on the front line until the war's end.

△ **Panzerkampfwagen IV**
Date 1936 **Origin** Germany
Weight 25 tonnes (27.6 tons)
Engine Maybach HL 120 TRM 12-cylinder petrol, 224 kW (300 hp)
Main armament 75 mm KwK 40 main gun

Originally an infantry support vehicle, the five-man Panzer IV went through a series of improvements to its armour and firepower that eventually turned it into an impressive main battle tank. The Panzer IV was the only German tank to remain in service throughout World War II.

Muzzle brake

88 mm KwK 43 main gun

△ **Panzer 38(t) Ausf E**
Date 1938 **Origin** Czechoslovakia
Weight 10 tonnes (11 tons)
Engine Praga EPA petrol, 93 kW (125 hp)
Main armament 3.7 cm KwK 38(t) L/47.8 gun

Acknowledging that the Czech Panzer 38(t) was superior to its own Panzers I and II, Germany continued 38(t) production after annexing Czechoslovakia. The 1,400-plus German 38(t)s built saw action in France, Poland, and the Soviet Union until 1942. The chassis was re-used in several tank destroyers.

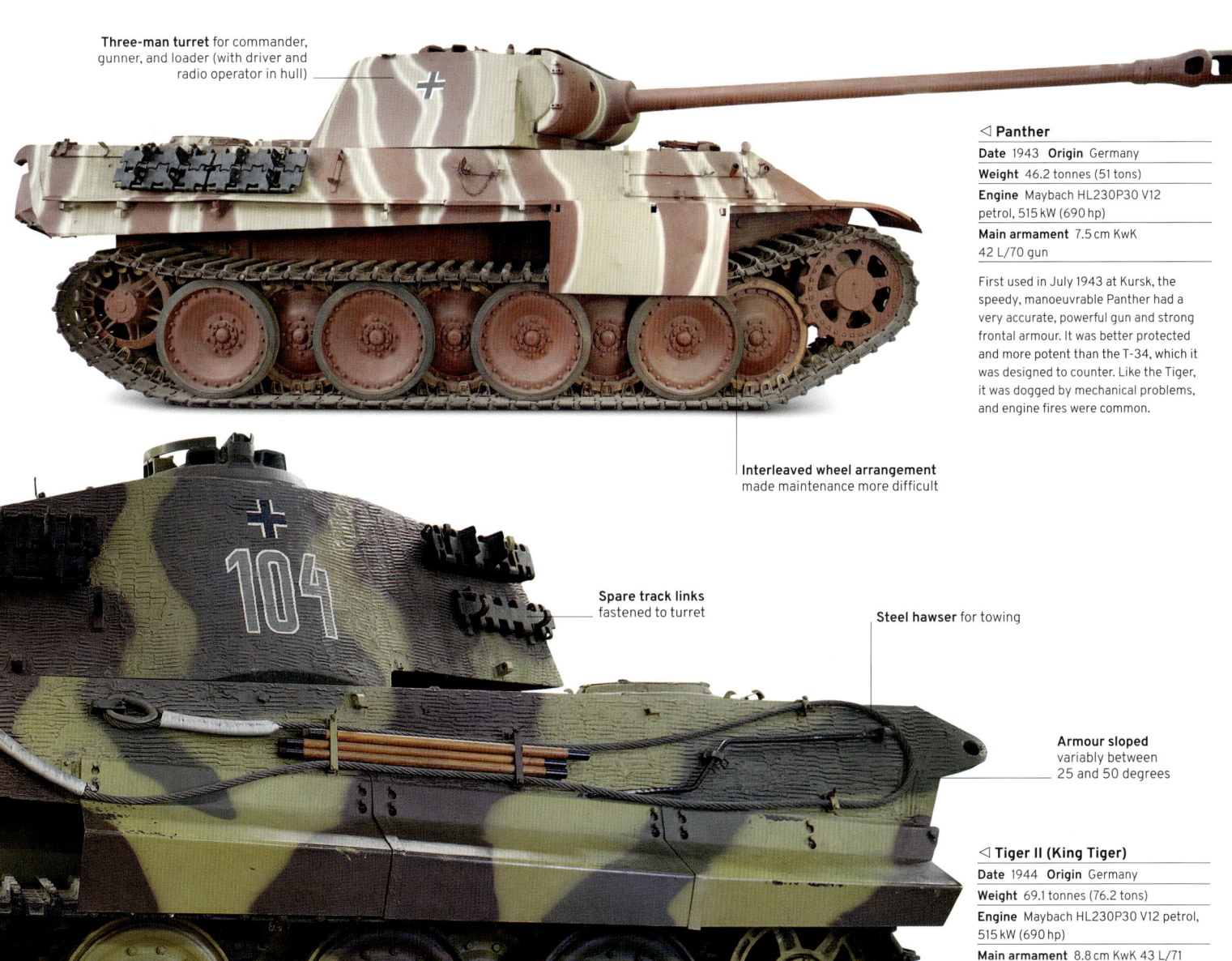

△ **Panzerkampfwagen III Ausf L**
Date 1939 **Origin** Germany
Weight 23.5 tonnes (25.9 tons)
Engine Maybach HL 120 TRM 12-cylinder petrol, 224 kW (300 hp)
Main armament 50 mm KwK 39 main gun

The Panzer III was Germany's main battle tank at the start of World War II. By the end of 1941, it was clear that it could not hold its own against the Soviet T-34. It was eventually relegated to minor combat roles, but the chassis was used for other armoured vehicles. This Ausf M mark had a crew of 5.

△ **M14/41**
Date 1940 **Origin** Italy
Weight 14.5 tonnes (16 tons)
Engine SPA 15T M41 diesel, 108 kW (145 hp)
Main armament 47 mm M35 L/32 gun

Lessons learned from deploying tanks in the Spanish Civil War enabled Italy to design a new generation of vehicles, which first saw action in North Africa in 1940. The well-armed M14/41 was a version of the M13/40 upgraded and optimized for desert use. The deficiency of its armour became apparent when exposed to the fire of Allied 2-pounders.

Breda 38 machine-guns

Three-man turret for commander, gunner, and loader (with driver and radio operator in hull)

◁ **Panther**
Date 1943 **Origin** Germany
Weight 46.2 tonnes (51 tons)
Engine Maybach HL230P30 V12 petrol, 515 kW (690 hp)
Main armament 7.5 cm KwK 42 L/70 gun

First used in July 1943 at Kursk, the speedy, manoeuvrable Panther had a very accurate, powerful gun and strong frontal armour. It was better protected and more potent than the T-34, which it was designed to counter. Like the Tiger, it was dogged by mechanical problems, and engine fires were common.

Interleaved wheel arrangement made maintenance more difficult

Spare track links fastened to turret

Steel hawser for towing

Armour sloped variably between 25 and 50 degrees

◁ **Tiger II (King Tiger)**
Date 1944 **Origin** Germany
Weight 69.1 tonnes (76.2 tons)
Engine Maybach HL230P30 V12 petrol, 515 kW (690 hp)
Main armament 8.8 cm KwK 43 L/71

With an 8.8 cm gun that was a threat even at long range, and frontal armour that could resist all Allied antitank weapons, the Tiger II was perhaps the most powerful tank in World War II. Engine unreliability hampered its effectiveness, while low production figures – only 489 were built – limited its impact.

Tiger I

With its powerful 88 mm gun, thick frontal armour, wide tracks, and enormous size, Germany's Tiger tank gained a fearsome reputation among Allied forces on the battlefields of World War II. Although the Tiger was dogged by technical glitches, it had an immense psychological effect on its opponents, and it remains the most mythologized tank of the war.

IN MAY 1941, after German weaponry had failed to pierce the armour of British Matilda 2 and French Char B tanks, Hitler ordered the production of a heavy tank. The result was the Tiger. It resembled earlier German tanks in its boxy shape and layout but was super-sized, weighing more than two Panzer IVs. This massive tank provided a stable platform for the accurate 88mm KwK 36 gun, for which it carried 92 rounds. During production, the engine was upgraded from 485 kW (650 hp) to 522 kW (700 hp), but engine and transmission still struggled with the vast weight, which reached 57.9 tonnes (63.75 tons) instead of the planned 50 tonnes (55 tons).

Rushed into service, the Tiger experienced a variety of teething problems that, combined with high manufacturing costs and a shortage of skilled crews, compromised its tactical effectiveness. It failed to have the desired battlefield impact: rather than punching through enemy lines as intended, it was mainly used defensively. However, its prowess was undeniable – even in this defensive role, it instilled terror in Allied tank crews.

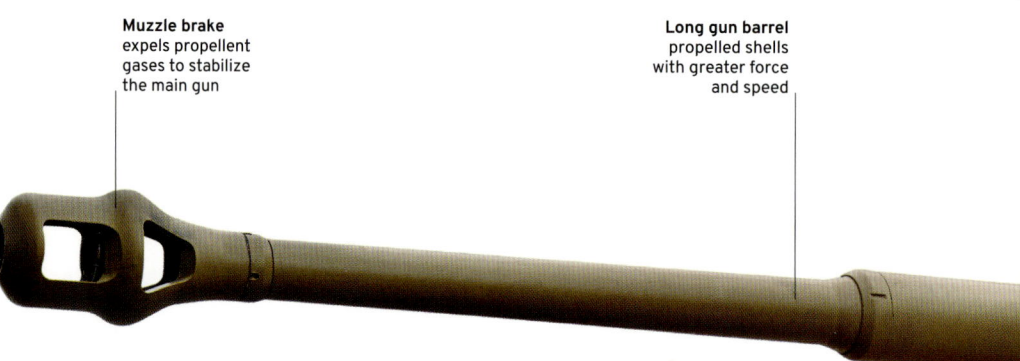

Muzzle brake expels propellent gases to stabilize the main gun

Long gun barrel propelled shells with greater force and speed

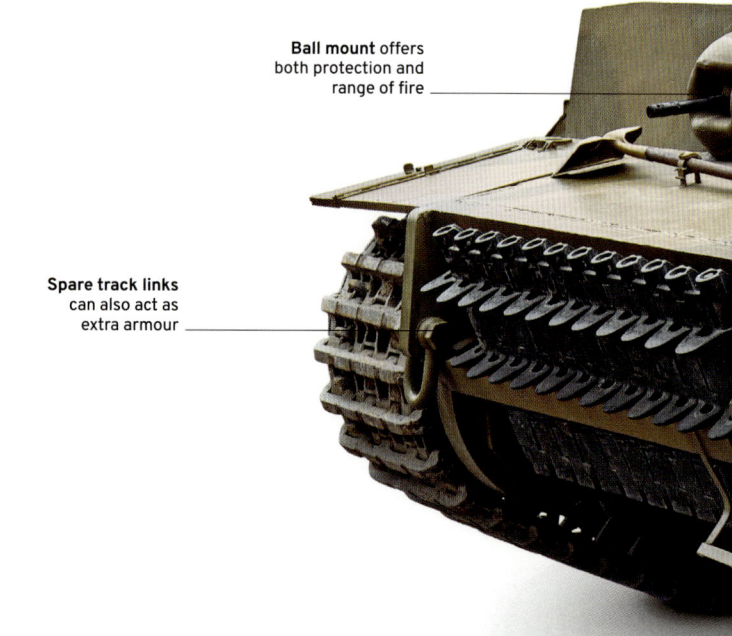

Ball mount offers both protection and range of fire

Spare track links can also act as extra armour

SPECIFICATIONS	
Model	PzKpfw VI Tiger Ausf E
Date	1942
Origin	Germany
Production	1,347
Weight	57.9 tonnes (63.75 tons)
Main armament	88 mm KwK 36
Engine	Maybach HL210P45 V-12 petrol, 485 kW (650 hp)
Secondary armament	7.92 mm MG34
Armour thickness	120 mm (4.75 in) max

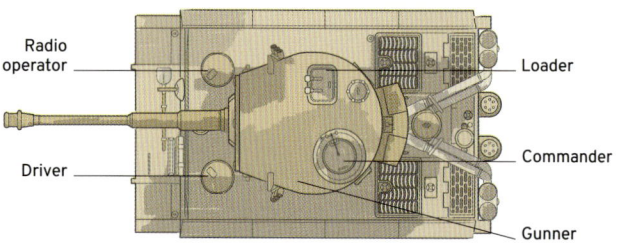

Radio operator, Driver, Loader, Commander, Gunner

Prized capture
Tiger 131, pictured here after restoration to running order, is an early example, equipped with the original HL210P45 engine rather than the later, more powerful version. It was seized by the Allies in Tunisia in April 1943 and, being the first complete Tiger captured, taken to Britain for extensive analysis.

TIGER I · 127

FRONT VIEW

REAR VIEW

131 deciphered
The number "131" reveals that this Tiger belonged to the 1st Company, the 3rd Platoon of its tank regiment, and that it was the 1st tank of its platoon.

Interleaved road wheels help to distribute weight evenly

EXTERIOR

Copying earlier German half-track designs, the road wheels are arranged in an interleaved fashion, in order to spread the immense weight of the tank. Suspension is provided by 16 torsion bars, with eight arms on either side, each arm holding three wheels. This arrangement required nine wheels to be removed in order to replace one of the inner wheels. The tank's size led to innovations such as removing outer road wheels and fitting thinner transport tracks for train travel. This tank, Tiger 131, still bears battle scars from the day of its capture.

1. National recognition symbol 2. Driver's vision port 3. Turret lifting lug 4. Smoke grenade dischargers 5. Radio operator's machine-gun 6. Track toolbox 7. Towing cables and wire cutters on hull 8. Feifel air filter tubes 9. Drive sprocket and interleaved road wheels 10. Commander's hatch 11. Turret pistol port

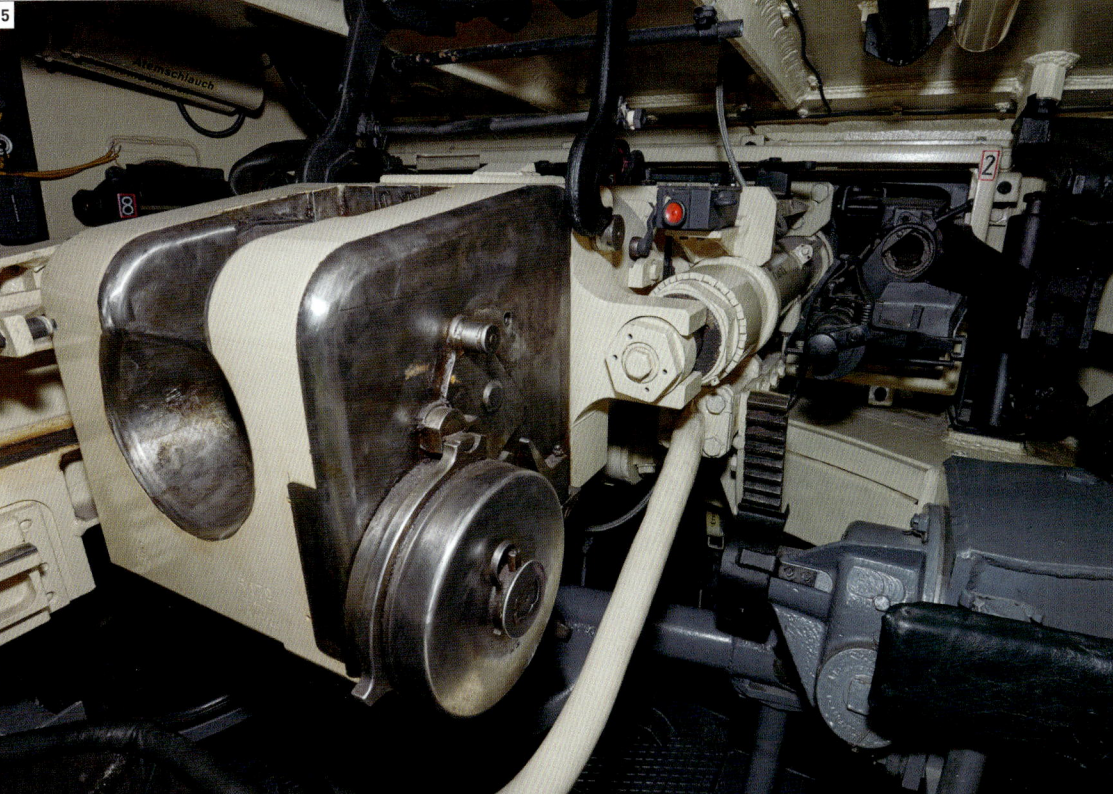

INTERIOR

The driver was stationed in the front of the main hull, to the left. On his right sat the radio operator, who operated the ball-mounted machine gun. On the turret's left-side, to the rear, sat the commander, with the gunner in front of him; the loader occupied the space to their right.

12. Looking down into commander's position 13. Turret traverse wheel 14. Commander's periscope 15. Loader's position and main gun breech 16. Driver's controls and vision port 17. Binocular gun sight 18. Gun recoil return gauge 19. Turret side vision port 20. Driver's instrument panel 21. Barrel elevation wheel 22. Co-driver's machine-gun

Allied Tanks

Although Allied tanks seldom reached the technical standard of their German counterparts, they were easier to mass produce. This was especially true of the American M4 Sherman, which played a key role in defeating German forces in Western Europe. Like other US Army tanks, it was robust and well built. In the 1930s, France produced some capable tanks, but it failed to use them effectively when Germany invaded in 1940. British tanks were often inadequate in combat situations, although later tanks such as the Comet performed well on the battlefield.

△ **SOMUA S35**
Date 1936	Origin France
Weight	19.5 tonnes (21.5 tons)
Engine	SOMUA V-8 petrol, 142 kW (190 hp)
Main armament	47 mm SA 35 L/32 gun

The three-man S35 equipped France's cavalry divisions. Its cast-steel armour gave better protection than riveted panels. The commander in the one-man turret had to load, aim, and fire the powerful gun, as well as instruct the crew.

△ **Char B1 bis**
Date 1936	Origin France
Weight	31.5 tonnes (34.7 tons)
Engine	Renault 6-cylinder petrol, 229 kW (307 hp)
Main armament	1 x 75 mm ABS 1929 SA 35 L/17.1 howitzer, 1 x 47 mm SA 35 L/32 gun

The most powerful French tank in 1940, the B1 bis mainly supported infantry. It carried a 75 mm howitzer for firing high explosives against enemy fortifications, and a turret-mounted antitank gun. The tank was prone to mechanical problems, and its heavy armour – up to 60 mm (2⅓ in) thick – limited both speed and range.

▷ **Valentine Mark II**
Date 1940	Origin UK
Weight	16.3 tonnes (18 tons)
Engine	AEC Type 190 diesel, 98 kW (131 hp)
Main armament	QF 2-pounder gun

The Valentine was the most-produced British tank of World War II, with more than 7,000 entering service. Some later versions replaced the 2-pounder gun with a 6-pounder. Used in North Africa, the Pacific, and Eastern Europe, this versatile tank spawned many specialized variants, including a bridgelayer and a flame-thrower.

△ **M3 Grant**
Date 1941	Origin USA
Weight	27.2 tonnes (30 tons)
Engine	Continental R-975 petrol, 254 kW (340 hp)
Main armament	1 x 75 mm M2 gun, 1 x 37 mm M5 gun

The M3 arose from the US Army's urgent need for a tank with a 75 mm gun. Waiting for a suitable turret design would delay production, so the gun was mounted in a sponson on the M3's hull, which limited the field of fire. The M3, known as the Lee in the US, used the successful engine and suspension from the M2 medium tank. British M3s, called Grants, had a modified turret.

ALLIED TANKS · 131

◁ **M3A1 Stuart**

Date 1942	**Origin** USA		

Weight 12.9 tonnes (14.2 tons)
Engine Continental W-670 9A petrol, 186 kW (250 hp)
Main armament 37 mm M6 L/56.6 gun

Widely used by the Allied powers in World War II, the Stuart was an improved version of the 37 mm-armed M2A4. It benefited from mass production techniques that made it reliable and easy to repair. Although obsolete as an offensive weapon by 1944, the Stuart continued to serve in a reconnaissance role.

▽ **M4A1 Sherman**

Date 1942 **Origin** USA
Weight 30.3 tonnes (33.4 tons)
Engine Continental R-975 petrol, 298 kW (400 hp)
Main armament 75 mm M3 L/40 gun

The M4 Sherman was the most important tank fielded by the Allies, equipping the armoured divisions of the US and Britain. It used the chassis from the M3 topped by a turret for the 75 mm gun. The M4A1, the first standard production Sherman, had a cast hull; the tank shown here was the second ever produced and is the oldest survivor.

△ **Comet**

Date 1944 **Origin** UK
Weight 33.5 tonnes (36.9 tons)
Engine Rolls-Royce Meteor Mark III V12 petrol, 447 kW (600 hp)
Main armament 77 mm HV gun

Developed from the earlier Cromwell, the Comet was more heavily armoured than its predecessor but equally mobile due to superior suspension. Arguably the best British tank of the war, it reached the front lines in limited numbers in early 1945, where its 77 mm gun proved effective against German Panthers and Tigers.

△ **M26 Pershing**

Date 1945 **Origin** USA
Weight 41.9 tonnes (46.2 tons)
Engine Ford GAF V8 petrol, 373 kW (500 hp)
Main armament 90 mm M3 L/53 gun

The powerful 90 mm gun of the M26 Pershing was effective against the German Panther and Tiger, but the tank's protracted development and production meant that only 20 vehicles reached Europe in time to see combat. The Pershing used the same engine as the M4A3 Sherman variant, but its great weight left it underpowered.

M4 Sherman

Although under-armoured and lacking a powerful enough gun to successfully take on the heavier German Panthers and Tigers, the Sherman was faster and had the supreme advantage of quantity through mass production. In the breakout from Normandy in 1944, American Shermans showed what they could do, sweeping across France at full tilt in large numbers, their progress halted only by supply issues.

THE M4 SHERMAN was designed in 1940 as the successor to the M3 Lee medium tank. US military strategy at the time saw tanks primarily as armoured cavalry that could dash through a breach in opposing formations and cause mayhem behind enemy lines. The speedy Sherman met these criteria perfectly. It was also robust, reliable, and easy to maintain. The Sherman made its combat debut in Egypt at the Second Battle of El Alamein in October 1942, and rapidly proved well suited to the rigours of war.

Eleven different plants across the US built the Sherman, most of them with no previous experience of tank manufacture. Together, these factories produced sufficient tanks – 63,181, including derivatives – to equip the US, British and Commonwealth, Russian, and other Allied armies. Shermans continued to operate in many national armies after World War II and were still serving in Paraguay as recently as 2016.

SPECIFICATIONS	
Name	M4A1 Sherman
Date	1940
Origin	USA
Production	49,234
Weight	30.2 tonnes (33.3 tons)
Main armament	75mm M3
Engine	Wright-Continental R-975 radial gasoline, 298 kW (400 hp)
Secondary armament	.30 Browning M1919 machine-guns
Armour thickness	118mm (4½ in) max

Extra stowage along the front glacis

FRONT VIEW **REAR VIEW**

M4 SHERMAN · 133

From Ohio to France
With 11 different factories manufacturing the Sherman around four main engine types, there was considerable variation between models. This M4A1, built in 1943 by the Lima tank works of Ohio, has upgraded armour. The tank served with US forces in World War II and was subsequently used as a training vehicle by the French Army.

HAVOC

"Havoc"
The initial letter of a tank's name indicated the company to which it belonged. This tank bears the markings H Company, 66 Armoured Regiment, 2nd US Armoured Division.

- **75 mm medium-velocity gun** (later upgraded to 76 mm)
- **Gun mantlet**
- **Barrel clamp**
- **Rubber-blocked track**
- **Additional side armour**
- **Hull** is cast rather than welded

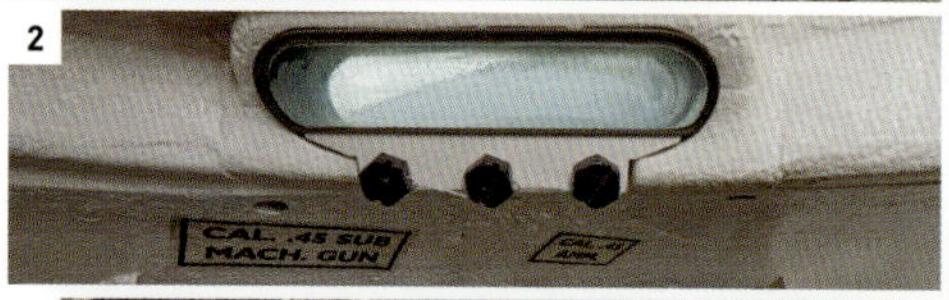

INTERIOR

Although later models included a second hatch, this M4A1 has the early turret design, which required commander, gunner, and loader to utilize the same hatch. Vision ports in the cupola gave the commander an all-round view of the battlefield from within the tank.

1. Looking down into the commander's position
2. Commander's vision cupola block   3. SCR 508 radio set   4. Turret interior showing commander's and gunner's positions   5. 75mm ammunition
6. 75mm gunsight   7. Azimuth indicator   8. Co-axial machine-gun   9. Main gun breech   10. Main gun elevation wheel   11. Driver's instrument panel
12. Driver's hatch   13. Driver's position

EXTERIOR

Analysis showed that stowed ammunition caused more fires, or "brew-ups", than the engine. Protecting ammunition was thus vital: extra side armour on the cast hull of this M4A1 helped to shield ammunition inside the tank. "Wet" ammunition storage (surrounding shell racks with water-filled jackets) was introduced on later models as an additional safeguard. Other modifications as the war progressed included wider tracks and an upgraded 76mm gun.

14. Allied Forces recognition symbol **15.** Headlamp **16.** Tow hook **17.** Co-driver's machine-gun **18.** Armoured roof fan cover **19.** Driver's periscope **20.** Driver's hatch (closed) **21.** Paired road wheels **22.** Front drive sprocket **23.** Spotlight **24.** Air filter **25.** Turret hatch and commander's cupola **26.** Engine with doors open

136 • 1918–1945

△ Matilda CDL
Date 1940	Origin UK
Weight 26.9 tonnes (29.7 tons)	
Engine 2 x AEC 6-cylinder diesel, 71 kW (95 hp)	
Main armament None	

The Canal Defence Light (CDL) was an adapted Matilda tank with a flickering 13-million candle power searchlight in its turret to dazzle enemy forces at night. The frequency of the light's flickering intensified the blinding effect.

Turret with searchlight

Vehicle body housing explosives

△ Goliath tracked mine
Date 1943	Origin Germany
Weight 0.4 tonnes (0.45 tons)	
Engine Zundapp SZ7 petrol, 9 kW (12.5 hp)	
Main armament 100 kg (220 lb) explosive	

The Goliath – a small, mobile bomb, only 1.63 m (5 ft 4 in) long and 0.62 m (2 ft) tall – was remotely controlled by an operator who remained in cover and directed the vehicle via a 650 m (2,130 ft)-long wire. Designed to destroy fortifications or clear minefields, the Goliath was vulnerable to small arms fire and rough terrain.

Armoured fuel trailer

△ Churchill Crocodile
Date 1943	Origin UK
Weight 40.6 tonnes (44.8 tons)	
Engine Bedford Twin-Six petrol, 261 kW (350 hp)	
Main armament Flame-thrower, 75 mm QF gun	

The Crocodile was a fully operational Churchill gun tank with a flame-thrower mounted at the front of its hull. Fuel for the flame-thrower was carried in a trailer. Flame-thrower tanks like the Crocodile were highly effective against fortifications: although they attracted heavy enemy fire, their presence often persuaded defending forces to surrender.

▷ Valentine Bridgelayer
Date 1943	Origin UK
Weight 19.9 tonnes (21.9 tons)	
Engine AEC A189 petrol, 101 kW (135 hp)	
Main armament None	

The bridge carried by this adapted Valentine tank could span 9.2 m (30 ft) and support 30-tonne (33-ton) vehicles. Bridgelaying tanks were first developed at the end of World War I, but did not see combat until World War II.

Short, wide barrel of 290mm mortar

◁ Churchill AVRE
Date 1943	Origin UK
Weight 39.6 tonnes (43.7 tons)	
Engine Bedford 12-cylinder petrol, 261 kW (350 hp)	
Main armament 290 mm Petard Mortar	

Developed in the wake of the ill-fated 1942 Dieppe Raid, the Armoured Vehicle Royal Engineers (AVRE) provided battlefield protection and destructive power for engineers. A versatile version of the Churchill tank, the AVRE could smash fortifications with its short-range mortar.

Canvas flotation screen provides buoyancy

△ Valentine Mk IX Duplex Drive
Date 1943	Origin UK
Weight 16 tonnes (17.6 tons)	
Engine GM 6046 diesel, 280 kW (375 hp)	
Main armament QF 6-pounder gun	

Duplex Drive (DD) tanks were developed to provide support for the infantry during the D-Day landings. Fitted with a propeller and a canvas screen, they could "swim" from ship to shore. Valentine DDs were used to train crews in the run-up to D-Day; similarly adapted Sherman M4 DDs were used for the actual landings.

Engineering and Specialist Vehicles

The difficulty of landing vehicles by amphibious assault was highlighted by the disastrous 1942 Dieppe Raid, when many Allied tanks failed to get off the beach. Successfully getting tanks ashore in a future invasion would thus be a challenge. Percy Hobart, British 79th Armoured Division commander, was tasked with developing vehicles to assist such landings. He based them on tank hulls, which gave the vehicles similar mobility and protection to tanks and made logistics easier. Nicknamed "Hobart's Funnies", they were used in northwest Europe, Italy, and the Far East.

ENGINEERING AND SPECIALIST VEHICLES • 137

Scissors bridge
folded on tank

Hydraulic arm
unfolds bridge

Chain flails
set off mines

△ **Sherman V Crab**
Date 1943 **Origin** USA
Weight 32.2 tonnes (35.5 tons)
Engine Chrysler A57 Multibank petrol, 317 kW (425 hp)
Main armament 75 mm M3 L/40 gun

Flail tanks, such as this Sherman V Crab, were used for clearing minefields – a dangerous job, especially when under enemy fire. The Crab had to travel at under 3.2 km/h (2 mph) in a straight line, while its spinning flail chains beat the ground with sufficient force to detonate any mines in the tank's path.

▽ **Churchill Armoured Recovery Vehicle (ARV)**
Date 1944 **Origin** UK
Weight 33.5 tonnes (37 tons)
Engine Bedford Twin-Six petrol, 261 kW (350hp)
Main armament None

Based on the Churchill tank and deployed by the Royal Electrical and Mechanical Engineers (REME), this armoured recovery vehicle – with a crew of three – gave mechanics protection as they sought to fix stricken vehicles or remove them from the battlefield. It carried a crane, towing gear, tools, and equipment for repairing damaged tank components.

Dummy gun

Crane for removing engines

▷ **StuG III**

Date 1940 **Origin** Germany

Weight 24.3 tonnes (26.8 tons)

Engine Maybach HL120TRM petrol, 224 kW (300 hp)

Main armament 7.5 cm StuK 40 L/48 gun

The most-produced German armoured vehicle, with over 11,000 built, the StuG or Sturmgeschütz ("assault gun") III was originally an infantry support vehicle armed with a short-barrelled, low-velocity 7.5 cm L/24 gun. Its low height and armour made it ideally suited to the role of tank-destroyer, and it was soon upgraded with the longer-barrelled L/48 antitank gun.

Drive sprocket transfers power from the engine to the tracks

▷ **M18 Hellcat**

Date 1943 **Origin** USA

Weight 17.8 tonnes (19.6 tons)

Engine Wright-Continental R-975 petrol, 298 kW (400 hp)

Main armament 76 mm M1A2 L/52 gun

A powerful engine, very thin armour, and torsion-bar suspension helped to make the M18 Hellcat one of the fastest ever armoured vehicles. Although its speed and agility met the criteria for a US tank destroyer, its lack of firepower limited its effectiveness, especially when confronted by heavier German tanks.

Allied and Axis Tank Destroyers

Tank destroyers and assault guns typically utilized the hulls of existing tank models. German and Soviet forces favoured turretless designs, which made the vehicles quicker and cheaper to manufacture than conventional tanks, and enabled them to carry a larger gun and heavier armour than the tank on which they were based. American tank destroyers prioritized mobility over firepower; intended to outmanoeuvre enemy tanks in counter-attacks, they retained the turret. In reality, all three countries used tank destroyers to support infantry and as artillery pieces.

▷ **SU-76M**

Date 1943 **Origin** USSR

Weight 10.4 tonnes (11.5 tons)

Engine 2 x GAZ-203 6-cylinder diesel, 63 kW (85 hp) each

Main armament 76.2 mm ZiS-3Sh L/42.6 gun

Able to destroy lighter German tanks, the SU-76M was a light assault gun and mobile artillery piece based on a stretched T-70 tank chassis. With only thin armour to protect the occupants and an open top, the SU-76M's crews were rather vulnerable. Production exceeded 12,600, making it the second most-produced Soviet armoured vehicle of the war, after the T-34 tank.

Muzzle brake reduces the gun's recoil

Camouflage scheme for Arctic warfare

ALLIED AND AXIS TANK DESTROYERS · 139

Idler wheel helps to maintain track tension

8.8 cm PaK 43/3 main gun

△ **Jagdpanther**
Date 1944 Origin Germany
Weight 46.7 tonnes (51.5 tons)
Engine Maybach HL230 P30 V12 petrol, 515 kW (690 hp)
Main armament 8.8 cm PaK 43/3 L/71 gun

Well armoured, mobile, and wielding a powerful gun, the Jagdpanther was an impressive mechanized weapon, especially when deployed in defensive or ambush roles. Based on the Panther chassis, its combat effectiveness was hampered by poor maintenance and crew training. Furthermore, only 392 examples of this forbidding tank-buster were produced – too few to affect the course of the war.

▽ **SU-100**
Date 1944 Origin USSR
Weight 31.5 tonnes (34.7 tons)
Engine Kharkiv Model V-2-34 diesel, 373 kW (500 hp)
Main armament 100 mm D-10S L/53.5 gun

Like the SU-85, from which it was developed, the SU-100 provided long-range antitank support to offensive formations. It also served as a backstop to defend against the heaviest German tanks. About 1,200 SU-100s were made in wartime; production and upgrades continued post war, keeping the vehicle in service around the world for decades.

External fuel tank

Commander's cupola

▽ **Jagdpanzer 38(t) Hetzer**
Date 1944 Origin Germany
Weight 16 tonnes (17.6 tons)
Engine Praga AC/2 petrol, 112 kW (150 hp)
Main armament 7.5 cm PaK 39 L/48 gun

The Hetzer was an ideal ambush vehicle, its compact size enabling it to wait concealed on the battlefield and surprise enemy forces. Based on the hull of the Panzer 38(t), it was smaller, lighter, and cheaper than other Jagdpanzers of the late war. Crews disliked it, due to the poorly laid-out and cramped interior. A total of 2,584 Hetzers were built.

▷ **ISU-152**
Date 1944 Origin USSR
Weight 47.2 tonnes (52 tons)
Engine Kharkiv Model V-2IS diesel, 388 kW (520 hp)
Main armament 152 mm ML-20S L/29 gun-howitzer

The USSR produced a range of self-propelled guns based on the chassis of its heavy tanks. For example, the SU-152 used the KV-1S, while the ISU-152 employed the later IS chassis. A lack of 152 mm barrels called for another variation – the ISU-122, armed with a 122 mm gun. With devastating firepower, they were well suited both to urban fighting and attack support.

Gun mantlet is heavily armoured

Hull based on Panzer 38(t)

Spare track links carried on front of hull

▷ **Jagdtiger**
Date 1944 Origin Germany
Weight 71.1 tonnes (78.4 tons)
Engine Maybach HL230 P30 V12 petrol, 515 kW (690 hp)
Main armament 12.8 cm PaK 44 L/55 gun

The Jagdtiger, the heaviest armoured vehicle of World War II, could defeat any Allied tank in long-range combat. Using the suspension from the Tiger, Jagdtigers were prone to malfunction and were often destroyed by their crews after breakdowns.

12.8 cm PaK 44 main gun

Soviet Tanks

When German forces invaded the Soviet Union in 1941, the Soviets initially suffered heavy losses of soldiers and tanks. To safeguard manufacturing facilities, tank production shifted east, beyond the Ural Mountains; British and American tanks helped plug the gap until the new factories were up and running. To increase output, production became standardized. Consequently, the tanks were simple in design and construction, which suited the limited skills of their crews, who were often inexperienced or poorly trained.

▷ Kliment Voroshilov-1 (KV-1)
Date 1939 **Origin** Soviet Union
Weight 48.3 tonnes (53.2 tons)
Engine Kharkiv Model V-2K, 373 kW (500 hp)
Main armament 76.2 mm ZiS-5 L/41.5 gun

The heavy KV-1 proved virtually immune to German antitank weapons when it entered combat in 1941. It was fitted with the same gun and engine as the T-34 but had poorer mobility due to its weight. This was one of the few tanks to continue in production after the Soviet factories moved east; around 4,700 KV-1s were built in total.

152 mm howitzer for breaching fortifications

Turret is tall, heavy, and box-shaped

△ Kliment Voroshilov-2 (KV-2)
Date 1939 **Origin** Soviet Union
Weight 53.9 tonnes (59.4 tons)
Engine Kharkiv Model V-2K, 410 kW (550 hp)
Main armament 152 mm M-10T L/20 howitzer

The Soviets believed that a tank armed with an artillery piece was vital to overcome well-fortified bunkers, having struggled in Finland in 1939–40 against such installations. The KV-2 was a KV-1 hull equipped with a howitzer. It was ineffective in practice, since the tall turret made the tank heavier, slower, and easier to target. When production ended in 1941, only 334 had been built.

▷ T-60
Date 1941 **Origin** Soviet Union
Weight 5.8 tonnes (6.4 tons)
Engine GAZ-202 6-cylinder, 52 kW (70 hp)
Main armament 20 mm TNSh cannon

The T-60 was a two-man Soviet scout tank used for reconnaissance. When the T-60 came up against German forces, it soon became evident that the tank was under-gunned and too lightly armoured. Since the turret was too small to accommodate a larger gun and efforts to thicken its armour reduced its mobility, it was replaced by the T-70.

20 mm cannon could only penetrate light armour

▷ T-34
Date 1941 **Origin** Soviet Union
Weight 31.4 tonnes (34.6 tons)
Engine Kharkiv Model V-2-34, 373 kW (500 hp)
Main armament 76.2 mm F-34 L/41 gun

Easy to operate due to its basic design, the T-34 was the mainstay of Red Army forces during World War II. Its relatively light weight and wide tracks were excellent for travelling cross-country over mud and snow.

45 mm armour on rear of hull

76.2 mm gun was more powerful than guns of many tanks of the time

Christie suspension system

SOVIET TANKS · 141

△ **T-70**

Date 1942	Origin Soviet Union

Weight 9.2 tonnes (10.1 tons)
Engine 2 x GAZ-202 6-cylinder, 52 kW (70 hp) each
Main armament 45 mm ZiS-19BM gun

A more heavily armed and armoured successor to the T-60, the T-70 still proved no match for Germany's advanced tanks. By 1943, the Soviets had decided to relegate light tanks to secondary roles, realizing that they had no useful place on the battlefield. An assault gun, the SU-76, was developed from the chassis of the T-70.

▷ **T-34/85**

Date 1944	Origin Soviet Union

Weight 32 tonnes (35.3 tons)
Engine Kharkiv Model V-2-34, 373 kW (500 hp)
Main armament 85 mm ZiS S-53 L/55 gun

By late 1943, the T-34 needed a revamp: it was being outgunned by other tanks, and its crews found it difficult to work effectively in the cramped two-man turret. Both issues were resolved in the T-34/85 ("85" denoting its improved 85 mm gun). The T-34/85 enjoyed a long postwar career with the Soviets and their client states, with one used as late as 2015 in Yemen.

▽ **Iosif Stalin-2 (IS-2)**

Date 1944	Origin Soviet Union

Weight 44.7 tonnes (49.3 tons)
Engine Kharkiv Model V-2IS, 388 kW (520 hp)
Main armament 122 mm D-25T L/45 gun

Galvanized by the need to counter the threat of Germany's Tiger and Panther heavy tanks, the Soviets produced the IS series – a development of the KV-1, with a new transmission and hull. When it entered service in 1944, the IS-2 replaced both the IS-1 and the 85mm–armed KV-85. Organized into several heavy tank regiments, IS-2s were used to spearhead attacks on German positions.

△ **Iosif Stalin-3M (IS-3M)**

Date 1945	Origin Soviet Union

Weight 46.5 tonnes (51.3 tons)
Engine Kharkiv Model V-2IS, 447 kW (600 hp)
Main armament 122 mm D-25T L/45 gun

Rapidly developed and rushed into service because of shortcomings in the IS-2's speed and armour, the IS-3 arrived too late to play a part in World War II. The IS-3 itself suffered from mechanical problems, but these were corrected in the improved IS-3M. The IS-3's sloping sides gave better protection, and this feature was adopted for subsequent postwar Soviet tanks.

T-34/85

The powerfully armed and well-protected T-34 was called the "best tank in the world" by German General Paul Ludwig Ewald von Kleist when his forces first encountered it in the summer of 1941. Speedy and nimble, hardy and easy to repair, and with a design suited to mass production, this medium tank and its variants were used in huge numbers.

MIKHAIL KOSHKIN'S design for the T-34 embodied lessons learned fighting the Japanese at Khalkhin Gol in 1939. His tank had thicker armour and a larger gun than its predecessors, the BT series, and a diesel engine that was less of a fire risk than earlier petrol engines, which had been vulnerable to incendiary devices. The first tanks rolled out of the factory in September 1940.

The T-34's armour of homogenous rolled and welded nickel steel offered good protection, while its 76mm high-velocity main gun – which was fired by the tank commander in the two-man turret – proved effective at armour penetration. In 1944, the up-gunned T-34/85 came into service, mounting an 85mm gun in an enlarged turret. Although crews were not always sufficiently trained, their bravery and the Red Army's growing awareness of how to use its tanks most effectively enabled T-34s to defeat more technically advanced adversaries.

Modifications made manufacturing quicker and cheaper, reducing the unit cost from 269,500 to 135,000 roubles. The need for simplicity was partly driven by production having to move to eastern Russia due to German advances. After the war, the tank was made in Czechoslovakia and Poland. Tens of thousands of T-34s saw service worldwide.

SPECIFICATIONS	
Name	T-34/85
Date	1940
Origin	Soviet Union
Production	84,700
Engine	Model V-2-34 V12, 373 kW (500 hp)
Weight	32 tonnes (35.3 tons)
Main armament	85 mm ZiS-53
Secondary armament	2 x 7.62 mm DT machine-guns
Armour thickness	60 mm (2.4 in) max

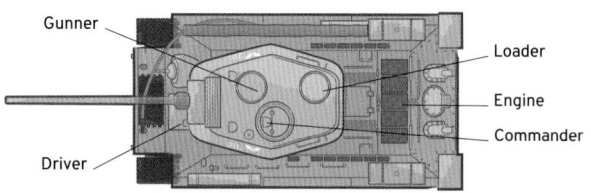

85 mm main gun was more powerful than on earlier T-34s

Co-axial machine-gun operated by the co-driver

Upgraded model
The up-gunned T-34/85's larger turret had space for three men – commander, gunner, and loader – allowing the functions of commander and gunner to be separated.

FRONT VIEW

REAR VIEW

Commander's cupola, added to later models

Battalion number
This T-34/85 was deployed in the second company (2) of the first battalion and was the command tank (11) of the first platoon. The small Russian letter on the right ("I" in English) is the initial of the first battalion's commander, Ivanov.

Fuel drum

Rubber-rimmed road wheels

Idler wheel set at the front

EXTERIOR

Although the finish on early T-34s was good, standards fell when manufacture of the tanks relocated east, to improvised factories beyond the Urals. The Red Army's leaders acknowledged that crude cast marks on the turret had little impact on the tank's fighting ability, so any time spent removing them would only lengthen the production process and increase costs.

1. Regimental insignia of 4th Guards Tank Corps 2. Driver's hatch (closed) 3. Co-driver's machine-gun 4. Spare track links 5. Road wheels 6. Exhaust 7. Fuel cap 8. Commander's (right) and gunner's (left) hatches 9. Axle joint 10. Commander's periscope 11. Fuel drum 12. Engine bay

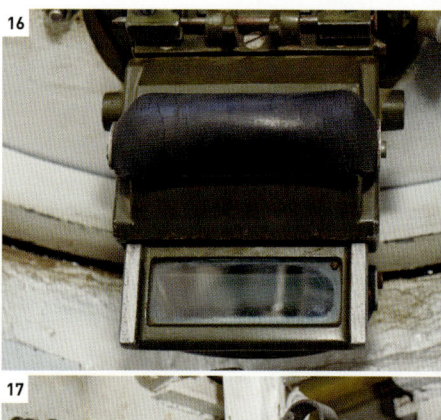

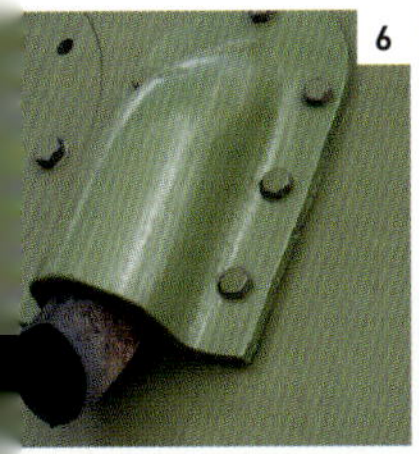
6

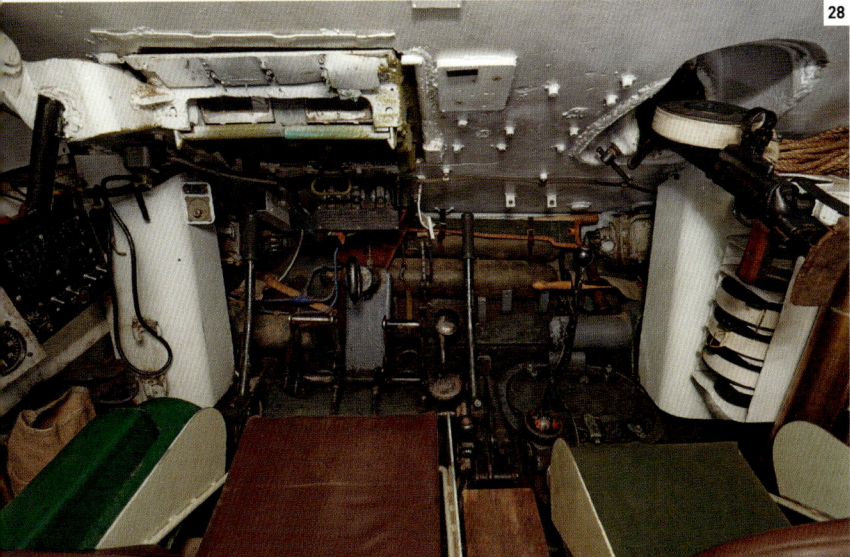

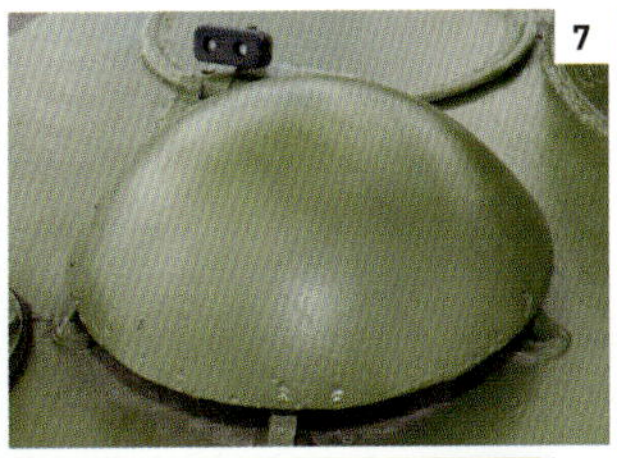
7

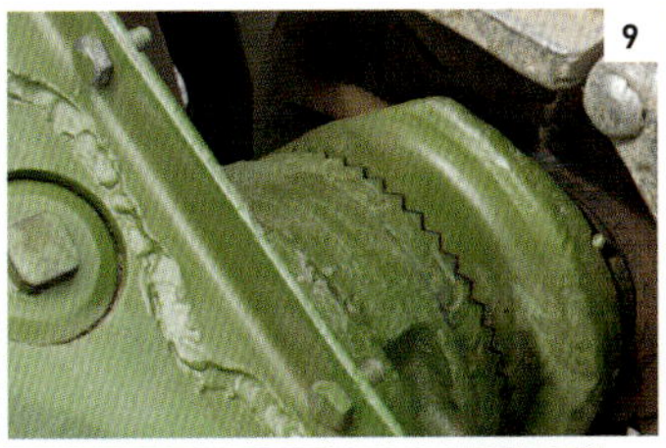
9

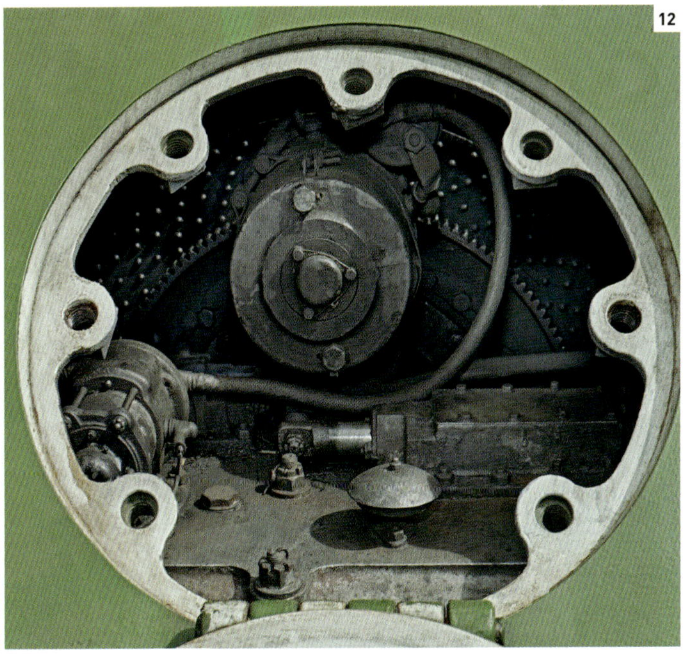
12

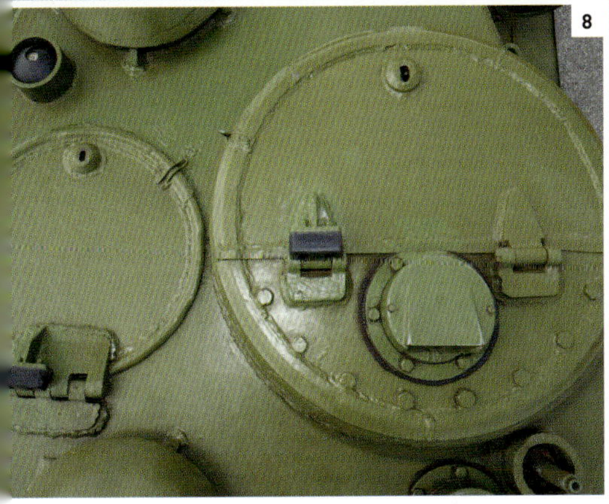
8

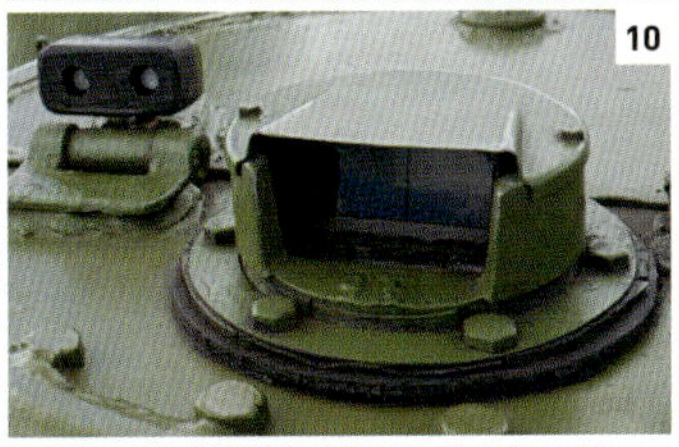
10

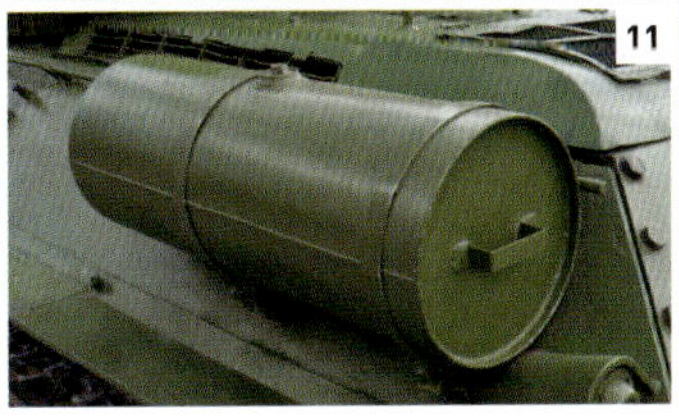
11

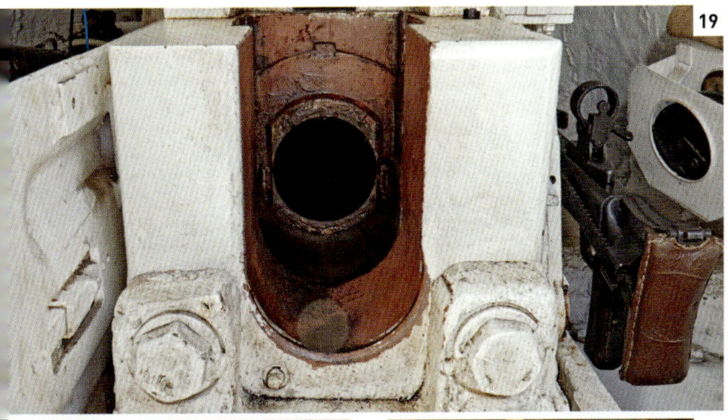
19

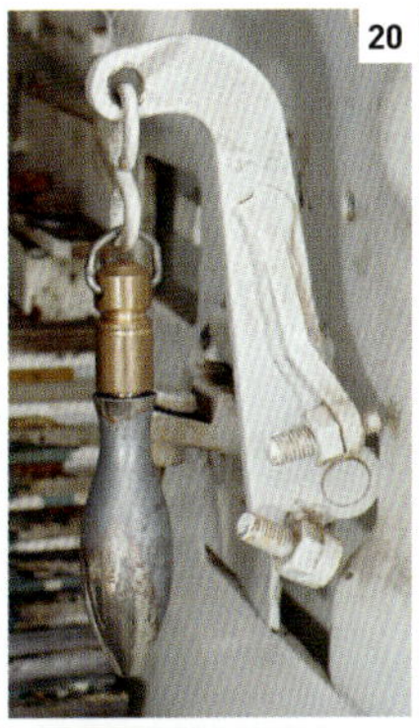
20

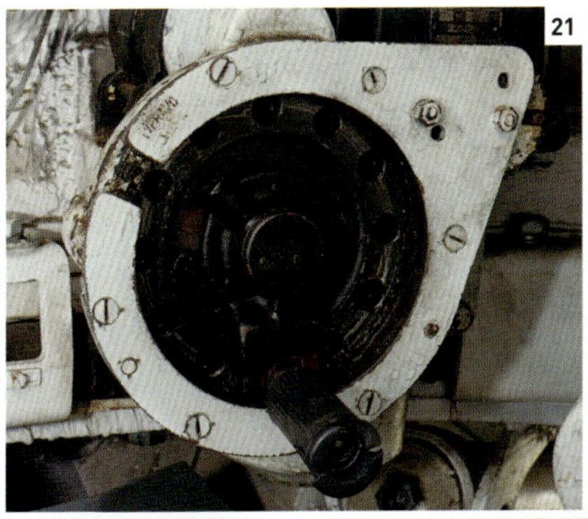
21

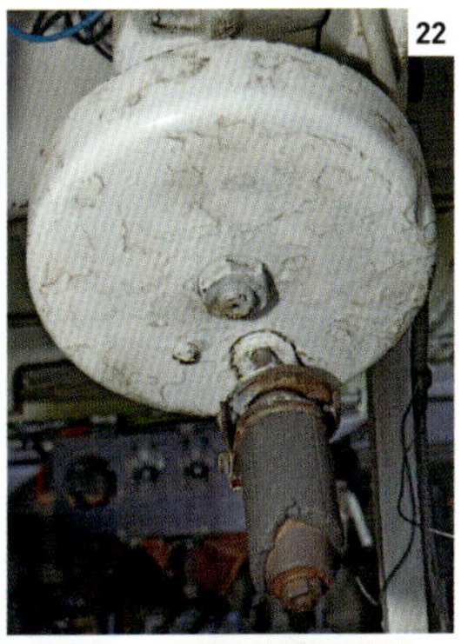
22

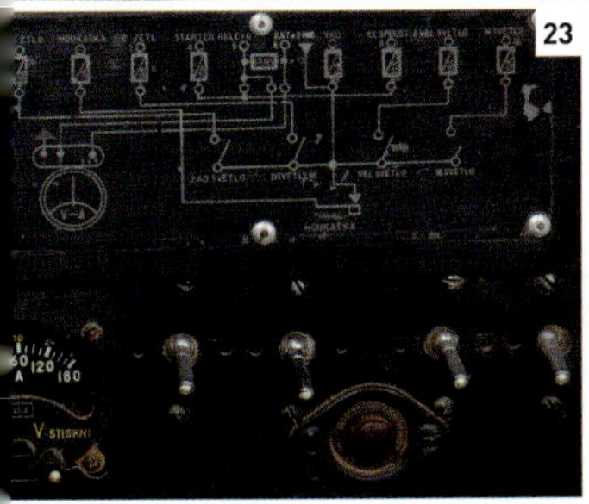
23

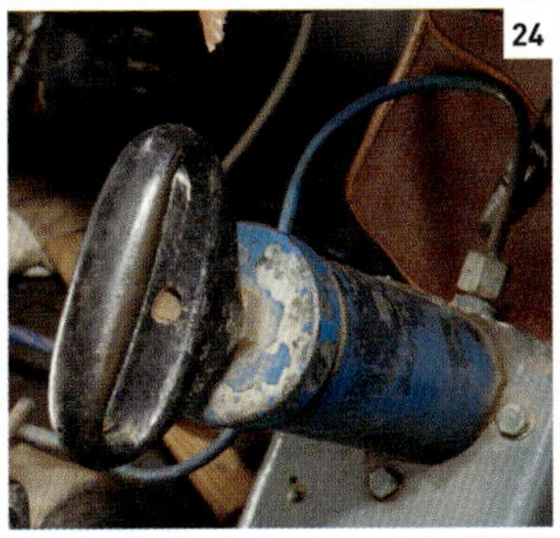
24

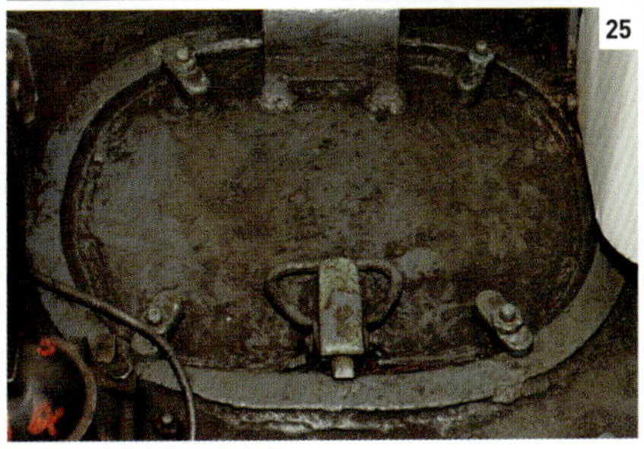
25

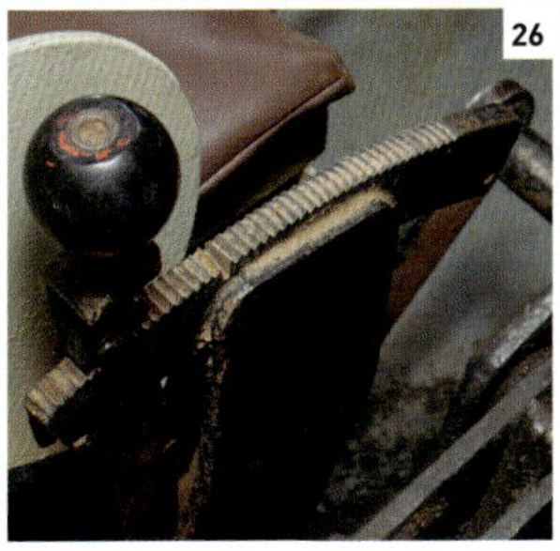
26

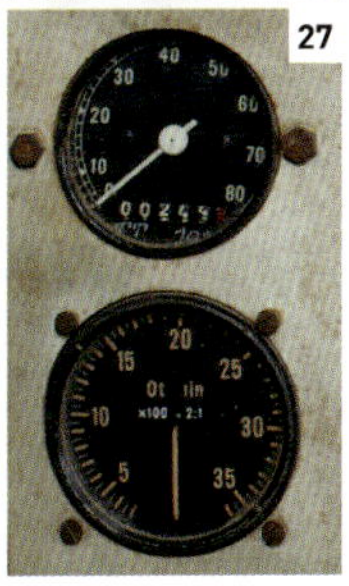
27

28

INTERIOR

Since tanks in wartime had an estimated service life of just a few months, the Soviets classified them as disposable munitions, alongside weapons such as hand grenades and shells. Consequently, little importance was given to crew comfort in the design of the T-34, and the interior of the tank was extremely basic but functional. The enlarged turret on the upgraded T-34/85 was slightly more spacious than that on earlier variants.

13. Looking down into commander's position **14.** Spare shells **15.** Commander's position showing main gun breech **16.** Gunner's periscope **17.** Co-axial machine-gun **18.** Radio **19.** Main gun breech (open) **20.** Fire extinguisher release **21.** Barrel elevation handle **22.** Turret traverse handle **23.** Instrument panel **24.** Pressure pump **25.** Escape hatch **26.** Gear lever **27.** Instrument dials **28.** Driver's position

▷ Universal Carrier, Mark II
Date 1939 **Origin** UK
Weight 4 tonnes (4.4 tons)
Engine Ford flathead V8 petrol, 63 kW (85 hp)
Main armament .303 Bren machine-gun

The Universal Carrier descended from British Carden-Loyd vehicles of the interwar era. It was effectively an amalgamation of several carrier developments into one "universal" design. This versatile vehicle was used to transport troops, weaponry, supplies, and artillery observation equipment, with some variants being made into gun platforms. Popular with infantry, it was one of the most-produced armoured vehicles in history.

Idler wheel at front of track

Armoured vision port gave view to the side

Fuel cans

◁ Daimler Mark II "Dingo"
Date 1940 **Origin** UK
Weight 3 tonnes (3.3 tons)
Engine Daimler 6HV petrol, 41 kW (55 hp)
Main armament None

Nicknamed the "Dingo", this small, popular, two-person scout car was highly mobile, thanks to the design of its transmission – shared with the Daimler Armoured Car – which offered five speeds both forward and reverse. Early Dingos had a sliding armoured roof and four-wheel steering; both features were omitted on later versions, although the solid rubber tyres were retained. Around 6,600 Dingos were made before production ended in 1945.

▷ Humber Scout Car
Date 1942 **Origin** UK
Weight 3.5 tonnes (3.9 tons)
Engine Humber 5-cylinder petrol, 65 kW (87 hp)
Main armament .303 Bren machine-gun

While the standard British scout car in World War II was Daimler's "Dingo", other companies were commissioned to produce similar vehicles to meet wartime demand. Humber made around 4,300 such vehicles. In the latter stages of World War II, Humbers were mainly allocated to armoured units, with Dingos generally being used by the infantry.

Machine-gun mount

Canvas canopy

△ CT15TA Armoured Truck
Date 1943 **Origin** Canada
Weight 4.6 tonnes (5.1 tons)
Engine General Motors 270 petrol, 75 kW (100 hp)
Main armament None

The CT15TA was based on the Canadian Military Pattern truck chassis. With a crew of two, it was used as a troop carrier and an ambulance, as well as a load carrier, but it was never intended as a vehicle for front-line combat.

Armoured Cars and Troop Carriers

World War II saw the widespread use of scout cars and armoured cars for reconnaissance and to provide support to infantry. Although fully tracked armoured infantry carriers were less common than half-tracks, the seemingly ubiquitous Universal Carrier fulfilled a multitude of support and combat roles for the Allies. Towards the end of the war, the highly successful tank-based Ram Kangaroo at last gave Allied infantry units the same mobility as their tank counterparts.

▷ Praying Mantis
Date 1943 **Origin** UK
Weight 5.3 tonnes (5.8 tons)
Engine Ford flathead V8 petrol, 64 kW (85 hp)
Main armament 2 x .303 Bren machine-guns

The Praying Mantis's body could be hydraulically raised over cover, allowing the two-man crew lying prone inside to fire at targets. This quirky attempt at a very-low-profile vehicle proved a failure, being difficult to operate and liable to make its occupants feel sick.

Compartment for driver and machine-gunner

Running gear – like the engine – was from the Universal Carrier

▽ M8 Greyhound
Date 1943 **Origin** USA
Weight 7.4 tonnes (8.2 tons)
Engine Hercules JXD petrol, 82 kW (110 hp)
Main armament 37 mm M6 L/56.6 gun

The M8 was originally designed as a wheeled tank destroyer, but it soon became a reconnaissance vehicle because of its light armament. Its six-wheel drive gave it a high speed on roads, but its suspension limited it across country. The vehicle was open-topped and thinly armoured.

△ Ram Kangaroo
Date 1944 **Origin** Canada
Weight 24.9 tonnes (27.5 tons)
Engine Wright-Continental R-975 petrol, 298 kW (400 hp)
Main armament .30 Browning M1919 machine-gun

Kangaroos were armoured personnel carriers made from converted tanks. Most were based on the Canadian Ram tank. This example could carry 11 soldiers. Kangaroos were widely used late in the war, as they allowed infantry to advance at the same pace as tanks, providing a high level of mobility and protection.

△ Sd Kfz 234/3 Schwerer Panzerspahwagen, 8-rad
Date 1944 **Origin** Germany
Weight 11.7 tonnes (12.9 tons)
Engine Tatra 103 diesel, 164 kW (220 hp)
Main armament 7.5 cm Kwk 51 L/24 gun

The Sd Kfz 234 was developed in the latter stages of World War II to replace the Sd Kfz 231 armoured car. It was equipped with a more powerful engine than its forerunner, thicker armour, and advanced suspension and steering that gave greater mobility. The four variants, including one with a turret, carried different armaments. This open-topped 234/3, equipped with a 7.5 cm gun, provided fire support to more lightly armed versions.

Aerial Combat Takes Centre Stage

Collectively, the combatant nations produced and fielded more than 700,000 military aircraft during World War II. The battle for the skies became as intense as the battle for supremacy on land, and air power gradually extended its strategic influence over all theatres of war, including the world's seas and oceans.

Combat aviation went through radical technological changes in the 1920s and 1930s. Biplanes were superseded by faster, stronger, cantilever-winged monoplanes with greater range and combat capabilities. New types of military aircraft were developed: two-engined medium bombers and four-engined medium-heavy bombers; dive-bombers; torpedo-bombers; high-performance fighters; transport aircraft; military seaplanes, and others. What the burgeoning air forces also needed was a tactical doctrine to guide their efforts.

Tactical positions

At the beginning of World War II, it was the Germans who appeared to take the lead in air combat tactics.

During the campaigns in Poland and Western Europe in 1939–40, German fighters such as the Bf 109 established air superiority, while Junkers Ju 87 Stuka dive-bombers acted as flying artillery in support of armour and infantry, and medium bombers such as the Heinkel He 111 delivered area bombardments against cities, troop concentrations, and logistics centres.

For a time, the tactics worked well, but the Germans did not adapt their approach as circumstances changed. Crucially, the Luftwaffe failed to

Daylight bombing
Flying in close formation to concentrate bomb strikes, US B-24 Liberator heavy bombers of the 15th Air Force hit the oil refinery at Pardubice, eastern Bohemia, on 24 August 1944.

Carrier operations
A Grumman F6F Hellcat prepares to take off from the flight deck of the USS *Yorktown*. During the battle for the Pacific, Hellcats shot down more than 5,200 enemy aircraft.

develop an effective long-range heavy bomber or an accompanying strategy, so it was unable to inflict decisive damage on distant industrial targets.

Long-range bombing
The same was not true of the Allies. Britain and, later, the US not only fielded endless squadrons of nimble fighters and formidable ground-attack aircraft, but they also produced large numbers of four-engined bombers, such as the British Avro Lancaster and the American Boeing B-17 Flying Fortress. From 1942, heavy bombers enabled the Allies to unleash a joint strategic bombing campaign of unprecedented proportions against German cities, the British bombing by night and the Americans by day. By 1943, bombing raids of more than 1,000 aircraft at a time were being launched. Allied losses were initially huge, but round-trip fighter escort from P-47 Thunderbolts and P-51 Mustangs gradually reduced the toll. The Germans were compelled to devote more and more resources to producing fighters to counter the raids, resulting in an ever-greater attrition of pilots and aircraft.

The German air force also lost the battle for air superiority and for tactical ground support. This was partly due to the Allies' far greater industrial output, but also because between 1942 and 1944 the Allies developed a brilliantly flexible system of ground-attack command. By 1944, German troops and vehicles could barely move across exposed highways or open spaces for fear of air attack.

Carrier war
In the Pacific theatre, the air war was radically different. The Pacific War opened with a Japanese air attack on the US Pacific Fleet at Pearl Harbor on 7 December 1941. Not only did this attack showcase the skill of the Imperial Japanese Navy Air Service (IJNAS), but it also demonstrated that aircraft carriers, from which the devastating attack was launched, were the future of naval warfare.

On the open waters of the Pacific, a struggle for supremacy began between the aircraft carriers of the United States and Japan. The fight was close until the Battle of Midway on 4–7 June 1942, in which the Americans destroyed all four of the Japanese fleet carriers: *Akagi*, *Kaga*, *Sōryū*, and *Hiryū*. It was a blow from which the Japanese Navy never recovered.

The US tapped into its enormous industrial capability to produce fleet carriers, escort carriers, and naval combat aircraft at rates far exceeding the capacity of a struggling Japan, and the attrition of Japanese aircraft and pilots became relentless. As the US regained Japanese-held territories and began to close in on the home islands, the Imperial Japanese Army Air Service (IJAAS) turned to kamikaze suicide missions. These self-sacrificing attacks could not stop the onslaught, nor could the Japanese prevent a strategic bombing campaign against the main islands that culminated in the dropping of atomic bombs on Hiroshima and Nagasaki in August 1945.

> **TALKING POINT**
>
> ### Japan's last resort
> The Japanese kamikaze campaign was an improvised effort to turn the tide of the Pacific War. The word kamikaze refers to the "divine wind", the storm that supposedly saved Japan from Mongolian invasion in 1281. From 1944, extreme nationalism merged with warrior *bushido* and Shinto spirituality to persuade hundreds of young pilots to voluntarily fly bomb-laden aircraft into enemy ships, killing themselves in the destruction of their target. Kamikaze was a desperate response to US air superiority and the increasing inexperience of Japanese pilots. It did not reverse American dominance, but it did inflict serious damage. The US lost 34 ships sunk, many more damaged, and 5,000 sailors killed from kamikaze waves, the worst attacks coming around the Philippines and Okinawa in 1944–45.
>
>
>
> **A recruitment poster** seeks new aviators for the Imperial Japanese Navy. As the war progressed, inexperienced pilots were sent on suicide missions in crude aircraft.

> "I do not **personally** regard… the cities of Germany as **worth the bones** of one British Grenadier."
>
> SIR ARTHUR HARRIS, MARSHAL OF THE RAF, SUPPORTING THE STRATEGIC BOMBING OF GERMANY, IN A LETTER OF 29 MARCH 1945

△ **Heinkel He111**

Date 1940 **Origin** Germany

Engine 2 x 999 kW (1,340 hp) Junkers Jumo 211 F-2 supercharged liquid-cooled inverted V12

Top speed 434 km/h (270 mph)

The He 111 was one of the most widely used German bombers of World War II. Poorly armed, it was vulnerable to fighters during daylight bombing raids, especially frontal attacks on the aircraft's "greenhouse" nose.

Dorsal turret armed with two .303 Browning Mark II machine-guns

Rear turret with four .303 in Browning machine-guns

△ **B-17G Flying Fortress**

Date 1940 **Origin** USA

Engine 4 x 895 kW (1,200 hp) Wright R-1820-97 Cyclone turbocharged air-cooled 9-cylinder radial

Top speed 462 km/h (287 mph)

The USAAF used the B-17 for precision daytime raids in World War II. The heavy defensive armament – vital for daylight operations – compromised the B-17's bomb capacity, reducing it to half that of the Avro Lancaster.

△ **Yokosuka D4Y3 Model 33 "Judy"**

Date 1940 **Origin** Japan

Engine 802 kW (1,075 hp) Mitsubishi Kinsei air-cooled 14-cylinder radial

Top speed 550 km/h (342 mph)

Few World War II dive-bombers could rival the speed of the carrier-borne D4Y, which was also used for Kamikaze attacks and reconnaissance missions, and as a night fighter. Design issues restricted production to just 2,038 aircraft.

.5 in waist machine-gun (one on each side)

Two .5 in machine-guns in dorsal turret

Forward gun turret

◁ **Consolidated B-24 Liberator**

Date 1941 **Origin** USA

Engine 4 x 895 kW (1,200 hp) Pratt & Whitney R-1830-65 Twin Wasp turbosupercharged air-cooled 14-cylinder radial

Top speed 467 km/h (290 mph)

More than 18,400 B-24s were built for Allied forces. The B-24 surpassed the B-17 in range, speed, and bomb capacity, and it was lighter too. However, it was unpopular with aircrews, being harder to fly than the B-17 and more likely to catch fire or crash when hit.

Bombers

Two types of bomber aircraft emerged in World War II: "tactical" bombers that struck at battlefield targets, and "strategic" bombers that flew long-range missions to destroy infrastructure or drop bombs onto industrial cities to disrupt manufacturing. The development of more powerful engines, radar-based guidance systems, and predictive bombsights made strategic bombers more effective. By 1944, the best of them could accurately deliver heavy bomb loads onto targets thousands of miles from their bases. However, they sustained huge losses – Britain's RAF Bomber Command alone lost over 8,325 aircraft during the war.

▷ **Junkers Ju 87D Stuka**

Date 1941 **Origin** Germany

Engine 1,044 kW (1,400 hp) Junkers Jumo 211J V-12

Top speed 390 km/h (240 mph)

The Ju 87 Sturzkampfflugzeug first saw combat in Spain in 1937, and later became a key element of German Blitzkrieg tactics. Its wailing siren had a terrifying effect as it dived to attack ground targets.

BOMBERS · 151

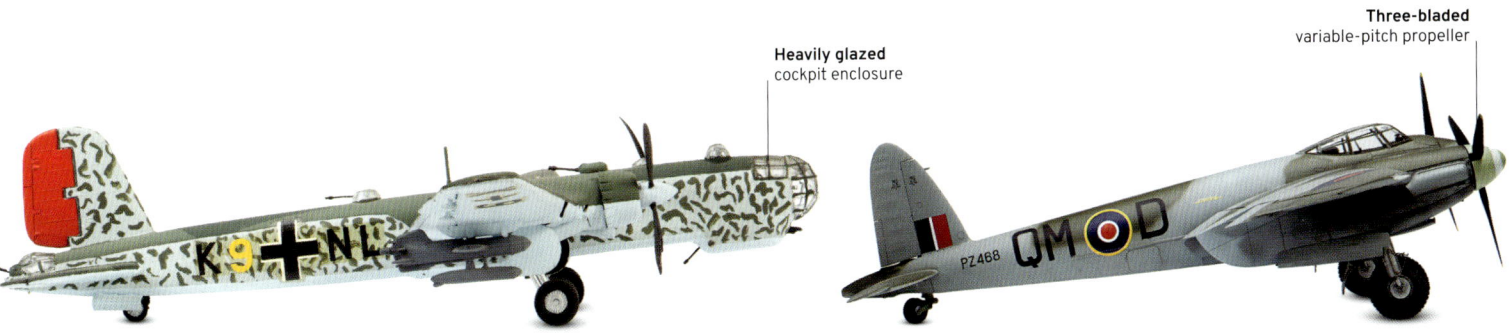

Bombardier's position

Rolls-Royce Merlin engines

Bomb bay doors (open)

Landing gear retracts hydraulically into recesses within the inner engine nacelles

△ **Avro Lancaster**
Date 1941 Origin UK
Engine 4 x 954 kW (1,280 hp) hp Rolls-Royce Merlin XX supercharged liquid-cooled V12
Top speed 460 km/h (285 mph)

The Lancaster, the RAF's main heavy bomber, had a huge bomb capacity of 6,350 kg (14,000 lb). It excelled as a night bomber, its four Rolls-Royce Merlin engines carrying the plane and its bomb load to targets in Germany and beyond.

Heavily glazed cockpit enclosure

Three-bladed variable-pitch propeller

△ **Heinkel He 177 Grief**
Date 1942 Origin Germany
Engine Two 1,939 kW (2,600 hp) Daimler-Benz DB 610 W-24s
Top speed 565 km/h (350 mph)

Germany's only purpose-built long-range heavy bomber of World War II, the Heinkel 117 had a troubled service history. It was beset by structural problems, an over-complicated engine, and the stipulation that it should also be able to function as a dive-bomber – a role it never successfully fulfilled.

△ **De Havilland Mosquito B.16**
Date 1942 Origin UK
Engine Two 1,275 kW (1,710 hp) Rolls-Royce Merlin 76 V-12s
Top speed 670 km/h (415 mph)

Made mostly of lightweight plywood, the Mosquito was fast enough and agile enough to outrun most enemy fighters. Serving in bomber, day- and night-fighter, anti-shipping, and reconnaissance roles, it became one of the most successful RAF aircraft of World War II.

Two-man cockpit

Fixed undercarriage

Fuselage and wings made mainly of aluminium alloys

△ **Boeing B-29A Superfortress**
Date 1944 Origin US
Engine Four 1,640 kW (2,200 hp) Wright R-3350-23 Duplex Cyclone radials
Top speed 575 km/h (357 mph)

The state-of-the-art Superfortress – the biggest, most capable Allied strategic bomber – had a pressurized fuselage and remotely controlled guns. In June 1944, Superfortresses began raids against targets in Japan, first from a base in China and later from the Mariana Islands. The aircraft is most famous for dropping nuclear bombs on the Japanese cities of Hiroshima and Nagasaki in August 1945.

Boeing B-17

Bristling with guns, able to defend itself against enemy fighters, and highly resistant to battle damage, the Boeing B-17 justified its name of "Flying Fortress". This extraordinary warplane, which could fly at an altitude of over 9,000 m (30,000 ft), became a symbol of America's ability to take the war to Germany, and massed ranks of Flying Fortresses took on most of the daylight bombing campaign.

WHILE ITS BOMB LOAD was comparable to that carried by the much smaller and faster de Havilland Mosquito, vast formations of B-17s could deliver a staggering tonnage of explosives. The B-17 was built in fewer numbers than the Consolidated B-24 Liberator, its contemporary, but a system of mass production ensured that for every Flying Fortress lost, US factories produced more than two new aircraft.

Despite cramped, uncomfortable conditions, hours in freezing temperatures, and often altitude sickness caused by the unpressurized cabin, the crew had to remain alert and ready to battle the Luftwaffe's fighters once over enemy territory. The immensely strong B-17 gained a reputation for being able to withstand a great deal of punishment and still get its crew back to base; because of this, the dependable Flying Fortress won the abiding affection of those who flew in it.

SPECIFICATIONS	
Model	Boeing B-17G Flying Fortress, 1940
Origin	USA
Production	12,731
Construction	Aluminium and steel
Weight	24,948 kg (55,000 lb) loaded
Wingspan	31.6 m (103 ft 9 in)
Engine	4 x 895 kW (1,200 hp) Wright R-1820-97 Cyclone turbocharged air-cooled 9-cylinder radial
Length	22.7 m (74 ft 4 in)
Top speed	462 km/h (287 mph)

Large fin stabilizes the bomber in flight

Waist gunner positions, one on either side, offer protection to the B-17's flanks

BOEING B-17 • 153

FRONT VIEW

REAR VIEW

Fighting machine
Originally known as "Sally B", this 1945 aircraft is the last remaining airworthy B-17 in Europe. It featured in the 1990 film *Memphis Belle*: the artwork added for the film is still visible on one side of the nose; the paintwork on the other side has now been restored to its "Sally B" design.

Large wings aid performance at high altitude

Top turret equipped with a pair of 0.5 in machine-guns

Nose section houses the bombardier and defensive armament

Retractable undercarriage

Wright Cyclone engine, noted for being rugged and reliable

EXTERIOR

Built to be tough and envisaged from the outset as a kind of "aerial battleship", Boeing's B-17 was part of a new generation of all-metal monoplanes with enclosed cockpits. Reporting on the prototype, a journalist noted that it resembled a "flying fortress" – the name immediately struck a chord with Boeing, who trademarked it.

1. Waist machine-gun position **2.** Transparent Plexiglas nose **3.** Wright Cyclone radial engine with Hamilton Standard hydromatic propeller **4.** Chin guns remotely controlled by bombardier **5.** Sperry swivelling ball turret **6.** Gun sight for tail-gunner's station **7.** Main wheel with oleo suspension

INTERIOR

With so much of the B-17's interior allocated to bombs and fuel, crew space was at a premium: the only place where a crew member could stand fully upright was the radio operator's station. Both bombardier and navigator had to crouch to reach their seats in the bomber's nose, while the tail gunner had to crawl to get to his remote position at the very rear of the aircraft. The ball-turret gunner, beneath the fuselage, had to be small enough to fit into his notoriously cramped station. On the flight deck sat the pilot and copilot, with the flight engineer above and behind them.

8. Front gun **9.** Bombardier's seat and Norden bombsight in nose compartment **10.** Fuselage interior with waist guns and oxygen tank **11.** Bomb bay, view from below – typically carried 2,722 kg (6,000 lb) of bombs **12.** Rear gunner's station in the tail

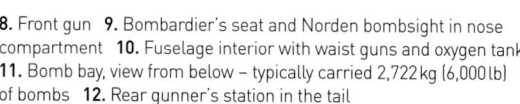

BOEING B-17 • 155

COCKPIT

Spacious and efficient, the B-17's "office" provided excellent visibility to the front and sides. The central console, between pilot and copilot, held the throttle controls, fuel switches, and controls for the fuel mixture and propeller-pitch. Behind this, located in the central panel, were the basic flight instruments – altimeter, airspeed indicator, turn-and-bank indicator, and rate-of-climb indicator. The pilot sat in the left-hand seat, with the copilot to his right. It was the copilot's responsibility to monitor the engine controls, which were on the right-hand side of the central panel.

13. The "office" – the B-17 flight deck **14.** Propeller-feathering controls **15.** Panel containing flight and engine instruments **16.** Copilot's control stick featuring Boeing logo **17.** Propeller pitch controls **18.** Throttle controls

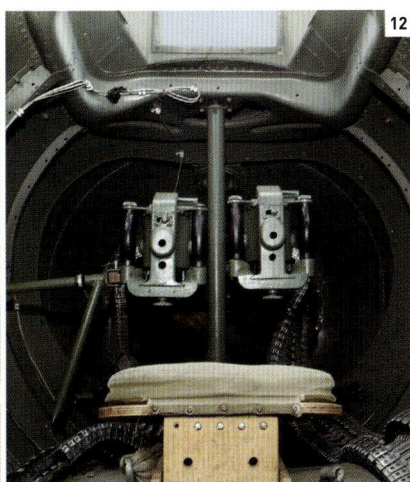

156 • 1918–1945

Rudder painted with tri-colour national markings

Metal skin fastened with rivets

△ **Dewoitine D.520**
Date 1940 Origin France
Engine 687.6 kW (935 hp) Hispano-Suiza 12Y 45 in-line V-12
Top speed 535 km/h (330 mph)

With a service ceiling of 10,500 m (34,500 ft) and a range of 1,530 km (950 miles), the D.520 was the most capable French fighter aircraft of World War II. It proved a match for Germany's Bf 109E, but only 400 had been produced before France surrendered in June 1940.

△ **Supermarine Spitfire MkII**
Date 1940 Origin UK
Engine 858 kW (1,150 hp) Rolls-Royce Merlin 45 supercharged liquid-cooled V12
Top speed 575 km/h (357 mph)

The MkII played a key role in the Battle of Britain, its light weight and aerodynamic profile giving the Spitfire superiority over opponents. Later variants remained in service until well after the end of World War II.

▷ **Focke-Wulf Fw 190**
Date 1941 Origin Germany
Engine 1,447 kW (1,940 hp) BMW 801S supercharged air-cooled 14-cylinder radial
Top speed 658 km/h (408 mph)

Designed by Kurt Tank, the Fw-190 – the first important fighter of World War II with a radial engine – remained technically superior until confronted by the Spitfire Mk IX. More than 20,000 of all variants were built.

Each wing housed a pair of 20 mm cannon and one or two machine-guns

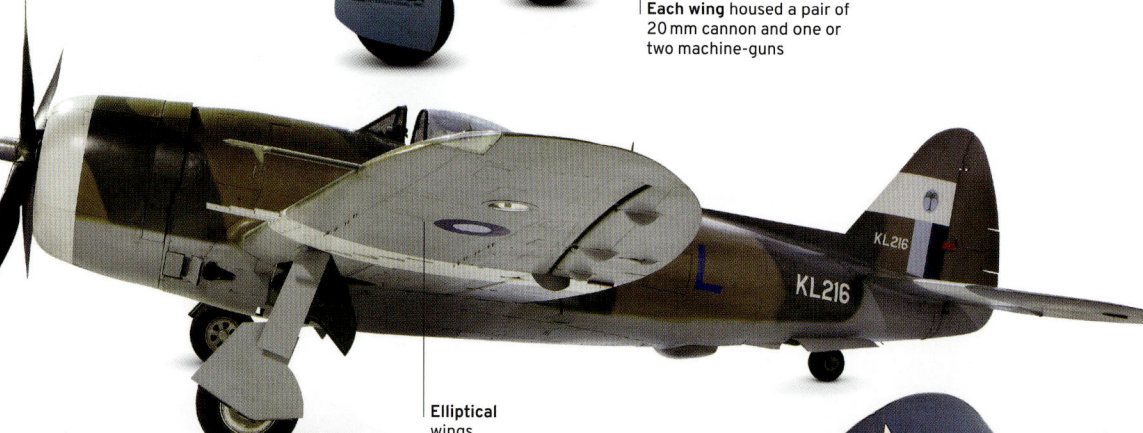

Elliptical wings

△ **Republic P-47 Thunderbolt**
Date 1942 Origin US
Engine 1,890.3 kW (2,535 hp) Pratt & Whitney R-2800-59W Double Wasp radial
Top speed 700 km/h (435 mph)

The Thunderbolt, nicknamed the "Jug" for its bulky shape, was an effective ground-attack fighter-bomber. Its ability to survive damage and its exceptional high-altitude performance, being able to out-dive any German aircraft, earned it the respect of pilots.

Fin and rudder designed to maximize manoeuvrability

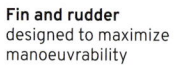

Retractable tail wheel

Fighter Planes

By the outbreak of World War II, the most able fighters could reach speeds exceeding 560 km/h (348 mph) and climb to 10,360 m (34,000 ft). Some combatant nations, such as Japan, initially favoured lightweight, lightly armoured planes, believing that manoeuvrability was all-important; others focused on protection and firepower. It was the latter that proved more effective. Such fighters were also easier to adapt to the ground-attack role, which became increasingly important as the war progressed.

FIGHTER PLANES · 157

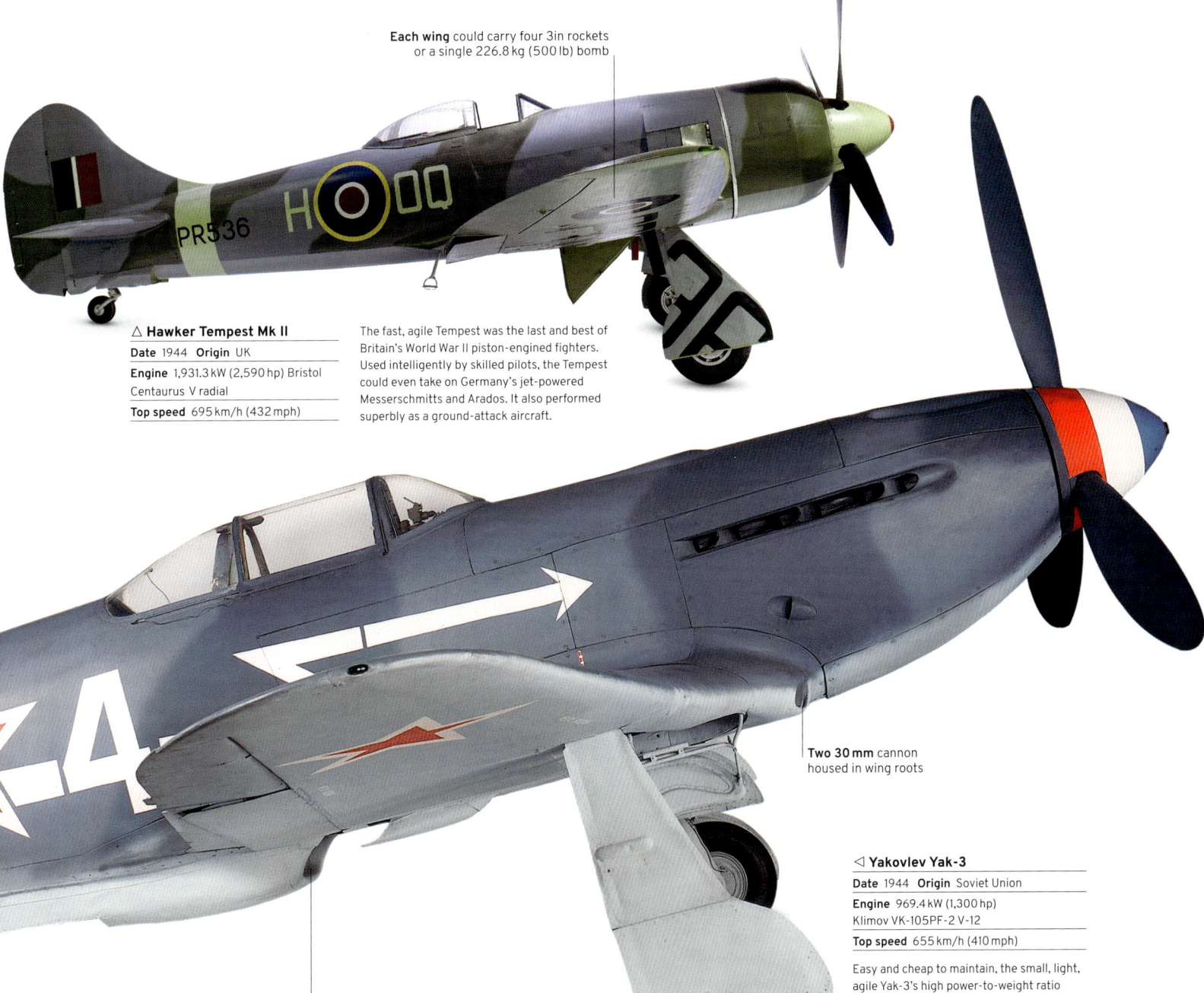

Fuselage is slender and tapered

△ **Nakajima Ki-43 Hayabusa "Oscar"**
Date 1942 **Origin** Japan
Engine 845.8 kW (1,150 hp) Nakajima Ha-115 14-cylinder radial
Top speed 530 km/h (330 mph)

Although slow by contemporary standards and poorly armed, the Hayabusa (Peregrine Falcon) was well-regarded by pilots for its manoeuvrability and superb climb rate, made possible by a weight of just 2.3 tonnes (2.5 tons). It was superior to opposing fighters in the war's early stages, but later suffered as Allied planes acquired heavier firepower.

Four-bladed Hamilton propeller

△ **North American P-51 Mustang**
Date 1943 **Origin** US
Engine 1,185.6 kW (1,590 hp) Packard Merlin V-1650-7 V-12
Top speed 705 km/h (438 mph)

The highly aerodynamic P-51 Mustang was produced in response to a request from the UK. It initially underachieved, but once re-fitted with a Packard-built Rolls-Royce Merlin engine, it played a huge part in the Allied air success. The Mustang became a mainstay of the USAAF, in both long-range escort and fighter-bomber roles.

Each wing could carry four 3in rockets or a single 226.8 kg (500 lb) bomb

△ **Hawker Tempest Mk II**
Date 1944 **Origin** UK
Engine 1,931.3 kW (2,590 hp) Bristol Centaurus V radial
Top speed 695 km/h (432 mph)

The fast, agile Tempest was the last and best of Britain's World War II piston-engined fighters. Used intelligently by skilled pilots, the Tempest could even take on Germany's jet-powered Messerschmitts and Arados. It also performed superbly as a ground-attack aircraft.

Two 30 mm cannon housed in wing roots

Air intake for engine

◁ **Yakovlev Yak-3**
Date 1944 **Origin** Soviet Union
Engine 969.4 kW (1,300 hp) Klimov VK-105PF-2 V-12
Top speed 655 km/h (410 mph)

Easy and cheap to maintain, the small, light, agile Yak-3's high power-to-weight ratio made it a formidable adversary in dogfights. Many pilots who flew the Mustang, the Spitfire, and the Yak-3 rated the Yak as the superior aircraft.

Supermarine Spitfire

Designed by R. J. Mitchell, creator of Supermarine's Schneider Trophy-winning racing floatplanes of the 1920s and early 1930s, the Spitfire is arguably the most famous aircraft of all time. Along with the Hawker Hurricane, this elegant, iconic fighter was instrumental in fending off the Luftwaffe during the Battle of Britain in 1940. Continuously modified and improved, the Spitfire remained in production throughout World War II.

MITCHELL'S SPITFIRE epitomized stressed-skin construction. Rather than fabric covering a wooden or metal frame, Mitchell used an eggshell-thin, aluminium-alloy outer surface to carry much of the load imposed on the aircraft. The striking elliptical wing shape was chosen for practical rather than aesthetic reasons, because it offered low drag yet still allowed room for eight 0.303-in Browning machine guns (later a combination of guns and 20-mm cannon) and the retracted undercarriage.

Superb handling characteristics ensured the Spitfire's immediate success. When flown to its limits in dogfights, the Spitfire could shake off a pursuer with a flick and half-roll and a quick pull out of the subsequent dive. It had the edge over the German Messerschmitt Bf 109 in speed, climb, and turning circle, although the Me 109 outperformed it at altitudes above 6,000 m (20,000 ft) and in steep dives.

The basic design of the Spitfire lent itself to continued development. By the time Mitchell's successor, Joseph Smith, had produced the final Spitfire variant – the Mk24 – in 1946, the aircraft possessed more than twice the horsepower of the prototype, and its maximum weight had increased by the equivalent of 30 passengers.

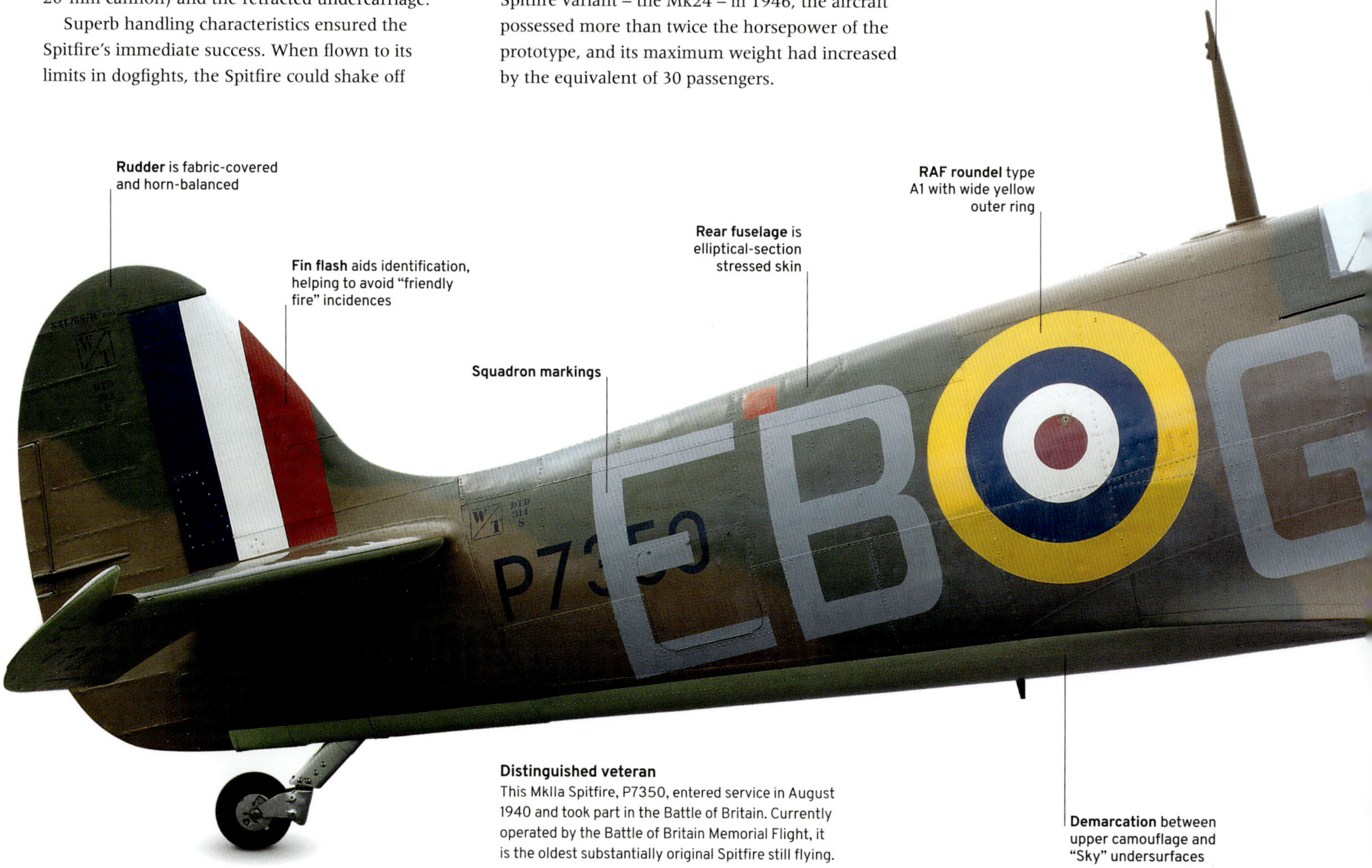

Aerial mast for high frequency (HF) radio

Rudder is fabric-covered and horn-balanced

Fin flash aids identification, helping to avoid "friendly fire" incidences

Squadron markings

Rear fuselage is elliptical-section stressed skin

RAF roundel type A1 with wide yellow outer ring

Distinguished veteran
This MkIIa Spitfire, P7350, entered service in August 1940 and took part in the Battle of Britain. Currently operated by the Battle of Britain Memorial Flight, it is the oldest substantially original Spitfire still flying.

Demarcation between upper camouflage and "Sky" undersurfaces

SUPERMARINE SPITFIRE • 159

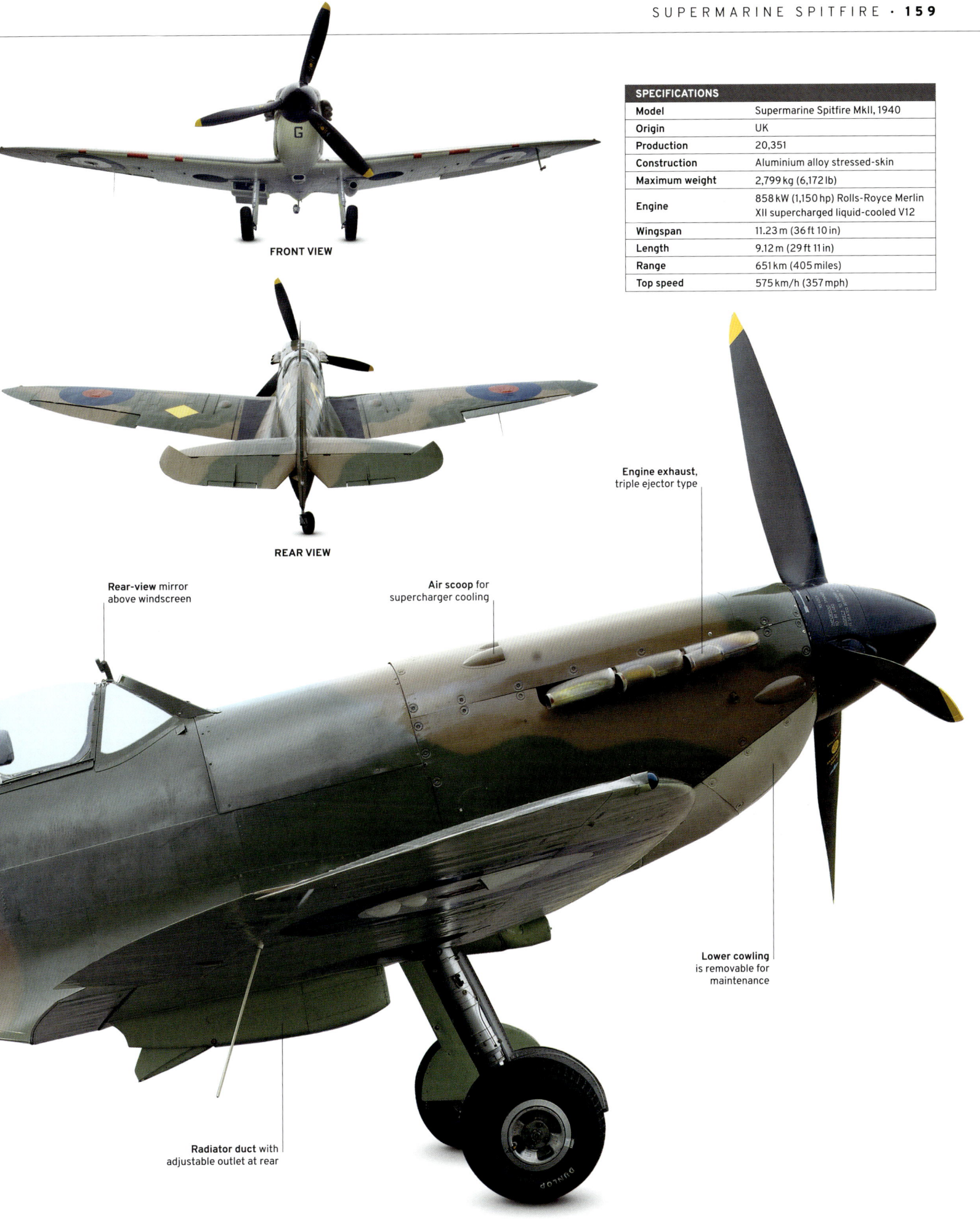

FRONT VIEW

REAR VIEW

SPECIFICATIONS	
Model	Supermarine Spitfire MkII, 1940
Origin	UK
Production	20,351
Construction	Aluminium alloy stressed-skin
Maximum weight	2,799 kg (6,172 lb)
Engine	858 kW (1,150 hp) Rolls-Royce Merlin XII supercharged liquid-cooled V12
Wingspan	11.23 m (36 ft 10 in)
Length	9.12 m (29 ft 11 in)
Range	651 km (405 miles)
Top speed	575 km/h (357 mph)

Engine exhaust, triple ejector type

Air scoop for supercharger cooling

Rear-view mirror above windscreen

Lower cowling is removable for maintenance

Radiator duct with adjustable outlet at rear

EXTERIOR

In a dogfight, speed can determine which pilot lives or dies, so the Spitfire's design tried to squeeze as many kilometres per hour as possible from the aircraft. Since streamlined surfaces reduce drag, flush-rivets were used on the wings – and, on later versions, on the fuselage too – to make the skin smoother. Adding ejector exhausts and a "Meredith Duct" around the radiator also increased speed by augmenting the main thrust from the propeller.

1. Ejector engine exhausts 2. Carburettor air intake
3. Pitot head measures airspeed 4. Radiator air intake
5. Tailplane fairing 6. Cartridge ejection chutes under wing
7. Fabric patch over machine-gun port to reduce drag (rounds break fabric when gun fires) 8. Starboard navigation light
9. Cockpit door with escape crowbar 10. Typical stencilling
11. IFF (Identification Friend or Foe) aerial grommet 12. Rudder trim-tab actuator 13. Tail light 14. Stencil for electrical bonding

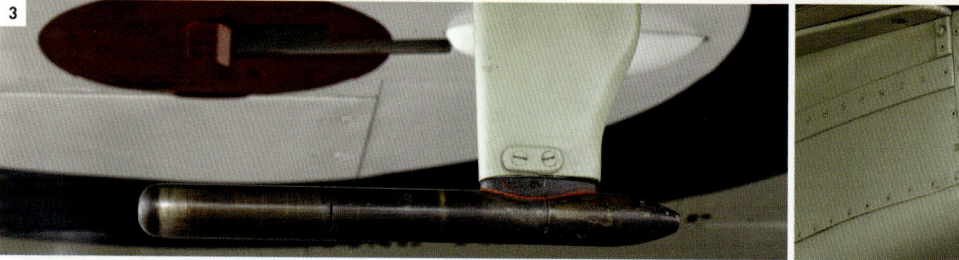
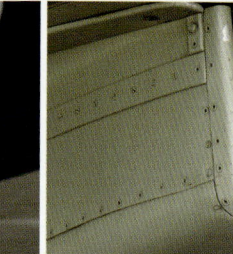
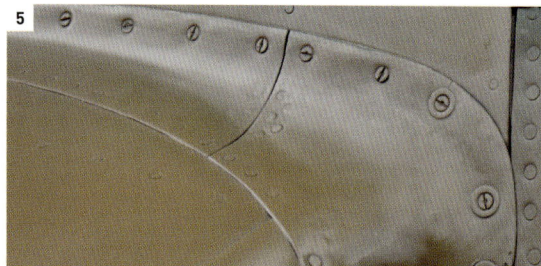

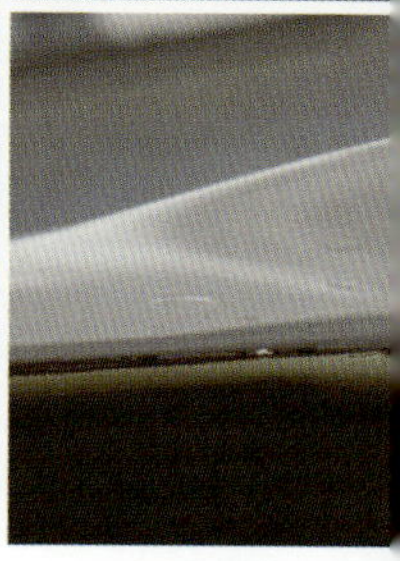

SUPERMARINE SPITFIRE • 161

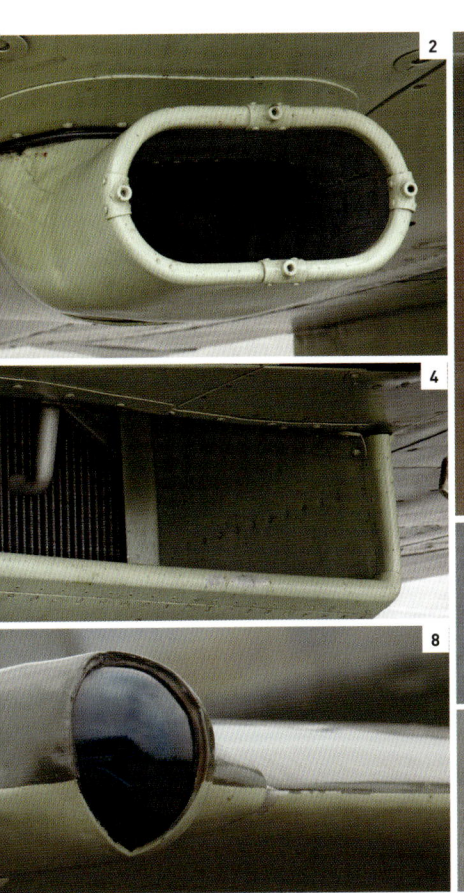
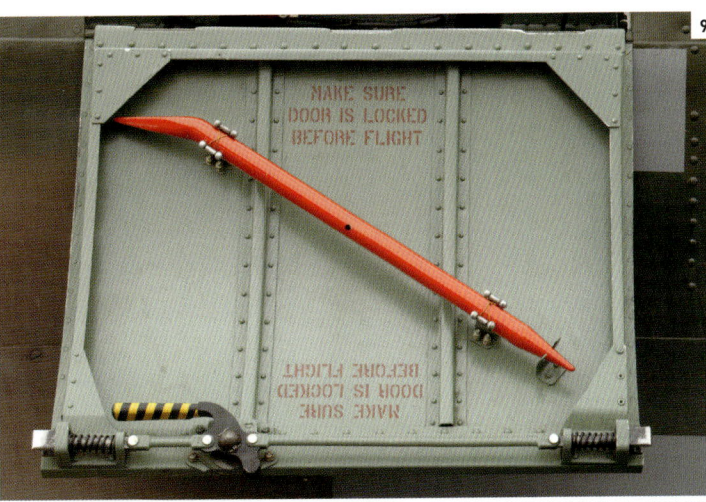
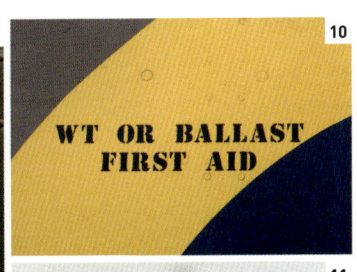
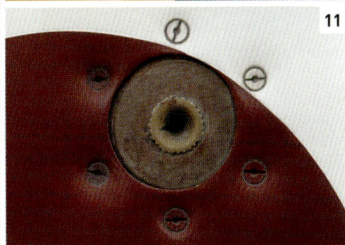
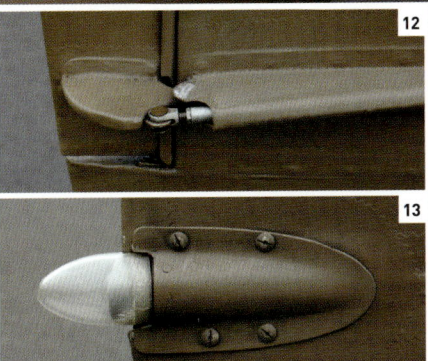
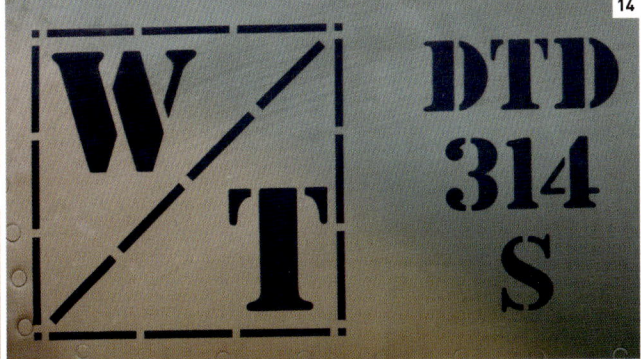

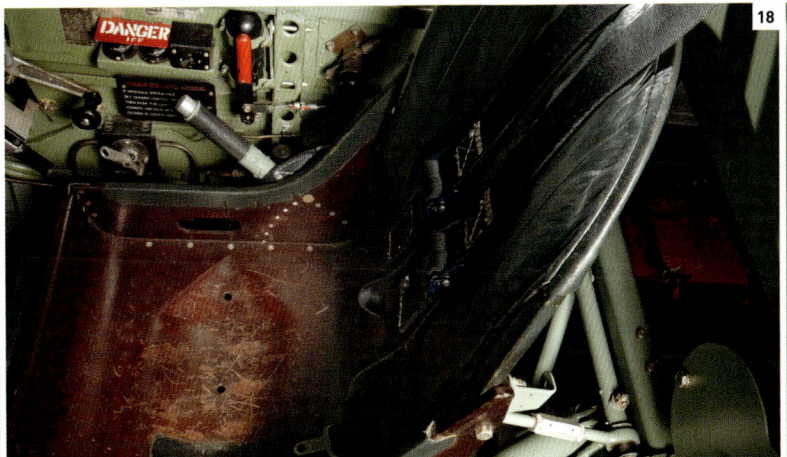

COCKPIT

Behind the control column was the "Basic Six" instrument panel (typical of most RAF aircraft of the time), comprising airspeed indicator, artificial horizon, vertical speed indicator, altimeter, heading indicator, and turn-and-slip indicator. To the right were the engine instruments; to the left, oxygen, undercarriage, and flap controls, and other instruments. The cockpit had no floor – just rudder pedals on which to rest the feet, with structure and systems beneath.

15. Instrument panel (with modern avionics in place of gun sight)
16. Control-column, with gun-button at top **17.** Undercarriage selector
18. Pilot's bucket-seat with height adjustment lever **19.** Gun-camera indicator **20.** Headrest and armour **21.** Rudder pedal

The Gliders of World War II

The use of airborne forces brought a new dimension to warfare, allowing troop and equipment landings behind enemy lines. Adverse weather conditions, however, could disperse parachutists over a wide area, leaving them isolated and vulnerable to attack. The glider provided a way to land groups of troops together and deliver a greater load of equipment. Towed by transport aircraft or heavy bombers, gliders, once released, were silent in their approach to a landing zone, enabling them to lead precision attacks, such as the German capture of Fort Ében-Émael in Belgium in 1940 and the British capture of the Orne River and Cael Canal crossings on the morning of D-Day in June 1944. Considered a one-use item, gliders were made of wood and could suffer major damage with rough landings, but they were relatively cheap to make and glider-borne infantry were quicker to train than paratroopers.

Glider pilots and airborne infantry receive instruction from RAF trainers, using troop-carrying Hotspur gliders, near Oxford in October 1942.

164 • 1918–1945

▷ **Messerschmitt Me262 Schwalbe**
Date 1942 **Origin** Germany
Engine 2 x 898 kg (1,980 lb) thrust Junkers Jumo 004 B-1 turbojets
Top speed 900 km/h (559 mph)

The first turbojet-powered combat fighter, the Me 262 quickly made an impact against the Allies' daylight bombing raids. However, it was hampered by a lack of dive brakes, as well as its engines' short life and inherent unreliability.

Four 30 mm cannon mounted in the nose

Small ailerons

Nose wheel was retractable

△ **de Havilland DH100 Vampire FB 6**
Date 1943 **Origin** UK
Engine 1,520 kg (3,350 lb) thrust de Havilland Goblin 3 turbojet
Top speed 882 km/h (548 mph)

First flown in 1943, the Vampire did not enter service until 1946. It was the RAF's second jet fighter, and the first made by British aircraft manufacturer de Havilland. Unusually, a large amount of wood (plywood and balsa) was used in its construction. The twin tail boom arrangement kept the tailplane clear of the exhaust.

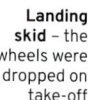

Swept-back wing form

Landing skid – the wheels were dropped on take-off

△ **Messerschmitt Me 163 Komet**
Date 1944 **Origin** Germany
Engine 1,700 kg (3,750 lb) Walter HWK 109-509A-2 liquid-fuel rocket
Top speed 960 km/h (600 mph)

The Komet was the sole rocket-powered fighter aircraft to see active service. With limited fuel, it could only make one or two firing passes at high-altitude bombers before having to glide back to base.

Engine mounted on top of fuselage

△ **Heinkel He162**
Date 1944 **Origin** Germany
Engine 798 kg (1,760 lb) thrust BMW 003 turbojet
Top speed 905 km/h (562 mph)

Intended to be cheap and simple enough to be flown by inexperienced pilots, the He162 was nicknamed the "Volksjager" (People's Fighter). A few He162s saw combat before the war's end; having been rushed through production, more were lost through design flaws than were shot down.

Bubble canopy provided the pilot with excellent visibility

Bullet-shaped fuselage

◁ **Lockheed P-80A Shooting Star**
Date 1944 **Origin** USA
Engine 2,087 kg (4,600 lb) thrust Allison J33-9 turbojet
Top speed 898 km/h (558 mph)

The first US jet fighter to see combat, the Shooting Star arrived in Europe too late for World War II service but, redesignated as the F-80, it featured extensively in the Korean War. Soon obsolete as a fighter, it was developed into the T-33 jet trainer, which remained in service until the 1970s with both the US Air Force and Navy.

Early Jets

Jet engines made their first appearance in aircraft in the latter stages of World War II. The advent of jet-propulsion technology required entirely new designs for combat aircraft. The new jet planes, which not only looked radically different from their piston-powered predecessors but also had significantly higher top speeds, changed aerial combat forever. Within a decade, piston-engined fighters had largely disappeared; most other propeller-driven military aircraft would soon go the same way.

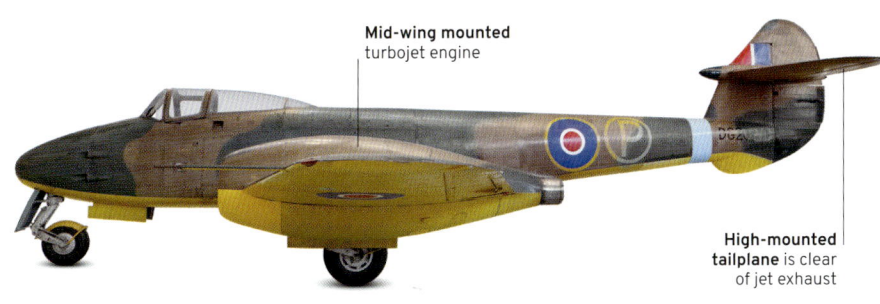

Mid-wing mounted turbojet engine

High-mounted tailplane is clear of jet exhaust

△ **Gloster Meteor**
Date 1944 **Origin** UK
Engine 2 x 1,590 kg (3,500 lb) Rolls-Royce Derwent turbojets
Top speed 965 km/h (600 mph)

This was the only Allied jet to enter combat in World War II, and it later served in Korea. It set new world records for speed, rate-of-climb, and endurance. The last Meteor variant was withdrawn as late as 1965.

Forward cockpit gave pilot no visibility to the rear

△ **Arado Ar 234B-2**
Date 1944 **Origin** Germany
Engine 2 x 500 kg (1,103 lb) thrust Junkers Jumo 004B-1 turbojets
Top speed 742 km/h (461 mph)

Germany's Ar 234 was the world's first jet bomber and reconnaissance aircraft. It was so fast that it easily outran Allied piston-engined fighters. To save weight, it was initially given a dolly and skid-type undercarriage; this proved impractical in service, so wheels were fitted instead.

Machine-guns located in the nose

Straight wings spanned 11.10 m (36 ft 5 in)

△ **Republic F-84C Thunderjet**
Date 1946 **Origin** USA
Engine 2,522 kg (5,560 lb) thrust Allison J-35 turbojet
Top speed 1,000 km/h (622 mph)

Republic developed the F-84 as a jet-powered successor to its P-47 Thunderbolt. As the company's first jet, it had a long and difficult gestation period. Despite this, the Thunderjet evolved into a highly competent fighter-bomber that saw front-line action in Korea. It was also the first plane flown by the Thunderbirds – the US Air Force aerobatic team.

Sea Battles in World War II

The naval war fought between 1939 and 1945 signalled the end of the era of the big-gun battleship. In its place came more technologically advanced submarines and aircraft carriers – the navy that could dominate the spaces above and below the waves could dominate the sea's surface.

British submarine
An S-class submarine moves through ice-covered waters off the east coast of England in 1940. In September 1939, when war began, Britain had 60 submarines in service.

The Atlantic theatre of war was defined by the battle between German U-boats and Allied convoys bringing desperately needed supplies from the US to Europe. At several key "happy times", as they were known in Germany, between 1940 and 1942, the U-boats were sinking Allied ships at a rapid rate, often faster than they could be built. From 1943, however, Allied antisubmarine technologies and tactics improved to the extent that by 1945 the German navy's U-boat arm had a 70 per cent crew fatality rate.

Although the undersea threat also had a profound impact in the Pacific theatre, where US Navy submarines alone accounted for more than 50 per cent of Japanese merchant losses, the ocean was, above all, the domain of the aircraft carrier. Ship-launched aviation projected power across the vast Pacific distances, well beyond the reach of naval guns. Between 1942 and 1945, the US built 17 large fleet

The navies of World War II included history's greatest battleships, in terms of physical size and firepower. However, despite their awesome gunnery and fearsome silhouettes, many were sunk by submarines or aircraft, or both.

On 14 October 1939, the British battleship HMS *Royal Oak* – a veteran of World War I – was torpedoed and sunk by the German submarine U-47 at Scapa Flow in Orkney, Scotland. Three battleships – the USS *Arizona*, *Oklahoma*, and *Utah* – were among the American losses from Japanese air attack at Pearl Harbor on 7 December 1941. Three days later, Japanese aircraft sank the British battleship *Prince of Wales* and battlecruiser *Repulse* off the east coast of Malaya. The German battleship *Tirpitz* was capsized at anchor in Norway on 12 November 1944 by British Lancaster bombers equipped with 5,400 kg (12,000 lb) "Tallboy" bombs. The largest, most heavily armed battleships that ever floated – the Japanese *Yamato* and *Musashi* – were both bombed to destruction by US Navy carrier aircraft in 1944–45. By the end of the war, battleships had become regarded as little more than liabilities.

Naval theatres

The nature of the naval war changed according to the theatre of operations. In the confines of the Mediterranean Sea, the war between 1941 and 1943 was primarily that of Allied and Axis shipping trying to resupply operations to North Africa and other coastal territories, harried by enemy air forces and submarines. Beyond the far north of Europe, from 1941 the Allied Arctic convoys – merchant ships with naval escorts – made freezing supply runs fraught with peril between Britain and the USSR through ice-choked seas, under heavy attack by German aircraft and U-boats.

Carrier power
The USS *Hornet* (CV-8), with five of its aircraft on deck, lies at anchor in the Pacific. The ship, a *Yorktown*-class carrier, was sunk in the Battle of the Santa Cruz Islands on 27 October 1942.

SEA BATTLES IN WORLD WAR II

> "The only thing that ever **really frightened** me during the war was the **U-boat peril**."
>
> WINSTON CHURCHILL, FROM HIS WORLD WAR II MEMOIRS

carriers, while Japan produced just six. By war's end, the US Navy also had around 37,000 aircraft, more than 10 times the Japanese number.

Coming ashore

Amphibious landings were another critical element of the sea war – an aspect of naval combat mastered by the Allies, who could not defeat Japan or Germany without putting troops and equipment on hostile shores. The Pacific theatre was essentially one great "island-hopping" campaign, while in Europe the operations at Sicily in July 1943 and Normandy in June 1944 delivered the largest amphibious landings in history and the springboard to ultimate victory.

Heavy fire
The USS *Iowa* (BB-61) fires its massive 406 mm (16 in) main guns across the Pacific around 1944. The guns were used mainly for shore bombardments of Japanese-held coastlines in preparation for amphibious landings.

TALKING POINT

Arctic convoys

Following the German invasion of the USSR in June 1941, the Allies sought to provide the beleaguered Soviets with essential war supplies via merchant convoys sailing from Britain and Iceland through the Arctic Ocean to the ports of Murmansk and Archangel. The supplies included trucks, aircraft, tanks, radios, tractors, railway engines, and even boots. Storms, pack ice, and sub-zero temperatures made the two-way journey highly dangerous, and if a sailor entered the water, life expectancy was about five minutes. In June 1942, convoy PQ17 lost 23 out of its 34 ships to German aircraft and U-boats on its way to the USSR. Out of all the Allied convoy campaigns the Arctic had the highest loss rate, 17 times greater than in the Atlantic, with nearly 3,000 sailors losing their lives.

A sailor on the British light cruiser HMS *Sheffield* operates an ice-covered signal projector in 1941. Ice build-up was a serious problem for the Arctic convoy ships.

Battleships and Cruisers

Major navies entered World War II focused on developing ever bigger, more capable battleships, with Germany's *Tirpitz* and *Bismarck*, the US's *Iowa*, and Japan's *Yamato* and *Musashi* all under construction at the war's start. Fast and powerfully armed, these huge ships were extraordinary fighting vessels. Such big-gun vessels undoubtedly played a key role in the war at sea; nevertheless, they also proved vulnerable to air attack, and aircraft carriers soon eclipsed them as the most valuable type of warship. Cruisers – typically described as "light" if armed with 6in guns, and "heavy" if they mounted anything larger – took part in surface engagements and escorted carrier and battleship groups. To combat the aerial threat, anti-aircraft cruisers emerged, with high-angle guns to protect against bombers.

Armoured conning tower

△ HMS Rodney
Date 1927	Origin UK
Displacement	45,925 tonnes (50,624 tons)
Length	216.4 m (710 ft)
Top speed	23 knots (43 km/h)

An unconventional arrangement of their main armament – all nine 16 in guns were located forward, in three triple turrets – characterized *Rodney* and its sister-ship *Nelson*. HMS *Rodney* played a key role in the sinking of the *Bismarck* in 1941 and bombarded coastal defences during the D-Day landings of 1944.

Three 6 in guns in each turret

Tripod mast with gunnery control platform

△ USS Northampton
Date 1930	Origin USA
Displacement	11,603 tonnes (12,790 tons)
Length	183 m (600¼ ft)
Top speed	32.5 knots (60 km/h)

The six *Northampton*-class armoured heavy cruisers saw much action in World War II. Three of the ships were lost, including *Northampton* itself, which was sunk by Japanese torpedoes during the short, hectic Battle of Tassafaronga on the night of 30 November 1942.

Two 8 in guns in turret

△ Takao
Date 1932	Origin Japan
Displacement	12,985 tonnes (14,314 tons)
Length	203.8 m (668½ ft)
Top speed	35.5 knots (66 km/h)

Built in the interwar years, the four *Takao*-class ships were upgraded prior to World War II. These ships were the largest, most effective of Japan's wartime heavy cruisers. Three were sunk at the Battle of the Philippine Sea in 1944; *Takao* was damaged, but survived – unrepaired – until the war's end.

▷ Bismarck
Date 1940	Origin Germany
Displacement	51,717 tonnes (57,008 tons)
Length	248 m (814 ft)
Top speed	29 knots (54 km/h)

Bismarck and its sister ship *Tirpitz* posed such a threat that the British Royal Navy deployed significant resources to keep them contained. In 1941, on *Bismarck*'s sole offensive operation, it sank the battleship HMS *Hood*. Pursued and attacked by British ships and aircraft, *Bismarck* was sunk by a combination of shell-fire, torpedo strikes, and scuttling. *Tirpitz* survived until 1944.

Turret housing two 38 cm guns

Three 152 mm guns in turret

Spotter aircraft

△ Vittorio Veneto
Date 1940	Origin Italy
Displacement	45,752 tonnes (50,434 tons)
Length	237.8 m (780 ft)
Top speed	30 knots (56 km/h)

During its five-year construction, the design specification for *Vittorio Veneto* altered significantly. One of only three fast Italian battleships to serve with the Italian navy during World War II, *Vittorio Veneto* carried its nine main guns in triple turrets, two forward and one aft.

▽ Yamato
Date 1941	Origin Japan
Displacement	71,113 tonnes (78,389 tons)
Length	263 m (863 ft)
Top speed	27 knots (50 km/h)

Despite being the largest and most powerfully armed battleships ever built, *Yamato* and its sister-ship *Musashi* proved vulnerable to air attack: both were sunk by carrier-launched US aircraft. *Shinano*, the third *Yamato*-class ship, was modified into an aircraft carrier during construction, but was sunk by the US submarine *Archerfish* while en route for fitting out.

BATTLESHIPS AND CRUISERS · 169

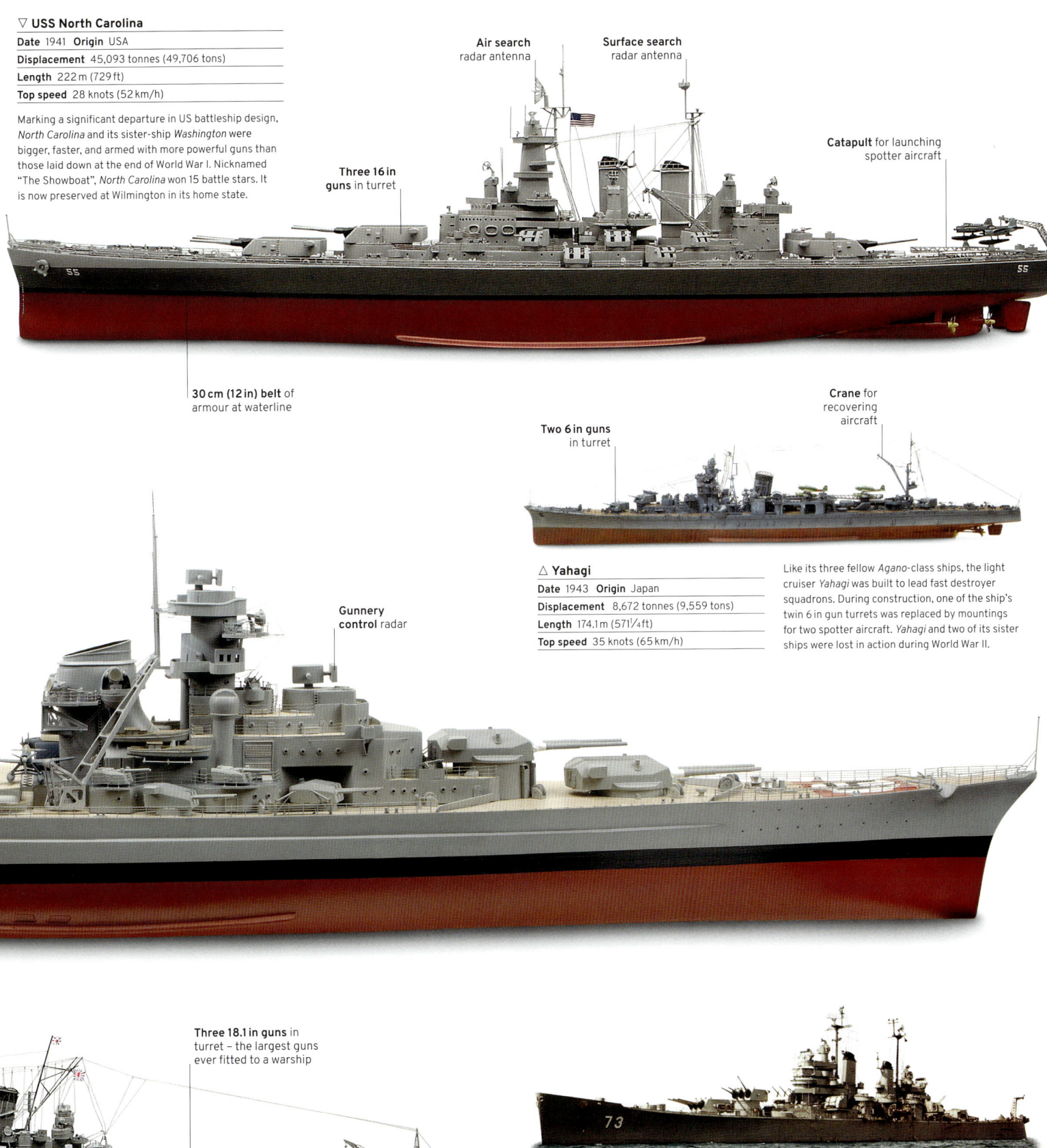

▽ USS North Carolina
Date 1941 **Origin** USA
Displacement 45,093 tonnes (49,706 tons)
Length 222 m (729 ft)
Top speed 28 knots (52 km/h)

Marking a significant departure in US battleship design, *North Carolina* and its sister-ship *Washington* were bigger, faster, and armed with more powerful guns than those laid down at the end of World War I. Nicknamed "The Showboat", *North Carolina* won 15 battle stars. It is now preserved at Wilmington in its home state.

△ Yahagi
Date 1943 **Origin** Japan
Displacement 8,672 tonnes (9,559 tons)
Length 174.1 m (571¼ ft)
Top speed 35 knots (65 km/h)

Like its three fellow *Agano*-class ships, the light cruiser *Yahagi* was built to lead fast destroyer squadrons. During construction, one of the ship's twin 6 in gun turrets was replaced by mountings for two spotter aircraft. *Yahagi* and two of its sister ships were lost in action during World War II.

△ USS Saint Paul
Date 1945 **Origin** USA
Displacement 15,966 tonnes (17,600 tons)
Length 205.3 m (673½ ft)
Top speed 33 knots (61 km/h)

In World War II, the US Navy optimized both its light and heavy cruisers for anti-aircraft duties. *Baltimore*-class heavy cruisers, such as the USS *Saint Paul*, were mainly used to protect carrier battle groups from air attack. *Saint Paul* later saw action during the Korean and Vietnam wars.

HMS Belfast

Ordered from Belfast shipbuilders Harland & Wolf in 1936 and launched in 1938, HMS *Belfast* was part of the British Royal Navy's response to the threat of Japan's *Mogami*-class cruisers. This light cruiser saw varied action during World War II, from escorting Arctic convoys and fighting German battleships, to bombarding the D-Day beaches and deployment to the Far East. HMS *Belfast* later took part in the Korean War, finishing its naval service years as an accommodation ship before being retired in 1963.

To prevent a naval arms race, definitions for warship types and limitations on their numbers were agreed in international treaties during the interwar years. As a category, cruisers fitted between larger battleships and smaller destroyers. By World War II, the roles of cruisers included scouting for the main fleet, attacking enemy ships and merchant vessels, and – having greater speed but less protection than battleships – cruising the wider oceans.

The 1930 London Naval Conference defined the light cruiser as having guns of less than 6.1 in (155 mm) and a displacement not exceeding 10,160 tonnes (11,200 tons). However, as *Town*-class cruisers, *Belfast* and its sister ship *Edinburgh* weighed 10,567 tonnes (11,648 tons) – the size restriction was ignored because Germany and Japan had failed to sign subsequent naval treaties.

In November 1939, just months after being commissioned, *Belfast* triggered a German mine. The subsequent rebuild turned *Belfast* into arguably the Royal Navy's most powerful cruiser. For the D-Day invasion of Normandy on 6 June 1944, *Belfast* was part of Bombardment Force E, supporting British and Canadian landings on Gold and Juno beaches; it remained there until the ground campaign moved out of range of her guns. The ship performed a similar role during the Korean War, firing over 8,000 rounds from her twelve 6 inch guns at land targets.

Draught marks indicate depth of the ship below the waterline

Turret (one of four) housing three 6 in guns

SPECIFICATIONS	
Model	HMS *Belfast*
Commissioned	1939
Class and type	*Town*-class light cruiser
Displacement	11,735 tonnes (12,936 tons)
Length	187 m (614 ft)
Propulsion	4 x Parsons geared steam turbines
Armament	12 x 6 in guns
Armour	114 mm (4½ in) max.
Maximum speed	32 knots (59 km/h)

Foremast

Unique ID
Moored on the River Thames in London, HMS *Belfast* is now a museum ship. *Belfast*'s unique Royal Navy pennant number – C (for Cruiser) 35 – is painted on its hull. Pennant numbers are used for identification.

Radar director for 6 in guns

Mainmast

Forward superstructure, including enclosed bridge

40 mm Bofors anti-aircraft gun

4 in HA/LA gun (anti-aircraft and low-angle)

EXTERIOR

Like many warships, *Belfast* was upgraded and improved during her service life. Although now partially returned to her wartime D-Day configuration, much of *Belfast*'s postwar refitting is still in evidence, including an enclosed bridge – constructed in 1956 as part of a modernization programme – to protect against nuclear, biological, and chemical (NBC) attack.

1. Name on hull 2. Ship's bell 3. Lifebuoy 4. Upper decks and bridge 5. Lattice mast with communications antennae and radar equipment 6. 40mm Bofors anti-aircraft guns and fire control (port side) 7. Radar director for 6in guns 8. 40mm Bofors anti-aircraft guns and fire control (starboard side) 9. Forward 6in gun turrets

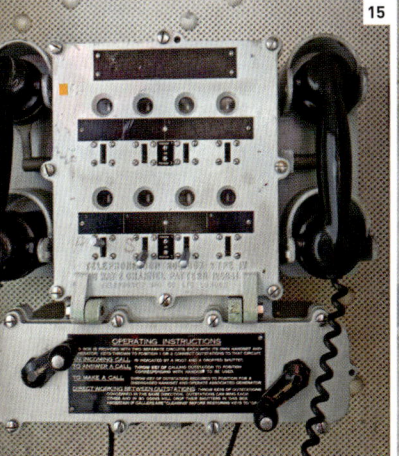

INTERIOR

Navigational, tactical, communication, and gunnery control systems were situated on the upper decks. Essential crew facilities included berths, a galley, bakery, and laundry, and a medical centre with sick bay, dental surgery, dispensary, and examination room. The mid-part of the lower decks was enclosed by a thick "box" of cemented armour to protect the boilers and turbines. Each gun turret was served by its own shell room in the hold; shells from a revolving carousel were hoisted up to the turret.

10. Compass platform (part of bridge)   **11.** Heating drainage controls.
12. Engine   **13.** Shell room with 6in munitions   **14.** Radar screen
15. Telephone control box   **16.** Laundry room   **17.** Pressure gauges
18. Fire-hose reel   **19.** Sick bay

Destroyers and Escorts in World War II

During World War I, the primary function of destroyers had been to defend the battle fleet against attack from similar ships or torpedo-boats, and to hunt submarines. For much of the interwar period, the size and numbers of naval vessels – including destroyers – were limited by international naval treaties, such as the Washington Treaty of 1922 and the London Treaty of 1930, although some nations exploited loopholes. By the late 1930s, Japan and Germany had rejected such restrictions. In World War II, with the concept of the battle fleet now obsolete, destroyers required a new role. Now larger, up-gunned, and armed with depth-charges, they were employed – along with a new generation of smaller escorts, including corvettes – to guard convoys of merchant ships against attack from submarines and aircraft.

Single 105 cm gun in each turret, fore and aft

△ **F-class escort ship**

Date 1936	Origin Germany
Displacement	712 tonnes (785 tons)
Length	75.9 m (249 ft)
Top speed	28 knots (52 km/h)

The ten German F-class ships built in the 1930s were conceived as fast fleet and convoy escorts that could also carry out anti-submarine and mine-sweeping duties. Unreliable power plants and poor performance in rough seas saw them withdrawn from front-line service later in the war.

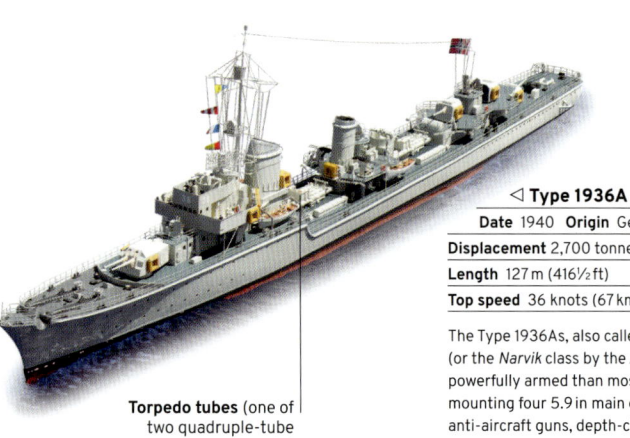

◁ **Type 1936A destroyer**

Date 1940	Origin Germany
Displacement	2,700 tonnes (2,976 tons)
Length	127 m (416½ ft)
Top speed	36 knots (67 km/h)

The Type 1936As, also called the Z23 class (or the *Narvik* class by the Allies), were more powerfully armed than most destroyers, mounting four 5.9 in main guns. As well as anti-aircraft guns, depth-charges, and torpedoes, they could carry up to 60 mines.

Torpedo tubes (one of two quadruple-tube arrangements)

Depth charges **4 in** gun

△ **HMS Acanthus**

Date 1940	Origin UK
Displacement	1,265 tonnes (1,394 tons)
Length	62.5 m (205 ft)
Top speed	16.5 knots (31 km/h)

Based on the design of commercial whale-catchers and powered by piston engines rather than turbines, *Flower*-class corvettes such as HMS *Acanthus* were the smallest purpose-built convoy escorts. *Acanthus* was armed with a single main gun, machine-guns, and depth charges.

Depth-charge launchers

Bridge

Two 4 in quick-firing guns on high-angle mount

△ **HMS Avon Vale**

Date 1941	Origin UK
Displacement	1,651 tonnes (1,820 tons)
Length	85.3 m (280 ft)
Top speed	27 knots (50 km/h)

This multi-role British ship was designed to defend merchant convoys against attacks by both submarines and aircraft. *Avon Vale* was the first of the second group of *Hunt*-class destroyer-escorts built for the Royal Navy during the early years of World War II.

▷ **Suzutsuki**

Date 1942	Origin Japan
Displacement	3,759 tonnes (4,144 tons)
Length	134.2 m (440¼ ft)
Top speed	33 knots (61 km/h)

Suzutsuki and its 11 *Akizuki*-class companions were built as fast, anti-aircraft escorts for carrier battle groups. The later addition of torpedo tubes and depth-charge launchers turned it into a general-purpose destroyer. *Suzutsuki* survived the war, along with five of the other *Akizuki*s.

DESTROYERS AND ESCORTS IN WORLD WAR II · 175

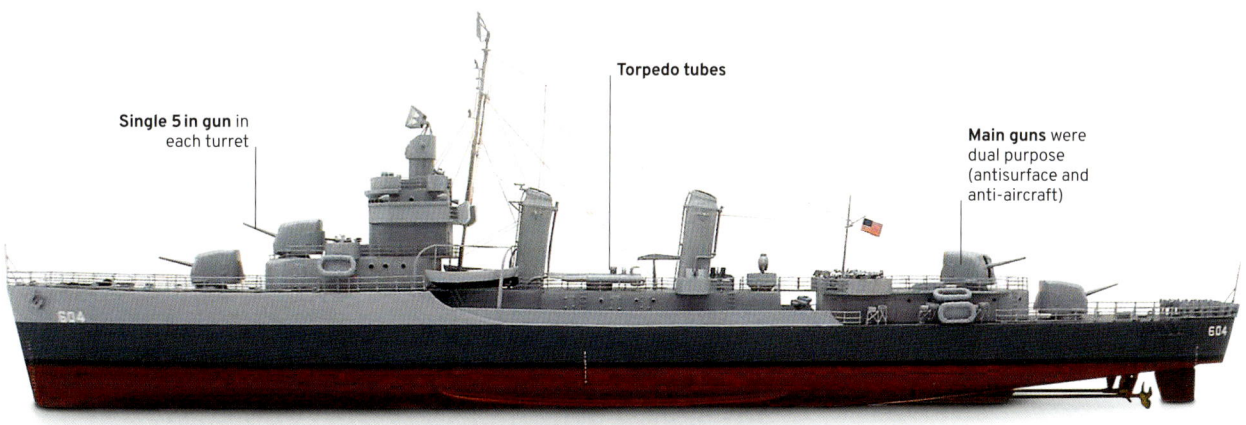

▷ **USS Parker**
Date 1942 **Origin** USA
Displacement 2,433 tonnes (2,682 tons)
Length 106.2 m (348½ ft)
Top speed 35 knots (65 km/h)

Parker was one of the later examples of the US Navy's *Benson/Gleaves*-class destroyers, which were the last to be designed before World War II. *Parker's* weaponry was reduced from five to four 5 in guns in single turrets, with light anti-aircraft guns installed in place of the fifth turret.

△ **USS Hazelwood**
Date 1943 **Origin** USA
Displacement 2,972 tonnes (3,276 tons)
Length 114.7 m (376½ ft)
Top speed 38 knots (70 km/h)

Designed in 1939 and built up until 1944, *Fletcher*-class destroyers such as the *Hazelwood* were the first to be built by the US without adhering to the limitations of the naval treaties. In all, 175 ships were produced. The *Hazelwood* and many other World War II survivors were reactivated out of reserve during the Korean War.

▽ **Buckley-class destroyer escort**
Date 1943 **Origin** USA
Displacement 1,700 tonnes (1,874 tons)
Length 93 m (306 ft)
Top speed 24 knots (44 km/h)

The US Navy's 102 *Buckley*-class vessels were prefabricated at US factories, then assembled on shipyard slipways. A further 46 were delivered to the Royal Navy, which classed them as frigates. *Buckleys* escorted convoys and engaged in antisubmarine warfare.

◁ **Type D escort ship**
Date 1944 **Origin** Japan
Displacement 752 tonnes (829 tons)
Length 69.5 m (228 ft)
Top speed 17.5 knots (32.5 km/h)

In 1943, Japan began mass producing escort ships to protect its convoys from Allied attacks. While simple in design, to aid speedy construction, Type Ds were robust, showing a surprising survival rate when struck by torpedoes or mines. However, they were often ineffective against Allied aircraft and submarines.

World War II Submarines

During World War II, when Germany's surface fleet was severely hampered by Hitler's prejudice against it, the Kriegsmarine's U-boats accounted for the bulk of German naval successes. Attacking escorted Atlantic convoys in "wolf packs" and sinking around 2,000 merchant vessels, the U-boats came close to bringing Britain to its knees. Improved technology, tactics, air cover, and intelligence eventually allowed the Allies to turn the tide decisively against the U-boats. In the Pacific, Allied submarines, primarily those of the US Navy, preyed on Japanese merchant vessels in order to weaken the economy of Japan. They also targeted troop transports and warships, landed raiding parties, and participated in evacuations.

◁ RN T-class (1937–44)
Date 1938–45	Origin UK
Displacement	1,341 tonnes (1,478 tons)
Length	83.8 m (275 ft)
Top speed	15.5 knots (29 km/h)

More than 50 T-class (or *Triton*-class) boats were built for Britain's Royal Navy in three groups between 1937 and 1944. The design saw considerable improvements, with the maximum dive depth of 91 m (300 ft) increasing to 106 m (350 ft) in the last group. Later builds remained in service until the 1960s.

▽ USS Gato
Date 1941	Origin USA
Displacement	1,549 tonnes (1,707 tons)
Length	95 m (311½ ft)
Top speed	20 knots (37 km/h)

Gato was the lead vessel of one of three closely related classes of "fleet boats" that accounted for most of the US Navy's wartime submarines (the other two classes being *Balao* and *Tench*). The vessels were modified extensively during and after the war. In the postwar years, *Gato* was used as a training boat until the 1960s. Many *Gato*-class boats were transferred to other navies in the 1970s, some remaining in service to the 1990s.

▷ German Type VIIC
Date 1940–44	Origin Germany
Displacement	761 tonnes (839 tons)
Length	67.1 m (220 ft)
Top speed	17 knots (31 km/h)

Type VIIs formed the backbone of Germany's submarine force. From ports in western France they harried Atlantic convoys and came close to shutting down the shipping routes that brought Britain much-needed supplies from North America. Around 660 Type VIIs were completed – more than any other submarine in history – with Type VIIC variants predominating.

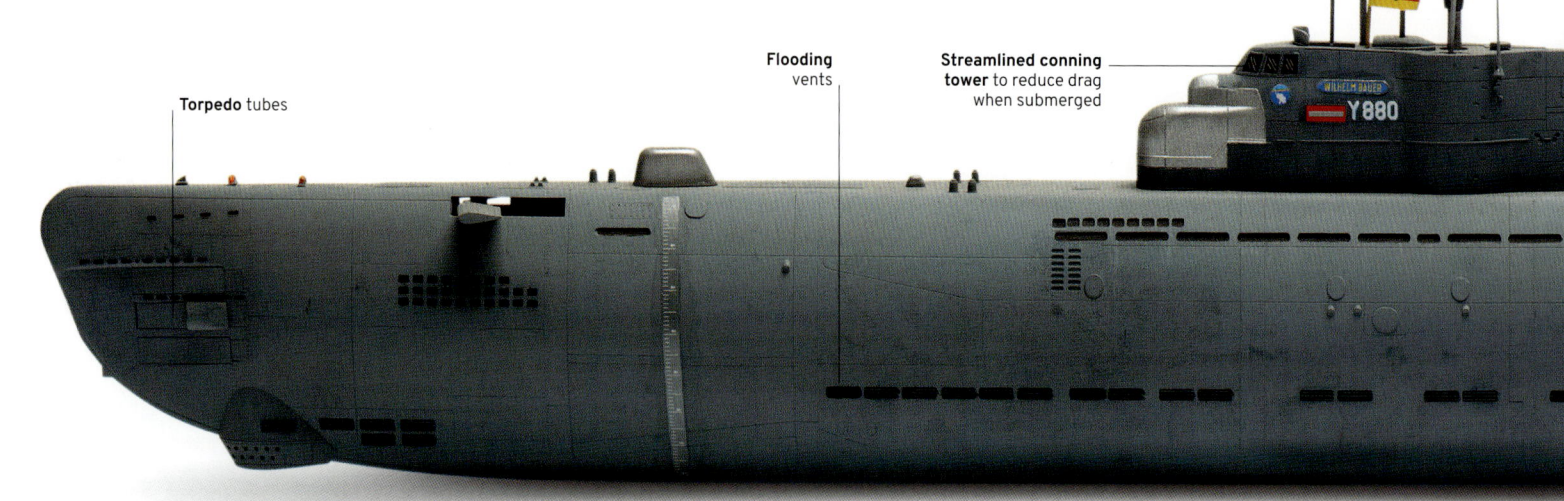

WORLD WAR II SUBMARINES • 177

Attachment point for tow cable

Engine exhaust

Propeller shrouded for protection

◁ **RN X-craft**
Date 1942–45 **Origin** UK
Displacement 27.2 tonnes (30 tons)
Length 15.7 m (51½ ft)
Top speed 6 knots (11 km/h)

With a crew of four, which included a diver, this midget submarine carried a pair of 2-ton mines, called "side-charges", along the sides of its hull. The mines were released to lie on the seabed below their intended targets. Just 23 X-craft were built for the British Royal Navy.

88 mm deck gun

"Jumping wires" allowed the submarine to pass under nets without getting snagged

Chains to prevent propeller fouling

Aichi M6A *Seiran* attack floatplane (one of three)

Compressed-air catapult for launching aircraft

Periscope array

25 mm anti-aircraft gun (one of 10)

5.5 in deck gun

△ **I-400**
Date 1944 **Origin** Japan
Displacement 5,309 tonnes (5,852 tons)
Length 122 m (410¼ ft)
Top speed 18.7 knots (35 km/h)

Airstrikes could be launched from the deck of this *Sen Toku*-class submarine aircraft carrier. Eighteen such boats were ordered by Japan to attack locks on the Panama Canal linking the Atlantic and the Pacific oceans; just three were built, one being converted into a tanker during construction. Not until the US Navy's *George Washington*-class nuclear-powered submarines appeared in the 1960s was their size surpassed.

Hull is more streamlined than previous designs

◁ **Wilhelm Bauer**
Date 1945 **Origin** Germany
Displacement 1,620 tonnes (1,786 tons)
Length 76.7 m (251½ ft)
Top speed 15.6 knots (29 km/h)

Originally U-2540, *Wilhelm Bauer* was a Type XXI – the war's most advanced submarine design. Many features introduced on the Type XXI are still found on modern submarines. Around 120 XXIs were commissioned, but none saw combat before the war's end. *Wilhelm Bauer* was scuttled in May 1945. Raised 12 years later and recommissioned, it is now a museum ship at Bremerhaven.

U-995 Submarine

For much of World War II, German U-boats – especially Type VIICs, the most numerous Axis submarines – were the scourge of Allied transatlantic convoys. Built at the Blohm and Voss yard in Hamburg and commissioned in September 1943, U-995 sank two warships and three merchant vessels on its nine patrols. U-995 was an upgraded Type VIIC, known as a VIIC/41, with a stronger pressure hull that enabled it to dive deeper than its predecessor.

SPECIFICATIONS	
Name	U-995
Commissioned	1943
Type	Type VIIC/41 submarine
Displacement	759 tonnes (837 tons)
Length	67 m (220 ft)
Propulsion	2 x 2,088–2,386 kW (2,800–3,200 hp) diesel; submerged: 2 x 559 kW (750 hp) electric
Armament	5 x torpedo tubes (14 torpedoes carried)
Top speed	17.7 knots (32.8 km/h)

Bridge, used for surface navigation and signalling; immediately below it is the conning tower, from where the ship was commanded during submerged attacks

Antisubmarine net deflector

Anti-aircraft guns

Adolf Hitler backed the idea of a powerful German navy, but only in 1939 did he approve Plan Z, a project to build ten battleships and four aircraft carriers by 1948. As a result, the war came too soon for the German navy. Its U-boat submarine fleet, led by Admiral Karl Dönitz, was not ready. Dönitz estimated he needed 300 U-boats to successfully campaign against Allied shipping, targeting mainly the supply convoys that crossed the Atlantic, but he had just 46 operational vessels when war began.

To build up U-boat numbers, construction was accelerated. Although 568 Type VIIC U-boats – the "standard" boat – were built from 1940 to 1945, there were never enough in service at any one time to dominate the sea lanes, despite experimenting with "wolf packs" – groups of submarines fighting together. Hitler also distracted the U-boats from their key task of sinking convoys by ordering them to patrol the Norwegian coast in case of invasion and to support the Italians in the Mediterranean Sea and Germany's Afrika Korps in North Africa.

In late 1940, with the use of captured bases on the western French coastline, the U-boats had their first "happy period", sinking significant quantities of British shipping. However, revised convoy tactics and the breaking of the German navy's Enigma codes in May 1941 led to higher level of U-boat detection by the Allies. Another "happy period" occurred after the US's entry into the war at the end of 1941, with ships sunk off the US coast and in the Caribbean. By spring 1943, air cover, better intelligence, the increased use of sonar and radar detection, and, once again, improved tactics, had led to fewer Allied losses and more U-boat sinkings.

U-995 was one of the 1,181 submarines that served with the German navy during World War II, of which 785, around two-thirds, were lost. In total, just under 3,000 Allied ships, warships, and merchant vessels were sunk by German U-boats.

Sole survivor
At the war's end, U-995 was one of 156 U-boats that surrendered; 116 were scuttled by the Royal Navy, but 30 were divided between Britain, the US, and the USSR for re-use. Britain gave U-995 to the Norwegian navy in 1948, and it served as the *Kaura* until 1965. Now a museum ship at Laboe, near Kiel, Germany, it is the only surviving Type VIIC U-boat.

Limber holes allowed water to flow freely between outer superstructure and pressurized hull

Bow diving plane (or hydroplane); one on each side

U-boat identification number (the U stands for *Unterseeboot*)

Torpedo tube opening (now covered)

EXTERIOR

U-995's distinctive external features are the bridge and conning tower, guns, and bulging saddle tanks (external ballast tanks outside of the pressure hull). It typically travelled on the surface, mainly at night to use the greater speed of its diesel engines and to charge the batteries needed by its electric motors when submerged. Anti-aircraft guns, important for protection should the U-boat be surprised on the surface, could also be used against smaller vessels if an expensive torpedo was considered wasteful.

1. Flak 38 20mm anti-aircraft guns **2.** Identification number **3.** Circular radio direction finder between attack periscope (left) and observation periscope (right), ship's logo beneath **4.** Stern view of twin rudders and twin propellers **5.** 3.7cm Flak M42U anti-aircraft gun **6.** Radar antenna **7.** Starboard moveable diving plane behind fixed fin **8.** Anchor **9.** Port saddle tank

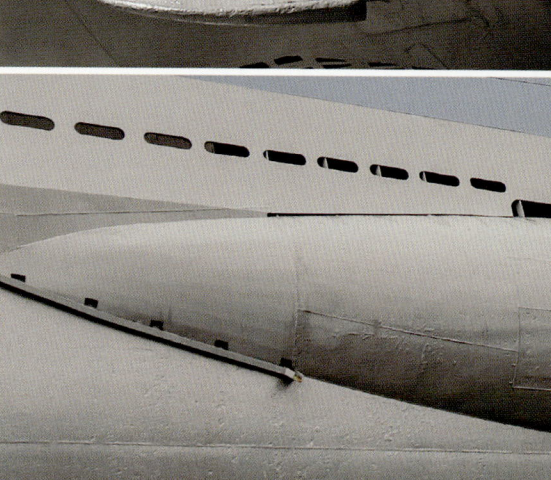

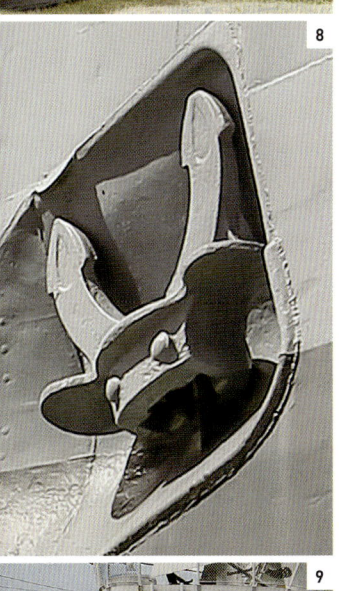

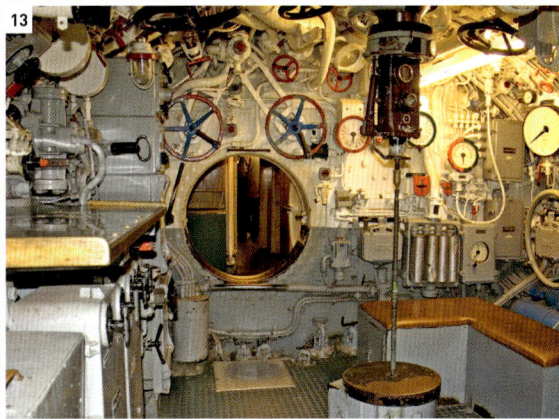

INTERIOR

The rear was dominated by the electric motors and diesel engines. In the centre, beneath the conning tower, was the control room, the ship's operational hub. Up front was the main torpedo room, with access to four tubes (there was a further tube at the stern). With a crew of up to 52, depending on the type of mission, living and working conditions were cramped – many of the men slept in the forward torpedo room – so maintaining morale and discipline was vital to ensure a successful patrol. Missions could last from 3 weeks to 6 months; fresh water for washing and shaving was limited, and most crew members grew beards.

10. View from aft through bulkhead door into control room 11. Engine order telegraph 12. Forward torpedo room 13. Control room interior, with chart table (left) and observation periscope (right) 14. Electric motor room 15. Forward torpedo launch tube hatches 16. Diesel engine room

Aircraft Carriers

The first ships to carry aircraft operated as floating bases for seaplanes. With subsequent experimentation, particularly during and after World War I, the aircraft carrier began to develop as a distinctive type of ship, equipped with a full-length flight deck and equipment for launching and recovering aircraft. By 1939, Britain's Royal Navy had a dozen such carriers in service or under construction; the Imperial Japanese Navy had a similar number, and the US Navy eight. The US Navy embraced the type most wholeheartedly in World War II, building large numbers of "fleet" carriers, and lighter, less-capable "escort" carriers – including many escort carriers for the British Royal Navy. During the war, carriers played a key role in winning crucial naval battles, keeping vital merchant shipping lanes open, and supporting amphibious landings.

△ HMS Furious
Date 1917 **Origin** UK
Displacement 23,255 tonnes (25,635 tons)
Length 239.7 m (786½ ft)
Top speed 30 knots (55 km/h)

During construction, *Furious* was modified from a light battlecruiser into a carrier by removing the forward turret and adding a short flying-off deck. It was later rebuilt from the main deck up and equipped with 36 aircraft. *Furious* served with distinction during World War II. In September 1944, now showing its age, it was withdrawn from frontline service and placed in reserve.

△ USS Saratoga
Date 1927 **Origin** USA
Displacement 43,745 tonnes (48,220 tons)
Length 270.7 m (888 ft)
Top speed 33 knots (61 km/h)

Saratoga and its sister-ship *Lexington* were begun as battlecruisers – part of a group of six ordered by the US Navy at the end of World War I – but chosen to be completed as carriers. In exercises, the pair helped to develop US carrier tactics prior to World War II. *Saratoga* won seven battle stars during her wartime service with the US Pacific Fleet.

◁ Akagi
Date 1927 **Origin** Japan
Displacement 43,435 tonnes (47,880 tons)
Length 260.7 m (855½ ft)
Top speed 31 knots (57 km/h)

Laid down as a battlecruiser, *Akagi* was finished as a carrier. Aircraft mainly took off from the lower hangar-deck levels and landed on the upper deck. Rebuilt in 1935–38 with an island superstructure and a single flight deck, *Akagi* took part in the attack on the US Pacific Fleet at Pearl Harbor in December 1941.

▽ USS Enterprise

Date 1938	Origin USA
Displacement	26,260 tonnes (28,945 tons)
Length	246.6 m (809 ft)
Top speed	32.5 knots (60 km/h)

A participant in nearly every Pacific carrier battle, the USS *Enterprise* – the second of three *Yorktown*-class vessels – won a record 20 battle stars. Despite such extensive involvement in combat, the *Enterprise* survived the war; however, her two sister ships, *Yorktown* and *Hornet*, were sunk in 1942.

▷ HMS Ark Royal

Date 1938	Origin UK
Displacement	28,165 tonnes (31,045 tons)
Length	243.8 m (800 ft)
Top speed	31 knots (57 km/h)

Ark Royal, Britain's first large, purpose-built aircraft carrier, introduced many elements – including steam catapults for launching aircraft, and hangars and a flight deck that were an integral part of the hull – that became standard on later carriers. Struck by a U-boat torpedo in the Mediterranean in 1941, having delivered aircraft to Malta, *Ark Royal* sank while being towed to Gibraltar.

◁ HMS Illustrious

Date 1940	Origin UK
Displacement	29,710 tonnes (32,750 tons)
Length	229.6 m (753½ ft)
Top speed	30.5 knots (56 km/h)

Illustrious was the lead ship of a class of three British fleet carriers laid down in 1937. The carrier trio served throughout the war, surviving multiple attempts to sink them. *Illustrious* pioneered armoured flight and hangar decks, but at the cost of a diminished capacity to store aviation fuel – a shortcoming that was never rectified.

△ USS Essex

Date 1942	Origin USA
Displacement	35,440 tonnes (39,065 tons)
Length	265.8 m (872 ft)
Top speed	32.7 knots (61 km/h)

No other group of ships played such a vital role in victory in the Pacific as the 24 *Essex*-class fleet carriers. The core of the US Navy's Fast Carrier Task Force, they all survived World War II. Rebuilt with angled flight decks, they went on to form the basis of the US postwar carrier fleet.

△ USS Guadalcanal

Date 1943	Origin USA
Displacement	11,075 tonnes (12,210 tons)
Length	156 m (512¼ ft)
Top speed	19 knots (35 km/h)

By employing mass production techniques, Henry Kaiser's shipyards could assemble ships more quickly and cheaply than other yards. Based on a freighter hull, *Guadalcanal* was built for the US Navy at Kaiser's yard in Vancouver, Canada. It was one of 50 *Casablanca*-class escort carriers.

Carrier and Maritime Strike Aircraft

The first planes to be operated from aircraft carriers were identical to those that used airfields on land, but by the mid-1920s aircraft were being specifically adapted for shipboard use. The designs of carrier- and land-based aircraft subsequently diverged, particularly during World War II, when it became apparent that carriers could be key to winning naval battles. Carrier-based aircraft included fighters to defend the mother ship and other vessels in the fleet, long-range reconnaissance aircraft, and dive-bombers and other specialist attack planes armed with torpedoes or bombs to strike targets at sea or on land.

△ **de Havilland DH98 Mosquito**
Date 1941   **Origin** UK
Engine 2 x 1,104 kW (1,480 hp) Rolls-Royce Merlin 21/21 + 23/23 water-cooled V12, later 2 x 1,260 kW (1,690 hp) 113 + 114
Top speed 589–670 km/h (366–415 mph)

Nicknamed the "Wooden Wonder", the Mosquito was fast, light, and highly versatile. It performed many roles during World War II, including missions against enemy shipping and submarines using rockets, bombs, and cannons.

△ **Grumman F4F Wildcat**
Date 1940   **Origin** USA
Engine 895 kW (1,200 hp) Pratt & Whitney R-1830-86 Twin Wasp radial
Top speed 515 km/h (320 mph)

Grumman adapted its mid-1930s F3F biplane fighter to create the F4F Wildcat, which had an improved tail, a more powerful engine, and a mid-mounted wing. Although not a match for the impressive Japanese Zero, the Wildcat proved a competent monoplane fighter.

△ **Douglas SBD-5 Dauntless**
Date 1942   **Origin** USA
Engine 895 kW (1,200 hp) Wright R-1820-60 Cyclone radial
Top speed 410 km/h (255 mph)

The rugged and dependable "Slow But Deadly" (SBD) sank more Japanese ships in World War II than any other American aircraft. It remained the US Navy's main dive-bomber until 1943. The SBD later evolved into the A-1 Skyraider, which was deployed in Korea and Vietnam.

Cockpit set well back to improve pilot's field of view
US Navy markings

△ **Vought F4U Corsair**
Date 1942   **Origin** USA
Engine 1,491.3 kW (2,000 hp) Pratt & Whitney R-2800-8 radial
Top speed 670 km/h (416 mph)

The Corsair had a very powerful engine and an inverted gull-wing design that allowed ground clearance for its huge propeller. It was World War II's most capable carrier-based fighter, also adept in a fighter-bomber role.

▽ **Mitsubishi A6M3 Zero**
Date 1942   **Origin** Japan
Engine 842.6 kW (1,130 hp) Nakajima NK1F Sakae 21 radial
Top speed 540 km/h (335 mph)

With superb agility and range, the Mitsubishi Zero (codenamed "Zeke" by the Allies) was Japan's best naval fighter; only in 1943 did Allied planes begin to surpass the Zero's combat abilities.

Elliptical wing shape of Spitfire was retained for all but the last Seafires

△ **Supermarine Seafire**
Date 1942   **Origin** UK
Engine 1,379.5 kW (1,850 hp) Rolls-Royce Griffon VI V12
Top speed 630 km/h (391 mph)

Seafire was a version of the Mark V Spitfire with modifications for shipborne use. It was developed to meet a shortfall in carrier aircraft supplied to the UK by the US, which also provided many carriers.

Wing housed three .5 in machine-guns

△ **Grumman F6F Hellcat**
Date 1943 Origin USA
Engine 1,641 kW (2,200 hp) Pratt & Whitney R-2800-10W Double Wasp radial
Top speed 610 km/h (379 mph)

The Hellcat's similarity to the Wildcat sometimes confused Japanese pilots. It was a costly mistake: the Hellcat was a new design, around 95 km/h (60 mph) faster than its lookalike and with better acceleration.

△ **Grumman F8F Bearcat**
Date 1945 Origin USA
Engine 1,790 kW (2,400 hp) Pratt & Whitney R-2800-34W Double Wasp radial
Top speed 680 km/h (422 mph)

The Bearcat – the last of World War II's "Cats" – had the same engine as the Hellcat, but it was about 20 per cent lighter, giving it a 30 per cent better climb rate and an extra 70 km/h (40 mph) on its top speed.

◁ **Hawker Sea Fury**
Date 1945 Origin UK
Engine 1,849 kW (2,480 hp) Bristol Centaurus XVIIC supercharged air-cooled 18-cylinder radial
Top speed 740 km/h (460 mph)

This "navalized" version of Hawker's cancelled Fury fighter had folding wings and an arrester hook. It was highly effective, even holding its own against jet fighters in the Korean War.

Folding wing

British navy markings

Three-bladed constant-pitch propeller

Glazed canopy provides all-round visibility

20mm cannon

Folding wingtips

Undercarriage wheels set far apart provide on-deck stability

Japanese navy markings

The Normandy Landings

The Allied invasion of Europe that began on 6 June 1944 – D-Day – was the largest amphibious operation ever attempted, landing around 156,000 troops and involving nearly 7,000 ships and other vessels, supported by almost 12,000 aircraft. Such an ambitious undertaking required a previously unmatched level of planning and preparation. Air superiority had been achieved against the Luftwaffe over France, and the German navy had been limited to a few fast attack boats in the channel ports. The objective was to successfully land enough soldiers and equipment to break through the German beach defences and then progress inland, and this led to the development of specialized landing craft and support vessels that had to be built in quantity. Tanks were adapted to swim ashore or carry additional equipment to demolish sea walls, clear minefields, or lay bridges.

Troops of the US 2nd Infantry Division pass a German bunker as they climb a bluff above the Easy Red sector of Omaha Beach, where supply trucks gather and landing craft and other vessels bring further men and equipment.

1945–1989
THE COLD WAR

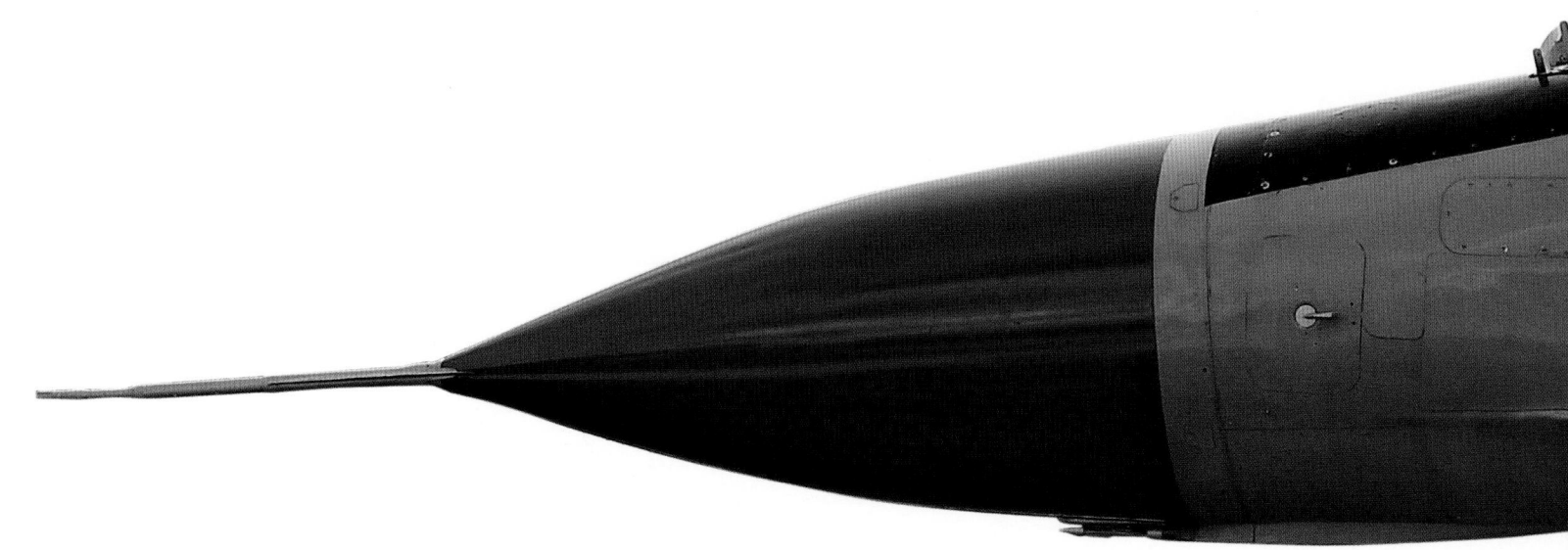

The Age of Technology

The Cold War was a nuclear standoff between the US and the Soviet Union, with numerous proxy wars fought in other nations around the world. The demands of this uncertain era and the arrival of computerization helped elevate military vehicle design to new heights.

As well as building up stockpiles of nuclear weapons, the two rival superpowers needed to develop the means of delivering the warheads to their targets. The primary instruments of nuclear warfare were initially long-range strategic bombers, which included huge aircraft such as the American B-52 Stratofortress and the Soviet Tupolev Tu-95. Over time, intercontinental ballistic missiles (ICBMs) took over the majority of the nuclear launch role, as well as submarine-launched ballistic missiles (SLBMs). However, heavy bombers remained on station on both sides of the Iron Curtain for the duration of the Cold War. The B-52 also found use in a conventional bombing role during the Vietnam War (1955–75).

The military vehicles of the Cold War were designed to operate in a nuclear age, and increasingly military vehicles of all types incorporated nuclear, biological, and chemical (NBC) protective features, intended to shield the crew from the effects of post-strike radiation or from nightmarish chemical or biological weapons. However, overall the postwar evolution of military vehicles was driven more by technological progress than by the threat of nuclear attack.

New power sources, new vehicles

The Cold War era saw great advances in rockets and jets. Successive breakthroughs in aircraft design and jet engines meant that by the 1960s some military aircraft were flying at two or even three times the speed of sound. This great leap in capability placed new demands on pilots. In World War II, if opposing fighters approached each other head-on at a distance of around 32 km (20 miles), their pilots would have had at least a minute or so before they needed to perform tactical manoeuvres. With the supersonic fighters of the Cold War, at the same distance they might have around 10 seconds.

The powerplant revolution extended to other domains and technologies too. During the 1950s and 1960s, the first nuclear-powered submarines and aircraft carriers entered service, their reactor engines offering almost indefinite range and endurance. The 1960s and 1970s also witnessed the development of the first production tanks and warships powered by gas turbine engines, which gave a higher power-to-weight ratio than internal combustion engines, albeit with less fuel efficiency at lower speeds.

Different types of vehicle also came to prominence in the Cold War era. The helicopter in particular rose to prominence, and was widely used in tactical military mobility. Over a decade of involvement in the war in Vietnam, for example, the US deployed more than 11,800 helicopters, which took on a

TALKING POINT

Berlin Airlift

At the end of World War II, the German capital Berlin was divided into four zones of occupation: French, British, US, and Soviet. In June 1948, a breakdown in political relations resulted in the Soviet Union imposing a land blockade on Allied West Berlin. In response, the USAF and RAF began an extraordinary 11-month, non-stop resupply operation to West Berlin via airlifts. By May 1949, when the blockade was finally lifted, in excess of 200,000 flights had delivered more than 2.3 million tonnes (2.54 million tons) of food, medicines, fuel, and other vital supplies to German citizens and Allied troops in West Berlin.

Berliners watch as a Douglas C-54 Skymaster comes in to land at Templehof airfield. At the very peak of the airlift, at Easter 1949, a plane landed in West Berlin almost every minute.

> "Today the **kind and quality of systems** which a nation develops can **decide the battle** in advance."
>
> US AIR FORCE GENERAL BERNARD "BENNIE" SCHRIEVER

Timeline

Building on the foundations of World War II, the Cold War era saw huge increases in the range, sophistication, and power of weapons and military technology. Computerization became widespread, and new powerplants, including jet engines, gas turbines, and nuclear reactors transformed propulsion.

- **1947** The T-54, the USSR's new postwar medium tank, enters service
- **1953** The US F-100D Super Sabre becomes the first fighter capable of supersonic speed in level flight
- **1954** The USS *Nautilus* (SSN-571), the world's first nuclear-powered submarine, is commissioned
- **1955** The US Air Force introduces the B-52 Stratofortress long-range strategic bomber
- **1956** In the US, the Bell UH-1 Iroquois helicopter enters production
- **1959** Production begins of the Soviet MiG-21, the Cold War's most numerous supersonic fighter
- **1959** The USS *George Washington* (SSBN-598), the first nuclear-ballistic-missile submarine, is launched
- **1960** The M113 armoured personnel carrier (APC) transforms US infantry transport

broad range of utility, support, and combat roles (it was the Vietnam War that inspired the helicopter gunship concept). Land vehicles were also changing. Tank fleets were increasingly rationalized, with advanced main battle tank (MBT) types, equipped with gyro-stabilized guns and composite armour, replacing both the medium and heavy tanks of the past. Army mechanization was fast-tracked by new generations of armoured personnel carriers (APCs) and infantry fighting vehicles (IFVs). IFVs could transport troops onto the battlefield, but they also had missile and gun armament to take on enemy armour, even MBTs. Military commanders of the Cold War now had far more technological force multipliers at their disposal.

Computerization and vehicles

Computers changed the capabilities of military vehicles most significantly during this era. The early computers of the 1940s and 1950s were the size of a room, but in the 1960s, developments in transistors and integrated circuits resulted in the miniaturization of computers, making them small enough to install in vehicles. Advances in computerization between the 1960s and 1980s transformed areas such as communications, fire-control, missile and bomb guidance, aircraft performance (through fly-by-wire technologies), rangefinding, surveillance, threat detection, and command-and-control systems. Later developments included satellite communications and battlefield data transfer.

Tank standoff
With Cold War tensions high, US M48 Patton tanks face Soviet T-55s across the famous Checkpoint Charlie, the border control point connecting East and West Berlin, in October 1961.

Equipped with these new technologies, military vehicles became ever more adaptive and lethal. The gunner of an M1A1 Abrams tank of the late 1980s had a ballistic fire-control computer that nearly guaranteed a first-round hit at a range of 3.2km (2 miles), while the pilot of an F-14 Tomcat could launch an AIM-54 air-to-air missile (AAM) at a target more than 128km (80 miles) away.

Electronic countermeasures (ECM) aircraft were able to detect and block enemy radar and radio transmissions over areas of hundreds of square kilometres. Even comparatively simple military trucks could now be equipped with a Global Positioning System (GPS) navigation computer, reducing the possibilities of navigational errors in confused battle spaces. Personnel also needed to adapt to this new technology: by the end of the Cold War in 1989, a level of technical skill and digital acumen in military vehicle operators had become a necessity in many of the world's armies.

US civil defence recruitment poster, 1951
The threat of global nuclear war was just as salient to civilian thinking as it was to military minds during the Cold War. Civil defence organizations sought to prepare citizens for the worst and mitigate the effects of a nuclear strike.

1966 The Soviet BMP-1, a tracked infantry fighting vehicle (IFV), enters service

1973 T-72 tanks, the next generation of Soviet MBTs, are introduced by the Red Army

1981 First flight of the Lockheed F-117 Nighthawk stealth aircraft

1985 The US M1A1 Abrams embodies a new approach to main battle tank (MBT) design

1967 The *Moskva* helicopter carrier enters service with the Soviet navy

1972 The McDonnell Douglas F-15 Eagle makes its maiden flight

1975 Commission of the nuclear-powered supercarrier USS *Nimitz* (CVN-68)

1981 US Army units receive the first Bradley infantry fighting vehicles (IFVs)

1983 The first of 16 Type 23 frigates is commissioned into the British Royal Navy

1991 *Arleigh Burke*-class destroyers enter US Navy service

Transporting Missiles

During the Cold War era, the annual November parade in Moscow served as a platform for the Soviet Union to display the strength of its armed forces both to its people and to the watching West. With the emergence of missiles as key determinants of military strategy and deterrence, missile-carrying vehicles became the most eye-catching features of these displays of military might. The Soviet Union required its missile arsenal, which ranged from surface-to-air missiles (SAMs) to huge intercontinental ballistic missiles (ICBMs), to have mobility for transportation and deployment. This inspired innovation among Soviet engineers, who began producing impressive designs for missile carriers, both wheeled and tracked, that could cope with rough, often muddy terrain, and harsh Soviet winters. These even included 16×16 wheeled configurations, which were among the largest vehicles ever built. Some missile carriers were designed for the safe transportation of these crucial weapons. Others were built as mobile launchpads for use in combat. Called transporter erector launchers (TELs), they were able to elevate to a firing position and launch one or multiple missiles.

Soviet 2k11 Krug TELs, each carrying a pair of SAMs, parade through Moscow's Red Square during the 1971 November parade.

Communist Bloc Tanks

The T-54, introduced soon after World War II, was the first of a series of Soviet tanks that were mass produced and exported to Warsaw Pact countries and Communist client states during the Cold War era, with derivatives also forming the basis of China's tank force. Intended for front-line breakthroughs and advances deep into enemy territory, these mobile tanks were low in profile, making them more difficult to hit – but also cramped inside. Many are still in service around the world, a testimony to their longevity: Russia even sent old T-54s and T-55s into combat after invading Ukraine in 2022.

△ **T-54**
Date 1947 **Origin** USSR
Weight 36 tonnes (39.7 tons)
Engine V-54 V12 diesel, 388 kW (520 hp)
Main armament 100 mm D-10T L/53.5 rifled gun

For the T-54, designers opted for torsion bars instead of Christie suspension. The tank was armed with the 100 mm gun that had proved its value on the earlier SU-100 tank destroyer. One of the most produced tanks in history, the T-54 has seen combat in Europe, the Middle East, Africa, and Asia.

100 mm rifled gun

Strong hull able to withstand a tactical nuclear blast at 300 m (984 ft)

Spare track links

▷ **T-55**
Date 1958 **Origin** USSR
Weight 36 tonnes (39.7 tons)
Engine V-55 V12 diesel, 433 kW (580 hp)
Main armament 100 mm D-10T2S L/53.5 rifled gun

The T-54 was developed into the T-55 by the addition of a more powerful engine and a nuclear, biological, and chemical (NBC) warfare protection system. With Soviet T-55 production continuing until 1981, later improvements included laser rangefinders and new sights. Many countries operating T-55s made their own upgrades, helping to extend the tank's lifespan into the 21st century.

▽ **Type 59-II**
Date 1959 **Origin** China
Weight 36 tonnes (39.7 tons)
Engine 12150L V12 diesel, 388 kW (520 hp)
Main armament 105 mm L7 rifled gun

By incorporating Chinese and Western technology, the Type 59 has diverged significantly from the Soviet-era T-54 tank from which it was originally developed. This Type 59-II variant is equipped with a British-designed gun, a gun-stabilization system, and NBC protection.

▷ **T-62**
Date 1962 **Origin** USSR
Weight 38 tonnes (41.9 tons)
Engine V-55-5 V12 diesel, 433 kW (580 hp)
Main armament 115 mm 2A20 L/49.5 smoothbore gun

Planned as a stopgap measure, the T-62 ended up becoming the mainstay of the Red Army into the 1970s. It had a larger hull than its forerunner, the T-55, added infrared night-vision, and a more powerful 115 mm gun – the first smoothbore gun in service and the first to fire Armour Piercing Fin Stabilized Discarding Sabot (APFSDS) projectiles.

COMMUNIST BLOC TANKS · 195

△ Type 62
Date 1962 **Origin** China
Weight 21 tonnes (23.2 tons)
Engine 12150L-3 V12 diesel, 321 kW (430 hp)
Main armament 85 mm Type 62-85TC rifled gun

Type 62 – essentially a scaled-down version of the Type 59 – was produced for use in regions of China where the large, heavy Type 59 found it difficult to operate successfully. The Type 62 had better ground pressure and mobility than the Type 59, although this came at the expense of its firepower and protection. The tank saw action during the Vietnam War.

▽ T-64B1
Date 1966 **Origin** USSR
Weight 39 tonnes (43 tons)
Engine 5DTF diesel, 522 kW (700 hp)
Main armament 125 mm 2A46 L/48 smoothbore gun

The T-64's advanced, complex design introduced many new features, the most notable being an autoloader for the gun. The T-64 was never exported, being built solely for the tank battalions that spearheaded the Soviet Army. The breakup of the Soviet Union left the T-64 factory in Ukraine, where the tank was further developed. The variant shown here is the T-64B1.

Twelve wheels driven by a V-46 diesel engine

◁ T-72M1
Date 1973 **Origin** USSR
Weight 41.5 tonnes (45.8 tons)
Engine V-46.6 diesel, 582 kW (780 hp)
Main armament 125 mm 2A46 L/48 smoothbore gun

Like the T-64, the three-man T-72 dispensed with a fourth crew member in favour of an automatic loader. It has received extensive upgrades over its long career: the latest models are fitted with distinctive Explosive Reactive Armour (ERA) panels and thermal hunter-killer sights. Export versions generally have less sophisticated systems and thinner armour.

Smoke grenade dischargers

Explosive Reactive Armour (ERA) on glacis plate

△ T-80U
Date 1976 **Origin** USSR
Weight 46 tonnes (50.7 tons)
Engine GTD-1250 gas turbine, 932 kW (1,250 hp)
Main armament 125 mm 2A46M1 L/48 smoothbore gun

An evolution of the T-64, the T-80 was deployed on Moscow streets during the attempted coup of 1991, and it has seen combat in Chechnya in 1995 and in Ukraine in the 2020s. This T-80U upgrade has a more powerful turbine than the original and a new turret protected by ERA panels.

Infrared searchlight for night operations

◁ Type 69-II
Date 1983 **Origin** China
Weight 36.7 tonnes (40.5 tons)
Engine 12150L-7BW V12 diesel, 433 kW (580 hp)
Main armament 100 mm smoothbore gun

Using the Type 59 as a template, Chinese manufacturers developed the Type 69 without help from the USSR. Shown here is the Type 69-II variant, which had an over-the-barrel laser rangefinder and an infrared searchlight next to the gun. Despite proving a significant export success, the Type 69 was not widely adopted by the Chinese military.

T-72

Designed for use if the Cold War had escalated into open conflict, the Soviet T-72 was relatively light compared to contemporary Western tanks, weighing just over 41 tonnes (45 tons). As with many Cold War-era Soviet tanks, it was believed to be less effective than its Western rivals in one-on-one encounters. However, it was fit for purpose, since Soviet commanders intended to use it in vast numbers for massed attacks that would swamp Western defences.

Smoothbore barrel, strong enough to ram through walls

125 mm gun, larger than those of contemporary Western tanks

FRONT VIEW

REAR VIEW

Sloping armour on front of hull

THE T-72 WAS SIMPLER in design and easier to maintain than its predecessor, the expensive and complex T-64. It incorporated features from earlier Soviet tank designs, including a frying pan-shaped turret, a reliable diesel engine, and a low profile.

Fed ammunition by an autoloader, the main gun could fire up to three shots in 13 seconds. The autoloader held 22 rounds in a circular, horizontal carousel, while a further 17 rounds were stored in the hull. Without the need for a manual loader, the T-72 could now function with just a commander, gunner, and driver. This, in turn, permitted a smaller, lighter design, since less crew space was needed. Guidelines stipulated that the three crew members could be no taller than 175 cm (5 ft 9 in), to ensure they could work in the T-72's cramped interior.

Having entered service with the Red Army in the 1970s, the T-72 is still used by over 40 countries. T-72s were also manufactured in Poland and Czechoslovakia, and the Soviets themselves produced versions of the T-72 specifically for export, often with lower standards of protection.

SPECIFICATIONS	
Name	T-72M1
Date	1973
Origin	Soviet Union
Production	Over 25,000
Engine	V46.6 V-12 diesel, 581 kW (780 hp)
Weight	41.5 tonnes (45.7 tons)
Main armament	125 mm 2A46M smoothbore
Secondary armament	12.7 mm NSVT machine-gun
Crew	3
Armour thickness	280 mm (11 in) max

Low-lying target
At little more than 2 m (6 ft) in height, the T-72 presents a difficult target for enemy forces. Using an autoloader for the 125 mm gun allowed a reduction in height, since there was no need for the turret to accommodate a standing crew member to load the gun.

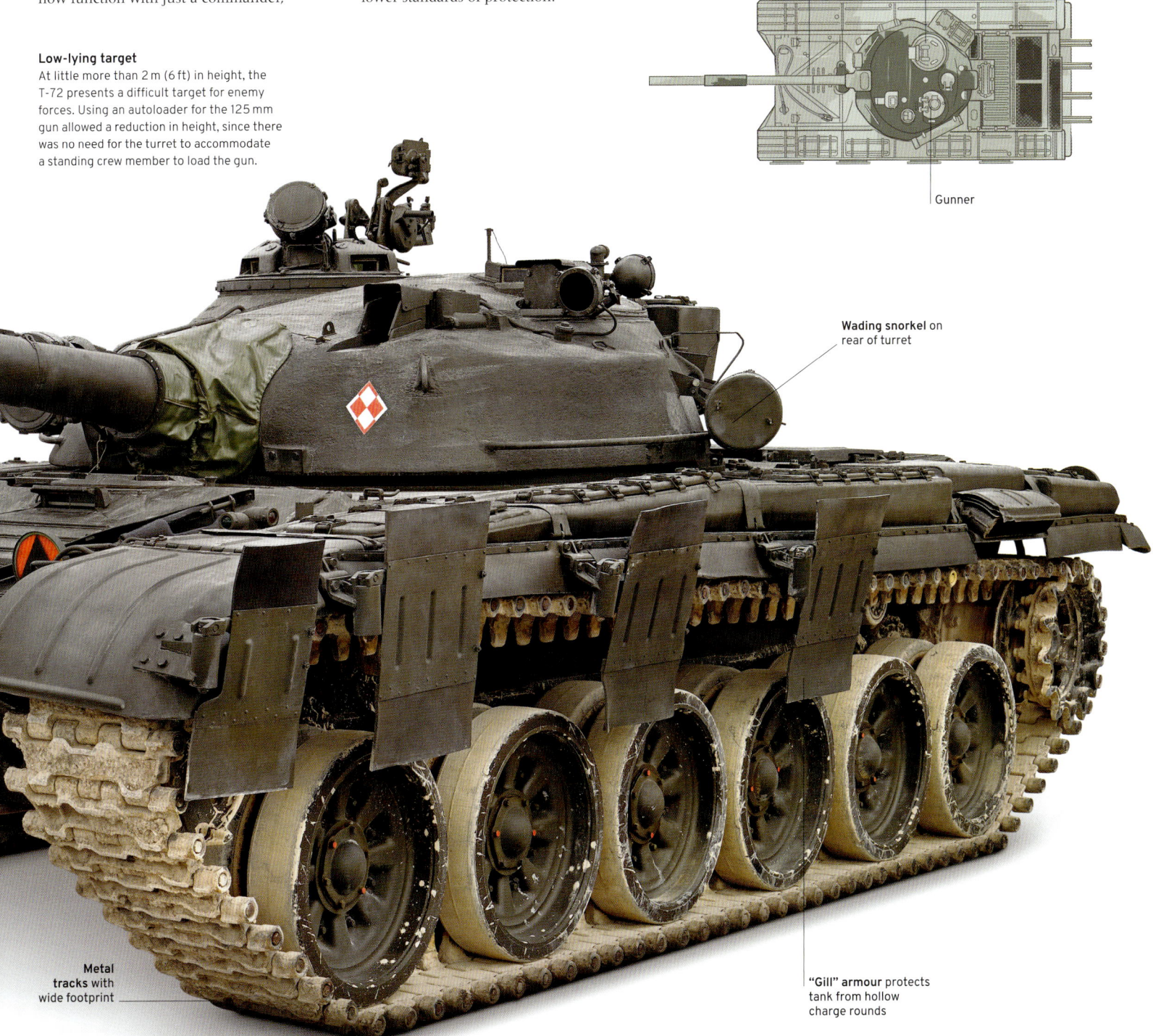

Wading snorkel on rear of turret

Metal tracks with wide footprint

"Gill" armour protects tank from hollow charge rounds

EXTERIOR

This T-72 from Polish service has been augmented along its sides by "gill" armour – rubber squares that can be angled forwards to detonate or disrupt hollow charge rounds before they strike the tank's main body. In addition to the 125 mm gun, the turret originally housed a 7.62 mm PKT co-axial machine-gun, while the external machine-gun bracket was mounted with an anti-aircraft 12.7 mm NSVT.

1. Polish national emblem **2.** Station keeping/convoy light **3.** Main gun sight **4.** Headlamp
5. Infrared light **6.** Machine-gun bracket **7.** Gunner's hatch (closed) **8.** Deep wading snorkel (stowed)
9. Commander's hatch (closed) **10.** Machine-gun ammunition boxes **11.** Engine exhaust
12. Additional "gill" armour **13.** Fuel drum brackets **14.** Rear reflector **15.** Spare track links on hull

INTERIOR

Although typically cramped and uncomfortable, the T-72's three-man crew compartment offered nuclear, biological, and chemical (NBC) protection. The tank's gunner had access to gunsights and a laser rangefinder for daylight fighting, as well as infrared sights for use in combat at night.

16. Looking down into commander's position
17. Commander's sight 18. Looking down into gunner's position 19. Gunner's sight
20. Commander's seat back and pistol case
21. Gun elevation handwheel 22. Driver's instrument panel 23. Driver's periscope
24. Main gun breech and autoloader
25. Gear lever 26. Left-hand steering lever
27. Looking down into driver's position

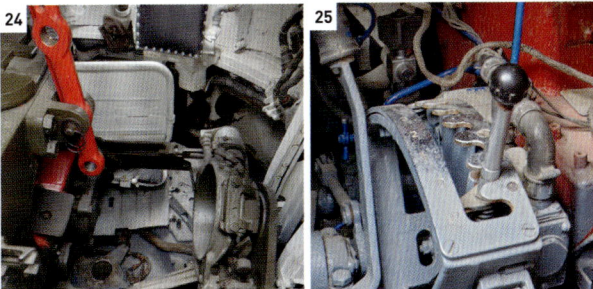

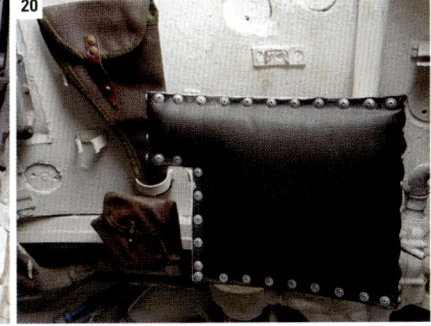

▷ **Centurion Mark 3**
Date 1948 **Origin** UK
Weight 50.8 tonnes (56 tons)
Engine Rolls-Royce Meteor Mark IVA petrol, 485 kW (650 hp)
Main armament Ordnance QF 20-pounder gun

The Centurion Mark 3 had an automatic stabilization system that enabled it to fire its powerful 20-pounder gun accurately while on the move. More than 4,400 Centurions were built, the majority of which were Mark 3s. This highly successful tank was exported to many countries and saw combat in Korea, India, Pakistan, and Vietnam.

Cupola for tank commander

Gun mantlet (armoured shield)

Headlamp

◁ **M41A1 Walker Bulldog**
Date 1951 **Origin** USA
Weight 23.2 tonnes (25.6 tons)
Engine Continental AOS-895-3 petrol, 373 kW (500 hp)
Main armament 76 mm M32 L/64 gun

The M41 replaced the M24 Chaffee light tank, which had been in service since late World War II. Still light enough to be transported by air, the M41 carried a significantly more potent gun. Widely exported, the M41 saw combat with US and South Vietnamese forces; a few nations still operate the M41.

▷ **M48 Patton**
Date 1952 **Origin** USA
Weight 44.7 tonnes (49.3 tons)
Engine Continental AV-1790-5B petrol, 604 kW (810 hp)
Main armament 90 mm M41 L/50 rifled gun

Development began on the M48 even before the M47, its predecessor, entered production. The M48 had an improved hull, turret, and suspension; later models were given an AVDS-1790 diesel engine and a 105 mm M68 gun. The M48 served with 26 nations and saw action in several conflicts; nearly 12,000 were built.

NATO Tanks

During the Cold War, NATO countries standardized many aspects of their militaries so that they could fight effectively together, but the alliance never produced a standard tank. Consequently, differing national doctrines led to contrasting designs: German Leopards, for example, emphasized mobility and were lightly armoured, while British Chieftains were better protected but less mobile. A key development was composite armour, consisting of layers of different materials, to replace steel, which was vulnerable to high-explosive antitank (HEAT) projectiles.

◁ **AMX-13**
Date 1953 **Origin** France
Weight 15 tonnes (16.5 tons)
Engine Sofam Model 8Gxb petrol, 186 kW (250 hp)
Main armament 75 mm SA 50 rifled gun

The AMX-13 was an air-portable light tank developed to support airborne forces. It was fitted with a front-mounted engine, an autoloader, and a two-part, oscillating turret whose entire upper section moved with the gun. The AMX-13, an export success, had many upgrades during its production, including 90 mm and 105 mm guns.

NATO TANKS · 201

◁ Chieftain Mark 11
Date 1966 **Origin** UK
Weight 55 tonnes (60.6 tons)
Engine Leyland L60 multifuel, 559 kW (750 hp)
Main armament 120 mm L11A5 L/55 rifled gun

The Chieftain replaced both the Conqueror and the Centurion in 1966, with the Mark 11 the final variant, in the 1980s. It was the first tank in which the driver drove in a semi-reclined position, enabling the tank's height to be reduced. Designed to defend against attacking Soviet forces, the Chieftain prioritized firepower and armour over mobility.

▽ Leopard 2A4
Date 1979 **Origin** West Germany
Weight 55.2 tonnes (60.9 tons)
Engine MTU MB 873 Ka-501 diesel, 1,119 kW (1,500 hp)
Main armament 120 mm Rheinmetall 120 L/44 gun

The 120 mm smoothbore gun, which would become standard on Western tanks, was introduced on the Leopard 2. The tank's turret incorporated composite armour, which meant it did not have to be sloped to be effective. The Leopard 2 is still in production and service; the 2A4, shown here, is the most common variant.

120 mm smoothbore gun was adopted by other Western tanks

Turret armour is vertical

Chobham-armour side skirt

◁ M1 Abrams
Date 1980 **Origin** USA
Weight 54.5 tonnes (60.1 tons)
Engine Textron Lycoming AGT1500 gas turbine, 1,119 kW (1,500 hp)
Main armament 105 mm M68 L/52 rifled gun

A replacement for the US Army's ageing M60, the M1's gas-turbine engine gave the new tank unmatched speed, but at the expense of very high fuel consumption. The M1 was clad in Chobham composite armour and equipped with a computerized fire-control system. Its armour was improved on later models, and the gun upgraded to a 120 mm smoothbore.

△ Challenger 1
Date 1984 **Origin** UK
Weight 62 tonnes (68.3 tons)
Engine Perkins CV12 V12 diesel, 895 kW (1,200 hp)
Main armament 120 mm L11A5 L/55 rifled gun

Designed for Iran but brought into service with the British Army when the contract was cancelled, the Challenger 1 was one of the first tanks with Chobham composite armour. Inside, it resembled a late-model Chieftain, but it carried a more powerful and more reliable engine, and it had hydrogas suspension. Challenger 1s first saw combat in the Gulf War of 1990–91.

Prague Spring

Tanks have been described as coming in two guises: as liberators or oppressors. The 4,600 Soviet tanks that rumbled into Czechoslovakia during 20–21 August 1968 were classic examples of the latter. The Prague Spring – leader Alexander Dubček's liberalization of the Communist-run country in an attempt to implement "socialism with a human face" – had drawn the ire of the Soviet Union. The Soviets responded by invading Czechoslovakia, aided by four other Warsaw Pact nations. Although resistance by the outraged population was mainly non-violent, more than 100 people died, hundreds were injured, and 300,000 fled the country. Prague, the capital, was the scene of huge protests against the occupying troops, many of whom were confused as to why they were there. Photographs of tanks facing citizen protesters were widely published in the West. They became a symbol of blunt Communist oppression, leading to taunts of "Workers of the World Unite, or I'll shoot you".

A T-62 tank, marked with a white invasion recognition cross, smashes the colonnades of Prague buildings as protesters look on during the 1968 invasion.

Leopard 1

First entering service in 1965, the German Leopard is without question one of the most successful tanks of the postwar era. Unlike the heavily armoured German tanks of late-World War II, the Leopard's design prioritized mobility over protection. For firepower, the Leopard was equipped with perhaps the most effective tank weapon of the time – the British 105 mm L7 gun, as used in the Centurion.

THE WEST GERMAN ARMY, which was formed in 1955, was at first equipped with American tanks. Two years later, Germany and France embarked on a joint tank-development project, but the partnership ended in 1962, with France pursuing a separate path to build its AMX-30. The Germans then followed their wartime practice of selecting the best model from prototypes built by different commissioned companies (or, in this case, groups of companies). In 1963, the contract for the new Standard Panzer – the tank that subsequently became known as Leopard 1 – was awarded to Krauss-Maffei of Munich.

The Leopard won many export orders, serving with the armies of 15 nations. From this relatively simple tank, numerous variants arose as new technologies were added, armour was augmented, and changes were made to suit individual countries' needs. On retirement, Leopards were often refurbished and sold in modified forms, including engineer-vehicle and recovery models.

SPECIFICATIONS	
Name	Leopard 1A1A2 (pictured)
Date	1965
Origin	West Germany
Production	6,486
Engine	MTU MB838 10-cylinder multifuel, 619 kW (830 hp)
Weight	42.4 tonnes (46.7 tons)
Main armament	105 mm L7A3
Secondary armament	2 x 7.62 mm MG3 machine-guns
Crew	4
Armour thickness	10–70 mm (0.4–2.8 in)

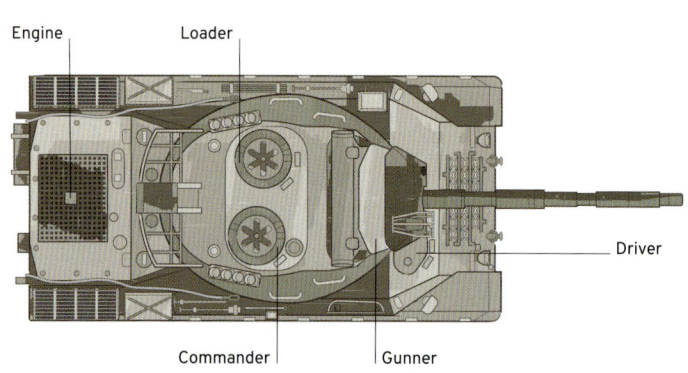

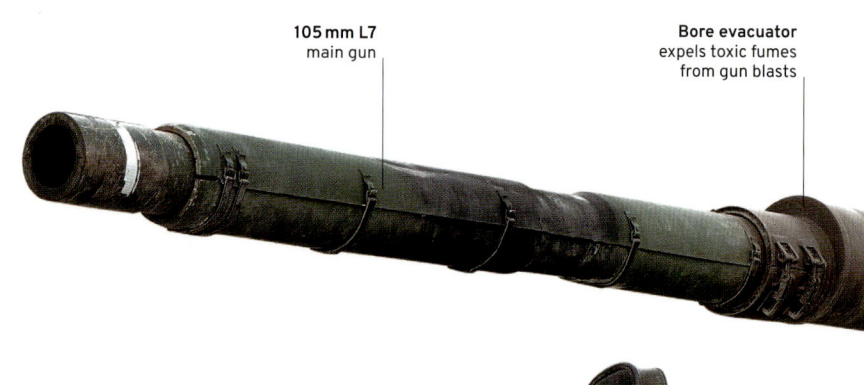

FRONT VIEW

REAR VIEW

- **Low-light TV/infrared** night light in protective cage
- **Commander's hatch**
- **Iron Cross,** the German Army emblem
- **Double pin tracks**

Upgraded Leopard
This 1980s version of the Leopard, the 1A1A2, has numerous upgraded features, including a gun-stabilization system, additional layers of turret armour, and improved gun sights and observation equipment.

INTERIOR

The engine occupied the rear of the Leopard's two interior compartments, which were separated by a firewall. At the front was the crew area: the tank commander sat in the turret, with the gunner in front of him, the loader to his left, and the driver sitting forwards and to the right.

15. Gunner's position   **16.** Looking down into commander's cupola
17. Commander's TRP 2A panoramic sight eyepiece   **18.** Loader's safety switch   **19.** Gunner's azimuth indicator dial   **20.** Commander's hydraulic hatch controls   **21.** 105mm gun breech   **22.** Looking down into driver's position   **23.** Gun stabilization system drift compensation box   **24.** Driver's controls   **25.** Intercom control panel   **26.** Driver's instrument panel
27. Gear lever   **28.** Fire extinguisher system

EXTERIOR

To make the Leopard 1 as light and mobile as possible, the tank's design reduced armour to a minimum. To mitigate this vulnerability, the hull's front-most section – the glacis plate – was angled at 60 degrees to the vertical to help deflect enemy projectiles. It also effectively thickened the hull by forcing projectiles to take a longer, diagonal route through its surface.

1. National recognition symbol 2. Headlight
3. Ice grousers 4. Holder for engine deck lifting tool (tool missing) 5. Driver's periscopes 6. Commander's TRP 2A panoramic sight head 7. Commander's cupola (closed) 8. Rangefinder aperture
9. Rear stowage bin 10. Drive sprocket
11. Gun cleaning rods 12. Smoke dischargers 13. Spare track link
14. Gun cradle above Leitkreuz blackout light

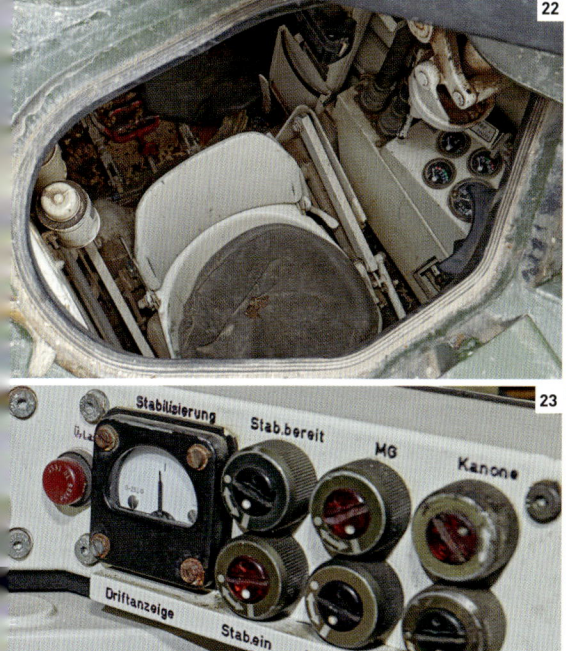

▷ **BTR-152**

Date 1950 **Origin** USSR
Weight 10.1 tonnes (11.1 tons)
Engine ZIS-123 petrol, 82 kW (110 hp)
Main armament 7.62 mm SGMB machine-gun

The six-wheeled BTR-152 carried 15 troops within its welded-steel body. Later models had an armoured roof and a central tyre-pressure regulation system. More than 12,500 BTR-152s of all variants, made for the Soviet military and for export, saw decades of service around the world.

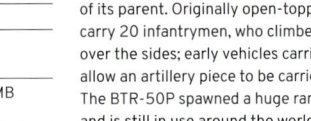

△ **FV603 Saracen**

Date 1952 **Origin** UK
Weight 10.2 tonnes (11.2 tons)
Engine Rolls-Royce B80 Mk 6A petrol, 119 kW (160 hp)
Main armament .30 Browning M1919 machine-gun

Able to carry 10 troops, the Saracen was armed with a .30 Browning machine-gun. Its drivetrain gave excellent mobility. There were command-vehicle and ambulance variants, and an internal security version was used in Northern Ireland. It was replaced by the FV432.

△ **BTR-50P**

Date 1954 **Origin** USSR
Weight 14.2 tonnes (15.7 tons)
Engine Model V6 diesel, 179 kW (240 hp)
Main armament 7.62 mm SGMB machine-gun

Based on the Soviet PT-76 light tank chassis, the BTR-50P shared the amphibious capability of its parent. Originally open-topped, it could carry 20 infantrymen, who climbed in and out over the sides; early vehicles carried a ramp to allow an artillery piece to be carried on the deck. The BTR-50P spawned a huge range of variants and is still in use around the world.

◁ **M113A1**

Date 1960 **Origin** USA
Weight 11 tonnes (12.1 tons)
Engine Detroit Diesel 6V-53 diesel, 158 kW (212 hp)
Main armament .50 Browning M2 machine-gun

The petrol engine that powered early M113s was soon replaced by a diesel. In the Vietnam War, US and South Vietnamese forces valued the mobility of their M113s, which they modified with extra machine-guns and armour. More than 80,000 M113s in over 40 variants served with at least 44 countries. Many users made their own upgrades to keep the vehicles operational in the 21st century.

▷ **FV432 Bulldog**

Date 1963 **Origin** UK
Weight 15.2 tonnes (16.8 tons)
Engine Rolls-Royce K60 No4 Mk 4F multifuel, 179 kW (240 hp)
Main armament 7.62 mm L7 machine-gun

The FV432 has been the standard British APC since the 1960s. Developed for service in Iraq and Afghanistan, the Bulldog, the latest variant, features extra armour, a new engine and transmission, and NBC (nuclear, biological, and chemical) protection. It is part of the FV430 family, which also includes mortar, ambulance, command, communications, and recovery vehicles.

Troop Carriers

Armoured personnel carriers (APCs) are generally intended as troop transports, with infantry dismounting to fight on foot when they encounter the enemy. In widespread use throughout the Cold War, APCs often shared automotive components with their more heavily armed tank counterparts, which made them cheaper to build and easier to maintain. Some states, such as the USSR, West Germany, and the UK, split their APC fleets, using tracked infantry fighting vehicles for front line action and wheeled vehicles to deliver reinforcements or perform defensive roles.

△ AAV7A1

Date 1971 **Origin** USA
Weight 25.3 tonnes (27.9 tons)
Engine Cummins VT400 diesel, 298 kW (400 hp)
Main armament .50 Browning M2 machine-gun, MK 19 40 mm Automatic Grenade Launcher

With capacity for 25 troops, the AAV7A1 (originally LVTP-7) was built as an amphibious tractor, or "amtrac", for the US Marine Corps. The latest of numerous upgrades incorporates automotive components from the M2 Bradley infantry fighting vehicle. Around 1,500 have been made, with worldwide sales.

△ Véhicule de l'Avant Blindé

Date 1976 **Origin** France
Weight 13 tonnes (14.3 tons)
Engine Renault MIDS 06-20-45 diesel, 164 kW (220 hp)
Main armament .50 Browning M2 machine-gun

This amphibious armoured personnel carrier can hold 10 infantry personnel. Designed to complement the tracked AMX-10P, the VAB has had a multitude of upgrades, including NBC protection. It continues in French service and has been used in UN peacekeeping roles. Variants include command-post, radar-carrier, and anti-aircraft missile launcher versions.

Pneumatic tyres

▽ Bv206

Date 1980 **Origin** Sweden
Weight 6.6 tonnes (7.3 tons)
Engine Ford V6 petrol, 101 kW (136 hp)
Main armament None

Light enough to be lifted by larger helicopters, the Bandvagn ("tracked vehicle") 206 is an articulated, all-terrain carrier. An armoured version, the Bv206S, provides protection for the occupants against small arms fire, and is in service with several national armed forces in troop-carrier and ambulance roles.

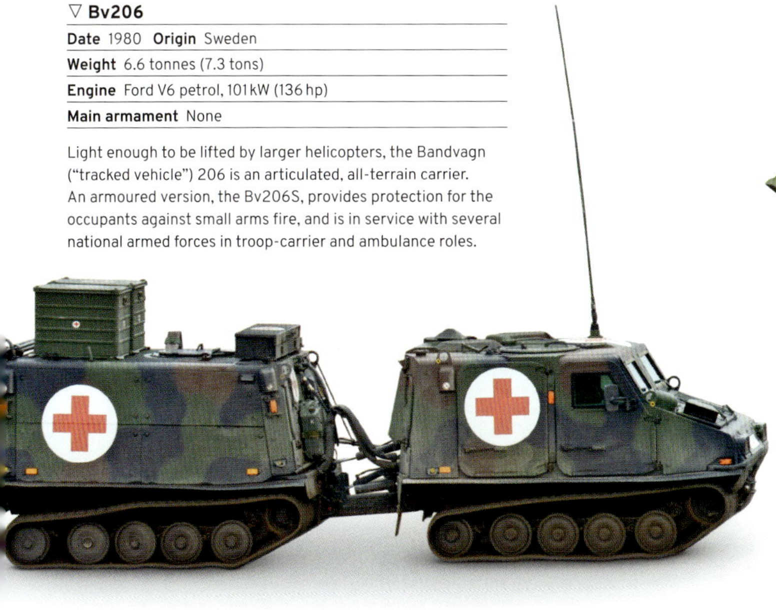

△ LAV-25

Date 1983 **Origin** USA
Weight 12.9 tonnes (14.2 tons)
Engine Detroit Diesel 6V53T diesel, 205 kW (275 hp)
Main armament 25 mm M242 cannon

The LAV-25, a version of the MOWAG Piranha-1 adapted for the US Marine Corps, is used mainly for reconnaissance, with antitank, command, and recovery variants. Upgrades include improved armour, suspension, and sights. It has a crew of three and can carry six troops.

Infantry Fighting Vehicles

The thin armour, light firepower, and limited mobility of armoured personnel carriers (APCs) left them vulnerable to attack. Military designers responded by developing a new generation of vehicles able to fight alongside tanks. These infantry fighting vehicles (IFVs) carried more potent guns and gave their occupants greater protection against conventional munitions and the atmospheric contamination expected on a nuclear battlefield. The Soviet BMP-1 set the template for IFV design. Western nations, concerned by this innovative vehicle, soon developed their own IFVs.

△ Schützenpanzer Lang HS.30
Date 1958 **Origin** West Germany
Weight 14.6 tonnes (16.1 tons)
Engine Rolls-Royce B81 Mark 80F petrol, 164 kW (220 hp)
Main armament 20 mm Hispano-Suiza HS.820 cannon

The low-profile Schützenpanzer Lang had capacity for five troops, who entered and left via roof hatches. To comply with the prevailing West German military doctrine that tanks, infantry, and troop carriers were to fight alongside each other, the vehicle was more heavily armed and armoured than contemporary APCs. Expensive upgrading resolved initial mechanical problems and unreliability.

73 mm gun can fire 8–10 rounds per minute

△ BMP-1
Date 1966 **Origin** USSR
Weight 13.5 tonnes (14.9 tons)
Engine UTD 20 diesel, 224 kW (300 hp)
Main armament 73 mm 2A28 smoothbore gun

The first true IFV, the well-armoured BMP-1 had a powerful main gun, an antitank missile launcher, and space for 10 troops, who could fire their weapons from inside the vehicle. However, it was cramped, vulnerable to mines, and its fuel tanks were located between the infantry's seats.

Smoke grenade dischargers

△ Marder 1
Date 1971 **Origin** West Germany
Weight 35 tonnes (38.6 tons)
Engine MTU MB 833 Ea-500 diesel, 447 kW (600 hp)
Main armament 20 mm Rheinmetall Rh202 cannon

Early versions of the Marder, the first Western IFV, had a remotely controlled machine-gun over the rear entry and firing ports for six troops. Thicker armour and a MILAN antitank missile launcher were added later. The Marder served with German forces during the Cold War, and subsequently in Kosovo and Afghanistan; vehicles supplied to Ukraine have seen action against Russian forces.

△ AMX 10P
Date 1973 **Origin** France
Weight 14.5 tonnes (16 tons)
Engine Hispano-Suiza HS 115 diesel, 194 kW (260 hp)
Main armament 20 mm Nexter M693 cannon

The AMX 10P was the inaugural French IFV. Its three-man crew and eight infantry passengers entered and exited via a ramp at the rear. Export destinations included Saudi Arabia, Singapore, and Indonesia, the latter receiving a marine-corps variant equipped with a 90 mm gun.

25 mm cannon has an effective range of 3 km (1 3/4 miles)

Rear stowage bin

▷ AIFV (Armoured Infantry Fighting Vehicle)
Date 1977 **Origin** USA
Weight 13.7 tonnes (15.1 tons)
Engine Detroit Diesel 6V-53T diesel, 199 kW (267 hp)
Main armament 25 mm Oerlikon KBA-B02 cannon

Based on the M113 APC, the AIFV had a gun turret, improved armour, an infantry capacity of seven, and firing ports. The Netherlands, the largest user, renamed it the YPR-765. Dutch forces operated over 2,000 vehicles in several variants; some saw action in Afghanistan.

▽ M2 Bradley

Date 1983	Origin USA

Weight 32.1 tonnes (35.4 tons)
Engine Cummins VTA-903T diesel, 447 kW (600 hp)
Main armament 25 mm M242 cannon

Despite a long and problematic development, and initial unreliability solved by costly modification, the M2 Bradley has since shown its worth in combat, with its TOW antitank missile launcher proving particularly effective. The three crew members and six troops enter and leave via roof hatches. Upgrades have improved its armour, sights, and electronic systems, and added space for a seventh soldier.

Radio antenna

Bar armour protects against RPGs

△ Warrior

Date 1986	Origin UK

Weight 28 tonnes (30.9 tons)
Engine Perkins CV-8 TCA diesel, 410 kW (550 hp)
Main armament 30 mm L21A1 RARDEN cannon

The Warrior originally had capacity for seven troops, but this upgraded version can carry only six. Other changes included giving the seats better protection against mine blasts and improving the suspension and crew visibility. Electronic counter-measures and extra armour were added for service in the Gulf, the Balkans, and Afghanistan. Repair, recovery, and command-post variants have since been developed.

Firing port (one of seven)

△ Type 89

Date 1989	Origin Japan

Weight 27 tonnes (29.8 tons)
Engine Mitsubishi 6SY31 WA diesel, 447 kW (600 hp)
Main armament 35 mm Oerlikon KDE cannon

In addition to its 35 mm cannon, the Type 89 carries a Type 79 antitank missile on each side of its turret. Developed during the 1980s and used solely by Japan, the Type 89 is similar to Soviet vehicles in that its seven infantry passengers enter through two rear doors; Western designs typically have a single door or ramp.

▷ BMP-3

Date 1990	Origin USSR

Weight 18.7 tonnes (20.6 tons)
Engine UTD 29M diesel, 373 kW (500 hp)
Main armament 1 x 100 mm 2A70 smoothbore gun, 1 x 30 mm 2A72 cannon

The Soviet-designed BMP-3 is heavily armed for an IFV. It is bigger and more spacious inside than the BMP-2 on which it is based. To get in and out, passengers must climb over the engine at the rear. Newer versions have explosive reactive armour (ERA) and active protection systems. BMP-3s have seen combat in Chechnya, Yemen, and Ukraine.

Transporting Special Forces

The birth of special forces in World War II called for transport tailored to the activities of these units, such as covert raids, behind-the-lines operations, or extracting personnel. Standard trucks, for example, might be modified to give greater range and more capacity for the bespoke weaponry and supplies of their special forces passengers, or enable them to cope with unusually challenging terrain. Likewise, the need for stealth and speed for the rapid insertion of troops led to the development of dedicated vehicles, boats, and aircraft.

Special forces became adept at adopting and adapting civilian technology. Manufacturers, in turn, gained kudos by working with special forces, and could sometimes incorporate military innovations into their products.

French naval commandos use a fast rigid inflatable boat (RIB) off the coast of Djibouti in 1985. The French military retained a base in Djibouti after the country's independence, which they used for hot-weather and desert training.

Tanks of Non-aligned Nations

In the Cold War, non-aligned nations often tried to plot a course between the two rival power blocs. Yugoslavia, for example, bought tanks from both sides; Switzerland and Sweden purchased from the West while they built up their own design and manufacturing ability; Finland bought Soviet tanks.

▽ **Type 61**
Date 1961 **Origin** Japan
Weight 35 tonnes (38.6 tons)
Engine Mitsubishi 12HM21WT diesel, 425 kW (570 hp)
Main armament 90 mm L/52 rifled gun

The Type 61 was Japan's first post-World War II tank. Rather than buying American tanks, which proved too large and heavy for Japanese crew and the country's terrain, a decision was taken to commission a home-grown vehicle. In all, 560 Type 61s were built; none were exported or saw combat.

△ **Strv 74**
Date 1958 **Origin** Sweden
Weight 22.5 tonnes (24.8 tons)
Engine 2 x Scania-Vabis 603/1 diesels, 127 kW (170 hp) each
Main armament 75 mm Strv 74 rifled gun

A modification of Sweden's 1940s-vintage m/42 tank, the Strv 74 was given a new, more powerful gun housed in a large but thinly armoured turret. The 225 Strv 74 conversions supplemented the Centurion in Swedish Army tank units until the late 1960s.

Muzzle brake

▷ **Vijayanta**
Date 1965 **Origin** India
Weight 39 tonnes (43 tons)
Engine Leyland L60 diesel, 399 kW (535 hp)
Main armament 105 mm L7A2 L/52 rifled gun

Built in India, the Vijayanta was a licensed version of the privately developed British Vickers Mark 1 export tank. Using the same gun as the Centurion, which was already in use in India, it had the engine and transmission from the Chieftain. Some 2,200 were built.

▷ **Strv 103 (S-Tank)**
Date 1967 **Origin** Sweden
Weight 39.6 tonnes (43.7 tons)
Engine Rolls-Royce K60 multifuel, 179 kW (240 hp) and Caterpillar 553 gas turbine, 365 kW (490 hp)
Main armament 105 mm Bofors L/62 rifled gun

The Strv 103's autoloading gun – fixed within the hull – was aimed by steering and adjusting the height of the hydropneumatic suspension. A low, turretless profile and a second, rear-facing driver made the Strv 103 extremely effective as an ambush vehicle, striking at the enemy then reversing to escape.

Barrel clamp

Towing hitch

◁ **Type 74**
Date 1975 **Origin** Japan
Weight 38 tonnes (41.9 tons)
Engine Mitsubishi 10ZF diesel, 537 kW (720 hp)
Main armament 105 mm L7 L/52 rifled gun

The Type 74 was Japan's response to the Soviet T-62, but a long gestation period meant it was slow to enter service. Its hydropneumatic suspension was able to raise, lower, or incline the vehicle to suit terrain being travelled over. Improved night vision systems and a laser rangefinder were among upgrades.

TANKS OF NON-ALIGNED NATIONS • 215

▷ **Merkava 1**
Date 1979 **Origin** Israel
Weight 59.9 tonnes (66 tons)
Engine Continental AVDS-1790-6A diesel, 671 kW (900 hp)
Main armament 105 mm M68 L/52 rifled gun

Lessons learned from the 1973 Yom Kippur War were incorporated into the design of the Merkava, which emphasized crew protection. The engine was front-mounted to allow for a door at the rear so that casualties could be evacuated or ammunition taken on board under fire. The Mark 1 was first used in Lebanon in 1982; significant redesigns resulted in the Mark 2 and 3. All three received further upgrades.

105 mm main gun

◁ **Strv 104**
Date 1985 **Origin** Sweden
Weight 54 tonnes (59.5 tons)
Engine Continental AVDS-1790-2DC diesel, 559 kW (750 hp)
Main armament 105 mm L7 L/52 rifled gun

In the 1950s, the Swedish Army bought around 600 British Centurions. With many upgrades carried out over the next 30 years, the eighty Strv 104 conversions were the most advanced. The Strv 104s had a more powerful engine, explosive reactive armour (ERA), modernized suspension, improved sights, and night vision. The tank was retired in 2003.

Driver's periscope

Wide tracks for winter conditions

Cold War Land Vehicles

During the Cold War era, many armies moved to full mechanization and motorization. As the world divided its allegiances between NATO and the Warsaw Pact, and new export markets opened, it became important to standardize vehicle types, features, and performance to ensure good interoperability between armed forces. The American M35 series 2½-ton 6×6 cargo truck, for example, was adopted by more than 45 nations worldwide. The new generations of military trucks and light vehicles progressively took advantage of advances in engine design, ergonomics, and off-road capability.

△ **Land Rover**
Date 1948 **Origin** UK
Engine 1.6-litre four-cylinder petrol, 37.3 kW (50 hp)
Payload c.500 kg (1,100 lb)

The Land Rover began as a four-wheel-drive civilian utility vehicle in 1948, but it was soon adopted and repurposed by the British military. Many specialist variants emerged during the 1950s and 1960s; seen here is a standard early model.

△ **M35 series 2½-ton 6×6 cargo truck**
Date 1949 **Origin** USA
Engine Reo or Continental petrol, 108.9 kW (146 hp)
Payload 4,500 kg (9,900 lb)

The M35 series trucks were produced between 1950 and 1988, during which time they experienced many combat deployments. The 6×6 configuration gave good off-road performance, while on-road these trucks could carry loads of up to about 4.5 tonnes (5 tons).

Blue flag signifies a lead vehicle in a military convoy

△ **Bedford RL Recovery Vehicle**
Date 1961 **Origin** UK
Engine 6-cylinder petrol, 82 kW (110 hp)
Payload 3,000 kg (6,614 lb)

The Bedford RL – and its numerous variant forms – served as the British Army's main medium truck during the early part of the Cold War. Produced from 1953 until the early 1970s, the RL was eventually replaced by the Bedford MK/MJ. When fitted out with wrecking gear, this rugged 4×4 could recover vehicles up to its own weight.

◁ **GAZ-66**
Date 1964 **Origin** USSR
Engine ZMZ-66-06 V8 petrol, 89.5 kW (120 hp)
Payload Approx. 2,000 kg (4,410 lb)

Developed by the Gorky Automobile Plant, this 4×4 was a core Warsaw Pact truck, with hundreds of thousands being built from 1964 to 1998 – many are still in use around the world. The truck embodied the typical Soviet vehicle traits of reliability and simplicity, although later variants acquired "frills" such as central tyre inflation.

COLD WAR LAND VEHICLES · 217

△ **Steyr-Daimler-Puch Pinzgauer**
Date 1975 Origin Austria/UK
Engine 4-cylinder petrol, 63.4 kW (85 hp)
Payload 1,000 kg (2,200 lb)

With a backbone-tube chassis and coil-sprung axles, this 4×4 (also available as a 6×6) had a top speed of 110 km/h (68 mph) and capacity for 10 passengers. A simple design and good cargo space won it popularity with European armies.

△ **Mercedes-Benz G Wagon Wolf**
Date 1979 Origin West Germany/Austria
Engine 2.3-litre M 102 E 23, 173 kW (232 hp)
Payload Approx. 1,000 kg (2,200 lb)

A vehicle popular with both civilian and military users, Mercedes' G-class was developed in West Germany and Austria from the early 1970s. When adopted by the Bundeswehr – the German armed forces – it acquired the "Wolf" nickname.

◁ **Humvee (High Mobility Multipurpose Wheeled Vehicle)**
Date 1985 Origin USA
Engine 6.2-litre Detroit Diesel V8, 160.3 kW (215 hp)
Payload 1,136 kg (2,500 lb)

The Humvee became the defining US military vehicle of the 1990s and 2000s. The Humvee has been produced in a wide range of configurations, including troop carrier, antitank missile platform, and ambulance variants.

Wide body profile
gives good stability

Entering the Jet Age

The first operational combat jets entered service towards the end of World War II, but were too late to influence the outcome of the air war. In the 1950s and 60s, however, jet power reset the parameters of combat aircraft, greatly increasing levels of performance and lethality.

Korean War jets
Two McDonnell F2H-2 Banshee jets cruise high over Wonsan Harbor, North Korea, looking for targets during the Korean War. The Banshee's maximum speed was 933 km/h (580 mph).

On 14 October 1947, in the skies over Muroc Dry Lake in the Mojave Desert of California, USAF captain Charles E. Yeager piloted an experimental Bell X-1 rocket-propelled aircraft to a speed of 1,127 km/h (700 mph). In doing so, Yeager became the first human to break the sound barrier in level flight. Yeager's adventure in speed was a seminal moment in the history of the jet age.

Going supersonic

During the second half of the 1940s, many air forces began to make the switch from piston-engined aircraft to jets, particularly in terms of their fighter complement. While the first generations of jet fighters, such as the British De Havilland Vampire and the Soviet Mikoyan-Gurevich MiG-9, were only capable of subsonic speeds, by the start of the 1950s, lessons learned from Yeager's landmark flight laid the foundations for supersonic jets to become a practical reality. The Korean War of 1950–53 saw the first clashes between transonic (close to the speed of sound) fighters, such as the North American F-86 Sabre and the Soviet MiG-15, both of which used turbojet engines and a swept-wing design.

As the 1950s progressed, increasing numbers of military aircraft acquired true supersonic capability in level flight, assisted by the adoption of newly developed afterburner technology. An afterburner is a device that injects fuel into the hot exhaust gases produced by the engine and burns it to provide additional thrust.

Among these supersonic pioneers were the American F-100 Super Sabre and F-105 Thunderchief, and the Soviet MiG-19 "Farmer" and MiG-21 "Fishbed". Not only were jets now becoming very fast – some could fly at Mach 2+ – but they also possessed astonishing climb rates, even with heavy ordnance loads. However, jets consumed large amounts of fuel. To prolong flights and extend ranges, effective methods of air-to-air refuelling were developed, whereby fuel could be transferred in-flight from a tanker aircraft to a receiving jet.

The fast new jet fighters changed the nature of air battles, because high speeds made line-of-sight gun combat increasingly difficult. As a result, the mid-1950s saw the start of a shift towards air-to-air missiles (AAMs).

Two examples were the Soviet RS-1U AAM, which "rode" a radar beam, and the American radar- and infrared-guided Hughes AIM-4F Super Falcon.

Heavy lift

The sheer power of jet engines made them ideal for heavyweight aircraft. Cold War air forces on both sides of the Iron Curtain raced to develop new strategic bombers capable of carrying massive thermonuclear devices across huge distances. The most successful of these designs was the Boeing B-52 Stratofortress, powered by eight Pratt & Whitney turbojets and with a wingspan exceeding 56 m (185 ft).

Manston Meteor
The Gloster Meteor F Mark I was Britain's first jet fighter and the Allies' only jet aircraft to perform combat missions in World War II. The RAF's 616 Squadron based at Manston in Kent, England, was the first to operate Meteors.

The B-52D variant, in service from 1956, could carry 19,090 kg (42,000 lb) of conventional or nuclear ordnance up to 13,418 km (8,338 miles) without refuelling. Such was the integrity of the aircraft design that the B-52 is still operational, more than 70 years after its introduction.

Other early jet bombers included the Soviet Myasishchev M-4 "Bison" and a trio of "V-bombers" developed by Britain during the 1950s as its strategic nuclear force: the Vickers Valiant, Handley Page Victor, and Avro Vulcan. The Vulcan, with its striking delta-wing, had exceptionally powerful performance. In 1960, the US introduced the Convair B-58 Hustler, the first operational bomber that could reach Mach 2.

By this time, the turbojet-powered logistical and support aircraft had also entered service. The Boeing KC-135 Stratotanker, for example, which was based on Boeing's 367-80 transport demonstrator, entered service with the USAF in 1957 as an air-to-air refuelling aircraft. In almost every domain of military aviation, the switch to jet power was taking place.

Flying wing
The Northrop YB-49 – a prototype jet-powered American heavy bomber – takes to the air for its first flight on 21 October 1947. Its "flying wing" design later led to the development of the B-2 Spirit, also known as the Stealth Bomber.

> "Flying fighters is **fun**. Flying bombers is **important**."
> USAF GENERAL CURTIS EMERSON LEMAY

TALKING POINT

Wernher von Braun

German engineer Wernher von Braun (1912–77) was drawn into rocket research by a fascination with the idea of space flight. In the mid-1930s, he experimented with installing rockets in aircraft: a Heinkel He 112 he converted was the first plane to be powered by a liquid-fuelled rocket engine. He also produced designs for a rocket-powered interceptor aircraft, but it was never built. In World War II, von Braun oversaw development of the V-2 ballistic missile. His work paved the way for the rocket planes introduced by Germany in the war's latter stages. After emigrating to the US at the war's end, he became a leading figure in the US space programme, rising to director of NASA's Marshall Space Flight Center in Alabama.

Wernher von Braun sits behind his desk at the NASA Space Flight Center in 1964. A charismatic public speaker, he became a well-known scientist and engineer in the US.

220 • 1945–1989

▽ **Mikoyan-Gurevich MiG-17**
Date 1951 **Origin** USSR
Engine 2,289–3,367 kg (5,046–7,423 lb) thrust Klimov VK-1F afterburning turbojet
Top speed 1,145 km/h (711 mph)

A modification of the Mig-15, this successful transonic (near speed of sound) fighter was kept effective into the 1960s by adding an afterburner. China built its Shenyang J-5 version from 1966 to 1986.

△ **Hawker Hunter F Mk1**
Date 1954 **Origin** UK
Engine 3,447 kg (7,600 lb) thrust Rolls-Royce Avon 113 turbojet
Top speed 1,130 km/h (702 mph)

Aided by its compact Rolls-Royce Avon engine, the long-serving Hunter was among the best of the early jet fighters. Designed by Sydney Camm, the Hunter's prototype set a world air speed record in 1953 of 1,171 km/h (727 mph).

Thin, stubby wings had span of just 6.9 m (21 ft 11 in)

△ **Lockheed F-104G Starfighter**
Date 1958 **Origin** USA
Engine 7,484 kg (16,500 lb) thrust General Electric J-79 turbojet
Top speed 2,125 km/h (1,328 mph)

The first fighter capable of sustained flight at speeds in excess of Mach 2, this aircraft was known as "the missile with a man in it". The Starfighter served both as a tactical fighter and a day-night interceptor.

▽ **Republic F-105D Thunderchief**
Date 1958 **Origin** USA
Engine 11,113 kg (24,500 lb) thrust Pratt & Whitney J-75 turbojet
Top speed 2,208 km/h (1,372 mph)

The largest single-seat, single-engined fighter-bomber ever made, Republic's Thunderchief could fly supersonic at sea level and reach Mach 2 at altitude. The "Thud", as it was known, was at the forefront of combat during the early part of the Vietnam War.

20 mm M61 Vulcan rotary cannon for air-to-air or air-to-ground engagements

Jet Fighters

One of the legacies of World War II was a tremendous advance in the development of the jet engine. Fighters and fighter-bombers in the postwar era increasingly had to be jet-powered to be competitive, and aircraft designs were continually evolving in the quest for supersonic speeds. Ever more powerful engines and an increasing understanding of supersonic aerodynamics, fuelled by Cold War paranoia and big military research and development budgets, saw top speeds rise from barely breaking the sound barrier in a dive to greater than Mach 2 – twice the speed of sound – in level flight.

▽ **Mikoyan-Gurevich MiG-21**
Date 1959 **Origin** USSR
Engine 5,740 kg (12,655 lb) thrust Tumansky R-11F-300 turbojet
Top speed 2,230 km/h (1,385 mph)

Although somewhat lacking in range and agility, the MiG-21, codenamed "Fishbed" by NATO, was an effective Mach 2-plus fighter-interceptor. Over 10,000 were built, more than any other supersonic fighter. A few are still in use around the world.

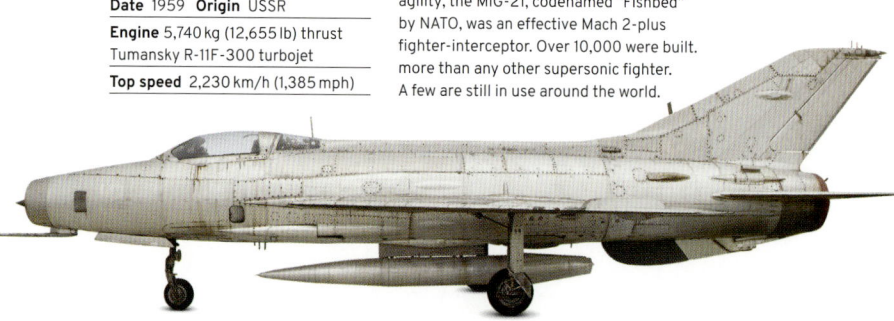

JET FIGHTERS · 221

△ **Chance Vought (F-8K) F8U-2 Crusader**
Date 1960 **Origin** USA
Engine 4,847–8,154 kg (10,700–18,000 lb) thrust Pratt & Whitney J57 afterburning turbojet
Top speed 1,975 km/h (1,225 mph)

The last US fighter with guns as its primary weapons, the carrier-borne F-8 Crusader was the US Navy's principal fleet-defence fighter in the late 1950s. Its wings tilted upwards to reduce take-off and landing speeds.

Stretched fuselage of IIIE allowed for a larger avionics bay and increased fuel capacity

△ **Dassault Mirage III**
Date 1961 **Origin** France
Engine 4,275–6,192 kg (9,436–13,668 lb) thrust SNECMA Atar 9C afterburning turbojet
Top speed 2,350 km/h (1,460 mph)

The delta-winged Mirage III interceptor was introduced by the French Air Force in 1961. The stretched IIIE fighter-bomber variant is shown here. Mirage IIIs have served with 21 nations.

Wings span 10.6 m (34 ft 11 in)

▽ **English Electric Lightning F6**
Date 1968 **Origin** UK
Engine 2 x 12,530–16,000 lb (5,684–7,257 kg) thrust Rolls-Royce Avon 301R turbojets
Top speed 2,400 km/h (1,500 mph)

With its stacked-engine design, the Lightning was the RAF's first supersonic jet and the only British-made Mach 2 fighter. The F1 entered service in 1960; the F6, seen here, had greater thrust and carried more fuel.

Military Transport Planes

Armies are perennially under pressure to carry out their operations faster and more efficiently, and – either for strategic or combat reasons – often on a wide geographic scale. This has led to the positioning of soldiers in bases around the globe, to establish garrisons that could be called upon in response to local events. The high cost of maintaining troops abroad prompted some nations to deposit tanks, vehicles, weaponry, and munitions in forward bases, and only transport troops to man the equipment when needed. While ships can carry larger loads, planes are a faster mode of ferrying personnel and military hardware – and speed may be a deciding factor in certain situations. Some military transporters have been converted from civilian aircraft, such as the Douglas C-47 Dakota (Skytrain), which began life as the DC-3 airliner; others, including the Lockheed C-130 Hercules, were designed specifically for military use, being able to take off from short, improvised runways and carry a heavy payload. Transport planes are costly to run and maintain, and they present large, relatively slow targets to an enemy, so no army can afford to rely on them as its sole means of moving troops and equipment.

A huge US Air Force Lockheed C-5 Galaxy transporter delivers a UH-60 Black Hawk helicopter to Latvia as part of a NATO exercise in 2017.

F-86 Sabre

Just as North American's P-51 Mustang had proved its worth helping the Allies win air superiority in World War II, the F-86 Sabre, the company's next major fighter, earned its combat spurs in the Korean War. In brutal dogfights in the skies above Korea, the Sabre had the edge over the Soviet Union's state-of-the-art, swept-wing MiG-15. One of the most graceful fighters ever built, the Sabre is the epitome of the "fighter pilot's fighter".

THE SABRE'S DESIGN combined a jet engine with a swept wing – two innovations in warplane technology introduced in the latter stages of World War II by Britain and Germany respectively. The engine of this low-wing fighter was fed by a flow of air from the nose intake, with exhaust gases venting via a tailpipe in the rear of the fuselage. A prototype, the XP-86, first flew in October 1947, exceeding Mach 1 the following year.

The Sabre entered USAF service as the F-86A in early 1949. Like most of its American fighter contemporaries, it was armed with six 0.5 in machine guns, each with a firing rate of approximately 1,100 rounds per minute. Thrust into frontline action after North Korean forces, backed by the Soviet Union and China, invaded South Korea in June 1950, the Sabre fought nose-to-nose in aerial duels against the Soviet MiG-15s of the communist forces. The nimble Sabre ultimately achieved a victory-to-loss ratio over its MiG adversary of better than four to one.

35-degree sweepback on both fin and tailplane

Wing is swept back by 35 degrees

Jetpipe is built to withstand high temperatures

Lateral airbrakes, one on either side of fuselage

Slotted wing flaps running from the fuselage to the ailerons extend to increase lift

SPECIFICATIONS

Model	North American F-86A Sabre, 1949
Origin	USA
Production	554
Construction	Aluminium and steel
Maximum weight	6,400 kg (14,108 lb)
Wingspan	11.3 m (37 ft 1½ in)
Engine	2,359 kg (5,200 lb) thrust General Electric J47-GE-7 turbojet
Length	11.4 m (37 ft 6 in)
Range	1,255 km (785 miles)
Top speed	1,102 km/h (685 mph)

REAR VIEW

FRONT VIEW

Designed for success
With its swept wing, gaping "mouth", bubble canopy, and well-proportioned overall design, the Sabre is one of the most distinctive and successful jet fighters in the history of aviation.

All-metal, flush-riveted stressed skin clads the oval-section fuselage

Bubble canopy provides excellent all-round visibility

M-3 machine guns, with 267 rounds per gun, mounted in nose

Hydraulic undercarriage is electrically controlled and sequenced

Nose-wheel door

EXTERIOR

The all-metal, flush-riveted, oval-section fuselage was aerodynamically efficient, and because the Sabre's engine was located within the fuselage and fed by a large intake in the nose, there were no drag-inducing engine pods or nacelles on the airframe. The result was a highly manœuvrable aircraft. The Sabre had a rather narrow-track undercarriage, due to the main wheels needing to retract into the fuselage.

1. Painted emblem **2.** Hydraulic nose wheel **3.** Recessed step for cockpit access **4.** One of three gunports on port side **5.** V-shaped windscreen (rounded on prototype) **6.** Pitot tube mounted on starboard wing **7.** Formation light set into starboard wing tip **8.** Fuel filler – maximum capacity is 87 gallons (397 litres) **9.** Port lateral airbrake **10.** Landing light (retracted) in wing **11.** Access panel for emergency engine disconnect **12.** External power receptacle and fuel filler on starboard side **13.** Fuel dump mast at rear of fuselage **14.** Stainless steel shroud for jetpipe **15.** Jetpipe

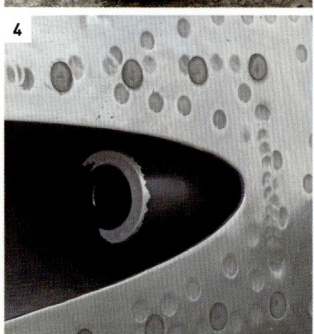
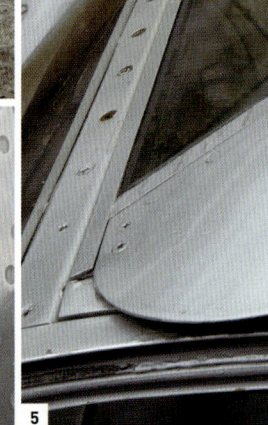

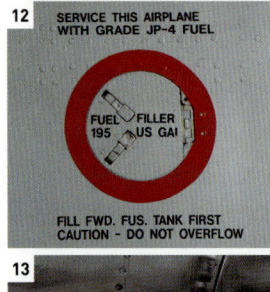
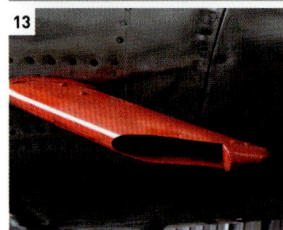

F-86 SABRE • 227

COCKPIT

The F-86A's bubble canopy – a holdover from North American's successful P-51 World War II fighter – gave the pilot unparalleled views in all directions. Inside the Sabre's well-designed cockpit, instruments were arranged in a neat and orderly fashion, with all flight controls placed within easy reach of the pilot. The controls for the engine, wing flaps, undercarriage, and airbrakes were on panels to the pilot's left, with the radio and electrical controls to his right.

16. Cockpit view 17. Gun sight with range (left) and span (centre) selectors 18. Flight instruments 19. Magnetic compass 20. Throttle and airbrake controls 21. Control column 22. Emergency hydraulic pump

Bombers and Ground-attack Aircraft

Cold War tensions led the West to fast-track the development of jet-engined bombers and ground-attack planes. The result was some truly impressive aircraft, such as the delta-wing Vulcan, the ultra-high-altitude Canberra, and the enormous Stratofortress. At first, Soviet jet-powered bomber design lagged behind Western efforts, since only turboprops had the range to reach the US and return. However, the USSR did produce the Tu-95 – the longest-range turboprop bomber ever in service, which is still operational today.

Straight wing design aided stability

Two-seat tandem cockpit

△ **English Electric Canberra**
Date 1951 Origin UK
Engine 2 x 3,357 kg (7,400 lb) thrust Rolls-Royce Avon RA7 109 turbojets
Top speed 933 km/h (580 mph)

Able to fly at high altitude and high speed, Britain's first jet bomber could evade early jet interceptors. In 1957, it set a new altitude record of 21,430 m (70,310 ft). Canberras served with many air forces.

Wing swept back at 35-degree angle

△ **Tupolev Tu-95 "Bear"**
Date 1956 Origin USSR
Engine 4 x 10,800 kW (14,483 shp) Kuznetsov NK-12M turboprops
Top speed 925 km/h (575 mph)

Combining sweptback wings and contra-rotating propellers, the Tu-95 has an exceptional range, able to fly around 15,000 km (9,320 miles) fully laden without refuelling. It is likely to remain in service until 2040.

Turboprop engine

Air intake for engines (two in each wing root)

△ **Avro 698 Vulcan**
Date 1956 Origin UK
Engine 4 x 7,711–9,072 kg (17,000–20,000 lb) thrust Bristol Siddeley Olympus turbojets
Top speed 1,040 km/h (646 mph)

The Vulcan, with its innovative delta-wing design, spearheaded Britain's nuclear deterrent. The aircraft delivered heavy payload capacity, high subsonic speed at altitude, and long range.

▽ **Sukhoi Su-7B**
Date 1961 Origin USSR
Engine 6,800–10,000 kg (15,000–22,000 lb) thrust Lyulka AL-7F afterburning turbojet
Top speed 2,150 km/h (1,336 mph)

The Su-7B developed from a fighter – the Su-7A – into a ground-attack version in the late 1950s. It was the first Soviet aircraft with an all-moving tailplane and movable-cone air intake.

Red star Soviet insignia

BOMBERS AND GROUND-ATTACK AIRCRAFT · 229

▽ Convair B-58 Hustler
Date 1960 **Origin** USA
Engine 4 x 4,400–7,076 kg (9,700–15,600 lb) thrust General Electric J79-GE-5A/B afterburning turbojets
Top speed 2,132 km/h (1,325 mph)

Although this delta-wing, Mach 2-capable nuclear bomber included many of the latest technological advances, crews found it difficult to fly. It was also more costly to operate than the Stratofortress and other bombers.

Afterburning turbojet engine (one of four)

Under-fuselage fuel pod

△ Boeing B-52 Stratofortress
Date 1955 **Origin** USA
Engine 8 x 5,488 kg (12,100 lb) thrust Pratt & Whitney J57 turbojets, later 7,711 kg (17,000 lb) thrust turbofans
Top speed 1,046 km/h (650 mph)

Operational since 1955, the B-52 was designed to carry nuclear warheads but evolved into a launch platform for cruise missiles and a conventional long-range bomber of awesome power. Upgraded B-52s are expected to serve into the 2040s.

▽ Grumman A-6 Intruder
Date 1963 **Origin** USA
Engine 2 x 4,218 kg (9,300 lb) thrust Pratt and Whitney J52-P-8B turbojets
Top speed 1,041 km/h (647 mph)

The Intruder was developed for the US Navy and Marine Corps as an all-weather long-range attack aircraft with high subsonic performance at low altitude. First flown in 1960, it entered service in 1963 and saw combat in the Vietnam War and the 1991 Gulf War.

Wings fold for carrier use

▽ Douglas A-4 Skyhawk
Date 1956 **Origin** USA
Engine 3,493 kg (7,700 lb) thrust Curtiss-Wright J65, later 3,856–4,218 kg (8,500–9,300 lb) thrust Pratt & Whitney J52 turbojet
Top speed 1,083 km/h (673 mph)

The compact, agile, and ultra-light ground-attack Skyhawk was designed in the early 1950s for the US Navy and Marine Corps. Its delta wing was so small it did not need to fold for storage on carriers.

In-flight refuelling probe

Single 20 mm Colt Mk 12 cannon, with 200 rounds of ammunition, in each wing root

△ Bell UH-1B Iroquois "Huey"
Date 1959 **Origin** USA
Engine 716 kW (960 shp) Lycoming YT53-L-5 turboshaft
Top speed 217 km/h (135 mph)

A prototype of the UH-1, the US Army's first turbine helicopter, flew in 1956; the UH-1B, shown here, was larger, heavier, and twice as powerful. Largely retired from the US military, some UH-1 variants still serve with other nations' forces. Over 16,000 were built.

△ Westland Wessex HAS3
Date 1967 **Origin** UK
Engine 1,193 kW (1,600 shp) Napier Gazelle 18 Mk165 turboshaft
Top speed 204 km/h (127 mph)

The HAS3 was a version of the original Wessex Mk1 upgraded for antisubmarine warfare. Its revolutionary Type 195 sonar system was more expensive than the helicopter itself.

△ Bell AH-1 Cobra
Date 1967 **Origin** USA
Engine 1,044 kW (1,400 shp) Lycoming T53-13 turboshaft
Top speed 315 km/h (196 mph)

The world's first dedicated helicopter gunship, the agile, heavily armoured Cobra, was developed for use in the Vietnam War. It combined a narrow, hard-to-hit fuselage with the dynamic components of the Huey.

△ Messerschmitt-Bölkow-Blohm MBB Bo105CB
Date 1970 **Origin** Germany
Engine 2 x 313 kW (420 shp) Allison 250-C20B turboshafts
Top speed 270 km/h (168 mph)

Germany's first domestically produced post-World War II helicopter, the Bo105 was also the first four–five-seat twin-engined utility design with rear loading capability. Its composite main rotor blades and rigid titanium rotor head gave exceptional manoeuvrability.

△ SA Gazelle
Date 1973 **Origin** France
Engine 440 kW (590 shp) Turbomeca Astazou IIIA turboshaft
Top speed 310 km/h (193 mph)

Initially produced by Sud Aviation and subsequently by Aérospatiale, the compact and agile Gazelle was used for observation, liaison, and pilot training. It was the first helicopter with a fenestron, or fantail – a ducted multi-blade tail.

Military Helicopters

Gas-turbine engines for helicopters were introduced in the mid-1950s. The new engines – which were lighter, more powerful, and more reliable than their piston forerunners – improved helicopter performance, lift capacity, and safety. They also opened up fresh roles for helicopters, from search and rescue (SAR) work and antisubmarine warfare (ASW) to infantry assault and medevac duties. During the Vietnam War, the first generation of pure combat helicopters emerged. Computerized fire-control and precision-guided munitions (PGMs) made these aircraft increasingly lethal as the century wore on, especially against armour.

◁ **Mil Mi-24 "HIND"**
Date 1973 **Origin** USSR
Engine 2 x 1,638 kW (2,197 shp) Isotov TV3-117 turboshafts
Top speed 310 km/h (193 mph)

The Hind – the most heavily armed attack helicopter of the Cold War, and still in service – has a rotary-barrel heavy machine-gun under the nose, as well as under-wing pylons for carrying a variety of missile types.

▽ **Sikorsky UH-60 Black Hawk**
Date 1979 **Origin** USA
Engine 2 x 1,163 kW (1,560 shp) GE T700 turboshafts
Top speed 294 km/h (183 mph)

The mid-1960s-designed Black Hawk utility helicopter entered production in 1976 and active service three years later. It has been used by the US Army mainly in its troop-carrier configuration, which carries 11 soldiers. The most recent version of the Black Hawk is the UH-60M.

▷ **Boeing CH-47D Chinook**
Date 1982 **Origin** USA
Engine 2 x 2,796 kW (3,750 shp) Honeywell T55-L-712 turboshafts
Top speed 296 km/h (184 mph)

The large, tandem-rotor CH-47 Chinook is one of the heaviest-lifting Western helicopters. The CH-47D and CH-47F variants of this long-lived helicopter – dating back to the 1960s – remain in service today.

▽ **Boeing Apache AH-64**
Date 1984 **Origin** USA
Engine 2 x 1,491 kW (2,000 shp) GE T700-GE-701D turboshafts
Top speed 303 km/h (188 mph)

The Apache was the first helicopter with day-and-night, all-weather battlefield capabilities. Able to engage heavy armour and troop movements, this heavy attack helicopter has advanced defensive systems.

The Helicopter Comes of Age

Adaptable to many roles, the helicopter replaced a variety of fixed-wing military aircraft. Able to take off from and land in small spaces such as jungle clearings, it was ideal for delivering or retrieving troops or launching attacks, and, with its capacity to hover, it proved a more stable platform for firing munitions than many planes. The US produced gunships for use in the Vietnam War, while the Soviet Union developed the concept of the "flying infantry-support vehicle" to carry troops and weaponry for ground attack. One of these, the heavily armoured Soviet Mil Mi-24, codenamed "Hind" by NATO, was fast in the air, able to carry a range of weapon pods, and featured titanium armour to minimize its weight. Used against mujahideen guerrillas after the Soviets occupied Afghanistan (1979–89), the Hind became the target for shoulder-launched missiles from man-portable air-defence systems (MANPADS).

Known as the "flying tank", the Soviet Mil Mi-24 was widely exported. It is seen here in Peruvian army service against guerillas and drug gangs in 1989.

AH-64 Apache

Designed to destroy tanks, armoured vehicles, and air-defence units, the twin-engined AH-64 Apache employs many of the technologies that dominate the modern battlefield. Developed for the US Army by Hughes Helicopters and now produced by Boeing, the Apache was introduced in 1984. In service with a number of nations, it performed well in the Gulf War of 1991 and the invasions of Afghanistan in 2001 and Iraq in 2003.

THE APACHE'S MAIN ARMAMENT consists of up to 16 Hellfire missiles carried on the stub wings. Using target-acquisition and fire-control systems, the crew simply select targets and fire. The missiles lock-on to their target and travel to their destination, which can be up to 8km (5 miles) away, without further input from the crew. This capacity, called "fire-and-forget", allows the Apache to take evasive action immediately after it has launched its weapons. The wings can also carry a pair of rocket pods, each able to launch 19 unguided 70mm rockets. The Apache's chain gun, under the nose, can fire 625 rounds per minute, fed from a 1,200-round magazine by an electrically driven chain mechanism.

To make the slow-flying Apache less vulnerable, the helicopter is equipped with sensors that warn of incoming threats, as well as infrared-radiation suppression systems, which impede its detection by heat-seeking enemy missiles. Decoy flares fired from near the tail by the automatic defence system confuse any missiles that do manage to target the helicopter.

SPECIFICATIONS	
Name	AH-64 Apache
Type	Attack helicopter
Length	17.8 m (58 ft 5 in)
Height	4.64 m (15 ft 3 in)
Engines	2 x GE T700-GE-701D turboshafts
Range	500 km (310 miles)
Armament	AGM-114 Hellfire missiles
Cruise speed	265 km/h (165 mph)
Maximum speed	303 km/h (188 mph)

Apache Longbow
The Apache is in service with a number of armed forces around the world. This is the AH1 – a version of Boeing's AH-64D Apache Longbow built under licence by AugustaWestland for the British Army.

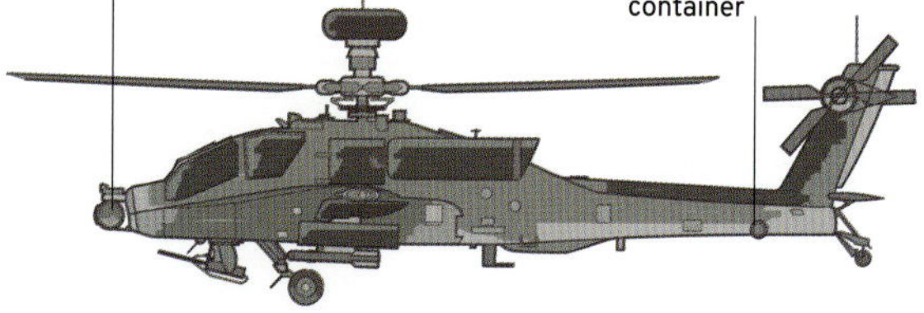

Mast-mounted Longbow radar gives a 360-degree electronic picture of the battlefield

Rotor blade is fully articulated

Turboshaft engine is protected by armour

HIDAS sensors

Stub wings

Wing pylons allow a range of different weapons to be carried

Target acquisition sensors

Flare container

Rocket pod

Missile launcher

EXTERIOR

The Apache's nose carries sensors for the Helicopter Integrated Defensive Aids System (HIDAS), which automatically detects and responds to enemy missiles. The main rotor blades, which attach to the hub via laminated steel straps, are easily folded or removed for transport. Wire cutters on the airframe can slice through power cables and telephone wires that might bring the aircraft down.

1. HIDAS sensors **2.** Main rotor assembly **3.** Wire cutter **4.** Decoy flare container **5.** Rocket pod **6.** M230 30mm chain gun **7.** Missile launcher (a training round is shown here)

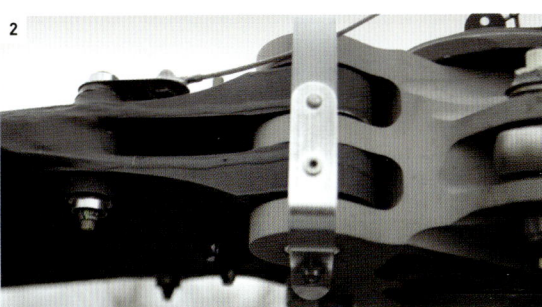

INTERIOR

The copilot/gunner sits in front of and below the pilot. Each crew member has a display that shows all the helicopter's systems. Both pilot and copilot are provided with flight and weapons controls in case one crew member needs to take full operation of the Apache. A "monocle" provides thermal (infrared) imaging and flight information in all conditions.

8. Control stick **9.** Canopy jettison handle **10.** Instrument panels **11.** Pilot's monocle

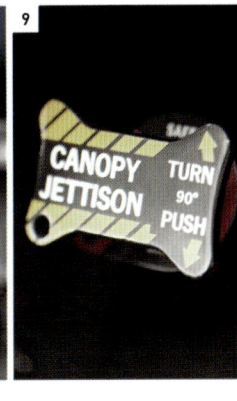

▷ Hawker Siddeley Harrier
Date 1970 **Origin** UK
Engine 9,752 kg (21,500 lb) thrust Rolls-Royce Pegasus 103 turbofan
Top speed 1,176 km/h (730 mph)

Equipped with vectored (directionable) thrust, the agile "Jump Jet" was the first successful vertical take-off and landing fighter. In the hands of a skilled pilot, it could be operated from any small clearing or ship deck.

Single-seat cockpit

Vectored thrust nozzle

Canard (forewing), one on either side, improved stability during landing and takeoff

◁ Saab 37 Viggen
Date 1971 **Origin** Sweden
Engine 7,348–12,750 kg (16,200–28,110 lb) thrust Volvo RM 8A/B afterburning turbofan
Top speed 2,231 km/h (1,386 mph)

The trailblazing Viggen was the first aircraft with both afterburners and thrust reversers, and the first to have a computer with integrated circuits. Easy to maintain, it was operable from a short stretch of road.

▽ McDonnell Douglas F-15 Eagle
Date 1972 **Origin** USA
Engine 2 x 7,915–11,340 kg (17,450–25,000 lb) thrust Pratt & Whitney F100-100/-220 afterburning turbofans
Top speed 2,660+ km/h (1,650+ mph)

Built as a response to the Soviet MiG-25, the twin-engined, multi-role F-15 Eagle emerged as one of the world's foremost fighter and strike aircraft, combining advanced avionics with immense power, high performance, and manoeuvrability.

Twin tail fins

Underwing fuel tank

Hughes APG-63 radar scanner in nose

Swing-wings pivot from a swept-back position for high-speed flight, to a more forward position for better low-speed manoeuvrability

▽ Grumman F-14 Tomcat
Date 1974 **Origin** USA
Engine 2 x 9,480 kg (20,900 lb) thrust Pratt & Whitney TF-30-P-414A afterburning turbofans
Top speed 2,485 km/h (1,544 mph)

Developed to guard US Navy carriers against long-range anti-ship missiles and enemy aircraft, the Tomcat remained in service until 2006, thanks to multiple upgrades to its weapons, engine, and radar.

Horizontal stabilizer is fully moveable

Two turbofan engines mounted in rear of aircraft

Front-line Aircraft

The introduction of turbofan engines, which produce more thrust than equivalent turbojets, provided extra power to front-line aircraft. A key advance in avionics was computerized "fly-by-wire" control, which allowed a previously unimaginable level of manoeuvrability. Offensive capabilities were boosted by "smart" weapons that could be guided towards their target with pinpoint accuracy, while the introduction of stealth technology on the F-117 Nighthawk was a milestone in the quest to avoid radar detection. Such innovations made developing all-new military aircraft increasingly costly.

▽ **General Dynamics F-16 Fighting Falcon**
Date 1974 **Origin** USA
Engine 7,781–12,973 kg (17,155–28,600 lb) thrust F110-GE-100 afterburning turbofans
Top speed 2,414 km/h (1,500 mph)

Fast and extremely agile, the lightweight F-16 was one of the first aircraft to use fly-by-wire controls. Built as an air-superiority day fighter for the USAF, the Fighting Falcon is still in production as a multi-role aircraft.

Ventral fin (port)

△ **Panavia Tornado GR1**
Date 1980 **Origin** UK/Germany/Italy
Engine 2 x 7,167 kg (15,800 lb) thrust Rolls-Royce Turbo Union RB199-103 turbofans
Top speed 2,337 km/h (1,452 mph)

The swing-wing, multi-role Tornado was designed to fly at a low-level and penetrate enemy defences. A joint UK, West German, and Italian development, it employed extensive fly-by-wire technology.

△ **Lockheed F-117 Nighthawk**
Date 1981 **Origin** USA
Engine 2 x 4,989 kg (10,800 lb) thrust General Electric F404-F1D2 turbofans
Top speed 993 km/h (617 mph)

The Nighthawk used sharply angled surfaces and a coating of radar-absorbent material to minimize its radar signature. Designed for night attacks with smart weapons, it could be flown on instruments alone.

V-shaped tail

▽ **Sukhoi Su-27**
Date 1984 **Origin** USSR
Engine 2 x 7,670–12,500 kg (16,910–27,560 lb) thrust Saturn/Lyulka AL-31F afterburning turbofans
Top speed 2,500 km/h (1,550 mph)

The twin-engined Su-27 has a good range, sophisticated avionics, and heavy armament. To minimize weight, large sections of this multi-role, super-manoeuvrable aircraft are made of titanium.

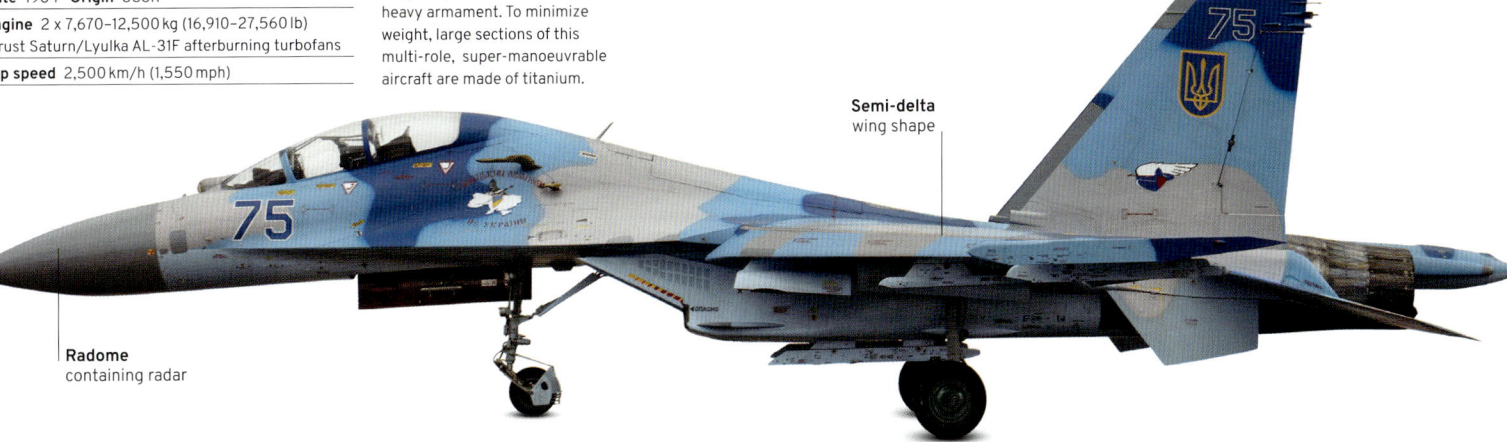

Semi-delta wing shape

Radome containing radar

Two-crew cockpit, with co-pilot behind pilot

Missile carried on wing pylon

Mikoyan MiG-29

Armed with the best short-range missiles of the day, the Soviet Mikoyan MiG-29 (codenamed "Fulcrum" by NATO) was one of the standout fighter-bombers of the 1980s and early 1990s. Exercises showed that it was almost impossible to defeat in a low-speed dogfight, its apparent invincibility down to astonishing agility aided by a pilot's helmet that could be used to aim weapons – the first appearance of this feature on a major fighter.

THE MIG-29 REPLACED the MiG-23 as the USSR's main tactical aircraft. Designed to counter the threat of American F-15s and F-16s, the tough, cheap-to-build MiG-29 prioritized raw performance over advanced electronics. As a result, early versions of the MiG-29 lacked a fly-by-wire system – an electronic interface between pilot and flight controls – which was standard on other agile fighters of the period.

In excess of 1,600 MiG-29s have been produced, including a carrier variant, and the planes have served with more than 40 air forces around the world. The most surprising operator was the US Air Force, which ran a secret training unit equipped with MiG-29s, bought in 1997 from Moldova. The latest advanced version of the aircraft, the MiG-35, made its debut in 2007. It can be fitted with thrust-vectoring control, making it the world's most manoeuvrable fighter.

SPECIFICATIONS	
Model	Mikoyan-Gurevich MiG-29, 1983
Origin	USSR
Production	1650
Construction	Largely aluminium; some composites
Maximum weight	18,480 kg (40,740 lb)
Engines	2 x 8,300 kg (18,300 lb) thrust Klimov RD-33 afterburning turbofans
Wingspan	11.43 m (37 ft 6 in)
Length	17.32 m (57 ft 10 in)
Range	1,500–2,900 km (810–1,566 miles)
Top speed	2,445 km/h (1,519 mph)

Instrument landing system (ILS) aerial for communicating with ground control

Tailplane is all-moving

Starboard ventral fin

B-8W rocket pods can be fitted for the ground-attack role

Perfect blend
The MiG-29 has a mid-mounted wing with blended leading-edge root extensions (LERX). The engines are underslung and separated by a large channel. Shown here is an early 9.12 model MiG-29 operated by the Ukrainian Air Force.

MIKOYAN MIG-29 • 239

FRONT VIEW

REAR VIEW

Upper wing air intake louvres feed air to the engine when on the ground to prevent debris being ingested

K-36 ejection seat operates at any speed or altitude

Infra-red search and track sensor and laser ranger to track targets

Glass-fibre radome protects radar antennae

Fairing for integral landing system

Air intake carries air to the engine when aircraft is in flight

THE EXTERIOR

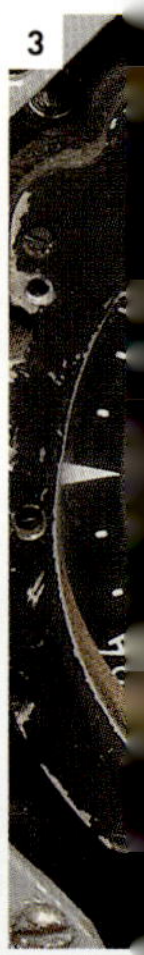

The muscular appearance of the MiG-29 is a product of its immensely strong airframe. The underslung engines and large leading-edge wing root extensions together contribute to the aircraft's superb high alpha performance – the ability to control the aircraft when the nose is raised at steep angles. The twin vertical tails are a legacy from the MiG-25; whereas the MiG-29's design emphasizes agility, its earlier cousin concentrated on speed.

10. Badge on tail **11.** Instrument landing system (ILS) aerial fairing **12.** Infrared search and track sensor/laser range finder **13.** Ultrahigh frequency (UHF) antenna **14.** Open cockpit compartment **15.** GSh-301 30mm cannon muzzle apertures **16.** Landing light on leg **17.** Air intake **18.** White "06" aircraft number **19.** Light under wing **20.** Landing gear **21.** B-8W rocket pod for 20 rounds of 80mm calibre **22.** Loading area for rocket pod at rear **23.** Variable area afterburner nozzle **24.** Port rudder

 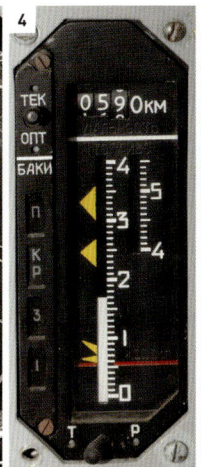 

COCKPIT

There is good visibility from the roomy cockpit. The control column lacks Hands on Throttle and Stick (HOTAS) technology, whereby buttons and switches on the throttle lever and joystick enable pilots to perform vital functions without letting go of the controls. Apart from the pilot's Shchel-3UM Helmet-mounted Display (HMD), all the MiG-29's displays are analogue dials – in contrast to the "glass" electronics of the American F/A-18 Hornet. The latest member of the family, the MiG-35, has three large multifunctional displays instead of analogue instruments (with four displays in the rear cockpit of the MiG-35D two-seater).

1. Cockpit **2.** Radar **3.** Heading setting indicator **4.** Fuel quantity display
5. Landing gear select and radar control panel **6.** Radar warning receiver
7. Combined oxygen panel **8.** K-36 ejection seat headrest **9.** Control stick

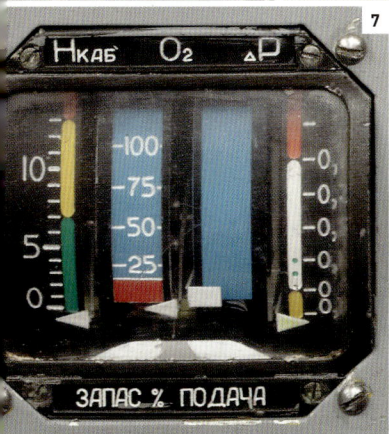  

 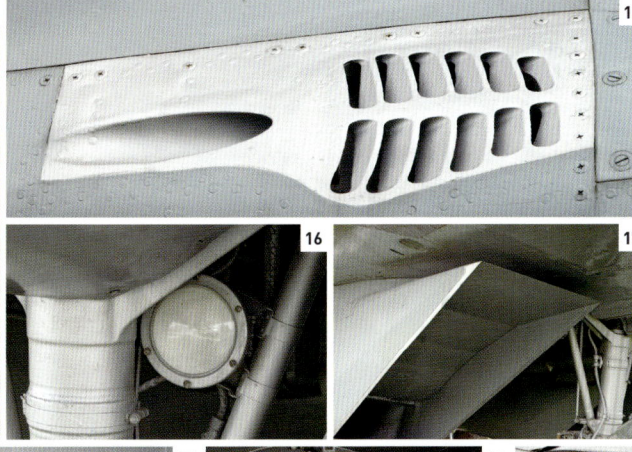 

Stealth Technology

Encounters with sophisticated surface-to-air missiles in the Vietnam War convinced the US Air Force of the need to make combat aircraft less visible to radar. After lengthy development as a "black project" by Lockheed's Skunk Works, the F-117 Nighthawk – the first military aircraft to be designed around stealth technology – made its maiden flight in June 1981. Although it entered service in 1982, its existence was kept secret until 1988. The aircraft's "F" (fighter) designation is misleading: lacking any air-to-air combat capabilities, it instead carried two 910-kg (2,000-lb) laser-guided bombs. The F-117 proved a crucial weapon, participating in US operations over Panama, the Gulf (1991 and 1998), and the Balkans. It was retired in 2008.

The F-117 – measuring 20 m (66 ft) long and with a wingspan of 13 m (43 ft) – had the radar footprint of a small bird. Coated with matt-black, radar-absorbent material (RAM), its angled surfaces scattered, rather than reflected, radar waves, while grilles over the engine air-intakes stopped radar bouncing back off the compressor blades. Omitting an afterburner and using long, heat-absorbent exhaust ducts reduced the aircraft's infrared signature.

A US Air Force F-117 Nighthawk flies low over the mountains of New Mexico during a training exercise.

The Changing Role of Navies

With the end of World War II, the days of large fleet engagements appeared to be over. As the Cold War intensified, however, the navies of the world found themselves with a new set of roles and responsibilities, keeping the strategic peace but also taking part in shooting wars.

The Soviet Union ended World War II comparatively weak in naval terms, certainly compared to the powerful US Navy. In July 1945, Soviet leader Joseph Stalin ordered a "still stronger and more powerful" naval service. This imperative energized naval production right through to the end of the 1960s, as the Soviet empire extended its reach over ever-greater portions of the world's oceans. The Soviets invested in new generations of surface vessels – from aircraft carriers, helicopter assault ships, and amphibious landing ships to missile-armed cruisers, destroyers, and frigates. They also built conventional and nuclear-powered submarines with ballistic-missile launch capability. By the 1970s, the Soviet navy rivalled that of the US, at least in terms of ship tonnage.

The US Navy appeared to be at a disadvantage. Its fleet strength contracted between 1964 and 1980: large numbers of World War II-era vessels were decommissioned, and funding was cut in the 1970s following the Vietnam War. However, the US Navy largely retained its technological superiority, and it substantially increased its strength during the 1980s under the "600-ship Navy" plan, which included a focus on Carrier Battle Groups (CBGs) and Marine expeditionary forces. During this decade, the under-funded Soviet navy became older and less functional.

Projecting power

At the strategic level, the Cold War was largely about power projection and deterrence. A key role of navies, in this context, was to police the sea lanes and oceans, attempting to establish dominance over maritime trade routes and contested waters while also containing the intrusions of the opposing navy. US and Soviet submarine fleets and electronic surveillance vessels conducted a shadowy struggle to monitor and provoke their opponents. This role was helped by the increase in range and endurance provided by nuclear powerplants.

Antisubmarine patrol
Maritime patrol aircraft such as this Lockheed P-3 Orion of the Royal Dutch Navy, were a major tool used to monitor and counter the threat of nuclear-missile submarines during the Cold War period.

Although the US and Soviet navies did not engage in direct conflict, they came close to it. The Cuban Missile Crisis, in October 1962, was a tense standoff over the Soviet deployment of ballistic missiles in Cuba. The US Navy blockaded access to Cuba, in a line stretching from Florida to Puerto Rico. Only diplomacy averted naval clashes and potential nuclear war.

The numerous proxy wars from the 1950s to the 1980s meant that the US Navy made regular deployments, ranging from low-key peacekeeping to full-scale combat operations. The Korean War (1950–53) saw the US Navy providing offshore fire support to the land campaign and facilitating the massive amphibious landings at Inchon in September 1950. In March 1966, during the Vietnam War, planes from the carriers of Task Force 77 conducted around 6,500 combat sorties over North and South Vietnam and Laos, flying from the Gulf of Tonkin and South China Sea; the US Navy's riverine and coastal war in Vietnam was equally intensive. The 1980s brought the Navy into various peacekeeping and combat operations across the Middle East, and in 1982 it facilitated a major amphibious landing on the Caribbean island of Grenada. Even as the Soviet Union collapsed in 1991, US carriers provided the central air attack component of Operation Desert Storm over Kuwait and Iraq.

Regional conflicts

The superpower struggle provided the wider context for naval roles between 1945 and 1991, but regional struggles also brought navies into operational use. During the 1971 India–Pakistan War, Indian Navy carrier aircraft and missile boats attacked Pakistani ships, harbours, and shore facilities. Two years later, in the Arab-Israeli Yom Kippur War, the first combat kills were made by surface-to-surface anti-ship missiles: five Syrian Arab Navy vessels were destroyed by Israeli Sa'ar-class missile boats.

The most influential naval battle of the Cold War era occurred in 1982. Argentina's amphibious invasion of the Falkland Islands (Islas Malvinas), a UK territory in the South Atlantic,

Submarine deterrent
The USS *Henry L. Stimson* (SSBN-655) was a *Benjamin Franklin*-class nuclear-powered submarine in service with the US Navy from 1966 to 1993. It carried 16 Polaris missiles armed with nuclear warheads.

> "You seldom hear of the fleets except **when there's trouble**, and then you hear a lot."
>
> ADMIRAL JOHN. S. MCCAIN JR, COMMANDER, UNITED STATES PACIFIC COMMAND, 1968–72

prompted the British to deploy a naval task force to reclaim the islands. Prior to the invasion, Britain had been planning major cuts in naval strength; now a task force of 127 ships steamed south, centred around the carriers *Invincible* and *Hermes*.

The subsequent naval war, while ultimately a British victory, was a close-run contest. The Royal Navy established surface superiority, sinking the cruiser ARA *General Belgrano* in a torpedo attack by the nuclear-powered submarine HMS *Conqueror*. However, strike jets flying from the Argentine mainland inflicted a terrible cost on the task force at sea and during the amphibious landing: the British lost seven craft, including two Type 42 destroyers and two Type 21 frigates. While the Falklands War prompted a global rethink of naval tactics, especially in terms of air defence for ships, it also illustrated that the age of expeditionary naval warfare was not over.

Floating air base
Aircraft carriers were powerful deterrents and projectors of power. Here, a US Navy Lockheed S-3A Viking, an antisubmarine warfare (ASW) plane, launches from the USS *Forrestal*.

TALKING POINT
Intelligence Gathering

Naval surveillance was an unceasing operation during the Cold War. Its primary objective was to monitor and analyse enemy naval deployments, whether surface ships or submarines. Some of this activity was covert; both sides used state-of-the-art electronic/signals intelligence (ELINT/SIGINT) vessels disguised as merchant ships, fishing trawlers, and scientific research ships. The US Navy also deployed the Sound Surveillance System (SOSUS), a wide-area network of underwater passive hydrophones that could detect the passage of Soviet submarines in key regions of the Atlantic and Pacific oceans.

A radar operator watches his screen in 1985 aboard the HSwMS *Carlskrona*, a Swedish minelayer that has also been used for intelligence gathering.

Cold War Frigates and Destroyers

Over the near five decades of the Cold War, frigate and destroyer design went through profound changes. Deck-mounted guns were retained, but their number and significance diminished as weapons portfolios switched to new generations of antiship, antisubmarine, and surface-to-air missiles. From the 1960s, surface- and air-search radars became increasingly advanced, with data flowing to integrated and computerized combat information centres. Vessels such as the US Navy's *Spruance*-class destroyers and the British Type 21 *Amazon*-class frigate moved from steam-turbine to gas-turbine propulsion, which delivered a high power-to-weight ratio and faster start-up times.

▷ **USS Herbert J. Thomas**
Date 1945 Origin USA
Displacement 3,516 tonnes (3,876 tons)
Length 119 m (391 ft)
Top speed 35 knots (65 km/h)

The *Herbert J. Thomas*, one of 98 *Gearing*-class destroyers, was designed initially to provide anti-aircraft and antisubmarine support for larger warships. The ship took part in both the Korean and Vietnam Wars, making effective use of its six 5-inch guns in three turrets.

Turret with two 4.5 in guns

△ **HMS Diamond**
Date 1952 Origin UK
Displacement 3,637 tonnes (4,010 tons)
Length 119 m (390 ft)
Top speed 30 knots (56 km/h)

As one of the *Daring*-class ships, *Diamond* was among the final conventional gun destroyers built for the British Royal Navy. Its guns were housed in three double turrets.

△ **Kola-class frigate**
Date 1951 Origin USSR
Displacement 1,900 tonnes (2,094 tons)
Length 96 m (315 ft)
Top speed 30 knots (56 km/h)

The Soviet *Kola*-class frigates were little different from World War II destroyers, albeit upgraded with more advanced radar and sonar equipment. Eight vessels in total were commissioned between 1951 and 1953.

▽ **HMNZCS Canterbury**
Date 1971 Origin UK
Displacement 3,038 tonnes (3,349 tons)
Length 113.4 m (372 ft)
Top speed 30 knots (56 km/h)

The *Canterbury*, one of the last *Leander*-class frigates, was built in Scotland and commissioned into the Royal New Zealand Navy. Its roles included peacekeeping in East Timor and relief efforts in the Pacific region.

Two 4.5 in guns

Flight deck for helicopter

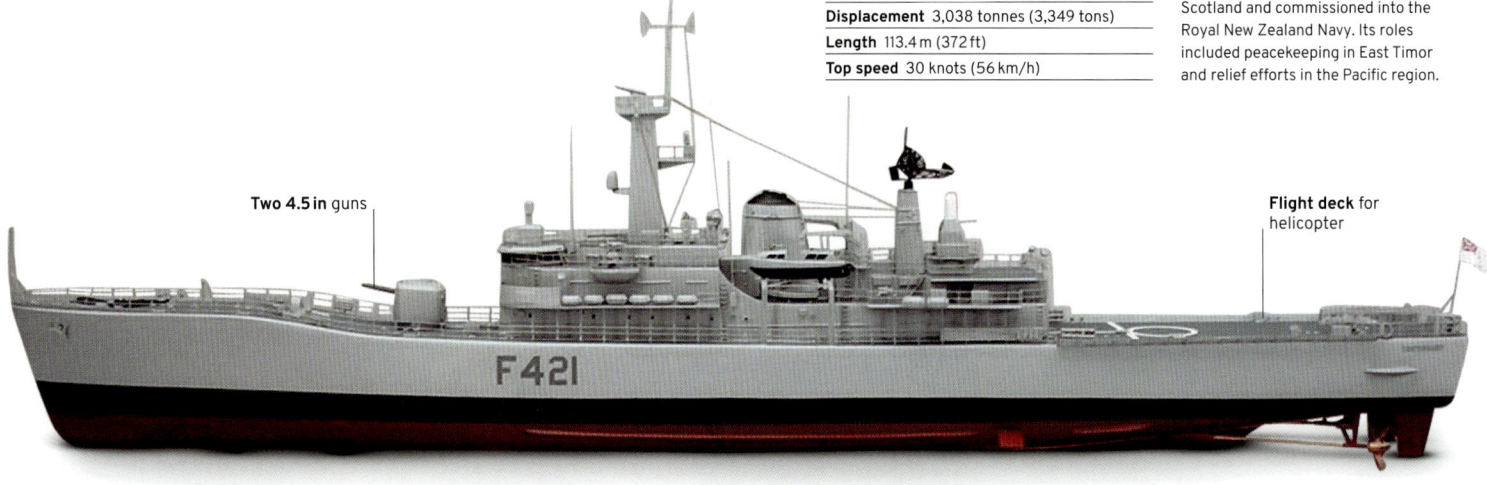

▽ **USS Pharris**
Date 1974 Origin USA
Displacement 4,264 tonnes (4,700 tons)
Length 133.5 m (438 ft)
Top speed 27 knots (50 km/h)

Launched as a *Knox*-class destroyer, and reclassified later as a frigate, the *Pharris* was armed with antisubmarine missiles and torpedoes. The ship was commissioned into the Mexican Navy in 2000.

Missile launcher

Missile launcher

COLD WAR FRIGATES AND DESTROYERS · 247

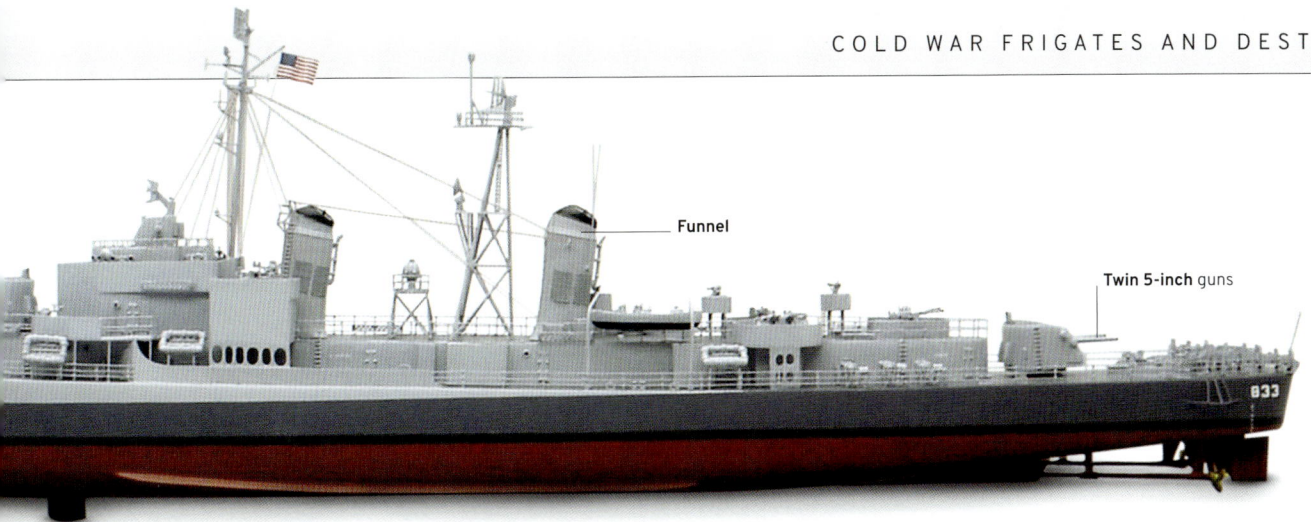

Funnel

Twin 5-inch guns

76 mm gun

◁ **Koni-class frigate**
Date 1975	Origin USSR
Displacement 1,900 tonnes (2,094 tons)	
Length 95 m (312 ft)	
Top speed 27 knots (50 km/h)	

The Soviet *Koni* class consisted of 14 antisubmarine frigates, built originally to replace the *Riga*-class ships but mostly sold for export. Type II variants included a revised superstructure to incorporate air-conditioning for use in warmer, non-European waters.

▷ **HMS Sheffield**
Date 1975	Origin UK
Displacement 4,420 tonnes (4,872 tons)	
Length 125 m (410 ft)	
Top speed 30 knots (56 km/h)	

The *Sheffield*, a Type 42 guided-missile destroyer, was armed primarily with the Sea Dart missile system. The ship took part in the Falklands War of 1982, and, while on patrol, was sunk by an Exocet missile fired by an Argentinian naval aircraft.

Radar scanner

Main mast

Target-illuminating radar

Sea Dart missiles

Antenna for aircraft navigation aid

▽ **USS Oliver Hazard Perry**
Date 1977	Origin USA
Displacement 3,658 tonnes (4,032 tons)	
Length 136 m (445 ft)	
Top speed 28 knots (52 km/h)	

Built to protect military and merchant convoys, the *Oliver Hazard Perry* was the lead ship in its frigate class. It was armed with anti-aircraft missiles and antisubmarine torpedoes.

76 mm gun

Sikorsky helicopter

USS Nautilus

Date 1954	Origin USA
Displacement	3,590 tonnes (3,957 tons)
Length	97.5 m (320 ft)
Top speed	22 knots (41 km/h)

Following the development of a successful nuclear propulsion plant by scientists and engineers at the Naval Reactors Branch of the US Atomic Energy Commission, *Nautilus* became the first operational nuclear-powered submarine in the world. In 1958, it made the first underwater transit of the North Pole. An attack submarine, *Nautilus* carried conventional torpedoes.

Bridge

Bow diving plane

▽ George Washington-class submarine

Date 1959	Origin USA
Displacement	6,055 tonnes (6,774 tons)
Length	116.3 m (382 ft)
Top speed	16 knots (30 km/h)

In service from 1959 until 1985, *George Washington*-class submarines were built to deploy the UGM-27 Polaris ballistic missile. Each submarine carried 16 of the A1 (later A3) variants of the missile in vertical launch tubes. The first Polaris test launch from a submarine was made on 20 July 1960.

Missile hatch (open)

Sail acts as a vertical stabilizer when the submarine is submerged

Streamlined shape to hull

▷ HMS Dreadnought

Date 1963	Origin UK
Displacement	3,556 tonnes (3,920 tons)
Length	81 m (266 ft)
Top speed	20 knots (37 km/h)

Equipped with six tubes for its 24 torpedoes, HMS *Dreadnought* was the British Navy's first nuclear-powered submarine. Its motive force came from an American Westinghouse S5W pressurized water reactor, which delivered 15,000 shp. Commissioned in 1963, HMS *Dreadnought* remained in service until 1980.

Nuclear-powered Submarines

Introduced in the 1950s, submarines powered by small nuclear reactors quickly proved they could surpass their diesel-electric rivals in speed, underwater endurance, and range. Some nuclear-powered submarines are attack submarines, designed to operate against surface ships or hunt down other submarines. Others, armed with nuclear ballistic missiles, are the most potent weapon systems ever developed. Lying beneath the waves, they can launch their deadly arsenal without warning, virtually immune from retaliatory action by the enemy. Their high level of concealment also gives them an invaluable second-strike capability.

Nuclear-Powered Submarines · 249

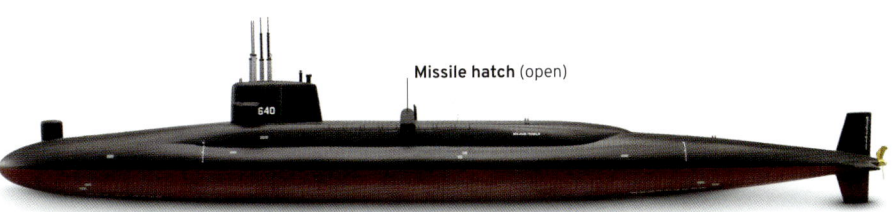

▷ **Benjamin Franklin-class submarine**

Date 1965	Origin USA
Displacement 7,443 tonnes (8,204 tons)	
Length 130 m (425 ft)	
Top speed 16 knots (30 km/h)	

This 12-ship class of ballistic missile submarine operated from the mid-1960s until the last vessel was decommissioned in 2002. The ships could reach dive depths of 400 m (1,312 ft) and could conduct submerged patrols lasting more than 60 days.

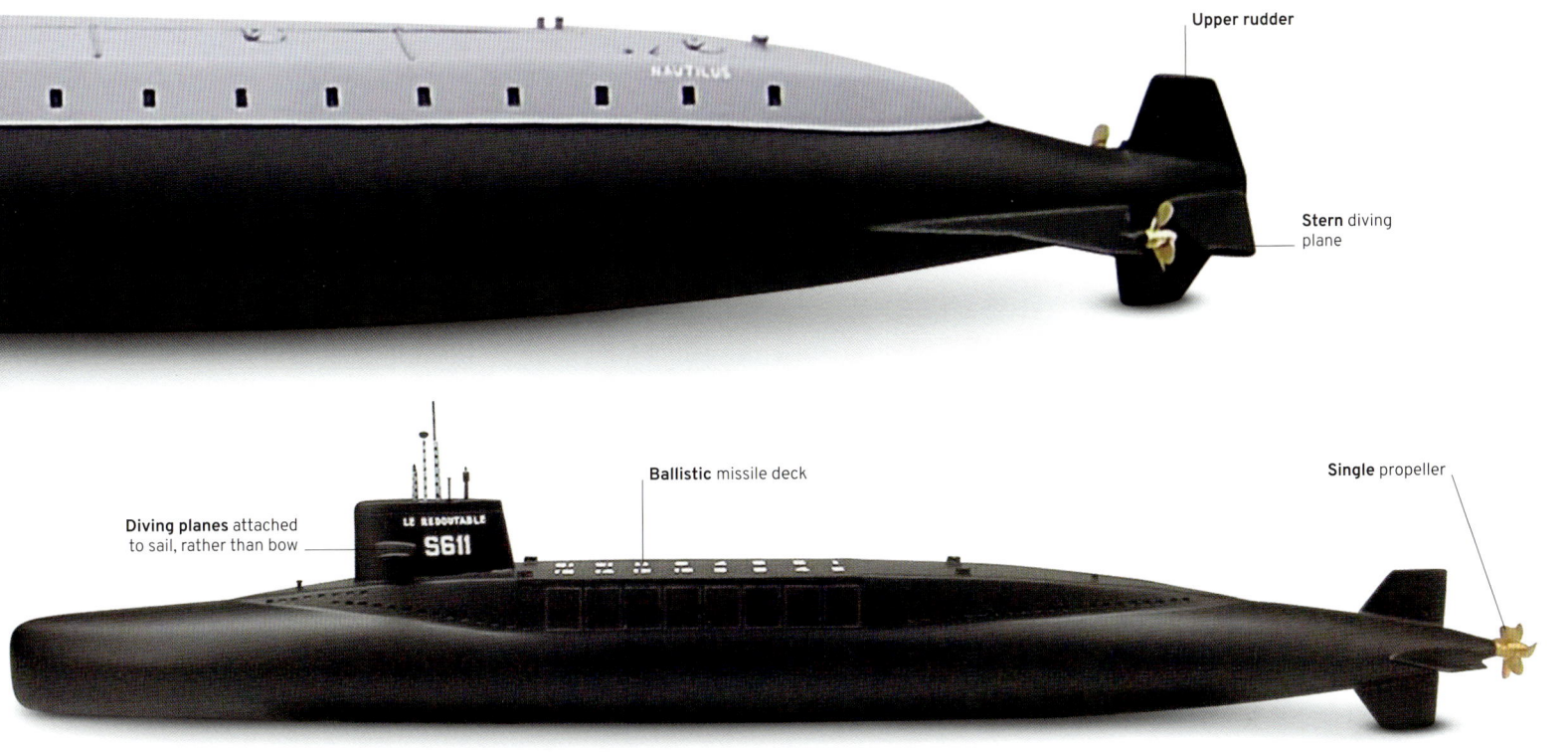

△ **Le Redoutable**

Date 1971	Origin France
Displacement 8,174 tonnes (9,010 tons)	
Length 128 m (420 ft)	
Top speed 18 knots (33 km/h)	

Le Redoutable was the lead vessel of its class and France's first ballistic missile submarine. Its original complement of M1 missiles had a range of 2,000 km (1,243 miles) when carrying a 450-kilotonne warhead.

▽ **Oscar-class submarine**

Date 1975	Origin USSR
Displacement 14,700 tonnes (16,200 tons)	
Length 155 m (509 ft)	
Top speed 15 knots (28 km/h)	

Construction of the *Oscar*-class of Soviet and Russian submarines began in 1975; the most recent of the series of 14 (to date) ships was commissioned in 2022. Modern *Oscar-II* variants are primarily designed to destroy enemy carriers using torpedoes and advanced anti-ship missiles.

△ **Novosibirsk**

Date 1984	Origin USSR
Displacement 2,362 tonnes (2,604 tons)	
Length 67 m (220 ft)	
Top speed 15 knots (28 km/h)	

A diesel-electric attack submarine of the *Kilo* class, *Novosibirsk* was armed with minelaying equipment and conventional torpedoes, as well as anti-ship and anti-aircraft missiles.

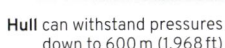

▷ **Trafalgar-class submarine**

Date 1986	Origin UK
Displacement 4,800 tonnes (5,290 tons)	
Length 85.4 m (280 ft)	
Top speed 20 knots (27 km/h)	

The seven *Trafalgar*-class submarines, alongside the preceding *Swiftsure* class, were a core element of Britain's nuclear submarine fleet from the 1980s until 2025. Several of the vessels made combat deployments from 2001, firing Tomahawk cruise missiles at targets in Afghanistan, Iraq, and Syria.

USS Nautilus

The world's first nuclear-powered submarine, the *Nautilus* entered service in 1954, during the early stages of the Cold War. Whereas conventional submarines could submerge for 12–48 hours, the *Nautilus* was able to stay under water for two weeks or more without having to surface or refuel. Nuclear submarines would soon dominate naval strategy, either as torpedo-carrying attack vessels or as nuclear missile carriers.

POWERED BY A NUCLEAR REACTOR, the *Nautilus* had unrivalled endurance under water: in 1955, it set a new record for a submerged voyage, covering 2,222 km (1,381 miles) in 90 hours. Three years later, it became the first submarine to travel below the polar ice cap to the North Pole. In addition to its reactor, the ship's innovations included dispensing with a deck gun, an inertial navigation system (on its 1958 sub-Arctic trip), and providing each crew member with a bunk – previous submarines used a shift system for bunks.

The *Nautilus*'s armament consisted of 24 Mk14 conventional torpedoes, some of which were kept in the tubes, ready for firing, with the rest being stored on racks in the torpedo bay. The *Nautilus* was equipped with electronic countermeasures systems that detected signals from other vessels and helped foil attempts to track the submarine from its own transmissions, while sonar was used to locate ships and other submarines, follow possible targets, and avoid collisions when submerged.

The *Nautilus* was not particularly fast beneath the waves, and by 1959 it was being superseded by vessels that could achieve higher subsurface speeds and reach greater depths, thanks to improved hull designs and the use of new materials. The *Nautilus* was retired in 1980 and is now a museum.

SPECIFICATIONS	
Name	USS *Nautilus*
Commissioned	1954
Type	Nuclear submarine
Displacement	3,590 tonnes (3,957 tons)
Length	97.5 m (320 ft)
Propulsion	STR nuclear reactor
Complement	13 officers, 92 enlisted
Armament	6 torpedo tubes
Maximum speed	23 knots (43 km/h)

Submarine sail
The *Nautilus* was commanded from the bridge, located at the top of the tower-like "sail", when travelling on the surface. The sail also housed the periscopes and antennas for radio and radar.

INTERIOR

Two planesmen in the control room operated the hydroplanes to adjust the ship's angle and depth under water; the helmsman, on their right, used the rudder to adjust the course. The attack centre, the heart of the submarine's role as a warship, housed controls for firing the torpedoes, two periscopes, and navigational equipment. Officers dined in the wardroom, the crew in the mess. Torpedoes were in the bow, with engines and the reactor towards the stern.

1. Control room **2.** Collision alarm **3.** Ballast tank water-level dials **4.** Hatch and vent display panel (to check closure prior to diving) **5.** Electronic countermeasures **6.** Sonar room **7.** Wardroom **8.** Galley **9.** Crew's quarters **10.** Attack centre **11.** Torpedo **12.** Torpedo bay

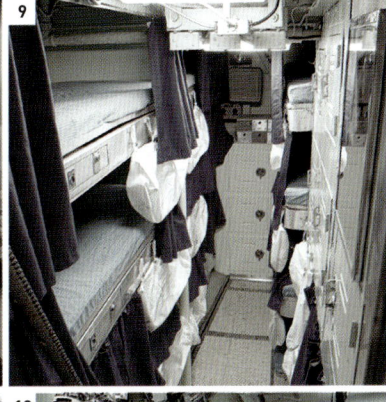

Military Patrol Boats

For millennia, inland waterways have been used as routes for travel and trade. In wartime, they can not only act as defensive barriers but also give access to enemy positions. During the Vietnam War (1954–75), the Mekong Delta, an area with few roads but a vast network of waterways, became a key conflict zone between the Viet Cong and US and South Vietnamese forces. The US Navy established Task Forces equipped with small Patrol Boats, Riverine (PBR) and larger Patrol Craft, Fast (PCF) to stop the transportation of enemy troops and supplies, enforce nighttime curfews, defend legitimate trade, and clear mines.

Operation Giant Slingshot, beginning in late 1968, aimed to block the flow of Viet Cong fighters infiltrating into South Vietnam from Cambodia via the Mekong Delta waterways. With around 50,000 local vessels estimated to be operating on these waterways, one of the main activities of the US patrol boats was carrying out stop-and-search inspections of sampans, junks, and other river traffic to prevent the smuggling of weapons.

With gunners poised and ready for action, US Navy PCF 43 cruises along a river in Vietnam during Operation Giant Slingshot in January 1969.

1989–PRESENT
THE HIGH-TECH AGE

Present War, Future War

Since the end of the Cold War, the development of military vehicles has been influenced both by current wars and by predictions of future conflicts. In both cases, digital technology continues to reshape the battlefield.

Gulf War strike aircraft
USAF F-15 Eagle and F-16 Fighting Falcon aircraft fly over burning Iraqi oil fields during the 1991 Gulf War in a display of the Coalition's air superiority.

Between 17 January and 28 February 1991, a large-scale US-led military coalition defeated the armed services of Iraq in Operation Desert Storm, the international effort to expel Iraqi occupation forces from Kuwait. The one-sided victory seemed to demonstrate the possibility of "Full Spectrum Dominance": a force being technologically superior across air, sea, land, space, and digital. The future, however, was to prove more complex.

From Gulf War to COIN war

The Gulf War was decided by aircraft, armour, ships, and artillery; there was little significant infantry fighting. The Coalition overran Iraq's largely outdated Soviet-style equipment. Ship-launched Tomahawk cruise missiles struck strategic targets with precision hundreds of kilometres from their launch point. Iraqi air defences were ineffective against a massive Coalition air campaign that wiped out Iraq's command-and-control network and huge volumes of equipment and vehicles, often using new generations of precision-guided munitions (PGMs). US M1 Abrams and British Challenger I tanks outgunned Iraqi T-72s and T-64s. The Coalition forces were coordinated by a powerful digital network of surveillance and communication.

The Gulf War seemed to prove that the weapons and vehicles of the Cold War still had relevance, especially when integrated into a "network-centric battlefield". However, from 2001, the US and its allies found themselves locked into two decades of counterinsurgency (COIN) warfare, principally in Afghanistan and Iraq. Based around armed resistance by local insurgents, COIN spawned new directions in vehicle design. The focus shifted to lighter,

> " There are **two dangers**... the over-reliance on **technology** and the failure to make the most of [its] **capabilities**."
>
> US MARINE CORPS, *WARFIGHTING*, 1997

Timeline

The Gulf War (1990–91), the War on Terror (2001–21), and the Ukraine War (2022–) tested and challenged the design of military vehicles, leading to transformational new tactics and technologies. Unmanned vehicles, stealth configurations, and the incorporation of artificial intelligence (AI) point the way to the future.

- **1991** The US Humvee light vehicle is used heavily in the 1991 Gulf War
- **1998** British Challenger 2 third-generation MBTs enter service
- **2005** The F-22 Raptor stealth fighter joins US Air Force squadrons
- **1995** The MQ-1 Predator unmanned combat aerial vehicle (UCAV) enters US service
- **2001** China introduces the Type 99 third-generation MBT into the People's Liberation Army (PLA)

faster types of armoured fighting vehicle (AFV) more suited to urban warfare. Land vehicle designs began to reflect the distinct threats posed by improvised explosive devices (IEDs) and rocket-propelled grenades (RPGs), with mine-resistant hull shapes, up-armoured light vehicles, and active armour protection systems. Ageing aircraft platforms such as the Fairchild Republic A-10 Thunderbolt II ground-attack aircraft and the B-1 Lancer bomber still proved effective, and drones were also widely used for surveillance and targeting. Aircraft carriers and missile-launching ships also took part, both for offshore strike missions and as surveillance platforms.

During the same period as the Global War on Terror (GWOT), which the US initiated after attacks in the US by the al-Qaeda terrorist group in 2001, new and more advanced military vehicle technologies emerged. China made astonishingly rapid steps in modernizing its armed forces: examples included its all-weather Chengdu J-20 stealth fighter; its first domestically produced aircraft carrier (the *Shandong*); the Type 039A/B *Yuan*-class submarine; and the Type 99A main battle tank (MBT). Internationally, many more naval vessels incorporated stealth designs and some also served as mounts for directed energy weapons (DEWs), such as lasers, and experimental electromagnetic railguns. Russia and other nations developed hypersonic scramjet-powered missiles that could fly erratic paths to their targets, evading air defences. In the background, warfare was changing.

New directions

In 2014, conflict broke out in eastern Ukraine between Ukraine's armed forces and Russian paramilitaries. This led to Russia's full-scale invasion of Ukraine in 2022, a conflict that has had major implications for future-warfare planning, not least for the procurement and development of military vehicles.

Some lessons learned have affirmed older technologies. During the era of COIN warfare in Afghanistan and Iraq, for example, there had been debates about the relevance of MBTs on the modern battlefield. The Ukraine conflict, however, has made extensive use of large fleets of heavy AFVs, and also of self-propelled artillery. Intense infantry combat showed the importance

> **TALKING POINT**
>
> ## Modern Communication Networks
>
> The lethality, performance, and utility of modern military vehicles is often dependent upon their integration into advanced battlefield communications networks. Even trucks and light vehicles might carry sophisticated voice/data systems, including monitors displaying real-time situational awareness of friendly and enemy forces. Satellite datalinks enable the secure transfer and receipt of large volumes of information, and enable exceptional precision in navigation and fire control. Jamming communications is also key: many advanced armies are investing in technologies designed to deny or disrupt enemy communications, while AI is being used to make communications more resistant to this.
>
>
>
> **US soldiers fold out** a vehicle-mounted antenna mast group (AMG), used as an amplifier and a communications relay for voice and data transmissions.

of infantry fighting vehicles (IFVs) for ingress and egress of the battlefield. Air power has remained influential, not least for launching long-range glide bombs beyond the range of air defences.

The most dramatic impact in the Ukraine War was made by drones, used in their millions to perform combat missions ranging from low-level surveillance through to armour-killing "suicide" missions. The majority of these are cheap, commercial drones converted for combat use. Increasingly, military drones have autonomous capabilities, such as AI-powered targeting systems.

Unmanned, autonomous technology is the future of military vehicles. It is being tested in every domain, and at all scales. The spectrum ranges from sofa-sized "robo-mules" designed to carry an infantry squad's equipment through to full-size autonomous or semi-autonomous tanks and warships. It is also likely that piloted combat aircraft will, in the future, be accompanied by autonomous "wingmen" to provide extra fighting capability.

Globally, the military world is shifting its focus from the COIN era to a new age of vehicular warfare. Future combat may well be as much about the fight between rival AI systems as it will be about battles of guns and missiles. As the digital decision-making process in warfare becomes ever faster, it points to a new generation of military vehicles in which the human being is optional – or, conceivably, even unnecessary.

Preparing for war in Ukraine
A Ukrainian T-80-type tank fires its smoothbore 125 mm (5 in) main gun during a training exercise in 2024, readying itself for frontline deployment in the war against Russia.

2007 Introduction of the US V-22 Osprey tiltrotor military transport and cargo aircraft

2007 Mine Resistant Ambush Protected (MRAP) vehicles are deployed in Iraq and Afghanistan

2010 Britain's Royal Navy commissions a new generation of nuclear submarine, HMS *Astute*

2014 The Turkish Bayraktar TB2 UCAV makes its first flight

2015 Russia begins production of the T-15 Armata advanced IFV

2016 The first US Navy *Zumwalt*-class multi-mission stealth ship is commissioned

2017 China introduces the Chengdu J-20 all-weather stealth fighter

2017 China launches its first domestically produced aircraft carrier, *Shandong* (17)

2019 The Sukhoi Su-57 becomes Russia's first stealth fighter

2020 Chinese Type 055 stealth guided-missile destroyers enter service

2022 Unmanned surface vehicles (USVs) conduct combat operations in the Ukraine War

2023 The B-21 Raider, the USAF's newest strategic bomber, makes its first flight

2024 US agencies begin tests of self-driving AFV designs

△ **Casspir**
Date 1979 Origin South Africa
Weight 10.9 tonnes (12 tons)
Engine Mercedes-Benz OM-352A diesel, 124 kW (166 hp)
Main armament None

With an enclosed armoured body and bullet-proof windows, South Africa's Casspir was designed for both riot control and fighting in the Border War. Its V-shaped underside protected against mines. This versatile, two-crew, 12-passenger vehicle was also used for recovery and mine clearance, and as a mortar carrier and tanker.

△ **Mamba**
Date 1989 Origin South Africa
Weight 6.8 tonnes (7.5 tons)
Engine Mercedes-Benz OM352 diesel, 92 kW (123 hp)
Main armament None

Unlike the Buffel, which it replaced, South Africa's Mamba has a roof and armoured windows. Mark I Mambas were two-wheel drive and carried five troops; later models were upgraded to four-wheel drive and had capacity for nine soldiers, combining high levels of protection with a non-threatening appearance. The Mamba's development has continued in the 21st century.

△ **Snatch Land Rover**
Date 1992 Origin UK
Weight 4.1 tonnes (4.5 tons)
Engine Land Rover 300Tdi diesel, 83 kW (111 hp)
Main armament None

The Snatch evolved from a series of armoured Land Rovers used in Northern Ireland, notably the "Piglet", fitted with a Vehicle Protection Kit (VPK), and the Glover Webb armoured patrol vehicle (APV). Deployed in Iraq and Afghanistan, the Snatch gave some protection against small arms fire and IEDs, but high crew casualties led to its withdrawal.

▽ **Mastiff**
Date 2006 Origin UK
Weight 23.6 tonnes (26 tons)
Engine Caterpillar C7 diesel, 246 kW (330 hp)
Main armament 7.62 mm or 12.7 mm machine-gun, or 40 mm grenade launcher

The Mastiff is Britain's version of the US Army's Cougar MRAP, which saved thousands of lives in Iraq and Afghanistan. Unlike the Cougar, the Mastiff is fitted with bar armour and replaces armoured side windows with armour plate.

Counterinsurgency Vehicles

The increasing use of landmines by insurgents and terrorist groups in the 1970s spawned vehicles specifically designed to protect against such devices. One solution was to raise the crew compartment higher and angle the underside to deflect the blast. The South African Border War of the 1980s saw the development of vehicles protected against both mines and direct fire. When the Improvised Explosive Device (IED) threat became a feature of war in Iraq and Afghanistan in the 21st century, these designs were the springboard for the development of Mine-resistant Ambush-protected (MRAP) vehicles.

COUNTERINSURGENCY VEHICLES • 259

△ **Bushmaster**

Date 2003	**Origin** Australia
Weight 15.4 tonnes (17 tons)	
Engine Caterpillar 3126E diesel, 224 kW (300 hp)	
Main armament Varies	

The Bushmaster can provide protection for a nine-man infantry section over long distances. Its armour and mine protection made it popular in Iraq and Afghanistan, and it has mortar, command, ambulance, air-defence, and route-clearance variants. It was supplied to Ukraine after Russia's 2022 invasion.

△ **Buffalo**

Date 2003	**Origin** USA
Weight 30 tonnes (33 tons)	
Engine Caterpillar C13 diesel, 328 kW (440 hp)	
Main armament None	

Longer and taller than other MRAPs, America's Buffalo is a transport for Explosive Ordnance Disposal (EOD) personnel. Operated from within the armoured hull, its 10 m (33 ft) articulated manipulator arm can uncover and disable IEDs. The Buffalo also serves with French, Canadian, Italian, and Pakistani forces.

▽ **Foxhound**

Date 2012	**Origin** UK
Weight 8.5 tonnes (9.4 tons)	
Engine Steyr M16 Monoblock 6-cylinder diesel, 157 kW (210 hp)	
Main armament Varies	

Britain's Foxhound – a replacement for the Snatch – carries a crew of six. Extensive use of advanced composite materials instead of metal reduces its weight, giving it unmatched manoeuvrability yet maintaining good blast protection.

Electronic mine-detecting system

Buffel

Entering service in 1978, South Africa's Buffel – "buffalo" in Afrikaans – was the first armoured personnel carrier (APC) specifically designed to protect its occupants against landmine explosions. It spawned a new generation of mine-resistant vehicles, many of which emulated the Buffel's most innovative design features.

THE BUFFEL ORIGINATED in South Africa during the South African Border War, a series of conflicts in South West Africa (now Namibia), Angola, and Zambia between 1966 and 1990. It was a development of South Africa's Bosvark ("bushpig") vehicle, which itself was a Mercedes Benz Unimog truck modified to give a very basic level of mine protection. Like the Bosvark, the Buffel used the U416-162 Unimog chassis.

A V- or boat-shaped hull to deflect mine blasts had featured on numerous earlier vehicles, including Britain's Saracen APC. The Buffel, however, was the first vehicle to prioritize the survival of the driver and passengers in its design brief. The hull and armoured sides not only offered high levels of protection in the event of mine detonations, but also shielded the passengers from small arms fire and shrapnel. The Buffel also provided good visibility to infantrymen travelling in the open-topped rear compartment.

The Buffel's revolutionary design inspired the Mine Resistant Ambush Protected (MRAP) concept in the 2000s. Many tens of thousands of MRAP vehicles were subsequently built by Coalition nations for use in Iraq and Afghanistan.

Armoured windscreen protects driver

Spare tyre stored on side of vehicle, away from blast zone

Mercedes 6-cylinder water-cooled diesel engine

Simple but tough
The first truly effective mine-resistant APC, the Buffel was based on the running gear of the very successful Unimog truck. This relatively simple yet incredibly tough vehicle was also produced in variants with closed infantry compartments and windows. As well as serving with South African forces, Buffels were exported to Sri Lanka and Uganda.

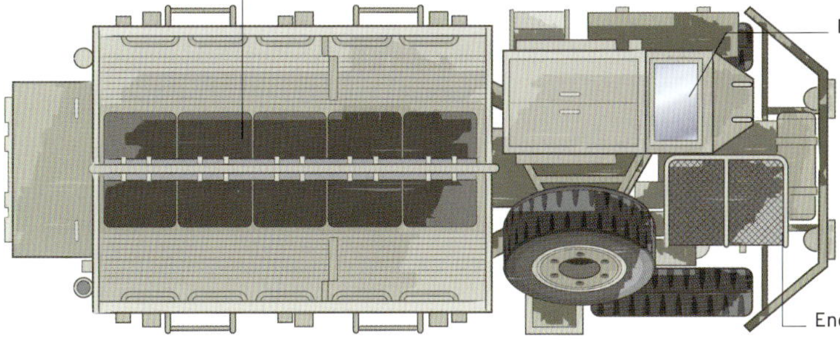

BUFFEL • 261

Infantry seats — Driver — Engine

SPECIFICATIONS	
Name	Buffel Armoured Personnel Carrier
Date	1978
Origin	South Africa
Production	Approx. 2,400
Engine	Mercedes-Benz OM-352 diesel, 93 kW (125 hp)
Weight	6.1 tonnes (6.7 tons)
Main armament	None
Secondary armament	None
Crew	1 + 10
Armour thickness	Hull: unknown; windscreen: 40 mm ($1^{3}/_{5}$ in) armoured glass

Roll bar offers protection if vehicle overturns

Steps for accessing rear compartment

Hull set high off the ground

FRONT VIEW

REAR VIEW

EXTERIOR

Soldiers entered the passenger compartment by climbing over the hinged sides, which could be dropped down to load equipment and supplies, while a roll bar protected the troops in the event of a tip-over. A 100-litre (22-gallon) tank supplied drinking water – essential for long-range patrols in the harsh climate of southern Africa – via a tap under the rear hull.

1. Headlight grill **2.** Front tow point **3.** Cab nose flap, open **4.** Bulletproof glass windscreen **5.** Winch for raising items, including tyres **6.** Main engine **7.** Main engine detail **8.** Main chassis frame **9.** Drinking water tap **10.** Rear light **11.** Suspension arms **12.** Vertical spring suspension **13.** 12.50 x 20 tyres, often filled with water to absorb blasts **14.** Rear tow hook **15.** Access steps

1

2

3

4

5

6

7

8

9

10

11

12

13

14

15

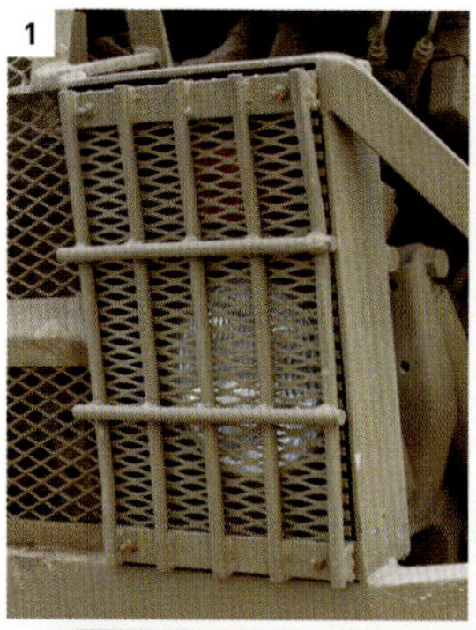

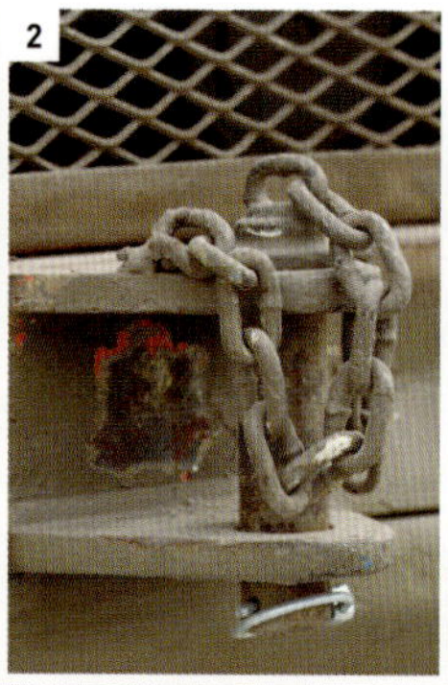

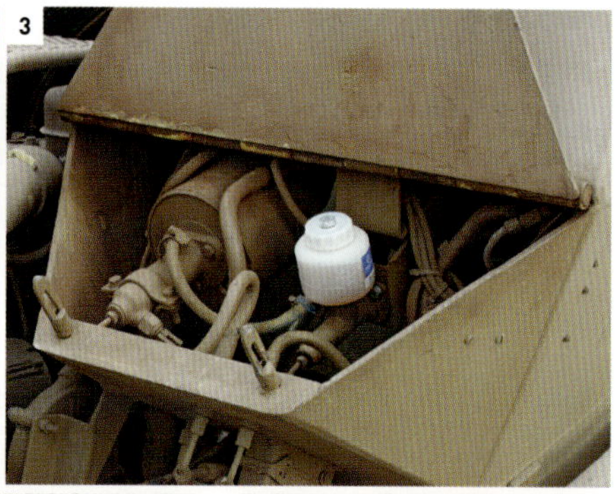

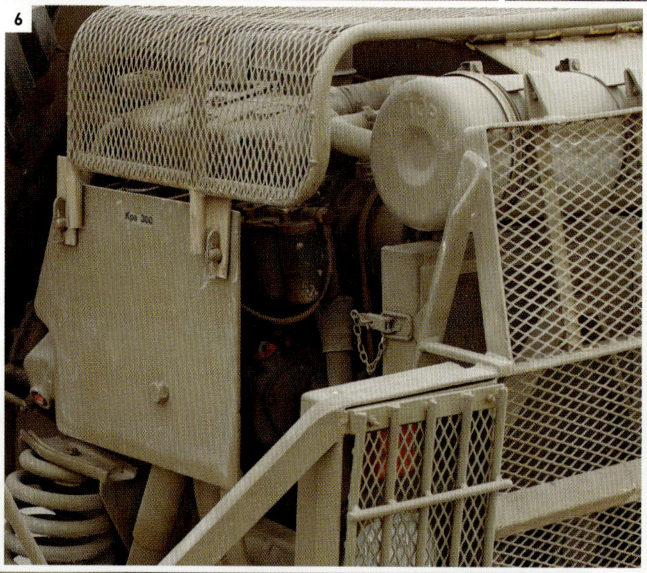

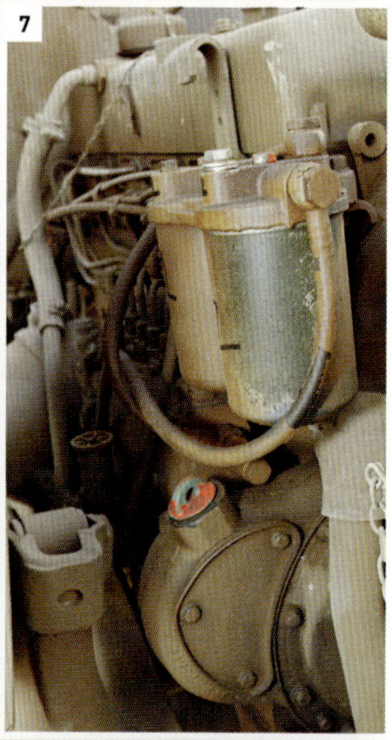

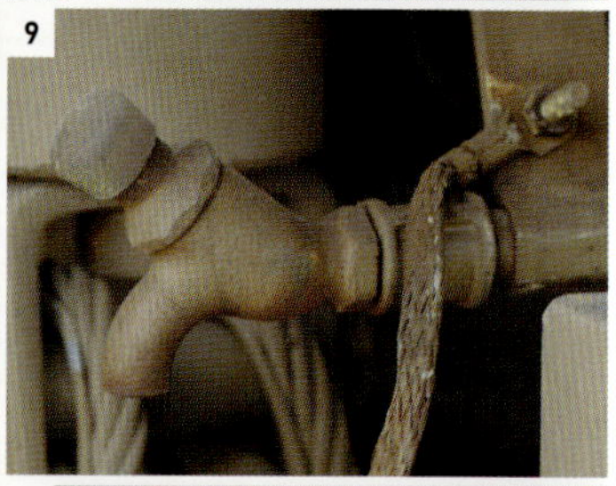

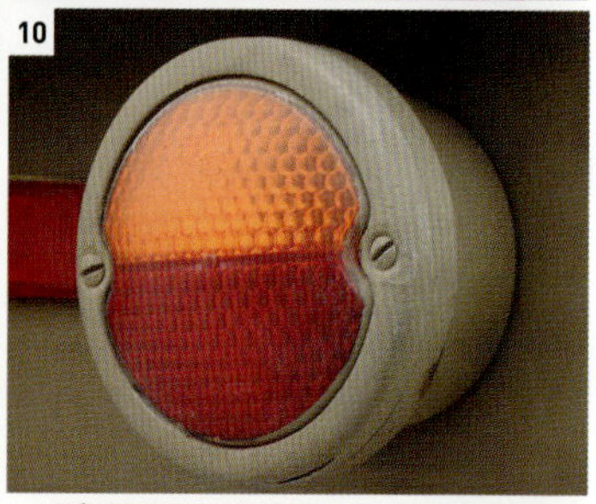

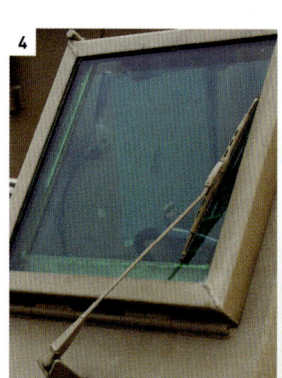

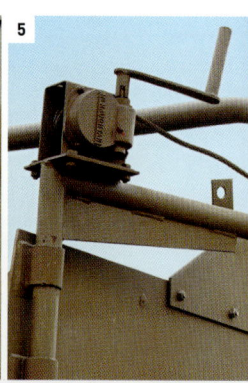

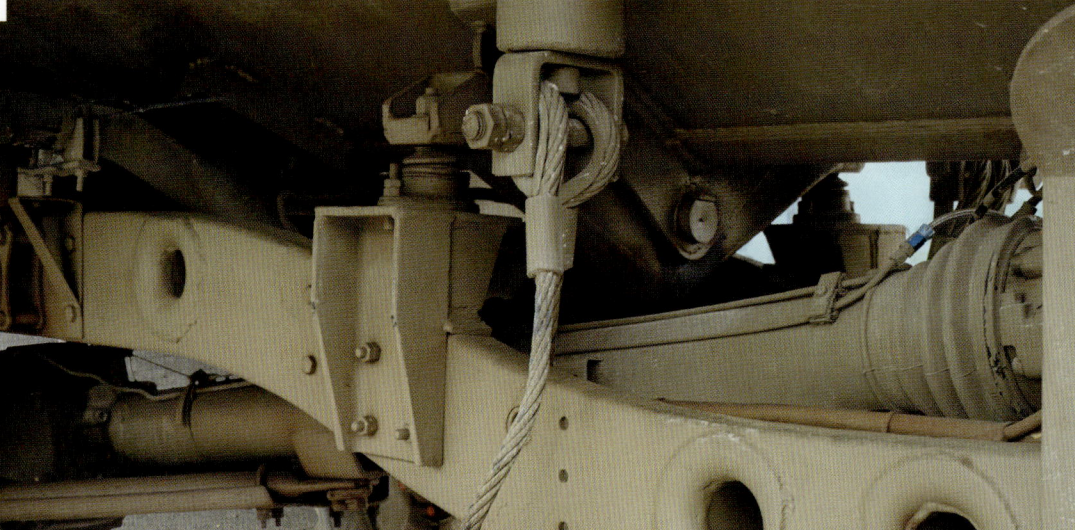

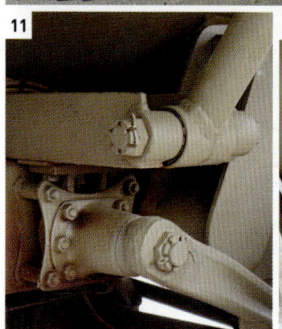

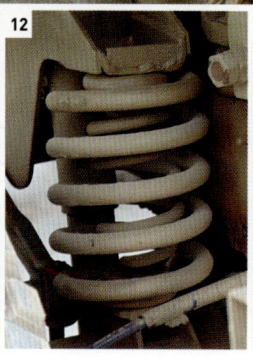

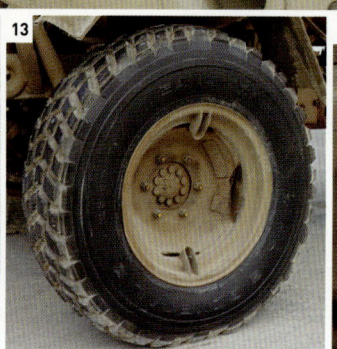

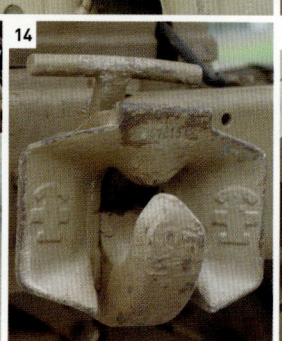

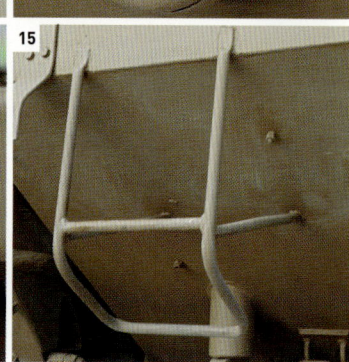

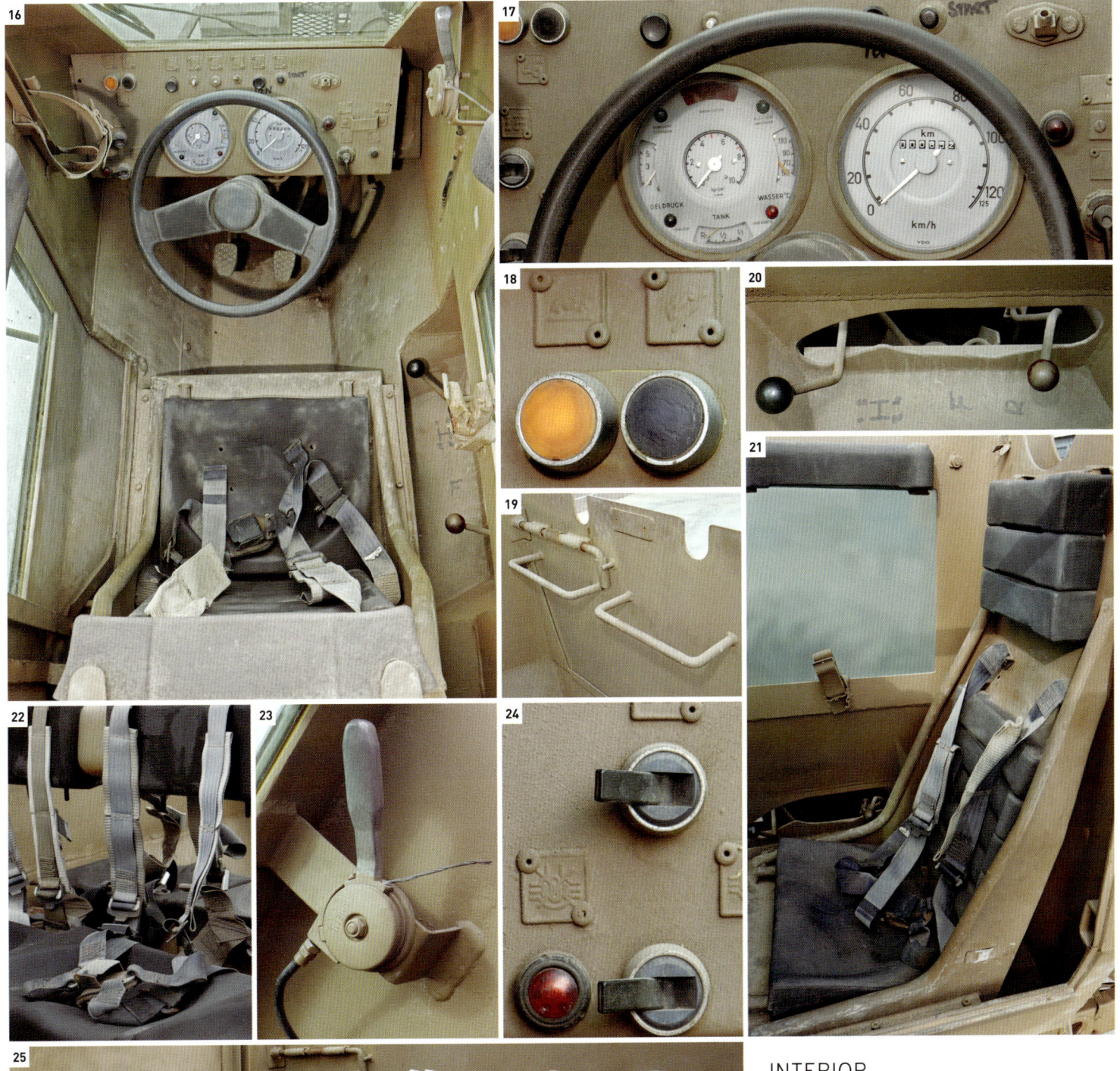

INTERIOR

The driver's position was set high off the ground behind the front axle, protected by bullet-proof windows to the front and sides. In the open-topped rear troop compartment were 10 back-to-back seats, each with a four-point seatbelt harness.

16. Looking down into driver's compartment
17. Instrument panel   18. Warning indicator lights
19. Hand and foot holds with bolt to release side panel
20. Gear and direction levers   21. Driver's seat
22. Safety harness   23. Choke lever   24. Driver's panel switches   25. Infantry seats

Modern Tank Warfare

The obsolescence of the tank has often been declared. The arrival of any new antitank technology has inevitably led to predictions of "the end of the tank", from the hand-held antitank weapons of World War II and the attack helicopters of the Cold War to modern drones. However, tanks have proved amazingly resilient, even in the modern era.

Due to tanks' high cost of manufacture, and the fact that there is no civilian market, few countries now retain the ability to build them. The vast amounts of time and money needed to develop a new tank – at best, around 10 years during the Cold War – mean that it is cheaper and easier to improve, upgrade, or rebuild older models. These upgrades continue to enable tanks to cope with the latest threats.

Russia's invasion of Ukraine in 2022 has raised the profile of tanks and other armoured vehicles, which are well suited to the war's tactical needs, such as the taking and holding of ground. The conflict's mass use of aerial drones and "top attack" weapons that destroy tanks' thinner upper armour from above has also presented a major threat. However, armoured vehicles continue to be effective on the battlefield with modifications such as protective cages to counter these new weapons.

A Ukrainian T-64 tank fires on Russian positions in the Donetsk region of Ukraine in January 2024. Ukraine continues to modernize its T-64s.

Troop Carriers

Since 1989, the development of Armoured Personnel Carriers (APCs) and Infantry Fighting Vehicles (IFVs) has been driven by technological advances and experience gained from conflicts such as the 1990–91 Gulf War and the two-decade "War on Terror". New generations of troop carriers, and upgraded older variants, have greatly increased lethality (the weapons carried) and survivability (the protection for the occupants). Improved digital fire-control systems, state-of-the-art sensors, and networked threat-detection enable rapid and often automated target engagement with the enemy. Better crew ergonomics, modular armour packages, and mine-resistant hulls have provided increased protection for crew and passengers.

Bullet-resistant front windows

40 mm cannon

△ XA-185
Date 1994 **Origin** Finland
Weight 13.5 tonnes (14.9 tons)
Engine Valmet 612 DWI diesel, 183 kW (246 hp)
Main armament 12.7 mm NSV machine-gun

The amphibious, six-wheeled XA-180, the first XA series vehicle, was introduced in 1984. The improved XA-185, which has served in peacekeeping roles and seen action in Afghanistan and Ukraine, has a more powerful engine. Further upgrades led to the non-amphibious XA-186, XA-188, and larger XA-203. XAs have been sold to Norway, Sweden, Estonia, Latvia, and the Netherlands.

△ CV90
Date 1993 **Origin** Sweden
Weight 22.8 tonnes (25.1 tons)
Engine Scania DI 14 diesel, 410 kW (550 hp)
Main armament 40 mm Bofors L/70 cannon

Developed in the late 1980s, Sweden's CV90 (or Stridsfordon 90) can carry between six and eight infantry personnel. Variants include command, forward-observation, anti-aircraft, and recovery vehicles. Export models are typically armed with a 30 mm or 35 mm cannon. Swedish, Danish, and Norwegian CV90s served in Afghanistan, and vehicles donated by Sweden to Ukraine since 2022 have seen combat against Russian forces.

▽ Piranha III
Date 1998 **Origin** Switzerland
Weight 22 tonnes (24.3 tons)
Engine Caterpillar C9 diesel, 298 kW (400 hp)
Main armament Variable

With sales to more than 12 countries, Piranha III variants range from electronic warfare, assault gun, and ambulance models to standard armoured personnel carriers. Derived from the Piranha, Canada's LAV-III is used by Canadian and New Zealand armed forces. The LAV-III also forms the basis of the US Army's Stryker family of carriers and combat vehicles.

Driver's hatch

INFANTERÍA DE MARINA

▷ BvS10 Viking
Date 2004 **Origin** Sweden
Weight 11.3 tonnes (12.5 tons)
Engine Cummins ISBe250 30 diesel, 205 kW (275 hp)
Main armament 40 mm CTAI CT40 cannon, 7.62 mm L7 machine-gun

Steered by hydraulic rams between the two cabs, the lightly armoured Viking has superb mobility on its rubber tracks, even over snow and sand. Operations in Afghanistan required extra armour to be added. The Viking was originally developed for the British Royal Marines from the smaller, unarmoured Bv206.

Crew compartment

Firing port

◁ VBCI
Date 2008 **Origin** France
Weight 29 tonnes (32 tons)
Engine Volvo diesel, 410 kW (550 hp)
Main armament 25 mm GIAT M811 cannon

Armed with a stabilized 25 mm cannon and designed for use as an infantry fighting vehicle, the three-man, eight-wheeled French VBCI can accommodate up to nine soldiers. The VBCI has been deployed in Lebanon, Afghanistan, and Mali. France currently operates 630, of which 110 are command posts.

▷ Schützenpanzer Puma
Date 2010 **Origin** Germany
Weight 43 tonnes (47.4 tons)
Engine MTU MT 892 Ka-501 diesel, 813 kW (1,090 hp)
Main armament 30 mm MK30-2/ABM cannon

The successor to the impressive Marder, the Puma houses its three crew and six infantrymen together in the hull; the turret is unmanned. Its modular armour can be increased to suit a higher threat level or, for air transport, reduced to lower the weight to 31 tonnes (34.2 tons).

Smoke grenade dischargers

◁ BMD-4M Airborne Assault Vehicle
Date 2014 **Origin** Russia
Weight 14 tonnes (15.4 tons)
Engine UTD-29 multifuel, 373 kW (500 hp)
Main armament 1 x 100 mm 2A70 smoothbore gun, 1 x 30 mm 2A72 cannon

The lightweight yet powerfully armed BMD-4M – derived from the BMD-4, which entered service with the Russian Airborne Troops (VDV) in 2004 – uses the engine and other automotive components from the earlier BMP-3 to ease costs, logistics, and maintenance. The BMD-MDM is an armoured personnel carrier variant.

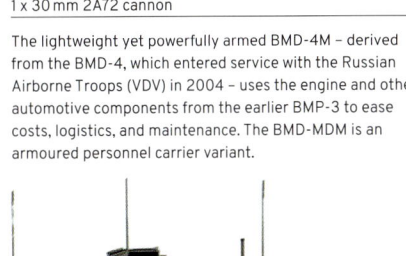

8x8 drive with hydropneumatic suspension

▷ Ajax
Date 2016 **Origin** UK
Weight 38 tonnes (41.9 tons)
Engine MTU 199 diesel, 597 kW (800 hp)
Main armament 40 mm CTAI CT40 cannon

The British Army's Ajax is an Intelligence, Surveillance, Target Acquisition, and Reconnaissance (ISTAR) vehicle with digital electronic architecture that allows it to share information with friendly forces. It is based on the ASCOD (Austrian Spanish Cooperation Development) armoured fighting vehicle. Command, specialist personnel carrier, engineering, reconnaissance, repair, and recovery variants are planned.

▷ M1A2 Abrams
Date 1992 **Origin** USA
Weight 63 tonnes (69.4 tons)
Engine Textron Lycoming AGT1500 gas turbine, 1,119 kW (1,500 hp)
Main armament 120 mm M256 L/44 smoothbore gun

The M1A1, which entered service in 1985, had superior suspension and transmission to the M1, and was up-gunned with a 120 mm smoothbore. The M1A2 added a commander's independent thermal viewer (CITV), which enabled the tank commander to look in a different direction to the gunner. The M1A2's electronics and computer systems were enhanced following experience in the Gulf.

△ T-90S
Date 1994 **Origin** Russia
Weight 48.6 tonnes (53.6 tons)
Engine ChTZ V92S2 V12 diesel, 746 kW (1,000 hp)
Main armament 125 mm 2A46M5 L/48 gun

Intended as a replacement for the T-72, from which it was developed, the T-90's upgraded onboard systems incorporated features from the T-80 and integrated the Shtora active protection system (APS). The largest user of the tank is India, which has 1,250 of the T-90S export version, followed by Russia, with around 550. The T-90 has seen combat in Ukraine and Syria.

△ Challenger 2
Date 1994 **Origin** UK
Weight 74.9 tonnes (82.6 tons)
Engine Perkins CV12 V12 diesel, 895 kW (1,200 hp)
Main armament 120 mm L30A1 L/55 rifled gun

The Challenger 2 has level 2L Dorchester armour modules on its hull and turret sides, electronic countermeasures, and heat and radar absorbent Solar Shield camouflage. Despite its name, the Challenger 2 has few parts that are compatible with the Challenger 1. Fitted with extra armour, Challenger 2s took part in the invasion of Iraq in 2003, by which time the British Army had 386.

▷ PT 91 Twardy
Date 1995 **Origin** Poland
Weight 45.9 tonnes (50.6 tons)
Engine PZL-Wola Type S12U multifuel, 634 kW (850 hp)
Main armament 125 mm D81TM smoothbore gun

An upgrade of the Soviet-designed, Polish made T-72M, the Twardy has a more powerful engine and transmission, additional Explosive Reactive Armour (ERA), and improved gun stabilization. Poland took delivery of 233 tanks, along with armoured recovery and engineering variants; 48 Twardys were bought by Malaysia, while India ordered more than 352 of the recovery variant from Poland.

▽ T-84
Date 1999 **Origin** Ukraine
Weight 51 tonnes (56 tons)
Engine KMDB 6TD-4 6-cylinder diesel, 1,119 kW (1,500 hp)
Main armament 125 mm KBA-3 cannon

Evolved post-1991 from the T-80UD – a Ukrainian diesel variant of the Soviet T-80 MBT – the T-84 entered service in 1999. It is armed with the 125 mm KBA-3 smoothbore cannon, fed by an automatic loader. The T-84's passive and reactive armour systems are augmented by active protection systems. In its modern Oplot variant, the T-84 outperforms many current Russian tanks in speed, survivability, and rate of fire.

Post-Cold War Tanks

At the end of the Cold War, many tanks were scrapped as nations reduced the size of their militaries. Vehicles under development in the late 1980s tended to be introduced slowly and in smaller numbers, while some existing tanks received upgrades, such as the introduction of the L/55 120 mm gun on the Leopard 2A6. Post-1989 conflicts have shown that, although heavy and difficult to deploy, tanks still have a battlefield role. In the 21st century, new vehicles have started to enter service, some with countries making their first forays into tank design.

POST COLD-WAR TANKS · 269

Spaced armour at front of turret
120 mm main gun

Tracks with rubber pads

△ **Leopard 2A6**
Date 2001 **Origin** Germany
Weight 62.4 tonnes (68.8 tons)
Engine MTU MB 873 Ka-501 diesel, 1,119 kW (1,500 hp)
Main armament 120 mm Rheinmetall 120 L/55 smoothbore gun

The 2A6 is substantially upgraded compared to the 2A4 of the Cold War era. The turret, now electrically driven rather than hydraulically powered, has distinctive wedge-shaped spaced armour, and it carries a more powerful L/55 gun. The gunner's sight has been relocated to the turret roof.

△ **Merkava Mark 4**
Date 2004 **Origin** Israel
Weight 65 tonnes (71.27 tons)
Engine MTU 883 V12 diesel, 1,119 kW (1,500 hp)
Main armament 120 mm IMI MG253 L/44 smoothbore gun

Like its Merkava forerunners, the Mark 4 prioritizes crew safety, with features such as automatic fire suppression, nuclear, biological, and chemical (NBC) warfare defence, and the Trophy active protection system (APS), which counters antitank threats. Electronic aids, such as a battle management system and automatic target tracking, enhance the tank's combat effectiveness. The Mark 4 has seen combat in Lebanon and Gaza.

△ **T-14 Armata**
Date 2015 **Origin** Russia
Weight Unknown
Engine ChTZ 12N360 V12 diesel, 1,119+ kW (1,500+ hp)
Main armament 125 mm 2A82-1M smoothbore gun

Based on the Armata Universal Combat Platform – a versatile platform for a range of armoured vehicles – the T-14 is much longer and taller than previous Soviet and Russian tanks. The crew of three sit at the front, while the unmanned turret houses the gun, autoloader, and sights, and both a hard- and a soft-kill APS.

Radio antenna

125 mm KBA-3 smoothbore cannon

120 mm main gun

◁ **Altay**
Date 2016 **Origin** Turkey
Weight 65 tonnes (71.7 tons)
Engine MTU MT 883 Ka-501 diesel, 1,119 kW (1,500 hp)
Main armament 120 mm L/55 smoothbore gun

A milestone for the Turkish armaments industry, the Altay is the country's first domestically designed tank. It is based on the South Korean K2 Black Panther but is mostly being developed and built by Turkish companies, including the sights and advanced fire-control system. Production is expected to total 1,000.

M1A2 Abrams

The Abrams was designed when engaging Soviet-bloc tanks in Europe was thought to be the most likely combat scenario. Since then, this American tank has seen action in very different locations and environments, yet time and again the Abrams has proved itself in battle. Made in large numbers – around 11,000 to date – the Abrams now equips seven national armies

AT THE TIME WORK BEGAN ON THE ABRAMS, the West displayed an ambivalent attitude towards tanks – the dilemma of potentially needing them and seeing other nations developing their own tanks, versus tightening military budgets and the restrictions they imposed on Western tank production and technology.

Viewed as a replacement for the M60, the first Abrams model carried a version of the British L7 105 mm gun, with ammunition stored separately in a blow-out compartment to protect the crew. The tank's small gas turbine engine was incredibly powerful but proved twice as thirsty as a diesel equivalent. After an American team was shown the latest British developments in Chobham armour in 1973, the tank was redesigned to adopt the new protection system. An upgrade of the laminate armour incorporating depleted uranium was later fitted to the M1A1 model, doubling the level of protection. The M1A1's armament was upgraded to the 120 mm German smoothbore gun, which gave it a huge advantage over Iraqi tanks in the 1991 Gulf War.

Improvements to the M1A2 model included a Commander's Independent Thermal Viewer, enhanced digital equipment, and a new fire control system. Street fighting in the Iraq War led to the development of the Tank Urban Survival Kit (TUSK) in 2006, which gives the tank better protection in built-up areas. With these upgrades, the Abrams will undoubtedly continue to be a powerful presence on the battlefield for decades to come.

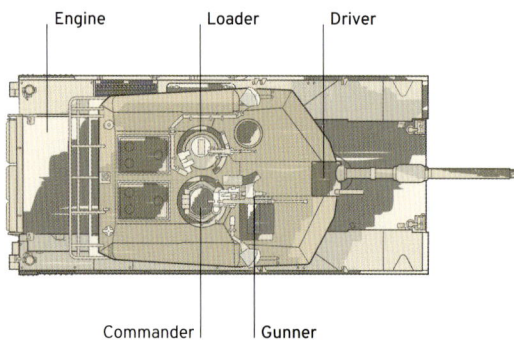

Commander's cupola, with open hatch

Engine compartment at rear

Armoured skirt

SPECIFICATIONS	
Name	M1A2 Abrams
Date	1992
Origin	USA
Production	Approx. 1,500
Engine	Textron Lycoming AGT1500 gas turbine, 1,119 kW (1,500 hp)
Weight	63 tonnes (69.4 tons)
Main armament	120 mm M256 smoothbore
Secondary armament	.50 Browning M2HB, 2 x 7.62 mm M240 MGs
Crew	4
Armour thickness	Unknown

FRONT VIEW

REAR VIEW

Machine-gun mount

Hi-tech destroyer
The M1A2 SEPv2 (System Enhancement Package), the latest incarnation of the Abrams, includes a Thermal Management System and upgrades to communications, display screens, sights, and other electronic systems. It also has an added auxiliary power unit.

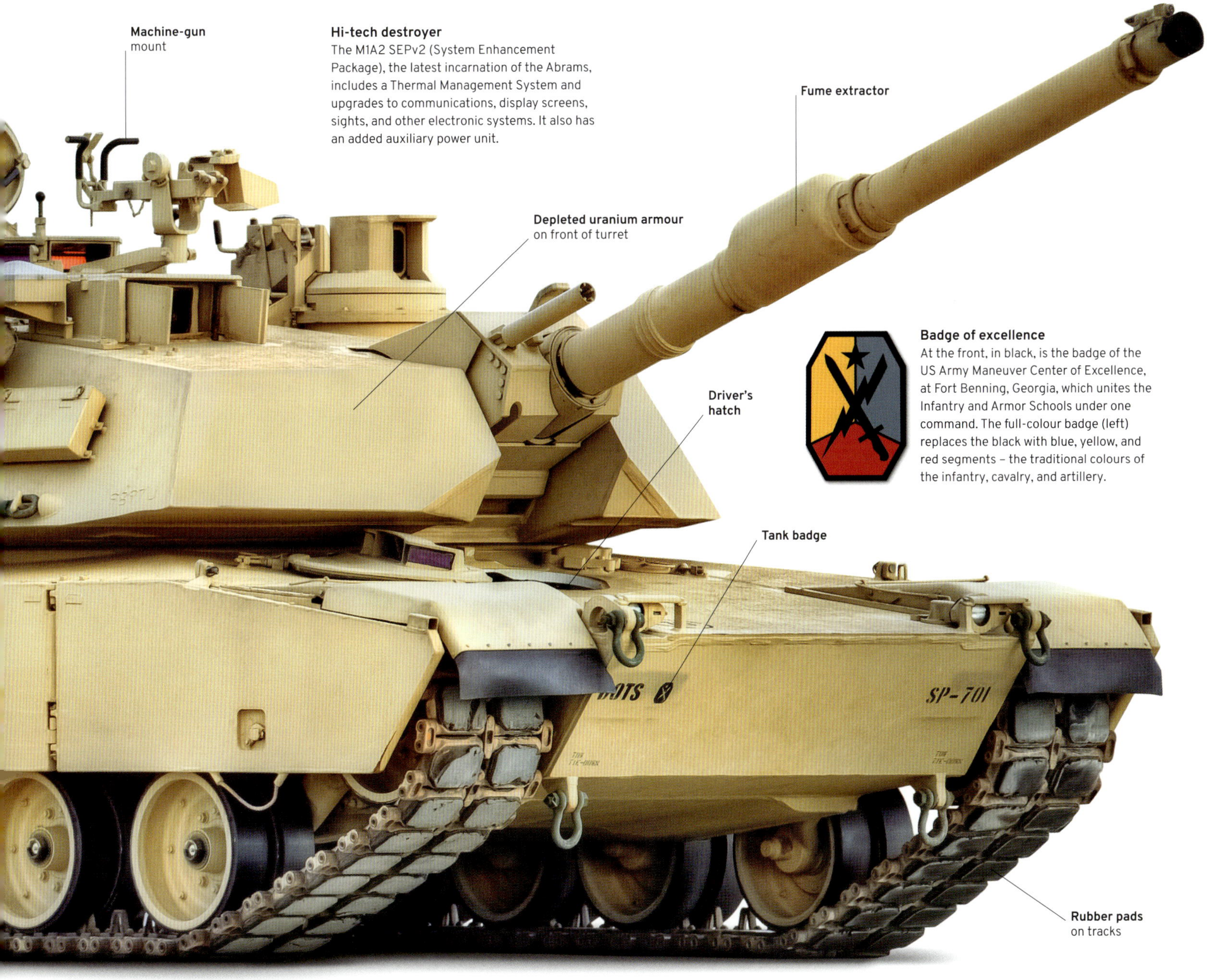

Fume extractor

Depleted uranium armour on front of turret

Driver's hatch

Badge of excellence
At the front, in black, is the badge of the US Army Maneuver Center of Excellence, at Fort Benning, Georgia, which unites the Infantry and Armor Schools under one command. The full-colour badge (left) replaces the black with blue, yellow, and red segments – the traditional colours of the infantry, cavalry, and artillery.

Tank badge

Rubber pads on tracks

INTERIOR

The M1A2's interior is lined with Kevlar, which protects the crew against spalling (splinters caused by the explosion of enemy projectiles). Ammunition is kept in armoured compartments, which feature blow-out panels. These minimize any damage should ammunition "cook off" in the heat of an explosion by ensuring that the force of the blast is directed away from the crew compartment.

1. Commander's station, looking right   2. Driver's station, looking forwards
3. Driver's steering and throttle T-bar control   4. Gunner's station   5. Gunner's primary sight eyepiece   6. Mounting for co-axial 7.62 machine-gun (not fitted)
7. Gunner's control handles   8. Top of main gun breech (closed)   9. Loader's station, looking left   10. Main gun breech (closed), showing case deflector tray
11. Bottom of main gun breech (open)

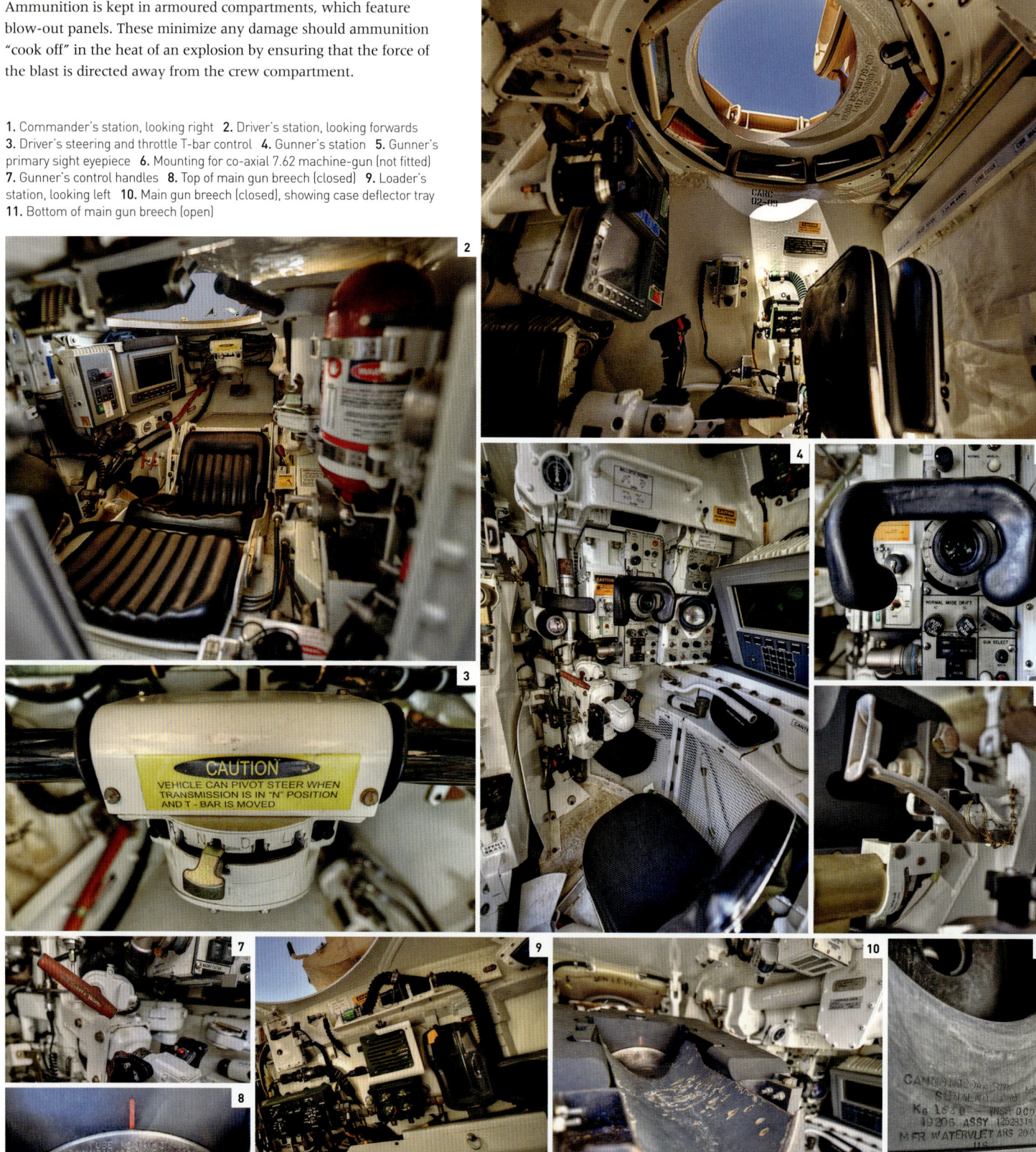

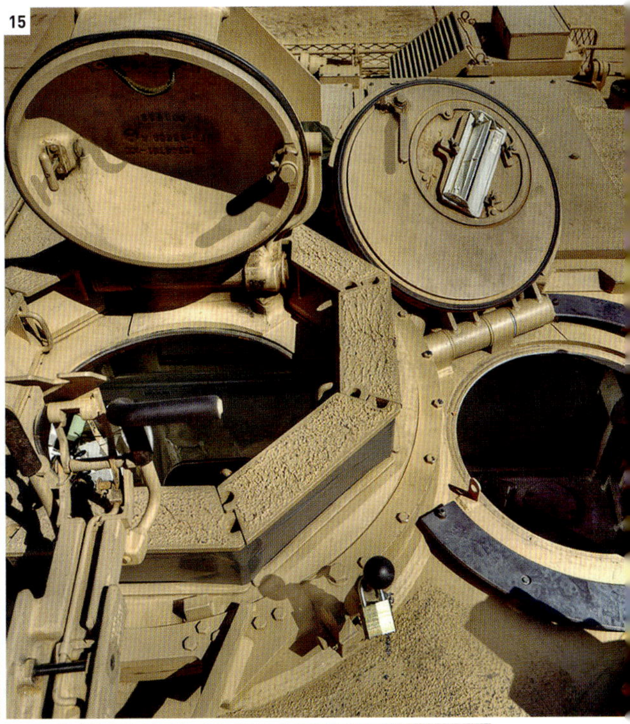

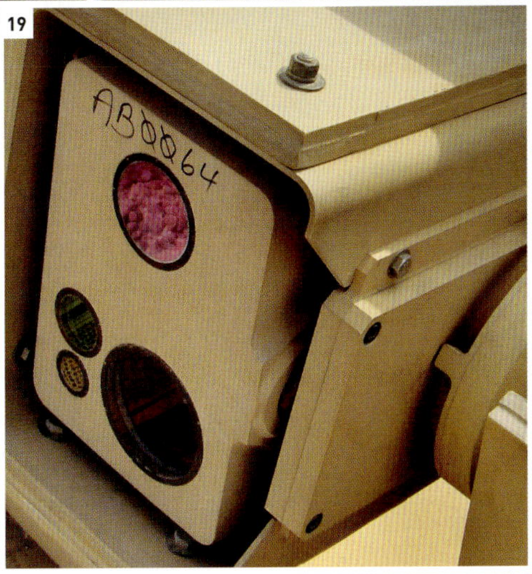

EXTERIOR

The M1A2 is one of the world's heaviest main battle tanks. The vast weight is partly due to the formidable composite armour, which is augmented by depleted uranium mesh on the turret and the front of the hull. This extraordinary armour is very effective against most current anti-tank weapons.

12. Towing eye **13.** Road wheel hub **14.** Road wheels and track **15.** Commander's (left) and loader's hatches **16.** Commander's cupola **17.** Track with rubber pads **18.** Loader's 7.62mm M240 machine-gun **19.** Common Remotely Operated Weapons Station sights **20.** Nuclear, biological, and chemical protection system vent **21.** Vapour Compression System Unit, part of the Thermal Management System **22.** Infantry phone **23.** Drive sprocket

Amphibious Warfare

The disembarkation of forces on an occupied coastline, such as the 1944 D-Day landings in Normandy, is a high-risk procedure. Many such amphibious assaults are complex "combined operations" using land, naval, and air assets in a coordinated way. Conditions such as weather, geography, and the nature of enemy defences further complicate the event.

For centuries, boats had been used to ferry soldiers and marines ashore, but in the wake of World War I and the Allies' disastrous experience of landing at Gallipoli in Turkey, the first dedicated landing craft were designed. World War II saw the production of a plethora of landing craft variations, along with amphibious vehicles and adaptations that allowed land vehicles to float or "wade" to help troops ashore. Today, many countries insist that their vehicles are amphibious and able to cross rivers and lakes, if not the open sea, while hovercraft – also known as Landing Craft Air Cushion (LCAC) – are able to access coastlines unreachable with conventional landing craft.

A US LCAC takes armour from ship to shore as part of the Bold Alligator amphibious assault exercise at Camp Lejeune, North Carolina, US, in 2017.

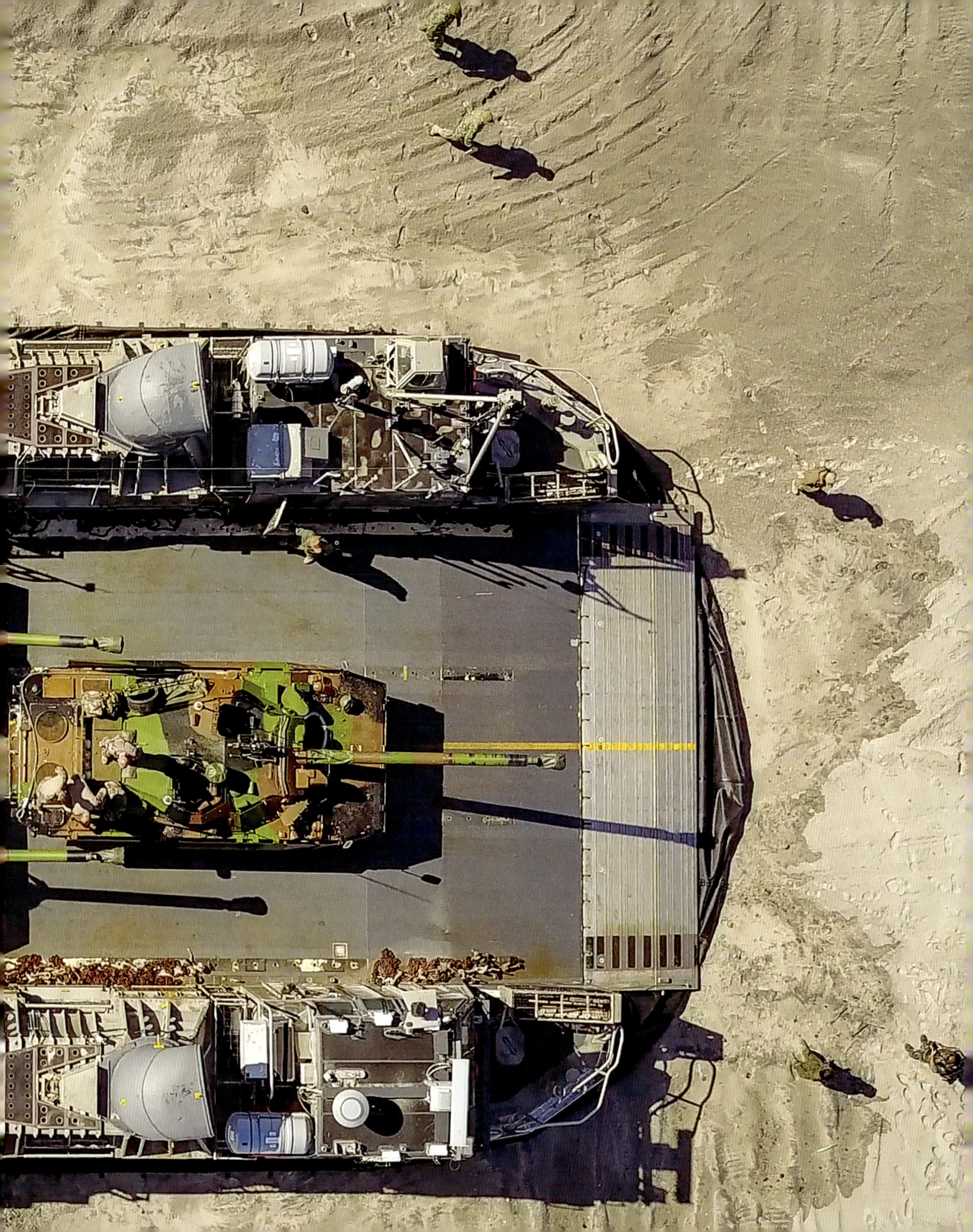

Warships in the Digital Age

From "stealth" hull profiles to autonomous pilots, the next generations of surface warship are designed to optimize lethality, survivability, and economy. The result is smaller and lighter vessels offering navies more tactical flexibility. At the same time, debates continue about the future of the biggest vessels, particularly aircraft carriers.

New generation
The USS *Zumwalt* was initially intended to provide fire support for ground forces. However, its proposed gun system was deemed too expensive and the ship was sent for refit with missile launchers for surface combat.

In October 2016, the USS *Zumwalt*, a new guided missile destroyer, was commissioned into service with the US Navy. The *Zumwalt*'s appearance was strikingly different to that of existing US Navy surface vessels: it had strange, angular hull lines that sloped inwards from the waterline, a pyramid-like superstructure, and a deck curiously free from the usual guns and equipment. The *Zumwalt* was part of the world's very first generation of "stealth" warships.

Stealth and signatures

When applied to warships, the term "stealth" refers to a profile and layout deliberately designed to minimize the ship's radar signature. This approach is backed by key tactical aspirations: a stealth warship might evade detection by electronic surveillance altogether, or its signature might be so reduced that the operators of enemy sensors confuse the ship with a minor civilian vessel. Despite the fact that the USS *Zumwalt* is 183 m (600 ft) long, its radar signature as it appears on a screen is described as resembling that of a small fishing boat. Such ships are harder to spot visually and when using sonar detection. Their stealth characteristics also mean that the vessels are less vulnerable to the tracking systems on antiship missiles, increasing their survivability. Stealth principles are now embedding themselves in many naval fleets. Examples include Swedish *Visby*-class corvettes, Chinese Type 055 guided-missile destroyers, French *La Fayette*-class frigates, and Japanese *Mogami*-class frigates.

Multiple hulls

Stealth is just one of many recent innovations in the design of warships. Another is the exploration of trimaran (or double-outrigger) hulls for use in littoral combat ships – vessels intended to operate extremely close to enemy coastlines. A trimaran hull features a main hull plus small outrigger hulls attached to either side of the boat by lateral beams. The main advantage of this configuration is that it considerably reduces the vessel's draught compared to that of a monohull (single-hulled) design, so the craft can operate in much shallower waters. Trimarans also have good seakeeping – the ability to remain stable under rough conditions at sea – without the need for heavy weighting at the bottom, as in a typical monohull vessel.

Weapons and systems

The future armaments of warships are also beginning to take shape, with new forms of offensive and defensive weaponry currently in development. Until comparatively recently, the US Navy was funding research into electromagnetic railguns as potential replacements for conventional guns. These weapons use electromagnetic forces to accelerate and launch inert rounds at astonishing speeds of around 7,240 km/h (4,500 mph), the projectiles relying on extreme kinetic energy alone to deliver their destructive effects. The railgun offers the possibility of warships without vulnerable explosive magazines on board, but severe issues with the power supply and barrel caused the US programme to be cancelled in 2021. Several other navies have pursued railgun technologies, however, so the weapon may yet appear on future warships.

Two major new fields in the design of naval weapons are hypersonic antiship missiles and directed-energy weapons (DEWs). The former are missiles that fly at Mach 5+, their extreme speed making them, with current technologies, almost impossible to defeat once in their final approach to target. Directed-energy weapons, by contrast, are weapons that fire laser or radio-frequency (RF) energy to destroy incoming threats, such as drones, small attack boats, and missiles.

An operational example of a DEW is the American High Energy Laser with Integrated Optical-dazzler and Surveillance (HELIOS). This has been integrated into the US Navy's influential Aegis Combat System, which tracks and engages multiple targets simultaneously. Several international navies have purchased Aegis, while others have developed systems with similar capabilities.

Ships without crews

One of the new frontiers of naval design is unmanned surface vehicles (USVs) and unmanned underwater vehicles (UUVs) – ships and submarines that are piloted remotely. Unmanned ships offer navies a number of important advantages. By operating without crews on board, they can be sent into dangerous situations without risk to human life, and they have almost unlimited endurance. Furthermore, without the need for crew quarters or stores, the ships can be smaller and cheaper to produce and the running costs are correspondingly lower. It is also easier to build such ships in "modular" formats, so they can be adapted quickly to new roles.

Uncrewed ship
This unmanned surface vehicle (USV) was developed by American company Leidos. Such vessels are becoming common in the US Navy. Note the trimaran hull design – ideal for littoral operations requiring shallow-draught vessels.

At present, most unmanned vessels in service are small littoral or support craft. However, the recent war in Ukraine has revealed their offensive potential. Ukrainian USVs packed with explosives were used in multiple assaults on Russian vessels, sinking or seriously damaging several ships, including the *Tarantul-III*-class missile corvette *Ivanovets* and the *Ropucha*-class landing ship *Olenegorsky Gornyak*. With the growing application of AI, the capabilities of unmanned warships will continue to expand, potentially transforming even small navies into advanced maritime fighting forces.

Cutting-edge carrier
Led by the USS *Gerald R. Ford*, US Navy ships sail in formation in the Mediterranean in 2023. The *Gerald R. Ford*-class is the most advanced US carrier type today. One of its key features is the Electromagnetic Aircraft Launch System (EMALS) for launching aircraft.

> **TALKING POINT**
>
> ## AI and Navies
>
> Already many of the world's navies are testing AI-powered digital systems aboard warships. The advantages of AI for navies include: the rapid acceleration in threat detection and defensive response, with the AI able to process thousands of sensor inputs in fractions of a second; greater speed and accuracy in the analysis of electronic data; improved coordination of fighting forces across a network; and more efficient management of supply, maintenance, and administration. The ultimate goal is to use AI to outperform by orders of magnitude enemies without AI or with inferior AI systems. The key question, however, is whether AI will support sailors or, in the long run, replace them.

> "**Transforming ourselves** and our great institution for the **dangerous decades** ahead is our imperative."
>
> ADMIRAL VERNON E. CLARK, US NAVY CHIEF OF NAVAL OPERATIONS, 2000–05

The Combat Information Center (CIC) of a modern US Navy carrier is the tactical focal point for command-and-control decisions during aircraft operations.

▽ Charles de Gaulle
Date 2001 **Origin** France
Displacement 42,500 tonnes (46,848 tons)
Length 261.5 m (858 ft)
Top speed 27 knots (50 km/h)

Construction of this nuclear-powered carrier started in 1989, but work stopped on four occasions due to financial issues. Commissioned in May 2001, five years late, the ship sailed to the Indian Ocean in November, where it flew missions into Afghanistan in support of the US-led Operation Enduring Freedom.

▽ USS Ronald Reagan
Date 2003 **Origin** USA
Displacement 103,056 tonnes (113,600 tons)
Length 332 m (1,092 ft)
Top speed 30 knots (56 km/h)

Carrying up to 60 aircraft and with a crew of 5,000, this *Nimitz*-class aircraft carrier is one of the largest ships afloat. The *Ronald Reagan* has spent much of its service career to date with the US Seventh Fleet, which is based in Japan.

▽ Cavour
Date 2008 **Origin** Italy
Displacement 27,100 tonnes (29,873 tons)
Length 244 m (801 ft)
Top speed 29 knots (54 km/h)

Originally equipped with Harrier jump jets, the *Cavour* now has a complement of F35 Lightnings. When acting as a support or amphibious landing ship, it can carry 24 tanks or other vehicles and 325 marines, and deploy heavy transport helicopters. The large hangar area was ideal for the role *Cavour* played in relief operations after the 2010 Haiti earthquake.

Island positioned amidships

▽ Juan Carlos
Date 2010 **Origin** Spain
Displacement 26,000 tonnes (28,660 tons)
Length 231 m (758 ft)
Top speed 21 knots (39 km/h)

The multi-role *Juan Carlos* can launch Harrier jump jets and helicopters, but its rear docking area, which can accommodate four landing craft, also enables it to act as an amphibious assault ship. The *Juan Carlos* has a large hangar space that can house aircraft or 46 Leopard tanks, and the ship can accommodate 900 soldiers.

▽ USS Gerald R. Ford
Date 2017 **Origin** USA
Displacement 101,600 tonnes (112,000 tons)
Length 337 m (1,106 ft)
Top speed over 30 knots (56 km/h)

On entering service, the US$13.5 billion *Gerald R. Ford* was the largest warship ever built, carrying up to 90 aircraft and a ship's complement of over 4,500. Among the new technologies it introduced was an electromagnetic aircraft launch system (EMALS). It always travels in a carrier strike group, which includes a cruiser, two destroyers or frigates, and a supply ship.

21st-century Aircraft Carriers

An aircraft carrier provides a mobile, seaborne air base. The most substantial carriers are the largest and most complex weapon systems ever built. Carriers are able to launch fast jets and helicopters for aerial missions or boats for amphibious assaults, and their facilities can be used for rescue and disaster recovery operations. While carriers are phenomenally costly naval vessels, they are also symbols of modern power and seen as symbolic of a nation's strategic international influence.

21ST-CENTURY AIRCRAFT CARRIERS · 279

Elevator moves aircraft between the deck and hangar

▽ **JS Kaga**
Date 2017	Origin Japan
Displacement	27,433 tonnes (30,240 tons)
Length	248 m (814 ft)
Top speed	over 30 knots (56 km/h)

Designed as a helicopter carrier but converted to carry aircraft such as the F35 Lightning, the *Kaga* and its sister ship the *Izumo* were the first aircraft carriers built by Japan since the end of World War II. They are part of a general build-up of Japanese military forces due to rising Sino-Japanese tensions in the Pacific region.

Twin islands (forward island controls ship functions, aft island controls flight operations)

◁ **HMS Prince of Wales**
Date 2019	Origin UK
Displacement	80,600 tonnes (88,800 tons)
Length	284 m (932 ft)
Top speed	32 knots (59 km/h)

The *Prince of Wales* is the second *Queen Elizabeth*-class carrier and currently flagship of the fleet. Able to carry 48 F35 Lightning II aircraft, it can also accommodate 250 marines as well as attack and transport helicopters. The ship's nine decks have a combined floor area of 16,000 square metres (19,136 square yards).

Island is located aft, giving more room for aircraft on deck

Flight deck has an electromagnetic aircraft launch system (EMALS) and advanced arresting gear (AAG)

E-2D Advanced Hawkeye airborne early warning and control system (AWACS) aircraft

Main flight deck has a 14-degree "ski jump" for takeoff

◁ **INS Vikrant**
Date 2022	Origin India
Displacement	45,000 tonnes (49,600 tons)
Length	262.5 m (861 ft)
Top speed	30 knots (56 km/h)

India has decided to deploy a three-carrier fleet: one vessel each for sea service east and west of the country, and one in reserve. The *Vikrant* can host up to 36 aircraft, both fixed-wing and rotary. It is the first carrier built in India, at a cost of US$3.1 billion.

USS George Washington

Commissioned in 1992 and boasting a flight deck covering 1.8 hectares (4.5 acres) – roughly the size of two-and-a-half soccer pitches – the USS *George Washington* is one of the US Navy's 10 *Nimitz*-class "supercarriers". The largest military vessels ever to take to the seas, these enormous aircraft carriers are the ultimate symbols of modern naval power.

SUPERCARRIERS SUCH AS the *George Washington*, the sixth US *Nimitz* class carrier, function as mobile strike platforms that can operate from anywhere in international waters. The *George Washington* can accommodate 85 aircraft, including fighter, strike, and transport planes, airborne early warning (AEW) aircraft, and helicopters.

The ship's dominant feature is the "island" superstructure. This command-and-control centre, located on the starboard side, houses the bridge and primary flight-control area. From here, officers monitor activities below. During flight operations, when four aircraft can be launched per minute, the deck is bustling with activity, with jets taking off and landing, and being refuelled, manoeuvred, and armed. Launch is aided by four catapults, two in the bows and two at the forward end of the angled deck: the landing deck is angled to port, to allow other activities to take place while aircraft return to the ship. When landing, a plane's tailhook must catch one of four high-tensile steel arrestor wires running across the flight deck. These decelerate the aircraft rapidly, bringing it to a halt within two seconds. A pilot increases the throttle when touching down, so that if the aircraft fails to catch the arrestor wires it still has sufficient speed to take off again and attempt another landing – a practice known as "touch and go".

Most aircraft are stored in the vast internal hangar, which stretches for much of the ship's length. Below deck are living quarters for the ship's personnel – the *George Washington* is a floating home for around 6,000 service men and women.

Floating battle station
Although designed primarily to offer an offensive strike capability via its jets, the *George Washington* is equipped with its own defences, such as anti-aircraft and antimissile weapon systems, and rapid-fire 20 mm guns.

USS GEORGE WASHINGTON • 281

Angled flight deck · Catapult tracks · Jet-blast deflector · Arrestor wire · Elevator · Island superstructure

SPECIFICATIONS	
Name	USS *George Washington*
Commissioned	1992
Class and type	*Nimitz*-class aircraft carrier
Displacement	105,870 tonnes (116,700 tons)
Length	332.8 m (1,092 ft)
Propulsion	2 × Westinghouse nuclear reactors
Complement	3,532 ship's company; 2,480 air wing
Armament	2 × Mk 57 Mod3 Sea Sparrow
Maximum speed	30 knots (56 km/h)

INTERIOR

The control rooms for the ship and for flying operations are based both in the island superstructure and below deck. In addition to the aircraft hangar, where aircraft are serviced and stored, the below-deck areas include the catapult and arrestor-gear machinery, 44 magazines, the nuclear power plant, and the engine room. Facilities for the thousands of crew and air wing personnel include messes, berths, medical facilities, and a gym.

1. Catapult mechanism instrument panel 2. Bridge 3. Hangar 4. Propeller shaft
5. Operating theatre 6. Arrestor-gear piston 7. Operations room 8. Reactor controls
9. No. 3 Pump room (sends aviation fuel to the flight deck) 10. Primary flight control
11. Engine bay (with F-14 Tomcat engine in foreground) 12. Bakery 13. Briefing room

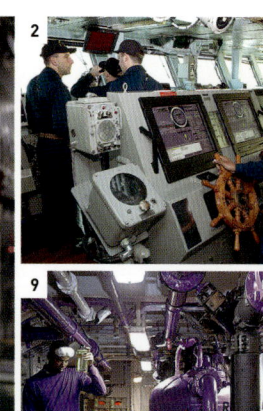

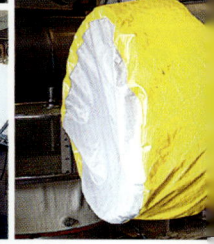

EXTERIOR

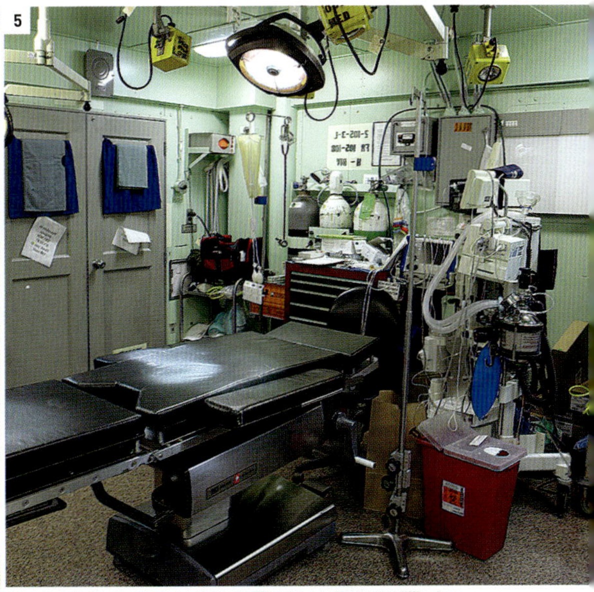

Four hydraulic elevators raise aircraft to the flight deck. The catapult shuttle, which launches the aircraft, attaches to a plane's undercarriage and is propelled along a track set into the flight deck by a steam-powered piston. During take-off, deflector shields prevent engine exhaust gases from causing damage or injury. Arrestor wires towards the stern halt jets as they land. Much of the ship's electronics, including radar and satellite communications equipment, is based on the island, which has the ship's number painted on its sides.

14. Preparing for take-off **15.** Catapult observation pod (retracts below flight deck) **16.** Catapult shuttle **17.** Shuttle track **18.** Jet-blast deflector **19.** Grumman F-14 tomcat landing **20.** Hydraulic elevator **21.** Island superstructure **22.** Aircraft weaponry **23.** Helicopter maintenance

◁ **USS Arleigh Burke**

Date 1991 Origin USA
Displacement 8,362 tonnes (9,218 tons)
Length 154 m (505 ft)
Top speed 30 knots (56 km/h)

A guided-missile destroyer, the *Arleigh Burke* is the lead ship of its class, incorporating stealth technology and the advanced AEGIS integrated total combat system. Armament includes Tomahawk cruise missiles.

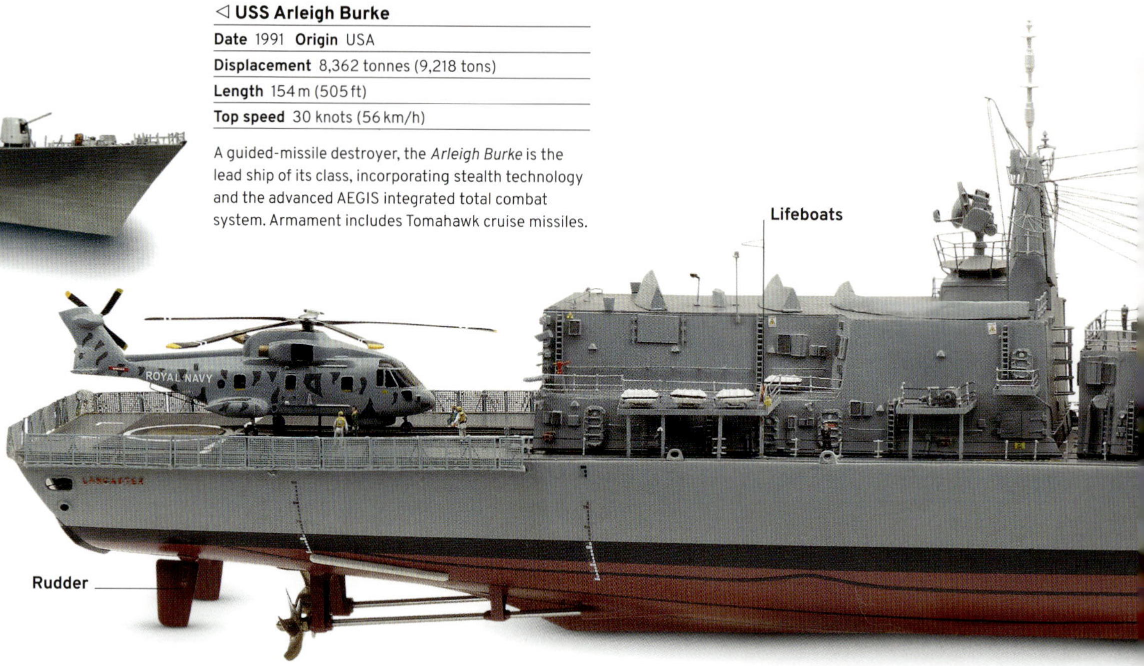

▷ **HMS Lancaster**

Date 1992 Origin UK
Displacement 4,900 tonnes (5,401 tons)
Length 133 m (436 ft)
Top speed 28 knots (52 km/h)

A Type-43 frigate that carries Sting Ray antisubmarine torpedoes, Sea Ceptor anti-aircraft and Harpoon antiship missiles, and a Wildcat helicopter, *Lancaster* has advanced attack and defence capabilities.

▽ **HMCS Vancouver**

Date 1993 Origin Canada
Displacement 4,770 tonnes (5,258 tons)
Length 134 m (440 ft)
Top speed 30 knots (56 km/h)

A multirole frigate, the *Vancouver* is the second *Halifax*-class series vessel of the Canadian Navy, built to deal with surface, aerial, and submarine threats, using missiles, torpedoes, and guns. It can also carry a Sikorsky helicopter.

Modern Destroyers and Frigates

While aircraft carriers and submarines are the most important weapons and key strategic deterrents of today's major naval forces, smaller escort vessels still have an important part to play. Since the Cold War, the distinction between destroyers and frigates has become less fixed, with both the (larger) destroyer and the (smaller) frigate favouring increasingly sophisticated guided-missile systems over guns as their main armament. Modern escort vessels may concentrate on either anti-aircraft or antisubmarine warfare but are usually equipped for both.

△ **Brandenburg-class frigate**

Date 1994 Origin Germany
Displacement 4,490 tonnes (4,949 tons)
Length 139 m (456 ft)
Top speed 29 knots (54 km/h)

The German *Brandenburg*-class frigates were built to perform a range of patrol and combat duties, including antisubmarine warfare, air defence, and flight coordination. Armed with torpedoes and Sea Sparrow and Harpoon missiles, each vessel also carries two Sea Lynx helicopters and powerful electronic countermeasures.

MODERN DESTROYERS AND FRIGATES · 285

Funnel

Sea Ceptor missile system

4.5 in Mark 8 gun

F229

▽ **Brahmaputra-class frigate**
Date 2000 Origin India
Displacement 3,850 tonnes (4,244 tons)
Length 126.5 m (415 ft)
Top speed 30 knots (56 km/h)

The three *Brahmaputra*-class guided-missile frigates, built in India for the Indian Navy, are a development of earlier *Godavari*-class ships. Their enhanced weaponry includes Kh-35 (SS-N-25 Switchblade) antiship missiles and Israeli-made Barak surface-to-air missiles.

Antiship surface-to-surface missiles

Missile-guiding radar

△ **Type 054A frigate**
Date 2008 Origin China
Displacement 3,963 tonnes (4,368 tons)
Length 134 m (440 ft)
Top speed 27 knots (50 km/h)

More than 30 Type 054A guided-missile frigates have been commissioned into China's People's Liberation Army Navy (PLAN). They employ stealth technology and advanced radar and electronic warfare systems, and can carry HQ-16 surface-to-air missiles and YJ-83 antiship cruise missiles, as well as antisubmarine rockets.

▽ **Admiral Gorshkov class**
Date 2018 Origin Russia
Displacement 5,400 tonnes (5,952 tons)
Length 135 m (443 ft)
Top speed 30 knots (56 km/h)

Also known as Project 22350, the *Admiral Gorshkov* class of frigates is one of the latest generations of Russian naval surface vessels. It incorporates stealth design and technologies and has a powerful array of armament, including Kalibr land-attack cruise missiles, Oniks antiship missiles, and Otvet antisubmarine missiles.

Helicopter hangar

Nuclear-powered Submarines

With their armament of submarine-launched ballistic missiles (SLBMs), nuclear-powered submarines are arguably the most powerful weapon system ever developed. Hidden deep beneath the waves, they are able to fire their highly destructive weapons without warning and are virtually immune from retaliatory action by the enemy. The submarines' high level of concealment also provides them with an invaluable capability to retaliate to a first nuclear strike and so act as an effective deterrent. More conventional attack submarines, powered either by nuclear reactors or diesel-electric motors, operate against surface vessels or hunt down other submarines.

△ Project 971 Shchuka-B (Akula-class)
Date 1984 **Origin** USSR
Displacement 7,385 tonnes (8,140 tons) (Akula I)
Length 110.3 m (362 ft)
Top speed 10 knots (19 km/h)

First deployed in 1986, this attack submarine type (designated *Akula*-class by NATO) was advanced for the time and underwent a series of upgrades lasting until the early 2000s. It features a double-hull system and eight torpedo tubes; seven original models were built, of which three are believed to still be in service.

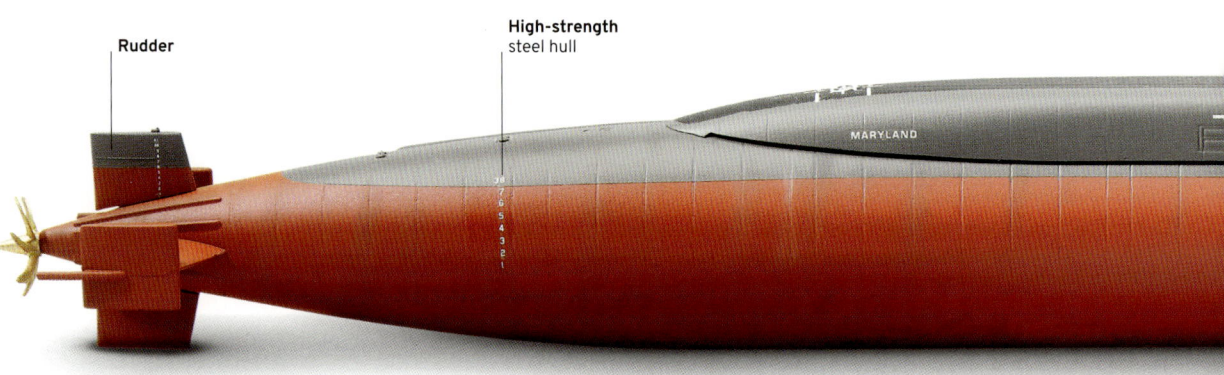

▷ USS Maryland (SSBN-738)
Date 1992 **Origin** USA
Displacement 15,208 tonnes (16,764 tons)
Length 171 m (560 ft)
Top speed 18 knots (33 km/h)

One of 14 *Ohio*-class ballistic missile submarines, *Maryland* is at the forefront of the US Navy's nuclear deterrent. It can carry up to 20 Trident missiles, with multiple warheads per missile and a range of 7,360 km (4,573 miles).

◁ HMS Vanguard (S28)
Date 1993 **Origin** UK
Displacement 15,900 tonnes (17,527 tons) submerged
Length 150 m (492 ft)
Top speed 25 knots (46 km/h) submerged

The lead vessel of its class, the *Vanguard* – the tenth Royal Navy ship to have that name – is armed with 16 Trident SLBMs, each capable of carrying up to 12 warheads. The submarine also has four tubes for Spearfish guided torpedoes.

△ Le Triomphant (S616)
Date 1997 **Origin** France
Displacement 12,640 tonnes (13,933 tons)
Length 138 m (453 ft)
Top speed 20 knots (37 km/h)

Le Triomphant is armed with 16 M51 SLBMs, each with up to ten warheads and a range of around 8,000 km (4,970 miles), and also has four torpedo tubes. It is the lead vessel of its class, which replaced the French navy's *Le Redoutable* class.

NUCLEAR-POWERED SUBMARINES · 287

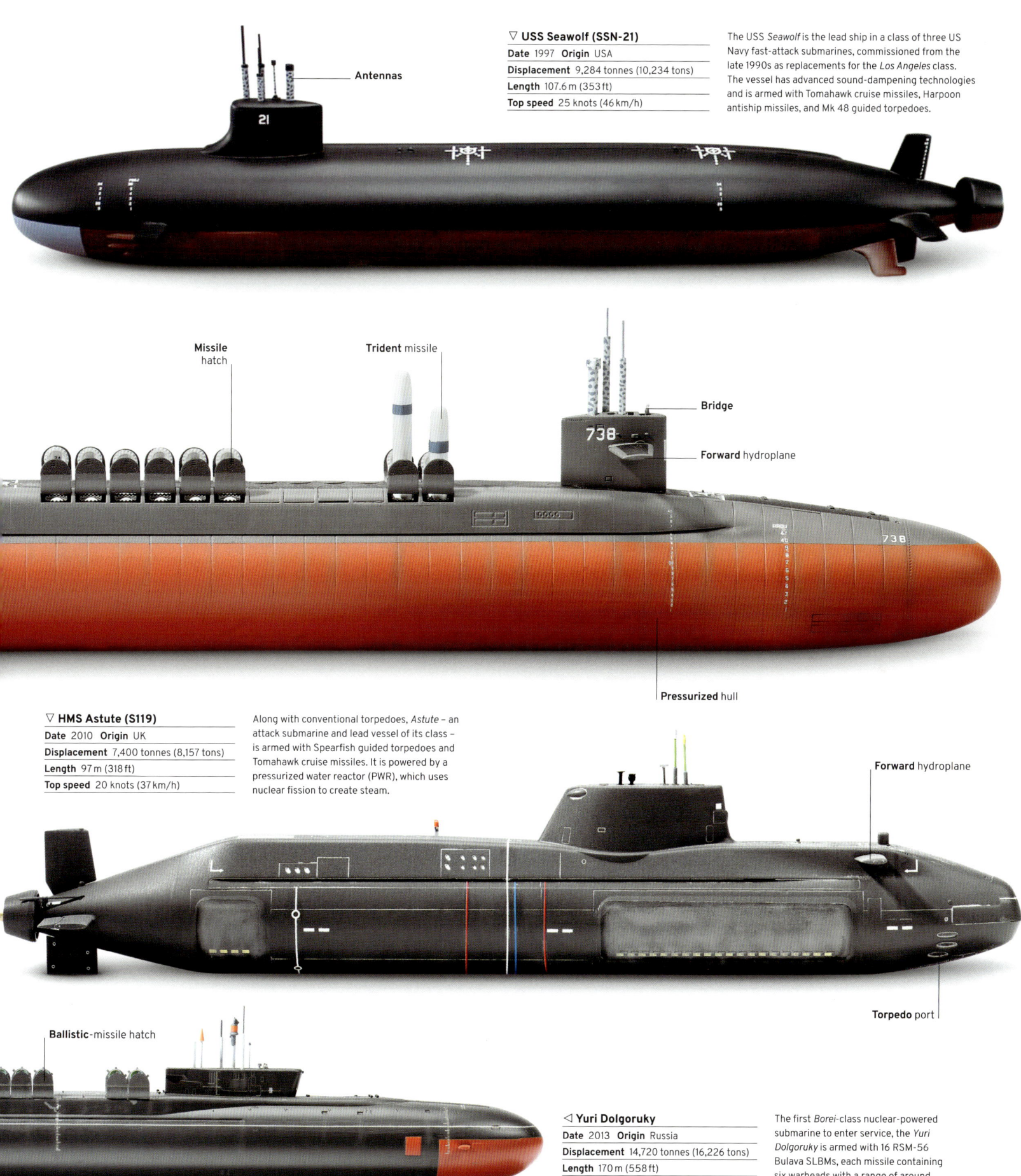

▽ **USS Seawolf (SSN-21)**
Date 1997 Origin USA
Displacement 9,284 tonnes (10,234 tons)
Length 107.6 m (353 ft)
Top speed 25 knots (46 km/h)

The USS *Seawolf* is the lead ship in a class of three US Navy fast-attack submarines, commissioned from the late 1990s as replacements for the *Los Angeles* class. The vessel has advanced sound-dampening technologies and is armed with Tomahawk cruise missiles, Harpoon antiship missiles, and Mk 48 guided torpedoes.

▽ **HMS Astute (S119)**
Date 2010 Origin UK
Displacement 7,400 tonnes (8,157 tons)
Length 97 m (318 ft)
Top speed 20 knots (37 km/h)

Along with conventional torpedoes, *Astute* – an attack submarine and lead vessel of its class – is armed with Spearfish guided torpedoes and Tomahawk cruise missiles. It is powered by a pressurized water reactor (PWR), which uses nuclear fission to create steam.

◁ **Yuri Dolgoruky**
Date 2013 Origin Russia
Displacement 14,720 tonnes (16,226 tons)
Length 170 m (558 ft)
Top speed 15 knots (28 km/h)

The first *Borei*-class nuclear-powered submarine to enter service, the *Yuri Dolgoruky* is armed with 16 RSM-56 Bulava SLBMs, each missile containing six warheads with a range of around 8,300 km (5,157 miles).

Tech in the Sky and Beyond

Autonomous, pilotless aircraft have already made a dramatic impact on the battlefield, and they may soon come to dominate air-to-air combat as well. Even further into the skies, governments are racing to establish space as a new frontier for military vehicles. The stakes are high as it seems increasingly likely that space will be a key theatre of war in future conflicts.

Militarization of space
A US Military Atlas V rocket carrying the Navy Mobile User Objective System 2 satellite launches from Cape Canaveral, Florida. The satellite, one of a constellation of five, is used mainly for defence communications purposes.

In 1903, the *Wright Flyer*, built by American brothers Orville and Wilbur Wright, made the first flight by a powered, controlled, heavier-than-air aircraft; aloft for 12 seconds, it travelled just 37 m (120 ft). Only a century later, there were aircraft that could exceed the speed of sound by many times, aircraft that could fly around the world or near the edge of space, aircraft able to lift tanks, and even aircraft that did not need pilots.

AI, autonomy, and drones

Around two decades on from the centenary of the *Wright Flyer*'s short "hop", digital technology – in particular artificial intelligence (AI) – is opening up new horizons in aviation, and it promises to transform air combat. In 2020, for example, the USAF ran tests in which human fighter pilots flew against AI pilots in five simulator combats. The AI won all five engagements. In September 2023, over Edwards Air Force Base in California, two real F-16s fought a non-lethal dogfight, one piloted by a human and one by AI, with the jets reaching speeds of 1,931 km/h (1,200 mph) and coming within 600 m (1,968 ft) of each other. The outcome remains confidential, but it appears that the AI-controlled F-16 – known as the X-62A VISTA (Variable In-flight Simulator Test Aircraft) – performed well.

Autonomous aircraft are now an accepted part of the future in military aviation. They offer all the advantages of uncrewed aircraft, such as 24-hour endurance, more space for ordnance and equipment, and the ability to withstand G-forces that would render a human pilot unconscious. To these, AI adds ultra-fast data processing and decision making, since the technology can draw on millions of tactical rehearsals to calculate the optimal manoeuvres for victory.

By 2024, the USAF was looking to sign its first contracts for autonomous fighters, and many other countries are near to doing the same. A key concept is Manned-Unmanned Teaming (MUM-T), which foresees piloted and unmanned AI aircraft working seamlessly together, the latter acting as AI-powered "wingmen".

The Ukraine War, which began in 2022, has seen advances in the development of semi- and fully-autonomous unmanned aerial vehicles (UAVs), popularly known as drones. The battlefield arms race has begun to shift towards the possibility of AI-controlled swarms of attack drones flexibly executing their mission profile, individually selecting targets through image-recognition software and destroying them with onboard weaponry. Current advanced drones such as the Helsing HX-2 have onboard AI that allows for dynamic adaptation to new threats and targets. Autonomous military aircraft is a future that has already arrived.

Space wars

Military technology now extends beyond Earth's atmosphere. Orbiting satellites fulfil a range of roles in support of the military, including communications, missile-launch early warning; space situational awareness (SSA); intelligence, surveillance, and reconnaissance (ISR); navigation; and meteorological forecasting. Correspondingly, satellites are now of vital military importance. America's Global Positioning System (GPS) satellite network, for example, delivers accurate positioning information to aid navigation, and is also used to direct many precision-guided munitions (PGMs). GPS can track the positions of friendly and enemy forces, facilitate secure data exchange (through high-precision timing), support supply chain

Cutting-edge fighter
The Lockheed Martin F-22A Raptor was at the forefront of fighter design on its introduction in 2005. Its features include stealth technology, super-manoeuvrability, and supercruise (supersonic flight without afterburners).

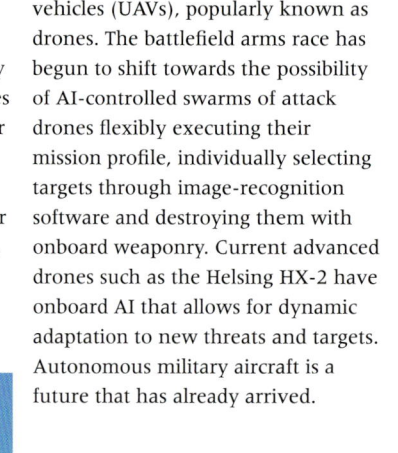

> "The potential for **autonomous air-to-air combat** has been imaginable for decades, but the reality has remained a **distant dream up until now.**"
> US SECRETARY OF THE AIR FORCE FRANK KENDALL, 2021–25

TECH IN THE SKY AND BEYOND

High-performance UAV
The Northrop Grumman MQ-4C Triton is a high-altitude, long-endurance unmanned UAV used by the US Navy and Australian Air Force for surveillance and reconnaissance. It can stay aloft for around 30 hours.

management, time-stamp electronic warfare, and underpin both nuclear and conventional command and control. Any disruption to the network of GPS satellites would have a severe impact on military operations 20,000 km (12,400 miles) below. Other countries have developed their own geolocation satellite networks as alternatives to GPS: China, for example, has the sophisticated BeiDou Navigation Satellite System, while Russia has its ageing GLONASS.

Attempts at disrupting geolocation satellites have already been made, and defence analysts and space authorities have noted satellites being moved into "threatening" positions in relation to other satellites, in order to interfere with their signals or orbits. Development is underway of military satellites with "advanced manoeuvring capability" that will be able to intercept their orbital rivals. There is also evidence that some countries are developing powerful conventional, nuclear, or directed-energy weapons (DEWs) that could destroy or disable dozens of satellites in an instant, leaving enemies without space-based positioning, timing, or observation. Such actions could also bring civilian life to a standstill, because many digital activities, from banking to navigation, rely on satellites.

The militarization of space, much like the use of AI in weapons technology, is still in its early days. Given the limits of physics and rocket propulsion, futuristic visions of dogfighting spacecraft are unlikely to become reality, and most military space vehicles are likely to be satellites. Exactly how these satellites will be used, what technology they will carry, and how they will interact with each other remain to be seen, but there is no doubt that they will be pivotal in the 21st-century arms race.

> **TALKING POINT**
>
> ## Driverless Land Vehicles
>
> Driverless vehicles may come to dominate land warfare as well as aerial combat. unmanned ground vehicles (UGVs) are remotely or autonomously driven military vehicles. Remote-control UGVs, which date back to World War II, have largely been experimental or peripheral, or used as expendable bomb-disposal tools. Today, however, UGVs with improved power supplies, powerful digital suites, advanced robotics, and AI are being adopted by armies. UGVs can perform reconnaissance, surveillance, mine clearance, medevac, and supply duties. Increasing numbers are being mounted with machine-guns or missile launchers. Armed UGVs are not standard, but they seem likely to become so one day.
>
>
>
> **Mounting a .50-calibre heavy machine-gun,** the tracked Titan Strike UGV – shown here on exercise – can deliver mobile suppressive fire in support of infantry units.

High-tech Fighters

The latest generations of fighter aircraft vie for supremacy in digital technology as well as in terms of airframes, manoeuvrability, and weaponry. Those developed since 2010 feature cutting-edge characteristics: a stealth design with reduced radar cross-section (RCS) and infrared-signature management; advanced avionics and target sensors; high manoeuvrability, often through thrust vectoring; electronic warfare systems (EWS); network-centric warfare (NCW) capabilities, with improved situational awareness (SA) and information sharing. The next generations of fighters are increasingly likely to be piloted by artificial intelligence (AI), either as fully autonomous (pilotless) aircraft or with a human-in-the-loop approach – either an onboard pilot or a ground controller.

▽ **Dassault Mirage 2000D**
Date 1995 **Origin** France
Engine 6,486–9,707 kg (14,300–21,400 lb) thrust SNECMA M53-P2 afterburning turbofan
Top speed 2,338 km/h (1,453 mph)

France's Mirage 2000D (the "D" stands for *diversifié*) is a two-seater multirole fighter and ground-attack aircraft. It is designed for long-range precision strikes and close air support missions.

△ **Boeing F/A-18E Super Hornet**
Date 1999 **Origin** USA
Engine 2 x 5,897–9,979 kg (13,000–22,000 lb) thrust General Electric F414-GE-400 afterburning turbofans
Top speed 1,915 km/h (1,190 mph)

Heavier than its F/A-18 Hornet predecessor – and with a greater range – the single-seater F/Z-18E is a multirole strike fighter. The aircraft can carry a variety of weapons, including missiles and precision-guided bombs.

Electro-Optical Targeting System (EOTS)

Thrust-vectoring capability

△ **Sukhoi Su-30 MkI**
Date 2002 **Origin** Russia
Engine 2 x 9,000–12,500 kg (19,842–27,558 lb) thrust Lyulka-Saturn AL-31FP vectoring turbofans
Top speed 2,124 km/h (1,320 mph)

This highly agile and sophisticated version of the Su-30, carrying both air-to-air and air-to-surface missiles, was developed jointly by Russia and India and is made for the Indian Air Force (IAF). More than 250 have been built, forming the backbone of the IAF.

▽ **BAe Harrier GR.9A**
Date 2004 **Origin** UK
Engine 10,795 kg (23,800 lb) thrust Rolls-Royce Pegasus Mk107 turbofan
Top speed 1,065 km/h (662 mph)

The GR.9A was the final version of BAe's vertical takeoff aircraft, fitted with a more powerful Pegasus engine, and avionics and weapons upgrades. It was withdrawn from service in 2010 on cost grounds.

Stealth airframe and materials

Three internal weapons bays

Underwing hardpoints

HIGH-TECH FIGHTERS · 291

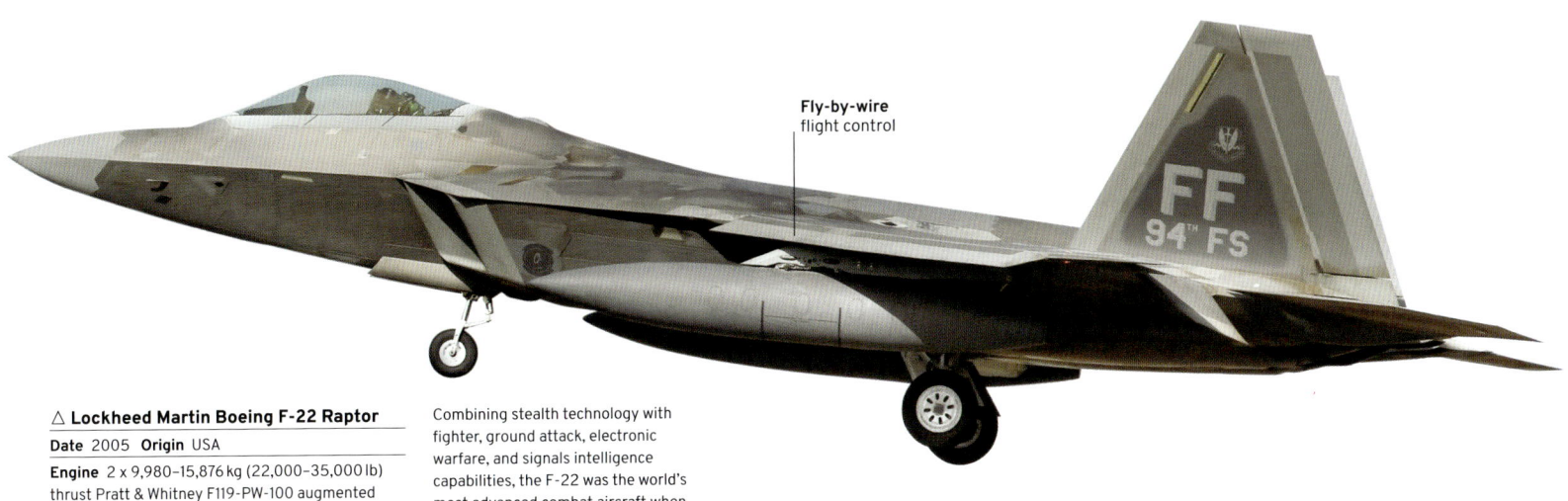

Fly-by-wire flight control

△ **Lockheed Martin Boeing F-22 Raptor**
Date 2005 **Origin** USA
Engine 2 x 9,980–15,876 kg (22,000–35,000 lb) thrust Pratt & Whitney F119-PW-100 augmented vectoring turbofans
Top speed 2,414 km/h (1,500 mph)

Combining stealth technology with fighter, ground attack, electronic warfare, and signals intelligence capabilities, the F-22 was the world's most advanced combat aircraft when it went into service. Production ended in 2012, with 187 jets operational.

Radar-absorbent materials

△ **Lockheed Martin F-35 Lightning II**
Date 2015 **Origin** USA
Engine 1 × 19,505 kg (43,000 lb) thrust Pratt & Whitney F135-PW-100 afterburning turbofan
Top speed 1,930 km/h (1,200 mph)

Like many modern fighters, the F-35 is a multirole aircraft, capable of ground attack as well as air superiority and interception missions, helped by advanced sensor technologies. It also includes variants designed for aircraft carrier operations.

△ **Chengdu J-20**
Date 2017 **Origin** China
Engine 2 × 14,515 kg (32,000 lb) thrust Shenyang WS-10C afterburning turbofans
Top speed 2,130 km/h (1,324 mph)

The Chengdu J-20 is an advanced all-weather stealth fighter. Its latest variants include thrust-vectoring control, advanced EWS, and the ability to collaborate with AI-controlled unmanned combat air vehicles (UCAVs).

△ **Sukhoi Su-57**
Date 2020 **Origin** Russia
Engine 2 × 15,000 kg (33,000 lb) NPO Lyulka-Saturn *izdeliye* 117 augmented turbofans
Top speed 2,135 km/h (1,327 mph)

A multirole stealth fighter, the Su-57 is designed for extreme manoeuvrability and has a large weapons payload. It is intended as the first of a family of similar aircraft.

Eurofighter Typhoon

The Typhoon is an advanced tactical fighter and one of the world's most exceptional military aircraft. Fast, agile, and bristling with sensors and weapons, this state-of-the-art aircraft makes a formidable opponent in dogfights. Considered by many to be second only to the F-22 Raptor in overall air-to-air combat capabilities, the Eurofighter Typhoon enjoys an advantage over the F-22 in aerial battles at close quarters.

THE EUROFIGHTER TYPHOON, the product of a collaboration between the UK, Germany, Italy, and Spain, took its maiden flight in 1994. Its canard delta configuration, with foreplanes (small wings) ahead of the main wings, typifies modern European fighters. Key to its extraordinary aerial performance is a lightweight construction – 82 per cent of the aircraft's surface is made of composite materials – combined with powerful turbofan engines.

Able to perform both fighter and bomber roles, the Typhoon first saw combat in 2011, using Enhanced Paveway II bombs against loyalist forces in Libya. Its manoeuvrability, acceleration, and climb rate surpass those of the F-15 Eagle and the F-16 Fighting Falcon, and make it a close rival to the F-22 Raptor. The Typhoon serves with five European nations – including those that developed it – and four Arabian Gulf states.

Carbon-fibre tail fin

Heat exchanger air intake

Adjustable petals of engine-nozzle

Towable radar decoy can be used to counter radar-guided missiles

External fuel tank mounted on wing

EUROFIGHTER TYPHOON

SPECIFICATIONS	
Model	Eurofighter Typhoon FGR4, 2007
Origin	UK, Germany, Italy, and Spain
Production	600+
Construction	Carbon-fibre composites, lightweight alloys, titanium, glass reinforced plastics
Wingspan	10.95 m (35 ft 10 in)
Length	15.96 m (52 ft 5 in)
Maximum weight	23,500 kg (52,000 lb)
Engines	2 x 9,060 kg (20,000 lb) thrust EJ200 turbofans
Range	3,790 km (2,350 miles) ferry range
Top speed	2,124 km/h (1,320 mph)

FRONT VIEW

REAR VIEW

Best in service
The Typhoon is the largest, most powerful, and fastest modern European fighter in service. Compared to the other Eurocanards – the Saab Gripen and the Dassault Rafale – it has larger wings and canards.

- **RAF roundel** with No.29 Squadron "colours"
- **Forward fuselage strake** improves airflow
- **Bubble canopy** gives good all-round visibility
- **Glass-fibre** reinforced plastic dome encloses radar
- **Louvres** for bleed air spill
- **Moveable canard** helps to control pitch and keep the aircraft stable
- **Nose wheel** retracts rearwards

EXTERIOR

A composite construction, and the fact that the engine face lies hidden deep within the fuselage, make the Typhoon relatively difficult to detect by radar. The wide horizontal spacing between the wings and the canard foreplanes allows more control torque to be exerted, which is one reason why the Typhoon has unparalleled agility at higher speeds. The variable lip of the "smiling" chin-mounted intake smooths the flow of air into the engine at higher angles-of-attack – the vertical angle of the aircraft relative to the direction of flight.

1. No.29 Squadron badge **2.** Air data sensors **3.** Canard foreplane (fully deflected) **4.** Port main undercarriage wheel **5.** Maintenance data panel (MDP) **6.** Cap on main body fuel tank **7.** Cap on wing-mounted fuel tank **8.** Low-visibility RAF roundel with No.29 Squadron "colours" **9.** Canopy release **10.** Laser warning receiver (LWR) **11.** Integrated tip stub launcher (ITPSL) including chaff dispenser **12.** Nozzle petals **13.** Engine bleed-air primary heat exchanger **14.** Navigation light **15.** Air conditioning system heat exchanger exhaust **16.** EJ200 afterburner section **17.** Missile approach warning system (MAWS) "sausage"

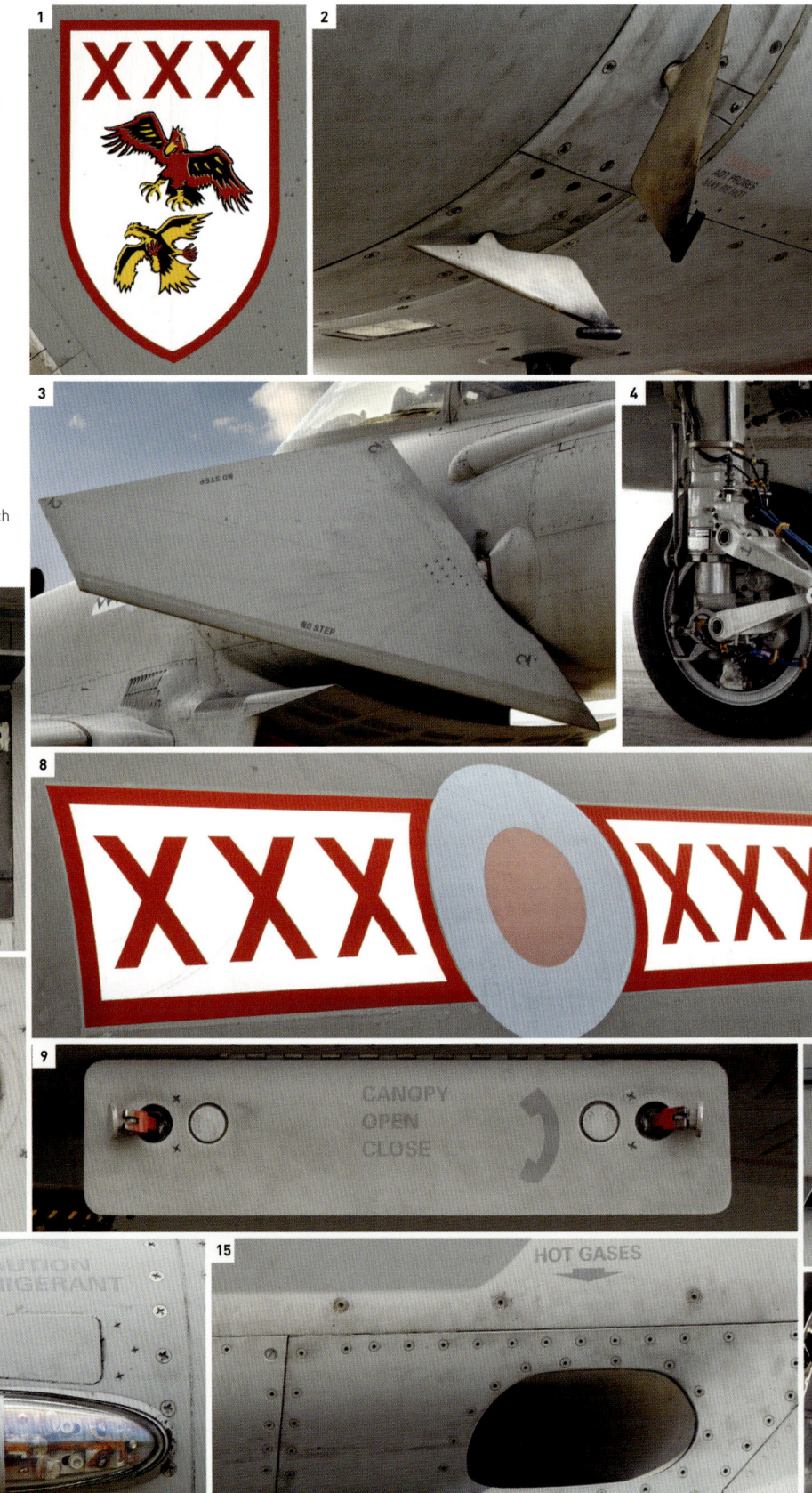

COCKPIT

Although it has a central control column rather than a sidestick, which is unusual for a modern Western fighter, the Typhoon is easy to fly and operate thanks to its pilot-aircraft interface. The pilot has voice control and the most advanced helmet in service: data presented on the visor can be used to designate targets. A wide-angle head-up display (HUD) and three large multi-functional displays (MFDs) enhance the ease of interacting with the Typhoon's systems.

18. Cockpit overview **19.** Manual data-entry facility (MDEF) **20.** Handle warning sign **21.** Electrical terminal (located in rear of cockpit) **22.** Throttle **23.** Starboard rudder pedal **24.** Control column handgrip **25.** Quick-release box for Martin-Baker M.16.A ejection seat harness **26.** Starboard side console panel

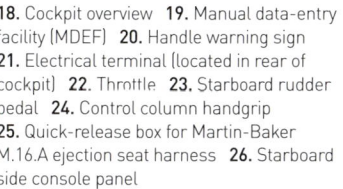

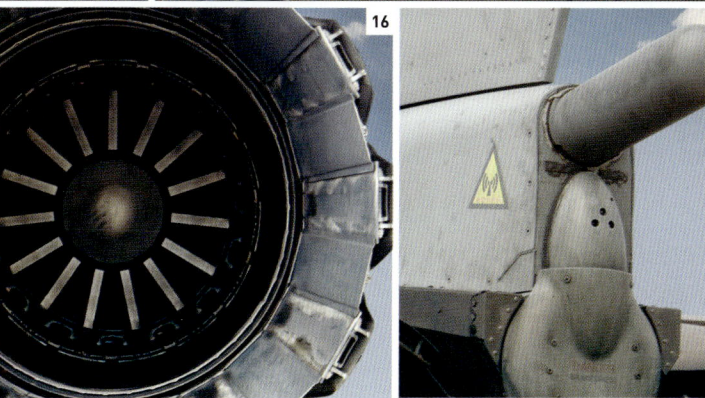

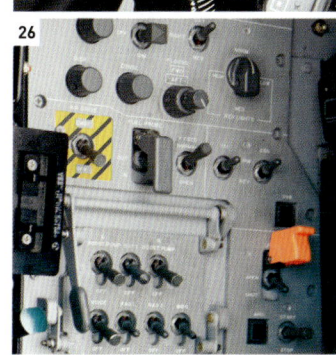

Drones in Modern Warfare

Unmanned aerial vehicles (UAVs) were first built during World War I on an experimental basis, although they never saw active service. By the 1930s, UAVs were being used as training targets, and in the Vietnam War they were deployed in large numbers for reconnaissance. Since then many nations have been developing UAVs, or "drones", for military and other purposes. The conflict in Ukraine, after Russia's invasion of 2022, saw rapid expansion in the use of drones, not only for the constant monitoring of enemy forces, but also as a new, relatively cheap weapon that could be mass produced. Commercial drones were converted, then manufactured in large quantities, to carry and drop bombs or deliver an explosive charge by crashing into a target. In response, electronic countermeasures were developed to disrupt the control signals of those flying the drones. This cat-and-mouse game of measure and countermeasure has meant that the technology of drones and the way they operate continue to change at an increasing tempo.

A Ukrainian soldier prepares a Vampire unmanned combat aerial vehicle (UCAV) for launch in February 2024. It can carry a 15 kg (33 lb) payload.

Drones

Unmanned aerial vehicles (UAVs) acquired the name "drones" (as in a drone bee) from the DH.82B Queen Bee, an unpiloted, radio-controlled target aircraft developed in Britain in the mid-1930s, although the origins of such vehicles date back to World War I. The role of UAVs diversified in the 1960s and 1970s, when they were mainly used for surveillance. It was from the 1990s, however, that UAVs revealed their full potential, not only as high-endurance reconnaissance platforms, but also as combat weapons delivering precision-guided munitions (PGMs) and, today, as single-use "suicide" drones.

▷ Northrop Grumman RQ-4 Global Hawk

Date 2001 **Origin** USA
Engine 3,447 kg (7,600 lb) thrust Rolls-Royce F137-RR-100 turbofan
Top speed 575 km/h (357 mph)

Able to survey through sandstorm and cloud, the Global Hawk was widely used in Iraq and Afghanistan. It can operate at high altitude for more than 30 hours, with a range of 22,780 km (14,155 miles)..

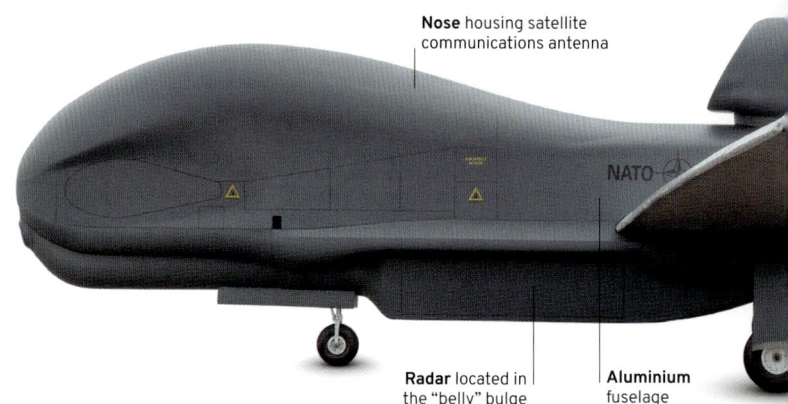

Nose housing satellite communications antenna

Radar located in the "belly" bulge

Aluminium fuselage

▽ General Atomics MQ-9 Reaper

Date 2007 **Origin** USA
Engine 671 kW (900 hp) Honeywell TPE331-10 turboprop
Top speed 463 km/h (288 mph)

The Reaper came into service with the US Air Force as the world's most advanced, and lethal, UAV. Turboprop powered, it is operated by a remote crew of two and carries a weaponry payload of 1,701 kg (3,750 lb), including up to eight Hellfire air-to-ground missiles.

C-band antenna for line-of-sight communication with ground control

Inverted-V tail with twin booms

Dome holds the aircraft's satellite communications system

Wingspan of 20 m (66 ft)

△ BAE Systems Mantis

Date 2009 **Origin** UK
Engine 2 x 283 kW (380 hp) Rolls-Royce M250B-17 turboshafts
Top speed 556 km/h (345 mph)

Designed to explore the military potential of UAVs, Mantis can fly itself and plot its own route, relaying data back to its base station via satellite. Capable of long-range missions, it has an endurance of at least 24 hours.

DRONES · 299

V-tail reduces radar and infrared signature

△ STC Orlan-10
Date 2010 **Origin** Russia
Engine 0.71 kW (0.95 hp) Saito Manufacturing FA-62B 1-cylinder 4-stroke
Top speed 150 km/h (93 mph)

The Orlan-10 has become one of Russia's most important reconnaissance drones, used in Ukraine, Syria, Libya, and Azerbaijan. It operates at fairly low altitudes of up to 5,000 m (16,404 ft), but can fly for 16 hours at a distance of up to 600 km (373 miles) from the command station.

Twin tail booms

△ Selex Galileo Falco Evo
Date 2012 **Origin** Italy
Engine 48–60 kW (65–80 hp) petrol
Top speed 216 km/h (134 mph)

Built originally for the Pakistan Air Force, this surveillance UAV has an operational time of 20 hours and a ceiling of 6,000 m (19,685 ft). It can carry a range of sensors and electronic warfare systems.

▽ Bayraktar TB2
Date 2015 **Origin** Türkiye
Engine 75 kW (100 hp) TM-100 petrol 2-stroke
Top speed 222 km/h (138 mph)

The Turkish Bayraktar TB2 is a combat-proven UAV, deployed in Syria, Libya, Azerbaijan, Ukraine, and parts of Africa. The drone has an operational altitude of 4,877 m (16,000 ft) and can carry a variety of precision-guided missiles.

T-shaped tail unit

▽ Ukrainian quadcopter
Date 2023 **Origin** Ukraine
Engine 4 electrically powered rotors
Top speed Unknown

Typical of the budget combat drones used in the Ukraine War, this Ukrainian quadcopter marries commercial drone technology with a shaped-charge high-explosive antitank (HEAT) warhead. The controller simply flies the drone into an enemy target to detonate the explosives.

Turboshaft engine delivering power to a propellor

Warhead tied to the body of the drone

MQ-9 Reaper

Part of the new wave of unmanned aerial vehicles (UAVs) that is changing the dynamics of modern warfare, the General Atomics Reaper can be deployed for surveillance and reconnaissance of ground targets. With a lengthy "loiter time", it is able to remain on station or provide an overwatch capacity to convoys or advancing ground forces. If required, it can fire precision-guided weapons at targets. The MQ-9 Reaper has a "crew" of two that operate it remotely – even from thousands of kilometres away.

Developed from General Atomics' Predator UAV, the Reaper first flew in 2001 and entered service with the US Air Force in 2007. A 708 kW (950 hp) turboprop engine gives the Reaper a cruising speed of 310 km/h (200 mph). When carrying extra fuel tanks, it can cover 2,590 km (1,610 miles) and linger over a target area for 30 hours, or 23 hours with a full weapons load.

Up to six pylons can mount laser-guided bombs, such as the GBU-12 Paveway II, air-to-ground missiles, like the AGM-114 Hellfire II, and the AIM 9 Sidewinder air-to-air missile. The Reaper can also carry Joint Direct Attack Munitions (JDAMs), which are standard bombs augmented to turn them into precision-guided weapons. Sensors may also be added to the pylons, depending on the nature of the mission.

The Reaper system can be transported in a container to a suitable launch site. It is controlled during its flight by a pilot and a sensor operator who may be many miles away in a home headquarters; their flight control adjustments, relayed by satellite, take 1.2 seconds. Extensively used by the US in Afghanistan and Iraq, the Reaper has also taken part in anti-pirate operations, carried out border-monitoring duties, and assisted search and rescue missions.

SPECIFICATIONS	
Model	MQ-9 Reaper
Origin	USA
Production	2007–
Maximum weight	2.2 tonnes (2.4 tons); full load 5.3 tonnes (5.8 tons)
Engines	Honeywell TPE331-10GD 708 kW (950 hp) turboprop
Wingspan	20 m (66 ft)
Length	11 m (36 ft)
Range	Standard 1,850 km (1,150 miles); extended 2,590 km (1,610 miles)
Top speed	480 km/h (300 mph)

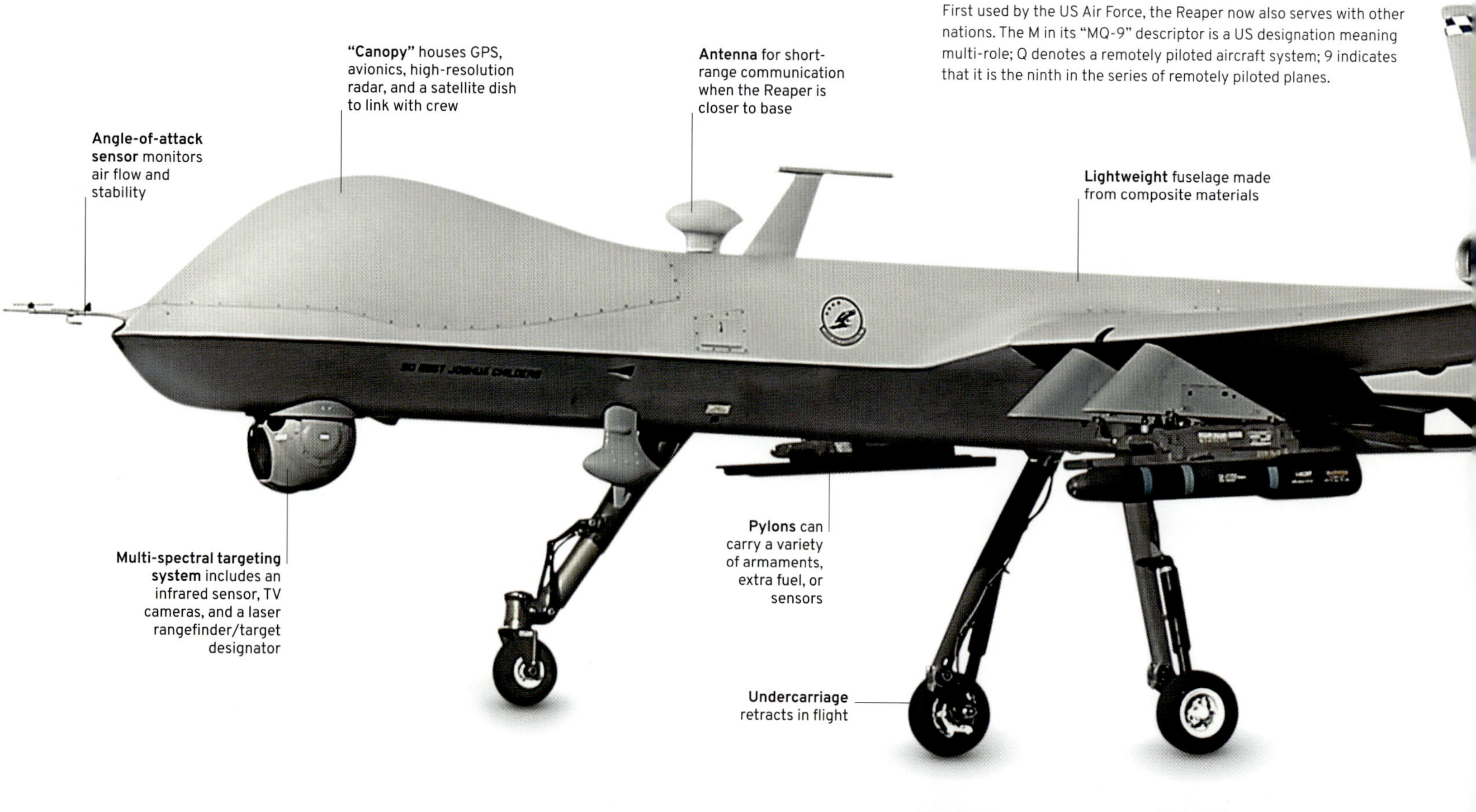

Remotely piloted aircraft
First used by the US Air Force, the Reaper now also serves with other nations. The M in its "MQ-9" descriptor is a US designation meaning multi-role; Q denotes a remotely piloted aircraft system; 9 indicates that it is the ninth in the series of remotely piloted planes.

Angle-of-attack sensor monitors air flow and stability

"Canopy" houses GPS, avionics, high-resolution radar, and a satellite dish to link with crew

Antenna for short-range communication when the Reaper is closer to base

Lightweight fuselage made from composite materials

Multi-spectral targeting system includes an infrared sensor, TV cameras, and a laser rangefinder/target designator

Pylons can carry a variety of armaments, extra fuel, or sensors

Undercarriage retracts in flight

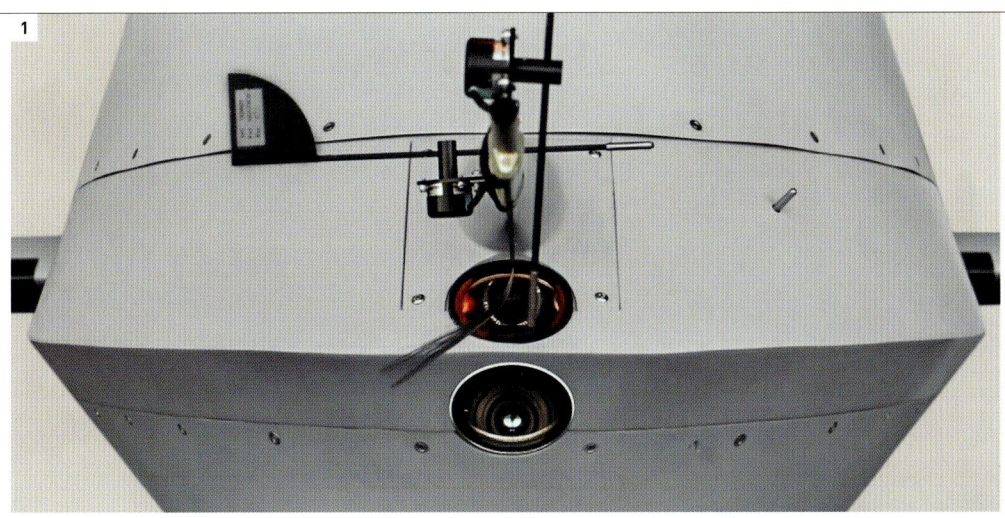

EXTERIOR

Although the MQ-9 Reaper's wingspan of 20 m (66 ft) is larger than that of many jet fighters, the aircraft can be disassembled and stored in a single container for shipment. Among the sensors on the MX-15 gimbal mount is a camera that it is claimed can read a car number plate from 3.2 km (2 miles) away. The Reaper has a two-tone grey paint scheme, darker on its upper surfaces, lighter underneath.

1. Nose: angle-of-attack sensor (above), camera (below) 2. Multi-spectral targeting system 3. Extended range fuel tank 4. Propeller 5. Pylons with GBU-12 Paveway II (left) and AGM-114 Hellfire (right) 6. Dorsally mounted engine vent 7. Wing-tip winglets (on some models)

Tailplanes are angled, rather than horizontal

Vertical stabilizer, with rudder, points downwards

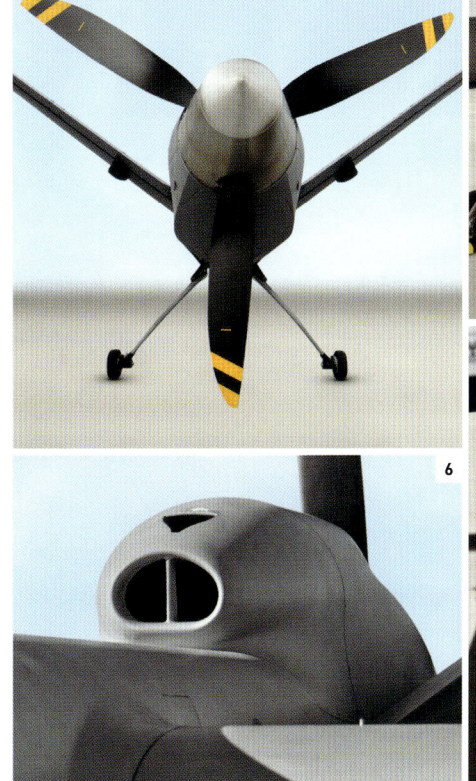

Seafaring Technology

Throughout history, the sea has provided a means of transporting goods around the world and finding fresh markets for trade. It also became a means for countries to spread their influence and acquire colonies by force. In times of war, ships built for trading journeys could be fitted with defensive weapons or converted to warships. Eventually, rivalries between powers such as Spain and Britain led to the establishment of permanent navies of purpose-built warships. Guns of bigger size and range led warships to increase in tonnage, and then to take on armour protection and new forms of propulsion. In the industrial era, warship technology became an even more urgent race to surpass rivals in speed, armour, and weaponry. Innovative technologies – such as submarines, mines, or aircraft that could be launched at sea, and radar and satellite surveillance – frequently threatened to make warships vulnerable, but in these cases counter-technologies were soon developed to limit or negate these threats. In the 21st century, as with many other areas of warfare, a new generation of unmanned craft is just starting to be deployed.

Talking point

Merchant ships in warfare

The expense of maintaining ships full-time for exclusively military purposes meant that for centuries merchant vessels were brought into military use when necessary, and military ships were sometimes converted to carry cargo or act in a dual role. During World War I and World War II, Britain's merchant navy had up to 200,000 sailors and carried supplies and troops all over the world. In recent times, civilian ships have been used for the ocean transport of large military forces during the Falklands War (1982), the Gulf War (1991), and the Iraq War (2003–11).

Trireme

Warships with banked rows of oars, each oar worked by an individual rower, were developed in the Mediterranean. Both the Greeks and the Phoenicians have been cited as the possible originators. Triremes – fighting vessels boasting three tiers of oars on each side – were in use by the 7th century BCE. Large numbers of oars freed triremes from dependency on the wind, allowing them to be more manoeuvrable in battle and to quickly build up speed for ramming attacks. A typical Athenian trireme had 170 oarsmen, which were usually citizens carrying out their military service.

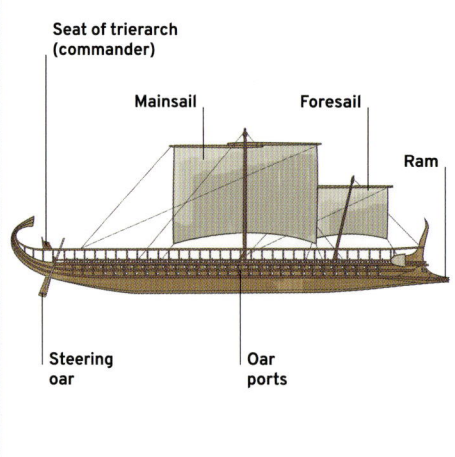

Longship

Scandinavian longships varied in detail due to variations in local materials and in the skills of builders. However, they all followed a general design: all were wooden, clinker built (with overlapping wooden hull planks), and had positions for oarsmen along each side, as well as a sail on a single mast for wind propulsion. Their shallow draught allowed them to travel up estuaries and inland along rivers. Viking longships made lengthy sea voyages, reaching Greenland and the North American mainland. The longship's design was so effective that it lasted for more than 1,500 years. The last longship was defeated in battle in 1429.

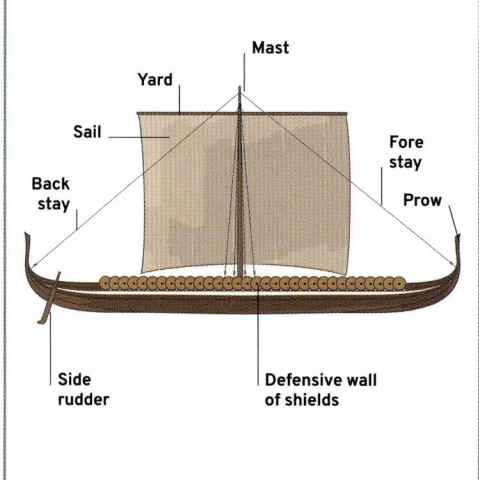

Galley

Developed from earlier Mediterranean vessels, the galley style of ship was built from antiquity through to the early 19th century. Galleys had a shallow draught and a narrow keel, and sat low in the water. While they had sails, galleys could also be powered by oars arranged in one or more banks. Galleys were used as trading vessels or warships – often as both on the same voyage, since ships had to protect themselves from pirates. Maritime powers such as Venice built fleets of galleys, with some vessels having a crew of up to 1,000. Castle-like structures were added on the rear to house weaponry and soldiers.

Ship of the line

Ships of the line were purpose-built, heavily armed, sail-powered battleships. They were introduced as the British Royal Navy and the Dutch navy devised tactics whereby ships would line up and fire a devastating broadside at the enemy. In such encounters, the ships with the most cannon to fire and with guns of greater size and range would have an advantage, and this led to ships of the line carrying up to 140 cannon. In the age of sail, from the 17th century to the mid-19th century, the number of ships of the line a nation possessed became an indicator of its naval power.

Pre-dreadnought

Steam-powered warships began to appear in the 1830s, and new "ironclad" ships saw action in the American Civil War of 1861–65. The design of Britain's *Majestic* class, launched in the 1890s, set a template for battleships that was mimicked by other navies. The ships had armour protection, coal-fired boilers, and sizable (12 in) guns in rotating, deck-mounted turrets. A naval arms race saw countries such as Japan and Russia commissioning similar battleships from British dockyards. This type of battleship, now known as a pre-dreadnought, became redundant after the launch of HMS *Dreadnought* in 1906.

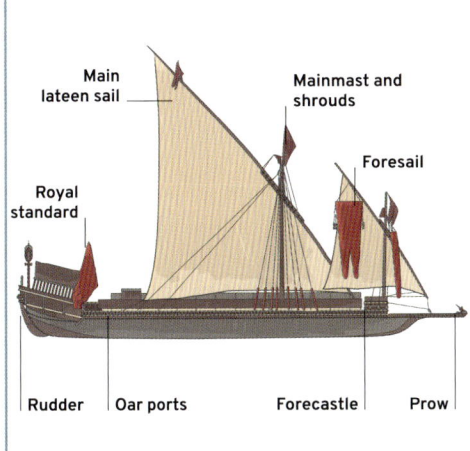
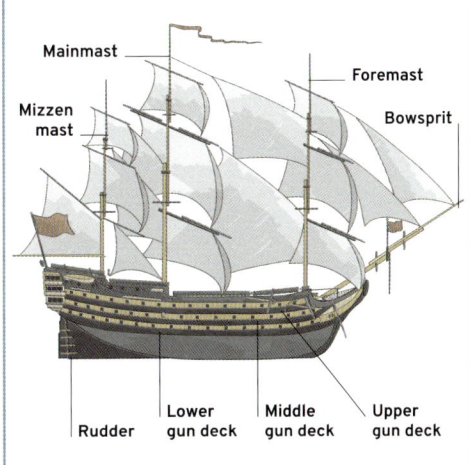
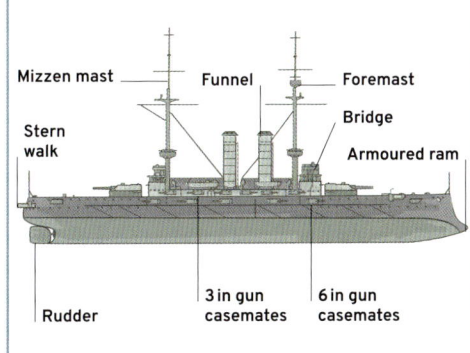

World War I battleship

With new steam turbines that gave it unprecedented speed, and an all "big gun" arrangement of ten 12 in guns in armoured turrets, HMS *Dreadnought*, commissioned in 1906, was a revolutionary battleship. Britain and Germany engaged in a race to develop ships of "dreadnought" specification, and other countries soon felt compelled to follow suit. Although the fleet actions of dreadnoughts in World War I were limited to the inconclusive Battle of Jutland (1916), Allied dreadnoughts saw some success in restricting the activity of the German fleet and blockading Germany from foreign supplies.

Nuclear-powered aircraft carrier

In 1961, the USS *Enterprise* became the first commissioned aircraft carrier to be powered by a nuclear reactor. The key advantage nuclear power brought to naval ships was that refuelling could be avoided and, in consequence, a warship could travel significantly further and carry out deployments of much longer duration. At present, only the US and France deploy nuclear-powered carriers, but other countries, notably China, are looking to join this select band. Currently the US has 12 nuclear-powered carriers in service; these carriers include the largest military machines ever built.

Modern destroyer

The destroyer started life at the end of the 19th century as a small, torpedo-carrying, light class of warship with limited range. However, as other warship types including battleships and cruisers became obsolete, the destroyer took on an increasing number of new roles. Today, the destroyer is the principal type of warship deployed by most modern navies. Equipped with stealth technologies, electronic warfare systems, helicopters, and missiles, destroyers now carry an enormous amount of weaponry compared to their predecessors, and they have grown in size to fulfil a range of roles.

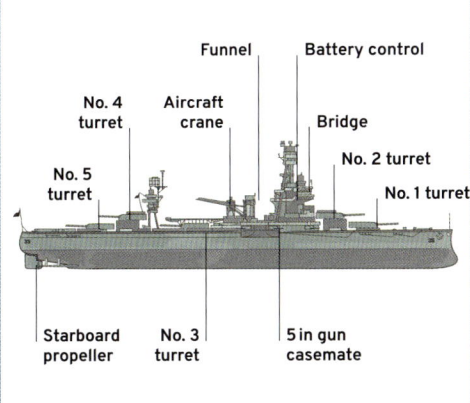
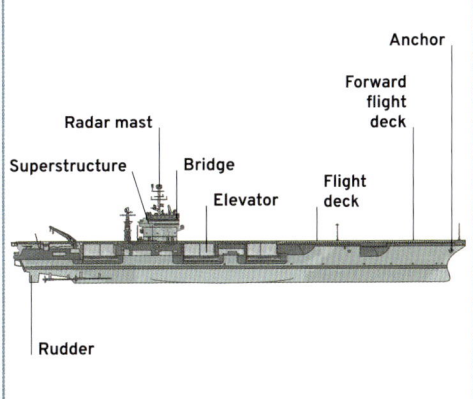
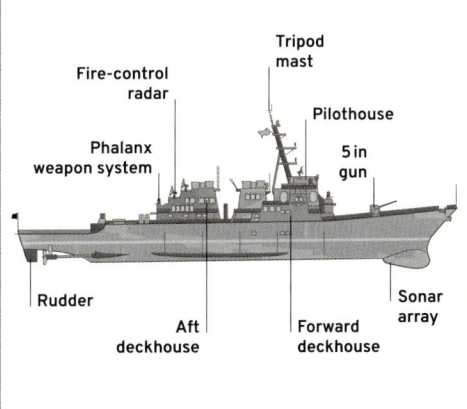

Protective Technology

The age of armour protection for vehicles began in earnest in the 19th century, when the hulls of wooden warships were reinforced with iron plates to defend against explosive and incendiary munitions. In World War I, protection extended to land vehicles, with steel plates fitted to armoured cars and tanks to shield crews from enemy fire. Increasingly powerful guns and armour-piercing rounds drove military vehicle designers to develop ever-more resistant armour. Much modern armour is "composite", consisting of nonmetallic materials such as ceramics or plastics incorporated into steel layers. Supplementary armour is extra layers of material added to the exterior of an armoured fighting vehicle.

THE DEVELOPMENT OF ARMOUR

The "ironclad" warships of the 19th century had armour of wrought-iron plates. Iron armour was superseded by steel, which is stronger and weighs less. Plates of rolled steel were made by passing cast billets between rollers until the metal was the desired thickness. This repeated compression aligned the grain in the metal, eliminating weaknesses and creating tough "homogenous" steel. Another development, face-hardening, reheated steel plates with carbon to give the steel a hardened surface, or "face". Metals such as chromium, molybdenum, nickel, and tungsten were added to produce steel-alloy armour with differing characteristics. The development of antitank rounds that could burn through armour, rather than penetrating it by kinetic energy, led to ceramic blocks being fitted to vehicles; these blocks give modern tanks their angular appearance. Such armour, known as "Chobham" after the UK town where it was developed, greatly increases protection to antitank rounds. The armour of today's vehicles varies according to their use and theatre of operation.

Tiger I, German heavy tank (1942)
World War II saw a race to create the most effective plate-armoured heavy tanks, and the Tiger I was among the most fearsome of these. Setting a tank's armour at an angle makes it likelier that rounds will deflect off the tank; it also increases the depth of armour to be penetrated. Surprisingly, the Tiger I had near-vertical armour, but the armour's thickness, rather than its geometry, made it impervious to many antitank weapons.

- **Thinnest armour** on top
- **Front hull armour** sloped at 13 degrees
- **Glacis armour** was heavily sloped
- **Underbelly armour** was relatively thin
- **Thin steel** track guards
- **Interleaved wheels** increased protection

Legend: 25 mm | 60 mm | 80–100 mm | 100–120 mm

Warships
Early 20th-century warships relied on heavy armour – Japan's *Yamato* had up to 650 mm (26½ in) of armour. Modern warships are lightly armoured, relying on stealth and electronic countermeasures.

Yamato battleship (1941)

Aircraft
Armour on planes and helicopters concentrates on vital areas, such as the cockpit; trying to make the entire aircraft immune to damage would increase its weight and impair performance.

Bell AH-1 Cobra (1965)

Land vehicles
Modern combat vehicles, such as Israel's Merkava Mark 4 tank, are both fast and manoeuvrable, being protected by composite armour, which is typically lighter than all-metal armour alternatives.

Merkava Mark 4 (2004)

Smoke grenades
Smoke has been used to obscure battlefield targets since ancient times. From the 1940s, smoke has typically been delivered by grenades discharged from launchers mounted on the outside of vehicles. A salvo of grenades can quickly form a smoke screen to conceal a vehicle's movement. Smoke grenades today work in both the visual and infrared parts of the spectrum, so targets are also hidden from both optical and thermal imaging systems.

EXPLOSIVE REACTIVE ARMOUR

A form of supplementary armour, explosive reactive armour (ERA) consists of relatively thin plates of armour with a backing of high explosive layers. When a plate is struck by a high-explosive antitank (HEAT) projectile, the jet of molten metal formed in the incoming round's warhead pierces the plate, but then detonates the high explosive layers beneath. The detonation blows the entire panel off the target vehicle before the HEAT round can penetrate the vehicle's main defensive armour below. ERA can, however, be defeated by "tandem charge" HEAT rounds. These use two charges, the second of which detonates just milliseconds after the first, by which time the vehicle's main armour has been exposed and is vulnerable.

BAR ARMOUR

The overall level of protection of light armoured vehicles can be increased inexpensively by fitting bar armour. An alternative form of supplementary armour, bar armour involves mounting a framework of hardened steel bars (usually horizontally) over vulnerable parts of a vehicle. Bar armour is not effective against kinetic-energy rounds, but it can defeat lightweight HEAT rounds such as those delivered by grenade launchers. The bars can trap or detonate the rounds before they reach the body of the vehicle itself, minimizing impact and protecting the occupants inside.

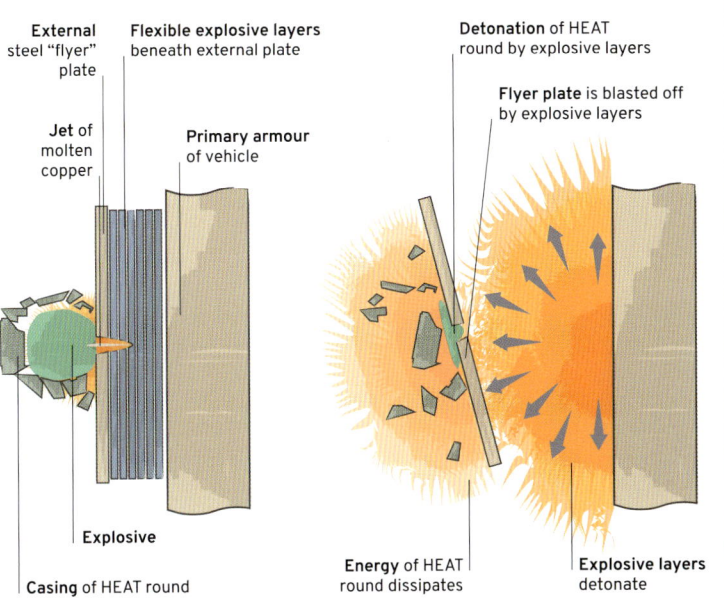

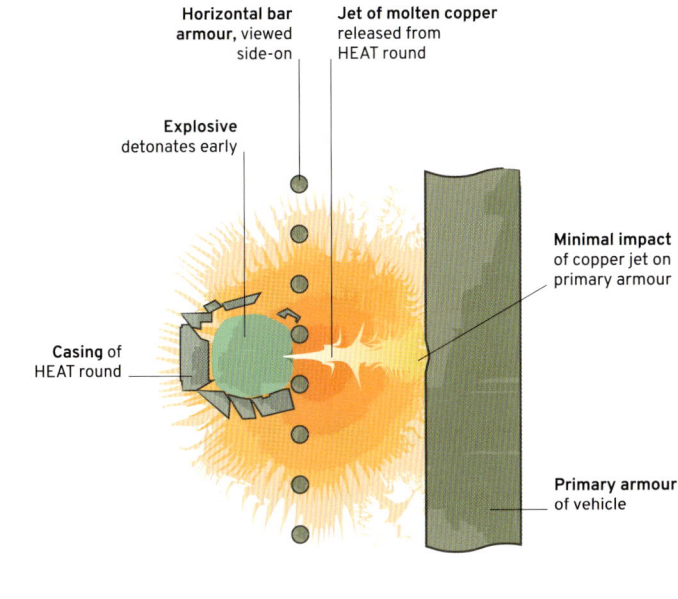

CAMOUFLAGE

Many modern military vehicles use camouflage patterns to disrupt their outlines and blend in with their surroundings, often mimicking natural habitats such as woodland, desert, or snowy terrain, or by using "dazzle" designs to obscure their direction of travel and distance from the enemy. Reducing a vehicle's heat footprint via thermal insulation and other means can help avoid detection, while radar-absorbant surfaces reduce long-range detectability.

Andrea Doria (1916) – dazzle camouflage

Pansarbil M40 (Lynx) (1939) – conventional camouflage

Lockheed F-117 Nighthawk (1981) – antiradar surfaces and design, reduced thermal footprint

Challenger 2 (1998) – thermal insulation

Flight Technology

Winged craft stay aloft due to a difference in air pressure above and below their wings. This differential, which results from the wings' aerofoil shape, produces lift – an upward force that acts together with weight, thrust, and drag (friction with the air) to produce flight. In level flight at constant speed, lift balances weight, and engine thrust balances drag. These basic principles are the same for modern jets as they were for the first heavier-than-air craft, while flight controls are also essentially the same as in the early days of aviation. The "stick-and-rudder" system, originally devised by French aviator Louis Blériot for his XI monoplane crossing of the English Channel in 1909, is still found in today's aircraft.

CHANGING WING SHAPES

To make aircraft wings as light as possible, early planes used very thin surfaces braced by wires. World War I biplane wings had thicker aerofoil shapes that induced less drag. Until the advent of later aircraft such as the Spitfire, unbraced cantilever monoplane wings had to be thick for high-speed flight. Swept-back "laminar-flow" wings, which reduced turbulence, proved the best for transonic (near the speed of sound) flight. Improved materials enabled them to be made even thinner for supersonic speeds.

Blériot XI (1909)
Typical of the early 1900s, the Blériot XI's wings had an aerofoil that was thin and cambered (curved) in cross-section. Roll was controlled by warping (twisting) the wings; bracing wires supported the bending load, which was kept to a minimum by the wings' short span.

Royal Aircraft Factory S.E.5a (1917)
By 1916, biplanes, which had two sets of wings, were routinely exceeding 160 km/h (100 mph) and performing aerobatics. Their flatter, lower-drag aerofoils could be kept relatively thin, because of the strength of the wire-braced biplane structure.

Supermarine Spitfire (1936)
The Spitfire had cantilevered wings that were self-supporting, with no bracing struts or wires. Very robust, shallow spars were combined with a stressed-metal skin to carry the load, resulting in a wing design that was thin yet strong.

North American F-86 Sabre (1949)
The Sabre was faster than the Spitfire, due in part to its swept-back, laminar-flow wings. The wings' aerofoil cross-section, with almost identical upper and lower surfaces, minimized drag by inducing smooth (laminar) airflow.

Lockheed F-117 Nighthawk (1982)
Very thin, sharp-edged, "over-swept" wings minimized the F-117's radar signature. Aerodynamic problems caused by this shape were addressed by computer-regulated fly-by-wire controls.

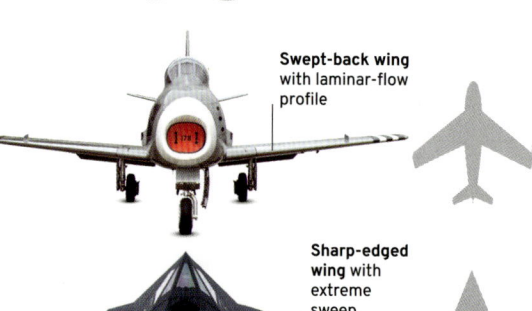
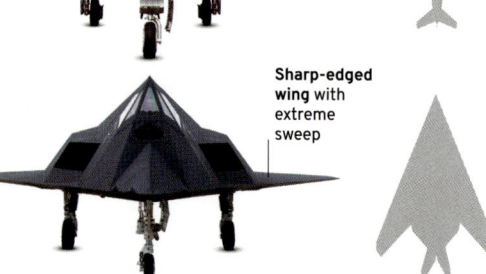

Monoplane wing with wire bracing

Biplane wing braced by wires and struts

Cantilevered wing with elliptical shape

Swept-back wing with laminar-flow profile

Sharp-edged wing with extreme sweep

LIFT AND BALANCING FORCES

A moving wing's aerofoil shape makes air flow faster over the top of it than underneath it, reducing the air pressure above the wing and generating lift. The angle at which the wing meets the oncoming air – the angle of attack – determines how much lift and drag are produced. If the critical angle is exceeded, the wing loses lift and stalling occurs.

FORCES

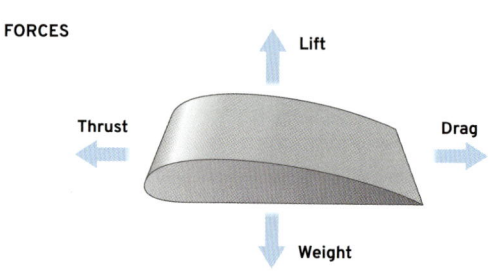

Lift / Thrust / Drag / Weight

MEDIUM ANGLE OF ATTACK

Wing angled upwards
Lift increases with angle of attack
Drag increases with angle of attack
Air above wing moves faster than air below

HIGH ANGLE OF ATTACK

Stalling occurs when critical angle is exceeded
Air flow is no longer smooth; air pressure above wing rises
Fall in air pressure differential reduces lift

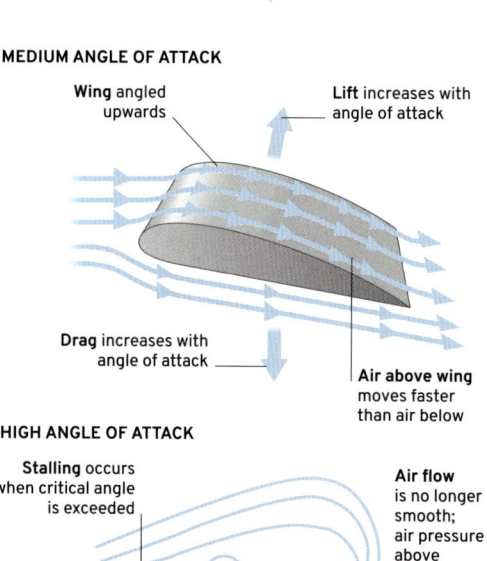

STICK-AND-RUDDER CONTROL

An aeroplane's controls rotate it around three axes. The up or down movement of the nose, called pitch, is controlled by tail-mounted elevators. The pilot moves the control stick forward or back to operate the elevators and make the plane dive or climb. Roll – the up or down rolling motion of the wing tips – is controlled by ailerons on the trailing wing edges; the pilot operates them by moving the stick sideways, which turns the plane. The vertically mounted rudder, operated by the pilot's foot-pedals, controls yaw, the side-to-side movement of the nose. The pilot uses the rudder to point the aeroplane in the desired direction. Large aircraft and fast jets may have powered controls, but they are still manoeuvred by the same basic stick-and-rudder input.

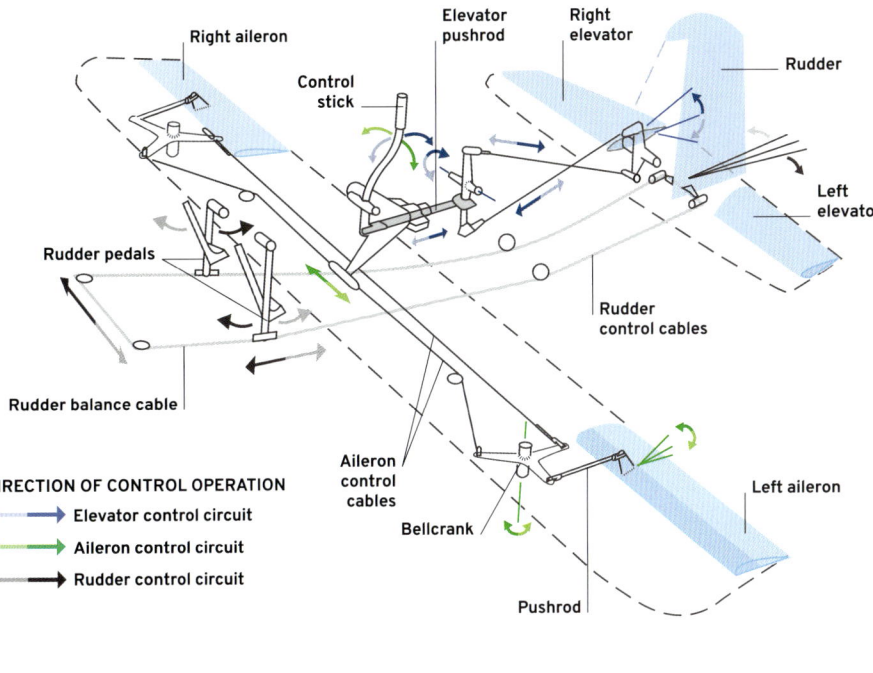

DIRECTION OF CONTROL OPERATION
- Elevator control circuit
- Aileron control circuit
- Rudder control circuit

Pitching up
To pitch upwards, the pilot pulls the control stick back, raising the elevators and causing the nose to rise. This increases the angle of attack, so the wing generates more lift and the aircraft begins to climb. The aircraft continues to pitch up until the pilot puts the stick to neutral, so that the elevators lie flat again.

Level flight
In level flight the tailplane, to which the elevators are attached, acts as a stabilizing surface that maintains the wings at a steady angle of attack. The elevators are kept flat, and during level flight the pilot will only move them up or down to compensate for the effects of air turbulence.

Pitching down
To pitch downwards, the pilot pushes the stick forwards. This lowers the elevators, causing the nose to drop. As the angle of attack decreases, lift reduces, and the aircraft descends. With weight now acting in the same direction as thrust from the propeller, the descending aircraft rapidly gains speed.

Turning
When the pilot moves the stick to one side, the aileron on that side rises, reducing lift; at the same time, the opposing aileron lowers, increasing lift on the other side. Since overall wing lift is now acting to the side, the aircraft starts to turn. The pilot moves the rudder to balance the different amounts of drag generated by the up- and down-pointing ailerons.

Glossary

4×4
A four-wheeled vehicle in which the engine's power drives all four wheels; in a 4×2, only two wheels are driven.

active protection system (APS)
A method of defeating antitank weapons that does not rely on armour. Active systems use projectiles to shoot down missiles. Passive systems use jamming and smoke to defeat missile guidance systems.

add-on armour
Additional external armour that can be fitted to an AFV to increase protection. Also known as appliqué armour.

aerofoil
A shaped surface, such as an aeroplane wing, tail, propeller, or helicopter rotor blade, that produces more lift than drag.

afterburner
A device that injects fuel into the hot exhaust gases produced by an engine and burns it to provide additional thrust.

aileron
A moveable control surface on an aircraft wing's trailing edge, used to control roll, the up or down movement of the wing tips.

airframe
The basic structure of an aircraft, including the fuselage, wings, and tail assembly but excluding the engines and other fittings.

amphibious vehicle
A vehicle that can travel both on water and on land.

angle of attack
The angle at which a wing (or a propeller or helicopter blade) meets the oncoming air. Aeroplanes usually fly with the front of their wings higher than the back, so that air deflects downwards, pushing the wings up.

armoured car
A lightweight wheeled AFV used for reconnaissance or armed escort duties.

armoured fighting vehicle (AFV)
A vehicle combining armoured protection, battlefield mobility, and offensive capability. AFVs include tanks, armoured cars, troop carriers, air-defence vehicles, amphibious vehicles, and self-propelled artillery.

armoured personnel carrier (APC)
A type of AFV, usually lightly armoured, that transports troops to the battlefield, where they disembark to fight.

arrestor wire
A cable stretched across the landing area of an aircraft carrier that engages the tailhook of a plane to bring the aircraft to a halt.

autoloader
A device that inserts shells into the breech of a tank's main gun, replacing the need for a crew member dedicated to this task.

bar armour
Add-on armour in the form of a mesh of steel bars fitted to the hull of an AFV to protect against rocket-propelled grenades (RPGs). Also called cage or slat armour. *See also* add-on armour.

barbette
An armoured cylinder supporting a gun turret on a warship.

battle management system
A computer-based system that gives near real-time information to aid the decision-making and effectiveness of commanders in the field and at headquarters.

battlecruiser
A class of heavily armed warship developed as a kind of fast battleship in the years leading up to World War I.

battleship
A large, heavily armoured warship with a main battery of large guns.

biplane
A plane with two sets of wings, braced by wires and struts to form a light, rigid structure. The biplane design produces more drag than a cantilever monoplane. *See also* monoplane.

bogie
A pivoting group of wheels (typically two or three pairs) beneath a vehicle.

bore
The internal diameter of a gun's barrel. *See also* calibre.

bore evacuator
See fume extractor.

breech
The rear end of a gun barrel, opened to load ammunition and closed for firing.

bridge
The main control centre of a ship, from where the captain and officers oversee the operations of the vessel.

bridge layer
A support vehicle that can deploy and retrieve a removable metal bridge to allow other military vehicles to cross obstacles such as rivers, craters, and trenches.

broadside
The simultaneous firing of all the guns on one side of a warship.

calibre
The internal diameter of a rifled gun barrel; since the 1950s, this has usually been expressed in millimetres (mm).

cantilever wing
A wing with no external support or bracing.

capital ship
A warship of the first rank in size and armament, such as a battleship.

caravel
A small, manoeuvrable ship with lateen sails developed in the 15th century.

carrack
A three- or four-masted sailing ship of the 15th and 16th centuries.

casemate
An armoured enclosure or compartment for guns on a warship.

cemented armour
Steel-alloy armour that had a hardened outer face for protection but was fibrous and flexible beneath to resist spalling.

Chobham armour
Composite armour, developed at Britain's tank research centre in Chobham, that includes ceramic tiles encased in metal mesh bonded to a backing plate with several elastic layers. Dorchester armour is a variant. *See also* composite armour.

Christie suspension
Tank suspension designed by J. Walter Christie in 1928. Each wheel had its own spring and could move freely vertically, allowing rapid travel over rough terrain.

co-axial machine-gun
A machine-gun mounted on the same axis as a vehicle's main gun and aimed using the same sights.

cog
A round-bottomed sailing ship developed in northern Europe in the Middle Ages.

combat engineer vehicle
An AFV, often fitted with mine-breaching devices, that is used to transport combat engineers around the battlefield. *See also* armoured fighting vehicle (AFV).

combat weight
The mass of a tank when fully equipped for battlefield action.

command vehicle
A vehicle from which a commander leads a unit; it may carry equipment such as multiple radios and map boards, and include desk space for officers and aides.

composite armour
Vehicle armour made up of layers of different materials, such as metals, ceramics, and plastics.

conning tower
A raised structure on a submarine from which an officer conned (conducted or controlled) the boat. Today, this structure is called sail, because submarines are now controlled from below deck. *See also* sail.

corvette
Originally a small, three-masted sailing warship, a corvette is a fast, lightly armed naval vessel.

counterinsurgency (COIN)
Operations against an enemy that does not operate as a distinct military force. Counterinsurgency vehicles are often armoured against mines or IEDs. *See also* improvised explosive device (IED).

cowl/cowling
The cover, often removable or partly removable, around a vehicle's engine. It is usually streamlined to reduce drag.

cruiser
In the 19th century, a steam warship, smaller than a battleship, able to operate in distant waters. Protected cruisers had armoured decks; armoured cruisers had a belt of armour around the hull. From 1930, cruisers were classed as light or heavy, according to their armament.

cupola
A mini turret on top of a tank's main turret, with ports that give the tank commander a (typically all-round) view of the battlefield.

destroyer
A type of warship conceived in the late 19th century to destroy torpedo boats, then adapted to fire torpedoes, and later used to escort warships and merchant convoys. Today, destroyers defend other ships from air, submarine, and surface attack.

diving plane
A control surface (also called a hydroplane) on a submarine that tilts the bow or stern up or down when submerging or surfacing, and helps control depth when submerged.

dogfight
A close-quarters battle between aircraft. It refers to individual duels, rather than to an attack by multiple planes in formation.

drag
The force (air or water resistance) that impedes the motion of a vehicle.

draught
The depth of a ship (to the lowest point of the hull) below the waterline.

dreadnought
A type of battleship, inaugurated by HMS *Dreadnought* in 1906, that surpassed previous ships for arms, armour, and speed.

drive sprocket
A toothed tank wheel that engages the track links to transfer torque from the engine and drive the track around.

drone
A more informal name for a UAV. *See also* unmanned aerial vehicle (UAV).

electronic countermeasures (ECM)
In modern warfare, any electronic devices designed to mislead the enemy's radar and other detection or targeting systems.

elevator
A control surface attached to the tailplane that affects the pitch of an aircraft (whether its nose points up or down, or is level).

explosive reactive armour (ERA)
See reactive armour.

fairing
A covering added to an aircraft, boat, or land vehicle to improve streamlining.

fire-control system
Technology that helps a weapons system to target, track, and hit targets with more speed and greater accuracy than a human operator could achieve. Fire-control systems today typically use sensors to detect the target, a computer to process data and calculate firing solutions, and stabilizing systems to ensure accuracy.

firing port
An opening on the side of an IFV through which infantry can fire without leaving the vehicle. *See* infantry fighting vehicle (IFV).

first-rate ship
A British designation for a ship of the line with more than 100 guns on three decks.

flame tank
A tank fitted with a flamethrower. Flame tanks are usually deployed for specialized operations, such as attacking fortifications.

flanking manoeuvre
An attempt to gain tactical advantage by moving an armed body around the side, or flank, of an enemy force.

flap
A control surface on the trailing edge of a wing that tilts downwards and/or extends backwards to increase the wing's lift.

fly-by-wire
A system that controls an aircraft's flight using electronics, rather than mechanical controls.

forecastle
On medieval ships, a raised structure at the front that served as a fighting platform for archers or marines; now a term applied to the front part of a ship's upper deck.

freeboard
The distance between the waterline and the deck of a ship.

frigate
Originally, a sail-powered warship that was faster than a ship of the line and had one gun deck. Modern frigates are used for escort and protection, especially against submarines and aircraft.

front-wheel drive (FWD)
The transmission of engine power only to a vehicle's front wheels. FWDs can be made lighter than 4×4 vehicles, since a drive shaft is not needed to send power to the rear wheels.

fume extractor
A vent in a tank gun barrel that stops toxic fumes released when a round is fired from entering the crew compartment. Pressure changes in the barrel expel fumes from the muzzle. Also called a bore evacuator.

fuselage
The main body of an aeroplane, excluding the wings and tail.

galleass
A large war galley developed in Venice in the 16th century to carry heavy guns.

galleon
The principal European warship of the 16th and 17th centuries, longer and narrower than the earlier carrack.

galley
A type of ship propelled primarily by oars, with a shallow draught, a long, narrow hull, and often a low freeboard. Used for more than 2,000 years, galleys had sails but relied heavily on the rowing of their oarsmen for manoeuvrability and speed.

gill armour
A type of spaced armour consisting of angled external rubber panels, as used on some Soviet tanks. *See also* spaced armour.

glacis plate
An angled plate at the front of a tank's hull that helps to deflect projectiles. The plate's slope ensures that any projectile that does strike it horizontally must pass through a greater thickness of armour.

ground-attack aircraft
An aircraft specialized for low-level strikes on ground targets; its attacks are more precise than those of a conventional bomber. Today, many military jets combine ground-attack capability with other roles.

grousers
Treaded or studded extensions to a tank's tracks that are added to give more traction on loose materials such as soil or snow.

guided munition
Unlike a bullet, whose trajectory is wholly determined by its propellant charge and gravity, the path of a guided munition can be altered and directed towards a target.

gun sight
An optical device used by gunners to aim with greater accuracy. Telescopic sights for tanks were adopted prior to World War II.

half-track
A vehicle steered by wheels at the front and propelled by tracks at the rear, combining the handling of a road vehicle with a tank's cross-country capabilities.

head-up display (HUD)
A transparent screen in the pilot's line of sight that projects information, such as combat status or flight performance data.

heavy tank
A class of tank designed for infantry support; usually more heavily armed and armoured than other tanks, but slower.

high-alpha performance
The ability of an aircraft to maintain controlled flight at high angles of attack, close to a stall, where the aircraft's nose is significantly higher than its flight path.

horsepower (hp)
A traditional unit of measurement of engine power; 1 hp is generally taken to be equal to 746 watts.

hydroplane
See diving plane.

hydropneumatic suspension
A type of suspension that uses oil and pneumatic pressure to keep a vehicle level and absorb shocks.

idler
An undriven end wheel on a tracked vehicle that serves to adjust the tension in the track.

improvised explosive device (IED)
A bomb made in an improvised manner, rather than being specifically designed and manufactured as an explosive device. Some IEDs use chemicals such as fertilizer as explosive materials, while others are adapted mines or artillery shells. Also called roadside bombs.

indirect fire
Fire aimed at a target the gunner cannot see. It usually requires a forward observer to correct the aim. Direct fire is firing at a visible target in the user's line of sight.

infantry fighting vehicle (IFV)
An AFV that carries troops to the battlefield and, being armed, can itself enter combat (unlike an APC). IFVs often have firing ports, and their armament may include antitank weapons. *See also* armoured personnel carrier (APC).

infrared
A type of electromagnetic radiation given off by warm objects. Night vision and thermal imaging devices use infrared sensors that can detect the heat signals of troops, vehicles, and other objects.

interrupter gear
A mechanism that allowed a machine-gun on an aircraft to fire through the arc of a spinning propeller. It paused the gun's fire when a blade was in line with its barrel.

ironclad
A type of mid-19th century warship, originally with armoured iron plates over a wooden hull, later with an all-metal hull.

joystick
A lever in an aeroplane's cockpit that is used to control the ailerons and elevators.

kamikaze
The suicide attacks of Japanese pilots who intentionally crashed their aeroplanes into enemy ships at the end of World War II.

knot
A unit of speed; 1 knot = 1 nautical mile per hour (1.85 km/h; 1$\frac{3}{20}$ mph).

landing gear
Wheels, skids, or floats on which an aircraft touches down when landing. Also called undercarriage.

laser rangefinder
A way of calculating a target's range from the time it takes for a laser pulse to reflect off the target and return to the rangefinder.

lateen sail
A triangular sail mounted at an angle on the mast. Lateen sails permitted ships to tack forward, even into light winds.

leaf spring
A basic form of suspension composed of overlaid arcs (or leaves) of steel that are fixed to the underside of a vehicle to form a shock-absorbing cushion onto which the axle presses. Also called a cart spring.

lift
The force exerted on a moving aerofoil that causes a wing to rise.

light tank
A thinly armoured tank designed for rapid movement rather than aggressive combat. Today, the light tank's role is largely confined to reconnaissance.

longship
A long, narrow, shallow-draught boat with a sail, oars, and a hull of overlapping planks, developed in Scandinavia.

Mach number
The ratio of an aircraft's speed to the speed of sound; an aircraft flying at Mach 3, for example, is travelling at three times the speed of sound.

machine-gun
A gun that uses the gas or recoil from its fired projectile to cycle its action and so give continuous automatic fire.

magazine
A device that holds ammunition and feeds rounds to a gun; also, an area (such as on a ship) where ammunition or other explosive material is stored.

main battle tank (MBT)
The principle form of modern tank, MBTs combine composite armour, powerful firepower, and good mobility. They are designed for armour-protected direct fire.

mantlet
A plate of armour that protects the area where the main gun of a tank emerges from the turret. This area is exposed to the enemy when the gun is fired, so the mantlet tends to be the thickest part of the tank's armour.

materiel
All the hardware needed by a military force to complete a specific mission, from munitions, weapons, and equipment to vehicles such as tanks, fighter aircraft, and warships.

medium tank
A class of tank that is almost as mobile as a light tank and almost as well protected as a heavy tank.

military logistics
The science of planning and carrying out the movement and maintenance of military forces, from setting up and sustaining supply chains to directing personnel and materiel to battlefields.

mine
An explosive laid underground or left floating on or just below the water's surface. Mines can be detonated by a variety of means, depending on their design, including by pressure, sound, magnetism, and remote control.

Mine Resistant Ambush Protected (MRAP)
A class of vehicle designed in response to IEDs. A V-shaped hull limits the effects of IED blasts, while armour protects against direct-fire attack. See also improvised explosive device (IED).

monitor
A class of 19th-century ironclad warship that took its name from the USS *Monitor*. Often applied to shallow-draught vessels used for shore bombardment.

monobloc
An engine in which the cylinders are cast together as a single unit, rather than separately, which improves mechanical rigidity and the reliability of the sealing.

monocoque
A method of constructing an aircraft, land vehicle, or boat. The outer shell, rather than internal supports, provides the main strength and load-bearing ability.

monoplane
An aeroplane with a single pair of wings. See also biplane.

muzzle
The forward, open end of a gun's barrel, from which fired munitions emerge.

muzzle brake
A device at the end of the barrel of a tank's main gun, or artillery piece, that vents propellant gases and reduces recoil.

nacelle
A streamlined casing that supports and surrounds an engine or other structure.

NATO
An acronym for the North Atlantic Treaty Organization, an international alliance of countries from North America and Western Europe formed in 1949 in opposition to the Soviet Union.

nautical mile
One nautical mile is equivalent to 1.85 km (1$\frac{3}{20}$ miles); 60 nautical miles = 1 degree of Earth's circumference.

NBC
Nuclear, biological, and chemical weaponry (often called weapons of mass destruction). Special protection systems are required if military personnel and equipment are to operate in areas where such weapons have been used.

optical rangefinder
An optical system that uses trigonometry to find a target's distance. Two prisms a known distance apart reflect images of the target into the operator's eyepiece. The operator adjusts the angle of the prisms until the two images appear as one; the distance is calculated from this angle.

ordnance
Weapons and ammunition, specifically relating to artillery.

outrigger
A structure that projects from the side of a boat. On an ancient Greek trireme, outriggers accommodated oarsmen.

pre-dreadnought
A battleship built or ordered in the period before HMS *Dreadnought* set new standards for armament, armour, and speed in 1906.

pylon
A structure that attaches engines, fuel tanks, or weapons to an aircraft.

radar
A system that detects and locates objects by sending pulses of radio waves that are reflected off the object back to the source.

rate of fire
The number of rounds that can be fired by a specific weapon in a given time, usually expressed in rounds per minute.

reactive armour
Add-on armour that reacts to incoming enemy projectiles to minimize damage. Explosive reactive armour (ERA) explodes if struck by armour-penetrating projectiles, damaging the projectile and dissipating its energy. See also add-on armour.

return rollers
Small wheels positioned above the road wheels of a tracked vehicle that ensure the top of the track runs straight between the drive sprocket and the idler. See also drive sprocket, idler, road wheels.

rifling
An arrangement of spiral grooves on the inside of a gun barrel. The rifling spins the fired projectile so that it travels through the air with greater accuracy.

road wheels
The main wheels that rotate within the tracks of a tank. They are unpowered and serve only to distribute the tank's weight.

rocket-propelled grenade (RPG)
An infantry antitank weapon that launches rocket-powered warheads. Most RPGs can be operated by a single soldier.

sail (submarine)
A tower-like structure on a submarine that houses the periscopes, and antennae for radar and communications. It serves as an observation post when at the surface and provides stability when submerged.

self-propelled gun (SP)
A mobile artillery piece – for example, a howitzer – that is mounted on a motorized chassis with wheels or tracks.

ship of the line
A well-armed sailing warship between the 17th and 19th centuries, built to fight in the line of battle, exchanging broadsides with the enemy's line.

smart weapon
A precision-guided munition that is directed to its target by laser or a satellite-linked GPS (global positioning system).

smoothbore
An unrifled gun barrel designed to fire fin-stabilized projectiles. These projectiles do not spin when fired, so they travel faster and have greater armour penetration.

sonar
A system that detects and locates objects by sending pulses of sound waves that are reflected off the object back to the source.

spaced armour
Armour consisting of a thinner plate in front of, and separated by a space from, a thicker plate below.

spalling
Flakes that break off when armour plate is struck by a projectile. Some tanks are fitted with special linings that protect against high-velocity spalling.

sponson
A gun platform projecting from the side of a tank or battleship.

stealth bomber
A bomber plane that makes use of stealth technology; the name most commonly refers to the American Northrop B-2 Spirit.

stealth technology
Technology that aims to make an aircraft invisible to radar and other modes of detection using angular radar-deflecting surfaces and radar-absorbing materials.

strategic bombing
The planned destruction of specific targets by aerial bombing, with the intention of weakening the economy and war-making capabilities of an enemy state, and sapping the morale of its people.

stressed skin
A rigid construction in which the skin or covering takes a portion of the structural load; intermediate between monocoque, whereby the skin bears all or most of the load, and a rigid frame, which has a covering that is not load-bearing.

supersonic
Faster than the speed of sound.

suspension
A system that cushions the structure and occupants of a vehicle as the wheels move over uneven terrain.

swept wing
A wing angled backwards towards the rear of an aeroplane to reduce drag. A swept wing also reduces lift, so it requires greater takeoff and landing speeds.

swing wing
A wing whose horizontal angle can be adjusted to give lower drag at high speeds and more lift at low speeds. The swing-wing mechanism itself adds to the aircraft's overall weight. Also called a variable geometry, or variable sweep, wing.

tailfin
The vertical part of an aeroplane's tail, to which the rudder attaches; the rudder controls yaw, the left or right movement of the aircraft's nose.

tailplane
The horizontal part of an aeroplane's tail, shaped like a small wing, that aids stability. The elevators attach to the tailplane. See also elevators.

tank
An AFV designed for front-line combat, featuring strong armour, heavy firepower, and tracks for battlefield manoeuvrability. See also armoured fighting vehicle (AFV).

tank destroyer
An AFV armed with a direct-fire gun or missile launcher designed specifically to target enemy armoured vehicles.

tankette
A tracked AFV resembling a small tank, used for light infantry-support duties and scouting. They were widely used after World War I and in World War II. See also tank.

thrust
The force that propels a powered aircraft through the air.

torpedo
A cylindrical, self-propelled missile that is launched from an aircraft, ship, or submarine. It follows an underwater path and explodes on contact with, or in the near vicinity of, its target.

torque
A measurement of the maximum twisting force generated by an engine. The higher the torque, the greater the capacity of the engine to perform work.

torsion bar suspension
Suspension that uses a twisting metal bar to cushion the vehicle's movement.

track
A continuous belt of linked steel plates (with or without rubber pads) that runs through or around the geared drive sprocket, idler, road wheels, and return rollers of a tank. See also drive sprocket, idler, return rollers, road wheels.

transmission
The electrical, hydraulic, or mechanical means by which a vehicle's engine power is converted into the rotary motion of the wheels or tracks.

transonic
Close to the speed of sound.

traverse
The ability of a gun or turret to rotate from the centre-line of its mount. Traverse is described in degrees: a gun or turret that fully revolves has a traverse of 360 degrees.

trireme
An ancient Greek galley with three banks of oars. (A galley with two banks of oars was called a bireme.) See also galley.

turbofan
A jet engine developed from the turbojet. In a turbofan, the turbine powers both the compressor and a large fan at the front, which directs some of the incoming air past the combustion chamber and turbine. This cool, unburned air mixes with the exhaust at the rear, producing extra thrust and reducing noise.

turbojet
The original jet engine. Fuel is burned in a combustion chamber in a stream of air that has passed through a turbine-driven compressor. The hot, pressurized gases produced by combustion expand and emerge from the rear of the engine as an exhaust jet, creating thrust.

turboprop
An engine similar to a turbojet, except that the turbine extracts most of the energy from the hot gases and uses it to drive a propeller, so a turboprop does not actually use "jet power" for propulsion.

turboshaft
While very much like a turboprop in design, a turboshaft engine turns a shaft that powers other machinery, rather than driving a propeller. Turboshafts are used in helicopters, boats, and tanks.

turret
A rotating upper section of a tank, which accommodates the main gun and most of the crew, or a rotating structure housing one or more guns on a ship. Some aircraft of the past had machine-gun turrets.

unmanned aerial vehicle (UAV)
A pilotless aircraft controlled either remotely or by systems in the aircraft itself. UAVs are used for targeted ground attacks and reconnaissance. Also called drones or remotely piloted vehicles (RPVs).

V-twin engine
An engine with two banks of cylinders arranged in a V formation for compactness.

V4, V6, V8, V10, V12, V16
Designations for engines with cylinders arranged in a V-formation, indicating how many cylinders each engine holds. Inline engines have cylinders arranged in a row.

Warsaw Pact
A defence treaty, signed in 1955, between the Soviet Union and its satellite states of Bulgaria, Czechoslovakia, East Germany, Hungary, Poland, Romania, and Albania. The Warsaw Pact was established as a counterweight to NATO. See also NATO.

"wet" ammunition storage
Surrounding shells with liquid containers to guard against ammunition fires.

Index

Page numbers in bold refer to main entries.

A

A/V Sturmpanzerwagen tank **57**
A7V tank 47
AAMs *see* air-to-air missiles
AAV7A1 (APC) **209**
Acanthus, HMS **174**
active protection system (APS) 268, 269
Adler von Lübeck **28**
Admiral Gorshkov-class frigate **285**
AEC Type Y truck 47
AEG G.IV **78**
AEGIS integrated total combat system 276, **284**
aerodynamics 96
aerofoil shape 306
Aéronautique Militaire 78
Aerostatic Corps 13
AEW *see* airborne early warning aircraft
Afghanistan, War in 232, 234, 257, 258, 260, 300
troop carriers 266, 267
afterburner technology 218
AFVs *see* armoured fighting vehicles
Agano-class ships 169
Agincourt, HMS **83**
AI *see* artificial intelligence
AIFV (armoured infantry fighting vehicle) **210**
Aigrette 33
AIM-54 (AAM) 191
Ain Zara, Battle of 66
air-to-air missiles (AAMs) 191, 218
airborne early warning aircraft (AEW) 280
Airco DH.9A "Ninak" **79**
aircraft 9
 airborne early warning (AEW) 280
 airship bombing raids **76–7**
 autonomous 288
 Boeing B-17 ("Flying Fortress") **152–5**
 bomber and ground-attack (Cold War) **228–9**
 bombers (World War I) 33, **78–9**
 bombers (World War II) **150–51**
 carrier and maritime strike aircraft (World War II) **184–5**
 Cold War 190, **218–21**, **236–7**
 early jets 96, **164–5**
 Eurofighter Typhoon **292–5**
 evolution of airborne warfare 33, **66–7**
 F-86 Sabre **224–7**
 fighter planes (World War I) **70–71**
 fighter planes (World War II) **156–7**
 flight technology **306–7**
 for special forces 212
 front-line aircraft (Cold War) **236–7**
 gliders (World War II) **162–3**
 high-tech fighters **290–91**
 jet fighters (Cold War) **218–21**
 long-range strategic bombers 190
 Mikoyan MiG-29 **238–41**
 military transport planes **222–3**
 monoplanes 97, **106–7**
 protective technology 304
 reconnaissance **68–9**, 70
 stealth technology **242–3**
 Supermarine Spitfire **158–61**, 306
 unmanned 288

aircraft *continued*
 World War I **66–7**, **70–71**, **78–9**
 World War II 97, **148–51**, **156–7**, **162–3**, **184–5**
aircraft carriers 9, 96, 184
 21st-century 257, 276, **278–9**
 Cold War 190, 244, 245
 USS *George Washington* **280–83**
 nuclear-powered **303**
 World War I 182
 World War II 97, 149, 166–7, **182–3**
airships 33, 66, **76–7**
Ajax (ISTAR) **267**
Akagi 182
Akizuki-class escort ships 174
al-Qaeda 257
Albatros D.V **71**
Altay tank **269**
Amazon-class frigates 246
ambulances 13, 48–9, 111
America-class ships 29
American Civil War
 rail transport 32, 34–5
 steamboat battles **44–5**, 303
 submarines 32, 44
American Expeditionary Force 69
American Revolutionary War 19
American Standard locomotive 34
ammunition trains 112
amphibious vehicles
 Cold War 244
 Normandy landings 167, **186–7**
 Schwimmwagen 121
 specialist vehicles 136
 Véhicule de l'Avant Blindé **209**
 World War II 97, 167
amphibious warfare 167, **274–5**
AMX 10P (IFV) **2109**
AMX-13 tank **200**
AMX-30 tank 204
Andrea Doria **83**
Antenna Mast Group (AMG) 257
anti-aircraft platforms 111
anti-aircraft weapons 66
antisubmarine warfare (ASW) 230
antitank weapons 264
Apache AH-64 helicopter **232–3**, **234–5**
APCs *see* armoured personnel carriers
APS *see* active protection system
APVs *see* armoured patrol vehicles
Arab-Israeli conflicts 244
Arabis-class sloops 89
Arado Ar 234B-2 **165**
Arctic convoys 166, **167**, 170
Arizona, USS 166
Ark Royal, HMS **183**
Arleigh Burke, USS 191, **284**
armour protected vehicles **304–5**
armoured car (rail) 113
armoured cars 33
 interwar 96, **98–9**
 World War I 47, **64–5**
 World War II 110, **146–7**
armoured fighting vehicles (AFVs) 33, 110–111, 257
armoured infantry fighting vehicle *see* AIFV
armoured patrol vehicles (APVs) 258
armoured personnel carriers (APCs) **208–9**, 210, 266
 Buffel **260–63**
 Cold War 191
 counter-insurgency vehicles **258–9**
armoured trains **34–5**

Armstrong Whitworth F.K.8 (Big Ack) **69**
artificial intelligence (AI) 257, **277**, 288, 289, 290
artillery 32, 33, 257
Astute, HMS (S119) 257, **287**
AT-62 tank **202–3**
Atlanta, USS **36–7**
Atlantic, war in the (World War II) 166
Atlas V rocket 288
atomic bombs **97**, 149
attritional warfare 8, 149
AugustaWestland 234
Austin
 7 car 123
 K3 120
Automitrailleuse de Découverte (AMD) Panhard modèle 1935 (armoured car) 99
auxiliary personnel 120
Aviatik B.I 66
Avon Vale, HMS **174**
Avro
 504K **70–71**
 698 Vulcan **228**
 Lancaster 97, 149, **150–51**
 Vulcan 219

B

B&O L Class No.57 *Memnon* **34–5**
B-1 Lancer bomber 257
BAe Harrier GR.9A **290**
BAE Systems Mantis **298–9**
Bainbridge-class destroyers 43
Baldwin Locomotive Works 113
 Baldwin Class 10-12-D **55**
 Baldwin "Spider" **55**
Ball, Albert 72
balloons 9, 13, 76
Bantam 123
Bapaume, Second Battle of 47
bar armour **305**
Barnwell, Frank 108
Bars-class submarine **93**
battlecruisers 82
battleships 80, 166
 1830–1918 **36–7**, **82–3**
 1918–45 **168–9**, 303
 see also ships
Bayraktar TB2 (UCAV) 257, **299**
Bedford
 QL 110
 RL Recovery Vehicle **216**
BeiDou Navigation Satellite System 289
Belfast, HMS **170–73**
Bell
 AH-1 Cobra helicopter **230**, 304
 UH-1B Iroquois "Huey" helicopter 190, **230**
Benjamin Franklin-class nuclear-powered submarines 244, **249**
Benson/Gleaves-class destroyers 175
Berliet
 CBA **49**
 CBA Surgical Truck **49**
Berlin Airlift **190**
Beta II airship **76–7**
Bewegungskrieg 111
Bf 109 148
biological weapons 172, 190, 194, 199, 208, 269, 273
biplanes 33, 66, 67, 96, 97
biremes 12
Bishop, Billy 72
Bismarck 97, **168–9**
Bisson 89
Black Sea Fleet 83

blackout kit 116
Blenkinsop, John 32
Blériot, Louis 306
Blériot XI **306**
blimps 76
Blitzkrieg **111**
Blockade of Europe (World War I) 81
blockades
 land **190**
 naval 9, **81**, 244
Blohm and Voss 178
BMD-4M Airborne Assault Vehicle **267**
BMP-1 (IFV) 191, **210**
boats
 amphibious warfare **274–5**
 for special forces 212
 military patrol boats **252–3**
 see also ships
Boeing
 367-80 transport demonstrator 219
 Apache AH-64 helicopter **230–31**, **234–5**
 B-17 Flying Fortress **152–5**
 B-17G Flying Fortress 149, **150**
 B-24 Liberator 148
 B-52 Stratofortress 190, 218, **229**
 B-52D 219
 B29-A Superfortress 97, **151**
 CH-47D Chinook helicopter **231**
 F/A018E Super Hornet **290**
 KC-135 Stratotanker 219
Boer War 35
Bolshevik Red Fleet 42
bomb disposal 289
bombing campaigns
 airship **76–7**
 atomic bombs **97**, 149
 Cold War 190, **228–9**, **238–41**
 strategic 66–7, 97, 149, 150
 Vietnam War 190
 World War I **66–7**
 World War II 9, 97, 148, 149, 150–51, 152
Borei-class nuclear-powered submarine 287
Bosvark 260
Bradley IFVs 191
Brahmaputra-class frigate **285**
Brandenburg-class frigate **284**
Braun, Wernher von **219**
Brest-Litovsk, Treaty of 89
bridge-building 111
Bristol
 Bulldog **108**
 Fighter F.2b **70**
Britain, Battle of 72, 158
British Railways
 LMS Stanier 8F **112**
 SR Class Q1 **113**
 WD Austerity **113**
Brunel, Isambard Kingdom 32
BSA 116
BTR-50P (APC) **208**
BTR-152 (APC) **208**
Buckley-class destroyer escort **175**
Buffalo **259**
Buffel **260–63**
buses 47, 48
Bushmaster **259**
Bv206 (APC) **209**
BvS10 Viking troop carrier **267**
Byzantine Empire 19

C

Cael Canal 163
caissons 13
Cambrai, Battle of 58, 63
camels 47
camouflage **305**

canard delta configuration 292
Canterbury, HMNZCS **246**
Cape St Vincent, Battle of 24
caravel-built hulls 13
caravels, Portuguese **23**
Carlskrona, HSwMS 245
carracks 22
Carrier Battle Groups (CBGs) 244
cars
   birth of 33
   World War I 47
   see also armoured cars
Carthaginians 12
Casablanca-class escort carriers 183
Casspir **258**
caterpillar tracks 63, 120, 121
cavalry 12
   World War I 47
Cavour **278**
Centurion
   Mark 3 tank **200**
   tank 204
Challenger 1 tank **201**, 256, 305
Challenger 2 tank 256, **268**
Chance Vought (F-8K) F8U-2 Crusader **221**
Char B1 bis tank 126, **130**
chariots 8, 12, **14–15**
Charles de Gaulle **278**
Charron, Girardot et Voigt 33
chemical weapons 172, 190, 194, 199, 208, 269, 273
Chengdu J-20 stealth fighter 257, **291**
Chesapeake, Battle of the 19
Chevrolet, Crossley-Chevrolet Armoured Car **99**
Chieftain Mark II tank **201**
Chinese, ancient 12, 15
Chobham armour 304
Christie, J. Walter 96
Christie M1931 tank **101**
Christie suspension system 96
Churchill
   Armoured Recovery Vehicle (ARV) **137**
   AVRE **136**
   Crocodile **136**
Clark, Admiral Vernon E. 277
Class V36 Shunter **112**
clinker-built hulls 13
Codrington, Vice-Admiral Sir Edward 27
cogs 22
COIN warfare *see* counterinsurgency (COIN) warfare
Cold War **190–91**, 196
   AH-64 Apache **234–5**
   bomber and ground-attack aircraft **228–9**
   changing role of navies **244–5**
   Communist Bloc tanks **194–5**
   F-86 Sabre **224–7**
   frigates and destroyers **246–7**
   front-line aircraft **236–7**
   helicopters **230–33**
   infantry fighting vehicles **210–211**
   jet fighters **218–21**
   land vehicles **216–17**
   Leopard 1 tank **204–7**
   Mikoyan MiG-29 **238–41**, **238–41**
   military patrol boats **252–3**
   military transport planes **222–3**
   NATO tanks **200–201**
   USS *Nautilus* **250–51**
   nuclear-powered submarines **248–9**
   Prague Spring **202–3**
   stealth technology **242–3**
   submarines **250–51**
   T-72 **196–9**
   tank warfare 264

Cold War *continued*
   tanks of non-aligned nations **214–15**
   transporting missiles **192–3**
   transporting special forces **212–13**
   troop carriers **208–9**
Comet tank **131**
command posts, mobile 111
command-and-control systems 191
communications 97, 191, 256, **257**
computerization, Cold War 190, 191
Conqueror, HMS 245
Consolidated B-24 Liberator **150**, 152
Constantinople, Siege of (717–18) 19
Constitution, USS **29**
Convair B-58 Hustler 219, **229**
convoys
   Arctic 166, **167**, 170
   Atlantic 84, 91, 166, 176, 178, 179
   escort ships **174–5**, 247
Coronel, Battle of 80
corvettes 174, 276, 277
counter-insurgency vehicles **258–9**
counterinsurgency (COIN) warfare 256, 257
Courbet **82**
Crimean War 32
Crossley-Chevrolet Armoured Car **99**
cruisers 80
   1830–1918 **36–7**
   1918–45 **168–9**
   HMS *Belfast* **170–73**
   Cold War 244
CT15TA Armoured Truck **146**
Cuban Missile Crisis 244
Curtiss P-40 Warhawk **109**
CV90 troop carrier **266**

D

D-Day landings 112, 136, 163, 168, 170, 186, 274
Daimler Mark II "Dingo" **146**
Dardanelles, Battle of the 80
Dassault
   Mirage 2000D **290**
   Mirage III **221**
   Rafale 293
data transfer, battlefield 191, 288
de Havilland
   DH.82B Queen Bee 298
   DH98 Mosquito **184**
   DH100 Vampire FB 6 **164**
   Mosquito 152
   Mosquito B.16 **151**
   Vampire 218
Delta, Battle of the 9
Derfflinger, SMS **83**
despatch riders 114
destroyers 33, **42–3**
   Cold War 244, **246–7**
   modern 257, 276, **284–5**, 303
   World War I **88–9**
   World War II **174–5**
Deutsche Reichsbahn DR Class 52 "Kriegslok" **112–13**
Dewoitine
   D27 **108**
   D.520 **156–7**
Diamond, HMS **246**
digital technology 256, 257, 288
directed energy weapons (DEWs) 257, 276, 289
dive-bombers 148
Djibouti 212
dogfights 70, 292
Dogger Bank, Battle of 80
Dönitz, Admiral Karl 179
Douglas
   A-4 Skyhawk **229**

Douglas *continued*
   C-47 Dakota (Skytrain) 222
   C-54 Skymaster 190
   SBD Dauntless **184**
Douhet, Giulio 96
Dreadnought, HMS (nuclear-powered submarine) 248
Dreadnought, HMS (warship) **82–3**, 303
dreadnoughts 32, **82–3**
Dresden, SMS **37**
drones, 9, 257, 264, 288, **296–7**, **298–9**
DRW C.V **68**
Dubček, Alexander 202

E

Eastern Front
   World War I 47
   World War II 110, 112
Edinburgh, HMS 170
Egyptians, ancient 8, 12, 14
El Alamein, Second Battle of 132
Electromagnetic Aircraft Launch System (EMALS) 277
electronic countermeasures (ECM) 191
electronic warfare systems (EWS) 285, 290
elephants, war 12
EMALS *see* Electromagnetic Aircraft Launch System
engineering, electrical and mechanical 96
engines
   evolution in warfare **32–3**
   gas-turbine 190, 230
   Harley-Davidson WLC 119
   internal combustion (ICE) 8, 33, 110
   interwar period 96
   jet 218–19
   Pierce-Arrow R Type 53
   reactor 190
   steam powered 32
   turbofan 237, 292
   turbojet 218–19
English Electric
   Canberra **228**
   Lightning F6 **221**
Enigma codes 179
Enterprise, USS **183**
Erhardt E-V/4 (armoured car) **65**
escort carriers **182–3**
escort ships
   Cold War 247
   modern **284–5**
   World War I **88–9**
   World War II **174–5**
Essex, USS **183**
Etrich Taube monoplane 66
Etruscans 14
Eurofighter Typhoon **292–5**
Explosive Ordnance Disposal (EOD) personnel 259
explosive reactive armour (ERA) 305

F

F-class escort ship **174**
Fairchild Republic A-10 Thunderbolt II ground-attack aircraft 257
Fairey Swordfish 97
Falklands War 80, 244–5, 302
Fenian Ram 42
Fiat
   15 Ter **48**
   2000 tank **56**
   Izhorski Fiat (armoured car) **65**
Fidonisy-class destroyers 89
field kitchens 110
flamethrowers 111

Flers-Courcelette, Battle of 33
Fletcher-class destroyers 175
Fleurus, Battle of 13
flight technology **306–7**
Flower-class corvettes 174
fluid mechanics 96
fly-by-wire technologies 191
Flyer 9, 33, 288
flying infantry-support vehicles 232
Focke-Wulf Fw 190 **156**
Fokker
   Dr.1 67, **70**
   D.VII **71**
   Eindecker fighter 107
Folland, Henry 72
foot mobility 8, 12
Ford 123
   Model T Ambulance **48–9**
Forrestal, USS 245
Fort Ében Émael 163
Foxhound **259**
France, allied landings 84, 112, 116, 163, 167, **186–7**, 274
Franco-Prussian War 32
freight locomotives, World War II **112–13**
frigates
   age of sail 28, 29
   Cold War 191, 244, **246–7**
   modern 276, **284–5**
Frunze, Mikhail 33
Fuji 37
Full Spectrum Dominance 256
Fuller, J.F.C. 96
Furious, HMS **182**
FV432 Bulldog (APC) **208**
FV603 Saracen (APC) **208**

G

galleasses 18
galleons 12, 13, 18, 22, **28**
galleys 12, 13, 18, 22, **303**
Gallipoli campaign 274
garrisons 12
gas masks, equine 47
Gato, USS **176**
Gavotti, Giulio 66
GAZ-66 truck 216
General Atomics
   MQ-1 Predator (UCAV) 256, 300
   MQ-9 Reaper **298**, **300–301**
General Belgrano, ARA 245
General Dynamics
   F-16 Fighting Falcon **237**, 256, 288, 292
   X-62A VISTA 288
geolocation satellites 288–9
George Washington, USS (supercarrier) 190, **280–83**
George Washington-class nuclear submarines 177, **248**
Gerald R. Ford, USS 277, **278–9**
Geranium, HMAS **89**
glide bombs 257
gliders, World War II 9, **162–3**
Global Positioning System (GPS) navigation 191, 288–9
Global War on Terror (GWOT) 256, 257, 266
Gloire 32
GLONASS 289
Gloster
   Gladiator **109**
   Meteor **165**
GMC
   CCKW military truck 97
   CCKW-352 110
Godavari-class ships 285

Goliath tracked mine **136**
Gorky Automobile Plant 216
Gotha bombers 66
Grand Fleet 80
Great Central Railway, GCR Class 8K **54**
Great Western 32
Great Western Railway, GWR Class 2301 "Dean Goods" **54–5**
Greek fire 19
Greek War of Independence 27
Greeks, ancient 12, 13, 18, **20–21, 22**, 302
Grenada 244
Gribeauval, Jean-Baptiste Vaquette de 13
ground attack aircraft **228–9**
Grumman
  A-6 Intruder **229**
  F-14 Tomcat 191, **236–7**
  F4F Wildcat **184**
  F6F Hellcat 149, **185**
  F8F Bearcat **185**
Guadalcanal, USS **183**
Guderian, General Heinz 96, 111
guided-missile destroyers and frigates 247, 257, 284, 285
Gulf War 234, 242, 244, 256, 266, 270, 302
gun carriages 12
gun sponsons 58
gun turrets, rotating 96
guns, railway **34–5**

H

H-class submarine **92**
Haig, Field Marshal Douglas 63
half-tracks 96, 110, **120–21**
Handley Page, Victor 219
Hannibal 12
Hanseatic League 28
Harland and Wolf 170
Harley-Davidson
  Model U US Navy version **114**
  WLA **115**
  WLC **115**, **116–19**
  XA **115**
Harris, Sir Arthur 149
Havock, HMS **42**
Hawker
  Hunter F Mk1 **220–21**
  Hurricane 72, 158
  Hurricane Mk1 106–7, **108–9**
  Sea Fury **185**
  Tempest Mk II **157**
Hawker Siddeley Harrier **236**
Hazelwood, USS **175**
heat-absorbent exhaust ducts 242
Heeresfeldbahn 54
Heinkel
  He111 148
  He162 **164**
  He177 Grief **151**
  He178 97
helicopter assault ships 244
helicopters, military 9, **230–31**
  Cold War 190–91
  Mil Mi-24 "Hind" **232–3**
Heligoland Bight, Battle of 80
Helsing HX-2 288
Henschel metre-gauge **55**
Herbert J. Thomas, USS **246–7**
Hermes, HMS 245
High Energy Laser with Integrated Optical-dazzler and Surveillance (HELIOS) 276
High Seas Fleet 80
high-explosive anti-tank (HEAT) projectiles 305
Hindenburg line 58

Hiroshima 97, 149, 151
Hitler, Adolf 124, 176, 179
Hittites 12, 14
Hobart, Percy 136
Holland, John Philip 42, 43
Holland, USS 42
Hood, HMS 168
Hornet, HMS 42, **88**
Hornet, USS 166, 183
horses
  in warfare 8, **12**
  World War I **47**, 48
  World War II 110
Hotspur gliders **162–3**
hovercraft 274
Hughes, AIM-4F Super Falcon (AAM) 218
Hughes Helicopters 234
Hull, USS **43**
hulls, multiple 276
Humber Scout Car **146**
Humvee (High Mobility Multipurpose Wheeled Vehicle) **217**, 256
Hunley, CSS 32
Hunt-class destroyers 174
Hussites 13
hydroplanes 251
hypersonic antiship missiles 276
hypersonic scramjet-powered missiles 257

I

I-400 submarine **177**
IEDs (improvised explosive devices) 257, 258
Illustrious, HMS **182–3**
Imperatritsa Mariya **83**
Imperial Japanese Navy Air Service (IJNAS) 149
Imperial Military Railways (IMR), armoured CSAR Class E4-10-2T **35**
Imperial Russian Navy 42
improvised explosive devices *see* IEDs
Indian Railways, Class AWE 113
Indiana, USS 37
Indians, ancient 15
India–Pakistan War 244
Industrial Revolution 8, 32
infantry
  mechanized 110
  supplies 46
  World War II 111
infantry fighting vehicles (IVFs) 191, **210–211**, 257, 266
infrared-radiation suppression systems 234
insurgents 258–9
intelligence gathering 66, **245**, 288
Intelligence, Target, Acquisition, and Reconnaissance vehicles (ISTAR) 267
interceptors 66
intercontinental ballistic missiles (ICBMs) 190, 192
internal combustion engines (ICE) 8, 33, 110
interrupter gear 66
interwar period
  aircraft carriers **182–3**
  armoured cars **98–9**
  battleships and cruisers **168–9**
  evolution of military vehicles **96–7**
  international naval treaties 174
Invincible, HMS 245
Iosif Stalin-2 (IS-2) **141**
Iosif Stalin-3M (IS-3M) **141**
Iowa, USS 167, 168
Iraq War 257, 258, 260, 270, 300, 302
Irish Republican Brotherhood 42

ironclads 32, 44, 303, 304
ISU-152 **139**
Italo-Turkish War 66, 78
Ivanovets 277
Iwo Jima, Battle of 82, 84, 96
Izhorski Fiat (armoured car) **65**

J

Jagdgeschwader 1 67
Jagdpanther **139**
Jagdpanzer 38(t) Hetzer **139**
Jagdtiger **139**
jamming, communications 257
jeeps **120–23**
Jellicoe, Admiral Sir John 81
jets
  early 9, **164–5**
  entering the jet age **218–19**
  jet fighters (Cold War) 190, **220–21**
Joint Direct Attack Munitions (JDAMs) 300
Juan Carlos **278**
Junkers
  Ju 87D Stuka **150–51**
  Ju87 148
Jutland, Battle of 80–81, 88, 303

K

Kadesh, Battle of 12
Kaga, JS **279**
Kagerō **43**
Kaiserliche Marine 80
kamikaze suicide missions **149**
Kendall, Frank 288
Kerch **89**
Khalkhin Gol, Battle of 142
kites, military 12
Kleist, General Paul Ludwig Ewald von 142
Kliment Voroshilov-1 (KV-1) **140–41**
Kliment Voroshilov-2 (KV-2) **140**
Knox-class destroyers 246
kŏbuksŏn (turtle ship) 18, **23**
Kola-class frigate **246**
Koni-class frigate **247**
Konig, Paul 81
Korean War
  cruisers 169, 170
  destroyers 246–7
  F-86 Sabre 224
  jet fighters 218
  naval warfare 244
Koshkin, Mikhail 142
Krauss-Maffei 204
Kriegsmarine 176
Krupp cemented armour 38
Kursk, Battle of 110
Kut-el-Amara, Siege of 67

L

L-class submarine **93**
La Fayette-class frigates 276
La France 33
Lancaster, HMS **284–5**
Lanchester
  Armoured Car (1915) **64–5**
  Armoured Car (1931) **98**
Lancia Ansaldo 1Z (armoured car) **65**
Land Rover **216**
landing craft 97, 186, 274
Landing Craft Air Cushion (LCAC) **274–5**
landmines 258, 260
Langley, USS 96

Larrey, Dominique-Jean 13
lasers 257, 276
lateen sails 13, 18
Latil TAR **48**
LAV-25 (APC) **209**
Le Redoutable **249**
Le Triomphant (S616) **286**
Leander-class frigates 246
Lebed XII **68**
Leichter Kampfwagen LKII **100**
Leichttraktor Vs.Ktz.31 **100**
Lend-Lease scheme 110, 112
Leonardo da Vinci 13, **16–17**
Leopard
  1 tank **204–7**
  2A4 tank **200–201**
  2A6 tank 268, **269**
Lepanto, Battle of 18
Leviathan 37
Lewis and Clark, USS 244
Leyland Armoured Car **99**
LFG Roland C.II (Walfisch) **68**
Liberty 3- and 5-ton trucks 47
Liberty merchant ships 97
Liddel Hart, Captain Sir Basil 97
light infantry vehicles 110
light reconnaissance vehicles 123
Lightning, HMS **42–3**
Lima tank works (Ohio) 133
limbers 13
Lincoln, Abraham 34
"Little Willie" tank 47, **56**
Lockheed
  C-5 Galaxy transporter **222–3**
  C-130 Hercules 222
  F-104G Starfighter **220**
  F-117 Nighthawk 191, **237**, 305, **306**
  F-117 Nighthawk helicopter **242–3**
  P-3 Orion 244
  P-80A Shooting Star **164**
  S-3A Viking 245
Lockheed Martin
  Boeing F-22 Raptor **291**
  F-22 Raptor 256, 288, 292
  F-35 Lightning II **291**
logistics
  aircraft ground support 149
  horses 12
  rail 32, 46, 47
  World War I 46
  World War II 110, **112–13**
London, Midland & Scottish Railway, LMS Stainer 8F **112**
London Naval Treaty 170, 174
London, Treaty of (1827) 27
longships 13, 18, **22**, 302
Los Angeles-class submarines 287
Ludendorff, General Erich 47
Luftwaffe 148–9, 152, 158, 186
Lutz, Oswald 111
LVG C.VI **69**

M

M1 Abrams tank **201**, 256
M1A1 Abrams tank 191, **201**
M1A2 Abrams tank 268, **270–73**
M2 Bradley (IFV) 209, **211**
M2A3 Light Tank **101**
M3 Lee (Grant) tank **130**, 132
M3A1 Scout Car **120**
M4 Sherman tank 96, 110–111, **132–5**
M4A1 tank **130–31**
M5 Half-track **121**
M8 Greyhound **146–7**
M14/41' tank **125**
M18 Hellcat **138**
M26 Pershing tank **131**

M35 2½ 6x6 cargo truck **216**
M41A1 Walker Bulldog **200**
M48 Patton tank 191, **200**
M113A1 (APC) 190, **208**
M1895 railway gun **35**
M1918 3 Ton Tank **57**
McCain, Admiral John S. Jr. 245
McCudden, James 72
McDonnell, F2H-2 Banshee 218
McDonnell Douglas, F-15 Eagle 191, **236**, 256, 292
main battle tanks (MBTs) 191, 256, 257
Malta, defence of 109
Mamba **258**
man-portable air-defence systems (MANPADS) 232
Manned-Unmanned Teaming (MUM-T) 288
Mannock, "Mick" 72
Maoris 23
Marder 1 (IFV) **210**
Mark I tank 33, 47, **56**
Mark IV tank 47, **57**, **58–61**
Mark V tank **62–3**
Mark VIII "International" tank **57**
Marshall, General George C. 123
Maryland, USS (SSBN-738) **286–7**
Mastiff **258–9**
Matchless G3/L North Africa version **115**
Matilda 2 tank 126
Matilda CDL **136**
MBP-3 (IFV) **211**
medevac 230, 289
Mediterranean Sea 22, 166
Medium Mark A Whippet (tank) **57**
Mekong Delta 253
Mercedes-Benz G Wagon Wolf **217**
merchant shipping 81, 97, 166, 174, 247
 in warfare **302**
Merkava 1 tank **215**
Merkava Mark 4 tank **269**, 304
Mesopotamia 12
Messerschmitt
 Bf 109 107, 158
 Bf 109E **109**
 Me 163 Komet **164**, 305
 Me 262 Schwalbe 97, **164**
 Messerschmitt-Böelkow-Blohm MBB Bo 105A helicopter **230**
Messines, Battle of 47
Mgebrov, Vladimir 64
Mgebrov-Renault armoured car **64**
Midway, Battle of 149
Mikasa **38–41**
Mikoyan-Gurevich
 MiG-9 218
 MiG-15 224
 MiG-17 **220**
 MiG-19 "Farmer" 218
 MiG-21 "Fishbed" 190, 218, **220**
 MiG-29 **238–41**
Mil Mi-24 "Hind" helicopter **231**, **232–3**
military transport planes **222–3**
mine clearance 289
Mine-resistant Ambush-protected (MRAP) vehicles 257, **258–9**, 260
Minerva Armoured Car **64**
mines *see* landmines; sea mines
missile carriers **192–3**
missiles
 air-to-air 191, 218
 antiship/antisubmarine 246, 247, 284, 285
 cruise 284, 285, 287
 guided 247
 hypersonic antiship 276
 hypersonic scramjet-powered 257
 intercontinental ballistic (ICBMs) 190, 192

missiles *continued*
 ship-launched 256, 257
 shoulder launched 232
 submarine-launched ballistic (SLBMs) 190, 244, 248, 286
 surface-to-air 246
 V-2 ballistic 219
Mitchell, R.J. 109, 158
Mitchell, William "Billy" 96
Mitsubishi A6M Zero **184–5**
Mobei, Battle of 12
Mobile Bay, Battle of 44–5
modern age
 21st-century aircraft carriers **278–9**
 amphibious warfare **274–5**
 Buffel **260–63**
 counter-insurgency vehicles **258–9**
 drones in modern warfare **296–9**
 Eurofighter Typhoon **292–5**
 high-tech fighters **290–91**
 M1A2 Abrams **270–73**
 modern destroyers and frigates **284–5**
 modern tank warfare **264–5**
 MQ-9 Reaper **300–301**
 nuclear-powered submarines **286–7**
 tanks **268–9**
 tech in the sky and beyond **288–9**
 troop carriers **266–7**
 USS *George Washington* **280–83**
 warships in the digital age **276–7**
Mogami-class cruisers 170
Mogami-class frigates 276
monoplanes 96, 97, **106–7**, 306
Moskva helicopter carrier 191
motorcycles, military 33, **114–15**
MRAP *see* Mine-resistant Ambush-protected (MRAP) vehicles
mules 47
Mullan, Michael 28
Murakano-class destroyers 43
Musashi 166, 168
Muyuan 12
Myastschev, M-4 "Bison" 219

N

Nagasaki 97, 149, 151
Nakajima Ki-43 Hayabusa "Oscar" **156**
Napoleon I, Emperor 9, 12, 13
Napoleonic Wars 12, 19, 76
Narval-class submarine **93**
Narvik class destroyers 174
NASA 219
Nash Motors Company 48
Nash Quad **48**
Nautilus, USS 190, **248–9**, **250–51**
naval blockades 9, **81**, 244
naval warfare
 AI and **277**
 Cold War **244–5**
 evolution of **18–19**
 modern **276–7**
 seafaring technology **302–3**
 World War I **80–81**
 World War II **166–7**
 see also ships
Navarin **37**
Navarino, Battle of **26–7**
Nazi Party 124
Nelson, Admiral Horatio 19, 24
Nelson, HMS 168
network-centric battlefield 256
Nieuport 12 **68**
Nimitz (CVN-68) supercarrier 191
Nimitz-class supercarriers 278, 280
"no man's land" 63
non-aligned nations, tanks **214–15**
Normandy landings 84, 116, 163, 167, **186–7**, 274
North Africa, Allied landings in 84

North American
 F-86 Sabre **224–7**, **306**
 F-100 Super Sabre 190, 218
 P-51 Mustang 97, 149, **157**, 224, 227
North British Locomotive Company 55
North Carolina, USS **169**
Northampton, USS **168**
Northrop
 B2-Spirit (Stealth Bomber) 219
 YB-49 219
Northrop Grumman
 B-21 Raider 257
 MQ-4C Triton 289
 RQ-4 Global Hawk **298–9**
Norton 116
 Big Four SWD **114**
Novik 88
Novosibirsk 249
NSU Kettenkrad HK 101 **115**
nuclear, biological, and chemical (NBC) protective features 190
nuclear bombs 151
nuclear-powered submarines **250–51**, **286–7**

O

O & K Feldbahn **54**
oars 12, 13, 18, 22–3, 302
oarsmen, Greek 20, 21
Okinawa, Battle of 82, 84
Oklahoma, USS 166
Olenegorsky Gornyak 277
Oliver Hazard Perry, USS **246–7**
Olympias Greek trireme **20–21**
Omaha Beach 186–7
Opel Blitz 110, **121**
Operation Desert Storm 244, 256
Operation Slingshot 253
Ordnance BL 12in gun Mk IX **35**
Orne River 163
Oscar-class submarine **249**
Ottoman Empire 12, 27, 66, 78, 83
outrigger hulls 276

P

Pacific War (World War II) 97, 149, 166–7, 176
Panavia Tornado GR1 **237**
Pansarbil m/40 (Lynx) **99**, 305
Panther tank **125**
Panzer 38(t) Ausf E tank **124**
Panzer I light tank 96
Panzer IV tanks 126
Panzer units 110, 111
Panzerkampfwagen I Ausf A **124**
Panzerkampfwagen III Ausf L **125**
Panzerkampfwagen IV **124**
parachutists 96, 163
paratroopers 163
paravanes 86
Paris, liberation of (1944) 122–3
Parker, USS **175**
Pathfinder, HMS 92
patrol boats, military **252–3**
patrol vehicles 99
PCF 43 (patrol boat) **252–3**
peacekeeping operations 244
Pearl Harbor 89, 149, 166, 182
Peerless Armoured Car **98**
People's Liberation Army Navy (PLAN) 285
Pershing Nord **55**
Persians, ancient 14–15
Peugeot modèle AC (armoured car) **64**
Pharris, USS **246**
Philippine Sea, Battle of the 168

Phoenicians 12, 302
Pierce-Arrow
 R Type **50–53**
 R8 49
Piranha III troop carrier **266–7**
Platz, Reinhold 71
Poliakarpov Po-2 **108**
Polikarpov, Nikolai 108
Pompée-class ships 29
powerplants, nuclear 190, 244
Prague Spring **202–3**
Praying Mantis **147**
precision-guided munitions (PGMs) 230, 256, 288
Prince of Wales, HMS (aircraft carrier) **279**
Prince of Wales, HMS (battleship) 166
Project 971 Shchuka-B (*Akula*-class) **286**
Project 22350 285
proxy wars 190, 244
Pruitki **42–3**
Prussia, rail transport 32
PT 91 Twardy tank **268**

Q

quadcopter **299**
Queen Elizabeth class super-dreadnoughts 82
quinqueremes 18

R

radar 191, 242, 245, 246, 276, 285, 302
radar cross-section (RCS) 290
radar-absorbent material (RAM) 242
radio trucks 111
radio-frequency (RF) energy 276
RAF *see* Royal Air Force; Royal Aircraft Factory
rail transport 8, 32
 armoured trains, railway guns **34–5**
 supply trains 46, 47
 World War I **46–7**
 World War I locomotives **54–5**
 World War II 33
 World War II logistics **112–13**
railguns, electromagnetic 257, 276
railroad battery 34
Railway Operation Division (ROD) 543
Ram Kangaroo **147**
Ramesses II, Pharaoh 12
Ramillies, HMS **80–81**
reconnaissance
 aircraft 9, 33, 66, **68–9**, 70, 97
 armoured cars 99
 drones 297
 modern 288
 UAVs 300
 UGVs 289
 vehicles 147
Reid, George W. 35
remote-control vehicles 289
Remount Department 47
Renault
 FT-17 tank **57**
 Mgebrov-Renault (armoured car) **64**
reparations 112
Republic
 F-84C Thunderjet **164–5**
 F-105 Thunderchief 218
 F-105D Thunderchief **220–21**
 P-47 Thunderbolt 149, **157**
Repulse, HMS 166
Revenge, HMS **28**
Richthofen, Manfred von (Red Baron) **67**, 70

Riddles, R.A. 113
Riga-class ships 247
rigging 13, 25
rigid inflatable boats (RIBs) **212–13**
riverine craft 13
road-building 111
robo-mules 257
robotics 289
rocket research 190, 219, 288, 289
rocket-propelled grenades (RPGs) 257
Rodney, HMS **168**
Rolls-Royce Armoured Car **98–9**
Romans 9, 15, 18, 22
Rommel, Erwin 111
Ronald Reagan, USS **278**
Ropucha-class landing ship 277
Royal Air Force (RAF) 66, 97
  Bomber Command 150
Royal Aircraft Factory 72
  B.E.2 66, **68–9**
  RAF F.E.2b **78**
  RAF R.E.8 **78**
  R.E.8 (Harry Tate) **69**
  S.E.5a 67, **71**, **72–5**, **306**
Royal Engineers 54
Royal Flying Corps (RFC) 67, 68, 72
Royal Navy 19, 24, 36, 80
  age of sail 28
  aircraft carriers and escort carriers 182
  E-class submarine **92–3**
  T/*Triton*-class submarine **176**
  World War I 92
  X-craft submarine **177**
Royal Navy Air Service 76
Royal Oak, HMS 166
Royal Tanks Corps 102
RS-IU AAM 218
Russian Civil War 42, 65
Russo-Japanese War 32, 43, 88

S

S-class submarine 166
S19, SMS **88**
S90, SMS **42**
SA Gazelle helicopter **230**
Saab
  37 Viggen **236**
  Gripen 293
sails 9, 12, 13, 18, 32, 302
  great age of sail **28–9**
Saint Paul, USS **169**
Salamis, Battle of 18
Salmson 2 **69**
SAMs *see* surface-to-air missiles
Santisima Trinidad 28
Saracen APC 260
Saratoga, USS 97, **182**
satellite communications 191, 257, 288–9
Scapa Flow 166
Schleswig War, First 32
Schlieffen Plan **46–7**
Schneider CA-1 tank **56**
Schriever, General Bernard "Bennie" 190
Schützenpanzer
  Lang HS.30 (IFV) **210**
  Puma troop carrier **267**
Schwartzkopf, Wolfgang 81
Schwimmwagen **121**
scout cars 146, 147
Sd Kfz
  231 6 rad Armoured Car **98**
  234/3 Schwerer Panzerspahwagen, 8-rad **147**
  251-8 Ausf C Half-track **120**
sea mines 44, 80, 81, 86
Sea Scouts 76
seaplanes 148

search and rescue (SAR) operations 230, 300
Seawolf, USS **287**
Selex Galileo Falco Evo **299**
self-driving vehicles 257
Sen-Toku-class submarine **177**
Seversky P-35/AT-12 Guardsman **108**
Sforza, Ludovico, Duke of Milan 16
Shangdong 257
Sheffield, HMS (guided-missile destroyer) **247**
Sheffield, HMS (light cruiser) 167
shells 80
Sherman
  M4 tank 96, 110–111, **132–5**
  M4A1 tank **130–31**
  V Crab **137**
ships 9
  aircraft carriers **182–3**, **278–9**
  battleships 1830–1918 **36–7**, **82–3**
  HMS *Belfast* **170–73**
  Cold War frigates and destroyers **246–7**
  Cold War navies **244–5**
  cruisers 1830–1918 **36–7**
  Demologos 13
  dreadnoughts **82–3**
  early warships **22–3**
  USS *George Washington* **280–83**
  great age of sail **28–9**
  Mikasa **38–41**
  missile-launching 256, 257
  nuclear-powered submarines **286–7**
  Olympias Greek trireme **20–21**
  protective technology 304
  seafaring technology **302–3**
  ships-of-the-line 28, 29, **303**
  stealth 276
  steamboat battles in American Civil War **44–5**
  superdreadnoughts **84–7**
  USS *Texas* **84–7**
  torpedo boats, destroyers and submarines 1830–1918 **42–3**
  uncrewed **276–7**
  HMS *Victory* **24–5**
  warships in the digital age **276–7**
  World War I **83**
  World War I destroyers and escorts **88–9**
  World War II destroyers and escorts **174–5**
  World War II sea battles **166–7**
  World War II submarines **176–7**
  see also aircraft carriers; amphibious vehicles; boats; submarines
Sicily, Allied landings 167
siege engines 12
Siegfried-class ships **36–7**
signalling 12
Sikorsky, UH-60 Black Hawk helicopter **222–3**, **231**
situational awareness (SA) 290
SM U-9 **92–3**
SM U-10 **92**
Smith, Joseph 158
smoke grenades **304**
Snatch Land Rover **258**
Sokoi **42–3**
Somme, Battle of the 47, 56, 63
SOMUA S35 tank **130**
sonar 250
Sopwith
  F.1 Camel **70**, 72
  Snipe 71
  triplane 70
sound barrier 218
Sound Surveillance System (SOSUS) 245
South African Border War 258, 260

Southern Railway, SR Class Q1 113
Soviet Union
  Cold War **190–91**, 244
  missile arsenal **192–3**
  Prague Spring **202–3**
  tanks **140–45**, **194–5**, **196–9**
space programme 219
space wars **288–9**
Spad XII 71
Spanish Armada 28
Spanish Civil War 109
special forces, transporting **212–13**
specialist vehicles, World War II 111
spoked wheels 12
Spruance-class destroyers 246
St Quentin Canal, Battle of 63
Stalin, Joseph 244
Stanier, William 112
static warfare, end of 97
STC Orian-10 **299**
stealth technology 219, **242–3**, 257, 276, 290, 291
steam power 8, 32, 303
steamships 13, 19, 32, **44–5**
Steyr-Daimler-Puch Pinzgauer **217**
stick-and-rudder control 306, 307
Stockton and Darlington Railway 32
strategic bombers 66–7, 97, 149, 150
Stridsvagn fm/31 armoured car **98**
Strv 74 tank **214**
Strv 103 (S-Tank) **214–15**
Strv 104 tank **215**
StuG III **138–9**
SU-76M **138**
SU-100 **139**
submarines 9
  1830–1918 **42–3**
  American Civil War 32, 44
  Cold War 190, **248–51**
  diesel-electric 33
  interwar period 96
  modern 257
  USS *Nautilus* **250–51**
  nuclear-powered 190, 244, **248–51**, **286–7**
  U-995 Submarine **178–81**
  U-boats 80, 81, 88, 92–3, 96, 166, 167, 176, **178–81**
  World War I 76, 80, 81, 88, **90–93**
  World War II 97, 166, 167, **176–81**
Sudomer, Battle of 13
Sukhoi
  Su-7B **228**, 305
  Su-27 **237**
  Su-30 Mki **290**
  Su-57 257, **291**
Sumerians 15
Supermarine
  Seafire **184**
  Spitfire 72, 96, **158–61**
  Spitfire MK1a **109**
  Spitfire Mk24 158
  Spitfire MkII **156**
supersonic jets 190, 218, 288
supplies
  air-drops 9, 67
  Berlin Airlift **190**
  Blockade of Europe **81**
  boats and 9
  horses and 8
  infantry 46
  UGVs 289
  World War I 46, 47, 67
  World War II 9, 97, 111
surface-to-air missiles (SAMs) 192, 246
surgical trucks 49
surveillance
  Cold War 191, 244, 245
  modern 256, 257, 276, 288, 289, 300
Suzutsuki **174–5**
synchronizer 66

T

T-14 Armata tank **269**
T-15 Armata tank 257
T-26 tank **100**
T-34 tank 97, **140**
T-34/85 tank **141**, **142–5**
T-35 tank **101**
T-54 tank 190, **194**
T-55 tank 191, **194–5**
T-60 tank **140**
T-62 tank **194**
T-64 tank 197, 256, **264–5**
T-64B1 tank **195**
T-70 tank **141**
T-72 tank 191, **196–9**, 256
T-72M1 tank **195**
T-80 tank 257
T-80U tank **195**
T-84 tank **268**
T-90S tank **268**
tactical bombers 150
Takao **168**
Tank destroyers, Allied and Axis **138–9**
Tank Urban Survival Kit (TUSK) 270
tanks
  Allied **130–31**
  Axis **124–5**
  Cold War 190, 191
  Communist Bloc **194–5**
  interwar technological developments 96
  Leonardo's "tank" 13, **16–17**
  Leopard 1 **204–7**
  light, medium and heavy (1918-39) **100–101**
  M1A2 Abrams **270–73**
  M4 Sherman 96, 110–111, **132–5**
  Mark IV 47, **56**, **58–61**
  modern tank warfare **264–5**
  NATP **200–201**
  non-aligned nations **214–15**
  Normandy landings 186
  post-Cold War **268–9**
  Prague Spring **202–3**
  protective technology 304
  Soviet **140–41**
  T-34/85 **142–5**
  T-72 **196–9**
  Tiger I **126–9**, 304
  Vickers Medium Mark II **102–5**
  World War I 8, 33, 47, **56–7**
  World War I tank battles **62–3**
  World War II 97, 110
Tarantul-III-class missile corvettes 277
Tarantula, USS **43**
Task Force 77 244
Tassafaronga, Battle of 168
taxis, Paris 48
Taylor, A.J.P. 46
technology
  and military mobility 8, 9
  Cold War **190–91**
  flight **306–7**
  present and future war 256, 257, **288–9**
  protective **304–5**
  seafaring **302–3**
Téméraire-class 74-gun ship of the line **29**
terrorists 258–9
Texas, USS **82**, **84–7**
thalamians 20
Thomas B. Jeffery Company 48
Thornycroft J Type **49**
Thornycroft, John 42, 43
thranites 20, 21
thrust 306
thrust vectoring 290
Tiger I tank **126–9**, **304**

Tiger II (King Tiger) tank **124–5**
Tirpitz 166, 168
torpedo boats 32, **42–3**, 80, 81
torpedo bombers 148
torpedoes 42, 44, 250, 251
    guided 287
    programmable 97
total war 97
tractors, artillery 33, 47
trade routes 9, 302
    Cold War 244, 253
    great age of sail 28
Trafalgar, Battle of 19, 24, 28, 29
Trafalgar, HMS **36**
Trafalgar-class submarine **249**
transonic fighters 218
transporter erector launchers (TELs) **192–3**
trench railways 54
trench warfare 63, 96
trimaran hulls 276
triremes 12, 13, 18, **20–21, 22**, 302
Triumph
    3HW **115**
    31W **114**
troop carriers
    Cold War **208–9**
    modern era **266–7**
    World War I **48–9**
    World War II **146–7**
troop transport
    air 9
    boat 9
    Cold War 191
    gliders 163
    military transport planes **222–3**
    rail 8, 32, 112
    World War II 9, 110
trucks
    Cold War 191, **216–17**
    for special forces 212
    ICE powered 33
    Pierce-Arrow R Type 49, **50–53**
    supply 97
    utility and troop (World War I) **48–9**
    World War I 33, 47
    World War II 97, 110, **120–21**
Tsushima, Battle of 32, 38, 43
Tupolev Tu-95 "Bear" 190, **228**
turtle ships (*kŏbuksŏn*) 18, **23**
Type 21 frigates 245
Type 23 frigates 191
Type 039A/B *Yuan*-class submarine 257
Type 42 destroyers 245
Type 054A frigate **285**
Type 055 stealth guided-missile destroyers 257, 276
Type 59-II tank **194**
Type 61 tank **214**
Type 62 tank **195**
Type 69-II tank **195**
Type 74 tank **214**
Type 89 (IFV) **211**
Type 95 Ha-Go tank **124**
Type 99 MBT 256
Type 99A MBT 257
Type 1936A destroyer **174**
Type D escort ship **175**
Type VIIC submarine **176–7**
Type XXI submarine 177

U

U-boats 80, 81, 88, 92–3, 96, 166, 167, 176, 178, 179
UAV *see* unmanned aerial vehicles
UC-1 Class submarine **90–91**
UCAV *see* unmanned combat aerial vehicles
UGV *see* unmanned ground vehicles
Ukraine War 256, 257, 264, 266, 277, 288, 297, 299
UN Relief and Rehabilitation Administration (UNRAA) 112
United States
    civil war steamboat battles **44–5**
    Cold War **190–91**, 244
United States Army Transportation Corps
    USATC S100 **112**
    USATC S160 **112**
Universal Carrier, Mark II **146**
Unmanned aerial vehicles (UAVs) 288, **296–9**
    MQ-9 Reaper **300–301**
unmanned combat aerial vehicles (UCAVs) 257
unmanned ground vehicles (UGVs) **289**
unmanned surface vehicles (USVs) 257, 276, 277
unmanned underwater vehicles (UUVs) 276
urban warfare 257
US Navy 80
Ushant, Battle of 24
USV *see* unmanned surface vehicles
Utah, USS 166
UUV *see* unmanned underwater vehicles

V

V-2 ballistic missiles 219
V-22 Osprey 257
V43, SMS **89**
Valentine
    Bridgelayer **136–7**
    Mark II tank **130**
    Mk IX Duplex Drive **136**
Vancouver, HMCS **284**
Vanguard, HMS **286**
VBCI troop carrier **267**
Vehicle Protection Kit (VPK) 258
Véhicule de l'Avant Blindé **209**
Velocette MAC-MDD **114**
Venetian galleys **22**
Verdun, Battle of 49
Versailles, Treaty of 96
Vickers
    Light Tank Mark VIB **101**
    Mark E, 6 Ton **100–101**
    Mikasa **38–9**
    Valiant 219
    Vickers Medium Mark II **102–5**
    Vimy **79**
Victory, HMS **24–5, 28–9**
Vietnam War
    cruisers 169
    destroyers 246–7
    drones 297
    heavy bombers 190
    helicopters 190–91, 230, 232
    military patrol boats **252–3**
    naval warfare 244
Vijayanta tank **214**
Viking longships 13, 18, **22**, 302
Vikrant, INS **279**
Visby-class corvettes 276
Voisin 8 **78**
Vought F4U Corsair **184**

W

W. H. Whiton 34
waka taua **23**
War Department Light Railways 54
war waggons 12, **14–15**
Ward, USS **88–9**
Warrior, HMS 32
Warrior (IFV) **211**
Warsaw Pact 202, 216
warships
    Cold War 190
    digital age **276–7**
    early **22–3**
    evolution of 8, 12, 13, **18–19**, 32
    present day **276–7**
    seafaring technology **302–3**
    World War I **80–81, 84–7**
    World War II 82, 84, 85, **166–73**
    see also naval warfare; ships
Washington Naval Treaty 96, 174
Washington, USS 169
Waterloo, Battle of 13
Western Front (World War I) 47, 66
Western Roman Empire 9
Westland
    Lysander **109**
    Wessex HAS3 helicopter **230**
Whippet tank **57**
White Motor Company, Model AEF Armoured Car **65**
Whitehead, Robert 42
Wickes-class destroyers 89
Wilhelm Bauer **177**
Willys 123
    MB "Jeep" 97, **120–21**
wind power 13
wing shape **306**
wireless communications 97
World War I
    aerial combat **148–9**
    aircraft 9, **66–7**
    airship bombing raids **76–7**
    amphibious warfare 274
    armoured cars 47, **64–5**
    artillery 32
    battleships 303
    Blockade of Europe **81**
    bomber aircraft 33, **78–9**
    destroyers **42–3**
    fighter aircraft **70–71**
    horses in 47
    locomotives **54–5**
    Mark IV tank **58–61**
    merchant shipping 302
    mobile warfare on land **46–7**
    monoplanes 107
    Pierce-Arrow R Type **50–53**
    RAF S.E.5A **72–5**
    rail transport 33
    railway guns **34–5**
    reconnaissance aircraft **68–9**
    requisitioned vehicles 47
    sea battles **80–81**
    submarine warfare 80, 81, **90–93**
    tank battles **62–3**
    tanks 8, 33, 47, **56–7**
    USS *Texas* **84–7**
    trucks 33, 47
    warships 83, **84–7**
World War II
    air power 9
    aircraft carriers 149, **182–3**
    Allied and Axis tank destroyers **138–9**
    Allied tanks **130–31**
    amphibious warfare 274
    Arctic convoys 166, **167**
    Atlantic convoys 84, 166, 176, 178
    Axis tanks **124–5**
    battleships and cruisers **168–9**
    Blitzkrieg 111
    Boeing B-17 ("Flying Fortress") **152–5**
    bombers **150–51**
    carrier and maritime strike aircraft **184–5**
    destroyers and escorts **174–5**

World War II *continued*
    early jets **164–5**
    engineering and specialist vehicles **136–7**
    fighter planes **156–7**
    gliders **162–3**
    Harley-Davidson WLC **116–19**
    HMS *Belfast* **170–73**
    logistics **112–13**
    M4 Sherman tank **132–5**
    merchant shipping 302
    military motorcycles **114–19**
    monoplanes **106–7**
    Normandy landings **186–7**
    sea battles **166–7**
    Soviet tanks **140–41**
    special forces 212
    submarines **176–7**
    Supermarine Spitfire **158–61**
    T-34/85 tank **142–5**
    tank warfare 110
    Tiger I tank **126–9**
    trucks, half-tracks, and light vehicles **120–21**
    U-995 submarine **178–81**
    warplanes **108–9**
    warships 82, 84, 85, **168–73**
Wright, Orville and Wilbur 9, 33, 288

X

XA-185 troop carrier **266**
xebec, Algerian **22**

Y

Yahagi 169
Yakovlev Yak-3 **157**
Yamato 166, 168, 304
Yeager, Charles E. 218
Yi Sun-sin, Admiral 18
Yokosuka D4Y3 Model 33 "Judy" **150**
Yom Kippur War 215, 244
Yorktown, USS 183
Yorktown-class vessels 183
Yuri Dolgoruky **286–7**

Z

Zeppelin airships 66
Zeppelin, Count Ferdinand von 76
Zeppelin-Staaken R.IV **78–9**
Zumwalt, USS 257, 276
Zündapp KS750 **114**
zygians 20

Acknowledgments

Dorling Kindersley would like to extend thanks to the following people for their help with making the book:

Senior Jackets Designer Suhita Dharamjit; Manish Upreti for DTP assistance; Vagisha Pushp for picture research assistance; Oliver Drake for proofreading; Helen Peters for indexing; Nic Dean for picture research; Nicholas Moran and Chris McNab for contents development; Steve Setford for additional text; Ciara Law for administrative assistance; Jane Ewart for additional design.

The publisher would like to thank the following for their kind permission to reproduce their photographs:

(Key: a-above; b-below/bottom; c-centre; f-far; l-left; r-right; t-top)

1 Dorling Kindersley: Dave King (c). **2-3 Dorling Kindersley:** Gary Ombler / Nationaal Luchtvaart Themapark Aviodome (c). **4 Dorling Kindersley:** Gary Ombler / Chris Till (bl); Gary Ombler / The Tank Museum, Bovington (br). **5 Dorling Kindersley:** Gary Ombler / Brooklands Museum (bl). **6 Dorling Kindersley:** James Mann / National Motor Museum, Beaulieu (bl); Gary Ombler / The Tank Museum, Bovington (br). **7 Alamy Stock Photo:** Inc (br). **Dorling Kindersley:** Gary Ombler / Shuttleworth Collection (bl). **8 Dorling Kindersley. 9 Shutterstock. com:** Frank L Junior (bl). **10-11 Alamy Stock Photo:** Newscom (c). **12 Alamy Stock Photo:** Album (cr); Niday Picture Library (clb). **13 Alamy Stock Photo:** Niday Picture Library (tc). **14 Alamy Stock Photo:** The Print Collector (cla, bl); Really Easy Star (cl); Zen Radovan (cra). **14-15 Alamy Stock Photo:** NMUIM (bc). **15 Alamy Stock Photo:** George Oze (tr); Zen Radovan (crb). **Bridgeman Images:** Dinodia (tl). **16-17 Getty Images:** De Agostini (c). **18 Alamy Stock Photo:** IanDagnall Computing (cl). **Getty Images:** DEA / G.Dagli Orti (tc). **19 Alamy Stock Photo:** GL Archive (tc); GRANGER - Historical Picture Archive (br). **20 Paul Lipke:** (bl). **Shutterstock.com:** Konstantinos Livadas (tl). **21 Dorling Kindersley:** Hellenic Maritime Museum, (all). **22 akg-images:** Eric Vandeville (clb). **Alamy Stock Photo:** Ian G Dagnall (cla); Chris Hellier (cr); piemags / rmn (br). **Bridgeman Images:** Luisa Ricciarini (tc). **23 Alamy Stock Photo:** Newscom (c); Prisma Archivo (tr). **© The Trustees of the British Museum. All rights reserved:** (bc). **24 Alamy Stock Photo:** Imagedoc (tl). **Getty Images / iStock:** gorgios (bc). **25 Alamy Stock Photo:** Detail Heritage (cl); simon evans (tr); World History Archive (ca); mauritius images GmbH (cra); Douglas Lander (c); Manfred Gottschalk (crb); Nikreates (bl); Maurice Savage (br, bc). **26-27 Getty Images:** Culture Club (c). **28 Alamy Stock Photo:** Graham Hunt (cl); INTERFOTO (tl). **Premier Ship Models:** (tr). **Shutterstock.com:** Hans C. Schrodter (br). **29 Alamy Stock Photo:** US Navy Photo (br). **Dorling Kindersley:** Gary Ombler / Fleet Air Arm Museum (tc). **Wikipedia. 30-31 Dorling Kindersley:** Gary Ombler / Musée des blindés, Saumur, France (c). **32 Alamy Stock Photo:** INTERFOTO (clb); Ivy Close Images (cr). **33 Alamy Stock Photo:** Shawshots (tc). **34-35 Dorling Kindersley:** Gary Ombler / B&O Railroad Museum (c). **34 Alamy Stock Photo:** Mouseion Archives (cl); Stocktrek Images, Inc. (bc). **35 Alamy Stock Photo:** Chronicle (tl, cr); Hum Images (cra); KGPA Ltd (br); GRANGER - Historical Picture Archive (bl). **36 Alamy Stock Photo:** History and Art Collection (cl); U.S. Department of Defense Archive (bc). **Wikipedia. 37 Alamy Stock Photo:** Chronicle (clb); Niday Picture Library (tr). **Wikipedia. 38-39 Dorling Kindersley:** Chester Ong / Mikasa Preservation Society (bc). **38 Getty Images:** Photos.com (tl). **40-41 Dorling Kindersley:** Chester Ong / Mikasa Preservation Society (all). **42-43 Board of Trustees of the Science Museum:** Science Museum Group (cr, bc). **42 Alamy Stock Photo:** dpa picture alliance archive (clb). **Library of Congress, Washington, D.C.:** (cla). **Wikipedia. 43 Alamy Stock Photo:** Smudge Whisker (clb). **Wikipedia. 44-45 Alamy Stock Photo:** Stocktrek Images, Inc. (c). **46 Alamy Stock Photo:** Chronicle (tr); Pictorial Press Ltd (bc). **47 Alamy Stock Photo:** American Photo Archive (tr); Trinity Mirror / Mirrorpix (br). **48 Alamy Stock Photo:** piemags / NSC (tl). **SomeBlokeTakingPhotos:** (cl). **48-49 Alamy Stock Photo:** wyrdlight (bc). **Snapshooter46:** (tc). **49 Alamy Stock Photo:** Associated Press (br). **Dorling Kindersley:** Gary Ombler / Milestones Museum (crb). **Fondation de l'Automobile Marius Berliet, Lyon, France:** (tr). **50 Alamy Stock Photo:** EMU history (tl). **54-55 Brian Stephenson/RAS. 54 Alamy Stock Photo:** 2ebill (br); Inc (cla). **55 Dorling Kindersley:** Gary Ombler / Harzer Schmalspurbahnen (tl). **Brian Stephenson/RAS. Wikipedia. 56 Alamy Stock Photo:** Chronicle (cr). **Bovington Tank Museum. Dorling Kindersley:** Gary Ombler / Musée des blindés, Saumur, France (cl); Gary Ombler / The Tank Museum, Bovington (bl). **57 Alamy Stock Photo:** Argus (clb). **Dorling Kindersley:** The Tank Museum, Bovington (bc); Gary Ombler / Musée des blindés, Saumur, France (cr); Gary Ombler / The Tank Museum, Bovington (cr). **Bill Strouse:** (crb). **58-59 Dorling Kindersley:** Gary Ombler / The Tank Museum, Bovington (bc). **58 Alamy Stock Photo:** De Luan (bl). **59 Dorling Kindersley:** Gary Ombler / The Tank Museum, Bovington (tl, tr). **60-61 Dorling Kindersley:** Gary Ombler / The Tank Museum, Bovington. **62-63 Alamy Stock Photo:** De Luan (c). **64-65 Wikipedia. 64 Bovington Tank Museum. TopFoto:** Roger Viollet (cl). **65 akg-images:** ullstein bild (tr). **Alamy Stock Photo:** PJF Military Collection (bc). **Bovington Tank Museum. 66 Dorling Kindersley:** Gary Ombler / Richard Simms (tr). **Getty Images:** Hulton Deutsch (bl). **67 Getty Images:** Evening Standard / Stringer (tc); ullstein bild Dtl. (br). **68 Alamy Stock Photo:** Ivan Batinic (cl); planecollection (bc). **Wikipedia. 68-69 Alamy Stock Photo:** David Osborn (ca). **69 Alamy Stock Photo:** Chronicle (cra, br); PF-(sdasm3) (tl); Antony Nettle (cr); History and Art Collection (clb). **70 Alamy Stock Photo:** Susan & Allan Parker (cl). **Dorling Kindersley:** Gary Ombler / Brooklands Museum (tc). **70-71 Dorling Kindersley:** Gary Ombler / Royal Airforce Museum, London (Hendon) (bc). **71 Dorling Kindersley:** Gary Ombler (tc); Gary Ombler / Royal Airforce Museum, London (Hendon) (cl). **72 Alamy Stock Photo:** Niall Ferguson (tl). **72-73 Dorling Kindersley:** Gary Ombler / Shuttleworth Collection (bc). **73 Dorling Kindersley:** Gary Ombler / Shuttleworth Collection (tl, tc). **74-75 Dorling Kindersley:** Gary Ombler / Shuttleworth Collection. **76-77 Getty Images:** Popperfoto (c). **78-79 Smithsonian National Air and Space Museum. 78 Alamy Stock Photo:** Antony Nettle (tr). **Canada Aviation and Space Museum:** (clb). **Phillip Capper:** (tr). **79 Dorling Kindersley:** Gary Ombler / Royal Airforce Museum, London (tc, c). **80 Getty Images:** Corbis Historical (cla); David Pollack / Corbis Historical (tr). **81 Getty Images:** Popperfoto (cra); Universal History Archive (bc). **82-83 Dorling Kindersley:** Gary Ombler / Fleet Air Arm Museum (cl). **82 Alamy Stock Photo:** PF-(bygone1) (br). **Wikipedia. 83 Alamy Stock Photo:** The History Collection (crb). **Getty Images:** Hulton Archive (cra). **SD Model Makers:** (tc). **84 Alamy Stock Photo:** Archive PL (tl). **88-89 SD Model Makers. 88 Alamy Stock Photo:** Chronicle (cra); The History Collection (cb). **Wikipedia. 89 Alamy Stock Photo:** Photo 12 (tl). **TopFoto:** World History Archive (crb). **Wikipedia. 90-91 Alamy Stock Photo:** GL Archive (c). **92 Alamy Stock Photo:** GL Archive (cla); INTERFOTO (clb). **Wikipedia. 92-93 SD Model Makers. 93 Alamy Stock Photo:** Hansrad Collection (br). **Wikipedia. 94-95 Dorling Kindersley:** James Mann / National Motor Museum, Beaulieu (c). **96 Getty Images:** Pictures from History (tc). **97 Alamy Stock Photo:** Shawshots (tr). **Getty Images:** Universal History Archive (br). **98 Paul Appleyard:** (tl). **Dorling Kindersley:** Gary Ombler / The Tank Museum, Bovington (cl). **Massimo Foti. Militaryfoto.sk:** (cr). **98-99 Dorling Kindersley:** The Tank Museum, Bovington (tc). **99 Alamy Stock Photo:** Martin Bennett (cl). **Arsenalen, The Swedish Tank Museum:** (br). **Dorling Kindersley:** Gary Ombler / The Tank Museum, Bovington (bl). **Shutterstock.com:** Sergey Ryzhov (tr). **100-101 Dorling Kindersley:** Gary Ombler / The Tank Museum, Bovington (tc). **100 Alamy Stock Photo:** Alexander Tolstykh (br); Universal Art Archive (bl). **Wikipedia:** JDankers (cl). **101 Cody Images:** (bl). **Dorling Kindersley:** Gary Ombler / The Tank Museum, Bovington (crb). **Library of Congress, Washington, D.C.:** Harris and Ewing Inc. (cra). **Chris Neel:** (tr). **Shutterstock.com:** Sergei Afanasev (clb). **102 Alamy Stock Photo:** piemags / ww2archive (tl). **Dorling Kindersley:** Gary Ombler / The Tank Museum, Bovington (clb, cb). **103 Alamy Stock Photo:** piemags / NBP (tr). **Dorling Kindersley:** Gary Ombler / The Tank Museum, Bovington (bc, tc). **104-105 Dorling Kindersley:** Gary Ombler / The Tank Museum, Bovington (all). **106-107 Getty Images:** Fox Photos (c). **108-109 Dorling Kindersley:** Gary Ombler / Yorkshire Air Museum (bc). **108 Dorling Kindersley:** Peter Cook / Planes of Fame Air Museum, Chino, California (cl); Gary Ombler / Sarl Salis Aviation (cr); Gary Ombler / Brooklands Museum (ca); Gary Ombler / Royal Airforce Museum, London (tl). **109 Dorling Kindersley:** Peter Cook / Planes of Fame Air Museum, Chino, California (cr); Gary Ombler / Royal Airforce Museum, London (Hendon) (tl); Gary Ombler / RAF Museum, Cosford (tr); Gary Ombler / Royal Airforce Museum, London (cl). **110-111 Getty Images:** Galerie Bilderwelt (tr). **110 Getty Images:** Hulton Archive / Stringer (ca); Keystone / Stringer (bl). **111 Getty Images:** George Rinhart (br). **112-113 Dorling Kindersley:** Gary Ombler / Eisenbahnfreunde Traditionsbahnbetriebswerk Stassfurt (bc). **112 colour-rail.com:** (tr). **Brian Stephenson/RAS:** (cl). **Wikipedia:** Rabensteiner (tl). **113 Alamy Stock Photo:** Islandstock (tl). **colour-rail. com. Dorling Kindersley:** Deepak Aggarwal / Rewari Steam Loco Shed (c). **Wikipedia:** (tr). **114 Dorling Kindersley:** James Mann / National Motor Museum, Beaulieu (br); Gary Ombler / National Motorcycle Museum (tc, ca). **115 Alamy Stock Photo:** CPC Collection (br). **Dorling Kindersley:** Dave King / National Motorcycle Museum, Birmingham (tl); Dave King / Motorcycle Heritage Museum, Westerville, Ohio (tr); Gary Ombler / Ian Stanley (cr); Dave King / James Mann / National Motor Museum, Beaulieu (bl). **116 Nationaal Archief, Den Haag:** Collectie Spaarnestad / Wout van de Hoef. (tl). **116-117 Dorling Kindersley:** James Mann / National Motor Museum, Beaulieu (bc). **117 Dorling Kindersley:** James Mann / National Motor Museum, Beaulieu (tc, tr). **118-119 Dorling Kindersley:** James Mann / National Motor Museum, Beaulieu. **120 Dorling Kindersley:** Ted Bear, The War and Peace Show (cl); The Tank Museum, Bovington (tr); Matthew Ward / Peter Barber-Lomax (bc). **121 Alamy Stock Photo:** ZarkePix (cla). **Dorling Kindersley:** Gary Ombler / By kind permission of The Trustees of the Imperial War Museum, London (cr); George Paice / War and Peace Show (br). **122-123 Getty Images:** AFP (c). **124 Alamy Stock Photo:** Azoor Photo Collection (bl). **Dorling Kindersley. Massimo Foti:** (tr). **124-125 Dorling Kindersley.**

125 Dorling Kindersley: The Tank Museum, Bovington (tl, tr, cl). **126 Getty Images:** ullstein bild Dtl. (tl). **127 Dorling Kindersley:** Gary Ombler / The Tank Museum, Bovington (all). **128-129 Dorling Kindersley:** Gary Ombler / The Tank Museum, Bovington (all). **130 Dorling Kindersley:** The Tank Museum, Bovington (cla, tr); Gary Ombler / The Tank Museum, Bovington (cb, bl). **130-131 Dorling Kindersley:** Gary Ombler / The Tank Museum, Bovington (bc). **131 Dorling Kindersley:** Gary Ombler / The Tank Museum, Bovington (tl, crb); Gary Ombler / I. Galliers / War and Peace Show (cra). **132 Dorling Kindersley:** Gary Ombler / Chris Till (bc, bl). **Getty Images:** Fred Ramage (tl). **133 Dorling Kindersley:** Gary Ombler / Chris Till (c). **134-135 Dorling Kindersley:** Gary Ombler / Chris Till (all). **136 Alamy Stock Photo:** Zachary Frank (clb); Fraser Gray (br). **Bovington Tank Museum:** (ca). **Dorling Kindersley:** Gary Ombler / The Tank Museum, Bovington (tl, tr). **137 Bovington Tank Museum. Dorling Kindersley:** The Tank Museum, Bovington (bl); Gary Ombler / The Tank Museum, Bovington (tc). **138-139 Dorling Kindersley:** The Tank Museum, Bovington (tl). **138 Dorling Kindersley:** The Tank Museum, Bovington (br); Gary Ombler / Gordon McKenna (c). **139 Dorling Kindersley:** The Tank Museum, Bovington (tr, cl, crb, br). **Dreamstime.com:** Victor Onyshchenko (cb). **140-141 Dorling Kindersley:** The Tank Museum, Bovington (tc). **140 Alamy Stock Photo:** Evgeny Haritonov (cl). **Dorling Kindersley:** Gary Ombler / Musée des blindés, Saumur, France (bc). **Shutterstock.com:** Karasev Viktor (cr). **141 Alamy Stock Photo:** Alexander Blinov (tr). **Dorling Kindersley:** Gary Ombler / The Tank Museum, Bovington (cr). **Getty Images / iStock:** G0d4ather (bl). **Shutterstock.com:** Yakov Oskanov (br). **142 Getty Images:** Victor Temin (tl). **143 Dorling Kindersley:** Gary Ombler / The Tank Museum, Bovington (all). **144-45 Dorling Kindersley:** Gary Ombler / The Tank Museum, Bovington (all). **146 Dorling Kindersley:** The Tank Museum, Bovington (tc, c); Gary Ombler / The Tank Museum, Bovington (cla); The War and Peace Show (bl). **146-147 Dorling Kindersley:** Jez Marren, The War and Peace Show (bc). **147 Dorling Kindersley:** Gary Ombler / The Tank Museum, Bovington (tc, cr, br). **148 Getty Images:** Mondadori Portfolio (bc). **149 Alamy Stock Photo:** CBW (tr); Hi-Story (br). **150 Dorling Kindersley:** Peter Cook / Planes of Fame Air Museum, Chino, California (cr); Gary Ombler / Flugausstellung (tl); Gary Ombler / Gatwick Aviation Museum (cb). **Shutterstock.com:** Ryan Fletcher (cl). **150-151 Dorling Kindersley:** Gary Ombler / RAF Battle of Britain Memorial Flight (tc); Gary Ombler / Gatwick Aviation Museum (bc). **151 Dorling Kindersley:** Gary Ombler / Gatwick Aviation Museum (cl, br); Gary Ombler / Scale Model World, Steve Abbey (cr). **152 Getty Images:** PhotoQuest (tl). **153 Dorling Kindersley:** Gary Ombler / B17 Preservation (all).

154-155 Dorling Kindersley: Gary Ombler / B17 Preservation (picture nos: 2,4,6,9,12,13,14,15,16,17 & 18). **154 Alamy Stock Photo:** Dave Block (clb); ZUMA Press, Inc (tr); Images-USA (crb); Albert Knapp (bc). **Shutterstock.com:** Frank L Junior (ca). **155 Alamy Stock Photo:** B. David Cathell (bl); ZUMA Press, Inc (bc). **156 Dorling Kindersley:** Peter Cook / Planes of Fame Air Museum, Chino, California (c); Gary Ombler / Royal Airforce Museum, London (clb); Gary Ombler / RAF Battle of Britain Memorial Flight (tr). **Rowhider:** (tl). **156-157 Dorling Kindersley:** Gary Ombler / Musee de l'Air et de l'Espace / Le Bourget (bc). **157 Dorling Kindersley:** Gary Ombler / Royal Airforce Museum, London (tr, c). **Shutterstock.com:** cpaulfell (tl). **158 Getty Images:** IWM (tl). **159 Dorling Kindersley:** Gary Ombler / RAF Battle of Britain Memorial Flight (all). **160-161 Dorling Kindersley:** Gary Ombler / RAF Battle of Britain Memorial Flight (all). **162-63 Getty Images:** Central Press (c). **164 Dorling Kindersley:** Gary Ombler / Royal Airforce Museum, London (Hendon) (tc); Gary Ombler / De Havilland Aircraft Heritage Centre (cla); Gary Ombler / RAF Museum, Cosford (cra). **Shutterstock.com:** Eugene Berman (bl). **164-165 Dorling Kindersley:** Peter Cook / March Field Air Museum, California (bc). **165 Dorling Kindersley:** Gary Ombler / Royal Airforce Museum, London (clb, tl). **Smithsonian National Air and Space Museum:** (c). **166 Alamy Stock Photo:** Trinity Mirror / Mirrorpix (cla). **Getty Images:** Bettmann (br). **167 Getty Images:** Corbis Historical (bc); IWM (cra). **168-169 Dorling Kindersley:** Gary Ombler / Fleet Air Arm Museum (cb). **SD Model Makers. 168 Alamy Stock Photo:** Chronicle (tr). **Dorling Kindersley:** Gary Ombler / Model Exhibition, Telford (cra). **SD Model Makers. 169 Dorling Kindersley:** Gary Ombler / Model Exhibition, Telford (cra). **SD Model Makers. Courtesy of U.S. Navy:** Naval History & Heritage Command (br). **170 Alamy Stock Photo:** brystock (tl). **172 Alamy Stock Photo:** Craig Buchanan (tr); Greg Balfour Evans (cl, cb); Stelios Michael (cr, clb); Andrew Duke (bl); Selwyn (fcr); Zoonar GmbH (br). **Getty Images:** Peter Dazeley (ca); Peter Dazeley (cra); NurPhoto (bc). **172-173 Alamy Stock Photo:** alias Ayub (tc). **173 Alamy Stock Photo:** Philip Bird (cl); imageBROKER.com (tc); Steve Vidler (tr); Selwyn (c); Zoonar GmbH (cr, bl); Frank Nowikowski (ca). **174 Alamy Stock Photo:** allanbellimages (cla); VTR (tr). **Dorling Kindersley:** Gary Ombler / Model Exhibition, Telford (cra); Gary Ombler / Fleet Air Arm Museum (cb). **174-175 Dorling Kindersley:** Gary Ombler / Model Exhibition, Telford (bc). **175 SD Model Makers. Courtesy of U.S. Navy:** Naval History & Heritage Command (cr). **Wikipedia. 176-177 Dorling Kindersley:** Gary Ombler / Model Exhibition, Telford (bc). **176 Dorling Kindersley:** Gary Ombler / Fleet Air Arm Museum (cb). **SD Model Makers. 177 Dorling Kindersley:** Gary Ombler / Scale Model World (ca); Gary Ombler / Scale Model World, Allan Toyne (cb). **SD Model Makers. 178 Archive Deutscher Marinebund (German Naval Association), Laboe. 178-179 Alamy Stock Photo:** Jürgen Wackenhut (bc). **180 Alamy Stock Photo:** Penelope Barritt (crb); mauritius images GmbH (tc); mauritius images GmbH (cl, bl); Michael Piepgras (cr); Phillip Berg (c). **180-181 Alamy Stock Photo:** mauritius images GmbH (tc); Zoonar GmbH (bc). **181 Alamy Stock Photo:** Penelope Barritt (clb); Paul Grove (tr); JB-2078 (cra, crb); Marek Slusarczyk (ca, cb). **Shutterstock.com:** rdp 15 (tc); rdp 15 (bc). **182 Dorling Kindersley:** Gary Ombler / Model Exhibition, Telford (ca). **SD Model Makers. 182-183 Dorling Kindersley:** Gary Ombler / Model Exhibition, Telford (clb). **183 SD Model Makers. 184-185 Ulrich Grueschow - MilitaryAircraft.de:** (bc). **184 Alamy Stock Photo:** Amy Lee (cr); chris mcloughlin (bl). **Dorling Kindersley:** Gary Ombler / RAF Museum, Cosford (tr); Gary Ombler / Old Flying Machine Company (clb). **Shutterstock.com:** Pulpits (cla). **185 Alamy Stock Photo:** Rick Pisio\RWP Photography (tl). **Dorling Kindersley:** Gary Ombler / Fleet Air Arm Museum (c). **186-187 Getty Images:** Bettmann (c). **188-189 Dorling Kindersley:** Gary Ombler / Ukraine State Aviation Museum (c). **190 Getty Images:** Bettmann (cl). **191 Alamy Stock Photo:** dpa picture alliance (tc). **Getty Images:** Buyenlarge (cb). **192-93 Getty Images:** Rolls Press / Popperfoto (c). **194 Alamy Stock Photo:** Colin C. Hill (bl); Oleksiy Maksymenko (tr). **Dorling Kindersley:** The Tank Museum, Bovington (br). **195 Dorling Kindersley:** Gary Ombler / The Tank Museum, Bovington (bl, cl). **Dreamstime.com:** Yykkaa (crb). **Bron Pancema:** (tl). **Shutterstock.com:** Karasev Viktor (tr). **196-197 Dorling Kindersley:** Gary Ombler / The Tank Museum, Bovington (c). **196 Dorling Kindersley:** Gary Ombler / The Tank Museum, Bovington (clb, bl). **Getty Images:** Ahmad Al-Rubaye (tl). **198-199 Dorling Kindersley:** Gary Ombler / The Tank Museum, Bovington (all). **200 Alamy Stock Photo:** Brent Beach (cl); Stocktrek Images, Inc. (bl). **Dorling Kindersley:** The Tank Museum, Bovington (crb, bc). **Shutterstock.com:** Kev Gregory (tc). **201 Alamy Stock Photo:** Dorset Media Service (tl). **Dorling Kindersley:** The Tank Museum, Bovington (br). **Getty Images / iStock:** Getty Images Plus (c). **202-203 Getty Images:** ullstein bild (c). **204-205 Dorling Kindersley:** Gary Ombler / The Tank Museum, Bovington (bc). **205 Dorling Kindersley:** Gary Ombler / The Tank Museum, Bovington (tr, tl). **206-207 Dorling Kindersley:** Gary Ombler / The Tank Museum, Bovington. **208 Alamy Stock Photo:** Panzermeister (clb). **Dorling Kindersley:** Gary Ombler / Musée des blindés, Saumur, France (tc); Gary Ombler / The Tank Museum, Bovington (cla). **Getty Images:** Leon Neal (br). **Shutterstock.com:** Art Konovalov (ca). **209 Dorling Kindersley:** Gary Ombler / Musée des blindés, Saumur, France (c). **Getty Images:** Michael Gottschalk (bl). **Jim Maurer:** (tl). **Shutterstock.com:** Leonard Zhukovsky (br). **210 Alamy Stock Photo:** Zoonar GmbH (cla). **Bri_J (Flickr):** (tr). **Massimo Foti. Shutterstock.com:** DLeng (clb); M.J.J. de Vaan (br). **211 Alamy Stock Photo:** dpa picture alliance archive (tc); ZapperSiR (cr). **Shutterstock.com:** Free Wind 2014 (br). **212-213 Getty Images:** Eric Bouvet (c). **214-215 Dorling Kindersley:** Gary Ombler / Musée des blindés, Saumur, France (bc). **214 Shutterstock.com:** Om_Joshi (cr); viper-zero (bl). **Wikipedia:** Johan Elisson (tr); PD-Self / Loss688 / Japan Ground Self-Defence Force (cl). **215 Dorling Kindersley:** Gary Ombler / Norfolk Tank Museum (c). **Shutterstock.com:** Dmitriy Feldman svarshik (tr). **216 Alamy Stock Photo:** Grzegorz Czapski (tr). **Stuart Mitchell:** (cr). **Shutterstock.com:** Art Konovalov (bl). **Wikipedia:** Steve F-E-Cameron (Merlin-UK) (cl). **217 Alamy Stock Photo:** Radharc Images (bc). **Bonhams:** (tl). **Wikipedia:** Darkone (tr). **218-219 Alamy Stock Photo:** De Luan (tc). **218 Getty Images:** Corbis Historical (cr). **219 Alamy Stock Photo:** Pictorial Press Ltd (br); U.S. Department of Defense Archive (bl). **220-221 Dorling Kindersley:** Peter Cook / The American Airpower Museum, Farmingdale, New York (c); Gary Ombler / City of Norwich Aviation Museum (tc). **220 Dorling Kindersley:** Gary Ombler / Flugausstellung (tl, br); Gary Ombler / Midlands Air Museum (cla). **221 Alamy Stock Photo:** Dean West (br). **Dorling Kindersley:** Peter Cook / Intrepid Sea, Air and Space Museum, New York (tr); Gary Ombler / Yorkshire Air Museum (cla). **222-223 Getty Images:** Anadolu (c). **224 Getty Images:** Interim Archives (tl). **225 Dorling Kindersley:** Gary Ombler / Golden Apple Operations Ltd (all). **226-227 Dorling Kindersley:** Gary Ombler / Golden Apple Operations Ltd (all). **228 Alamy Stock Photo:** Allstar Picture Library Ltd (cl); horsemen (ca). **Dorling Kindersley:** Gary Ombler / Yorkshire Air Museum (tr); Gary Ombler / Ukraine State Aviation Museum (bl). **228-229 Alamy Stock Photo:** Nir Ben-Yosef (bc). **229 Alamy Stock Photo:** Bob Graham (cr); Tami Ruble (tc). **Dorling Kindersley:** Peter Cook / Pima Air and Space Museum, Tuscon, Arizona (cla). **230 Dorling Kindersley:** Gary Ombler / Flugausstellung (cr); Gary Ombler / Royal International Air Tattoo 2011 (clb). **Getty Images:** Athanasios Gioumpasis (tl). **230-231 Alamy Stock Photo:** Konstantinos Koronakis (br). **Dorling Kindersley:** Gary Ombler / Fleet Air Arm Museum (tc). **231 Alamy Stock Photo:** Stocktrek Images, Inc. (ca). **Dorling Kindersley:** Gary Ombler / Royal International Air Tattoo 2011 (cb). **Getty Images / iStock:** ILya Oslyakov (tc). **232-33 Getty Images:** Patrick Aventurier (c). **234 Alamy Stock Photo:** Avpics (bc); Lloyd Horgan (tl). **235 Dorling Kindersley:** Gary Ombler / RAF Wittering, Cambridgeshire (all). **236 Dorling Kindersley:** Gary Ombler / Flugausstellung (tl); Gary Ombler / Nationaal Luchtvaart Themapark Aviodome (cla); Gary Ombler / Imperial

ACKNOWLEDGMENTS

War Museum, Duxford (c). **236-237 Dorling Kindersley:** Peter Cook / Pima Air and Space Museum, Tuscon, Arizona (bc). **237 Dorling Kindersley:** Gary Ombler / Royal International Air Tattoo 2011 (tl, cb); Gary Ombler / Flugausstellung (cla). **238 Shutterstock.com:** VanderWolf Images (tl). **239 Dorling Kindersley:** Gary Ombler / Ukraine State Aviation Museum (all). **240-241 Dorling Kindersley:** Gary Ombler / Ukraine State Aviation Museum (all). **242-243 Alamy Stock Photo:** Stocktrek Images, Inc. (c). **244 Alamy Stock Photo:** Dino Fracchia (tr); JJ (br). **245 Alamy Stock Photo:** CHM (bc); Classic Picture Library (tr). **246-247 SD Model Makers. 246 Alamy Stock Photo:** NB / ROD (bl). **Dorling Kindersley:** Gary Ombler / Fleet Air Arm Museum, Eric Dyke (cla). **SD Model Makers. The US National Archives and Records Administration. 247 SD Model Makers. Wikipedia:** Javier Bueno Iturbe (cl); Nathalmad (cra). **248-249 SD Model Makers. 248 Getty Images:** Science & Society Picture Library (br). **SD Model Makers. 249 Model by Ingemar Caisander:** (clb). **Dorling Kindersley:** Gary Ombler / Fleet Air Arm Museum (crb). **SD Model Makers. 250 Alamy Stock Photo:** Ewing Galloway (tl). **The US National Archives and Records Administration:** (bc). **251 Dorling Kindersley:** Gary Ombler / Historic ship Nautilus and Submarine Force Museum, Connecticut (all). **252-253 Getty Images:** U.S. Navy (c). **254-255 Alamy Stock Photo:** Grobler du Preez (c). **256 Alamy Stock Photo:** World History Archive (tc). **257 Alamy Stock Photo:** American Photo Archive (cr). **Getty Images:** Anadolu (bl). **258 Alamy Stock Photo:** Grobler du Preez (tr). **Shutterstock.com:** Grobler de Preez (tl). **Witham Specialist Vehicles Ltd:** Ministry of Defence, UK (cl). **259 Alamy Stock Photo:** Aviation Visuals (tr); Hot Shots (cr). **Ministry Of Defence UK © Crown copyright 2021:** Sgt Wes Calder RLC (tl). **260 Wikipedia:** Chamal Pathirana (b). **264-265 Getty Images:** Global Images Ukraine (c). **266 Alamy Stock Photo:** Esa Hiltula (cla). **Shutterstock.com:** Stefan Holm (tr). **Wikipedia:** Outisnn (bc). **267 Alamy Stock Photo:** Sergei Butorin (cb); Imago (cr); Mike Needham @ digitally_challenging (br). **Getty Images:** Ludovic Marin (ca); Leon Neal (r). **268 Alamy Stock Photo:** Sergii Popsuievych (br). **Shutterstock.com:** Karolis Kavolelis (tc); StockPhotoLV (cb); OlegDoroshin (cl). **269 Alamy Stock Photo:** Associated Press (bc); Oleg Zaslavsky (cl). **Combat Camera Europe:** (tc). **Getty Images / iStock:** vicnt (cr). **270-271 Image courtesy of General Dynamics Ordnance and Tactical Systems:** (bc). **270 Alamy Stock Photo:** 501 collection (tl). **271 USAASC:** (tl); photo by SGT Richard Wiley, 2nd Armoured Brigade Combat Team, 3rd Infantry Division, Public Affairs (tr). **272-273 U.S. Army photo:** (all). **274-275 Getty Images:** Fred Marie / Art in All of Us (c). **276 Courtesy Leidos, Inc.:** © Salty Dingo 2023 (bc). **Courtesy of U.S. Navy:** (cla). **277 Getty Images:** Park Ji-Hwan (br). **Courtesy of U.S. Navy:** US Navy Sixth Fleet (tc). **278 Alamy Stock Photo:** Stocktrek Images, Inc. (cr); Martin Witte (clb). **Getty Images:** michaelbwatkins (tr). **Shutterstock.com:** Joris van Boven (cla). **278-279 Alamy Stock Photo:** U.S. Department of Defense Archive (bc). **279 Alamy Stock Photo:** Rob Arnold (cla); Stocktrek Images, Inc. (tc). **Getty Images:** Hindustan Times (bc). **280-281 NAVY.mil:** Photographer's Mate 3rd Class Summer M. Anderson (c). **280 Alamy Stock Photo:** ZUMA Press, Inc (tl). **282-283 Dorling Kindersley:** Gary Ombler / USS George Washington and the US Navy (all). **284-285 Dorling Kindersley:** Gary Ombler / Fleet Air Arm Museum (tc). **284 Alamy Stock Photo:** one-image photography (c); Focke Strangmann (br). **Getty Images:** Mark Wilson (tl). **285 Alamy Stock Photo:** Associated Press (bc); PJF Military Collection (cl); dpa picture alliance (cr). **286-287 Dorling Kindersley:** Gary Ombler / Fleet Air Arm Museum (c, bc). **286 Dorling Kindersley:** Gary Ombler / Fleet Air Arm Museum (clb, bl). **287 Dorling Kindersley:** Gary Ombler / Fleet Air Arm Museum (cb). **SD Model Makers. 288 Alamy Stock Photo:** Andrew Harker (bl); NASA Photo (tr). **289 Alamy Stock Photo:** CNP Collection (tc); PA Images (br). **290 Alamy Stock Photo:** Marco McGinty (cla). **Dorling Kindersley:** Gary Ombler / Royal International Air Tattoo 2011 (tr); Gary Ombler / RAF Museum, Cosford (b). **290-291 Alamy Stock Photo:** Malcolm Haines (c); James Hancock (bc). **291 Alamy Stock Photo:** Kris Christiaens (br); Gary Stedman (tc). **Getty Images:** Dibyangshu Sarkar (cl). **292 Alamy Stock Photo:** Avpics (tl). **293 Dorling Kindersley:** Gary Ombler / RAF Coningsby (all). **294-295 Dorling Kindersley:** Gary Ombler / RAF Coningsby (all). **296-297 Alamy Stock Photo:** Ukrinform (c). **298 U.S. Air Force:** Lt. Col. Leslie Pratt (c). **298-299 Getty Images:** Anadolu (c). **299 Getty Images:** Global Images Ukraine (br). **Wikipedia:** Mike 1979 Russia (tr). **300 Alamy Stock Photo:** US Air Force Photo (tl). **Getty Images:** Isaac Brekken (bc). **301 Alamy Stock Photo:** American Photo Archive (br); Contraband Collection (cl); ZUMA Press, Inc (tr); Wildfire Image (cra); Michael Fitzsimmons (crb); Operation 2024 (bc). **New York National Guard:** (cb). **302 Alamy Stock Photo:** piemags (bl). **304 Dr. Zachi Evenor:** (bl). **Getty Images:** Shaul Schwarz (br). **SD Model Makers. 305 Arsenalen, The Swedish Tank Museum:** (crb). **SD Model Makers. 306 Dorling Kindersley:** Gary Ombler / Shuttleworth Collection (tc, ca); Gary Ombler / RAF Battle of Britain Memorial Flight (c); Gary Ombler / Golden Apple Operations Ltd (cb)

Endpapers: Shutterstock / 19srb81

DK LONDON

Senior Art Editors Katie Cavanagh, Helen Spencer
Senior Editors Hugo Wilkinson, Victoria Heyworth-Dunne
Editors John Andrews, Steve Setford
Senior Production Editor Andy Hilliard
Senior Production Controller Laura Andrews
Managing Editor Gareth Jones
Managing Art Editor Luke Griffin
Art Director Maxine Pedliham
Design Director Phil Ormerod
Publishing Director Georgina Dee

DK DELHI

Senior Editor Janashree Singha
Senior Art Editor Nidhi Mehra
Project Art Editor Shipra Jain
Art Editor Arshti Narang
Managing Editor Soma B. Chowdhury
Senior Managing Art Editor Arunesh Talapatra
Senior Pre-Production Designer Harish Aggarwal
Pre-Production Designer Raman Panwar
Pre-Production Image Editors Vikram Singh, Ashok Kumar
Pre-Production Manager Balwant Singh
Pre-Production Image Manager Pankaj Sharma
Project Jacket Designer Juhi Sheth
Senior Jacket Coordinator Priyanka Sharma Saddi
Creative Head Malavika Talukder

Consultant David Willey
Contributors Chris McNab, David Willey

First published in Great Britain in 2026 by
Dorling Kindersley Limited
20 Vauxhall Bridge Road, London SW1V 2SA

The authorized representative in the EEA is
Dorling Kindersley Verlag GmbH. Arnulfstr. 124,
80636 Munich, Germany

Copyright © 2026 Dorling Kindersley Limited
A Penguin Random House Company
10 9 8 7 6 5 4 3 2 1
001–350185–Feb/2026

All rights reserved.
No part of this publication may be reproduced, stored in or introduced into a retrieval system, or transmitted, in any form, or by any means (electronic, mechanical, photocopying, recording, or otherwise), without the prior written permission of the copyright owner.

DK values and supports copyright. Thank you for respecting intellectual property laws by not reproducing, scanning or distributing any part of this publication by any means without permission. By purchasing an authorised edition, you are supporting writers and artists and enabling DK to continue to publish books that inform and inspire readers.
No part of this publication may be used or reproduced in any manner for the purpose of training artificial intelligence technologies or systems. In accordance with Article 4(3) of the DSM Directive 2019/790, DK expressly reserves this work from the text and data mining exception.

A CIP catalogue record for this book
is available from the British Library.
ISBN: 978-0-2417-4512-0

Printed and bound in UAE

www.dk.com

This book was made with Forest Stewardship Council™ certified paper – one small step in DK's commitment to a sustainable future. Learn more at www.dk.com/uk/information/sustainability